Military Strategy Classics of Ancient China

English & Chinese

The Art of War, Methods of War 36 Stratagems & Selected Teachings

Texts by

Sun Tzu, Wu Qi, Wei Liao, Sima Rangju, & Jiang Ziya

Edited by

Shawn Conners

Translated by

Chen Song

Special Edition Books

Military Strategy Classics of Ancient China: The Art of War, Methods of War, 36 Stratagems & Selected Teachings

Texts by Sun Tzu, Wu Qi, Wei Liao, Sima Rangju, Jiang Ziya

Edited by Shawn Conners

Translated by Chen Song

Copyright © 2013 by Special Edition Books
All rights reserved. No part of this book may be reproduced or utilized in any form or by any means, electronic or mechanical, including photocopying, recording, or by any information storage and retrieval system, without permission in writing from the publisher, except that brief passages may be quoted by reviewers provided full credit is given.

First Edition — March 2013

Published by
Special Edition Books

ISBN 13: 978-1-937021-03-0
ISBN 10: 1-937021-03-3

Military Strategy Classics of Ancient China

Introduction for Western Readers

Wearing the attire of a Confucian scholar, Wu Qi attended an audience with Lord Wen of Wei to discuss military matters.

Lord Wen of Wei announced, "I do not have much interest in military matters."

Wu Qi replied, "From plain visible facts, I can deduce the hidden. From the past, I can foretell the future. How can your Lordship sincerely say that he has no interest in this subject?"

Interest in military superiority has existed among warriors, commanders, scholars and students, since the dawn of civilization. In the West, the ancient classic stories of Beowulf, Homer and Julius Caesar are, even centuries later, required reading in high schools and universities. This familiarity with the military achievements of the greatest warriors in our collective history is not limited to military scholars. Students taking *Latin* are required to read the military strategies of Julius Caesar: *Gallia est omnis divisa in partes tres*. Students of civics and law classes will learn from Machiavelli that *the ends justify the means*. Students of history will read the military exploits of Philip of Macedon, his son Alexander; Napoleon Bonaparte and his aide, Baron de Jomini; as well as Generals Lee and Grant from the American Civil War. Successful leaders in both Eastern and Western civilization have been, as Wu Qi rightly guessed, very much interested in military strategy.

As was the case in ancient Western civilization, the ancient Chinese Yellow River valley civilization has been engaged in military activity since the dawn of their recorded history[1]. The area is home to the

---

[1] The first recorded document is believed to be dated c. 6000 BCE.

Introduction

longest continuing civilization known to scholars. It is written that in the 29th century BCE, the first Great Sovereign of China, Fu Xi (伏羲) was born. According to legend, the land was swept by a great flood and only Fu Xi and his sister Nüwa survived. They then retired to the mythological Kunlun Mountain to pray for Heavenly guidance. Fu Xi and Nüwa used clay to create human figures, and with the divine power entrusted to them, made the clay figures come alive. Fu Xi then came to rule over his descendants for more than 100 years. Fu Xi taught his subjects to cook, to fish with nets, and to hunt with weapons made of iron.

The ancient Chinese were involved in frequent wars of unification, expansion and defense of their territories. They developed warfare on a sophisticated level to meet these demands. China produced massive infantry-based armies and navies which battled for control of the rivers of China.

As the implements of war were analyzed and improved upon, infantrymen employed a variety of more efficient weapons made of iron. Dagger-axes came in various lengths from nine to eighteen feet, and were used as thrusting spears with a slashing blade. A typical heavy infantryman may have been equipped with armor consisting of a leather jerkin covered with narrow bronze plates and a hardened leather helmet. His main weaponry would be a pole-arm with an iron head and a bronze dagger-axe for a secondary weapon. Heavy infantry would have been formed into large, close formations for battles.

The Qin later began producing stronger iron swords, crossbows and the compound bow. Another Chinese innovation allowed a crossbow to be rendered useless simply by removing two pins, preventing enemies from capturing a working model. The stirrup was also adopted at this time. Stirrups gave cavalry men greater balance and crucially allowed them to leverage the weight of the horse in a charge, without being unseated.

Qin army formations and tactics can be understood somewhat from the Terracotta Army of Qin Shi Huang found in the tomb of the First Emperor. There were over 8,000 soldiers, 130 chariots with 520 horses and 150 cavalry horses, the majority of which are still buried in the pits near Qin Shi Huang's mausoleum. The formations revealed that light infantry were first deployed as shock troops and skirmishers. They were followed by the main body of the army, consisting of heavy infantry. Cavalry and chariots were positioned behind the heavy infantry, used for flanking or charging. In order to counter the threat from the nomadic invaders of the time, the Qin began construction of the Great Wall, the building of which would last for centuries. The walls and fortifications would ultimately be 5,500 miles long, when counting all of its branches.

Later, more significant Chinese military inventions and improvements would follow. In the 9th century of the Common Era, the Chinese were the first to develop gunpowder, followed in the 10th century by the invention of the first gunpowder firearms. The first guns were spear-like weapons made of bamboo, called fire lances (火枪). These short-ranged, one-shot, disposable weapons were often held in racks on city walls and gave Chinese defenders a tremendous tactical and psychological advantage when fired in volleys. They were ideal for dealing with enemies trying to scale city walls, or for holding the enemy at bay behind a breached gate. They were in widespread use by the time of the Song Dynasty in the 12th century.

As was the case in Western counterpart, the Roman Empire, successive leaders extended China's boundaries primarily by military conquest. However, by the time of the Han Dynasty and the opening of the "Silk Road" trade routes, the teachings of Confucius had become the accepted canon of moral and political thought in China. Confucian scholars revised a variety of Chinese classic military texts to bring the writings more in line with Confucian ideals. This practice was continued by scholars of Buddhism and Taoism. Some of the classic texts of China

Introduction

therefore contain anachronous or historically questionable content. So important was the perception of a ruler being anointed by Heaven, that some of the texts may now contain material much different than originally recorded, such as in the *Three Strategies of Huang Shigong*.

Before the discovery of the First Emperor's tomb in 1972, students wishing to read historic military accounts of ancient China in *The Art of War* by Sun Tzu or *The Book of Wuzi* by Wu Qi might have had to order the book from a rare book store, or from mainland China itself. Today, *The Art of War* has become required reading for many students in legal disciplines, the field of business management, and basic Eastern philosophy classes. A modern survey of the business section of a local book store might yield titles such as, *The Art of War for Managers*, *Sun Tzu and the Art of Business* and *The Art of Command by Wei Liaozi*. Strategic wisdom from Sun Tzu, Wei Liao and other Chinese generals has become part of our lexicon, such as the axioms: *All warfare is based on deception* by Sun Tzu, and *Sheath a dagger in a smile* from the *Thirty Six Stratagems*.

Chinese cinema, novels and martial arts techniques have also permeated Western culture to a profound degree. Many of the names of the ancient *Worthy* of China may seem familiar to even casual lay readers. The recent international proliferation of Chinese *wuxia*[2] has brought classic Chinese novels such as *Water Margin* and *The Romance of the Three Kingdoms* to Western audiences. The battles won by Sun Tzu and Jiāng Zǐyá have become the epic backdrop for modern international films, such as *Hero* (2002), *Red Cliff* (2008), and *The Warring States* (2011).

Military Strategy Classics of Ancient China presents modern translations of eight of the more important and relevant military texts which have survived the ages, and gained new prominence among Western students of Eastern military strategy and the martial arts philosophy. Exact dating of each text has never been agreed upon; however, the eight texts are presented in close approximation to chronological order, from the 11th century BCE through the 7th century of the Common Era. Each text in Chen Song's groundbreaking translation is presented in modern English, followed by Chinese characters.

---

[2] Wuxia is a broad genre of Chinese fiction concerning the adventures of martial artists and military heroes in literature, opera, films, television series, and video games.

Included Texts

The Six Secret Teachings (六韜) is a well-known and somewhat revolutionary text on civil and military strategy traditionally attributed to the legendary figure Jiāng Zǐyá (also known as Tai Gong Wang) presented in the format of a dialogue between King Wen (Zhou Chang) and Jiāng Zǐyá. This text is the earliest of the collected works in this edition, and the use of divination and astrology differs significantly from this work and later works. The text is believed to have been originally written in the Zhou Dynasty (c. 11th century BCE) with sections added as late as the Warring States period.

The Art of War (孙子兵法) Sun Wu (also known as Sun Tzu) expounds on the importance of military strategy and tactics, in particular the topics of assessing the opponent, positioning forces, and careful analysis of the enemy, in each of nine situations and terrains. Each of the 13 chapters is transcribed as a lesson by Sun Tzu, traditionally starting with the phrase "Master Sun said." *The Art of War* is still considered one of the most important military texts ever compiled. It is believed to have been written during the late Spring and Autumn period or the early Warring States period (c. 470 BCE).

The Methods of War (司马法) is a military text attributed to Sima Rangju which discusses concepts of military theory, as well as administration and propriety: laws, regulations, discipline, tactics, and strategy. It is alternatively known as *Sima Fa*, *Sima Art of War*, *Methods of Sima*, or *Principles of Sima*. The title "Da Sima" is translated in this edition as "Minister of War". It is believed to have been developed in the state of Qi during the mid-Warring States period (c. 430 BCE).

The Book of Wuzi (吴子) is a classic Chinese work on military strategy attributed to Wu Qi. It is also sometimes referred to as the *Wuzi*, *Wuzi Art of War* or *The Book of Wu Qi*. In an ongoing dialogue, Lord Wen of Wei (魏文侯) and his son, Lord Wu of Wei (魏武侯) ask Master Wu Qi questions about war theory and strategy, seeking to clarify earlier teachings and analyze historic military maneuvers. It is believed to have been written during the middle of the Warring States period (c. 420 BCE).

Introduction

The Book of Wei Liaozi (尉繚子) is a text which considers military strategy, while discussing both a civil and a military approach to conducting state affairs. Recommendations are included for ruling over the army, managing differing types of cities, and how to preserve the state. Also discussed are the judicial responsibilities of both the general and the ruler. Although the authorship is debated, it is believed to have been written from the perspective of a military general named Wei Liao during the late Warring States period (c. 400 BCE).

The Three Strategies of Huang Shigong (黄石公三略) is a military text which focuses on personnel concerns and logistics: concepts of government, the administration of forces; the characteristics of a capable general; and implementing a system of rewards and punishments. Although called *The Three Strategies of Huang Shigong*, there is no agreement on the historical author. It has been variously attributed to Huang Shigong and Jiāng Zǐyá, author of the *Six Secret Teachings*. Other scholars believe it may be a complete forgery. It is believed to have been written during the Han Dynasty (c. 210 CE).

The Thirty Six Stratagems (三十六计) is a text used to illustrate a series of stratagems used in conflict, politics and war, often through improvised or deceptive means. The stratagems are divided into six groups: stratagems of *advantage, opportunity, attack, confusion, deception* and *disadvantage*. Each individual stratagem is presented with examples from Chinese history. The stratagems were originally taken from a much larger collection in the *Book of Qi*, written during the Southern Qi Dynasty (c. 452–498 CE).

Questions and Replies: Tang Taizong and Li Jing (唐太宗李卫公问对) is an ongoing set of dialogues between Tang Dynasty Emperor Taizong and Li Jing, a prominent Tang general. In analyzing military strategy, centuries after the Warring States period, Tang Taizong and Li Jing discuss previous military works such as Cao Cao's *Xin Shu*, Wu Qi's *Book of Wuzi*, Sun Tzu's *The Art of War*, Sima Rangju's *Methods of War* and Jiāng Zǐyá's *The Six Secret Teachings*. Although no clear authorship has been established, the text is believed to have been written in the late Tang Dynasty (c. 599-649 CE).

Notes on the Texts

Where possible, the most widely-known spelling variant of proper names is used, rather than rigidly adhering to Wade-Giles or Pinyin transcription standards. Alternate variations are presented for reference. This is done for ease of reference and efficient electronic text searches.

"Zi" (子; "Tzu" in Wade-Giles transliteration) was used as a suffix for the family name of a respectable man in ancient Chinese culture. It is a rough equivalent to "Sir" and is commonly translated into English as "Master". In the case of Sun Wu, "Sun" is the family name. Sun Wu is also "Sun Tzu", "Sun Zi" and "Sunzi". Similar variations occur with Wu Qi (Wuzi) and Wei Liao (Wei Liaozi).

Sima Rangju, Sima Fa, Tian Chang and the "Ssu-ma" all refer to the same individual, in the context of this compilation. This text on military strategy has historically been referred to as *Methods of Sima*, or *Principles of the Sima*, although occasionally it is referred to as the shortened: "Methods" or "Principles". The title, "Da Sima" is translated as "Minister of War." In this translation, the title is rendered as "Methods of War".

In ancient military texts of China, *Direct* and *Indirect* actions are often discussed. These strategies are also occasionally referred to as "Orthodox" and "Unorthodox" in earlier translations of Chinese texts.

For the presentation of numbers, numeric values of less than 100 are spelled using words, such as "six" and "thirty six", while numeric values greater than 100 are presented in numeric format, such as "120" or "10,000".

For dates, the original texts use the BC/AD calendar era method of date notation. The introductory information, footnotes, references and supplemental material use the BCE/CE methods of notation.

Introduction

Timeline of Chinese Dynasties

2070 - 1600 BCE	Xia Dynasty – Tribal government
1600 - 1122 BCE	Shang Dynasty – City-States ruled by Priest Kings
1122 - 256 BCE	Zhou Dynasty – Feudalism; Mandate of Heaven proclaimed
221 - 207 BCE	Qin Dynasty – Legalism replaced Feudalism
206 BCE - 220 CE	Han Dynasty – Confucianism made state philosophy
220 CE - 589 CE	(Dark Ages) – North/South Division; North ruled by invaders
589 CE - 618 CE	Sui Dynasty – Reunification of empire
618 CE - 907 CE	Tang Dynasty – Civil service exams made path to government
960 CE - 1270CE	Song Dynasty – North occupied by non-Chinese invaders
1279 - 1368 CE	Yuan Dynasty – Mongol conquest
1368 - 1664 CE	Ming Dynasty – Chinese restoration; Great Wall built
1664 - 1911 CE	Qing Dynasty – Manchu conquest and rule
1839 - 1842	Opium War with Britain; ceding of Hong Kong
1885	Sino-French War over Vietnam
1894	Sino-Japanese War over Korea
1900	Boxer Uprising
1911	Republican Revolution

Military Strategy Classics of Ancient China

Historic Maps

Shang Dynasty

1600 BCE – 1100 BCE

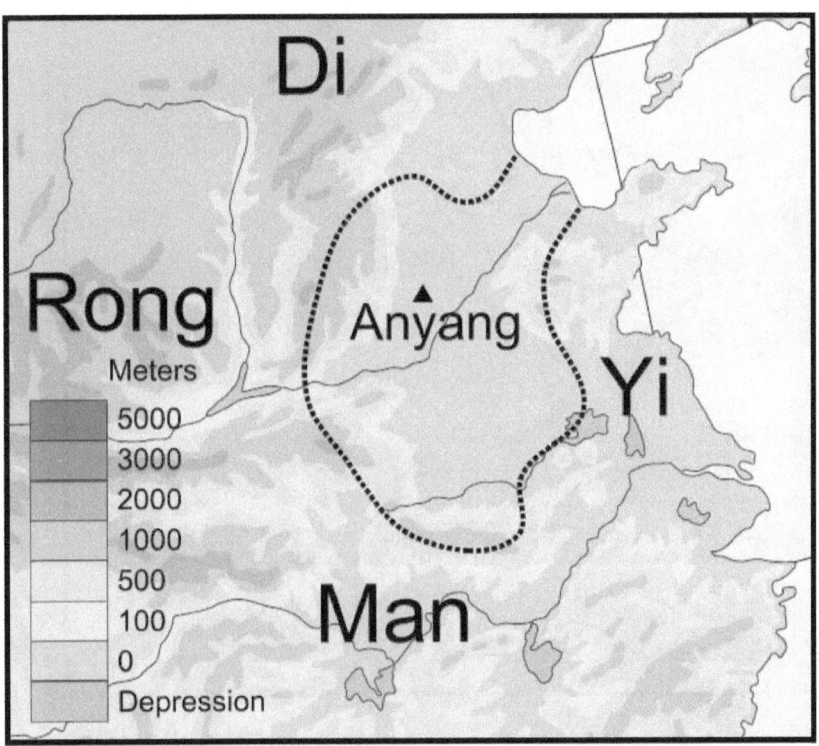

Zhou Dynasty

1100 BCE– 221 BCE

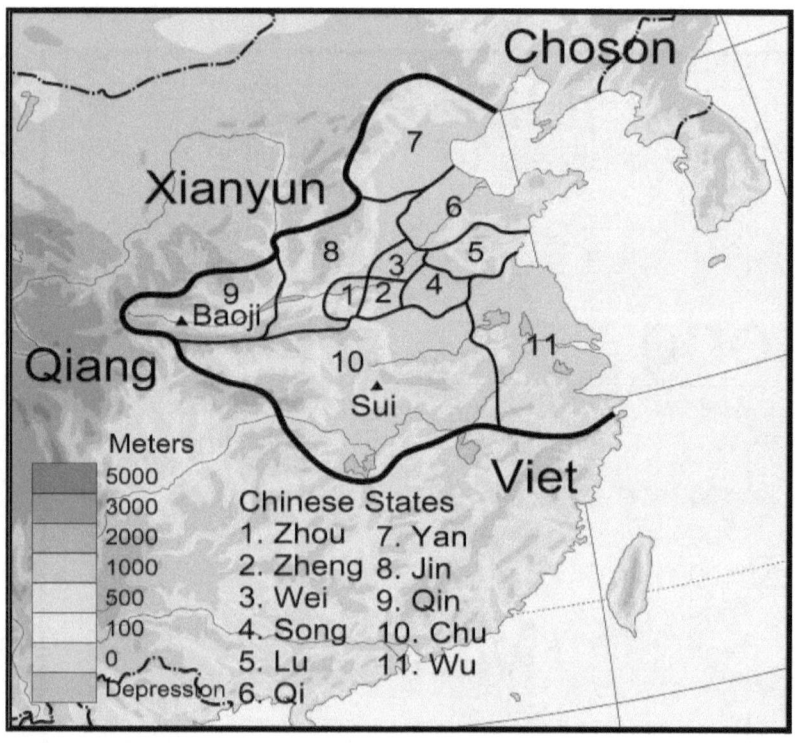

Military Strategy Classics of Ancient China

Han Dynasty

206 BCE – 220 CE

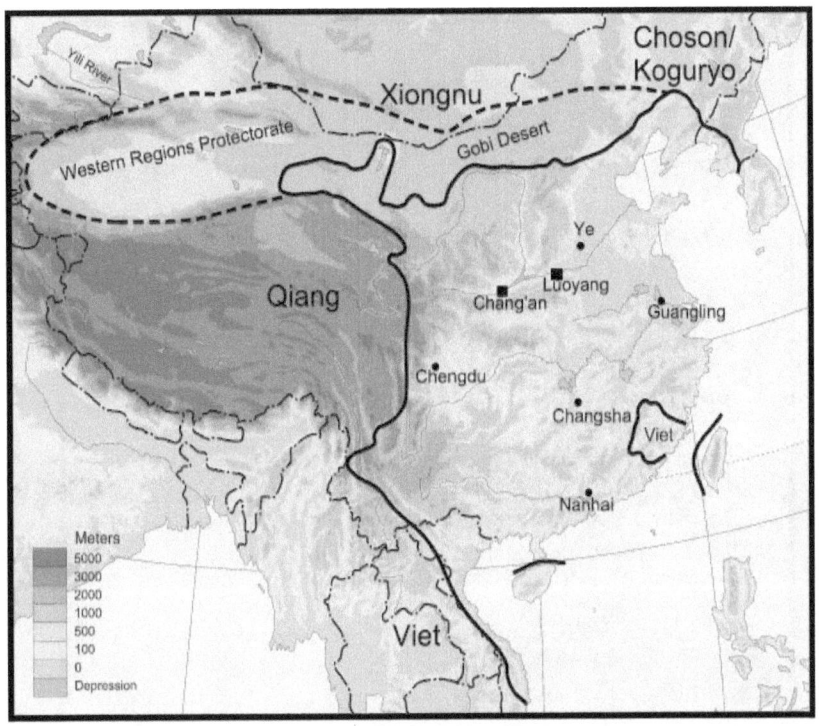

Introduction

Dark Ages/Period of Division

220 CE – 589 CE

Table of Contents

Introduction for Western Readers – by Shawn Conners		i
I.	**Jiang Ziya – Six Secret Teachings,** 姜太公六韜	1
	1. Civil Teaching	1
	2. Military Teaching	22
	3. Dragon Teaching	32
	4. Tiger Teaching	59
	5. Leopard Teaching	73
	6. Hound Teaching	83
II.	**Sun Tzu - The Art of War,** 孙子兵法	97
	1. Assessment and Planning	97
	2. Waging War	100
	3. Attack Strategies	103
	4. Positioning the Army	106
	5. Forces	108
	6. Weaknesses and Strengths	111
	7. Military Maneuvers	115
	8. Variation and Adaptation	119
	9. Troop Deployment and Movement	121
	10. Terrain	126
	11. The Nine Battlegrounds	130
	12. Attacking with Fire	137
	13. Intelligence and Espionage	140
III.	**Sima Rangju – Methods of War,** 司马法	143
	1. Benevolence as Foundation	143
	2. Duty of the Son of Heaven	148
	3. Determining Ranks	155
	4. Formational Discipline	163
	5. Employing the Masses	170
IV.	**Wu Qi – The Book of Wuzi,** 吴子兵法	173
	1. Part 1	
	a. Importance of Seeking Talent	180
	b. Knowing the Enemy	181
	c. Managing Troops	188
	2. Part 2	
	a. Selection of Generals	193
	b. Responding to Changes in War	198
	c. Motivating Talent	203

V.	**The Book of Wei Liaozi**, 尉繚子		207
	1. Heavenly Positions		207
	2. Military Discussion		209
	3. Discussion of Regulations & Systems		212
	4. Combat Superiority		217
	5. Tactical Balance of Power in Attack		222
	6. Tactical Balance of Power in Defense		227
	7. Twelve Cultivations		229
	8. Military Discussions		230
	9. General as Officer of the Law		237
	10. Officers & Rulers		239
	11. Foundations of Governance		241
	12. Tactical Balance of Power in Warfare		245
	13. Heavy Punishment		247
	14. Army Organizations		248
	15. Exit and Entry		249
	16. Rewards & Punishment in War		250
	17. Regulating & Ordering the Troops		251
	18. Regulating Movement of Troops		252
	19. Orders of a General Before the Start of War		254
	20. Vanguards		255
	21. Military Instructions I		257
	22. Military Instructions II		261
	23. Army Orders I		265
	24. Army Orders II		268
VI.	**The Three Strategies of Huang Shigong**, 黄石公三略		273
	1. The Upper Strategy		273
	2. The Middle Strategy		287
	3. The Lower Strategy		291
VII.	**The Thirty Six Stratagems**, 三十六計		299
	1. Stratagems of Advantage		299
	2. Stratagems of Opportunity		308
	3. Stratagems of Attack		315
	4. Stratagems of Confusion		323
	5. Stratagems of Deception		330
	6. Stratagems of Disadvantage		338
VIII.	**Questions & Replies: Tang Taizong and Li Jing**, 唐李对问		351
	1. Part 1		351
	2. Part 2		372
	3. Part 3		393
IX.	**Bibliography**		395

Military Strategy Classics

of

Ancient China

English & Chinese

The Art of War, Methods of War

36 Stratagems & Selected Teachings

Six Secret Teachings

Jiang Ziya

六韬

The Six Secret Teachings *(六韬) is a well-known and somewhat revolutionary text on civil and military strategy traditionally attributed to the legendary figure Jiāng Zǐyá (also known as Tai Gong Wang), presented in the format of a dialogue between King Wen (Zhou Chang) and Jiāng Zǐyá. This text is the earliest of the collected works in this edition, and the use of divination and astrology differs significantly from this work and later works. The text is believed to have been originally written in the Zhou Dynasty (c. 1100 BCE) with sections added as late as the Warring States period.*

Chapter 1 - Civil Teaching
King Wen's Teacher - The Meeting

In preparation for a hunting trip, the Royal Scribe performed a divination for his master, King Wen (Zhou Chang), and declared: "On the north bank of the Wei River, you will find a great bounty. It will be neither a dragon, nor a tiger nor a bear, but a great Sage who is heaven-sent to be your mentor. By following his teachings, my lordship and his descendants will flourish."

King Wen asked: "Truly, this is the omen?"

The Scribe replied: "My ancestor divined a harbinger similar to that of today for Emperor Shun, who then found Yao Tao to assist him."

King Wen fasted for three days before mounting his chariot and driving his hunting horses to the northern bank of the Wei River. There he found Jiāng Zǐyá (Tai Gong Wang) sitting on the grassy shore, fishing. King Wen approached him and then asked courteously: "Do you like fishing?"

Jiāng Zǐyá said: "I have heard that gentlemen and villains alike take pleasure in realizing their ambitions. My fishing is similar to your ambitions."

周文王将去打猎，史编占卜以后说：''你到渭水北岸打猎，将有巨大的收获，所得的既不是龙、彲，也不是虎、罴，而是预兆得到有公侯才干的人，他是天赐给你的导师，辅佐你的事业日益昌盛，并将加惠于你的后代子孙。''

文王问："占卜的预兆果真有这样好吗？史编说："我的远祖史畴曾为舜占卜而得到皋陶，那时的预兆和今天的很相似。"
文王于是斋戒三天，然后，乘猎车，驾猎马，到渭水北岸打猎，终于见到了太公正坐在长满茅草的岸边钓鱼。文王上前慰劳并询问："你喜欢钓鱼吗？"
太公说："我听说君子乐于实现自己的抱负，小人乐于做好自己的事情。我现在的钓鱼与这个道理很相似，并不是喜欢钓鱼。"

Three Authorities

King Wen inquired, "How is it similar?"

Jiāng Zǐyá replied: "Fishing is similar to enlisting talent. There are three baits that will attract talent: generous salaries, concern for life and death, and opportunity for recognition. For every fish there is an appropriate lure. All those who fish wish to be successful. The philosophy of fishing has deep meaning. It contains many truths, many profound principles."

文王问："怎么个相似法呢？"
太公说："比如君主收罗人才就和钓鱼一样，操有三种权术：用厚禄收罗人才，好象用饵钓鱼一样；用重赏收买死士，好象用香饵钓鱼一样；用不同的官位授予不同的人才，好象用不同的诱饵钓取的取不同的鱼一样。凡是垂钓的都是为了得鱼，钓鱼的道理也很深奥，从中可以看了大的道理。"

Fishing, Nation and Attracting Talent

King Wen said: "I would like to hear about these principles."

Jiāng Zǐyá said: "When the water is deep and flows continuously, fish will spawn there. This is in the nature of things. When the roots are deep, the tree can grow tall and produce lush vegetation and fruit. This is in the nature of things. When men of true worth come together for a common purpose and speak the truth, great accomplishments can result. This is in the nature of things. Speaking is merely representations of thought. Speaking the truth is of utmost importance. I would like to speak the truth without adornment; will it displease you?"

King Wen said: "A man of true benevolence can accept the truth however outrageous. What makes you think I would be adverse to the idea? Please continue."

Jiāng Zǐyá continued: "When the fishing line and bait are small, only small fish will be caught. When the line and bait are of medium size, medium size fish will be caught. When the line is strong and the bait generous, large fish will be caught. When men accept salaries from the ruler, they will submit to him. When a ruler provides adequate rewards, men will perform to the limit of their capabilities for him. If a ruler treats the families as the foundation of the state, the state will be his. If a ruler uses the state as the base to conquer the kingdom, the kingdom will be his."

文王说:"我想听听这深奥的道理!"
太公说:"泉源深,水流就不息,水流不息,鱼类就能生存,这是自然的道理;树根深,枝叶就茂盛,枝叶茂盛,就能结出果实,这也是自然的道理;君子情意相投,就会亲密合作,亲密合作,事业就能成功,这也是自然的道理。言语应付,是把真情掩饰起来了,能说真情实话,才是最好的事情。现在我说的都是至情之言,毫不隐讳,你恐怕会有反感吧?"
文王说:"只有仁德的人才能接受最直率的规劝,才不厌恶真情实话。我怎么会那样呢?"
太公说:"钓丝细微,鱼饵可见,小鱼会来上钩;钓丝适中,鱼饵味香,中鱼会来上钓;钓丝粗长,鱼饵丰富,大鱼会来上钩。鱼要贪吃香饵,就会被钓丝牵着;人要食君俸禄,就会服从君主使用。所以用香饵钓鱼,鱼可供烹食;以爵禄取人,人可竭尽其力;以家为基础而取国,国可为你所有;以国为基础而取天下,天下可全部征服。"

Shang Dynasty, Zhou Dynasty

"For many generations, with much exuberance, the vast Shang Dynasty has gathered much wealth and achieved prosperity but in the end it will all evaporate. Quietly the Zhou Dynasty has laid a foundation for a future greatness that will brightly shine in all directions. It is subtle and mysterious. That is how the Sage attracts the hearts of people, subtly, through his virtues. The plans of the Sage wondrously provide that the desires of all will be met, that everyone gets what he seeks; thus the ruler achieves his goals by embracing the people.

太公慨叹地说:"幅员广大、历代多代的[商王朝],它所积聚起来的东西,终归要烟消云散。不声不响,暗中准备的[周国],它的光辉必定会普照四方。微妙啊!
圣人的德化,就在于独创地、潜移默化地收揽人心。欢乐啊!圣人考虑的事情,就在于使人人各得其所,从而建立起收揽人心的方法。"

Gaining the Kingdom and Populace

King Wen asked: "How can a ruler embrace the people in such a manner that they will give him their allegiance?"

Jiāng Zǐyá said: "This cannot be done by a single means but by constantly showing the Way of Heaven to all people. A ruler who shares the wealth of the kingdom with all the people will gain the kingdom. A ruler who monopolizes the profits will lose the kingdom. All Heaven has its four seasons, and the Earth its resources. A ruler capable of sharing the resources with people is truly benevolent. Whenever a ruler has true benevolence, all under Heaven will give him their allegiance. A ruler; who saves the people from dangers, eliminates their hardships, relieves their misfortunes; is a virtuous ruler. Whenever a ruler has true virtue, all under Heaven will give him their allegiance. A ruler, who shares weals and woes, likes and dislikes with the people; is righteous ruler. The people will follow a righteous ruler. All people fear death and take pleasure in life. They appreciate virtue and pursue profit. Helping all the people become prosperous is the Way of Heaven. Whenever a ruler walks the Way, all under Heaven will give him their allegiance."

King Wen bowed and said: "This is true wisdom. I dare not refuse Heaven's edict and mandate." He then invited Jiāng Zǐyá to return with him in his chariot to his palace and henceforth be his teacher.

文王问："制定什么样的收揽人心的方法才能使天下归心呢？"
太公说："天下不是一个人的天下，而是天下人的天下。能和天下人同享天下利益的，就可以取得天下；独占天下利益的，就会失掉天下。天有四时，地有财富，能和人民共同享受的，就是仁爱，谁有仁爱，天下就归顺谁。免除人们的死难，解决人们的困难，消除人们的祸患，解救人们危急的，就是恩德，谁施恩德，天下就归顺他。和人民同忧同乐，同好同恶的，就是道义，谁讲道义，天下就归附谁。人们都厌恶死亡而乐于生存，欢迎恩德而追求利益，能使天下人都获得利益的，就是王道，谁实行王道天下就归顺谁。"
文王再一次拜谢以后，说："先生讲的太恰当了，我怎能不接受上天的旨意呢！"
于是，把太公请上车一起回到国都，并拜他为师。

Fullness and Emptiness

King Wen asked Jiāng Zǐyá: "In the world there are many different states in many divergent conditions, some full, others empty, some ordered and others in chaos. What causes these differences? Are they the result of differences in the moral character of the rulers? Or are they the result of natural changes and transformation of Heaven (astrology)?"

Jiāng Zǐyá answered: "When a ruler lacks moral character, then his state will be in danger and the affairs of the people will be in chaos. When a ruler has strong moral character, then his state will be secure and peaceful and the affairs of the people will be well-ordered. The fortune and misfortunes of the state depend on the character of its ruler, not with natural changes and transformation of Heaven."

King Wen said: "It would please me to hear more about the Sages of antiquity."

Jiāng Zǐyá said: "When Emperor Yao[1] governed the kingdom, people referred to him as a worthy ruler."

King Wen asked: "How did he govern the kingdom?"

Jiāng Zǐyá replied: "When Emperor Yao ruled the world, he did not bother with personal adornments of gold, silver, pearls and jade. He did not bother with clothes that were brocaded, embroidered or elegantly decorated. He did not bother with collecting strange, rare or unusual things. He did not bother with idle amusements or licentiousness. He did not bother with lavishly decorating the palace or the state buildings. He did not even bother to trim the reeds that grew about his courtyard. He wore a deerskin robe and simple clothes to cover his body and ward off the cold. He ate coarse food: unpolished grain and thick soup made from ordinary vegetables. He was careful not to disturb the labor of the people or disrupt the seasons for agriculture and sericulture with conscription. He moderated his own personal desires, curbed own his willfulness and directed the affairs of state with minimal interference in the everyday affairs of the people.

"He honored those officials who upheld the laws, who were loyal, honest and of high integrity, and gave them generous salaries. He showed his love and respect for those among the people who were filial and compassionate. He comforted and encouraged those who labored in agriculture and sericulture. He distinguished virtuous from the evil by honoring the virtuous. He promoted fair laws and strong enforcement to prohibit artifice and to promote virtuousness.

"If there was someone with merit who he personally disliked, in spite of his dislike, he would still reward him. If there was someone guilty of wrongdoing who he loved, in spite of his love, he would still punish him. He saw to the needs of the widows, orphans and solitary elders. He gave aid and restitution to those who had suffered misfortune.

"The resources he allotted to himself were very meager. The taxes and services he required of his people were very small. As a result the whole country was prosperous and happy and never suffered from hunger and cold. The people revered him. They looked upon him as if he were the sun and moon and gave their allegiance to him as if he were truly their father."

King Wen nodded and said: "Great indeed is the worthy and virtuous ruler!"

文王问太公说："天下纷杂，有时强盛，有时衰弱，有时安定，有时混乱，会这样，是什么原因？是君主贤与不贤的关系呢，还是天命变化的结果呢？"

---

[1] Emperor Yao (堯) (c. 2356 BCE – 2255 BCE) was a legendary Chinese ruler, one of the Three Sovereigns and the Five Emperors.

太公说："君主不贤则国家危亡而人民变乱；君主贤明则国家太平而人民安定。所以国家祸福在于君主贤与不贤，而不在于天命的变化。"
文王说："可以把古时圣贤君主的事迹讲给我听听吗？"
太公说："从前帝尧统治天下，上古的人都称他是贤君。"
文王说："他是怎样治理国家的？"
太公说："帝尧为君主时，不用金银珠玉装饰，不穿锦绣华丽的衣服，不观赏珍贵稀奇的物品，不珍藏古玩宝器，不听淫佚的音乐，不粉饰宫廷墙垣，不雕饰甍桷椽楹，不修剪庭院茅草，以鹿裘御寒，以布衣遮体，吃粗粮饭，喝野菜汤，不因劳役而误农时，约束心志而从事清静无为。官吏中忠正守法的，就升迁爵位，廉洁爱民的
就增加禄。人民中有孝敬父母、抚爱幼小的就敬重他；尽力从事农桑的就慰勉他。区别善恶良莠，表彰善良人家，提倡公正节操，以法制禁止奸邪诈伪。对厌恶的人，他有功必赏；对喜爱的人，他有罪必罚。赡养鳏寡孤独的人，救济祸患伤亡的家。至于帝尧自己则是生活俭朴，征用赋税劳役很少，所以天下万民富足安乐而没
有饥寒的面容。百姓爱戴他象景仰日月一样，亲近他象亲近父母一样。"
文王说："伟大呀！帝尧这位贤君的德行！"

Affairs of State

King Wen said to Jiāng Zǐyá: "I would like to learn more about properly administering the affairs of state. I wish to be an honorable ruler who has the respect of the people in a peaceful land. What should I do?"

Jiāng Zǐyá said: "Love the people."

King Wen asked: "What do you mean: love the people?"

Jiāng Zǐyá said: "Act in the interest of the people; do not harm them. Protect their lives; do not kill them. Help them prosper; do not rob them. Promote their welfare; do not burden them. Give them happiness; do not cause anger. Grant them cause to have joy; do not create sorrow

King Wen asked: "Can you explain the reason in this?"

Jiāng Zǐyá replied: "When the ruler helps the people maintain productive positions in society, he has profited them. When the farmers can attend to the necessary labor for each season, he has helped them to produce. When the ruler reduces punishments and fines, he has given them a better life. When he has imposed only light taxes, he has given them grants. When a ruler keeps expenditures for his palaces, mansions, terraces and pavilions to a minimum, and allows the people to spend instead on their needs, he gives them happiness. When his officials are not corrupt, cruel or capricious, he makes the people happy.

"But if the ruler allows the people lose their productive positions in society, he has harmed them. If the farmers are not able to attend to the seasons duties, he has destroyed them. If the people are innocent but he punishes them, he has slain them. If the ruler imposes heavy taxes, he robs them. If the ruler builds numerous palaces, mansions, terraces and pavilions, thereby diminishing the people's strength, he has made it bitter for them. If his officials are corrupt, cruel and capricious, he makes the people angry."

"Thus, the ruler who excels at administering the affairs of state governs the people the way parents treats their beloved children, as an older brother treats his beloved younger brother, with tenderness. When he sees that the people suffer from hunger and cold, he is troubled for them. When he sees them in distress and suffering, he grieves for them.

"A ruler should impose rewards and punishments as if he were imposing them upon himself. He should impose taxes as if he were imposing them on himself. This is the way he loves the people."

文王问太公道：我想知道治国的根本道理，想要使君主受到尊敬，人民得到安宁，应当怎么办呢？
太公说：惟有爱民罢了！
文王说：应当怎样爱民呢？
太公说：要给与人民利益而不要损害他们，要促进人民生产而不要破坏他们，要保护人民的生命而不要杀害他们，要给与人民实惠而不要掠夺他们，要使人民安乐而不使他们痛苦，要使人民喜悦而不使他们愤怒。
文王说：请你再解释一下其中的道理！
太公说：不使人民失去职业，就是给了人民利益；不耽误农时，就是促进了人民的生产；不惩罚无罪的人，就是保护了人民的生命；少收赋税，就是给了人民实惠；
少建宫室台榭，就能使人民安乐；官吏清廉不苛扰盘剥，就能使人民喜悦。反之，如果使人民失去职业，就是损害了他们的利益；耽误农时，就是破坏了他们的生
产；人民无罪而妄加惩罚，就是杀害；对人民横征暴敛，就是掠夺；多修建宫室台榭，就会增加人民的痛苦；官吏贪污苛扰，就会使人民愤怒。
所以善于治国的君主，统驭人民要象父母爱护子女，兄长爱护弟妹那样，见其饥寒扰为他忧虑，见其劳芳就为他悲痛，施行赏罚就象自己身受赏罚一样，征收赋税就象夺取自己的财物一样。这些就是爱民的道理。

Great Forms of Propriety - Forms of Propriety between Ruler and Officials

King Wen asked Jiāng Zǐyá: "What is the proper form of behavior between a ruler and his officials?"

Jiāng Zǐyá replied: "A ruler should try to understand and appreciate the circumstances facing his officials and his people. The officials should be respectful and dutiful. To understand his officials and his people, the ruler should try to be close to them. For the officials to be dutiful, they should not conceal anything from their ruler.

"The ruler should be benevolent. The officials should wholeheartedly perform their official duties to the best of their abilities. The benevolence of the ruler should be all encompassing, like the Heaven. The determination of the officials in the performance their duties should be as solid as the Earth. One Heaven, one Earth; that is how propriety should be observed."

文王问太公说：君主与臣民之间的礼法怎样呢？
太公说：作为君王最重要是能洞察下情，作为臣民，最重要是能谦恭驯服。君主要洞察下情，就不能疏远臣民；臣民要谦恭驯服，就不能隐瞒意见。君主要普施恩德，臣下要安分守职。普施恩德，要象天空那样覆盖万物；安分守职，要象大地那样稳重厚实。君主效法天，臣下效法地，这就构成了君臣之间的礼法。

Great Forms of Propriety - Disposition of the Ruler

King Wen asked: "How should a powerful ruler comport himself?"

Jiāng Zǐyá replied: "His manner should be tranquil and composed. He should be dignified and soft-spoken. He should be courteous and open to the advice of his officials. He should be unbiased and selfless. He should be courteous, fair and just in his treatment of all his subjects and in conducting the affairs of state."

文王问：君主应该怎样临朝执政呢？
太公说：君主要安详稳健而气质宁静，要柔和有节而胸有成竹，要善于与臣民协商问题而不固执已见，对人要谦虚而无私，处事要公正而不偏。

Great Forms of Propriety - Listening to Options

King Wen asked: "How should a ruler deal with advice about the affairs of state?"

Jiāng Zǐyá replied: "He should give all advice his most careful consideration. He should not casually accept or reject any advice. Casually accepting advice makes a ruler appear apathetic. Casually rejecting advice makes it difficult to obtain needed advice in the future. In his reflections, the ruler should appear as a high mountain; when looked up to, its height cannot be perceived. The ruler should appear as a deep abyss; its depth cannot be fathomed. When he deliberates a ruler should be enlightened, composed and just; that is the ideal."

文王问：君主应该怎样倾听意见呢？

太公说：不要轻率接受，不要简单拒绝。轻率接受，容易丧失主见；反面拒绝，容易闭塞言路。君主要象高山那样，使人仰慕效法，要象深渊那样，使人莫测其深。英明正确，镇静公正，就是准则。

Great Forms of Propriety - Improving Wisdom

King Wen asked: "How can a ruler achieve wisdom?"

Jiāng Zǐyá replied: "He must use all his senses to the utmost. He must use his eyes to see clearly. He must use his ears to hear acutely. He must use his mind for deep deliberations. When he uses his eyes to see clearly, there is nothing under heaven that will be invisible to him. When he uses his ears to hear acutely, there is nothing under heaven that he will not hear. When he uses his mind for deep deliberations, there is no detail under heaven that will escape his consideration. Just as the spokes that converge on the hub of a wheel, his senses will be focused and he will know all."

文王问：君主怎样才能洞察一切呢？

太公说：眼睛贵在能看清事物，耳朵贵在能听到消息。头脑贵在能考虑周详。如能使天下人的眼睛都去看，就没有看不见的事物；使天下人的耳朵都去听，就没有听不到的消息；使天下人的心思都去考虑，就没有考虑不周的事情。四面八方的情况都汇集到君主那里，君主自然就能洞察一切而不受蒙蔽了。

Lessons from Sages

King Wen was in bed, seriously ill. He summoned Jiāng Zǐyá and the Crown Prince to his side. With a sigh, he said: "Heaven is about to abandon me. Zhou's state affairs will soon be entrusted to you. Today I hope that you, my teacher, can discuss some great principles that I can pass down to my future generations."

Jiāng Zǐyá said: "My King, what do you wish to know?"

King Wen asked: "I would like to hear about the former Sages, how they fell, how they rose?"

Jiāng Zǐyá said: "If one sees 'good', but is remiss in doing it; if opportunity arises but action is not taken; if you know something is wrong, but never sanction it, these are the three conditions which caused the Sages to fall. If one is soft and quiet when treating himself, dignified and respectful when treating others, strong yet genial when handling things, tolerant and resolute when opportunities arise; these are the three principles which cause Sages to rise. Thus when righteousness overcomes the covetous, the state will flourish. When the covetous overcome the righteous, the state will fail. If cautiousness overcomes carelessness, it is good for the state. If carelessness overcomes cautiousness, the state is destroyed."

文王卧病在床，召见太公望，太子发也在床边，文王叹息说：唉！上天将要抛弃我了，周国的社稷，就托付给你。现在我想请你讲些至理名言，以便明确地传给子孙。
太公问：你要问什么呢？
文王说：先圣治国的至理名言，为什么被废弃，为什么能推行？其原因可以讲给我听吗？
太公说：见到善事却怠惰不为，时机到来却迟疑不决，知道不对却泰然处之，这三种情况就是先圣治国之理废弃的原因。能柔能静以待己，能恭能敬以待人，能强能弱以接物，能忍能刚以待机，这四种就是先圣治国之道能推行的原因。所以正义胜过私欲，国家就昌盛；私欲胜过正义，国家就衰亡；谨慎胜过懈怠，国家就吉祥； 懈怠胜过谨慎，国家就会灭亡。

Six Characteristics

King Wen asked Jiāng Zǐyá: "What circumstances could cause a ruler of the state to lose his position?"

Jiāng Zǐyá answered: "He is not fastidious about with whom he associates. The ruler should note the six characteristics when selecting capable men and three 'treasures' of the state."

King Wen asked: "What are these six characteristics?"

Jiāng Zǐyá explained: "The first is *benevolence*, the second is *righteousness*, the third is *loyalty*, the fourth is *trustworthiness*, the fifth is *courage*, the sixth is *strategizing*. These are the six characteristics to consider when selecting capable men."

King Wen asked: "How does one apply these criteria to selecting capable men?"

Jiāng Zǐyá replied: "Make him rich and observe whether he commits offenses. Place him in a high position and see if he becomes arrogant. Entrust him with high office and see how he remains. Present him with a problem to solve and see if he conceals anything. Put him in danger and see if he is becomes fearful. Require him to manage an emergency and see if he is handles it well."

"If he becomes wealthy and does not commit offenses, then he is benevolent. If he is placed in a high position but does not become arrogant, then he is righteous. If he is entrusted with high office and he remains obedient, then he is loyal. If he deals with the problem without concealing anything, he is trustworthy. If he is placed in danger and does not become fearful, then he is courageous. If he is required him to manage an emergency and handles it well, he is capable of making plans and strategizing. But, remember, the ruler cannot entrust the three 'treasures' to other people, otherwise he will lose his authority."

King Wen asked: "What are the 'three treasures'?"

Jiāng Zǐyá replied: "Agriculture, Production and Commerce are referred to as the 'three treasures'. If the farmers are gathered into districts, then grains will be plentiful. If the craftsmen are gathered into districts, then tools will be sufficient. If the merchants are gathered together, then material goods will be sufficient.

"If the 'three treasures' are settled each in their places, the populace will not worry. There will not be chaos in the districts, and also not be confusion among clans. The officials should not be richer than the ruler. No cities should be larger than the capital of the state. When the six characteristics are observed, the ruler will flourish. When the 'three treasures' are established, the state will be secure."

文王问太公道：统治国家和人民的君主为什么会失掉他的国家和民呢？
太公说：那是用人不慎的缘故。人君应当选拔具备六项德行标准人才和抓住三件重大的事情。
文王说：什么是具备六项标准的人才呢？
太公说：一是仁爱，二是正义，三是忠实，四是诚信，五是勇敢，六是智谋。这些就是所说的具备六项标准的人才。
文王问：怎样谨慎选拔符合六项标准的人才呢？
太公说：使他富裕，看他能否不逾越礼法；给他高位，看他能不骄不傲；付与他重大任务，看他是否能坚定不移地去完成；命他去处理问题，看他是否能不隐瞒欺骗；让他身临危难，看他能否临危不惧；使他处理突然事变，看他是否能应付自如。富裕而不逾越礼法的人，是仁爱的人；尊贵而不骄傲的人，是正义的人；能坚定不移地完成重大任务的人是忠实的人；处理问题能不隐瞒欺骗的人，是诚信的人；能够临危不惧的人，是勇敢的人；能对突然事变应付裕如的人，是有智谋的人。君主不要把处理三件大事的权力交给别人，交给别人，君主就丧失自己的权威。
文王问：你指的那三件大事呢？
太公说：这三件大事就是大农、大工、大商。把农民组织起来，聚居一乡，互助合作，粮食自然会充足；把工人组织起来，聚居一乡，互相协作，用具自然会充足；
把商人组织起来，聚居一乡，互通有无，财货自然会充足。三种行业，各得其所，人民无忧无虑。不要打乱这种区域经济，不要拆散他们家族组织。臣民不得富于君主，城邑不得大于国都。
具备六项标准的人才得到重用，国君的事业就会昌明隆盛；三种经济事业完善，国家就能长治久安。

Preserving Territories

King Wen asked Jiāng Zǐyá: "How does one preserve the integrity of the state's territory?"

Jiāng Zǐyá said: "Do not alienate your kinsmen. Do not neglect the people. Be friendly and courteous towards nearby states, and control all that is under you. Do not loan your authority of state to other men. If you loan your authority of state to other men, then you will lose it. Do not harm those of lower position to benefit those of higher position. Do not abandon the fundamental in favor of the inconsequential. At midday when the sun is shining brightly, you should dry things. When you grasp a knife, you must cut. When you raise an axe, you must attack.

"If, during the warmth of the day, you do not dry things out in the sun, this is a lost opportunity. If you grasp a knife but do not cut anything, you will lose the opportunity for gain. If you raise an axe and do not attack, your enemies will attack you.

"If small streams are not blocked, they will become great rivers. If you do not extinguish the smallest flames, you will be helpless when they turn into great fires. If you do not pull up the two-leaf sapling, you may someday have to use an axe to remove a great tree.

"Consequently, the ruler must develop wealth within his state. Without material wealth, he has nothing of value to spread beneficently or means to bring his relatives together. Should he alienate his relatives, it will cause harm. Should he loses the common people, he will lose his kingdom.

"You should not loan sharp weapons to others. If you loan out sharp weapons, you will be hurt by them, and will not live out your allotted span of years."

King Wen then asked: "What do you mean when you speak of 'benevolence and righteousness'?"

Jiāng Zǐyá replied: "Honor and respect the common people; assemble and unite your relatives. If you honor and respect the common people, they will be in harmony. And if you assemble and unite your relatives, they will be happy. This is the way to establish the essential cords of benevolence and righteousness.

"Do not allow other men to diminish or steal your authority. Rely on your natural wisdom, observe common conventions. Those who submit and defer to you should be treated generously and virtuously. Those who oppose you should be broken with force. If you honor and respect the people and trust them, the state will be peaceful and in harmony"

文王问太公说：应该怎样守卫国土呢？

太公说：不可疏远宗族，不可怠慢民众，安抚近邻，控制四方。治国大权不可旁落，大权旁落，君主就会失去威权。不要损下益上，不要舍本逐末。太阳到了正午，
要抓紧时机曝晒；拿起刀子就要抓时机宰割；拿起斧子就要抓紧时机砍伐。到了中午不曝晒就会丧失机；拿起刀子不宰割也会丧失时机；拿起武器不杀敌，反会被敌所害。细小的水流不堵塞，将会扩展成江河；微弱的火星不扑灭，将会酿成熊熊大火；刚萌芽的两片嫩叶不撷除，将来就必须用斧头去砍。所以君主必须讲求富国之道，国不富就谈不上行仁政，不行仁政就不能团结宗亲。疏远了宗亲就会受害，失去了人心就会失败。不要把统御国家的权力付托给别人，大权旁落，自己就会为人所害而身死国亡。

文王问：什么是仁义呢？

太公说：所谓仁、义就是尊重民意，团结宗亲。尊重民意就能得到人民拥护；团结宗亲就能得到他们的爱戴。这些就是行仁义的准则。不要让人篡夺了你的权力，要
根据自己的明察顺乎常理去处理事情。对于顺从你的人，要给与恩德而信任他，对于反对你的人要用武力消灭他。遵循上述原则不变，天下就会拥护而顺从了。

Preserving State

King Wen asked Jiāng Zǐyá: "How does a ruler preserve his state?"

Jiāng Zǐyá answered: "You should observe a vegetarian diet for seven days, and then I shall speak to you about the essential principles of Heaven and Earth, what the four seasons produce, the Way of true humanity and knowledge, and the nature of the people's impulses."

King Wen observed a vegetarian diet for seven days, then facing the north, bowed twice and requested Jiāng Zǐyá's teaching.

Jiāng Zǐyá said: "Heaven brings forth the four seasons; Earth produces the myriad of all things. Under Heaven, there are the people, and the Sage acts as their shepherd. The nature of spring is birth when the myriad of things begin to flourish. The nature of summer is growth when the myriad of things mature. The nature of autumn is gathering when the myriad of things are full. The nature of winter is storing away when the myriad of things are still. When they are full, they are stored away; after they are stored away, they again revive. No one knows where it ends; no one knows where it begins. The Sage accords with it and models things based on it. Thus when the realm is calm and well ordered, the benevolence and sagacity of the Sage are hidden. When the realm is disrupted and in turbulence, his benevolence and sagacity will be evident. This is the Way.

"In his special position between Heaven and Earth, the authority of the Sage is vast and substantial. If the Sage governs the people in a normal fashion, the people will be at peace. But should the people become agitated, this will create impulses. When impulses stir then conflict will arise, and there will then be a struggle for authority. The Sage will have gathered his forces and power in the dark, and when the opportunity arises, will come out. One, who ventures to be the first leader to overthrow tyranny and rid the land of evil, will unite all under Heaven with him. When things return to normal and become calm again, the ruler should not continue to strive, but instead be calm and hold fast. The ruler who thus preserves the state will share in the splendor of Heaven and Earth."

文王问太公道：怎样保卫国家呢？
太公说：请先行斋戒，然后再告诉你关于天地间事物运动的规律，四季万物生长的变化，圣人治国的道理，民心转变的根由。文王斋戒七天，以弟子礼再度拜问太公。
太公说：天有四时，地生万物。天下有人民，人民由圣王来治理他们。春天的规律是滋生，万物都欣欣向荣；夏天的规律是成长，万物都繁荣茂盛；秋天的规律是收
获，万物都饱满成熟；冬天的规律是收藏，万物都潜藏不动。万物成熟就应收藏起来，收藏起来[明年又]播种生长，[循环往复]是没有终点的，也没有起点。圣人可以参照这个规律，作为治理天下的普遍原则。
所以天下大治，仁人圣主就隐而不露；天下大乱，仁人圣主就拨乱反正，建功立业。这是必然的规律。
圣人处在天地间，他的地位作用是很大的。他按照常理教育人民，使人民安定。民心不安，就是动乱发生的原因，动乱一旦发生，天下就有权力得失之争了。这时圣人就秘密地发展力量，时机成熟就公开地进行讨伐。首先倡导除暴安民，天下必然响应。当形势已恢复正常时，既不要进而争功，也不要退而让位。这样守国，他的威望就可与天地同光了。

Honoring the Worthy

King Wen asked Jiāng Zǐyá: "Among my subjects, who among them should be elevated, who should be assigned inferior positions? Who should be selected for employment and who should be dismissed? Which activities should be banned and which need to be controlled?"

Jiāng Zǐyá said: "Elevate the Worthy and place those who are unworthy in inferior positions. Choose those who are sincere and trustworthy, eliminate those who are deceptive and artful. Throughout your realm you should prohibit violence and chaos, and put an end to extravagance and lethargy. Accordingly, the wise ruler recognizes the 'six hazards' and 'seven harms'."

King Wen said: "I would like to know more about these hazards and harms."

Jiāng Zǐyá said: "As for the 'six hazards': First, if your subordinates build extravagant mansions with pools and terraces, and they indulge themselves in idle pleasures and female companions, it will injure the King's honor.

"Second, when the people are not engaged in farming and silk production, but instead give rein to their poorer judgments, loiter about, disdain and transgress the laws and prohibitions, and are not following the instructions of the officials, it will injure the King's influence.

"Third, when officials form cliques and factions which obfuscate the worthy and wise, and obstruct the ruler from feeling the pulse of the state, it will injure the King's authority.

"Fourth, when scholars are contentious and pompously display 'high moral standards', assuming that such behavior is an expression of their disposition; when they have private relationships with other feudal lords, thereby slighting their own ruler, it will injure the King's military capability.

"Fifth, when subordinates are contemptuous of the administrators, disdain titles and positions, and are loath to face hardship for their ruler, it will injure the loyalty of meritorious subordinates to the king.

"Sixth, when the strong clans encroach upon the weak, wantonly seize what they will; when they insult and ridicule the poor and weak, it will injure the endeavors of the common people.

"As for 'the seven harms': First, those men who are without wisdom or strategic planning ability should not be rewarded and honored with rank; likewise, those who are strong and courageous, but who regard war lightly, and take unnecessary chances on the battlefield; men such as these, the King must be careful not to employ as his generals.

"Second, there are those who have a reputation but lack substance: Those who constantly waver in what they say and believe; those who conceal the good and spread the bad; those who always seek short-cuts; with men such as these the King should be careful not to entrust with his plans.

"Third, there are those who make their appearance simple, wear plain clothes, exhibit disregard for office in order to seek fame, exhibit disregard for wealth in order to gain profit. These are 'fakes' which the King should be careful to avoid.

"Fourth, there are those who wear strange adornments and their clothes are very elaborate. They listen often to the disputations of others and they speak speciously about unsound ideas, displaying them as a sort of personal ornamentation. They appear to dwell in poverty and live in tranquility while disparaging the customs of the world. These are cunning people and the King should be careful not to favor them.

"Fifth, there are those who with slander, obsequiousness and pandering seek office and rank. They tend to be reckless, treating death lightly, out of their greed for wealth and position. They are not moved by major affairs but respond solely out of avarice. With lofty talk and specious discussion, they will try to ingratiate themselves with the ruler. The King should be careful not to engage them.

"Sixth, there are those who have buildings elaborately carved and inlaid, who promote artifice and flowery adornment over the interests of agriculture and commerce. The king must impede them.

"Seventh, there are those who defraud the people, who practice sorcery and witchcraft, who advance unorthodox ways and circulate inauspicious sayings which befuddle good people. The King must stop them.

"If the people do not give their best, they are not our people. If the officers are not sincere and trustworthy, they are not our officers. If the ministers do not offer their loyalty, they are not our ministers. If the officials are not of high integrity and do not love the people, they are not our officials. If the chancellor cannot enrich the state and strengthen the army, harmonize yin and yang, ensure security for the ruler of the state with ten thousand chariots, properly control the ministers, establish targets and priorities, make clear rewards and punishments, and give pleasure to the people, he is not our chancellor.

"The Way of the King is like the head of a dragon. He dwells in the heights and looks out far. He sees deeply and listens carefully. He displays his form but conceals his nature. He is like the heights of Heaven, which cannot be perceived. He is like the depth of an abyss, which cannot be fathomed. Thus, if the ruler should have cause to be angry but does not become angry, evil subordinates will rise. If the ruler should execute the law but does not, chaos will appear. Thus the wise ruler knows that if strategic interests are not tended and military power is not exercised, enemy states will grow strong and bold."

"Excellent!" said King Wen.

文王问太公说：作为君主，应当尊崇什么人，抑制什么人，任用什么人，除去什么人，严禁什么事，制止什么事呢？
太公说：作为君王，应当推崇德才兼备的人，抑制无德无才的人，任用忠诚信实的人，除去奸诈虚伪的人。严禁暴乱的行为，制止奢侈的风气。所以君主用人时，应当警惕六种坏事，七种坏人。
文王说：我想听听这些道理！
太公说：所谓六种坏事就是：

第一，大臣中若有大修宫室池榭，搞游玩观赏，歌舞行乐的，就会败坏君主德政。
第二，人民中若有不从事农桑，意气用事，仿效游侠，违犯禁令，不服官吏教导的，就会败坏君主教化。
第三，群臣中若有营私结党，排挤贤智，蒙蔽君主开目的，就会损害君主权威。
第四，士民中若有自高自大，气焰嚣张，里通外国，不尊重君主的，就会损害君主威严。
第五，群臣中若有轻视爵位，藐视上级，并以替君主冒险犯难为耻辱的，就会打击功臣的积极性。
第六，强宗大族争相掠夺，欺压贫弱，就会损害人民生计。
所谓七种坏人就是：
第一，没有智略权谋，为了获得重赏高官，强横恃勇，轻率处战，企求侥幸立功的，君主切勿用他做将帅。
第二，有名无实，当面一套，背后一套，掩人之善，扬人之恶，到处钻营取巧的，君主必须慎重，不能与他共谋大事。
第三，外表朴素，衣着粗劣，自称"无为"，实是沽名，自称无欲，实是图利，这是虚伪的人，君主切不可亲近他。
第四，冠带奇特，衣着讲究，博闻善辩，空谈高论，以此装点门面，处在简陋僻静的地方，专门诽谤时俗，这是奸诈的人，君主切不可宠用他。
第五，谗言谄媚，不择手段，以求官爵；鲁莽拼命，不计后果，贪取俸禄；不顾大局，见利就行，高谈阔论，取悦人主，对于这种人君主切不要任用他。
第六，凡从事雕文刻镂、技巧华饰的奢侈工艺而妨害农业生产的人，君主必须加以禁止。
第七，用骗人的方术，奇特的技艺，巫蛊左道，符咒妖言，迷惑善良人民的人，君主必须禁止。
所以人民不尽力去务农，就不是好人民；士不忠诚，就不是好的士；臣不直谏，就不是好臣；官吏不公平廉洁爱护人民，就不是好官吏；宰相不能富国强兵，妥善处
理各项问题，确保君权的稳固，整饬群臣的纲纪，核查名实，严明赏罚，使万民乐业，这就不是好宰相。做君主的方法要象龙头一样，高瞻远瞩，洞察一切，深刻地
观察问题，审慎地听取意见，仪表庄严肃穆，衷情隐而不露。使人觉得他象天那样高而不可穷极，象渊那样深而不可测量。因此，君主对应该斥责的人不加斥责，奸
臣就会兴风作浪；当杀的而不杀，大乱随着就会发生，当用兵讨伐而不讨伐，敌国就会强大起来。
文王说：好啊！

Promoting the Worthy

King Wen asked Jiāng Zǐyá: "How does it happen that a ruler exerts himself to advance the Worthy but is unable to obtain any results from such efforts, and in fact, the world grows increasingly chaotic, even to the point that he is endangered or perishes?"

Jiāng Zǐyá answered: "If one advances the Worthy but does not actively employ them, this is attaining the 'advancing the Worthy' in principle but lacks the substance of 'advancing the Worthy.'"

King Wen asked: "Where then is the error?"

Jiāng Zǐyá said: "The error lies in employing men who are popularly praised rather than employing men who are truly Worthy."

"How is that so?" King Wen asked.

Jiāng Zǐyá replied: "If the ruler takes those who the world commonly praises as being Worthy and those who the world condemns as being worthless, then those in the larger cliques will advance, and those in the smaller ones will decline. If such a situation persists, groups of evil individuals will band together and obscure the Worthy. Loyal subordinates will perish even though they are innocent. Perverse subordinates will obtain rank and position through false reputations. In this way, if such chaos continues to persist in the world, the state will be in constant danger and cannot avoid destruction."

King Wen asked: "How then does one truly advance the Worthy?"

Jiāng Zǐyá replied: "Your chief general and your chancellor should divide the responsibility for selecting appropriate men, selecting then based on the requirements of the positions and the talents of the applicants. In accord with the requisites of the position, they will assess the substance required. In selecting men, they will evaluate their abilities, matching the talent with the position. When the requisite matches the reality, then the Way (the Tao) for advancing the Worthy will have been realized."

文王问太公说：君主致力于选用贤能，但又收不到实效，社会反而更加混乱，以致国家陷于危亡，这是什么道理呢？
太公说：选拔出贤能但不加以任用，这是有举贤的虚名，而无用贤的实效！
文王说：产生这种过失的原因在哪里呢？
太公说：其过失在于君主好用一般人所称赞的人，因而就得不到真正的贤人了。
文王说：为什么呢？
太公说：如果君主认为一般人所称赞的是贤人，一众人所诋毁的是不贤的人，那么党羽多的就会被任用，党羽少的就会被排挤。这样奸邪势力就会结党营私而埋没贤人，忠臣无罪而被置于死地，奸臣用虚名骗取爵位，所以社会愈加混乱，国家也就不能避免危亡了。

文王说：怎样举贤呢？

太公说：将相分工，根据各级官吏应具备的条件选拔贤能，再根据各种官职应具备的条件考核在职人员，甄别其才智的高低，考查其能力的强弱，使其德才与官位相称，官位与德才相当。这就掌握着举贤的原则与方法了。

Rewards and Punishment

King Wen addressed Jiāng Zǐyá: "Rewards are the means to encourage the good, and punishments the means to discourage evil. By rewarding one man, how may I stimulate a hundred, and by punishing one man, how may I rectify the multitude."

Jiāng Zǐyá replied: "In general, in employing rewards and punishments, credibility and certainty are essential. When reward is certain to be meted out for good deeds and punishments inevitable for bad ones, then wherever the eyes see and the ears hear, and even where they do not see or hear there will no one who will not believe in the inevitability of your justice. Since the ruler's sincerity must extend to Heaven and Earth and penetrate to the spirits, how much more so should it be to men?"

文王问太公说：奖赏是为了鼓励好人好事，惩罚是为了惩戒坏人坏事。我想奖赏一人以鼓励百人，惩罚一人以警戒众人，应该怎么办？

太公说：用赏贵在守信，用罚贵在必行。如能对于你所见、所闻的事都做到赏信罚必，那么，那些你所未见未闻的事，也都自然会潜移默化了。[赏信罚必就是诚信，]诚信可以畅行于天地，上达于神灵，何况对人呢！

Using Troops - Unity of Troops

King Wen asked Jiāng Zǐyá: "What is the correct way to employ troops?"

Jiāng Zǐyá said: "In general, of all the principles of employing troops, none surpasses unity. Unified troops can move like one entity, can depart like one entity. The Yellow Emperor said: 'Unification approaches the correct way of using troops and touches on the pinnacle of using troops.' Its employment lies in the seizing opportunity; its manifestation lies in the disposition; its success lies with the ruler. Thus the Kings from antiquity termed weapons evil implements, and only when they had no alternatives, did they employ them.

"Although the Shang Emperor knows about existence, he knows not about perishing. He knows pleasure but not disaster. The secret of existence does not lie in existence, but in understanding perishing. The secret of pleasure does not lie in pleasure but in understanding disaster. Now that you have already considered the sources of such changes, why should you concern yourself with the future flow of events?"

文王问太公道：用兵的规律是什么呢？
太公说：一般用兵的规律，没有比统一意志更为重要的了，军队能统一意志，就能行动自由[所向无敌]了。黄帝说："军队意志统一就基本符合了战争的规律，就几乎能用兵如神。"运用这种[统一意志的]力量在于不失时机，发挥这种力量在于因势利导，能否具有这种力量，都在于君主的所作所为。所以古代圣王把战争称为凶器，只在不得已时才使用它。
当今商王只知道其国家还存在，而不知他已面临危亡；只知纵情享乐，而不知他已面临祸殃。国家能否长存，在于能否居安思危；君主能否长乐，在于能否乐不忘忧。现在你已思虑到存亡的根本问题，还忧虑什么枝节问题呢？

Using Troops - Deceptions to Gain Upper Hand

King Wen said: "In the event that two armies should directly encounter each other, when the enemy cannot come forward and we cannot go forward. Each side will normally go about establishing fortifications and defenses without daring to be the first to attack. If I should wish to launch an attack, but lack sufficient advantage, what should I do?"

Jiāng Zǐyá said: "You should make an outward display of confusion while making sure to actually be well-ordered; Show an appearance of hunger while actually being well-fed; Make an outward display of lacking fighting spirit, but rally and maintain the highest morale; Have some troops come together, others split up; some assemble, others scatter to create an outward display of lacking discipline; Make secret plans and keep your intentions a mystery; Raise the height of fortifications, and conceal your elite troops for ambush purposes. If the officers and men are quiet and not heard to making any sounds, the enemy will not know of our preparations. Then we can implement the strategy: 'Feign an attack in the east and attack in the west'."

King Wen said: "Should the enemy know of our true situation and have a thorough knowledge of our plans, what should I do?"

Jiāng Zǐyá said: "The main technique for military conquest is to carefully investigate the enemy's intentions and quickly take advantage of them, such as; launching a sudden attack where it is least expected."

文王说：两军相遇，敌人不能来攻我，我亦不能去攻敌人，双方均设置坚固的守备，谁都不敢率先行动，我想袭击他，又没有有利的条件，这时该怎么办呢？
太公说：[在这种情况下]要外面假装混乱，而内部实际严整；表面伪装缺粮，而实际储备充足；军队实际战斗力强，而装着战斗力弱。使军队或合或离

[假装没有节制]，或聚或散[假装没有纪律]。要隐匿计谋，秘密企图，高筑壁垒，埋伏精锐，隐蔽静肃，使敌不知道我的企图，以便声东击西。

文王说：敌人若已知道我的情况，了解我的计谋，怎么办呢？

太公说：作战取胜的方法，在于周密察明敌情，抓住有利的时机，而出其不意地打击它。

Chapter 2 - Military Teaching
Opening Instructions - When to Start a War

King Wen summoned Jiāng Zǐyá to the capitol: "Alas! The Shang King is extremely perverse. He judges the innocent guilty and has them executed. I would like to assist the people and rectify this evil, how should I proceed?"

Jiāng Zǐyá replied: "You should cultivate your virtue and morals, submit to the guidance of Worthy men, extend beneficence to the people, and through this extension, make an observation of the ground sentiments. If sentiment is at its worst, you cannot initiate the movement to revolt. If there is chaos in the society, your planning cannot precede it. Only when there are chaos and misfortune from nature and in society, then and only then can you make plans. You must look at the Shang King's public performance, and his behavior when not under the public eye, and only then will you know his mind. You must look at his external activities, and also his internal activities, and only then will you know his thoughts. You must observe who he distances himself from and who he gets close to, and only then will you know his true feelings."

文王在酆召见太公，说：唉！商纣王暴虐到了极点，随意杀害无罪的人，请你帮助我拯救天下人民，你看怎么办呢？
太公说：君主先要修德，要礼贤下士，要施惠于民，以观察天道的吉凶，当天道还没有灾害征兆的时候，不可先倡导征讨；人道没有出现祸乱的时候，不可先策划兴师。必须看到既出现了天灾，又发生了人祸时，才可以策划征伐。[必须全面地分析情况，]既要看到他公开的言行，还要看到他秘密的活动，才能知道他的想法；
既要看到他表面的行动，又要看到他内部的谋划，才能了解他的意图；既要看到他疏远什么人，也要看到他亲近什么人，才能掌握他情感上的倾向性。

Uniting the Whole State

"If you apply the principles of Tao (the Way), the Way will be attained. If you apply the correct action, the correct result will be attained. If you establish the proper forms of administration, proper policies and systems can be effected and implemented easily. If you use your full strength, the strong can be conquered. If you can achieve victory without fighting, then your army will not suffer any losses, you will have entered into the realm of ghosts and spirits. How marvelous! How subtle!

"If you are one with the people and suffer the same maladies, you and they will aid each other; if you share the same ambitions, you will help each other succeed; if you have the same likes and dislikes you will seek them out together. In this way, without employing soldiers you will win; without using any battering rams, you will have attacked, without digging any moats and ditches, you will have defended."

执行吊民伐罪的政治主张就可取得成功；遵循统一天下的路线前进，统一的目的就可达到；顺应民意以建立军队和国家的制度，新的制度就能建立起来；争取建立优势力量，就可用于战胜强大的敌人。战争取得全胜而不必经过战斗，使全军没有伤亡，真可谓用兵如神了。微妙啊！微妙啊！能与人同疾苦就能互相救援，同理想就能互相成全，同憎恶就能互相帮助，同爱好就有共同的追求。这样，就是没有军队也能取胜，没有冲车、机弩也能进攻，没有沟垒也能防守。

Governing the State

"The wise should act unwise; the greatest plans seem as though not planned at all (secrecy); the greatest courage is not courage alone; the greatest gain is not to profit on your own. If you profit all under you, all will open themselves to you, accepting you. If you harm all under you, all under you will be closed from you. All under Heaven is not the property of one man but of all under Heaven. If you want all under Heaven, it is as if pursuing some wild animal, and then all under Heaven will want a piece of meat. It is similar to you and all under you riding in the same boat to cross over the water, after completing the crossing you will all have profited. However, if you fail to make the crossing, then you will all suffer the harm. If you act as if you're all on the same vessel, the empire will be open to your aim and none will be closed to you.

"He, who does not take from the people, takes the people. He, who does not take from the state, takes the state. He, who does not take from anything under Heaven, will take all under Heaven. He who does not take from the people, the people will profit. He who does not take from the states, states will profit. He who does not take from all under Heaven, all under Heaven will profit. Such actions lie in being unseen; such affairs lie in being unheard; and victory lies in what cannot be known. How marvelously subtle!"

有大智的人不夸耀他的智慧，有深谋的人不暴露他的谋略，有大勇的人不只凭血气之勇，图大利的人不只顾自己利益。为天下谋利益的天下人都欢迎他，使天下人受害的，天下人都反对他。天下不是那一个人的天下，而是天下人的天下。想取得天下的人，就象猎取野兽一样，天下人都有分享猎物的心，也好象同船渡河一样，渡过了，大家就达到了共同的目的；失败了，大家都受害。这样做，天下人都只有欢迎他的理由而没有反对他的理由了。不掠夺人民利益的，可以取得人民的拥护；不掠夺别国利益的，可以取得别国的拥护；不掠夺天下利益的，可以取得天下的拥护。不掠夺人民利益的人，人民归向你，这是人民给你的利益；不掠夺别国利益的，别国归向你，这是别国给你的利益；不掠夺天下利益的，天下人归向你，这是天下人给你的利益。所以这种方法妙在使人不可见，事机秘密妙在使人不可闻，胜利妙在使人不可知。真是微妙呀！微妙呀！

The Demised State

"When an eagle is about to attack, it will fly low and draw in its wings. When a fierce wild cat is about to strike, it will lay back its ears and crouch down low. When the Sage is about to move, he will display a blank countenance.

"Now there is the case of Shang, where the people were confused and suspicious of each other. The Shang Emperor's indulgence in pleasure and sex were boundless.[2] This is a sign of a doomed state. I have observed their fields - weeds and grass overwhelm the crops. I have observed their people - the perverse and crooked overcome the honorable and upright. I have observed their officials - they are violent, perverse, inhumane and evil. They overthrow the laws and make chaos of the punishments. People from all ranks have not awakened to this state of affairs. It is time for their state to perish.

"When the sun appears, the myriad of all things is illuminated. When great righteousness appears, the myriad of all things will profit. When the great army appears, the myriad of all things will submit. Great is the virtue of the Sage! Listening by himself, seeing by himself, this is his pleasure!"

猛禽将要袭击目标，必先敛翅低飞；猛兽将要捕捉猎物，必先贴耳伏地；圣人将要采取行动，先示人以愚钝的样子。现在的商朝人民，疑虑相告，动乱不已，而商王仍然荒淫无度，这是亡国的征兆。我观察他的田地里，野草盖过了禾苗；我观察的群臣，荒诞邪僻的压倒了公平正直的；我观察他的官吏，都是暴虐残酷，违法乱刑，他们上下还执迷不悟，这是该亡国的时候了。日月当空就能普照万物，采取正义的行动对万民有利，大军出动就能使天下降服。伟大啊，圣人的德操，独到的见地，人所不及，自有乐在其中！

Civil Instructions - How a Sage Governs

King Wen asked Jiāng Zǐyá: "What does the Sage govern?"

Jiāng Zǐyá said: "What worries does he have? What constraints? The myriad of things will realize their positions naturally. What constraints, what worries? The myriad of things all flourish naturally. No one should realize the transforming influence of government, similar to how no one realizes the effects of the passing of time. The Sage takes 'action-less' action and the myriad of things are transformed. What is exhausted? When things reach the end, they return again to

---

[2] King Zhou (紂王) was the pejorative posthumous name given to Di Xin (帝辛) or Emperor Xin, the last king of the Shang Dynasty. He may also be referred to by adding "Shang" (商 Shāng) in front of any of his names. Note that Zhou (紂) is a completely different character from the "Zhou" (周) used by the succeeding Zhou Dynasty. In Chinese, 紂 also refers to the part of a saddle or harness most likely to be soiled by the horse.

the beginning. Relaxed and complacent, he turns about seeking it. Seeking it, he gains it and must store it. Having already stored it, he cannot but implement it. Having already implemented it, he does not turn about and make it clear that he did so. Now because Heaven and Earth need not let everyone know how they work, they are forever able to give birth to the myriad of things. The Sage does not pronounce what he is doing and he is able to attain a glorious name."

文王问太公说：圣人治理天下应该遵循什么原则呢？
太公说：圣人无需去忧虑什么，也无需去制止什么，万物自会各得其所；不去制止什么，不去忧虑什么，万物自会繁荣滋长。政令的推行，要使人们在不知不觉中潜移默化，就象时间在不知不觉中自然推移一样。圣人遵循无为而治的原则，万物被他潜移默化，就象四季推移一样，周而复始，永无穷尽。从容优闲，无为而治的思想，君主必须反复探索；既已探索到了，那就不可不存之于心中；既已存于心中，那就不可不在政治上去实行；既已实行了，也就无需明告于天下。因为天地并不须宣告自己的规律，而万物就自会按其规律长生；圣人也不须宣告无为而治的思想，而自会显示出其辉煌的成就。

Civil Instructions - Three Greats of Governance

"The Sages of antiquity assembled people together as families, assembled families to compose states, and assembled states to constitute the realm of all under Heaven. They divided the realm and enfeoffed worthy men to administer the states. They officially designated this order the 'Great Order'.

"They promulgated the government's instructions and accorded with the people's customs. They transformed the multitude of 'crooked' behaviors into 'straight', changing their form and appearance. Although the customs of various states were not the same, they all took pleasure in their respective places. The people loved their rulers, so they termed this transformation as the 'Great Settlement'.

"Ah, the Sage concentrates on educating and transforming without notice, the Worthy focus on rectifying themselves. The stupid man cannot be transformed, others cannot rectify him, therefore he contends with other men. When the ruler creates too many rules, punishments become excessive. When punishment is excessive, the people are troubled. When the people are troubled, they leave and wander off. No one, of whatever position, can be settled in his life, and generations on end have no rest; this they termed the 'Great Loss'."

古时圣人把人们聚集起来组成家庭，把许多家庭组成国家，把许多国家组成天下；分封贤人为各国诸侯，把这种制度叫做"大纪"。然后宣扬政教，顺应民俗，把邪僻行为化育为正直的风气，以移风移俗；各国之习俗虽不相同，但各自都喜爱本土，人人都敬其长上，这叫做"大定"。唉，圣王用清静无为的政治来治理天下，贤君用正己正人的规范来治理国家，愚君既不能正己又不能正人，所以与氏相手；君主政令烦多，就会使用多种刑罚；刑多，人民就会忧惧；民惧，就会流散逃亡。上下不安生业，长期动乱不休，这叫做"大失"。

Civil Instructions - Governing the Populace

"The people of the world are like flowing water. If you obstruct the water, it will stop. If you open a way, it will flow. If it is quiet, it will be clear. How spiritual! When the Sage sees the beginning, he knows the end."

King Wen asked: "How does one be at harmony with them?"

Jiāng Zǐyá said: "Heaven has its constant forms and the people have their normal lives. If you work together with them, then the relationship will be tranquil. The pinnacle is to accord with them, the next-highest is to transform them. When the people are transformed, and follow their government, then affairs can be completed, even when no actions are taken. The people are enriched, even if no one gives to them. This is the virtue of the Sage."

King Wen said: "I agree with all that you have said. From dawn until midnight, I will think about it, never forgetting it, employing it as our constant principle."

天下人心的向背象流水一样，阻塞它就停止，开放它就流动，不搅动它就保持清彻。哦!人心变化真是神妙莫测！有圣人看到它的萌芽，就能推断它的结果。
文王说：怎样使天下安静呢？
太公说：天有一定的变化规律，人有经常从事的生业，能与人民：共安生业，天下就会安静。最好的政治是顺应人心来治理人民，其次；是宣扬政教以感化人民。人民被潜移默化而服从政令，上天"无为"却能生长万物，人民也不需要施与，生活自能富裕，这就是圣人的德政。
文王说：你说的深合我意，我一定朝思夕念，永志不忘，用它作为治理天下的原则。

Civil Offense

King Wen asked Jiāng Zǐyá: "What are the methods of civil offense tactics?"

Jiāng Zǐyá replied: "There are 12 methods of civil offense tactics."

"In regard to your target: First, accord with what he likes in order to accommodate his wishes. This will feed his arrogance and he will invariably mount some perverse plan. We can then use the situation to our advantage and be able to eliminate him.

"Second, be close with those he loves in order to fragment his reputation. When men have two different inclinations, their primary loyalty invariably declines. When his court no longer has any loyal ministers, the state will inevitably be endangered.

"Third, bribe his assistants; secretly foster a deep relationship with them. While they stand in his court physically, their thoughts and inclinations will be directed outside it. The state will certainly suffer harm.

"Fourth, foster his licentiousness and his indulgence in entertainment in order to dissipate his will. Present to him generous gifts of pearls and jade, ply him with beautiful women. Speak deferentially, listen respectfully, follow his commands, and agree with him in everything. He will never imagine you might be in conflict with him and will unleash his treacherous ways.

"Fifth, treat the ruler's loyal officials generously, but reduce your gifts to the ruler. When the ruler himself comes as emissary, delay him, appeal to his vanity but do not actually assist him. When he sends other men as emissaries, treat them with sincerity, embrace and demonstrate trust in them. The ruler will then again feel you are in harmony with him. If you can to obtain the loyalty of his officials by treating them generously, his state can then be plotted against.

"Sixth, make secret alliances with his most respected ministers. Sow discord between the ruler and his officials who are not in court. Make it advantageous for his talented people assist other enemy states. Entice other enemy states to encroach upon his territory. Few states have faced such a situation and survived.

"Seventh, if you wish to obtain his trust, you must offer him generous gifts. Gather in his assistants, loyal associates and loved ones, by secretly showing them the gains they can realize by allying with you. Have his assistants slight their work, and then his preparation will be futile.

"Eighth, present him with great treasures, and pretend to conspire with him. When your plans are successful and profit him, he will have faith in you because of his profits. This is what is called 'being closely embraced'. The result of being closely embraced is that he can be easily manipulated. When someone rules a state but is externally manipulated, he will inevitably be defeated.

"Ninth, honor him and praise him. Avoid anything that will cause him personal discomfort. Display the proper respect owed to a great power, and you will surely be trusted. Glorify and praise him; magnify his image; proclaim his virtues; humbly embellish him as a Sage. Then his state will suffer great misfortune.

"Tenth, be courteous and submissive to him so that he will trust you. Thereby you may learn about his true situation. Embrace his ideas and respond to his affairs as if you were his brother. Once you have achieved full knowledge of his affairs, you can subtly control him. Thus, when the time comes, it will seem as if all Heaven wants him to be destroyed.

"Eleventh, disrupt his channels of information. There will be found no one among his subordinates who does not value rank and wealth or hate danger and misfortune. Secretly express great respect towards them, and gradually bestow valuable gifts in order to subvert his best talent. Build your own resources until they become very substantial, but present an appearance of shortage. Secretly bring in wise and able counselors, and entrust them with planning great strategy. Attract courageous generals, and encourage their fighting spirit. Even when they are adequately rich and honored, continue to add to their riches. When your faction has been fully established, you will have attained the objective of 'blocking his information channels'. If one is the head of a state, but his information channels are blocked, how can he control his state?

"Twelfth, support his self-indulgent and immoral officials in order to confuse him. See that he is provided beautiful women and licentious music in order to befuddle him. Send him hunting dogs and outstanding horses in order to tire him. From time to time, allow him to exercise great power in order to entice him to greater arrogance. Then investigate his transgressions and plot with the world against him.

"By full implementation of these twelve methods, they will become a military weapon. Once the signs that your plans have been achieved are obvious, that is the time to attack."

文王问太公说：文伐的方法如何？
太公说：文伐的方法有十二种：
一是，依照敌人的喜好，顺从他的心愿，使他滋长骄傲情绪必会去做些邪恶的事情，我再巧妙地加以利用，就必能将他除掉。
二是拉拢敌君的近臣，以削弱敌国的力量。敌之近臣既然怀有二心，其忠诚程度必然降低。敌人朝中没有了忠臣，它的国家就必定处于危亡的境地。
三是，贿赂敌国的近臣，和他建立深厚的情谊，他们身居国内心向国外，敌国就必将发生祸害了。
四是，助长敌国君主过份的享乐行为，扩大他的荒淫意趣。用大量珠玉贿赂他，赠送美女讨好他。言词卑下，曲意听认。顺从其命令，迎合其心意。这样，他就忘记与我作斗争而放肆发展其邪恶的行为了。
五是，对敌国的忠臣要尊敬，少给他些礼物。他当使者前来交涉时，要故意拖延他，不要听从他的意见。极力促使敌君改派他人来替代，然后给他透露一些真实情况，表示亲近他信赖他以结友好。如能这样地用不同的方法去对待敌国忠臣与奸佞，就可以谋取他的国家了。
六是，收买敌国君主左右的大臣，离间他边远的大臣，使其有才干的大臣都帮助外国，再加以外国的入侵，这个国家就很少有不灭亡的了。

七是，要想使敌国君主对我深信不疑，就必须赠送他大量礼物，收买他左右亲信的大臣，暗中给他们好处，使其君臣忽视生产，造成其国家积蓄空虚。

八是，赠送敌国君以重宝，进而与他同谋别国，所图谋的又对他有利。由于对他有利，他必然信任我，这就密切了敌国君主与我的关系。关系越密切，敌国君主必为我所利用。他有国而被外国利用，其国必亡。

九是，用煊赫的名号颂扬他，不让他受到危难，给他势倾天下的感觉，必恭必敬地顺从他；以至高无上的名位尊崇他，先夸耀他的功绩显荣，再恭维他德比圣人，这样他必然会狂妄自大而对于国事懈怠废驰了。

十是，对他要表示恭顺诚信，以取得他的友情和信任；顺承他的意图办事，好象兄弟一般地亲密；既已得到他的友情和信任，就进一步微妙地控制他；时机一到，就象上天叫他灭亡一样而把他消灭了。

十一是，闭塞敌国君主视听的方法；凡是臣民没有不渴望富贵而厌恶危难与灾祸的，用暗中许给尊贵的官位，秘密送给大量财宝的方法，收买敌国的英雄豪杰。国内

积蓄很多，外表却装作穷困。暗中收纳智士以制定谋略；收纳勇士以提高士气。要满足他们取得富贵的愿望，而不断发展壮大，结成自己的党徒，聚集起力量。这样

做就能闭塞人的视听而秘密壮大自己了。敌人虽有国家，但耳目已为人所闭塞，那还能够保住他的国家呢？

十二是，扶植敌国的乱臣，以迷乱其君主的心智；进献美女淫声，以迷惑其君主的意志；送他良犬骏马，使他沉溺在犬马游猎之中而神形疲惫；又常报以有利的形势，使他高枕无忧；然后，观察有利时机与天下人共谋而奇取他的国家。

以上十二种计谋能善为运用，就可成全武功。所谓上察天时，下察地利，等到各种有利的征侯都已显露时，就可举兵征伐了。

According with the People

King Wen asked Jiāng Zĭyá: "What should one do so that he can best govern the populace?"

Jiāng Zĭyá said: "When your greatness spreads over all the populace, only then will you be able to govern it completely. When your trustworthiness spreads over the populace, only then will you be able to make covenants with it. When your benevolence spreads over the populace, only then will you be able to embrace it. When your grace has spread over the populace, only then can you preserve it. When your authority covers the populace, only then will you be able not to lose it. Govern without doubt, similar to the revolutions of Heaven or the changes of the seasons; nothing can change them. Only when these six are complete will you be able to establish complete governance over the populace.

"Accordingly, one who profits the populace will find them open to him. One who harms the populace will find them closed to him. If one gives life to the populace, they will regard him as virtuous. If one kills the populace, they will want to be rid of him. If one acts in accordance with the wishes of the populace, they will be accessible to him; if one impoverishes the populace, they will regard him as their enemy. One who gives peace to the populace, the populace will rely on; one who endangers the populace, the populace will view as a disaster. The populace is not the realm of one man. Only that ruler who can run the State according to the Way can dwell in the ultimate position of authority."

文王问太公，说：具备什么条件才可以治理天下呢？
太公说：器量盖过天下，然后才能包容天下；诚信盖过天下，然后才能约束天下；仁慈盖过天下，然后才能怀柔天下；恩惠盖过天下，然后才能保有天下；权力盖过天下，然后才能不失天下；遇事果决不疑，就象天体运行不能改变，就象四时变化不能更易一样。这六个条件具备了，然后就可以治理天下了。
所以为天下人谋利益的，人民就拥护他；使天下人受祸害的，人民就反对他；关心为天下人谋生存的，人民就怀念他的恩德；杀戮天下人的，人民就要毁灭他；顺应天下人意愿的，人民就归向他；造成天下人穷困的，人民就仇视他；使天下人安居乐业的，人民就依靠他；使天下人遭受危难的，人民就逃离他。天下不是一个人的天下，只有有道的人，才能做君主。

Three Doubts

King Wu (Zhou Gong Wu, second son of King Wen) inquired of Jiāng Zǐyá: "I want to attain our aim of overthrowing the Shang, but I have three doubts. I am afraid that our strength will be inadequate to attack the strong, unable to estrange his close supporters within the court and unable to cause discord between Shang and his people. What should I do?"

Jiāng Zǐyá replied: "Be familiar with the situation, be very cautious in making plans, and employ your material resources. Now in order to attack the strong, you must nurture their arrogance, and exaggerate it to make it worse. What is too arrogant will certainly fail; what is too extended must have deficiencies. Attack the strong through growing his arrogance. Cause estrangement of his favored officials by using their favorites, and cause disharmony with his people by means of your people.

"Now in the way of planning, thoroughness and secrecy are treasured. You should become involved with him in numerous affairs and ply him with temptations of profit. Conflicts will then surely rise.

"If you want to cause his close supporters to become estranged from him, you must do it by using what he favors - making gifts to those whom he favors, giving them what they want. Tempt them with what they find profitable, use them to sow discord between the ruler and close supporters, and causing the close supporters to be unable to attain their ambitions. Those who covet profits will be extremely happy at the prospects, and they will continue seeding doubts among the close supporters and the ruler.

"Now without doubt, the Way for attacking is to first obfuscate the King's clarity and then attack his army, destroying his greatness and eliminating the misfortune of the people. Debauch him with beautiful women, entice him with profit. Nurture him with (food) flavors and provide him with the company of female musicians. Then, after you have caused his subordinates to become estranged from him, you must cause the people to grow distant from him, while never letting him know of your plans. Appear to support him and draw him into your trap. Do not let him become aware of what is happening, for only then can your plan be successful. When bestowing your beneficence on the people, you cannot begrudge the expenses, similar to the proper care of cows and horses. Frequently make gifts of food and clothing and follow up by loving them.

"The mind is the means to open knowledge; knowledge is the means to open up the source of wealth; and wealth is the means to open up the people. Gaining allegiance of the people is the way to attract worthy men. When one is enlightened by sagely advisers, he can govern all under Heaven."

武王问太公说：我想建功立业，但有三点疑虑：恐怕力量不足以进攻强敌；恐怕不能离间敌人的亲信；恐怕不能瓦解敌人的军队。对此怎么办呢？
太公说：一是因势利导；二是慎用计谋；三是使用钱财。要进攻强敌，必先助长它的恃强蛮横，使他更加猖狂自大。过于强横，必遭挫折；过于骄傲，必致失误。要进攻强大敌人，必先助长它的强暴；要离间敌人亲信，必先收买敌人亲信；要瓦解敌人军队，必先收揽敌国民心。运用计谋，以周密最为重要。许给敌人一些好处，给与敌人一些利益，使他们互相争夺。
要想离间敌国君主所亲信的忠臣，应从他所宠爱的佞臣着手，用他们所想得到的东西送他，许给他们以丰厚的利益。利用他们[去播弄是非]，使其君主疏远忠臣，使这些忠臣不能得志。那些佞臣因为得到我们给与的利益很高兴，就会去制造敌人相互间的怀疑，而达到我离间他们的目的。
一般攻击强大敌人的方法是，首先蒙蔽敌国君主的耳目，然后才能进攻他强大的军队，摧毁他庞大的国家，以达到为民除害的目的。[蒙蔽敌人耳目的方法是：]用女色腐蚀他，用厚利引诱他，用美味养他，用淫乐迷乱他。既离间了他的亲信，也就会使他疏远人民，不让他发觉这是谋，推推拉拉把他引入了我们的圈套，而他还不明白我的意图，然后就可成事了。施恩惠于人民，不要吝惜财物，人民和牛马一样，经常喂养它们，就能使它们和你亲近。思考研究可以产生智慧，智慧可以产生财富，财富可以养育民众，民众中就可以涌现出贤才，大批贤才涌现出来就可以辅住君主统治天下。

Chapter 3 - The Dragon Teaching
King's Wing

King Wu asked Jiāng Zǐyá: "When the King commands the army he must have 'legs and arms' (top assistants) and 'feather and wings' (aides) to bring about his military greatness and spirituality. How should this be done?"

Jiāng Zǐyá said: "Whenever one mobilizes the army, the commanding general should be the one giving orders. He must have an understanding of all aspects, not depending on one technique alone. In accord with their abilities, assign duties - each one taking charge of what they are good at, constantly changing and transforming the duties assigned with the times, to create the essential principles and order. Thus the general has seventy two assistants in order to respond to any events. Prepare the number according to the method, being careful that they know the orders and principles. When you have all the different abilities and various skills, then the myriad of affairs will be complete."

King Wu asked: "May I ask about the numbers?"

Jiāng Zǐyá said: "Trusted aide, one: in charge of advising about secret plans for responding to sudden events; observe the signs from Heaven so as to eliminate sudden change; exercising general supervision over all planning; and protecting and preserving the lives of the people.

"Advisors, five: responsible for preparing measures of security and against danger; anticipating the unforeseen; evaluating performance and ability of generals; announcing rewards and punishments; appointing ranks to officers; making difficult decisions; and determining what is advisable and what is not.

"Astrologers, three: undertaking responsibility for the stars and calendar; observing the weather; predicting auspicious days and times; investigating signs and phenomena; verifying disasters and abnormalities; and knowing Heaven's mind with regard to the moment for completing or abandonment.

"Topographers, three: in charge of gathering information on the terrains that the army will pass by; precipitous and easy passages, both near and far; and water and dry land, mountains and defiles, so as not to lose the advantages of terrain.

"Military Strategists, nine: responsible for discussing divergent views; analyzing the probable success or failure of various operations; selecting the weapons and then training men in their use; and identifying those who violate the ordinances.

"Supply Officers, four: responsible for calculating the requirements for food and water; preparing the food stocks and supplies, and transporting the provisions along the route; and supplying the fives grains so as to ensure that the army will not suffer any hardship or shortage.

"Guerilla Officers, four: responsible for picking men of talent and strength; disbursing weapons and armor; for setting up lightning fast attacks, so that the enemy does not know where they come from.

"Signal Officers, three: responsible for the pennants and drums, for clearly signaling to the eyes and ears; for creating deceptive signs and seals to issue false designation and orders; and for stealthily and hastily moving back and forth, going in and out like spirits.

"'Limbs and Arms' (capable assistants), four: responsible for undertaking heavy duties and handling difficult tasks; for the repair and maintenance of ditches and moats; and for keeping the walls and ramparts in order to defend against and repel the enemy.

"Liaison Officers, two: responsible for gathering what has been lost and supplementing what is in error; receiving honored guests; holding discussions and talks; mitigating disasters; and resolving difficulties.

"Officers of Authority, three: responsible for implementing the unorthodox and deceptive; for establishing the different and unusual things that people do not recognize; and for putting into effect inexhaustible transformations.

"Information Gatherer, seven: responsible for going everywhere, listening to what people are saying; and observing the officers in all directions, and gathering information on the army's true circumstances.

"'Claws and Teeth', five: responsible for raising military greatness; for stimulating and encouraging the army, causing them to risk danger and attack the enemy's elite troops without ever having any doubts or second thoughts.

"'Feathers and Wings', four: responsible for flourishing the name and fame of the army; for shaking distant lands with its image; and for moving all within the four borders in order to weaken the enemy's spirit.

"Roving Officers, eight: responsible for spying on enemy spies; manipulating the emotions of the enemy population; and observing the enemy's thoughts. Basically they perform the function of spies and double agents.

"Astrological Zealots, two: responsible for spreading slander and falsehoods and for calling on ghosts and spirits in order to confuse the minds of the populace.

"Medical Officers, three: in charge of the medicines; managing blade wounds; and curing the various illnesses.

"Accountants, two: responsible for accounting for the provisions and foodstuffs within the Three Armies' encampments and ramparts; for the fiscal materials employed; and for receipts and disbursements."

武王问太公说：君主统帅军队必须有辅佐的人，以造成他非凡的威望，这该怎么办呢？

太公说：一般用兵时统帅军队都以将帅作为司令，司令，重在通晓和掌握全面情况，而不在于专精某项技术。他应该量才录用各种人材，取其各种专长，使之根据情

况变化处理各项事务，这是统帅军队的根本所在。所以将帅要有助手七十二人，以便集中各种人才的智慧。只有这样去设置助手，才能做到全面而详细地掌握情况，

正确决择。使具有各种专门技术的人，都能发挥其智慧，各项任务也都可以圆满地完成了。

武王问：请你再逐条详细地讲讲怎样？

太公说：腹心一人。主管：参赞谋略，应付突然事变，观测天象，消除祸忍，总揽大计，保全民命；

谋士五人。主管：谋划安定危局的措施，考虑尚未出现的形势变化，鉴定将士的品德才能，宣布赏罚，授予官位，决断疑难的问题，裁定事情的可否；

天文三人。主管；观察天象，观测气候，推算时间，考察吉凶的征兆，查验灾害和意外事件，观察天意的顺逆。

地利三人。主管：察明军队行军和驻止时的地形状况，分析利害消长，距离远近，地形险易、江河水情以及山势险阻等，使军队作不失地利；

兵法九人，主管：探讨敌我形势的异同，分析作战胜负的条件，配备和训练各种兵器的使用，揭发非法行为；

通粮四人。主管：计划给养，筹备储存，保证粮食运输，筹集五谷，使军队供应不发生困难；

奋威四人。主管：选拔有才能的勇士，配发适用的兵器装备，组织突击部队以便风驰电掣，出其不意地打击敌人；

伏鼓旗三人。主管：军中的旗鼓，统一视听信号，[以便指挥顺畅]；并制造假符节，发布假号令，[以迷惑敌人，]忽来忽往，神出鬼没。

股肱四人。主管：规划保卫重地，守护要害工程，修筑沟堑壁垒，以备守御；

通材三人。主管：指出将帅的过失，弥补他的疏漏，应对宾客，讨论问题，消除祸患，解决纠纷；

权士三人。主管：施行诡诈奇谋，安排绝术奇技，不让敌人识破，进行无穷的变化，

耳目七人。主管：在与敌人往来接触中，听风声，看动静，查明天下形势和敌军情况；

爪牙五人。主管：宣扬我军的军威，激励三军的斗志，使之冒险犯难，冲锋陷阵而无所疑惧；

羽翼四人。主管：宣扬将仲的威名声誉，震骇远方，动摇邻国，削弱敌军的斗志；

游士八人。主管：察出敌方奸细，探知敌国变乱，操纵敌国人心，观察敌方意图，进行间谍活动；

术士二人。主管：使用奇诈，假托鬼神，瓦解敌军斗志；

方士二人。主管各种药物，治疗创伤，医治疾病；

法算二人。主管计算军队营垒、粮食和财用出入的数量及情况。

Discussion of Generals

King Wu asked Jiāng Zǐyá: "What should a general be?"

Jiāng Zǐyá replied: "Generals should have the five important characteristics and should not have the ten flawed characters."

King Wu asked: "Can you please elaborate?"

Jiāng Zǐyá elaborated: "What we refer to as the five important characteristics are *courage*, *wisdom*, *benevolence*, *trustworthiness* and *loyalty*. If he is courageous, he cannot be overwhelmed. If he is wise, he cannot be forced into turmoil. If he is benevolent, he will love his men. If he is trustworthy, he will not be deceitful. If he is loyal, he will always have the interest of the state.

"What are referred to as the ten flawed characters are as follows: being courageous and treating death lightly; being hasty and impatient; being greedy and lusting for gains; being benevolent but unable to inflict punishment; being wise but afraid; being trustworthy and assuming others are also honest; being unscrupulous and incorruptible but not loving men; being wise but indecisive; being resolute and self-reliant; being fearful and very dependent on people.

"One who is courageous and treats death lightly can be antagonized and destroyed. One who is hasty and impatient can be destroyed by dragging the war. One who is greedy and loves profit can be bribed. One who is benevolent but unable to inflict suffering can be worn down. One who is wise but fearful can be threatened.

"One who is trustworthy and likes to trust others can be deceived. One who is scrupulous and incorruptible can be insulted. One who is wise but indecisive can carry surprise attack against him. One who is resolute and self-reliant can use words to pay obeisance to him. One who is fearful and likes to entrust responsibility to others can be tricked.

"Thus Sun Tzu[3] made the statement: 'War is of vital importance to the state, it is a matter of survival or extinction.' And thus were created the sayings: 'The fate of the state lies in the hands of the general' and 'the general is the pillar of the state.' Thus, this position is what all former Kings valued. Thus in commissioning a general, you cannot but carefully evaluate and investigate his character.

"Thus it is also said that two armies will not be victorious, nor will both be defeated. When the army ventures out beyond the borders, before they have been out ten days - even if a state has not perished - one army will certainly have been destroyed and the general killed."

King Wu exclaimed: "Marvelous!"

武王问太公说：评论将帅的原则是什么？
太公说：将帅需有五项才德和无十种缺点。
武王说：请问它的具体内容？
太公说：所谓五种才德是，勇敢、明智、仁慈、诚信和忠实。勇敢就不可侵犯，明智就不可扰乱，仁慈就能得众心，诚信就不欺骗别人，忠实就能一心为国。
所谓十种缺点是：有勇猛而轻于牺牲的，有暴躁而急于求成的，有贪婪而好利的，有仁慈而流于姑息的，有聪明而胆小怕事的，有诚信而轻信别人的，有廉洁而近于刻薄的，有多谋而犹豫不决的，有坚强而刚愎自用的，有懦弱而依赖别人的。勇敢而轻于牺牲的，可以激怒而战胜他。急躁而急于求成的，可以持久作战拖垮他。贪婪而好利的，可以贿赂他。仁慈而流于姑息的可以袭扰疲惫他。聪明而胆小怕
事的，可以胁迫他。诚信而轻信别人的，可以欺骗他。廉洁而近于刻薄的，可以轻悔他。多谋而犹豫不决的，可以突然袭击他。坚强而刚愎自用的，可以用言词奉
承：他[使他轻举妄动，疏忽大意，然后打败他]。懦弱无能而好依赖别人的，可以愚弄他。
战争，是国家的大事，它关系着国家的存亡，国家的命运就掌握在将帅的手里。将帅，是国家的辅佐，为历代君王所重视，因此任命将帅不可不反复审察。所以说：
战争的双方不可能都取得胜利，也不可能都失败。只要军队一越出国境，不出十日，不是一方亡国就必然是另一方破军杀将。
武王说：好极了！

Selecting Generals

---

[3] The mention of Sun Tzu in this text supports the widely accepted theory that the text of the *Six Secret Teachings* was modified later in the Warring States Period, while still retaining the basic military thought of the earlier Qi dynasty.

King Wu asked Jiāng Zǐyá: "If a King wants to raise an army, how should he go about selecting and generals and determining qualifications?"

Jiāng Zǐyá said: "There are fifteen cases where a general's external appearance and internal character are not coherent. These are:
1. He appears to be a gentleman but is actually immoral.
2. He seems kind-hearted but is a thief.
3. His countenance is reverent and respectful, but his heart is insolent
4. Externally he is incorruptible and circumspect, but he lacks respect.
5. He appears perceptive and sharp, but lacks such talent.
6. He appears profound but lacks all sincerity.
7. He appears adept at planning but is indecisive.
8. He appears to be decisive and daring, but is incapable.
9. He appears guileless but is not trustworthy.
10. He appears confused and disoriented, but on the contrary is loyal and substantial.
11. He appears to engage in specious discourse but is a man of merit and achievement.
12. He appears courageous but is afraid.
13. He seems severe and remote, but on the contrary easily befriends men.
14. He appears forbidding, but on the contrary is quiet and sincere.
15. He who appears weak and insubstantial, yet when dispatched outside the state there is nothing he does not accomplish, no mission that he does not execute successfully.

"Those who the world disdains, the Sage values. Ordinary men cannot see through them; only great wisdom can discern them. This is because the general's external appearance and internal character do not always visibly cohere."

King Wu asked: "How does one know this?"

Jiāng Zǐyá replied: "There are eight forms of tests by which you may know it. First, question them and observe the details of their reply. Second, verbally confound and perplex them and observe how they react. Third, send a spy out to test their loyalty. Fourth, clearly and explicitly question with what you already know to see their character. Fifth, appoint to positions of financial responsibility to observe their honesty. Sixth, test them with beautiful women to observe their uprightness and character. Seventh, confront them with difficulties to observe their courage. Eighth, get them drunk to observe their conduct. When all eight have been fully explored, then their character, values and morals can be distinguished."

武王问太公说：帝王起兵想选拔英明而有权略的人为将，并知道他的才能高下，应该怎么办？

太公说：士的外表和内情不符的有十五种情况：有的外似贤良而内实不肖，有的外似善良而实为盗贼，有的外似恭敬而内实不逊，有的外似谦谨而内不至诚，有的外

似精干而内无才学，有的外似浑厚而内不诚实，有的外多计谋而内不果断，有的外似果断而内无作为，有的外似老实而内无信用，有的外似动摇而内实忠诚，有的言行过激而作事却有功效，有的外似勇敢而内心惧怕，有的外表严肃而内实平易近人，有的外貌严厉而内心温和厚道，有的外表虚弱、貌不惊人，但受命出使没有到不

了的地方，没有完不成的任务。[那些外貌不扬，而内在品质好的人，]往往为天下人所看不起，却独为圣人所器重，一般人不知道他们内在的才华，非有高明的见

识，是不能看清这些人的实情的。这就是士的外表和内在才华不相一致的情况。

武王问：用什么办法可以真正了解他们呢？

太公说：有八种考验方法：一是提出问题，看他知道得是否详尽清楚；二是详尽追问看他应变的能力；三是用间谍考察，看他是否忠诚；四是明知故问，看他有无隐瞒，借以考查他的品德；五是让他管理财物，看他是否廉洁；六是用女色试他，看他的操守如何；七是把危难的情况告诉他，看他是否勇敢；八是使他的酒，看他能

否保持常态。这八种考验方法都用了，一个人的贤与不贤就能区别清楚了。

Appointing Generals

King Wu asked Jiāng Zǐyá: "What is the process of appointing the commanding general?"

Jiāng Zǐyá said: "When the state encounters danger, the ruler should avoid the Main Hall, summon the general and charge him as follows: 'The security or endangerment of the state all lie with the army's commanding general. At present such-and-such state does not act properly submissive. I would like you to lead the army forth to respond to it.'"

"After the general has received his mandate, command the Grand Scribe to bore the sacred tortoise shell to divine an auspicious day. Thereafter, to prepare for the chosen day, observe a vegetarian regimen for three days, and then go to the ancestral temple.

"After the ruler has entered the gate to the temple, he stands facing the west. The general enters the temple gate and stands facing north. The ruler personally takes the head of the Axe of Authority, saying: 'From this to Heaven above, will be controlled by the General of the Army.' Then taking the handle of Axe of Authority, he handed it to the general, saying: 'From this to the depths below, will be controlled by the General of the Army. When you see weaknesses in the enemy, you should advance; when you see that they are strong, you should halt. Do not assume that having the numerical advantage, we can treat the enemy lightly. Do not commit yourself to die just because you have received a heavy responsibility. Do not, because you are honored, regard other men as lowly. Do not be opinionated and contravene the masses. Do not take verbal facility to be a sign of certainty. When officers have not yet been seated, do not sit. When the officers have not yet eaten, do not eat. You should share hardship with them. If you behave in this way the officers and masses will certainly exhaust their strength in fighting to the death.'

"After the general has received his mandate, he bows and responds to the ruler: 'I have heard that a country cannot follow the commands of another state's government, while an army in the field cannot follow central government control. A general with two minds cannot properly serve his ruler; a general in doubt cannot respond to the enemy. I have already received my mandate and taken sole control of the awesome responsibility of the Axe of Authority. I do not dare return alive, without success. I would like to request that you condescend to grant complete and sole command to me. If you do not permit it, I dare not accept the post of the commanding general.' The King then grants it, and the general formally takes his leave and departs.

"Military matters are not determined by the ruler's commands; they all proceed from the commanding general. When the commanding general approaches an enemy and decides to engage in battle, he is not of two minds. In this way, there is no Heaven above, no Earth below; no enemy in front and no ruler to the rear. For this reason, the wise make plans for him, the courageous fight for him. Their fighting spirit soars to the sky; they are swift like galloping steeds. Even before the blades clash, the enemy surrenders submissively.

"War is won outside the borders of the state, but the general's merit is established within it. Officials are promoted and receive the highest rewards; the populace rejoices; and the general is credited. For this reason, natural systems will run smoothly; the grains will grow abundantly; and the whole state will be secure and peaceful.

King Wu said: "Excellent!"

武王问太公说：任命主将的方式如何？
太公说：凡国家遇有危难，国君就避开正殿，在偏殿召见主将命令。他说：
　　"国家安危全靠将军，现在某国背叛，望将军率军征讨。"
主将接受了任命，国君就命太史占卜，斋戒三天，前往太庙，钻龟甲，择吉日，授给斧钺。[到了吉日]国君进入太庙门，面向西站着，主将进太庙门，面向北站着。国君亲自拿着钺的头部，把钺柄交给主将说："从此，军中上至于天的一切事情全由将军管理。"又亲自拿起斧柄，把斧的刃部交给主将说："从此军中下至于渊的一切事情全由将军管理。"见敌虚弱就前进，见敌坚强就停止，不要以为我军众多就轻敌，不要以为任务重大就拚命，不要以为身居高位就轻视别人，不要固执己见而违背众意，不要把诡辩游说当成真理。士卒没有坐，你就不要先坐；士卒没有吃，你就不要先吃，冷热都要与士卒同。这样，士卒们必能尽死力作战。
主将接受任命后，再拜并回答说："据我所知，国事不应受外部的干预，作战不能由君主在朝廷内遥控指挥。臣怀二心就不能忠心耿耿地侍奉君主，将帅受君主的牵制，疑虑重重就不能专心专意地去对付敌人。我既已奉命掌握军事大权，[不获胜利]不敢生还。请你允许我照上面的话去做！你不允许，我就不敢担任主将。" 国君允许了他，主将就辞别君主率军出征。
从此军中一切事务，不听命于国君而听命于主将，临敌决战，意志统一。这样，主将就能上不受天时限制，下不受地形限制，前无敌人敢于抵抗，后无君主从中牵制。就能使有知谋的人都为他策划，有勇力的人都为他战斗，士气昂扬直冲霄汉，行动迅速如快马奔腾，兵未交锋而敌已降服。战争取胜于国外，功名显扬于国内，官吏都得到晋升，士卒都得到奖赏，百姓欢欣鼓舞，将帅没有罪过。从此风调雨顺，五谷丰登，国家安宁。
武王说：好啊！

General's Military Greatness

King Wu asked: "How does the general create and establish his military dominance? How can he be enlightened? How can he make his prohibitions effective and get his orders implemented?"

Jiāng Zǐyá said: "The general creates military dominance by punishing the higher authority or ranks, and becomes enlightened by rewarding the lower ranks. Prohibitions and laws are made effective by implementing punishments carefully. Therefore, if executing one man can impact the whole army, kill him. If by rewarding one man, the masses will be pleased, reward him. In executing, the effect is greater when performed on the high ranking; in rewarding, effect is greater when bestowed on the low ranking. When you kill the powerful and the honored, it shows that punishment is not limited to only the low ranking. When rewards extend down to the cowherds, grooms, and stablemen, it shows that rewards are not limited to only the high ranking. When punishments reach the highest rank and rewards penetrate to the lowest rank, then your military dominance has been established."

武王问太公说：主将用什么来树立威信，用什么来体现明察，用什么来做到所禁必止，所令必行？
太公说：主将以诛杀地位高的人来树立威信，以奖赏地位低的人来体现明察，以严明惩罚来作到所禁必止，所令必行。因此，杀一人能使全军震惊的：就杀他，赏一人能使万人欢喜的，就赏他。诛杀，重在诛杀地位高的人；奖赏，重在赏赐地位低的人。能诛杀那些有权有势的人物，说明刑罚能及于最上层；能奖赏到牛僮、马夫等饲养人员，说明赏赐能达到最下层。刑罚能及于最上层，赏赐能达到最下层；这就说明主将的威信能够贯彻上下了。

Motivating the Army

King Wu asked Jiāng Zǐyá: "When we attack, I want the soldiers to contend with each other to scale the wall first, and compete with each other to be in the forefront when we fight in the field. When they hear the sounds of the gongs to retreat, they will be angry; when they hear the sounds of the drums to advance, they will be happy. How can we accomplish this?"

Jiāng Zǐyá said: "A general has three techniques for attaining victory."

King Wu asked: "May I ask what they are?"

Jiāng Zǐyá said: "If in winter, the general does not wear a fur robe, in summer, does not carry a fan, and in rain does not set up a canopy, he is called a 'general of propriety.' Unless the general himself submits to these observances, he will not have the means to know the cold and warmth of officers and soldiers.

"If, when they advance into ravines and obstacles, or encounter muddy terrain, the general always takes the first steps and leads the army, he is termed a 'general of action.' If a general does not personally set an example through action, he has no means to know the labors and hardships of the officers and soldiers.

"If, only after the men are settled in their encampment does the general retire; only after all the cooks have finished their cooking, does he go inside to eat; and if the army does not light up, he also does not light up, he is termed as a 'general who can control desires.' Unless the general himself practices controlling his desires, he has no way to know the hunger or fullness of the officers and troops.

"The general shares heat and cold, labor and suffering, hunger and fullness with the officers and men. Therefore, when the soldiers hear the sound of the drum, they are happy, and when they hear the sound of the gong, they are angry. When attacking at a high wall or crossing a deep lake, under a hail of arrows and stones, the officers will compete to be the first to scale the wall. When the blades clash, the officers will compete to be the first to go forward.

"It is not because they like death and take pleasure in being wounded, but because the general knows their feelings of heat and cold, hunger and fullness, and clearly displays his knowledge of their labor and suffering. And therefore, they are willing to try to serve!"

武王问太公说：我要使全军官兵攻城时争先登城，野战时争先冲击，听到停止号令就愤怒，听到前进号令就欢喜，应该怎么办？

太公说：将帅有三个克敌制胜的要领。
武王说：请讲讲它的具体内容！
太公说：将帅冬天不穿皮衣，夏天不用扇子，雨天不张伞蓬，这样就是礼将；将帅不能以身作则，就无从体会士卒的冷暖。越过险阻地形，通过泥泞道路，将帅必先下车(马)步行，这样就是力将；将帅不身体力行，就无从体会士卒的劳苦。军队宿营就绪，将帅才进宿舍，军队的饭菜都已做好，将帅才能就餐，军队没有照明，将帅也不照明，这样就是止欲将；将帅不能克制自己，[与士卒共甘苦]，就无以体会士卒的饥饱。由于将帅能同士卒共寒暑、共劳苦、共饥饱，所以全军官兵听到
前进号令就欢喜，听到停止号令就愤怒。即使面临高城深池，箭石如雨，士卒也能争先登城，[野战时]，刚一交锋，也都能争先冲击。士卒并不是愿意牺牲，乐于
伤残，而是因为将帅深深地关怀他们的冷暖、饥饱，体贴到他们的辛苦，因而他们甘愿尽力报效啊！

Secret Tallies

King Wu asked Jiāng Zǐyá: "If we lead the army deep into the territory of the feudal lords and the army suddenly suffers some delay or requires urgent action – perhaps a situation to our advantage or one to our disadvantage – and I want to communicate between those nearby and those afar; respond to the situation from the central government, in order to meet the needs of the army – how should we do it?"

Jiāng Zǐyá said: "The ruler and his generals have a system of secret tallies, altogether consisting of eight types:
1. There is a tally signifying a great victory over the enemy, one foot long.
2. There is a tally for destroying the enemy's army and killing their general, nine inches long.
3. There is a tally for capturing enemy cities, eight inches long.
4. There is a tally for driving the enemy back and reporting deep penetration, seven inches long.
5. There is a tally to alert the army to prepare for stalwart defensive measures, six inches long.
6. There is a tally for supply requests and additional soldiers, five inches long.
7. There is a tally signifying the army's defeat and the general's death, four inches long.
8. There is a tally signifying the army's defeat and injuries to the army, three inches long.

"Further, for those who bring in the information late, or if the information from the tally should leak out, execute all those who heard and told about it. These eight tallies, which only the ruler and general should secretly know, provide a technique for covert communication that will not allow outsiders to know the true situation. Thus, even though the enemy has the great wisdom of a Sage, no one will comprehend their significance."

"Excellent!" said King Wu.

武王问太公道：率领军队深入敌国境内，全军突然遭遇紧急情况，或者有利，或者有害。我想从近处通知远方，从国内策应外地，以满足三军需要，应该怎么办？

太公说："君主与将帅间有预定的秘密通信工具叫阴符，概分八类：有我军大胜，全歼敌人的，其长一尺；击破敌军，斩杀敌将的，其长九寸；占领城市、夺取城邑的，其长八寸，击退敌人，报告远方的，其长七寸；警告军民必须坚守的，其长六寸；请领粮食，增加兵力的，其长五寸；军队失败，将领伤亡的，其长四寸；战斗不利，士卒伤亡的，其长三寸。凡是奉命传递阴符的人，如有延误时限、泄露机密的，传播的人和听传播的人，都一律处死。上述八类阴符是君主与将帅秘密掌握，用来暗通信息的。这种对内对外都严守秘密的通信方法，即使敌方有绝顶聪明的人也不能识破这种秘密。

武王说：好啊！

Secret Letters

King Wu asked of Jiāng Zǐyá: "The army has been led deep into the territory of the feudal lords, and the commanding general wants to implement changes, and make complicated plans. These matters are quite complex, and the simple tally is not adequate to clearly express them. As they are separated by some distance, verbal communication cannot get through. What should we do?"

Jiāng Zǐyá said: "Whenever you have secret affairs and major considerations, letters should be employed, rather than tallies. The ruler sends a letter to the general; the general uses a letter to query the ruler. The letters are composed 'as one unit and then divided'. They are sent out in three parts, with only one person knowing the contents. 'Divided' means it is separated into three parts. 'Sent out in three parts, with only one person knowing' means there are three messengers, each carrying one part; and when the three are put together, only then does one know the contents. This is then referred to as a 'secret letter'. Even if the enemy has sagacious wisdom, they will not be able to recognize the contents."

"Excellent!" said King Wu.

武王问太公说：率领军队深入敌国境内，国君主将想要与敌交战，根据情况进行灵活的机动，以求取得出其不意的胜利，事情繁乱，阴符难于说明，彼此相距又很遥远，语言不通，怎么办？

太公说：所有密谋大计，应当用阴书，不用阴符，国君用阴书指示主将，主将用阴书请示国君。这种书信都是"一合而再离，三发而一知"。"一合而再离"就是把
一封书信分为三部分；"三发而一知"就是用三个人送信，每人送一部分，相互参差，即使送信的人也不知道书中的内容，这就叫做阴书。敌人无论怎样聪明，也不能识破我的秘密。
武王说：好啊！

Army's Disposition

King Wu asked Jiāng Zǐyá: "What is the Way of aggressive warfare?"

Jiāng Zǐyá replied: "The Army's attacking disposition should change in accordance with the enemy's movements, and changes coming from the confrontation between the two armies. Indirect and direct tactics are produced from the inexhaustible resources of the mind. Thus the greatest affairs are not discussed, and employment of troops is not spoken about. Moreover, words which discuss ultimate affairs are not to be discussed openly. The employment of troops is not so definitive as to be visible. They go suddenly, they come suddenly. Only when one can exercise sole control over the army, without being governed by other men, is such a one a military weapon.

"If your plans are heard, the enemy will make counterplans. If you are perceived, they will plot against you. If your objectives are known, they will put you in difficulty. If you are fathomed, they will endanger you.

"Thus one who excels in warfare has already won before the deployment of forces. One who excels at eliminating the misfortunes of the people manages them before they appear. Conquer the enemy; be victorious by being formless. The superior fighter has won before engaging in battle. Thus one who fights and attains victory in using blades is not a good general. One who makes preparation after the battle has been lost is not a superior Sage. One whose skill is the same as the masses is not a superior craftsman.

"In military affairs, nothing is more important than certain victory. In employing the army, nothing is more important than obscurity and silence. In movement, nothing is more important than the unexpected. In planning, nothing is more important than not being knowable. To be the first to gain victory, initially display some weakness to the enemy and only afterward do battle. Then your effort will be half, but the achievement will be doubled.

"The Sage observes signs from the movements of Heaven and Earth, and knows its principles. He observes the movement of the sun and the moon and understands their seasonal activity. He follows the cycles of day and night, taking them as his constant. All things have life and death in accordance with the principles of

Heaven and Earth. Thus it is said that if one fights before understanding the situation, even if his army is more numerous, he will certainly be defeated.

"One who excels at warfare will await events in the situation without making any movement. When he sees he can be victorious, he will arise; if he sees he cannot be victorious, he will desist. Thus it is said, that he does not have any fear, he does not vacillate. Of the many various types of harms that can befall an army, indecision is the greatest. Of the disasters that can befall an army, none surpasses doubt.

"One who excels in warfare will not lose an advantage when he perceives it, or be doubtful when he meets the opportunity. One who loses an advantage or lags behind the time for action will, on the contrary, suffer from disaster. Thus the wise follow the time and do not lose an advantage; the skillful are decisive and have no doubts. He strikes like a sudden clap of thunder, which does not give time to cover the ears; strike like a flash of lightning, which does not give time to close the eyes. Advance as if suddenly startled; employ your troops as if deranged. Those who oppose you will be destroyed; those who come near will perish. Who can defend against such an attack?

"Now when matters are not discussed and the general preserves their secrecy, he is superior. When things are not manifest but he discerns them, he is wise. Thus if superior and wise, no enemies will act against him in the field, nor will any state stand against him."

"Excellent!" said King Wu.

武王问太公说：进攻的原则是什么？
太公说：作战的形势是随着敌人的行动而变化的，临机应变产生于两军对阵的时候，奇正运用来源于将帅智慧与思虑。所以，机要的大事不能泄露，用兵的策略不可外传，重大决策不容纷纷议论，作行动不可暴露于敌，忽往忽来，独断专行而不受制于人，这是用兵重要原则。一般作战，敌人探听到我军兴兵，就要研究应付的策略；敌人发现了我军行动，就要设法破坏我军行动；敌人了解了我军企图，必致为敌所困扰；敌人摸清了我军规律，必致为敌所危害。所以善用兵的人，取胜于展开
军队之前；善于除害的，消灭祸患于萌芽前；善于取胜的人，取胜于无形之中；最好的作战是不战而屈人兵。所以用死拚硬斗来取胜的将领，不算是好的将领；在失
败之后来设防的，不是聪明的人。智慧与一般人相同的，不是国家的导师；技术与一般人相同的，不能算是能工巧匠。用兵最重要的是所攻克，作战最重要的是保守
机密，行动最重要的是出敌不意，计谋最要的是不被识破。凡是未战而先胜的，都是先示弱于敌，而后进战，这样可以事半而功倍。

圣人观察天地的变化，反复探索其原因，根据日月的运行，遵季节的变化，比照昼夜长短等自然现象，掌握了普遍的规律，就知道万物的生死枯荣是随着天地的变化而变化的必然性。所以说，没有摸清敌人情况就去作战，虽然军队众多，也必定失败。

善于打仗的人，军队处于待机状态时不受干扰，看到有胜利把握就进攻，没有胜利把握就停止。所以说，不要惧怕，不要犹豫，用兵的害处，犹豫最大，军队的灾

祸，莫过于狐疑。善于打仗的人，看到有利的情况决不放过，遇到有利的战机决不迟疑。因为失去有利条件和错过有利时机而动，反而会使自己受害。因此，明智的

将冲抓住战机就不放过，机智的指挥者，一经决定就不犹豫。所以才能象迅雷一样使人不及掩开，象闪电一样使人不及闭眼，前进如惊马奔驰，战斗如狂风骤雨，阻

挡它的就被击破，靠近他的都被消灭，谁能抵抗得了这种军队呢！

将帅用兵，能不声不响而胸有成竹的叫做神，情况尚未明朗而看出端睨的叫做明。所以懂得神明的道理，作战就没有势均力敌的手，面前就没有敢于抵抗的敌国了。

武王说：好啊！

Indirect Troops

King Wu asked Jiāng Zǐyá: "In general, what is most essential in the art of employing the army?"

Jiāng Zǐyá replied: "The ancient saying, 'excelling at warfare' does not mean they excelled in waging war above Heaven, nor waging war below Earth. Their success and defeat in all cases proceeded from their spirit-like disposition. Those who attained it flourish; those who lost it perished.

"Now when our two armies, opposing each other, have deployed their armored soldiers and established their battle arrays, releasing some of your troops to create chaos in the ranks is the means by which to fabricate deceptive changes.

1. Deep grass and dense growth are the means by which to stage a concealed escape.
2. Valleys with streams and treacherous ravines are the means by which to stop chariots and defend against cavalry.
3. Narrow passes and mountain forests are the means by which a few can attack a large force.
4. Marshy depressions and secluded dark areas are the means by which to conceal your appearance.
5. Deploying on clear, open ground without any concealment is the means by which to fight with strength and courage.

6. Being as swift as a flying arrow, attacking as suddenly as the release of a crossbow are the ways by which to destroy brilliant plans.
7. Setting up ingenious ambushes and preparing indirect troops, stretching out distant formations to deceive and entice the enemy are the means by which to destroy the enemy's army and capture its general.
8. Dividing your troops is the means by which to attack their circular formations and destroy their square ones.
9. Taking advantage of their fright and fear is the means by which one can attack ten.
10. Taking advantage of their exhaustion and encamping at dusk are the means by which ten can attack 100.
11. Unorthodox technical skills are the means by which to cross deep waters and ford across rivers.
12. Strong crossbows and long weapons are the means by which to fight across water.
13. Distant observation posts and far-off scouts, explosive haste and feigned retreats are the means by which to force the surrender of walled fortifications and compel the submission of towns.
14. Drumming and setting up a great tumult are the means by which to implement unorthodox plans.
15. Attacking during high winds and heavy rain are the means by which to strike the front and seize the rear.
16. Disguising some men as enemy emissaries is the means by which to sever supply lines.
17. Forging enemy commands and orders and wearing the same clothes as the enemy are the means by which to be prepared for retreat.
18. Warfare which is invariably in accord with righteousness is the means by which to incite the masses and be victorious over the enemy.
19. Honored ranks and generous rewards are the means by which to encourage the obeying of orders.
20. Severe punishments and heavy fines are the means by which to force the weary and indolent to advance.
21. Happiness and anger, bestowing and taking away, civil and martial measures, at times slowly, at others rapidly – all these are the means by which to order and harmonize the army, to govern and unify subordinates.
22. Occupying high ground is the means by which to be alert and assume a defensive posture.
23. Holding defiles and narrows is the means by which to be solidly entrenched defensively.
24. Mountain forests and dense growth are the means by which to come and go silently.
25. Deep moats, high ramparts, and large reserves of supplies are the means by which to fight a prolong wall.

Thus it is said, 'One who does not know how to plan for aggressive warfare cannot be spoken with about the enemy. One who cannot divide and move his troops cannot be spoken with about unorthodox strategies. One who does not have a deep understanding of both order and chaos cannot be spoken with about changes.'

"Accordingly it is said: 'If the general is not benevolent, then the army will not be close or support him. If the general is not courageous, then the army will not be fierce. If the general is not wise, then the army will be in doubt. If the general is not perspicacious, then the army will be confounded. If the general is not quick-witted and acute, then the army will lose the opportunity. If the general is not constantly alert, the army will be weak in defense. If the general is not strong and forceful, then the army will fail in their duty.'

"Thus the general is the Master of Fate. The army is ordered because of him, and they are disordered because of him as well. If one obtains someone who is Worthy to serve as general, the army will be strong and the state will prosper. If one does not obtain a Worthy as general, the army will be weak and state will perish."

"Excellent!" said King Wu.

武王问太公说：用兵的法则，其大要如何？
太公说：古代善于用兵的人并不是能战于天上，也不是能战于地下，其成功与失败，都在于能否造成神妙莫测的态势，得此势的就胜利，不得此势的就失败。当两军对峙出兵列阵时，放纵士卒，混乱行列，目的是引诱敌人；占领草木茂盛的地区，是为了便于隐蔽撤退；占领溪谷险阻的地形，是为了阻止敌人战车和骑兵的行动；
占领险隘关塞山林地区，是为了便于以少击众；占领低湿幽暗的地区，是为了隐蔽队形；占领平坦开阔的地区，是为了比勇斗力；行动快如飞箭，猛如发机，是为了
以迅雷不及掩耳之势，打乱敌人的计划；巧妙埋伏，设置奇兵，虚张声势，诱骗敌人，是为了歼灭敌军、俘虏敌将；从多方面袭击，是为了打破敌人圆阵或方阵；乘
敌惊慌失措进攻，是为了达到以一击十的目的；趁敌疲劳农宿袭击，是为了达到以十击百的效果；利用奇妙的渡江手段，是为了克服江河障碍；使用强弩和长兵器是
为了便于越水作战；在远方设关卡、派斥侯，快速行动、不拘常法，是为了袭取敌人城邑；故意鼓噪喧嚣前进，是乱敌耳目、施行奇计妙策，冒着大风大雨前进，是
为了达到攻前袭后多方进击；伪称敌使者游行于敌后的，是为了切断敌人粮道；诈用敌人号令、敌人服装的，是为了便于准备撤退；作战时先对官兵喻以大义，激励
士气战胜敌人的方法；加封官爵，加重奖赏，是为了劝勉兵执行命令；实行

严刑重罚，是为了督促疲弊的军队坚持战斗；有怒，有赏有罚，有礼有威，有慢有快，是
为了协调全军意志，统一动；占领高大而又视界开阔的地形，是为了利于警戒和守御；守住阻要地，是为了固守；占领山林深草的地形，是为了隐蔽军队行动构筑深 沟高全，多储粮秣，是为了持久作战。
所以说，不懂攻战的策略，就谈不上对敌作战；不会机动使用力，就谈不上出奇制胜；不精通军队治乱的原因，就谈不上应变。所说，将帅不仁爱，军队就不拥护；
将帅不勇敢，军队就没有战斗力；将帅不机智，军队就会迟疑；将帅不英明，军队就会大败；将帅考虑问题不精细，军队就会失掉战机；将帅缺乏警惕，军队就会疏
于戒备；将帅领导不坚强，军队就会失职败事。所以将帅是军队的主宰，将帅精明军队就严整，将帅无能军队就混乱。有了精明能干的将帅，就会兵强国昌；没有精 明能干的将帅，就会兵弱国亡。

Five Notes

King Wu asked Jiāng Zǐyá: "From the sound of the pitch pipes, can we know the fluctuations of the army, foretell victory and defeat?"

Jiāng Zǐyá said: "Your question is profound indeed! Now there are twelve pipes, with five major notes: *Gong, Shang, Jiao, Zheng* and *Yu*. These are basic, orthodox sounds, unchanged for over thousands of generations. The spirits of the five notes is similar to the five elements. Metal, wood, water, fire and earth – each according to their conquest relationship, can be employed to counteract each other – the five notes can be used to know more about the enemy.

"In antiquity, during the period of the Three Sage Emperors, they used the nature of vacuity and non-action to govern the hard and strong. They didn't have characters for writing; everything proceeded from in accordance to the behavior of the five elements. The behavior of the five elements is in accordance to Heaven and Earth. The division into the six *jia* is a realization of marvelous and subtle spirit.

"Their method was, when the day had been clear and calm – without any clouds, wind or rain – to send light cavalry out in the middle of the night, to approach the enemy's fortifications. Stopping about 900 paces away, they would all lift their pipes to their ears and then yell out to startle the enemy. There would be a very small, subtle sound that would respond in the pitch pipes.

"If the *Jiao* note responded among the pipes, then we should attack from the west. If the *Zheng* note responded in the pipes, then we should attack from the north. If the *Shang* note responded in the pipes, then we should attack from the south. If the *Yu* note responded in the pipes, then we should attack its center. If none of the notes responded, it is then *Gong*, and we should attack from the east.

"These signs of the five notes are evidence to assist in the conquest, the subtle moments of success and defeat."

"Excellent!" said King Wu.

Jiāng Zǐyá continued: "These subtle, mysterious notes all have external indications."

"How can we know them?" King Wu asked.

Jiāng Zǐyá replied: "When the enemy has been startled into movement, listen for them. If you hear the sound of the drums, then it is the *Jiao*. If you see the flash of lights from a fire, then it is *Zheng*. If you hear the sounds of metal, of spears and halberds, then it is *Shang*. If you hear the sound of people sighing, it is *Yu*. If all is silent, without any sound, then it is *Gong*. These five are the signs of sound and appearance."

武王问太公说：从律管发出的五音，可以知道三军的消长，胜负的征兆吗？
太公说：深奥啊！这个问题。十二律管主要有五个音阶——
宫、商、角、徵、羽，这是它的基本声音，千年万代不会改变的。五微妙变化是自然的常法，借此可以推知敌情变化，金木水火土各生克取胜。用兵之道也是以其胜攻不胜啊！
古代三皇用"虚无"以制刚强，当时没有文字，一切都按王行生克行事。五行生克的道理是天地自然法则，六甲之分是非常微妙的。运用五音五行的方法是：当天气晴朗，没有阴云风雨时，半夜派遣轻骑前往敌人营全，距敌九百步以外，都拿着律管对着耳朵。对敌方大声疾呼以震惊它，敌方会有回声反应于律管中，反应来的声音是微弱的。律管中如有"角"声反应，应当从西方去打它；律管中如有"徵"声反应，应当从北方去打它；律管中如有"商"声反应，应当从南方去打它；律管中如有"羽"声反应，应当从敌人中央去打它；所有律管都没有回声是"宫"声的反应，应当从东方去打它。这是五行生克的应验，辅助制胜的征兆，胜败的关键。
武王说：好啊！
太公说：五音微妙，都有外在的征候！
武王问：怎么知道的？
太公说：当敌人惊动时就听音并观察。听到鼓声是角声的反应；见到火光是徵声的反应；听到金铁矛戟兵器声是商声的反应；听到敌人的呼啸声是羽声的反应；寂寞无闻的是宫声的反应。这五种音和色是相符合的。

Army's Indications

King Wu asked Jiāng Zǐyá: "Before engaging in battle I want to first know the enemy's strengths and weaknesses, to foresee indications of victory or defeat. How can this be done?"

Jiāng Zǐyá replied: "Indications of victory or defeat will be first manifest in their spirit. The enlightened general will investigate, for that will be evidenced in their behavior. Clearly observe the enemy's coming and going, advancing and withdrawing. Investigate his movements and periods at rest, whether they speak about portents, what the officers and troops are talking about. If the army is exhilarated and the officers and troops fear the laws; respect the general's commands; rejoice with each other in destroying the enemy; proud of each other's courage and ferocity; and praise each other for their military greatness and martial demeanor – these are indications of a strong enemy.

"If the army is startled a number of times, the officers and troops no longer maintaining good order; they terrify each other with stories about the enemy's strength; they speak to each other about the disadvantages; they are anxiously listening and talking to each other; they talk incessantly of ill omens, spreading doubts and confusing each other; they fear neither laws nor orders and do not regard their general seriously - these are indications of weakness.

"When the armies are well ordered; strong fortified defenses – with deep moats and high ramparts – and they enjoy the advantages of high winds and heavy rain; the army is untroubled; the signal flags and pennants point to the front; the sound of the gongs and bells crisp and clear; and the sound of the small and large drums clearly rises – these are indications of having obtained spiritual assistance, foretelling a great victory.

"When their formations are not solid; their flags and pennants confused and entangled with each other; they go contrary to the advantages of the high wind and heavy rain; their officers and troops are terrified; and their morale is low while they are not unified; their war horses have been frightened and run off, their military chariots have broken axles; the sound of their gongs and bells sink down and is murky; the sound of their drums is dull and not rousing – these are indications foretelling a great defeat.

"In general, when you attack city walls or surround towns, if the color of the city's aura is like dead ashes, the city can be slaughtered. If the city's aura drifts out to the north, the city can be conquered. If the city's aura goes out and drifts to the west, the city can be forced to surrender. If the aura goes out and drifts to the south, it cannot be taken. If the city's aura goes out and drifts to the east, the city cannot be attacked. If the city's aura goes out and drifts back in, the city's ruler has already fled. If the city's aura goes out and overspreads our army, the soldiers will surely fall ill. If the city's aura goes out and just rises up without any direction, the army will have to be employed for a long time. If, when you attack a walled city or surround a town for more than ten days without thunder or rain, you must hastily abandon it, for the city must have a source of great assistance.

"Those are the means by which to know whether you can attack and then go on to mount the attack, or whether you should not attack and therefore stop."

"Excellent!" said King Wu.

武王问太公说：我想在战前先知敌人的强弱，预见胜败的征侯应该怎么办？
太公说：胜败的征侯，首先在敌人精神上表现出来，明智的将帅是能够察觉的，而精神效果又反映在人的行为上。周到地侦察敌人出入进退的情况，观察它的动静，言语中的吉凶预兆，士卒间传播的消息。凡是全军喜悦，士卒畏惧法令，尊重将帅命令，相互以破敌为喜，相互以勇猛为荣，相互以威武为誉，这是军队坚强的象征。如果全军不断地惊动，士卒意志不统一，相互以敌人的强悍来恐吓，相互传捎不利的情况，相互探听消息，谣言不止，相互欺蒙，不畏惧法令，不尊重将帅，这是军队虚弱的象征。
三军整齐，阵势巩固，深沟高垒，又有顺着大风大雨的有利件，三军未动而旅旗前指，金铎声高扬而清晰，鼙鼓声婉转而响亮，这得到神明的帮助，取得大胜的征候。行阵不稳固，旌旗纷乱而方向明，又有逆着大风大雨的不利条件，士卒恐惧，士气衰竭而涣散军马惊骇乱奔，兵车断轴毁坏，金铎声低沉而混浊，鼙鼓声沉闷而 响，这是大败的征候。
凡攻城因邑：城上的"气"如果是死灰色，城可被毁灭；城上的气出而向北，城可被攻克；城上的气出而向西，城可能投降；城上的气出而向南，该城就坚不可拔；
城上的气出而向东，该城不可进攻；城上的气出而又入，守城的主将必然逃亡败北；城内的气出而覆盖我军上空，对我军必定不利；城内的气高升而不停止，是用兵
长久的征恢。凡是攻城因邑，如果过了十天仍不打雷下雨，必须迅速撤去，因为城中必有贤能的辅佐。这就可以知道为什么可攻就攻，不可攻就停止的道理了。
武王说：好啊！

Agriculture Implements

King Wu asked Jiāng Zǐyá: "The Empire has achieved peace and is settled, and the state is not engaged in any conflict, can we dispense with maintaining the implements of war? Can we forego preparing for defense?"

Jiāng Zǐyá replied: "The implements for offense and defense are fully found in ordinary human activity. Digging sticks serve as *chevaux-de-frise* (defensive structures used to obstruct cavalry), obstacles to movement. Oxen and horse-pulled wagons can be used in the encampment and as covering shields. The different hoes can be used as spears and spear tipped halberds. Raincoats of straw and large umbrellas serve as armor and protective shields. Large hoes, spades, axes, saws, mortars and pestles are tools for attacking walls. Oxen and horses are the means to transport provisions. Chickens and dogs serve as lookouts. The cloth that women weave serves as flags and pennants.

"The method that the men use for leveling the fields is the same for attacking walls. The skill needed in spring to cut down grass and thickets is the same as needed for fighting against chariots and cavalry. The weeding method used in summer is the same as used in battle against foot soldiers. The grain harvested and the firewood cut in the fall will be provisions for the military. In the winter, well filled granaries and storehouses will ensure a solid defense.

"The units formed in the fields and villages will provide the tallies and good faith that bind the men together. The villages have officials and the offices have chiefs, similar to an army having a general who can lead. The villages have walls surrounding them, which are not crossed; they provide the basis for the division into platoons. The transportation of grain and cutting of hay provide for the state storehouses and armories. The skills used in repairing the inner and outer walls in the spring and fall, can be used to build ramparts and fortifications.

"Thus the tools and skills for employing the military are completely found in ordinary human activity. One who is good at governing a state will take them from ordinary human affairs. Then they must be made to accord with the good management of livestock, to the opening up of wild lands, and the settling of the people where they dwell. The husband has a number of acres that he farms, the wife a measured amount of material to weave – this is the way to enrich the state and strengthen the army."

"Excellent!" said King Wu.

武王问太公说：天下安定，国家没有战争，野战、攻城的器械，可以不要整备吗？防守的设备，可以不要设施吗？
太公说：战时的战攻守御器材全可在平时的人民生产生活用具筹集，耒耜，可用为作战的障碍器材；马、牛、车、舆，可用作为的营垒和屏障器材；锄耰，可用为作战的矛戟；蓑衣、雨伞、斗笠，可用为作战的盔甲和大小盾牌；钁锸、斧、锯、杵臼，都可用为攻城器材；牛马，可用来转运粮食；鸡可用来报时，犬可用来警戒，妇纺织的布柿，可用作指挥旗帜；男子平整土地技术，可用于攻城业；春季割苹斩棘的方法，可用为同战车骑兵作战的技术；夏季耘锄草的方法，可用为同步兵决战的技巧；秋季收割庄稼柴草，就是储备战时粮秣；冬季粮食装满仓库，就是为域时长期坚守作准备；同村同里的人，平时相编为伍，可用为战时管理军队的依据；里有
吏，官有长，如同军队有将帅；里有围墙不得相越如同军队的驻地区分；运输粮食、收割饲草，如同战时充实仓库；春秋两季筑城郭、修沟渠，如同战时增强壁垒滚沟。所以说，作战的准备完全寓于农事之中。所以治理国家必

须使人民繁殖六畜，开垦田地，安定住所，男子种田有一定的亩数，妇女纺织有一定的尺度，这就是富国强兵的方法。
武王说：好啊！

Army's Equipment

King Wu asked Jiāng Zǐyá: "When the king mobilizes the army, are there any rules for determining the army's equipment, such as the implements for attack and defense, including type and quantity?"

Jiāng Zǐyá said: "A great question, my King! The implements for attack and defense each have their own categories. These implements will affect the effectiveness of the army: the source of military greatness of the army."

King Wu said: "I would like to hear about them."

Jiāng Zǐyá replied: "As for the basic numbers when employing the army, if commanding 10,000 armed soldiers, the rules for the various types of equipment and their employment are as follows.

"Thirty six Large Charging Chariots, with teams of skilled officers, strong crossbowmen, spear bearers, and halberdiers - for each side of the large chariots; altogether twenty four people in each chariot. The chariots have eight-foot wheels. On it, pennants and drums are set up. According to the Art of War, such chariots are referred to as 'Shaking Fear'. They are used to penetrate solid formations, to defeat strong enemies.

"Seventy two Large Flank Chariots, equipped with teams of skilled officers, strong crossbowmen, spear bearers, and halberdiers comprise the flanks. They have five-foot wheels and winch-powered linked crossbows which fire multiple arrows for self-protection. They are used to penetrate solid formations and defeat strong enemies.

"144 Flank Supporting Small Chariots, equipped with winch-powered linked crossbows to fire multiple arrows for self-protection. They have deer wheels and are used to penetrate solid formations and defeat strong enemies.

"Thirty six Crossbow Large Chariots, equipped with skilled officers, strong crossbowmen, spear bearers, and halberdiers comprising the flanks, with 'flying duck' and 'lightning's shadow' arrows for self-protection. 'Flying duck' arrows have red shafts and white feathers, with bronze arrowheads. 'Lightning's shadow' arrows have green shafts and red feathers, with iron heads. In the daytime, they display pennants of red silk six feet long by six inches wide, called 'Blinding Light'. At night, they hang pennants of white silk, also six feet long by six inches wide, called 'Meteors'. They are used to penetrate solid formations, to defeat infantry and cavalry.

"Thirty six Great Attack Chariots, carrying Praying Mantis Martial Warriors; they can attack both horizontal and vertical formations and can defeat the enemy. Light Chariots for repelling mounted invaders, also called 'Lightning Chariots'. The Art of War refers to them as mounting 'thunder attacks'. They are used to penetrate solid formations, to defeat both infantry and cavalry attacking at night.

"170 Spear and Halberd Chariots for repelling night invaders from the front flank. Each carries three Praying Mantis Martial Knights. The Art of War refers to them as mounting 'thunder attacks'. They are used to penetrate solid formations, to defeat both infantry and cavalry.

"Iron truncheons with large square heads weighting twelve catties (1 stone = 120 catties), and shafts more than five feet long: 1,200 of them. These are also termed 'Heaven's Truncheon'. The Great Handle Fu Ax with an eight-inch blade weighing eight catties, and shafts more than five feet long: 1,200 of them. These are also termed 'Heaven's Ax'. Also the Iron Square Head Pounder, weighing eight catties, with a shaft of more than five feet: 1,200. These are also termed 'Heaven Pounder'. They are used to defeat infantry and hordes of mounted invaders. The Flying Hook is eight inches long. The curve of the hook is five inches long and the shaft is more than six feet long: 1,200 of them. They are thrown into the masses of soldiers to hook the soldiers.

"To defend the army, deploy chariots equipped with wooden Praying Mantises and sword blades. Each chariot is twenty feet across, altogether twenty of them. On open and level ground the infantry can use them to defeat chariots and cavalry. Wooden caltrops which stick out of the ground, about two feet five inches: 120 of them. They are employed to defeat infantry and cavalry, to urgently press the attack against invaders, and to intercept their flight.

"Short-axle Quick-turning Spear and Halberd Chariots: 120 of them. They were employed by the Yellow Emperor to vanquish Chi You. They are used to defeat both infantry and cavalry, to urgently press the attack against the invaders, and to intercept their flight.

"For narrow roads and small bypaths, set out iron caltrops eight inches wide, having hooks four inches high and shafts of more than six feet: 1,200. They are for defeating retreating cavalry.

"If, in darkness of night, the enemy should suddenly press an attack, and there are bound to be clashes, stretch out a ground net and spread out two arrow headed caltrops connected together with weaving women-type caltrops on both sides. The points of the blades should be about two feet apart: 12,000 sets.

"For fighting in wild expanses and in the middle of tall grass, there is the square-shank, arrow-shaped spear: 1,200 of them. The method for deploying these spears is to have them stick out of the ground one foot five inches. They are used to defeat infantry and cavalry, to urgently press the attack against invaders and to intercept their flight.

"In narrow roads and small bypaths, and constricted terrains, set out iron chains: 120 of them, to defeat infantry and cavalry, urgently press the attack against the invaders, and intercept their flight. For protection and defense of the gates to fortifications, there are small mobile shields with spear and halberd tips affixed: twelve of them and winch-drive, multiple arrow crossbows for self-protection.

"For the protection of the army, there are Heaven's Net and Tiger's Drop, linked together with chains: 120 of them. One array is fifteen feet wide and eight feet tall. For chariots with Tiger's Drop and sword blades affixed, the array is fifteen feet wide and eight feet tall: 520 of them.

"For crossing over moats and ditches, there is the Flying Bridge. One section is fifteen feet wide and more than twenty feet long: eight of them. On top, there are swivel winches to extend them by linked chains.

"For crossing over large bodies of water, there is the Flying River: eight of them. They are fifteen feet wide and more than twenty feet long and are extended by linked chains.

"There is also the Heavenly Float with Iron Praying Mantis, rectangular inside, circular outside, four feet or more in diameter, equipped with winches: thirty two of them. When the Heavenly Floats are used to deploy the Flying River to cross a large lake, they are referred to as 'Heaven's Huang' and also termed as 'Heaven's Boat'.

"When in mountain forests or occupying the wilds, connect the Tiger's Drops to make a fenced encampment. Employ iron chains, lengths of more than twenty feet: 1,200 sets. Also employ 600 large ropes with rings, girth of four inches, length of more than forty feet; 200 sets of midsized ropes with rings, girth of two inches, length of forty feet or more; and 12,000 sets of small braided cords with rings, length of twenty feet or more.

"Wooden canopies for covering the heavy chariots, called 'Heaven's Rain', which fit together along serrated seams, each four feet wide and more than four feet long: one for each chariot. They are erected by using small iron posts.

"For cutting trees, there is the Heavenly Ax, which weighs eight catties. Its handle is more than three feet long. Procure 300 of them. Also procure the mattock with a blade six inches wide and a shaft more than five feet long: 300 of them.

"Copper rams for pounding, more than five feet long: 300. Eagle claws with square shafts, iron handles, and shafts more than seven feet long: 300. Square-shafted iron pitchforks with handles more than seven feet long: 300. Square-shafted double-pronged iron pitchforks with shafts more than seven feet long: 300. Large sickles for cutting grass and light trees with shafts more than seven feet long: 300. Great oar-shaped blades, weight of eight catties with shafts more than six feet long: 300. Iron stakes with rings affixed at top, more than three feet long: 300. Large hammers for pounding posts, weight of five catties, handles more than two feet long: 120.

"Armored soldiers: 10,000. Strong crossbowmen: 6,000. Halberdiers with shields: 2,000. Spearmen with shields: 2,000. Skilled men to repair offensive weapons and sharpen them: 300. These then are the general numbers required for each category when raising an army."

King Wu said: "So it shall be."

武王问太公道：君王起兵征伐，军队武器装备和攻守器材，其种类和数量有一定标准吗？
太公说：这的确是个大问题啊！攻守战具的种类、数量，各有不同，这是有关军队威力强弱的大问题。
武王说：我想知道得详细些。
太公说：凡统率甲士万人，其所使用的武器器材的大概标准是：武冲大战车三十六辆，以"材士"使用强弩、矛、戈在两旁护卫，每车用二十四人推行。其车轮高八尺，车上竖旗设鼓。兵法上把这车辆叫做"震骇"，可用它攻破坚阵，击败强敌。
武翼大橹矛戟战车七十二部，以有技能而勇敢的武士使用强弩、矛、戟为两旁护卫。这种车装有五尺高的车轮，并附有绞车连弩，可用它攻破坚阵，击败强敌。提翼小橹战车一百四十四部，并附有绞车连弩，这种车装有独轮，可用它攻破坚阵，击败强敌。
大黄参连弩大战车三十六辆，以"材士"使用强弩矛戟在两旁护卫，并附有"飞凫"、"电影"两种旗帜。飞凫用红色的竿，白色的羽，以铜矛头为旗竿头；"电影"用青色的竿，红色的羽，以铁矛头为旗竿头。白天用大红色的绢作旗子，其长六尺，宽六寸，名为"光耀"；夜间用白色的绢作旗子，其长六尺，宽六寸，名为"流星"。这种战车可用以攻破坚阵，击败强敌。
大扶胥冲车三十六辆，以螳螂武士乘于车上，可用它纵横冲击，击败强敌。轻快的车骑也叫电车，兵法称它为电击。它可用以攻破坚阵，击败故人乘夜来袭的步骑。矛戟扶胥轻车一百六十辆。每车乘螳螂武士三人，兵法称这种为霆击，可用它攻破坚阵，击败敌人的步骑。
大方头铁棒也叫天掊，重十二斤，柄长五尺以上，共一千二百把。长柄斧也叫天钺，刃长八寸，重八斤，柄长五尺以上，共一千二百把。方头铁锤也叫天槌，重八斤，柄长五尺以上，共一千二百把。可用以击败敌人的步、骑兵。飞钩，长八寸，钩尖长四寸，柄长六尺以上，共一十二百枚。它可用以投到敌方钓取敌人。

军队防守时，应使用"木螳螂剑刃扶胥"每具宽两丈，共一百二十具，也叫行马。在平坦的地形上步兵可用它阻止敌人的车。骑的行动。设置木蒺藜，要高于地面二尺五寸，兵一百二十具。可用它阻止敌人的步、骑，拦阻势穷力竭的敌人和截断逃跑的敌人。轴旋短冲矛戟战车共一百二十辆，黄帝曾用以打败蚩尤。可用它击败敌人的步、骑，拦阻势穷力竭的敌人和截断逃跑的敌人。

在隘路、小道，可以布设铁蒺藜。铁蒺藜刺长四寸，宽八寸，每具长六尺以上，共一千二百具，可用它拦阻敌人的步兵和骑兵。敌人在能见度很低的时候宽突然前来挑战，白刃相接，这时应张设地罗，布置两镞蒺藜和参连织女，各具的芒尖相距二寸，共一万二千具。在旷野深草地区作战，配备方胸铤矛，共一千二百把。设置铤矛的方法，是使它高出地面一尺五寸。以上这些，都可用以阻止敌人的步、骑、拦阻势穷力竭和敌人和截断逃跑中的敌人。在隘路，小道和低洼的地形上，可张设铁锁链，共一百二十具。它可用以阻止敌人的步骑，拦阻势穷力竭的敌人和截断逃跑的敌人。守卫管门用矛、戟、小橹各十二具，并附有绞车连弩。

军队驻守时应设天罗虎，落锁连，每部宽一丈五尺，高八尺，共一百二十具。虎落剑刃扶香，每具宽一丈五尺，高八尺，共五百二十具。

为渡沟堑装备的飞桥，每间宽一丈五尺，长两丈以上，飞桥上装有转关辘轳，共八具，使用铁环和长绳架设。渡江河使用浮桥，浮桥用宽一丈五足、长二丈以上的桥板八段拼成，用铁环长绳联结起来。天浮和铁螳螂内成圆形，外径四尺以上，两者用铁环绳索联接，共三十二套。浮桥板就架在天浮上，渡大水，这就叫天潢，也叫天船。军队在山林地扎营，应用木材结成栅寨，必须准备长二丈以上的铁链一十二百条；带铁环的粗大绳索，铁环大四寸，绳长四丈以上，共六百条；带铁环的中等绳索，铁环大二寸，绳长四丈以上，共三百条；小号绳索长二丈以上，共一万二十条。天下雨时，辎重车要盖上车顶板，还要盖上用麻编结而成的篷布，篷布宽四尺，长四丈以上，每车一具，用小铁桩固定在车顶上。砍伐树木使用大斧，重个斤，柄长三尺以上，共三百把；大锄，刃宽六寸，柄长五尺以上，共三百把；"铜筑因为全"，长五尺以上共三百把："鹰爪齐胸铁耙"，柄长七尺以上，共三百把；齐胸铁又柄长七尺以上，共三百把；齐胸两枝铁叉，柄长七足以上，共三百把。除草木使用的大镰，柄长七尺以上。共三百把；大橹刃，重八斤，柄长六尺，共三百把；带环的铁板长三足以上，共三百个；铁锵钟头重五斤，柄长二尺以上，共一百二十把。军队万人，需要强弩六千张，戟和大盾两千套，矛和盾两千套，修理攻城器具和磨快兵器的能工巧匠三百人，以上是作战所需要的兵器器材的大略数目。

武王说。应当这样！

Chapter 4 - The Tiger Teaching
Three Formations

King Wu asked Jiāng Zǐyá: "In employing the army, there are the Heavenly Formation, the Earthly Formation and the Human Formation. What are these?"

Jiāng Zǐyá replied: "When you accord your formation to celestial objects like the sun and moon, the stars, the planets and the handle of the Big Dipper - one on the left, one on the right, one in front and one to the rear - this is referred to as the Heavenly Formation.

"When you accord your formations to the hills and mounds, rivers and streams, giving you advantage at the front, rear, left and right, this is referred to as the Earthly Formation.

"When you create your formation according to the type of chariots and horses and the strategies you are using, this is referred to as the Human Formation."

"Excellent!" said King Wu.

武王问太公说：用兵时有所谓天阵、地阵、人阵，是什么意思？
太公说："根据日月星辰斗杓等天象位置来布阵，就叫天阵。利用立陵水泽等地形为依托来布阵，就叫地阵。根据所使用的兵种和战法来布阵，就叫人阵。
武王说：好啊！

Fast Battles

King Wu asked Jiāng Zǐyá: "If the enemy surrounds us, severing both our advance and retreat, breaking off our supply lines, what should we do?"

Jiāng Zǐyá replied: "These are the most distressed troops in the world! If you employ them explosively, you will be victorious; if you are slow to employ them, you will be defeated. In this situation, deploy your troops into 'Four Martial Assault Formation'. Use your military chariots and valiant cavalry to assault and startle their army, and attack them with haste. Then you can thrust across them."

King Wu asked: "After we have broken out of the encirclement, if we want to take advantage of it to gain victory, what should we do?"

Jiāng Zǐyá said: "The Left Army should assault to the left and the Right Army should assault to the right. But do not get entangled in protracted fighting with the enemy over any one road. The Central Army should alternately attack from the front and attack the rear. Even though the enemy is more numerous, their general can be driven off."

武王问太公说：如果敌人包围了我军，遮断交通，断绝粮道，应该怎么办？
太公说：这是处境最困难的军队。在这种情况下，急速突围就能胜利，拖延时日就要失败。突围的队形要把军队结成"四武冲阵"，使用强大的战车和骁勇的骑兵，打击和震骇敌军，疾速突击，这样就可以横行无阻地突围了。
武王说：如果我军已突出重围以后，还想乘势击败敌军，对此怎么办？
太公说：以左军迅速向左攻击，右军迅速向右攻击，不要和敌人争夺道路，以免分散兵力，同时以中军轮翻突击，或击敌前或抄敌后。敌军虽多，也能打败。

Certain Escape

King Wu asked Jiāng Zǐyá: "Suppose we have led our troops deep into the territory of the feudal lords where the enemy unites from all quarters and surrounds us, cutting off our road back home and severing our supply lines. The enemy is numerous and extremely well-provisioned, and gained the terrain advantage. We want to get out - how can we?"

Jiāng Zǐyá said: "In the matter of staging a certain escape, your equipment is the key, while courageous fighting is of foremost importance. If you investigate and learn what parts of the enemy's fortifications are weakly defended, and the places where there are no men, you can then stage a certain escape.

"Order your generals and officers to carry the black pennants and take up the implements of war. Require the soldiers to put wooden gags into their mouths. Then move out at night. Men of courage, strength and swiftness, who will risk extreme danger, should occupy the front, to level the enemy's fortifications and open a passage for the army. Skilled soldiers and strong crossbowmen should compose an ambushing force which will remain in the rear. Your weak soldiers, chariots and cavalry should occupy the middle. When deployment is complete, slowly advance, being very cautious not to startle or frighten the enemy. Have the Large Charging Chariots group defend the front and rear, and the Large Flank Great Chariots protect the left and right flanks.

"If the enemy should be startled, have your courageous, strong risk-takers fervently attack and advance. The weaker troops, chariots and cavalry should bring up the rear. Your skilled soldiers and strong crossbowmen should conceal themselves in ambush. If you determine that the enemy is in pursuit, the men lying in ambush should swiftly attack their rear. Make your fires and drums numerous to confuse the enemy, and attack as if coming out of the very ground or dropping from Heaven above. If the army fights courageously, no one will be able to withstand us!"

King Wu said: "In front of us lies a large body of water, or broad moat, or deep water hole which we want to cross. However, we do not have equipment, such as boats and oars. The enemy has fortifications and ramparts which limit our army's advance and block off our retreat. Patrols are constantly watchful; passes are fully defended. Their chariots and cavalry press us in front; their fighters attack us from the rear. What should we do?"

Jiāng Zǐyá said: "Large bodies of water, broad moats and deep water holes are usually not defended by the enemy. If they are able to defend them, their troops will certainly be few. In such situations, you should use the Flying River with winches and also Heaven's Huang to cross the army over. Our courageous, strong and skilled soldiers should move where we indicate, rushing into the enemy, breaking up his formations, all fighting to the death.

"First of all, burn the supply wagons and provision, and clearly inform the men that those who fight courageously will live, while cowards will die. After they have broken out and crossed the bridges, order the rear elements to set a great conflagration visible from afar. The troops moving forth must take advantage of the cover afforded by grass, trees, hillocks and ravines, ready to spring an ambush.

The enemy's chariots and cavalry will certainly not dare to pursue them too far. Using the flames as a marker, the first to go out should be ordered to proceed as far as the flame and then stop to re-form into 'Four Martial Assault Formation'. In this way, the army will be fervent and sharp and fight courageously, and no one will be able to withstand us."

"Excellent!" said King Wu.

武王问太公说：领兵深入敌国境内，敌人从四面合围我军，切断我军退路，断绝我军粮道。敌军既众，粮食又多，占领了险阻地形，守备坚固，我想突围而出，应该怎么办？
太公说：突出敌人包围的方法，兵器材器最为重要，而首先必须奋勇战斗。查明敌人兵力薄弱的地方，以及无人防守的处所，乘虚而击，就可以突出包围。突围的部署，将士们都拿着黑旗，持着器械，口中衔枚，乘夜行动。使勇敢有力、行动轻捷、敢于冒险犯难的将士在前面，攻占某些敌人营垒，为我军打开通路，让有技能而勇敢的武士使用强弩，隐伏在后面掩护，老弱士卒和车骑在中间行进。部署完毕后，沉着行动，谨慎从事，不可惊慌，使用武冲大战车在前后护卫，用武翼大橹矛戟 战车在左右掩护。
如果敌人发觉我军突围行动，我先头部队就迅速向前突击，老弱士卒和车时限在后面，材士使用强弩隐蔽地埋伏起来。当敌来追我时，我伏兵就迅速攻击它的后尾，并多用火光、鼓声乱敌耳目，使其感到我军好象是从地而出，从天而降，全军奋勇战斗，敌人就不能阻截我军的突围了。
武王说：假如面前遇到大河、宽沟、深坑，我军要想渡过，而没有准备船只，敌人屯兵筑垒，阻止我军前进，堵塞我军归路，其斥候又戒备很严，险要地形都在敌人手中，敌人的战车、骑兵又在前面拦阻，勇士又在后面袭击，对此怎么办？

太公说：凡是大河、宽沟、深坑，敌人一般是不设防的，即使防守，兵力也必定很少。这样，就可以用浮桥、折叠桥和船只渡过我军，以勇力材士按照指定方向，冲锋陷阵，拼死战斗。先焚烧我的辎重，烧掉我的粮食，再明确告诉将士，勇斗的就有生路，怯战的就是死亡。已经脱出危险的就令我军后卫部队设置烟火信号，派出远方斥候，占领丛林、坟茔和险阻的地形，准备阻击敌人。这样，敌人的战车骑兵必然不敢长驱远追了。其所以用火作为信号，是令先突围的到达有火的地方，就编成"四武冲阵"。这样，我三军将士都精锐而勇斗，敌人就无法阻止我军了。

武王说：好啊！

Planning for the Army

King Wu asked Jiāng Zǐyá: "Suppose we have led the army deep into the territory of the feudal lords, where we encounter deep streams or water in large valleys, ravines and defiles. Our army has not yet fully forded them when Heaven lets loose a torrent, resulting in a sudden flood surge. The rear cannot maintain contact with the front portion. We don't have equipment to cross the river and the supply has been cut off. I want to finish crossing, to keep the army from becoming bogged down. What should I do?"

Jiāng Zǐyá said: "If the leader of the army and commander of the masses does not first establish his plans, the proper equipment will not be prepared. If his instructions are not precise and trusted, the officers and men will not be trained. Under such conditions, they cannot comprise a conqueror's army.

"In general, when the army is involved in a major campaign, everyone should be trained to use the equipment. For attacking a city wall or surrounding a town, there are armored assault chariots, overlook carts, and battering rams, while for seeing inside the walls, there are the 'cloud ladders' and 'flying towers'. If the advance of the army is stopped, then there are Large Charging Chariots, for defending both front and rear. For severing roads and blocking streets, there are the skilled soldiers and strong crossbowmen controlling the two flanks. If you are encamping or building fortifications, there are the Heaven's Net, the Martial Drop, the *chevaux-de-frise*, and the caltrops.

"In the daytime, climb the cloud ladder and look off into the distance. Set up five colored pennants and flags. At night, set out 10,000 fire-cloud torches, beat the thunder drums, strike the war drums and bells, and blow the sharp sounding whistles.

"For crossing over moats and ditches, there are the Flying Bridges with mounted winches and cogs. For crossing large bodies of water, there are boats called

Heaven's Huang and Flying River. For going against the waves and up current, there are the rafts and the rope pulled River Severance. When the equipment to be used by the army is fully prepared, what worries will the commander-in-chief have?"

武王问太公说：领兵深入敌国境内，遇到深溪大谷和难以通过的河流，我军还没有渡完、忽然天降暴雨，流水大涨，后面的军队被水隔断，既没有船只。又没有水草、粮食的供给，在这种情况下，我想完全渡过去，使三军不至停留过久，应该怎么办？

太公说：大凡率领军队行动，如果计划不预先制定，器械不预作准备，平时训练不周到，士卒动作不熟练，这就不能算是王者的军队了。凡军队在有军事行动的时候，没有不熟练使用各种器械的。如攻城围邑，就用"轒辒"、"临车"、"冲车"；观察城内就用"云梯"、"飞楼"；三军进止，就用"武冲"、"大橹"在前后掩护；断绝交通，遮断街道，就用材士强弩，控制两侧；设置营垒就用"天罗"、"武落"、"行马"、"蒺藜"；白天就登上云梯瞭望远方，并设立五色旌旗；夜晚就设置烟火，升击"雷级"，敲小鼓，摇大铃，吹胡品，用为指挥信号；越沟壕，就用"飞桥"、"转关"、"辘轳""锄铻"；渡大河，就用"天潢"、"飞江"；逆流而行，就用"浮海"、"绝江"。如果军队应用的器材都具备了，主将还忧虑什么呢？

Approaching the Border

King Wu asked Jiāng Zǐyá: "Both the enemy and our army have reached the border where we are in a standoff. They can approach, and we can also advance. Both deployments are solid and stable; neither side dares to move first. We want to go forth and attack them, but they can also come forward as well. What should we do?"

Jiāng Zǐyá said: "Divide the army into sections. Have our advance troops deepen the moats and increase the height of the ramparts, but none of the soldiers should go forth. Array the flags and pennants, beat the leather war drums, and complete all the defensive measures. Order our rear army to stockpile supplies and foodstuffs without causing the enemy to know our intentions. Then send forth our elite troops to secretly launch a sudden attack at their rear, striking where they do not expect it, attacking where they are not prepared. Since the enemy does not know our real situation, they will not advance."

King Wu asked: "Suppose the enemy knows our real situation and has fathomed our plans. If we move, they will be able to know what we are up to. Thus they send forth their elite troops, concealed in the deep grass, to ambush us on the narrow roads. What should we do?"

Jiāng Zǐyá replied: "Each day, the vanguard should go forth and instigate skirmishes with them, in order to psychologically wear them out. Have our older and weaker soldiers to drag brushwood to stir up the dust, beat the drums and shout, and move back and forth - some going to the left, some to the right, never getting closer than 100 paces from the enemy, to create an illusion that we have a large army. Their general will certainly become mentally fatigued, and their troops will become fearful. In this situation, the enemy will not dare come forward. Then our advancing troops will sometime continue forward to attack their interior, other times their exterior. With our army all fervently engaging in battle, the enemy shall certainly be defeated."

武王问太公说：我军和敌人在国境上互相对峙，敌可以来攻我，我可以去攻敌，彼此阵势都很坚固，谁也不敢首先行动，我想前去袭击敌人，又担心敌人前来袭击我军，应该怎么办？

太公说：在这种情况下，应把我军区分为前中后三部分，令我前军深沟高垒，不要出战，列旌旗，击鼙鼓，作充分的战斗准备。令我后军多积粮食，不要使敌人知道我军企图。然后，派遣精锐部队偷袭敌人后方，出其不意，攻其不备地袭扰敌人，使敌人无法了解我军情况，就不敢前来进攻了。

武王问：如果敌人察知我军情况，明瞭我军企图，我一行动敌人就知道我要做什么，因而派他的精锐部队埋伏在深草地里，拦阻我必经的隘路，袭击我防备不周的地方，对此怎么办？

太公说：令我前军，每天前往挑战，以懈怠敌人的斗志；令我老弱士卒，拖动树枝，扬起灰尘，击鼓呐喊，往来不停，以壮我军声势。我挑战部队或出现在敌人右

边，或出现在敌人左边，距离敌人不超过百步，在我不断扰乱下，敌人的将帅必定疲于应付，敌人的士卒必定发生恐慌。这样，敌人就不敢前来了。我军反复不停的扰乱，或袭击他的内部，或打击他的外部，然后，全军疾速投入战斗，敌人就一定会被打败了。

Maneuvering

King Wu asked Jiāng Zǐyá: "Suppose we have led our troops deep into the territory of the feudal lords and are confronting the enemy. The two deployments encamp across from each other, are equal in numbers and strength, and neither dares to move first. I want to cause the enemy's general to become terrified; their officers and men to become dispirited; their battle array to become weak; their reserve army to want to run off; and those deployed in front to be shaken. I want to beat the drums, set up a clamor, and take advantage of it to attack and cause the enemy to run off. How can we do it?"

Jiāng Zǐyá said: "In this case, send our troops out about ten miles from the enemy's rear and have them conceal themselves on both flanks. Send your chariots and cavalry out about 100 miles and have them assume positions to cut across both enemy's front and rear. Multiply the number of flags and pennants, and increase the number of gongs and drums. When the battle starts, beat the drums, set up a clamor and have your men all rise up together. The enemy's general will surely be afraid and his army will be terrified. Large and small groups cannot come to each other's rescue; upper and lower ranks cannot help each other; and the enemy will definitely be defeated."

King Wu asked: "Suppose the enemy has gained the terrain advantage, thus we cannot conceal troops on the flanks, and moreover our chariots and cavalry have no way to cross behind them and assume positions to cut off the enemy's front and the rear. The enemy anticipates my plans and makes preemptive preparations. Our officers and soldiers are dispirited, our generals are terrified. If we engage in battle, we will not be victorious. What then?"

Jiāng Zǐyá replied: "An interesting question. In this case, five days before engaging in battle, dispatch distant patrols to observe their activities and analyze their forward movement in order to prepare an ambush and await them. We must meet the enemy on 'death' ground'. Spread our flags and pennants out over great distances, disperse our arrays and formations. We must race forward to meet the enemy. After the battle has started, make a sudden retreat, beating the gongs to signal it. Withdraw about three miles, beyond the ambush, then turn about and attack. Your concealed troops should simultaneously arise. Some should penetrate the flanks; others attack their vanguard and rear guard positions. If the army fervently engages in battle, the enemy will certainly run off."

"Excellent!" said King Wu.

武王问太公说：领兵深入敌国境内，敌我势均力敌，两军相对，众寡强弱相等，谁也不敢首先行动。在这种情况下，我想使敌人将帅恐惧，士卒悲叹，行阵不稳，后阵的想逃，前阵的动摇，然后，擂鼓呐喊乘势进击，从而使敌人逃跑，应该怎么办？
太公说：想做到这样，就须派遣部队绕到敌后十里的地方，在道路两旁设置埋伏，另组织成车和骑兵远出百里，迂回到敌军的深远后方，令各部队多备旌旗，增设金鼓，战斗发起时，擂鼓呐喊，各军同时进攻，这样敌军将帅必然恐惧，士兵必然惊骇，以至大小部队互不救援，官兵不相照顾，这样，敌军必定会被打败。
武王说：如果敌方地势不使我军在其两旁设伏，我车骑无法迂回到敌人的深远后方，同时敌人又发觉了我军的企图，并预先有了准备，这时我士卒悲观，将帅恐惧，就是进战也不能取胜，应该怎么办？
太公说：你所问的确实很微妙啊！象这种情况，在战前五天就应向远方派遣斥候，窥探敌人的动静，观察敌军前来的征候，预设伏兵等待他。必须在对敌人最不利的
"死地"与敌军遭遇，使我先头部队疏散旌旗，行列不整，我以一部兵力向敌前进，刚一交锋即行撤退，故意鸣金收兵，后退三里再回头反击，这时伏

兵乘机而起，或突击敌军两旁，或抄袭敌军前后，全军备力作战，敌人必败而逃走。
武王说：好啊！

Gongs and Drums

King Wu asked Jiāng Zǐyá: "Suppose we have led the army deep into the territory of the feudal lords where we are confronting the enemy. The weather has been either extremely hot or very cold, and it has been raining incessantly day and night for ten days. The ditches and ramparts are all collapsing; defiles and barricades are unguarded; our patrols have become negligent; and the officers and men are not alert. Suppose the enemy comes at night, and our army is unprepared while the upper and lower ranks are confused and disordered. What should we do?"

Jiāng Zǐyá said: "In general, for the army, alertness makes for solidity, laziness results in defeat. Order our guards on the ramparts to unceasingly challenge everyone. Have all those bearing the signal flags, both inside and outside encampment, watch each other, responding to each other's orders with countersigns, but do not allow them to make any noise. All efforts should be externally oriented.

"3,000 men should comprise a detachment. Instruct and constrain them with warning, requiring each of them to exercise vigilance at his post. If the enemy approaches, when they see our state of readiness and alertness, they will certainly turn around. As a result, their strength will become exhausted and their spirits dejected. At that moment, send forth our elite troops to follow and attack them."

King Wu asked: "The enemy, knowing we are following him, conceals elite troops in ambush while pretending to continue to retreat. When we reach the ambush, their troops turn back and attack us, some attacking our front, others our rear, whiles some press towards our fortifications. Our army is terrified, and in confusion, fall out of formation and leave their assigned positions. What should we do?"

Jiāng Zǐyá said: "Divide into three forces, then follow and pursue them, but do not cross beyond their ambush. When all three forces have arrived, some should attack the front and rear, while others should penetrate the two flanks. Make your command clear. Fervently attack, advancing forward, and the enemy will certainly be defeated."

武王问太公说：领兵深入敌国境内，敌我兵力相当，适值严寒或酷暑，或又日夜大丙，旬日不止，因而壕全全部损毁，险隘矣塞不能守备，斥候麻痹懈怠，士卒疏于戒备，这时，敌人乘夜来袭，三军皆无准备，上下又疑虑混乱，对此怎么办？

太公说：凡军队，有戒备就能巩固，若松懈就要失败。在我军营垒上口令呼应之声不绝，哨兵手持旗帜，与营垒内外联络，相互传送号令，金鼓之声不可断绝，对外表示已做好战斗准备，以三千人为一屯，谆谆告诫，严加约束，使各自慎重守备。若敌人来犯，发现我军戒备森严，即使追近我军阵前，也必退去，这时，我应乘敌 力尽气衰之际，派遣精锐部队紧随敌后猛击敌人。

武王说：敌人知道我要跟踪追击，于是埋伏了精锐士卒，然后假装退却不止，当我军进刮伏兵地区时，敌人就回头配合其伏兵向我反击，有的攻我前队，有的击我后队，有的追近我营垒，因而我军大为恐慌，行列陷于混乱，各自擅离在阵中的位置，对此怎么办？

太公说：在这种情况下应把我军分为三队，分向敌人跟踪追击，不要进入伏击圈，在到达敌伏击圈前就要三队同时追到敌人，有的攻击敌人前后，有的攻击敌人两侧，并须严明号令，使士卒疾速进击，敌人必被打败。

Severed Routes

King Wu asked Jiāng Zǐyá: "Suppose we have led the army deep into the territory of the feudal lords where, confronting them, we have each assumed defensive positions. The enemy has severed our supply routes and occupied positions cutting across both our front and rear. If I want to engage them in battle, we cannot win; but if I want to maintain our position, we cannot hold out for long. What should we do?"

Jiāng Zǐyá replied: "In general, when you venture deep beyond the enemy's borders, you must investigate the configuration and strategic advantages of the terrain and concentrate on seeking out terrain advantages. Rely on mountains, forests, ravines, rivers, streams, woods, and trees to create a secure defense. Carefully guard passes and bridges and moreover be certain you know the advantages of terrain conveyed by the various cities, towns, hills, and mounds. In this way, the army will be solidly entrenched. The enemy will not be able to sever our supply routes, nor be able to occupy positions cutting across our front and rear."

King Wu asked: "Suppose after our army has passed through a large forest or across a broad marsh and are on flat, accessible terrain, due to some miscommunication, our allies are not here and the enemy suddenly falls upon us. If we engage them in battle, we cannot win; if we assume a defensive position, it will not be secure. The enemy has outflanked us on both sides and occupied positions cutting across our front and rear. The army is terrified. What should be done?"

Jiāng Zǐyá replied: "Now the rule for commanding an army is always to first dispatch scouts forward so that when you are 200 miles from the enemy, you will already know their position. If the terrain is not to our advantage, then use the

Large Charging Chariots to serve as a cover and advance. Also establish two rear guard armies to the rear. The distance between the main forces and the rear guard armies can be as far as 100 miles away, or as near as fifty miles away. Thus when the alarm sounds or an urgent situation arises, both front and rear will know about it, and the army will always be able to complete their deployment into solid formation, never suffering any destruction or harm."

"Excellent!" said King Wu.

武王问太公道：领兵深入敌国境内，与敌对峙，这时敌人截断了我军粮道，迂回到我军后方，从前后两方面夹击我军。我想和他作战恐怕不能取胜，我想防守又恐怕不能持久，这该怎么办？
太公说：凡是深入敌国境内，必须观察地理形势，务求控制有利地形。依托山林、险阻、水表、林木以求阵势的巩固，严守关隘桥梁，还应掌握城邑、丘墓于有利地形。这样，我军防守就能坚固，敌人既不能绝我粮道，也不能迂回到我的后方，从两面夹击我军了。
武王说：我军通过大的森林、广阔的沼泽地及平坦地形时，友军队失误未到，突然与敌遭遇，要想进战怕不能取胜，想防守怕巩怕不能巩固，这时敌人包围我军两侧，超越我军远后方，我三军大为恐惧，对此怎么办？
太公说：统军作战的方法，当先向我前进远方派出斥候，在距离敌人尚有二百里时，就需要确实了解敌军所在的位置。如果地势对我行动不利，就用武冲车在前面掩护行进，并编两支"踵军"在后跟进，踵军和主力的距离远的可达百里，近的可达五十里，一旦遇急情况，前后可以互相救援。我三军如能经常保持这种完善而巩固
的部署，也就不至于遭受严重的伤亡和失败了。
武王说：好啊！

Occupying the Enemy Territories

King Wu asked Jiāng Zǐyá: "Suppose, being victorious in battle, we have deeply penetrated the enemy's territory and occupy his land. However, large walled cities remain that cannot be subjugated, while their second army holds the defiles and ravines, standing off against us. We want to attack the cities and besiege the towns, but I am afraid that their second army will suddenly appear and strike us. If their forces inside and outside unite in this fashion, they will oppose us from both within and without. Our army will be in chaos; the upper and lower ranks will be terrified. What should be done?"

Jiāng Zǐyá said: "In general, when attacking cities and besieging towns, the chariots and cavalry must be kept at a distance. The encamped and defensive units must be on constant alert in order to obstruct the enemy both within and without. When inhabitants have their food cut off - those outside being unable to transport anything in to them - those within the city walls will be afraid, and their general will certainly surrender."

King Wu said: "Suppose that when the supplies inside the city are cut off - external forces being unable to transport anything in - those in the city clandestinely concoct secret plans, and then sally forth at night, throwing all their forces forward. Some of their chariots, cavalry and elite troops assault us from within; others attack from without. The officers and troops are confused, the army defeated in chaos. What should be done?"

Jiāng Zǐyá said: "In this case, you should divide your forces into three armies. Be careful to evaluate the terrain's configuration and then strategically place them. You must know in detail the location of the enemy's second army, as well as his large cities and other fortifications. Leave them a passage in order to entice them to flee. Pay attention to the defense of the escape passage. The enemy will be afraid, and if they do not enter the mountains or the forests, they will return to the large towns, or run off to join the second army. Use our chariots and cavalry to attack the front of the escaping troops; do not allow them to escape. Since those remaining in the city will think that the first to go out have a direct escape route, their well-trained troops and skilled officers will certainly move forth, with the old and weak remaining. Do not engage in battle. Just sever their supply routes, surround and guard them, and you will certainly outlast them.

"Do not set fire to what the people have accumulated; do not destroy their palaces or houses, nor cut down trees at gravesites and altars. Do not kill those who surrender nor slay your captives. Instead, show them benevolence and righteousness, extend your generosity to them. Announce to the people that the fault lies in only the ruler. In this way, the entire city will then submit."

"Excellent," said King Wu.

武王问太公说：乘胜深入敌国，占领其地，还有大城未能攻下，而敌人城外另有一支部队固守险要地形，与我相持。我想围攻，又恐其城外部队猝然逼近，会合其城内守军向我夹击，以至三军大乱，上下大骇，应该怎么办呢？
太公说：凡攻城围邑时，须把战车、骑兵配置在离城较远的地方，担任守卫和警戒，以隔绝敌人的内外联系。这样，城内日久粮绝外面不得输入，城内军民就会发生恐怖，守城的将领就会投降。
武王问：城内敌人断粮，城外粮食不得输入，这时敌人互相连系密谋突围，乘夜出城拼命死战，以车骑锐士或冲入我营内，或攻击营外，使我士卒惶惑，三军败乱，对此怎么办？
太公说：遇到这种情况，应把我军分为三支部队，并根据地形屯驻部队。首先查明敌城外部队状况及所据守的地区和附近大城别堡的关系位置，然后为被围敌人留出一条道路，以诱其外逃，但须严密戒备，不使敌人跑掉。由于被围敌人恐惧，不是想逃到深山密林，就是想撤到另一大城。这时我军应以

一支部队，赶走敌人城外的

"别军"；以另一支部队，用战车和骑兵在距城较远的地方，阻击敌人突围的先头部队，不让他们脱逃。在这种形势下，守城敌军就会误认为其先头部队已突围成

功，打通了撤退的道路，其精锐士卒必会继续从城内外逃，城内只剩下老弱残兵了。然后用我第三支部队，以车骑直驱敌后，敌人必不敢继续突围，我军也不要急于

进攻，只要断绝其粮道，把他围困起来，日子一久，敌人就会投降。攻克城邑后，不要焚烧粮食，不要毁坏房屋，不要砍伐坟地的树木和里社的丛林，不要杀戮投降

的，不要虐待被俘的，对敌国人民要表示仁义，施以恩德。对其士民宣告：有罪的只是无道君主一人。这样，天下就会心悦诚服了。

武王说；好啊！

Fire Warfare

King Wu asked Jiāng Zǐyá: "Suppose we have led our troops deep into the territory of the feudal lords where we encounter deep grass and heavy growth which surround our army on all sides. The army has traveled several hundred miles; men and horses are exhausted and have halted to rest. Taking advantage of the extremely dry weather and a strong wind, the enemy ignites fires upwind from us. Their chariots, cavalry and elite forces are concealed in ambush to our rear. The army becomes terrified, scatter in confusion and run off. What can be done?"

Jiāng Zǐyá said: "Under such circumstances, use the cloud ladders and flying towers to look far out to the left and right, to carefully investigate front and rear. When you see the fires arise, then set fires in front of our own forces, spreading them out over the area. Also set fires to the rear. If the enemy comes, withdraw the army and take up entrenched positions on the blackened earth to await their assault. In the same way, if you see flames arise to the rear, you must move far away. If we occupy the blackened ground with our strong crossbowmen and skilled soldiers protecting the left and right flanks, we can also set fires to the front and rear. In this way, the enemy will not be able to harm us."

King Wu asked: "Suppose the enemy has set fires to the left and right and also to the front and rear. Smoke covers our army, while his main forces appear from over the blackened ground. What should we do?"

Jiāng Zǐyá replied: "In this case, assuming you have prepared a burnt section of the ground, go into 'Four Martial Assault Formation' and have strong crossbowmen cover the flanks. This method will not bring victory, but will also not end in defeat."

武王问太公说：领军深入敌国境内，茂密的草丛区围绕在我军前后左右，我已行军数百里，人困马乏，宿营休息。敌人趁天干风紧，在上风放火，其车骑锐士又埋伏在我军的后面，以致三军恐怖，散乱逃跑，对此怎么办？

太公说：在草地宿营要利用云梯、飞楼，登高盼望前后左右，发现敌人放火，就顺着风向也在我军较远的前方放起火来，扩大火焚面积。同时又在我军后方放起火

来，[以便淹出一块"黑地"，]若是敌人来攻，我就可以把军队撤到这块黑地坚守。前未围攻的敌人此时还在我军后面，他看到火起，定会退走。我军在黑地内布

阵，用材士强弩掩护两翼，[敌人再行火攻]，我又如法在前后放火，如此反复进行，敌人就无法加害于我了。

武王问：敌人既在我的左右放火，又在我的前后放火，以至烟覆盖了我军，而敌军突然向我据守的黑地逼近，对此怎么办？

太公说：遇上这种情况，可将我军结成"四武冲阵"，以强弩掩护我的左右，这种办法虽然不能取胜，也不会失败。

Empty Fortifications

King Wu asked Jiāng Zǐyá: "How can I know whether the enemy's fortifications are empty or full, whether they are coming or going?"

Jiāng Zǐyá said: "A general must know the ways of Heaven, the advantages of terrain and human affairs. You should mount high and look out far in order to see the enemy's changes and movements. Observe his fortifications, and then you will know whether they are empty or full. Observe his officers and troops and then you will know whether they are coming or going."

King Wu asked: "How will I know it?"

Jiāng Zǐyá said: "Listen to see if his drums are silent, if his bells make no sound. Look to see whether there are many birds flying above the fortifications, if they were not startled into flight. If there are no dust clouds overhead, you will certainly know the enemy has tricked you with dummies.

"If enemy forces precipitously go off - but not very far - and then return before assuming proper formation, they are rushing their officers and men too quickly. When they act too quickly, the forward and rear are unable to maintain good order. When they cannot maintain good order, the entire battle disposition will be in chaos. In such circumstances, quickly dispatch troops to attack them. Even if you use a small number to strike a large force, they will certainly be defeated."

武王问太公说：怎样知道敌人营垒的虚实和敌军调动的情况呢？

太公说：为将帅的必须上知"天道"，下知"地理"，中知"人事"。登高瞭望段营垒，以观察敌人的动静。瞭望敌人的营垒就知道他内部的虚实；观察士卒的动态，就知道他调动的情况。

武王问：用什么办法知道这些呢？

大公说：如果听不到敌人鼓声，也听不到铃声，瞭望敌营垒上有许多飞鸟而不惊惧，空中也没有尘烟飞扬，必然是敌人的空营，而守营的只是些假人。如果敌人仓猝撤退不远，还没有停下来而又返回的，这是调动军队太忙乱的现象。太忙乱，他的前后就没有秩序，没秩序，行列就会混乱。象这样情况，我可疾速出兵打击他，虽然以少击众，也必会取得胜利。

Chapter 5 - The Leopard Teaching
Forest Warfare

King Wu asked Jiāng Zǐyá: "Suppose we have led our troops deep into the territory of the feudal lords where we encounter a large forest which we share with the enemy in a standoff. If we assume a defensive posture, I want it to be solid, or if we fight, to be victorious. How should we proceed?"

Jiāng Zǐyá said: "Divide the army into the 'Four Martial Assault Formation'. Have the troops placed at a strategic position and station the archers and crossbowmen outside, with those carrying spear-tipped halberds and shields inside. Cut down and clear away the grass and trees, and extensively broaden the passages in order to facilitate our movement in the battle site. Set our pennants and flags out on high and carefully maneuver the army without letting the enemy know our true situation. This is referred to as 'Forest Warfare'.

"The method of Forest Warfare is to form the spear bearers and halberdiers into groups. If the woods are not dense, cavalry can be used in support. Battle chariots will occupy the front. When there is opportunity, they will fight; when not opportune, they will desist. When there are numerous ravines and defiles in the forest, you must deploy your forces in the 'Four Martial Assault Formation' in order to be prepared, both front and rear. If the army attacks swiftly, even though the enemy is numerous, they can be driven off. The men should fight and rest in turn, each with their section. This is the main outline of Forest Warfare."

武王问太公说，领兵深入敌国境内，遇到森林地，与敌人各占森林一部对峙时，我想要防御就能固，进攻就能胜，应该怎么办？
太公说：将我军区分为"四武冲阵"，配置在便于作战的地方，弓弩手布在外层，戟楯放在内层，砍去草木，开辟道路，以便利战斗行动；高挂旗帜，以便联络，严格控制掌握全军，同时不使敌人察知我军的情况，这就是森林地战斗。森林地作战的方法：应将我军使用矛我的士卒编为混合小分队，在森林中树木稀疏的地方以骑
兵辅助作战，把战车配置在前面，发现有利的情况就打，没有发现有利的情况就不打。如森林中有许多险阻地形，就必须设置"四武冲阵"，以防敌袭击我军前后，
战斗时务使全军急剧地进行战斗，敌人即便众多，也可被我打败，部队要轮番作战轮番休息，各按编组行动，这是森林地战斗的原则。

Surprise Battle

King Wu asked: "When our enemy makes a military incursion into our country, encroaches upon our land, loot our cattle, advance in large numbers and come near to our city, the soldiers are in deep fear, our people are detained as prisoners;

under such a situation, what could I do if I want to defend solidly or fight victoriously?"

Jiāng Zǐyá said: "Such an enemy, who attacks suddenly; their cattle are surely lacking in food, and the soldiers are lacking food, so they are attacking fiercely. In this case, we should order our distant army to select an elite team and attack our enemy quickly from their rear flank. We must make detailed and precise calculations to determine the operational time, as they must join us in the darkness of night. Our whole army should fight our enemy swiftly and violently, though there are a lot of them, the commanders would still be detained by us."

King Wu said: "Our enemy is divided into three or four parts, either invading into our territory and lands, or stopping to plunder our cattle. The enemy's army has not fully arrived; instead, they use parts of the troops to cause us fear. What should we do in such a case?"

Jiāng Zǐyá said: "We should make careful observations of the situation; we must make military preparations before the enemy army fully arrives; we must go into a state of combat readiness. Build the fortress four miles outside our city; the drums and the flags should be placed perfectly. Other than that, we should also assign part of our army as an ambush. Order the troops on top of the fortress to concentrate their bows, set up a secret exit every hundred steps, and use wooden barriers to lock it up. The chariots and cavalry should be placed at the outside of the fortress. The elites in the army should be used for the preparation of the ambush. If the enemy comes, let our lightly armed troops fight our enemy; pretend defeat, then retreat. Order our defense army to set up flags and hit drums; make defensive preparations, so the enemy will think that we focus our forces to defend our city. Therefore, they should come forward into our city. At the same time, I will have our ambushing army come into action, attack the enemy's battle array or attack our enemy from the outside. At this time, our whole army should bravely and quickly attack our enemy from the front and the back; with this, we could make the brave unable to defend, and the speedy unable to retreat. This kind of strategy is called sudden attack. However large our enemy's troops are, they will still be defeated."

"Excellent!" said King Wu.

武王问太公说：敌人深入我国，长驱直入，侵占土地，抢掠牛马，蜂涌前来，追我城下，我士卒大为恐惧，人民被拘禁为俘虏，这种情况下，我想以守能固，以战能胜，应该怎么办？
太公说：象这样的敌军叫做突然来袭的敌军，他的牛马必然缺饲料，他的士卒必然没有粮食，只是凶猛地向我进攻，在这种情况下，应令我远方的军队，挑选精锐的
士卒，迅速袭击敌人的后方，详细计算确定作战时间，务必在夜暗与我会合，三军迅速猛烈地与敌战斗，敌人虽多，敌将也可被我俘虏。

武王说：敌军分为三、四部分，或者进攻以侵占我土地，或者驻止以掠夺我牛马，他的大军还没有完全到达，而以一部分兵力迫近我城下，以致我军恐惧，应该怎么办？

太公说：仔细观察情况，在敌人尚未完全到达前，就应先完成战备，严阵以待。在距城四里的地方构筑营垒，金鼓旗帜，都完全布设起来，另派一部分为伏兵。令我

营垒上的部队多集中强弩，每百步设一突门，用行马封锁。战车、骑兵配置在营全外面。勇锐士卒隐蔽埋伏。敌人如果来到，使我轻装部队与敌交战后佯败退走。令

我守军在城上立旗帜，击鼙鼓，作好防守准备，敌人以为我主力守城，必然逼近城下。这时我突然出动伏兵，冲入敌人阵内，或攻击敌人阵外，此时全军勇猛迅速地

出去，既攻击敌人正面，又攻击敌人后方，使敌人勇敢的无法抵抗。轻快的来不及逃跑。这种戏法称为"突战"。敌人虽然众多，也必被我打败。

武王说：好啊！

Strong Enemy

King Wu asked Jiāng Zǐyá: "Suppose we have led the army deep into the territory of the feudal lords until we are opposed by the enemy's assault forces. The enemy is numerous while we are few. The enemy is strong, while we are weak. The enemy approaches at night - some attacking the left, others the right. The whole army is shaken. We want to be victorious if we choose to attack or solid if we choose to maintain a defensive posture. How should we act?"

Jiāng Zǐyá said: "In this situation, we refer to them as 'Shaking Invaders'. It is more advantageous to go out and fight; you cannot be defensive. Select skilled soldiers and strong crossbowmen, together with chariots and cavalry to comprise the left and right flanks. Then swiftly striking his forward forces and quickly attacking his rear as well. Some should strike the exterior, others the interior. Their troops will certainly be confused, their generals afraid."

King Wu asked: "Suppose the enemy has blocked off our forward units some distance away and is pressing an attack on our rear. He has broken up our elite troops and cut off our skilled soldiers. Our interior and exterior forces cannot communicate with each other. The army is in chaos, all running off in defeat. The officers and troops have lost their will to fight, the generals and commanders have no desire to defend themselves. What should we do?"

Jiāng Zǐyá said: "Illustrious is your question, my King! You should make your commands clear and be careful about your orders. You should have your courageous and crack troops, who are willing to confront danger, sally forth - each man carrying a torch and two men to a drum. You must know the enemy's location then strike both the interior and exterior. When our secret signals have been communicated, order them to extinguish the torches and stop beating all drums. The interior and exterior should respond to each other, each according to the appropriate time. When our army fervently attacks, the enemy will certainly be defeated and vanquished."

"Excellent!" said King Wu.

武王问太公说：领兵深入敌国境内，与敌人突击部队接触，敌众我寡，敌强我弱，而敌人又利用夜暗前来，既攻我的左翼，又攻我的右翼，全军震动，我想使进攻能胜利，防御能牢固，应该怎么办？
太公说：这样的敌人叫做"震寇"。我军利于出战，不宜防守，须挑选材士强弩，以战车、骑兵为左右翼，迅速攻击敌人正面，急剧袭击敌人侧后，既要攻击敌人阵外，又要攻入敌人阵内，这样，敌军必然混乱，敌军将冲也必然惊惶失措而被打败。
武王说：敌人在远处阻截我的前方，急速攻击我的后方，遮断我精锐的救兵，阻绝我应援的材士，使我内外失去联系，以致三军扰乱，散乱逃走，士卒没有斗志，将吏无心固守，应该怎么办？
太公说：高明啊，君王所提出的问题！在这种情况下，应该明审号令，出动我勇猛精锐的士卒，使每人携持火炬，二人同击一鼓，必须探知敌人的准确位置，然后部署军队，有的攻击敌人外部，有的冲入敌人内部。部队都佩带暗号，互相识别，扑灭火炬，停息鼓音，以便内外策应，大家都按预先约定的信号准确执行，全军猛烈的战斗，敌必败亡。
武王说：好啊！

Martial the Enemy

King Wu asked Jiāng Zǐyá: "Suppose we have led the army deep into the territory of the feudal lords where we suddenly encounter a martial and numerically superior enemy. If his martial chariots and valiant cavalry move and attack our left and right flanks, and our army becomes so shaken, that their flight is unstoppable, what should I do?"

Jiāng Zǐyá replied: "In this situation, you have what is termed as a 'defeated army'. Those who are skillful in employing their forces will manage a victory. Those who are not will perish."

King Wu asked: "What can one do?"

Jiāng Zǐyá replied: "Have our most skilled soldiers and strong crossbowmen, together with our martial chariots and valiant cavalry, conceal themselves on both sides of the retreat route, about three miles ahead and behind our main force. When the enemy pursues us, launch a simultaneous chariot and cavalry assault from both sides. In such circumstances, the enemy will be thrown into confusion and our fleeing soldiers will stop by themselves."

King Wu continued asking: "Suppose the enemy's chariots and cavalry are squarely opposite ours, but the enemy is numerous while we are few, the enemy strong while we are weak. Their approach is disciplined and spirited and our formations are unable to withstand them. What should we do?"

Jiāng Zǐyá replied: "Select our skilled soldiers and strong crossbowmen, and have them lie in ambush on both sides, while the chariots and cavalry deploy into a solid formation and assume position. When the enemy passes our concealed forces, the crossbowmen should fire en masse into their flanks. The chariots, cavalry, and skilled soldiers should then urgently attack their army - some striking the front, others striking the rear. Even if the enemy is numerous, they will certainly flee."

"Excellent!" said King Wu.

武王问太公说：领兵深入敌国境内，突然遭遇敌人，人数甚多而且勇猛，并以武冲大战车和骁勇的骑兵包围我的两翼，全军震惊，纷纷逃跑，不可阻止，对此怎么办？
太公说：这样行动的军队叫做"败兵"。处理得好可以因此而胜取，处理不好也会因此而灭亡。
武王说：具体该怎么办呢？
太公说：埋伏我的材士强弩，并以武冲大战车和骁勇的骑兵配置在其两翼，伏击地域一般距离我主力前后约三里，敌人若来追击，就出动我的战车、骑兵，冲击敌人的两侧。这样敌人就会混乱，我逃跑的士卒就会自动停止。
武王说：敌我双方的战车、骑兵相遇，敌众我寡，敌强我弱，敌人前来，阵势整齐，士卒精锐，我要与敌对阵而战，难以抵挡，对此怎么办？
太公曰：挑选我材士强弩伏于两侧，战车骑兵布成坚阵防守。如敌人通过我埋伏的地方，就集中弓弩射击他的两翼，出动战车、骑兵和勇锐士卒，猛烈的攻击敌军，既要攻他的正面，又兵攻他的侧背，敌人虽然众多，必定被我打败。
武王说：好啊！

Crow and Cloud Formation in Mountains

King Wu asked Jiāng Zǐyá: "Suppose we have led the army deep into the territory of the feudal lords, where we encounter high mountains with large, flat rock outcroppings on top, with numerous peaks, all devoid of grass and trees. We are surrounded on all sides by the enemy. Our army is afraid, the officers and troops are confused. I want to be solid if we are to defend our position, and victorious if we choose to fight. What should we do?"

Jiāng Zǐyá replied: "Whenever the army occupies a mountain, they are trapped on high by the enemy. When they hold the land below the mountain, they are imprisoned by the forces above them. If you have already occupied the top of the mountain, you must prepare the Crow and Cloud Formation. The Crow and Cloud Formation should be prepared on both the yin and yang sides of the mountain. Some will encamp on the yin side; others will encamp on the yang side. Those occupying the yang side must prepare against attacks from the yin side. Those occupying the yin side must prepare against attack from the yang side. Wherever the enemy can ascend the mountain, your troops should establish defense lines. If there are roads passing through the valley, sever them with your war chariots. Set your flags and pennants up high for easier communication. Be cautious in commanding the army; do not allow the enemy to know your true situation. This is referred to as a 'Mountain City.'

"After your lines have been set, your officers and troops deployed, rules and orders already issued, and tactics - both direct and indirect - already planned, deploy your assault formation at the outer perimeter of the mountain, and have them occupy advantageous positions. Thereafter, have your chariots and cavalry go into the Crow and Cloud Formation. When your army fervently attacks the enemy, even though the latter are numerous, their generals can be captured."

武王问太公说：领兵深入敌国境内，遇到高山巨石，山顶高耸，没有草木，四面受敌，全军恐惧，士兵迷惑，我想以守就固，以战就胜，对此怎么办？太公说：凡是军队配置在山顶，容易为敌所孤立，不得自由下山，配置在山麓，容易为敌所困，而不得自由行动。既然在山地作战，那就必须布成乌云之阵。所谓乌云之阵，[就是控制机动部队，支援各方作战的兵力部署，]同时对山南山北各个方面都要戒备，既要守山的北面，又要防守山的南面。军队占领山的南面，要戒备山的北面，占领山的北面，要戒备山的南面。占领山的左面，要戒备山的右面；占领山的右面，要戒备山的左面。凡是敌人能攀登的地方，就要派兵戒备，交通要道和能通行的谷地，就用战车阻绝，高挂旗帜，以便联络，谨饬三军，严阵成待，不使敌人察知我军情况，卒所占领的山地构成坚固的防御，就叫做。"山城"。行列已经排定，士卒已经列阵，法令已经颁行，奇正方略已经确定，各部队都编成"冲阵"，配置在比较突出的高地，便于作战的地方，再把战车骑兵布成乌云之降，当敌来攻时，我全军急剧战斗，敌军虽多，必被打败，其将领也可俘获。

Crow and Cloud Formation in Marshes

King Wu asked Jiāng Zǐyá: "Suppose we have led the army deep into the territory of the feudal lords where we are confronting the enemy across a river. The enemy is well equipped and numerous; we are impoverished and few. If we cross the water to attack, we will not be able to advance; while if we want to outlast them, our supplies are too few. We are encamped on infertile ground. There are no towns in any direction and moreover no grass or trees. There is nothing the army can plunder, while the oxen and horses have neither fodder nor a place to graze. What should we do?"

Jiāng Zǐyá said: "The whole army is unprepared; the oxen and horses have nothing to eat; the officers and troops have no supplies. In this situation, seek opportunity to trick the enemy and quickly get away, setting up ambushes to your rear."

King Wu said: "The enemy cannot be deceived. My officers and troops are confused. The enemy has occupied positions cutting across both our front and rear. Our army is defeated and in flight. What then?"

Jiāng Zǐyá replied: "When you are searching for an escape route, gold and jade are necessary. You must obtain intelligence from the enemy's emissaries. You must obtain the intelligence cautiously, and in great detail."

King Wu asked: "Suppose the enemy knows I have laid ambushes, so their main army is unwilling to cross the river. The general of their second army then breaks off some units and dispatches them to ford the river. My army is shaken. What should I do?"

Jiāng Zǐyá said: "In this situation, divide your troops into assault formations, and have them occupy advantageous positions. Wait until all the enemy's troops have emerged, and then spring your concealed troops, rapidly striking their rear. Have your strong crossbowmen on both sides shoot into their left and right flanks. Have your chariots and cavalry go into the Crow and Cloud Formation, arraying them against their front and rear. Then your army should vehemently press the attack. When the enemy sees us engaged in battle, their main force will certainly ford the river and advance. Then spring the ambushing forces, urgently striking their rear. The chariots and cavalry should assault the left and right. Even though the enemy is numerous, they can be driven off.

"In general, the most important thing in employing your troops is that, when the enemy approaches to engage in battle, you must deploy your assault formations and improve their positions. Thereafter, divide your chariots and cavalry into the Crow and Cloud Formation. This is the 'indirect' way of employing your troops. What is referred to as the Crow and Cloud Formation is like the crows dispersing and the clouds forming together. Their changes and transformation are endless."

"Excellent!" said King Wu.

武王问太公说：领兵深入敌国境内，与敌隔河对峙，敌人资材充足，兵力众多，我军资材贫乏，兵力寡少，我想渡河进攻，却无力前进，我想拖延时日，却粮食缺
乏，不能持久。而且我军处在荒芜贫瘠的地方，附近没有城邑也没有草木，军队无处掠取物资，无处放牧牛马，对此怎么办？
太公说：军队没有器械，牛马没有饲料，士卒没有粮食，在这种情况下应该寻找机会，欺骗敌人，迅速转移，并在后面设置伏兵，[反击敌之追击]。

武王问：如果敌人不受我诈骗，我军士卒迷惑，敌人进到我军前后，我三军溃退，对此怎么办？

太公说：这时寻求出路的方法：主要是用金玉货财，贿赂敌之军使，此事必须精密细致不使敌察觉最为重要。

武王问：敌人已知我有伏兵，大军不肯渡河，另派小部队渡河，我军大为惶恐，对此怎么办？

太公说：在这种情况下，军队应该部署为"四武冲陈"，配置在便于作战的地方，待其全部渡河后，发动伏兵，猛烈袭击其侧后，强弩由两旁射击敌人左右。把我战车、骑兵分布为"乌云之陈"，戒备前后，使三军急剧战斗。敌人见我军打击他已渡河的小部队，其大军必然会渡河前来，这时指挥我伏兵猛烈袭击敌后，战车、骑兵冲击敌人两翼，这样，敌人虽多，定会被打败，其将必逃。用兵的主要原则是，当面临战斗时，必须设置"四武冲陈"配置在便于作战的地方；然后使用战车和骑兵分布成"乌云之陈"，这就是出奇制胜的方法。所谓"乌云"，就是乌散云合、变化无穷的意思。

武王说：好啊！

Few and Many

King Wu asked Jiāng Zǐyá: "If I wish to attack a large number with only a few, or attack the strong with the weak, what should I do?"

Jiāng Zǐyá said: "If you wish to attack a large number with only a few, you must do it at sunset, setting an ambush in tall grass, pressing them on a narrow road. To attack the strong with the weak, you must obtain the support of a great state and assistance of neighboring states."

King Wu asked: "We do not have any terrain with tall grass, and moreover there are no narrow roads. The enemy has already arrived; we cannot wait until sunset. I do not have the support of any great state or the assistance of neighboring states. What then?"

Jiāng Zǐyá said: "You should set out specious formations and false enticements to lure and confuse their general, to redirect his path so that he will be forced to pass tall grass. Make his route long so you have time to ready your engagement at sunset. When his advance units have not yet finished crossing the water, his rear units have not yet reached the encampment, release our concealed troops, vehemently striking his right and left flanks, while your chariots and cavalry stir chaos among his forward and rear units. Even if the enemy is numerous, they will certainly flee.

"To serve the ruler of a great state, to gain the submission of the officers of neighboring states, make gifts generous and speak deferentially. In this fashion, you will obtain the support of a great state and assistance of neighboring states."

"Excellent!" said King Wu.

武王问太公说：我想以少击众，以弱击强，应该怎么办呢？
太公说：要以少击众，必须利用日春，把部队埋伏在深草地带，在隘路截击敌人。要以弱击强，必须有大国的协助，邻国支援。
武王说：我方没有深草地带可设伏，又没有隘路可利用，敌人到达时间又不在日暮，我方没有大国的协助，也没有邻国的支援，应该怎么办呢？
太公说：用虚张声势，引诱诈骗手段迷惑敌将，诱使敌人迂回行进，通过深草地带；诱使敌人多绕远路延误时间，迫使他在日暮时与我交战，乘敌人先头部队还没有全部渡水，后续部队还来不及宿营的时机，出动我伏击部队猛烈袭击敌人两翼，并令我战车和骑兵扰乱敌人的前后，敌兵虽多，也会被打败。敬事大国君王，礼交邻国贤士，多送金钱，言辞谦逊，就能与大国结盟，得到邻国的援助了。
武王说：好啊！

Divided Valley

King Wu asked Jiāng Zǐyá: "Suppose we have led the army deep into the territory of the feudal lords where we encounter the enemy in the midst of a steep valley. I have mountains on our left and a body of water on the right, while the enemy has the mountains on their right and the body of water on their left. Both of us divide the valley in our standoff. If we want to be solid if I choose to defend, or be victorious if I choose to attack, how should I proceed?"

Jiāng Zǐyá said: "If you occupy the left side of a mountain, you must urgently prepare against an attack from the right side. If you occupy the right side of a mountain, then you should urgently prepare against an attack from the left. If the valley has a large river, but you do not have boats and oars, then you should use the Heaven's Huang to cross the whole army over. Those who have crossed should widen the road considerably in order to improve your fighting position. Use the Martial Charge Chariots to cover the front and rear; deploy your strong crossbowmen into ranks to solidify all your lines and formations. Employ Martial Charge Chariots to block off all the intersecting roads and entrances to the valley. Set your flags out on high ground. Such posture is referred to as a 'Chariot Citadel'.

"In general, the method for valley warfare is for the Martial Charge Chariots to be in the forefront and the Large Covered Chariots to act as a protection. Your skilled soldiers and strong crossbowmen should cover the left and right flanks. 3,000 men will comprise one detachment, which must be deployed in the assault formation, seeking advantageous positions. Then the Left Army should advance at the left, the Right Army at the right, and the Center Army to the front - all three armies attacking and advancing together. Those having already fought should return to their detachment's original positions; the units fighting and resting in succession until you have won."

"Excellent!" said King Wu.

武王问太公说：引兵深入敌国，与敌在险阻狭隘的地方相遇，我军占领的地形是左山右水，敌军占领的地形是右山左水，各据险要，相互对峙，[在这样的情况下]各想守必固，战必胜，应该怎么办？

太公说：我军占领山的左侧时，应迅速成备山的右侧；占领山的右侧时，应迅速成备山的左侧。险要地带中的大江没有船只利用时就应用浮游器材渡过我军。已渡江的先头部队应迅速开辟前出道路，抢占便于作战的地形以利主力进入战场。用武冲大战车掩护我军的前后，广泛配置强弩，以使阵形坚固。在通向几个方向的交通枢

纽和两山之间的谷口，用武冲天战车阻绝，并在高处插上旗帜，这就构成了"车城"。对险要地带进攻的打法是以武冲大战车为前导，以大盾牌为防护，使材士强弩保障我左右两翼，步兵每三十人为一屯，编成"四武冲阵"，配置在便于作战的地形上；左军用于左翼，右军用于右翼，中军用于中央，三军并肩攻击前进，或轮番作战，轮番休息；已战的回到集结地域，未战的依次进攻，直到取得胜利为止。

武王说：好啊！

Chapter 6 - The Hound Teaching
Dispersing and Assembling

King Wu asked Jiāng Zǐyá: "If the King, leading the army, has dispersed the army to several locations, and the commanding general wants to have them reassemble at a specific time for battle, how should he use rules, rewards and punishments to achieve it?"

Jiāng Zǐyá answered: "In general, the masses of the military will always be subjected to making changes between dividing and reuniting. The commanding general should first set the place and day for battle, then issue full directives and particulars to the generals and commanders setting the time, indicating whether to attack cities or besiege towns, and where each should assemble. He should clearly instruct them about the time and day for battle. The commanding general should then establish his encampment, array his battle lines, put up a gnomon (part of a sundial) at the official gate, clear the road and wait. When all the generals and commanders have arrived, compare their arrival with the designated time. Those who arrived before the appointed time should be rewarded. Those who arrived afterward should be executed. In this way, both the near and distant will race to assemble, and the whole army will arrive together, uniting their strength to engage in battle."

武王问太公说：君王统兵出征，三军分驻数地，主将要按期集中军队与敌交战，并申令全军，明定赏罚，应该怎么办？
太公说：用兵的方法，由于三军众多，必然有分散和集中作战部署上的变化。主将要预先确定作战的地点和日期，然后用战斗文书晓喻诸将吏，明确规定要围攻的城
邑，各军应集中的地域，作战的日期，到达的时间。然后主将设营布阵，在营门立表，以观测日影，计算时间，禁止行人，等待将吏到达。将吏到达时间，要核对其
是否按时到达；先期到达的赏，过期到达的杀。这样，不论远近，都会按期赶来会集，三军全部到达后，就能集中力量与敌交战了。

Martial Sharpness

King Wu asked Jiāng Zǐyá: "In general, when employing the army, it is essential to have military chariots, courageous cavalry, and elite troops as vanguards, and then use a perceived opportunity to strike the enemy. In which situations can we strike?"

Jiāng Zǐyá answered: "Anyone who wants to launch a strike should carefully monitor and look for 14 situations in the enemy's actions. When any of these changes becomes visible, attack, for the enemy will certainly be defeated."

King Wu asked: "May I know the 14 changes?"

Jiāng Zǐyá said:
1. When the enemy has begun to assemble they can be attacked.
2. When the men and horses have not yet been fed, they can be attacked.
3. When the seasonal and weather conditions are not advantageous to them, they can be attacked.
4. When they have not secured advantageous terrain, they can be attacked.
5. When they are fleeing, they can be attacked.
6. When they are not vigilant, they can be attacked.
7. When they are tired and exhausted, they can be attacked.
8. When the general is absent from the officers and troops, they can be attacked.
9. When they are traversing long roads, they can be attacked.
10. When they are fording the river, they can be attacked.
11. When the troops have not had any leisure time, they can be attacked.
12. When they encounter the difficulty of precipitous ravines or are on narrow roads, they can be attacked.
13. When their battle array is in disorder, they can be attacked.
14. When they are afraid, they can be attacked.

武王问太公说：用兵的要领，必须有威武的战车，矫健的骑兵，能冲锋陷阵的精锐士卒，作为前锋部队，发现敌有可农之机就打。那么，究竟什么时机方可以打呢？

太公说：要打击敌人，应当抓住十四种对敌不利的情况，发现这种情况的一种就打，故人必被打败。

武王说：你可以把这十四种对敌不利的情况讲给我听吗？

太公说：敌人刚集结、立足未稳时可以打；人马饥饿时可以打；天候季节对敌不利可以打；地形对敌不利可以打；敌奔走赶路时可以打；敌人没有戒备时可以打；部队疲劳时可以打；将离士卒时可以打；长途跋涉后可以打；敌军渡河时可以打；敌军忙乱时可以打；通过险阻隘路时可以打；行列散乱时可以打；军心惊怖时可以打。

Selecting Warriors

King Wu asked Jiāng Zǐyá: "What is the way to select warriors?"

Jiāng Zǐyá replied: "Within the army, there will be men with great courage and strength who are willing to die, and may even take pleasure in suffering wounds. They should be assembled together and called 'Warriors who Risk the Blade'. Those who have very fierce dispositions, who are robust and courageous, strong and explosive, should be assembled together and called 'Warriors who Penetrate the Lines'.

"Those who are extraordinary in appearance, bear long swords, and advance with measured tread in good order should be assembled together and called 'Courageous Elite Warriors'.

"Those who can straighten iron hooks, have great strength, and can go into the enemy's line and smash gongs and drums and destroy flags and pennants, should be assembled together and called 'Warriors of Courage and Strength'.

"Those who can scale heights and cover great distances, who are light-footed and excel at running should be assembled together and called 'Invading Warriors'.

"Those who, while serving the ruler, lost their authority and want to gain merit again, should be assembled together and called 'Warriors who Fight to Death'.

"Those who are relatives of slain generals, the sons or brothers of generals, who want to avenge their deaths, should be assembled together and called 'Warriors who See Death Lightly'.

"Adopted sons, slaves or former prisoners-of-war, who want to cover up their pasts and achieve fame, should be assembled together and called the 'Incited Dispirited'.

"The lowly, poor and angry, who want to satisfy their desires, should be assembled together and called 'Warriors Committed to Death'.

"Those who have been imprisoned and then spared corporal punishment, who want to escape from their shame, should be assembled together and called 'Warriors Fortunate to be Used'.

"Those who combine skill and technique, who can bear heavy responsibilities, should be assembled together and called 'Warriors Awaiting Orders'.

"These are the army's selected warriors and one should pay great attention to the selection process."

武王问太公说：选编士卒的方法怎样？
太公说："军队中有勇气大、不怕死、不怕伤的，把他们编为一队，叫做"冒刃之士"，有锐气旺盛、年壮勇猛、强横凶暴的，把他们编为一队，叫做"陷阵之士"；有姿态奇异各用长剑，步伐稳健能在行列中整齐行动的，把他们编为一队，叫做"勇锐之士"；有臂力过人能伸直铁钩、强壮有力能冲入敌阵摧破敌人金鼓、撕破敌人旗帜的，把他们编为一队，叫做"勇力之士"；有能越高城，行远路，轻足善走的，把他们编为一队，叫做"寇兵之士"，有因王公大臣失势，而要重立功劳的，把他们编为一队，叫做"死斗之士"，有阵亡将帅的子弟，要为其父兄报仇的，把他们编为一队叫做"敢死之士"，有曾被招赘、被俘虏，要求扬名遮丑的，把他们编为一队，做"励钝之士"；有因贫穷而愤怒，要求立功受赏的，把他们编为一队，叫做"必死之士"；有刑徒免罪，要掩盖其耻辱的，把他们编为一队，叫做"幸用之士"，有才技胜人，能任重致远的，把他们编为一队，叫做"待命之士"。这是军队中选士的方法，不可不详加考虑啊！

Teaching Combat

King Wu asked Jiāng Zǐyá: "When we have assembled our body of men to form an army, and wish to train both the officers and men fully with the way of combat; how should we proceed?"

Jiāng Zǐyá said: "For leading the whole army, you must have the appropriate gongs and drums by which to order and assemble the officers and men. The generals should clearly instruct the commanders and officers, teaching them the use of weapons, mobilization, and stopping, all to be in accord with the movement of flags and signal pennants.

"Thus when teaching the commanders and officers, when ten individuals have completed their study of combat instructions, have each of them extend their study to ten men. Then, ten men who have completed their study of combat instructions will extend them to 100. And from 100 who have completed their study, it will be extended to a 1,000; And from 1,000 to 10,000, and from these 10,000 to the whole army.

"When all have completed their study of combat, have the whole army practice together. In this fashion, you will be able to realize a Great Army and establish your military authority throughout the realm."

"Excellent!" said King Wu.

武王问太公说：编成全军部队，要使士卒的动作娴熟，其训练方法如何？
太公说：统率三军必须用金鼓来指挥，这是为了统一军队的行动。将帅必先明确告诉官兵怎样操练，而又要反复讲解清楚，训练他们操作兵器熟悉战斗动作，和依照
各种族帜指挥信号的变化而变更行动的方法。所以训练军队时，先进行单人教练，单人教练完成了，再十人合练；十人学战，教练完成了，再百人合练；百人学战，
教练完成了，再千人合练；十人学战，教练完成了，再万人合练，万人学战，教练完成了，再三军合练以训练大军作战的方法。各项教练完成了，就可会集成百万大军，组成强大的军队，立威于天下。
武王说：好啊！

Forces' Equivalents

King Wu asked Jiāng Zĭyá: "When chariots and infantry engage in battle, one chariot is equivalent to how many infantrymen? When cavalry and infantry engage in battle, one cavalryman is equivalent to how many infantrymen? When chariots and cavalry engage in battle, one chariot is equivalent to how many cavalrymen?"

Jiāng Zĭyá replied: "Chariots are the wings of the army; they are the means to penetrate solid formations, to press strong enemies and to cut off their flight. Cavalry are the army's keen observers; they are the means to pursue a defeated army, to sever supply lines and to strike roving forces.

"Thus when chariots and cavalry are not engaged in battle with the enemy, one cavalryman is not able to equal one foot soldier. However, after the masses of the army have been arrayed in opposition to the enemy, when fighting on easy terrain, the rule is that one chariot is equivalent to eighty infantrymen. One cavalryman is equivalent to eight infantrymen. Then, one chariot is equivalent to ten cavalrymen.

"The rule for fighting on difficult terrain is that one chariot is equivalent to forty infantrymen. One cavalryman is equivalent to four infantrymen. One chariot is equivalent six cavalrymen.

"Chariots and cavalry are the army's strong weapons. Ten chariots can defeat 1,000 men; 100 chariots can defeat 10,000 men. Ten cavalrymen can drive off 100 men, and 100 cavalrymen can drive off 1,000 men. These are the approximate numbers."

King Wu asked: "What are the ranks of the chariot and cavalry officers who command the various units and the numbers in the corresponding units?"

Jiāng Zĭyá replied: "As for the chariots – there is a leader for five chariots, a captain for ten, a commander for fifty and a general for 100.

"For battles on easy terrain, five chariots comprise one line. Each line is forty paces apart; the chariots from left to right should be ten paces apart, with detachments sixty paces apart. On difficult terrain the chariots must follow the roads, with ten chariots comprising a company and twenty a regiment. Front to rear spacing should be twenty paces, left to right six paces, with detachments thirty six paces apart. If they venture off the road more than two miles in any direction, they should return to the original road.

"As for the number of officers in the cavalry: there is a leader for five men, a captain for ten, a commander for 100 and a general for 200. The rule for fighting on easy terrain: five cavalrymen will form one line, and front to back their lines should be separated by twenty paces with a left to right distance of four paces and with fifty paces between detachments. On difficult terrain, the rule is: that each line of five cavalrymen will deploy front to back, ten paces; left to right, two paces; between detachments, twenty five paces. Thirty cavalrymen comprise a company; sixty form a regiment. For every ten cavalrymen, there is a captain. In action, they should not move out of the range of 100 paces, after which they should circle back and return to their original positions."

"Excellent!" said King Wu.

武王问太公说：用车兵对敌步兵战斗，一辆战车相当于几名步兵？几名步兵相当于一辆战车？用骑兵与步兵战斗，一名骑兵相当于几名步兵？几名步兵相当于一名骑兵？用战车对骑兵战斗，一辆战车能当几名骑兵？几名骑兵相当于一辆战车？

太公说：战车是加强军队战斗力的，用以攻坚陷阵，截击强敌，切断其退路的。骑兵是军队中窥探敌人，乘敌之隙的，用以跟踪追击，断敌粮道，袭击散乱流窜的敌

人的。因此车骑使用不恰当，在战斗中一名骑兵还不能抵挡一名步兵。全军布列成阵，骑步配合得当，那么在平坦地形上作战，一辆战车可以抵挡步兵八十名，步兵

八十名相当于一辆战车，一名骑兵可以抵挡步兵八名，八名步兵相当于一名骑兵，一辆战车可抵挡骑兵十名，十名骑兵相当于一辆战车。在险阻地形上作战，一辆战

车可抵挡步兵四十名，四十名步兵相当于一辆战车；一名骑兵可抵挡步兵四名，四名步兵相当于一名骑兵；一辆战车可抵挡骑兵六名，六名骑兵相当于一辆战车。战车和骑兵是军队中威烈快速的冲击力量。十辆战车可以击败敌千人，百辆战车可以击败敌万人，十名骑兵可以击退敌百人，百名骑兵可以击退敌千人，这些是大约的 数字。

武王说：战车和骑兵应配置的军官数量和作战方法怎样？

太公说：战车应配备军官的数量是，五车设一长，十车设一吏，五十车设一率，百车设一将。在平坦地形上作战的战法，五车为列，前后相距四十步，各车间隔十

步，队间距离和间隔各六十步。险阻地形上作战的战法，战车必须沿道路行进，十车为一聚，二十车一屯，车与车前后距离二十步，左右宽约六步，队间距离和间隔

各十六步，活动范围前后左右各二里，各车战斗后仍由原路返回。骑应配备军官的数量是，五骑设一长，十骑设一吏，百骑设一率，二骑设一将。在平坦地形作战的

战法，五骑为一列，前后相距二十步，左右间隔四步，队间距离和间隔各五十步。在险阻地形上作战时，后相距十步。左右间隔二步，队间距离和间隔各二十五步，

三十骑为一屯，六十骑为一辈。活动范围前后左右各百步，战斗后各返原来位置。武王说：好啊！

Chariot Warriors

King Wu asked Jiāng Zǐyá: "How should one go about selecting warriors for chariots?"

Jiāng Zǐyá said: "The rules for selecting warriors for chariots are to pick men under forty years of age, who are five feet and seven inches or taller; whose running ability is such that they can pursue a galloping horse, who can race up to it, mount it and ride it forward and back, left and right, up and down, and all around; They should be able to quickly furl up the flags and pennants and have the strength to fully draw an eight-picul crossbow; They should practice shooting front and back, left and right, until thoroughly skilled. They are termed 'Martial Chariot Warriors'. With them, you must be most generous."

武王问太公说：怎样选拔车上武士？
太公说：选拔车上武士的标准，取其年龄四十以下，身长七尺五寸以上；跑起来追得上奔跑的马，能在奔驰中跳上战车，并能对前后、左右、上下各方应战力能掌握旗帜，拉满八石弩，熟练地向左右、前后射箭的人，这种人称为武车士，待遇不可不优厚。

Cavalry Warriors

King Wu asked Jiāng Zǐyá: "How should one go about selecting warriors for the cavalry?"

Jiāng Zǐyá said: "The rules for selecting warriors for the cavalry are to take only those who are under forty, those who are at least five feet and seven inches tall, who are strong and quick, who surpass the average; Men, who while racing a horse, can fully draw a bow and shoot; men, who can gallop forward and back, left and right, and all around, both advancing and withdrawing; Men who, while racing a horse, can jump over moats and ditches, ascend hills and mounds, gallop through narrow confines, cross large water bodies, and race into a strong enemy, causing chaos among their masses. These are called the 'Martial Cavalry Warriors'. With them, you must be most generous."

武王问太公道：怎样选拔骑士？
太公说：选拔骑士的标准，取其年龄四十以下，身长七尺五寸以上，身强力壮，敏捷快速，超过一般人的，能在乘马疾驰中挽弓射箭，对前、后、左右各方应战或回
旋进退，越过沟堑攀登高地，冲过险阻，横渡大水，追逐强敌，打乱众多敌人的，这种人称为武骑士，待遇不可不优厚。

Battle Chariots

King Wu asked Jiāng Zǐyá: "What is the best way to use battle chariots?"

Jiāng Zǐyá replied: "The infantry's value may be maximized by knowing changes and movement; the chariot's value may be maximized by knowing the terrain's configuration; the cavalry value may be maximized by discovering the unknown short-cuts and side roads. Thus these three bodies share the same goal, but their employment differs. In chariot battles, there are ten types of fatal situations in which defeat is likely and eight on which victory can be achieved."

King Wu asked: "What are the ten fatal situations?"

Jiāng Zǐyá replied: "1. If after advancing, there is no way to withdraw, this is fatal terrain for chariots:
2. If after passing beyond narrow defiles, you pursue the enemy some distance, this is terrain which will exhaust the chariots.
3. If the land in front makes advancing easy, while that to the rear is treacherous, this is terrain that will entrap the chariots.
4. If you penetrate into narrow and obstructed areas from which escape will be difficult, this is terrain on which the chariots may be cut off.
5. If the land is collapsing, sinking, and marshy, with black mud sticking to everything, this is terrain which will 'labor' the chariots.
6. If the left is precipitous while the right is easy, with high mounds and sharp hills. This is terrain contrary to the use of chariots.
7. If luxuriant grass runs through the field, and there are deep, watery channels throughout. This is terrain which thwarts the use of chariots.
8. If our chariots are few in number, the land easy, and we are outnumbered by enemy infantry, this is terrain on which our chariots may be defeated.
9. If there are water filled ravines and ditches to the rear, deep water to the left and steep hills to the right, this is terrain on which chariots may be destroyed.
10. If it has been raining day and night for more than ten days without stopping and if the roads have collapsed so that it not possible to advance or to escape to the rear. This is the terrain that will sink the chariots.

"These ten are the deadly terrains for chariots. Thus they will cause the stupid general will be captured and allow the wise general to escape."

King Wu asked: "What are the eight conditions of terrain that may yield victory?"

Jiāng Zǐyá replied: "1. If the enemy's ranks - front and rear - are not yet settled, you may strike into them.
2. If their flags and pennants are in chaos and their men and horses are frequently shifting about, you may strike into them.
3. If some of their officers and troops advance while others retreat, others move to the left, and yet others move to the right, then you may strike into them.
4. If their battle array is not yet solid and their officers and troops are looking around at each other, they you may strike into them.

5. If as they advance, they appear full of doubts, and as they withdraw, fearful, then you may strike into them
6. If the enemy's whole army becomes suddenly frightened, all of them rising up in great confusion, then you may strike into them.
7. If you are fighting on easy terrain and twilight has not ended, then you may strike into them.
8. If, after traveling far, at dusk they are camping and their whole army is terrified, you may strike into them.

"These eight circumstances constitute conditions in which the chariots will be victorious. If the general is clear about the ten fatal situations where defeat is probable and the eight favorable situations where victory is possible, then even if the enemy should surround him - attacking with 1,000 chariots and 10,000 cavalry from the front and the flanks – the wise general will invariably be victorious."

"Excellent!" said King Wu.

武王问太公说：战车怎样作战？
太公说：步兵作战贵在熟悉情况变化，车兵作战贵在熟悉地形状况，骑兵作战贵在熟悉别道捷径，车骑步同是作战部队而用法不同。车兵作战有十种死地、八种有利的情况。
武王问；什么是十种死地？
太公说：可以前进而不能退回，这就是战车的死地。越险阻，长途追逐敌人，这就是战车的竭地。前面平坦，后面险阻，这就是战车的困地。陷入危险而难于出来，
这就是战车的绝地。毁塌积水粘泥地带，这就是战车的劳地。左面险阻右面平坦，还要爬坡，这就是战车的逆地。盛草连垄，还要渡过水泽，这就是战车的拂地。车少地平，而又战车与步兵配合不当这是战车的败地。后有沟渠，左有深水，右有高坡，这就是战车的坏地。昼夜大雨，连日不停，道路毁坏，前不能进，后不能退，
这就是战车的陷地。这十种都是战车的"死地"。所以愚将由于不了解这十种死地而被擒，智将由于了解之十种死地，就能避开它。
武王又问：八种有利的情况是什么？
太公说：敌人的前后行阵尚未排列完毕就乘机攻破它。敌人旌旗紊乱，人马不断调动，就来机攻破它。敌士卒有的向前，有的退后，有的往左，有的往右，混乱不已，就乘机攻破它。敌阵势不稳定，士卒前后相互观望，就乘机攻破它。敌前进犹豫，后退害怕，就乘机攻破它。敌三军突然惊乱，轻举妄动，就乘机攻破它。敌与我战于平坦地形上，日暮还未结束战斗，就用战车攻破它。敌长途行军，宿营很晚，三军惧战，就乘机攻破它。这八种情况都是对战车作战有利的情况。将帅明白了十种"死地"和八种"胜地"，敌人即便四面包围，用千乘万骑向我正面压迫，两侧突击，也不可怕，无论多少次战斗都必定取得胜利。

武王说：好啊！

Cavalry in Battle

King Wu asked Jiāng Zǐyá: "How can the cavalry best be employed in battle?"

Jiāng Zǐyá responded: "For the cavalry, there are ten circumstances that can produce victory and nine that will result in defeat."

King Wu asked: "What are the ten circumstances that can produce victory?"

Jiāng Zǐyá replied: "When the enemy first arrives, before their lines and deployment are settled, when the front and rear not yet united, if our cavalry strikes into their forward cavalry, with simultaneous attacks to their left and right flanks. They will certainly flee.

"When the enemy's lines and deployment are well-ordered and solid, when their officers and troops are eager to fight, our cavalry should outflank the enemy but not go too far off. Some of our cavalry should be seen to race away and some race forward. They should be fast as the wind, as explosive as thunder, so that their dust turns the daylight as murky as dusk. Our flags and pennants and even our uniforms should be changed several times to exaggerate our strength and confuse the enemy. Then they can be conquered.

"When the enemy's lines and deployment are not solid, if their officers and troops do not want to fight, press them both front and rear, make surprise attacks on their left and right. If you then outflank and encircle them, they will certainly be afraid.

"When, at sunset, if the enemy wants to return to his camp and their army is frightened, if we can outflank them on both sides, urgently striking their rear, pressing them up to the entrance to their fortifications, and then, we do not allow them to go in. They will certainly be defeated.

"When the enemy lacks the advantages of ravines and defiles for securing their defenses, if you penetrate deeply into their territory and sever their supply lines, they will certainly be hungry.

"When the land is level and easy and the enemy cavalry approaches us from all four sides, if then our chariots and cavalry strike into them, they will certainly become disordered.

"When the enemy flees, with the officers and troops scattered and in chaos, if our cavalry outflanks them both on sides and obstructs them to the front and rear, their general can be captured.

"When the enemy is returning to his camp at dusk and his soldiers are very numerous, his lines and deployment will certainly become disordered. Our cavalry should be formed platoons of ten and regiments of 100. Our chariots should be grouped into squads of five and companies of ten. Our flags and pennants should be set out in great profusion, intermixed with strong crossbowmen. Then, units of our cavalry should attack their two flanks, others cut off the front and rear, and then the enemy's general can be taken prisoner. These are the ten circumstances in which the cavalry can be victorious."

King Wu asked: "What are the nine circumstances which will lead to defeat?"

Jiāng Zǐyá said: "If our the cavalry penetrates the ranks of the enemy but does not destroy their formation, and then the enemy feigns flight, only to turn their chariots and cavalry about to strike our rear - this is a situation in which our cavalry will be defeated.

"If we pursue a fleeing enemy into confined ground far into their territory without stopping, then the enemy may ambush both our flanks and sever our rear - this is a circumstance in which the cavalry will be surrounded and defeated.

"If we go forward when there is no road back, if we enter when there is no way out, this is known as 'Heaven Trap' or 'Earthly Cave'. It is fatal terrain for the cavalry.

"If the way by which we enter is constricted and the way out is distant; weaker enemy forces can attack our strong ones; and their few can attack our many - this is terrain on which our cavalry can be exterminated.

"If there are great mountain torrents, deep valleys, tall luxuriant grass, forests and trees - these are conditions which will exhaust the cavalry.

"If there is water on both left and right, while ahead are large hills, and to the rear there are high mountains, and if our army is fighting between the bodies of water while the enemy occupies both the interior and exterior ground - this is terrain that presents great difficulty for the cavalry.

"If the enemy has cut off our supply lines, and if we advance, we would not have a route by which to return - this is terrain that is troublesome for the cavalry.

"If we are sinking into marshy ground, and advancing and retreating must both be through quagmires - this is terrain that will labor the cavalry.

"If on the left, there are deep water sluices, and on the right, there are gullies and hillocks, but the ground appears level - good terrain for advancing, retreating, and enticing an enemy - this is a terrain that is a pitfall for the cavalry.

"These nine circumstances comprise fatal terrain for cavalry, which an enlightened general may use to keep the enemy far off and allowing time for him to escape, and for the ignorant general, it is the means for him to be entrapped and defeated."

武王问太公说：骑兵怎样作战？
太公说：骑兵作战有"十胜"和"九败"。
武王问：十胜怎样？
太公说：敌人初到，行阵未定，前后不相联系，我骑兵应立即击破其先头骑兵部队，夹击其两翼，敌必溃逃；敌人阵势，整齐坚固，士卒战斗情绪很高，我骑兵部队
应缠住敌人两翼不放，有时奔驰过去，有时奔驰回来，快速如风，猛烈如雷，使尘土飞扬迷漫，白昼如同黄昏，不断更换旗帜，改变服装，[使敌人疑虑重重，]敌
军就可以被打败；敌人行阵不稳固，士卒没有斗志，就迫近敌人前方和后方，袭击其左右从两翼夹击它，敌人必会震恐；敌人日暮回营三军震骇·我骑兵应夹击其两
翼，急速袭击其后尾，迫近其营垒入口，阻止其进入营垒，敌人在慌从中必会溃败；敌人没有险阻地形可以固守，我骑兵应长驱立入，切断其粮道，敌人必会陷于饥
饿；敌处于平坦地形，四面受到威胁，我骑兵协同战车四面围攻它，敌人必会溃乱；敌人败逃，士卒散乱，我骑兵或由其两翼夹击，或袭击其前后，敌将帅也就可以
被擒；敌人日暮退回营垒，部队很多，队形一定混乱，就令我骑兵十人为一队，百人为一屯，战车五辆为一聚，十辆为一群，多插旗帜，配以强弩或者打击其两翼，
或者断绝其前后，敌将帅也可以被俘获。这就是骑兵作战的十种取胜的战机。
武王问："九败"是什么？
太公说：用骑兵攻击敌人，如果不能突破敌阵，敌人假装跑，而以战车和骑兵攻我后方，这就使我骑兵处于失败的境地了；击败退之敌，越过险阻，长驱深入而不好
止，敌人埋伏在我两旁，绝我后路，这就使我骑兵处于被围的境地了；"前进后，无法退回，进后，无法出来，这叫陷入"天井"之内，困于"地穴"之中，这就使
骑兵处于灭亡的境地了；进路狭窄，出路迂远，敌可以弱击强，以少击众，这就使我骑兵处于覆灭的境地了；大涧深谷，林木茂盛，活动困难，这会使我骑兵处于精
疲力竭的境地；左右有水，前有大山，后有高岭，我三、军在两水之间作战，敌人内守山险，外据水要，这就使我骑兵处于艰难的境地；敌人断我粮道

，我只有进路
而没有退路，这就使我骑兵陷于困难的境地；沼泽地、低湿泥泞地，这是使骑兵疲劳的患地；左有深沟，右有坑凹，一高一低，看起来就象平地，无论进退都会招致
敌人来攻，这就是骑兵作战的陷地。这九种都是骑兵的"死地"。这是明智的将帅所竭力避开的地方，昏庸的将冲所以陷于失败的原因。

Infantry in Battle

King Wu asked Jiāng Zǐyá: "How should the infantry engage in battle with chariots and cavalry?"

Jiāng Zǐyá replied: "When the infantry engages in battle with chariots and cavalry, they must use the terrain to their advantage, using hills and mounds, ravines and defiles. The long weapons and strong crossbow should occupy the forward positions; the short weapons and weak crossbow should occupy the rear, firing en salvo. Even if large numbers of the enemy's chariots and cavalry should arrive, they must maintain a solid formation and fight intensely, while our most skilled soldiers and strongest crossbowmen prepare against attacks from the rear."

King Wu said: "If there are no hills or mounds, ravines or defiles and the enemy arrives in strength. If their chariots and cavalry outflank us on both sides, and if they are making repeated attacks against our front and rear positions. And finally, if our army is terrified and trying to flee in chaotic defeat, what can be done?"

Jiāng Zǐyá replied: "The army should be ordered to establish a four sided formation with the oxen and horses placed in the center. Defensive barricades and anti-personnel devices should be readied. When the enemy is seen to begin to advance, the men should deploy the spiked barricades, the *chevaux-de-frise* and caltrops at the periphery. At the back of these barricades, they should dig ditches five feet deep and five feet wide, creating what is called the 'Cage of Fate'.

"The chariots should be deployed as ramparts and pushed forward and back. Then, whenever they stop, they will be useful as battlements. Our skilled soldiers and strong crossbowmen should defend the left and right flanks. The army should be under orders to fight tirelessly to exhaust the enemy and crush him."

"Excellent!" said King Wu.

武王问太公说：步兵怎样与战车、骑兵作战？
太公说：步兵与战车、骑兵作战，必须依托丘陵、险阻的地形列阵，把长兵器和强弩配置在前面，把短兵器和较弱的弩配在后面，轮流战斗，更番休止。敌战车和骑兵大量到达，我只有坚守阵形，顽强战斗，并使材士强督戒备后方。

武王说：我方没有丘陵，又无险阻可利用，敌人到达的兵力既多又强，战车骑兵包围我两翼。突击我前后，我三军恐惧，溃败逃跑，对此怎么办？

太公说：令我士卒制作行马和木蒺藜，把牛车、马车都集中起来编为一队，步兵列成"四五冲阵"。观察到敌军即将到来，就在他来的方向，广泛布设蒺藜，并挖掘

环形的壕沟，深宽各五尺，这叫做"命笼"。步兵带着行马进退，用车辆组成营垒推着它前后移动，停止下来就成为营寨，用材士强弩戒备左右，然后号令全军急剧 地战斗，不得懈怠。

武王说：好啊！

Terracotta chariot with horses

The Art of War

Sun Tzu

孙子兵法

The Art of War (孙子兵法) *Sun Wu (also known as Sun Tzu) expounds on the importance of military strategy and tactics, in particular the topics of assessing the opponent, positioning forces, and careful analysis of the enemy, in each of nine situations and terrains. Each of the 13 chapters is transcribed as a lesson by Sun Tzu, traditionally starting with the phrase "Master Sun said." The Art of War is still considered one of the most important military texts ever compiled. It is believed to have been written during the late Spring and Autumn period or the early Warring States period (c. 470 BCE).*

Chapter 1
Assessment and Planning

War is of immense importance, because the outcome will determine the survival of the nation and its people. Thus, the initial assessment of war is of the utmost importance.

战争是国家大事，它关系到军民的生死、国家的存亡，一定要认真的研究。

There are five major areas one should look at, and compare them with those of the enemy, to understand the situation. Then assess the chances of victory. They are: political intelligence, weather, terrain, generalship, and legal doctrine.

所以，要从五方面作分析，比较敌我双方的情况，来了解战争的情势：一是道，二是天，三是地，四是将，五是法

Political intelligence refers to the ruler's capability to unite the whole nation. In this way, the people are prepared to co-exist and brave danger together with the ruler.

所谓"道"，是指民众与国君同一意愿。民众可以在战争中和国君出生入死

Weather represents day or night, light level, temperature, and seasonal changes. Terrain refers to the route or battlefield conditions; high or low, distant or near, easily accessible or treacherous, width, and ease of defense or attack.

天是指阴晴，昼夜，暑寒，四季变化。'地'是指地势的高度，距离，险恶易行，广阔狭隘，或者容易攻守。

Generals should be assessed by their wisdom, trustworthiness, benevolence, courage and discipline.

'将'是指将军的智能谋略，信能赏罚，仁能附众，勇能果断，严能立威。

Army organization structure refers to the army organization and control, systems and procedures, and command and control of deployment of resources.

所谓"法"，是指军队的编组制度，将吏的管理和后勤支援。

Generals who are able to assess these five factors well would be able to win, and those who cannot would fail. Thus in planning, the general must be able to examine, assess and compare the following dimensions with those of his enemies to determine the chances of victory.

Which ruler has a higher political intelligence? Which general is more capable? Which side has advantages created by the weather and terrain? Which side is capable of executing orders effectively and efficiently? Which army is better equipped, stronger and larger in numbers? Which side has better training? Which side is more enlightened in the administration of rewards and punishment? Based on the comparison, I would be able to see which side will emerge the winner and which would emerge the loser.

这五方面，将帅一定得知道，知道的越祥细，胜算就越大，不只是越祥细，而且还需要和敌方做比较，才可知胜算。如：哪一方的国君政治贤明？哪一方的将帅指挥与韬略高明？哪一方得天时地利？哪一方能贯彻执行法令？哪一方的军队较强？哪一方的兵士训练有素？那一方赏罚严明？根据以上，便可知谁胜谁负。

A general who adopts my strategies would be able to win the battle; he must be retained. Generals who do not adopt my strategies would not be able to win the battle, they must be removed. Besides adopting the proposed plans and strategies, the general must create or take advantage of situations to push for victories.

如果将帅听从我计谋，运用他可得胜利，应该留用。如果将帅不听从我计谋，运用他必失败，应该弃之不用。将帅采取了计策，可也需要利用战争走势，以辅佐作战取胜。所谓"势"是根据有利条件而采取相应措施或行动。

All warfare is based on deception. When you are capable, feign that you are incapable. When you are near, feign that you are far. When you are far away, feign that you are near.

战争也需要诡诈。能而假装不能,要用兵或计谋而假装不用,要去近处而假装去远处,要去远处而假装去近处。

If the enemy is greedy, use baits to lure him. If the enemy is in disarray, attack him. If the enemy is strong and has no weaknesses yet, be well-prepared to seize the opportunity to attack. If the enemy is superior in numbers and high in morale, avoid engaging. If the enemy is easily angered, arouse anger. If the enemy looks down on you, increase the arrogance further. If the enemy is resting, harass him so that the troops are not well-rested. If the enemy's organization is strong, insinuate discord among them. Attack places where the enemy troops are not well-prepared or where they will least expect an attack. This is how a war should be fought, in order to win. These strategies should not be disclosed before execution.

对于贪利的敌人,用利诱使他;对于处与混乱状态的敌人,乘机攻取他;对于实力充实的敌人,须要防备他;对于兵力强大的敌人,须要避开他;对于容易发怒的敌人,尽量激怒他;对于鄙视我方的敌人,使他更加骄傲;对与在休息的敌人,要设法使他疲劳;对于内部团结的敌人,尽量分离他们;要在敌人没有防备时发动攻击,攻击敌人意想不到的的地方。这是兵家取胜之法,不可在执行前外传。

In conclusion, those who have considered careful details during planning and assessment will win, while those who have considered fewer details will lose. The more details considered, the higher the chances of winning, and vice versa. By observing the planning and assessment process, I am able to see whether victory or defeat is expected.

凡是未战之前预计能够取胜,是因为筹划周密、取胜条件充分。未战之前预计失败,是因为筹划不周密、取胜条件不够充分。筹划地越周密,胜利条件越充分,就越有胜算;筹划不周,而胜利条件不充分,就肯定失败,更不须要提不筹划会有什么后果。我们根据这些就可看出谁胜谁负。

Chapter 2
Waging War

In general, before the start of the military campaign, one would need 1,000 speedy chariots, 1,000 heavy wagons and 10,000 armored and equipped soldiers. Supplies have to be transported for thousands of *li*[1], and there is a need to provide for expenses both at home and at the battlefront. Examples of such expenses are entertainment of visitors and emissaries, procurement of materials like glue and paint, and maintenances fees for armor and other equipment. These expenses would amount to 1,000 pieces of gold daily. An army of 10,000 could only be raised when a sufficient amount of supplies is raised.

凡用兵作战，一般上需要动用战车千辆，辎重车千辆，铠甲十万个，还要越境千里运送粮草；拢总内外开销，如招待宾客费用，补给胶漆等材料，修补铠甲的费用，每日须耗费千金。准备齐了后方可出动十万大军。

The purpose of raising an army is to achieve swift and decisive victory. If victory cannot be achieved quickly, the army will become lazy, and lose their fighting spirit. When they attack city walls, they would be greatly exhausted. If the army is out on a military campaign for too long, the nation's resources would be greatly depleted. When the army is in bad shape and the resources of the nation are exhausted, other neighboring warlords would capitalize on these weaknesses by launching an attack. Even if there are clever and capable strategists or advisors, they would not be able to reverse the situation.

While blunders are known to occur during military operations, one has yet to witness a successful military operation where there are long delays. No one has seen a military campaign where the longer the campaign, the more beneficial it is to the nation.

Someone who does not fully understand the inherent danger of deploying troops would also not understand the advantages of using them.

用这军队，须要求速胜，否则旷日持久会使军队疲惫，锐气受挫，而攻城则力量耗尽，出兵长久则使国家财政受到影响。一旦陷入持久战，战力下降，士气受挫，财务资源耗尽的情况，诸侯会乘机起兵攻打。到时即使有智者也不能挽回局面。只有听说过用兵拙而速胜，没看过用兵细巧久战而得胜。战争持久而国家有利的例子更是没有。所以，不能完全了解用兵之害处，则不能完全了解用兵有利之处。

---

[1] *Li* are Chinese miles, although the actual distance for one *li* is about 500 meters.

The general who is well-versed with warfare does not require additional conscription of soldiers, or require supplies to be delivered more than three times. Military weapons and equipment should be prepared and obtained from the nation, and food and other supplies should be obtained from the enemies instead so that the army will always be well-fed and have ample supplies.

A nation could become poor due to multiple transportations of supplies over long distances, impoverishing the people. The prices of food and supplies in the area which the army is located would inflate. This rise in prices would erode the wealth of the people. The nation would impose greater tolls and taxes on the people to cover costs. When the strength of the army is exhausted, and wealth of the nation depleted, every household would be emptied of provisions.

The wealth of the people would be reduced by seventy percent. As for the nation, it would incur the loss of equipment and livestock; chariots, horses, helmets, bows and arrows, spears and shields, oxen and heavy wagons. These losses would be about sixty percent of the nation's assets.

善于用兵作战的将军，不会再征集兵队，粮草不运输超过两回；武装配备取用于我国，粮食则征用敌国，这样军队的粮食需求便可满足了。国家会因为多次运输军队需求而贫穷，多次运输也使百姓贫困。靠近驻军的地方，物价必然上升，而致使百姓和国家财竭，致使国家急需征税。战场上军力用尽，国内各家空虚，百姓的财产将会用去十分之七。政府的财力也会因为车辆的损坏，马匹的疲惫，盔甲、箭弩、戟盾、矛橹的补充和运输用的牛和车的征用，而损失十分之六。

Hence, a wise general would always make a point to use the supplies and provisions of the enemy. Consuming one cartload of the enemy's provisions is equivalent to twenty cartloads of our own. Consuming one piculs of the enemy's food is equivalent to twenty piculs of our own.[2]

所以明智的将军，务求用敌方的粮食。因为用敌方一种粮食，就等于我方二十种粮食。用敌方一石饲料，等于我方二十石饲料。

In order to kill the enemy, you need to make your troops hate them. To motivate your troops to plunder enemy resources, you need to reward them with material goods. In a chariot battle, the first person who is able to capture more than ten enemy chariots should be rewarded. We should then remove and replace the banners on captured chariots with ours and use it together with ours. Captured soldiers should be treated well. Only in this way, can we win the enemy and become stronger in the process.

---

[2] A picul was an ancient unit of measurement literally translated as "a shoulder load". It was equal to approximately 123lbs or 60kg.

能让士兵奋勇杀敌是怒气，
能让士兵勇于夺取敌方物资是奖赏。在车战中，凡得战车十辆以上，奖赏最先夺取战车者，更换车上旌旗，并编入我方战车部队。优待被俘虏的敌方士兵和使用他们。这就是所谓能胜过敌人，又壮大我方的方法。

In war, it is better to go for swift victories rather than engaging in a prolonged campaign. Thus a general who is adept in warfare is also the controller of people's fate and nation's survival.

所以用兵作战宜速胜，不宜持久作战。熟悉用兵之法的将军，是掌握人民生死命运的人，国家安危的主宰。

Chapter 3
Attack Strategies

In war, to capture the whole nation intact is the best strategy; to ruin or shatter the nation is a weaker option. To capture the whole division intact is the best strategy; to destroy it is a weaker option. To capture the whole battalion intact is the best strategy; to destroy it is a weaker option. To capture the whole company intact is the best strategy; to destroy it is a weaker option. To capture the whole section intact is the best strategy; to destroy it is a weaker option.

凡用兵打战之法，使敌国完整降服是上策，攻破它是次一等；使全敌军降伏为上策，击溃它是次一等；使敌军全旅降伏为上策，击溃它是次一等；使敌军全卒降伏为上策，击溃它是次一等；使敌军全伍降伏为上策，击溃它是次一等；

Thus, to fight a hundred battles and win a hundred battles is not a reflection of the ultimate strategy. The ability to subdue the enemy without ever doing battle is a reflection of the ultimate strategy.

因此即使百战百胜，并非最高明；只有不用战斗而使敌方降伏，才是最高明的。

The supreme plan is to attack the enemy's strategies and plans, by thwarting them. Next is to attack the enemy's strategic alliances. The next option is to attack enemy troops. Attack the enemy's cities when it is the only option available.

故上兵伐谋，其次伐交，其次伐兵，攻城之法为不得已。

The preparation of shields, weapons and equipment would take at least three months to complete. The preparation of the observation ramps would take another three months at least. Such long preparation may cause the general in charge to lose his patience and rationality. Thus he may launch an assault on the walls like ants, resulting in one third of his troops being killed, and the attacked city is still not conquered. This is the disastrous consequence of such an assault.

若要攻城，需制造攻城的大盾和四轮车，准备攻城器械，须三个月才完成；构筑攻城的土山又另须三个月。将帅不胜忿怒，
而下令攻城，驱使士兵像蚂蚁一样爬梯攻城，那士兵会死了三分之一，可是城却未攻下。这是攻城之灾。

The general who is adept at warfare will be able to subdue his enemy's troops without engaging in battles, to capture the enemy's city without launching assaults, or to conquer the enemy's city without a prolonged campaign. He will always focus on using the least amount of the nation's resources to conquer his objectives whole and intact, while contesting for supremacy. Thus his troops are not worn out and his victories are complete. In essence, this is the art of strategic attacks.

善于用兵与谋略的将帅，不战而使敌兵屈服，不攻而夺城，不久战而毁灭敌国；他必会以全胜作为考量来争天下。这样一来军队不会疲惫，士气不会受挫，而能取得全胜。这就是谋攻之法则。

When you outnumber your enemy ten to one, surround him. When you outnumber your enemy five to one, attack him. When you outnumber your enemy two to one, divide him. When the troops are comparable, there is a possibility of engaging him. When the enemy is larger in number, be able to escape from him. When greatly inferior in numbers than the enemy, be able to avoid him. Because, regardless of how resilient the smaller troop is, it will definitely be captured by the stronger and larger troops.

用兵法则是，我方有十倍于敌人的兵力就包围他，我方有五倍于敌人的兵力就攻击他，我方有两倍于敌人的兵力就分散他，我方与敌人有相等兵力就须设法战胜他，我方兵力比敌人少就须摆脱他，我方实力比敌人弱就须避免与他决战。因为不管弱小的军队再怎么顽强，也是会成为强大敌人的俘虏。

The general, being an official, serves the nation. If he is thoughtful and detailed in his work, the nation would be strong and mighty. If he is full of flaws, the nation would be weak and vulnerable.

将帅是国家重要的辅助者。如果相依无间，国家一定强盛；如果相依有隙，国家一定衰弱。

There are three ways in which the ruler can adversely affect his army's campaign. The ruler can give the order to advance, without knowing that his army should not advance. The ruler can give the order to retreat, without knowing that his army should not retreat. This is equivalent to interfering or hindering military command and movement.

The ruler who is ignorant of the army affairs participates and interferes in its affairs. This causes confusion in the officers and men.

The ruler ignorant of the command system, and authority within the army, interferes in the execution of responsibilities. This causes apprehension and suspicion among the officers and men. If the army is caught in confusion and apprehension, the neighboring warlords may take the opportunity to attack. It is like using a confused and chaotic army to entice your enemy to attack you.

国君不利于军队有三种情况：不了解军队为何不可前进，而硬是要它前进，不了解军队为何不可撤退，而硬是要它撤退，此乃束缚军队；不懂得军队内部，而干预军队行政，使将士们迷惑不解；不懂得用兵权谋，而干预军队指挥，使将士们产生疑虑。将士们既迷惑又疑虑，各诸侯国乘隙进攻之灾难会临头。这好比自乱军心，自取灭亡。

There are five ways to predict victory. He who knows when to launch an attack, and when not to, will win. He who knows when to vary the size of his troops according to battle situations will win. He who is able to unite his whole army as one will win. He who is well-prepared and far-sighted and awaits his enemy will win. He who is capable and does not have to contend with the interference of his ruler will win. These are the five ways to decide if a victory can be secured.

有五种情况可知得胜利或否：知道什么情况可以战，知道什么情况不可以战，能得胜；懂得运用兵力多与寡者，能得胜；君，将于兵上下同心，可得胜；以有准备对没准备，可得胜；将军有才能而君主不牵制，可得胜。这就是知可否得胜之法。

He who knows well his enemy, and himself, will not be defeated easily. He who knows himself, but not his enemy, will have an even chance of victory. He who neither knows himself nor his enemy is bound to suffer defeat in all battles.

所以说，了解自己，了解对方，百战不败。了解自己，不了解对方，胜败各占一半。不了解自己，不了解对方，每战必败。

Chapter 4
Positioning the Army

In ancient times, those who were skillful in warfare ensured that they would not be defeated and then waited for opportunities to defeat the enemy. The ability to prevent defeat is your responsibility, while the opportunities for victory depend upon the enemy. Thus, those who are adept at warfare can ensure that they will not be defeated by the enemy, but will not be able to ensure victory over the enemy. Thus, one is able to predict victory but not necessarily be able to achieve it.

从前善于打仗的人，先创造不会被敌人战胜的条件，来等待可以战胜敌人的机会。不被战胜的主动权在自己，可战胜敌人的条件是敌人创造的。所以善于打仗的人，能做到不被敌人轻易取胜，可是不能肯定敌人必会被打败。所以说，胜利可以预知，但不能强求。

If the enemy cannot be overcome, defend. If the enemy can be overcome, attack. If resources are not available, or are in short supply, then defend; and, vice versa. Those who are able to defend are able to use the surroundings to conceal troops well. Those who are able to attack are able to attack in ways that are out of the ordinary. As such, they are not only able to ensure the greatest security and protection; they would also be able to achieve complete victories.

当不可能战胜敌人时，应该进行防御。当可以战胜敌人时，应该进攻。采取守势是因为资源不足，采取攻势是因为资源充足或有余。善于防守者，深深隐蔽自己兵力于各种地形之下；善于攻击者，高度发挥自己的力量，像从天而降，所以能保存自己又获得全胜。

To predict a victory that cannot surpass the common military knowledge is not the hallmark of a great military strategist. To win a battle that is praised by many, is not the hallmark of great military strategist either. Predicting and achieving such victories is like lifting a hair, which does not indicate that one has great strength; or being able to see the moon and the sun does not mean one has great eyesight. And also similarly, to be able to hear the roar of the thunder does not mean one has sharp hearing. Ancient sages' definitions of generals who are adept at war are those who excelled in securing victories by choosing enemies who are easiest to overcome. Thus, one who is adept at warring wins without being known for his wisdom, reputation, courage or merit.

预见胜利，不超过一般人的见识，不算高明中的高明，经过激烈战斗而后取胜，天下人都说好，也不算高明中的高明。这就像是举得起秋毫算不得力大，能看得见日月算不得眼明，听得见雷声算不得耳灵。古时候善于打仗之人，选择能容易获胜的敌人，所以所得的胜利，既没智慧的名声，也没勇武的战功。

He wins battles with confidence, and without making mistakes. He does not make mistakes, because he adopts measures that lead to victories. Victory is already secured because the enemy is already in a position of defeat. Therefore, the person adept at warfare, will put himself in a position where the odds of defeat are the smallest, and grabs every opportunity to defeat the enemy. As such, a would-be victorious army ensures victory before engaging the enemy. A would-be defeated army will engage his enemy first, before looking for chances of victory. The person adept in warfare not only cultivates his moral code but maintains law and order. In this way, he is able to govern and determine victory and defeat in war.

所以他们取得胜利不会有差错。之所以没有差错是因为他们的作战措施是建立在必胜的基础上，战胜已处于失败地位的敌人。善于打仗的人，先立于不败之地，而又不放过任何能胜敌人的机会。打胜仗的军队，先创造取胜的条件，而后同敌人作战。打败战的军队先同敌人交战，而后希望侥幸取胜。善于作战的人，修明政治，确保法制，所以能够掌握胜败的决定权。

Now in warfare, evaluations must be made as follows: first, estimate the degree of difficulty; second, assess the scope of the operation; third, calculation of one's own forces; fourth, comparison of forces; and fifth, establish the chances of victory. Based on the characteristics of the terrain, the degree of difficulty is estimated. Based on the degree of difficulty, the scope of the operation is assessed. Based on the scope of the operation, the calculation of one's own forces is made. Based on the calculation of one's own forces, comparisons are evaluated against those of the enemy. Based on the evaluations, the chances of victory can then be established.

军事上，有五个范畴，一是"度"，二是"量"，三是"数"，四是"称"，五是"胜"。根据地形，可看出战役的难度，而从难度可看出战役所需要资源量，而从资源数量可看出所需的兵士数量，又从兵士数量作比较，判断谁强谁弱，就可知谁胜谁负。

Thus, a victorious army is like a gladiator matched against a weakling. A defeated army is like a weakling matched against a gladiator. The person adept in warfare is able to command and direct his troops to fight like an avalanche, streaming down mercilessly from thousands of feet high. Such is the disposition of a powerful and victorious army.

所以，胜利的军队与失败的军队相比，就像用"镒"称"铢"那样占有绝对优势；失败的军队较之以胜利的军队，就像用"铢"称"镒"那样处于绝对劣势。军事实力强大的胜利者指挥军队作战，就像决开在八千尺高处的溪中积水那样，一种力量的表现。

Chapter 5
Forces

Managing a large force can be similar to managing a small force. It is a matter of organization and structure. To direct and control a large force can be similar to directing and controlling a small force. It is a matter of communication and formations. The fact that the whole army can withstand an enemy attack without conceding defeat is because of the apt use of the "*direct* and *indirect*".[3] The strength of the troops can be increased to a level similar to using solid stones to hurl at eggs. This is done by avoiding the enemy's strengths and attacking its weaknesses.

要管理人数众多的军队如同人数少的军队，是靠军队的组织；要指挥人数众多的军队如同指挥人数少的军队，是靠规定好的信号。统帅全国军队，即使遭受敌人攻击，也不致失败，是因为"奇正"运用正确。军队可以攻击，如同以石击卵，是因为军队避实击虚。

In battle, use the *direct* forces to match the enemy, and use the *indirect* forces to win the enemy. Thus, the person who is adept at using *indirect* force can use it in such infinite ways, like the ever-changing forces and elements of nature, and the ceaseless flow of water in rivers and streams. *Direct* and *indirect* forces are like the end and the beginning, and also like the ever changing role of the sun and moon. They perish and resurrect like the changing of the four seasons. There are only five basic notes, but their combinations and permutations can create so many musical scores, that one is not able to hear them all. There are only five basic colors, but their mixes and matches produce so many visuals that one is not able to view them all. There are only five basic flavors, but their mixtures and blends produce so many tastes that one is not able to taste them all. In war, there are only the *direct* and *indirect* forces. However the combinations and changes between the two are infinite. Their interactions and combinations are like two never-ending, interlocking rings, where possibilities of its beginning and ending cannot be determined.

大凡作战，是以"正"兵求合，而以"奇"兵求胜。所以善于出奇制胜者，其战法变化如天地运行变化无穷，像江河那样奔流不歇。终而复始，犹如日月的运行；去而又来，好似四季的更迭。乐音不过五个音节，可是五个音节的变化，却听不胜听。颜色不过五种，可是五色的变化，却看不胜看。滋味不过五种，可是五味的变化，却尝不胜尝。作战不过"奇"和"正"，可是"奇""正"相互的变化，就像圆环旋转那样，无始无终，能穷尽吗？

---

[3] In ancient military texts of China, "Direct" and "Indirect" actions are often discussed. These strategies are also occasionally referred to as "Orthodox" and "Unorthodox.

When the gushing torrential water tosses stones and pushes boulders, it is because of the force of its momentum. When the ferocious strike of an eagle breaks the body of its prey, it is because of the timing of the strike. Thus the forces and momentum of the adept in warfare are overwhelming and ferocious, and his timing of the engagement is precise and swift. His stance is like a fully stretched bow and the timing is like the release of the trigger.

川急的流水飞快的奔泻，以至能把石头漂动，那是因为水势强大的关系。凶猛的飞鸟飞快的突击，以至能捕杀猎物，那是因为节奏恰当的关系。所以善于指挥作战者，他所制造的态势险峻，发出的节奏短促。险峻的态势犹如张满的弓弩，短促的节奏犹如击发弩机。

In the midst of disorder and turmoil in war, while the troops have to fight under chaotic situations; they must remain orderly and in control. In the midst of confusion and chaos in fighting, one must still be able to marshal the troops from all directions and deploy them such that they cannot be defeated.

旌旗纷纷，人马纭纭，在混乱的状态下作战，须使自己的军队不发生混乱。战车转动，步卒奔驰，在迷蒙不清的情况下，必须把军队部署得四面八方都能应付自如。

To feign disorder, one must possess strict discipline. To feign cowardice, one must possess great courage. To feign weakness, one must possess great superiority. Order and disorder depend on organization and structure. Courage and cowardice depend on posture and circumstances. Strengths or weaknesses depend on the formation and dispositions of the army.

以乱诱敌的基础在于治，以怯欺敌的基础在于勇，以弱致敌的基础在于强。严整或混乱，是由组织编制好坏造成的；勇敢或怯弱，是由态势优劣所造成的；强大或弱小，是由实力大小对比所造成的。

Thus the person, who is adept at warfare, manipulates the enemy by creating circumstances that will make them conform. Entice the enemy with baits he cannot resist. Keep him on the move and ambush him.

所以善于调动敌方者，制造假象迷惑敌人，敌人必会依从其调动。用敌人必取之利诱敌。用利诱的话，必须用重兵等待敌人，给一重击。

Thus, the person who is adept at warfare uses the battle circumstances and does not solely depend on his troops to seek victory. As such, he is able to select the right men and trust them to exploit the battle circumstances. The person who knows how to exploit battle circumstances is able to command his troops like rolling logs and boulders. The characteristics of the logs and boulders are such that they are not dangerous when not moving, but have destructive effects when moving. If they are square they cease to move, but when they are round, they roll. Thus the person who is adept at warfare can resemble that of moving logs, and boulders moving down the mountain, when he uses battle situations.

所以善于用兵作战者，总是设法造成有利的态势，而不苛求于将吏。他能选择人才去创造或利用有利态势。善于用势者，指挥其部队如同滚动木头和石头一般。木头和石头放在平地就稳，放在斜坡就容易滚动，方的容易静止，圆的灵活滚动。善于用势者，指挥其部队如同像转动圆石从万丈高山飞滚下来之势。

Chapter 6
Weaknesses and Strength

Those who arrive first at the battleground will have sufficient time to rest and prepare against the enemy. Those who arrive late to the battleground will have to rush into battle when they are already exhausted.

凡先占据会战地点等候敌人可安逸，后到达会战地点而仓促参战则疲惫。

Thus the person adept in warfare seeks to control and manipulate his enemy instead of being manipulated and controlled. He can cause his enemy to arrive on his own accord by luring him with benefits. He can deter his enemy from coming by creating dangers and harm.

所以善于作战者，使敌人被自己所调动，而不被敌任所调动。能使敌人自己来，是因为利益。能使敌人不要来，是因为有害处。

Thus when the enemy is well-rested, disturb and tire him. When the enemy is well stocked with food, starve him. When he is encamped and comfortable, make him move. Attack places where the enemy needs to rush to defend. Move quickly along routes where the enemy least expects.

当敌人安逸时，使他们疲劳。当敌人饱食时，使他们饥饿。当敌人扎营安定时，使他们移动。出动于敌人必救之地，活动于敌人意想不到之地。

An army can travel for a thousand *li* without being exhausted if it moves along places where there are no enemies. To be certain to capture what you attack is to attack a place where the enemy does not defend, or where his defense is weak. To be certain to hold on to what you defend is to defend a place, such that the enemy does not have the courage to attack, or where the defense is made invulnerable to attacks. Thus, the person who is adept at offence, attacks places which the enemy does not know how to defend. The person adept at defense protects places such that the enemy has no idea how to attack. Such is the intricacy, and subtlety of an expert in warfare that he appears to be invisible and without trace. Such is the mystery of the expert in warfare that he is not heard or detected.

行军千里而不觉疲劳，是因为行于无敌人阻碍之地。攻打敌人而必取，是因为攻击敌人不能守的地方。防守能稳固，是因为防守让到敌人不知如何攻击。所以，善于攻者，让敌人不知如何防守。善于守者，让敌人不知如何攻击。微妙啊微妙，微妙到无形可见；神奇啊神奇啊，神奇到无声可闻。所以这样的人可成为敌人的主宰。

He is able to advance without resistance because he accelerates along areas that are not defended by the enemy. He is able to retreat without being pursued because he withdraws at a much faster speed than the enemy.

前进而不受到抵御，是因为攻击其防守薄弱之处；撤退而不受敌人阻止，是因为迅速撤退到远处，使敌人赶不上。

Thus, when I desire to go into battle, even if the enemy is behind high walls and deep moats, he will have no choice but to engage me because I attack where he needs to rescue or protect. When I do not desire to go into battle, even though I may be occupying any ground and not erecting any form of defense, the enemy will still be unable to start a battle with me. This is because I contradict the normal rules of engagement and prevent him from reaching his desired destination.

所以如果我想打，敌人虽然有高垒深沟，也不得不与我战，因为我进攻敌人必定会救援的地方；如果我不想作战，即使画地界而防守，敌方也不会与我作战，因为我已把他引向别处或阻止他抵达目的地。

Thus, if I can uncover the dispositions of the enemy while remaining concealed myself, I can keep my forces concentrated and united, and force those of the enemy to be divided and dispersed. If I can concentrate and unite my troops at one place, while those of the enemy are scattered at ten different places, then I can use my entire force against one tenth of his. Thus, I will be able to have numerical strength over him. If I can use a larger and stronger force to attack a smaller and inferior enemy force, those enemies will surely be defeated. If the enemy does not know where I am going to attack, he will have to defend many places. The more places he needs to defend, the more dispersed his force will be. Thus, I am able to engage a small part of his troops with my full force. If he strengthens the front, the rear will be weakened. If he strengthens the rear, his front will be weakened. If he defends his left, his right will be exposed. If he defends his right, his left will be exposed. If he tries to defend everywhere, he will be vulnerable everywhere.

若知敌人兵形而我方兵形不被敌方所知，则我方兵力可集中在一处而敌方兵力被分散。我方集中在一处，敌方分散在十处，这就是说我方有十倍于兵力攻击敌人，造成我方有优势。能以众击寡，那么正面作战的敌人就少了。我与敌方交战的地点不为人知，敌方所要防备的地方就多；敌方所要防备的地方多，则我方所攻击的地方敌人就会少；前方设防则后方薄弱，后方设防则前方薄弱，左方设防则右方薄弱，右方设防则左方薄弱，处处设防，则处处薄弱。

The inferiority or weakness in numbers is normally associated with the defending side. The superiority or strength in numbers is associated with the attacking side.

劣势，是居于防守的一方；优势，是居于攻击的一方。

If you know the terrain of the battleground and the exact date of engagement of battle, your army can travel a thousand *li* and still be ready for battle. If you do not know the location of the battleground and the exact date of engagement, then your left flank will not be able to rescue your right flank, and the right flank will not be able to rescue your left flank. The front will not be able to rescue the rear and the rear will not be able to rescue the front. This problem is compounded even more, considering that the farthest force may be ten *li* away or the nearer force only several *li* apart.

预先知道作战地点和时间，才能千里行军而又可交战。不预先知道作战地点和时间，则左翼不能救右翼，右翼不能救左翼，前方不能救后方，后方不能救前方，更何况是远在数十里，或近在数里？

Based on my analysis and evaluation, the army may have superiority in numbers, but does this mean that it has the definite advantage in winning battles? Thus I say: victories can be created by us. Although the enemy may have a larger and stronger force, he can be prevented from engaging me. Therefore, scheme to discover the plans of the enemy so as to know their likelihood of success. Provoke him so as to know his reasons and basis for movement and actions. Know his dispositions so as to know the vulnerability of the ground he is occupying. Throw some contests against the enemy so as to know his area of his strengths and weaknesses.

依我看，越国的兵力虽多，但对它争取胜利会有什么帮助呢？胜利可以造成的，敌人虽多，但可以使它无法与我争斗。通过策略可知敌我双方优劣，通过挑动可知敌人活动之道理，同过调查可知地形，通过较量来得知双方实力强弱。

The ultimate skill in the deployment of troops is to ensure that it has no fixed or constant formation and disposition. Without ascertainable formations, even the most well-placed and observant spy will not be able to probe and comprehend, and the wisest strategist will not be able to uncover your plans or plot against you. The victory gained as a result of adapting to the circumstances of the enemy will never be understood by the troops. Everyone may know the formation that I used to secure victory. However, no one will know the ways, methods and reasons behind how I went about creating that victory.

所以部署兵队最高境界，是无任何形。无形，则深入我方的间谍刺探不到情报，敌方谋略者也想不出对策。运用多变战术引导众人取得胜利，众人也不了解如何取胜。人们知道我取得胜利的态势，可是不知我如何创造此态势。

Therefore, the victory gained from each battle comes about because strategies and tactics are never repeated. Rather, they should vary according to the circumstances, with infinite possibilities. The principle underlying military deployment may be likened to water. It is the inherent characteristic of flowing water to flow from high places and hasten its movement in low places. In the same way, the disposition and deployment of an army should be to avoid strengths and attack weaknesses. Just as water controls its flow according to the characteristics of the terrain, an army should try to create its victory according to the situations of the enemy. So, in the conduct of war, there are no fixed situations and conditions, just like water has no constant shape and configuration. The persons who gains victories by adapting to the changing conditions and situations of the enemy can be considered a legend in warfare. Thus, there is no guaranteed victory among the five elements of nature. There is no permanency for each of the four seasons. There are days which are short and days which are long. There are changes in the shape of the moon throughout a month.

所以作战胜利都不是重复旧方式，而是适应不同的态势而不变化无穷。兵力的部署应该像流水，水的流向从高向低，进攻敌人应该避开敌人坚实之处，而趋向薄弱之处。流水的方向是由地势决定，军队作战也应该根据不同敌人而决定制胜策略。所以军队作战没有固定的态势，如同水也没有固定的形状。能够根据敌人的变化而取得胜利者，可称之为"神"。所以五行相生相克，没有固定常胜，四季变化也没有固定的开始与结束，白昼有长短，月亮有圆缺。

Chapter 7
Military Maneuvers

In any military campaign, the general will first receive orders from his ruler. He then assembles the troops and mobilizes the people. He must harmonize these diverse groups and build their relationships and comradery. However, none of these are more difficult than military maneuvers. The difficulty about the art of maneuvering is to convert difficult and torturous routes into direct accesses, and to turn disastrous circumstances into advantageous situations.

一般用兵法则是，将帅从君主领命，招募士卒，组织与训练一支军队，和部署建立同生共死的关系等等。但这些并不难，而最难的是争取有利战机。争取有利战机的困难在于把迂回的路变为直路，把不利条件变为有利。

Thus, advance by using indirect routes, and lure the enemy by offering enticements as bait. As such, while you may set off later than your enemy, you will be able to arrive earlier than him. The one who knows how to do this understands the use of *direct* and *indirect* strategies.

用迂回的道路前进，并用利来引诱敌人，这样一来即使比敌人晚出发，也还能先到达战场。这就是懂得弯路和直路的道理。

In maneuvering there are advantages to be gained and dangers and calamities as well. One who attempts to mobilize a complete and fully equipped army, so as to go after advantages and gains will be late in seizing them. One who sends a lightly equipped army to go after advantages and gains is likely to suffer severe losses of stores and supplies.

An army may bundle up and keep wearing armor, in order to rush its movement forward through nights and days without rest, so that double the distance can be covered. It can travel 100 *li* to contend for advantages against the enemy. However, such an army is likely to risk having the generals of its three divisions captured. This is because the stronger and fitter men will be in front while the weaker ones are far behind. As a result, only one tenth of it will reach the destination. It can travel 50 *li* to contend for advantages against the enemy. In this case, the general of the vanguard will be humiliated and defeated. This is because only half the troops will arrive at the destination. It can travel 30 *li* to contend for advantages against the enemy, but only two thirds of the troops will arrive at the destination.

It follows that an army without heavy equipment and supplies will perish. An army without sufficient food and grain will die. An army without sufficient stockpiles and reserves will not survive.

军争有其有利的一面，也有其危险的一面。如果携带所有辎重与敌争利，则赶不上。若放弃所有辎重与敌争利，则辎重损失。因此，卷起盔甲，昼夜不停，加速赶路，走上一百里与敌争利，三军将领有可能被俘虏，体力好的士卒在前，体力不好的在后，一般只有十分之一的部队会抵达；若是五十里与敌争利，则上将军受折损，一般只有二分之一的部队会抵达；若是三十里与敌争利，一般只有三分之二的部队会抵达。所以军队没有足够辎重就会灭亡，没有足够粮食就会灭亡，没有足够物资积蓄就会灭亡。

Thus, if the schemes and ploys of the neighboring warlords are not known, one should not be keen to enter into any alliances with them. Those who do not know the conditions of the forested mountains, the dangerous terrain of mountain paths, and the treacherous nature of swamps and marshes will not be able to conduct the movement of troops. Those who do not use local guides will not be able to gain the advantages of the terrain.

所以，如果不知各诸侯的打算，则不可与之结交；如果不掌握地形，则不可行军；如果不用乡导，则不能得地利。

Thus, war is based on who applies deception best. Move when there are advantages. Create changes in situations through the dispersion and concentration of forces. Thus, when in movement, be as swift as the wind. When in slow marches, be as majestic as the forest. When raiding, be as ferocious as the fire. When not in movement, be as steady as the mountains. When in concealment, be as inscrutable as the darkness. When attacking, be as overwhelming as the roar of thunder and merciless as the strike of lightning. When looting and plundering the villages, share the bounty with the troops; when occupying conquered territories, also share the bounty. Consider and deliberate carefully before deciding on any action. Those who can master beforehand the skill of using the *indirect* and *direct* approaches, strategies and schemes will win. Such is the art of maneuvering military forces.

所以用兵打战要靠权变才能成功，有利可图则动，以分散或集中军队为变换战术。军队行动应该，快如疾风，慢如森林，掳掠如火，不动如山，不可窥测如阴暗，攻击冲锋如雷电；掳掠乡邑，所得分发给兵众；扩张领土，分发所得之利；权衡利害得失而后动。预先得知迂直之计能得胜。此乃军争之法。

According to the *Military and Political Guide*, "In battles, as verbal communication cannot be heard clearly, cymbals and drums are used as commands." As visual communication and eye contact are hampered, banners and flags are used as signals. Now the purpose of using cymbals, drums, flags and banners is to draw attention of the troops and focus them for combat under the direction of the commander. Once the troops are united as one body, the courageous ones will not advance forward by themselves and the cowardly ones will not retreat by themselves. This is the art of directing larges forces in battles.

Military Strategy Classics of Ancient China

<<军政>>
说:"作战中用口令指挥无效,所以应该用金鼓;因为看不见,所以应该用。"

金鼓和金鼓,是用来统一全军行动的。全军统一,则勇者不会擅自前进,怯懦者不会擅自后退。这就是指挥军队的方法。

For battles at night, use more torches and drums. For battles in the day, use more banners and flags. These different means of communication can be designed to influence the judgment of the enemy.

夜战多用金鼓和火把指挥,白天作战则多用旌旗指挥军队,也可用它们误导敌人。

Thus, they serve to destroy the morale of the enemy's army. With regard to the generals of the enemy, they serve to rob them off their decisiveness. At the beginning of a military campaign, the fighting spirit of the forces is high. As the campaign progresses, the spirit of the forces become sluggish and tiredness sets in. Towards the end of the campaign, thoughts of returning home will set in. Therefore, the adept at warfare avoids engaging the enemy when their morale is high, and only attacks them when their spirits are sluggish, and the soldiers are homesick. This is how to control the morale factor.

所以可以使三军士气衰歇,可是将军决心动摇。在早晨士气旺盛,中午士气低落,傍晚士气衰歇。善于用兵者,避敌人旺盛锐气,待敌人士气衰歇才攻击,此乃掌握士气用兵之法。

Use orderliness and stability to confront chaos and disorder. Use calmness and steadfastness to deal with noisiness and chaos. This is control of the psychological factor.

用自己的整齐对待敌人的混乱,用自己的冷静对待敌人的喧哗,这是掌握用兵时的心理方面。

Use proximity to battlefields to counter enemies who come from afar. Use well rested troops to counter tired and exhausted enemies. Use well fed troops to counter enemies that are hungry. This is control of the physical factor.

以自己的近对待敌人的远,以自己的安逸对待敌人的疲劳,以自己的饱食对待敌人的饥饿,这就是掌握用兵时体力的方面。

Never engage an approaching enemy who displays orderly flags and banners. Never engage an advancing enemy which shows an impressive and organized formation. This is control of the change factor.

不拦截旗帜整齐的敌军部队,不攻击阵容强大的敌军部队,这就是掌握机动变化。

Thus the art of applying military maneuvers includes the following:

1. Do not advance against an enemy who is encamped on high ground.
2. Do not engage an enemy who is assaulting downwards from high ridges.
3. Do not pursue an enemy who only pretends to retreat in desperation.
4. Do not attack the agile and motivated elite force of the enemy.
5. Do not fall for bait offered by the enemy.
6. Do not intercept an enemy who is returning to his home country.
7. In surrounding an enemy, always leave him an escape route.
8. Do not pursue a desperate enemy relentlessly

These are the ways and art of maneuvering and deploying troops.

用兵之方法是:
敌人在高处,不可攻击;不要迎战背后有高地依恃的敌人;不要追击假装撤退的敌人;不要攻击气势正盛的敌人;不要捡拾敌人以利诱我的饵食;不要截阻或追击想回家的敌军;包围敌人时,应该留一个逃生活口;敌人被困时,不可过度施压。

Chapter 8
Variation and Adaptation

In a military campaign, the general first receives orders from his ruler. He then assembles the troops and mobilizes the citizens. When on treacherous ground, you must never encamp. When on focal ground, you must attempt to ally with neighboring states. When on isolated ground, you must not stay there. When on constricted ground, you must plan and strategize. When on deathly ground, you must fight relentlessly.

大凡用兵的法则，首将先领命与君主，后征集兵队，编成军团，出征时，若在"圯地"不可扎营，若在"衢地"应结交邻国，若在"绝地"不可久留，若在"围地"要巧出计谋，若在"死地"要拼死奋战。

There are some routes and paths that must not be taken. There are some armies and troops that must not be assaulted. There are some cities that must not be attacked. There are some grounds that must not be contested. There are some military orders that need not be obeyed. Thus, the general who knows how to vary and adapt to changing situations so as to gain advantages is one who is skillful in applying the art of war. The general who is familiar with the terrain but does not know how to vary and adapt to changing situations will not be able to take advantage of what that terrain has to offer. In military command, if the general cannot master the art of variations and adaptability, he will not be able to deploy his troops to maximum advantage, despite understanding the five strategic considerations.

有些道路不宜走，有些敌军不宜打，有些城池不宜攻，有些要地不宜争，有的国君命令可以不执行。所以，将帅能够精通以上各种机变的运用，就是懂得用兵。将帅不能够精通机变的运用，虽然了解地形，也不能得到地利。将帅不能够精通机变的运用，虽然知道"五利"，也不能充分发挥军队的战斗能力。

Thus, the wise strategist will always weigh and consider the favorable and unfavorable factors in his deliberations. By factoring the favorable factors, the mission can be accomplished with confidence. By factoring the unfavorable factors, disasters and crises can be averted.

所以，聪明的将帅在考虑问题时，必定会兼顾到利害两方面条件。考虑到利，可以提高胜算，成功的信心。考虑到害，可以避免祸患和排除疑虑。

Control the neighboring warlords through the use of intimidation and threats. Harass and wear down the neighboring warlords through incessant creation of troubles and activities. Hasten and direct the movements of the neighboring warlords through the offer of benefits and baits.

要使各国诸侯屈服，就用诸侯最害怕的事威胁他；要使各国诸侯劳役，就用他不得不去做的事去驱使他；要使各国诸侯趋向你要的方向，就用小利去引诱他。

Thus, in the conduct of war, one must not rely on the failure of the enemy to come, but on the readiness of oneself to engage him. One must not rely on the failure of the enemy to attack, but on the ability of oneself to build an invincible defense.

用兵之法是，不要寄望敌人不会来，而要依靠自己，充分军备，严阵以待；不要寄望敌人不会进攻，而要依靠自己，使自己不易攻破。

Thus, there are five dangers that will plague any general. If he is reckless, he can be killed. If he is cowardly and desperate to live, he can be captured. If he is easily angered, he can be provoked. If he is sensitive to honor, he can be insulted. If he is overly compassionate to people, he can be disturbed and harassed. These five characteristics are the greatest potential pitfalls and mistakes of a general, and the cause of disasters in any military operation. The destruction of an army and the deaths of generals are caused by these five dangers, thus they should be examined thoroughly.

将帅有因性格上的缺陷而造成的危险；有勇无谋，只知道拼死，可能被诱杀；贪生怕死，临阵畏怯，可能被俘虏；急躁易怒，可能因被羞辱而败亡；在乎名声，可能受不了羞辱而败亡；一味爱民爱士卒，可以容易被烦扰。以上五点是将帅可能范下的错，而会殃及兵队。军队覆灭，将帅被杀，都是由着五种危险引起，所以不可不慎重，不可不深思。

Chapter 9
Troop Deployment and Movement

In the deployment of troops and in the analysis and assessment of the enemy, certain principles must be kept in mind. After crossing the mountains, move and stay close to the valleys. For a commanding view and to ensure better chances of survival, occupy high grounds. When the enemy has occupied high ground, do not attempt an assault. These are the principles for deploying troops in mountainous terrain.

凡军队行军作战和战场观察判断敌情时要注意以下原则：通过山地时，要靠近有水草的谷地；驻止时，要选择山地，使视野宽阔，但是如果敌人已占领高地则不要仰攻。这是在山地行军的法则。

After crossing a river, get as far away from its bank as possible and move on. When an invading force of the enemy is crossing a river, never engage it in the midst of the river itself. Rather, let half of its force cross the river first; then attack it, so that you can gain the advantage. If you are eager to attack an invading enemy, never engage him at the point where he plans to cross a river. For a commanding view and to ensure better chances of survival against the enemy, occupy high ground. Never move upstream to engage an enemy. These are the principles for deploying troops in marine battles.

横渡江河，要在离江河稍远的地方驻扎；如果敌人渡水来进攻，不要在水中攻击，应该等半数渡江河过后才攻击，这样才有利；如果要更敌军决战，不要靠近水边列阵；沿江河驻扎军队也应该驻扎在高处，使前面视野辽阔；不要在敌军下游驻扎或布阵；这些是江河地带行军法则。

When crossing salty swamps and marshes, move away quickly; never linger there. If you need to engage the enemy in salty swamps and marshes, stay close to areas that are lush with grasses and have your rear to the forest. These are the principles for deploying troops in salty swamps and marshes.

通过盐碱沼泽地带，要迅速离开，不可久留；如果在盐碱沼泽地带与敌军交战，必须靠近水草、背靠树林；这些是在盐碱沼泽地带行军的法则。

On level terrain, occupy positions that allow you ease of maneuvers. By ensuring that the right flank and support forces are on higher grounds, the danger is confined to the front, as the rear is secured and safe. These are the principles for deploying troops on level terrain.

在平陆地带驻军，要选择地势平坦的地方，主要是翼侧和后方依托高地，前低后高，这就是在平原地带行军作战法则。

By mastering the principles of the four different situations for deployment of troops, the Yellow Emperor was able to conquer the other warlords of the surrounding areas. In general, an army prefers to take up positions on high ground and detests occupying low ground. It favors positions that are bright and sunny and detests places that are dark. It prefers to nourish its troops by locating in areas where food and supplies are in abundance. An army that does not suffer from disease and sickness is bound to win more battles.

以上四种"处军"法则的好处，是黄帝能战胜"四帝"的重要原因。大凡驻军都喜欢高地而厌恶低处，偏向阳亮之地，厌恶阴湿之地，接近水草以保持供应，这样一来军队不易生病，也就给胜利多一个保障。

When in hilly areas, you need to be cautious and alert by camping on the sunnier side, and have the right flank and rear guard on higher ground. In this way, the troops will benefit because you are able to exploit the advantages of the terrain.

丘陵、堤防驻军，必须驻扎在向阳的一面，并且要把主要翼侧和后方依托着它。这样对于用兵有利，得到地形给于的辅助。

When there is rain upstream and the river is foaming, you must wait for the water to subside before trying to cross the river.

河流上游暴雨，看到水沫冲来，要渡河者应该带水势平稳以后再渡。

In any terrain, there are treacherous gullies, natural wells, natural prisons, natural nets, natural traps and natural crevices. Move quickly away when encountering them and never even be close to them. I will keep a distance from them, but will force the enemy near them. I will face them directly but will force the backs of the enemy towards them.

凡是遇到"绝涧"、"天井"、"天牢"、"天罗"、"天陷"、"天隙"等地形，必须迅速离开而不要靠近。我远离它，而是敌军靠近它。我面向它，敌方背对它。

The surrounding areas along the route that an army takes may have treacherous paths and ponds covered with grasses and reeds, marshlands, forested mountains and areas with thick undergrowth and vegetation. So in moving through such areas, it must be extra vigilant and embark on detailed and thorough searches. They provide good areas for ambushes laid by the enemy, or where his spies are hidden.

军队在行军时，在难以行走的路、湖沼、芦苇丛生的低洼地区、草木繁茂的山林地区，必须仔细反复的搜索，因为这些地方都容易隐藏伏兵或奸细。

When the enemy is nearby and yet is able to remain silent, he is relying on the strategic advantages conferred by the terrain. When the enemy attempts to provoke you into battle from a distance, he is trying to lure you forward to engage him. When the enemy camps on a level and accessible ground, there must be advantages and reasons to do so.

敌军离我方近，却能保持安静，那是他倚仗占据险要地形。敌军离我方远，却来挑战，那是企图诱我前进。敌军之所以占据平地，定有他的好处和用意

When the forest trees show signs of movement, the enemy may be approaching. When there are many obstacles of bundled grasses and hay along the way, the enemy may be trying to arouse your suspicion. When the birds suddenly rise in flight, there are likely ambushes nearby. When frightened animals rush out from the forest, the main force of the enemy is at hand.

树林里很多树在摇动，可能是敌军来袭；在草丛中设有许多遮蔽物，是敌人企图迷惑我；鸟群突然飞起，表示下面有埋伏；走兽到处跑，表示敌人大举来袭；

When the dust rises high and concentrated, the enemy chariots are approaching. When the dust rises low and is widespread, the enemy infantry is approaching. When the dust shows sign of scattering in different streaky directions, the enemy is sending out troops to cut and gather firewood. When the dust rises and settles occasionally in small patches, the enemy is setting up camp.

飞尘高而尖，可能是敌军战车向我开来；飞尘低而广，可能是敌军士卒向我奔来；飞尘疏散而细长，可能是敌人在打柴；飞尘少而时起时落，可能是敌军在扎营；

When the envoy of the enemy speaks humbly and lowly while preparations are being intensified, the enemy is planning to attack. When the envoy of the enemy speaks arrogantly and aggressively with threats to attack, the enemy is preparing to withdraw. When the envoy of the enemy asks for a truce when there is no prior agreement or understanding, the enemy is scheming.

敌方使者言辞谦卑而实际上又积极备战，表示是要向我进攻；敌方使者言辞强硬而军队有向我逼近，表示他要撤退；敌方使者在没有前提下求和，其中必有阴谋；

When the light chariots leave the main force to take up flank positions, the enemy is gearing up formation for the battle. When there is much movement among the soldiers and chariots of the enemy, rushing to take up positions, his reinforcements have arrived. When half of the enemy troops are advancing while the other half is withdrawing, he is attempting to lure you.

敌战车先出而占据翼侧，是在布列阵势；敌军急速奔走并摆开兵车列阵，是祈求与我决战；敌军半近半退，是要引诱我军

When the soldiers of the enemy are leaning against their weapons, they are hungry and short of food. When the enemy soldiers assigned to get water start to drink first, they are extremely thirsty and in need of water supplies. When the enemy sees an obvious advantage but does not want to seize it, he is severely tired and exhausted. When the birds gather around the enemy campsite, the site is empty. When the enemy soldiers scream and yell at night, they are in great fear. When the army of the enemy is disorderly and chaotic, the authority of the general is not respected. When the banners and flags of the enemy are shifted around frequently, the troops are in disarray. When the junior officers of the enemy are short-tempered and easily angered, they are tired and detest their responsibilities. When the enemy kills horses for food, there are no provisions in his camp. When the cooking utensils are hung away and the soldiers refuse to return to camp, the enemy is in a desperate situation.

敌军倚着兵器而站立着，是因为饥饿缺粮；打水的敌兵急于饮水，是因为干渴缺水；敌军见利不取，是因为疲劳过度。地方营寨上有鸟停集，那表示营寨是空的；敌营夜间有人惊呼，说明敌军心里恐惧；敌军纷扰无次序，是其将帅无威严；敌军旗帜摇动而不整齐，是因为其阵形已经混乱；敌军官吏急躁易怒，是因为过度疲劳困倦；敌人用粮食喂马，杀牲口吃，收起炊具，不返回营寨，是准备拼命突围的"穷寇"；

When the officers and men gather in small groups to speak softly and subdued tones, the general has lost their support. When the rewards are given out excessively, the general is lacking ideas. When punishments are carried out excessively, the general is in great distress. A general who behaves ruthlessly at the initial stage, and then begins to fear his own troops subsequently, is one who is neither intelligent nor capable. When the envoy of the enemy arrives with praises and gifts, they are signs that the enemy desires a truce. When the enemy arrives with much anger and ferocity, yet for a long time refuses to engage in battle, or to withdraw, one must be very vigilant and study his behavior and motives carefully.

当兵士官吏成群结队，窃窃私语，将帅低声下气同部下讲话，表示敌将失去人心；一而再奖励士兵，表示敌军已没办法；一而再重罚部属，表示敌军陷入困境；将帅先对士卒凶暴，后害怕部下，是最不精明的。敌人借故派使者来谈判，措词委婉态度谦和，表示他想休战；敌军盛怒前来，但久不交战，又不离去，必须谨慎地观察其意图。

The strength of an army does not depend on superiority of numbers. Do not advance compulsively based on having large forces. Concentrate the strengths of your forces sufficiently and judge the moves and motives of the enemy accurately, so as to capture him. He who lacks strategic foresight and insight and underestimates his enemy will definitely end up being captured.

打战不在于兵力越多越好,只要不轻敌冒进,并集中兵力,了解敌情,就可以战胜敌人。无深谋远虑而又轻敌的将帅必定被人俘虏。

When the men are punished before their loyalty is secured, they will be rebellious and disobedient. If disobedient and rebellious, it is difficult to deploy them. When the loyalty of the men is secured, but punishments are not enforced, such troops cannot be used either.

将帅在士卒尚未亲近依附时,就冒然处罚士卒,士卒肯定不服,不服则难使用。士卒已经亲近依附,但不执行军纪军法,这样的军队也不可使用。

Thus, the general must be able to instruct his troops with civility and humanity and unite them with rigorous training and discipline so as to secure victories in battles. When orders are regularly enforced and used to train the soldiers, they will be obedient. When orders are not regularly enforced nor used to train the soldiers, they will not be obedient. When orders are regularly enforced, it is because of the mutual trust and confidence between the commander and his men.

所以将帅应该以文明与人性来喝令士卒,用军纪、军法来来统一士卒。这样的军队打起战来会取得胜利。平时能认真贯彻命令、教育士卒,士卒就能养成服从的习惯;平时不认真贯彻命令、不教育士卒,士卒就会养成不服从的习惯;平时能认真执行命令,是由于将帅与士卒相互取得信任的缘故。

Chapter 10
Terrain

There are different kinds of terrain, such as: communicative ground, entrapping ground, indifferent ground, constricted ground, key ground and distant ground.

地形有"通""挂""支""隘""险""远"等六种。

An area that is easily accessible to me and the other side is considered as a communicative ground. On a communicative ground, the priority is to occupy a high and sunny position that is convenient and beneficial for overseeing the supply routes for food and rations. In this way, advantages in battle are gained.

我可以去、敌可以来的地域,叫做"通"。在通形地域,要抢先地势高而又向阳,沟通并保护粮道,这样与敌交战就比较有利。

An area that is easy to enter but difficult to retreat from is called an entrapping ground. On an entrapping ground, when the enemy is ill-prepared in defense, one can launch attacks to capture successfully. However, if the enemy proves to be well prepared and the assault fails, one is hard put to beat a retreat, and is thus placed in a very disadvantageous position.

可以前进,难以后退的地域称作为"挂"。在挂形地域,敌人若无防备,就可以出击取胜;若敌人有所防备,出击而不能胜,又难以退回,就不利了。

An area that is not advantageous for occupation for both sides is called an indifferent ground. On an indifferent ground, should the enemy throw out bait, one must never take it, nor launch an attack. Instead, one should pretend to retreat and, in turn, lure the enemy out. When half of his troops have been drawn out, it is then advantageous to launch an attack.

敌我双方出击都不利,此地域称作为"支";在支地,纵然敌人如何引诱我方,我方都不可出击;可引兵离去,诱使敌人前出一半时,我军突然出击,就有利。

On a constricted ground, one must be the first to occupy it; one should then fortify the strategic access points with troops and await the arrival of the enemy. If the enemy occupies the constricted ground first and has already fortified the strategic access points, refrain from attacking. Only attack the strategic access points when they are weak and not fortified.

在隘形地域,若我方先占领,应当用重兵占领隘口;若敌人先占领,并以重兵把守隘口,不可攻击,若没重兵把守,就因该迅速攻击隘口。

On key ground, first occupy and then camp on higher, sunnier ground to await the arrival of the enemy. If the enemy occupies the key ground first, he has to be lured away. One must not follow to attack him.

在险形地域者，如果我军先到达，应占据地势高而向阳的地方，等待来犯的敌人；如果敌军先占据，就应引敌军离去，而不追击。

On a distant ground, if both forces are equally matched, it becomes difficult for one to provoke the other into battle, as there is no advantage to be gained in a direct battle.

在远形地域，双方势均力敌，不宜挑战，勉强求战，于我不利。

The natural laws of terrain underlie these six types of ground. It is the general's responsibility to study and examine their characteristics thoroughly.

以上六点，是利用地形的法则；观察地形是当将帅的一大责任。

An army suffers from flight, insubordination or collapse. It may also suffer from ruin, disorganization and rout. The six calamities mentioned are not due to natural causes but are the fault of the general.

军队失败的六种情况是"走""弛""陷""崩""乱"和"北"。这六种情况，非天灾，而是将帅的过失。

Even when all other conditions and characteristics are comparable, if an army insists on attacking an enemy force ten times its size, the result will be flight. When the soldiers are strong and courageous but the officers are weak and cowardly, the result will be insubordination. When the officers are strong and brave but the soldiers are weak and timid, the result will be collapse. When the senior officers are angry and insubordinate because of the general's failure to recognize their capabilities, and they engage the enemy in a spirit of resentment and act out of their own will, the result will be ruin. When the general is weak and lacks discipline, when his orders and instructions are not enlightened, when his officers and men do not have clear lines of responsibilities, and when the command structure and formations are confusing, the result is disorganization. When the general, unable to assess the enemy's character, allows a smaller force to strike a larger one, pitting its weakness against the enemy's strengths, and having no elite troops at the front, the result will be rout. The above six situations are definite causes of defeat. It is again the responsibility of the general to study these situations thoroughly.

在敌我条件相当的情况下，如果攻击十倍于我的敌人，因而失败，这称作为"走"。兵卒强悍而将吏懦弱，因而失败，称作为"弛"。将吏强悍而兵卒懦弱,因而失败，称作为"陷"。偏将怨怒而不服从指令，遇到敌人，擅自率军出战，主将又不肯定他们能否取胜，因而失败，称作为"崩"。主将软弱又不威严，训练没有章法，吏卒无所遵循，布阵杂乱无章，因而失败，这称作为"乱"。将帅不能判断敌情，以少击众，以弱击强，作战又没有精锐作骨干，因而失败，这称作为"北"。以上六种情况，必然造成失败，观察军队是否有以上的情况是当将帅的一大责任。

Advantages of terrain are exploited to complement the deployment of troops. The general must be able to also assess the enemy so as to secure victories. He must be able to determine the characteristics of terrain to understand its dangers, distance, scope and coverage in the use of battle. Those are the moral responsibilities of the supreme commander. He who knows these factors and applies them in battle will win. He who does not know these factors, nor applies them will be defeated in battle.

地形是用兵作战的辅助条件。正确判明敌情，研究地形险易，计算道路远近，这是将帅的责任。懂得这些并能用来指导作战，就必然胜利。不懂得这些道理去指挥作战，就必然失败。

If an assessment of the battle situations is one of definitive victory, the general must engage in battle even though the ruler has issued orders not to do so. If an assessment of the battle situation is one of definitive defeat, the general must not engage in battle, even though the ruler has issued orders to do so. The loyal general is thus able to advance in battle without thought of seeking personal fame or glory. He retreats without fear of punishment. His concerns are always on protecting the welfare of the people and the upholding of interest of the ruler. Such a general is a precious talent that is favored by the nation.

所以如果根据战场实际确有必胜把握，即使国君命令不许打，也可以坚决去打；如果根据战场实际不能取胜，即使国君命令打也可以不打。所以，进不求名誉，推不避罪责，只求保护民众和维护国君的根本利益，这样的将帅，是国家最宝贵的财产。

When the general regards his troops as infants, they will be willing to follow him through the greatest threats and gravest danger. When the general treats his troops like beloved sons, they will be willing to support and die for him. An army may be so overly pampered by the general that it cannot be useful, so excessively loved that it cannot be commanded and so disorderly that it cannot be disciplined. Such an army is like a bunch of spoiled and arrogant brats, and cannot be deployed.

将帅对待士卒能够像对待婴儿那样关切，士卒就可以随将帅赴汤蹈火；将帅对待士卒像对待自己的儿子那样，士卒就会与将帅共患难、共生死。但是，对待士卒如果厚待而不能使用，溺爱而不能命令，违法乱纪也不能严肃处理，这样的军队就像娇惯的子女一样，不能用来作战。

If I know that my troops are capable of attacking the enemy, but do not know if the enemy is invulnerable to being attacked, the chance of victory is half. If the enemy is vulnerable to attack, but I am unaware that my troops are incapable of the task, the chance of victory is only half. In war, I may know that the enemy is vulnerable to attack and my troops are capable of attacking. But, if I do not know that the terrain is not favorable for the conduct of such assault, then the chance of victory is half.

只了解我军能打,而不了解敌军不可以打,胜利的可能性只有一半;了解敌军可打,而不了解我军不能打,胜利的可能性也只有一半;了解敌军可打,也了解我军能打,而不了解地形不利于作战,胜利的可能性仍然只有一半。

Thus, he who is adept at warfare, when deploying his troops for battle, is never confused or misguided. When he mounts a military campaign, he never runs out of strategies or plans. Thus it is said: Know the enemy, know yourself; your victory will not be threatened. Know the weather, know the terrain, and your victories will be limitless.

所以真正懂得用兵的人,行动起来目的明确而不迷惑,采取措施或谋略变化无穷而不呆板;所以,了解敌人,了解自己,争取胜利不会有危险;懂得天时,懂得地利,胜利可保全。

Chapter 11
The Nine Battlegrounds

In the deployment of troops, there are nine types of ground:

1. Dispersive ground
2. Frontier ground
3. Key ground
4. Communicative ground
5. Focal ground
6. Serious ground
7. Treacherous ground
8. Constricted ground
9. Death ground

用兵的方法，有散地，有轻地，有争地，有交地，有衡地，有重地，有圮地，有围地，有死地。有

When the warlords are fighting in their own territory, it is on dispersive ground. When a force has just made a shallow penetration into the territory of the enemy, it is considered to be on frontier ground. A terrain is equally advantageous for the general and the other side to occupy is considered key ground.

诸侯在自己境内作战，叫做散地。进入敌国但入境不深，叫做轻地。我军得到有利，敌军得到也有利的战地，叫做争地。

An area that is easily accessible to me and to the other side is considered communicative ground. When a territory is surrounded by three other states, and when its seizure by any of the states is crucial to the determination of supremacy over the rest, then the surrounding territory is considered focal ground. When an army has penetrated deep into the territory of the enemy, leaving behind hostile fortified cities and towns, it is considered to be on serious ground.

我可以往，敌可以来的地区，叫做交地。与多国交接，先到达就可以得天下之众的地区，叫做衢地。进入敌国而且入境深，经过的城邑多的地区，叫做重地。

When an army is moving along forested mountains, dangerous mountain passes, swamps, marshlands, difficult paths and roads, it is considered to be on treacherous ground. An area that can only be reached through narrow passes, that allows retreat only through dangerous and crooked paths and where a small force of the enemy is sufficient to strike a larger force of yours, is classified as constricted ground. An area in which one can only survive through fearless fighting, and will definitely perish if one does not, is called a death ground.

山林、险阻、沼泽，一切难以行走的道路，叫做圮地。进口狭隘，退路迂曲，敌军能以其少胜我多的地区，叫做围地。迅速作战则能生存，不迅速作战则覆灭的地区，叫做死地。

Therefore, when on dispersive ground, do not engage in battle. When on frontier ground, do not stop advancement of troops. When the enemy is occupying key ground, do not launch assaults. When on communicative ground, ensure that your forces are not separated. When on focal ground, you must attempt to befriend and ally with neighboring states. When on serious ground, forage on the supplies and resources of the enemy. When on treacherous ground, hurry the movement of the troops. When on constricted ground, plan and strategize. When on death ground, fight relentlessly.

所以散地不宜作战，轻敌不宜停留，争地不宜进攻，交地行军不可间断，衢地当四面结交诸侯，重地当掠取粮物，圮地当迅速通过，围地当设制计谋，死地应拼死而战。

It is said that the skillful military strategists of the past were able to ensure that the front and rear troops of the enemy could not reinforce each other on time. They ensured that the larger and smaller forces of the enemy would not be able to support nor rely on one another. They ensured that the officers and men of the enemy would not be able to rescue each other. They ensured that the commands and orders of the enemy from top to bottom would not be accepted nor obeyed. As a result, the troops of the enemy would be scattered and unable to concentrate. Even when they manage to gather together, they could never have a complete and orderly army. Move only when there are advantages to be gained. Cease when there are no advantages to be gained.

古代善于用兵的将帅，能使敌人前面和后面不相衔接，主力和非主力不相策应，官兵不相救援，上级与下级失去团结，士卒溃散难以集中，即使兵力集中也不能保持整齐。对我方有利就行动，对我方无利就停止。

When I am asked: What can be done to an approaching enemy that is superior in numbers, orderly and well-commanded? I would suggest: Be first to capture something the enemy treasures most and he will accede to your demands.

试问：如果敌人人数众多而且又阵势严整地前来与我作战，应用什么方法对付？ 回答是： 先夺敌人要害就能使他听从于我。

Speed is of the essence in the use and deployment of troops in war. Exploit the enemy who is unprepared. Travel routes that he does not expect nor is concerned about. Attack your enemy in places expected least.

用兵关键在于速度，乘敌人尚未赶到，走敌人意想不到的道路，去攻击敌人没有防备的地方.

The principles governing an invading force are as follows: when you have penetrated deep into the territory of the enemy, your forces must be highly focused and concentrated so that the enemy will not be able to overwhelm you. You must be able to forage and live off the resources of the enemy, so that your troops will have adequate food and supplies. Nourish and nurture the troops prudently and do not tire them unnecessarily. Unite the spirit and morale of the troops and conserve and accumulate their combat prowess. When deploying the troops, use strategies and plans that are beyond the predictions of the enemy.

一般对敌国进攻的规律是，越深入敌境，士卒的意志越须专一，让防守之敌越是不能抵御；掠取富饶的乡村，三军就有足够粮食；注意休整军队，不使之过于劳累，鼓足士气，养精蓄锐；部署兵力，设制计谋，使敌人无法揣测我方意图。

Place your troops in positions where they cannot escape and they will fight fearlessly unto death, with no thought of fleeing. This is because when they are not afraid to die, the officers and men will give their utmost for battle. When the troops are trapped in dangerous and treacherous situations, they will lose their sense of fear. When they have nowhere to flee, they will be firm and resilient in their fighting spirit. When they have penetrated deep into hostile territory, they will be extra cautious in action. When there is no other choice left, they will fight fearlessly. Thus, such an army requires no instruction to be vigilant and ready for combat. The troops require no asking in order to do what is expected of them. No discipline is needed to gain their close rapport and support. No other orders are needed to obtain their trust and reliance. Such an army forbids superstitious practices and casts away doubts and rumors, thus enabling it to confront death without any fear.

把军队投之于无路可走的境地，士卒就会宁可战死也不会败退，而既然宁死不退，就会竭尽全力。军队陷于危险的境地就会无所畏惧，而无路可走，军心就会稳固。如敌境越深就会越拘束，迫不得已就会奋战到底。所以不用训练也会戒备，不用强求也能做到，不用约束也会亲附，不用命令也会遵守，禁绝占卜，祛除疑虑，即使战死也不会逃跑。

My officers and men do not have excess wealth; but it is not because they detest the accumulation of material possessions. They do not fear for their lives, but it is not because they do not yearn for longevity. On the day when the orders for war are issued, the troops will weep; those sitting down will have their tears and mucus wetting their garments. Those lying down will have their tears streaming down their cheeks. However, when thrown into positions of no escape, they will display the fearless courage of Zhuan Zhu and Cao Gui.[4]

我军士卒没有多余的钱财，并不是他们不爱钱财，不贪生怕死，也不是不想长寿。作战命令下达的时候，士卒们坐着的泪湿衣襟，躺着泪流满面，把他们投之于无路可走的绝地，他们就会向专诸、曹刿一样勇敢。

Thus the army adept in warfare may be likened to the snake, Shuai Ran. The Shuai Ran is a snake found in the Chang Mountains. When you strike its head, its tail will attack you. When you strike its tail, its head will attack you. When you strike its body, both its head and tail will attack you.

所以，善于用兵的将帅，就好像率然一样。率然是恒山的一种蛇，打它的头，尾巴就会来救应，打它的尾巴，头就会来救应，打它的身子，头和尾巴都会来救应。

When I am asked: Can the deployment of troops have the same capability as the Shuai Ran? My answer is: It is possible. It was said that the people and soldiers of the kingdom of Wu and Yue hated one another tremendously. However, if they were placed in the same boat facing strong and threatening winds, they would cooperate and help one another like a left hand and a right hand. Thus it is not sufficient to rely on tying up the horses and burying the wheels of the chariots as a means to control the army. The effective deployment of both the strong and weak forces depends on the understanding and exploitation of the terrain. Thus the adept in warfare leads his army as if he was leading a single person; this is inevitable.

试问军队也能像率然一样吗？答案是可以。吴国人与越国人是相互仇视的，但当他们同乘一条船渡河而遇到风险时，他们互相救援，就像一个人的左右手。所以用联马埋车轮以示死战，是靠不住的，使士卒齐心协力勇往直前如同一人，是治理军队的方法。所以善于用兵的将帅，能使军队携起手来像一个人一样，这是由于客观形势迫使军队不得不这样。

The art of generalship is to be calm and somber in thought, inscrutable and comprehensive in strategizing; and strict, just and fair in the management of military affairs. He must be able to keep information away from the knowledge of his officers and men, so that they will not know his plans. He changes his methods of doing things and alters his strategies so that no one can see through his plans and schemes. He changes his campsites and travels by unexpected routes so that no one can guess his motives. The shrewd and capable general, on a specific military mission, is like someone who leads his men to scale great heights and, at

---

[4] Zhuan Zhu refers to Duke Zhuang of Lu. Cao Gui was a military scholar who stood against Bao Shuya, during a battle in the Spring and Autumn period (c. 630 BCE).

the most crucial moment, removes the ladder that leads them up. He would lead his army deep into the hostile territory of the enemy and then reveal his real intention after burning the boats and breaking the cooking pots. He would lead the army like a flock of sheep, herding them in one direction, and then switching back to another without them understanding what he is trying to accomplish. To assemble all the divisions of the army and expose them to great danger is what a general is expected to do.

将帅用兵，要做到冷静而沉稳，端庄稳重，严正而有条理。要能蒙蔽士卒而耳目，使他们对军事新行动毫无所知。经常变换作战内部署，改变计划，使人们什么也搞不清楚。经常改换宿营地，故意迂回行军，使人们什么也无法推测。将帅与他们约期会战，就像登高而抽取梯子一样，断其归路。将帅与士卒深入别国境内，然后才告之于作战目的，下令作战。这就像驱赶羊群赶过来，赶过去，不知道要上哪儿去。聚集三军士卒，把他们头置于危险的境地，这就是统帅军队应当做的事情。

The variations and changes of the various types of ground, the advantages pertaining to defensive and aggressive actions and the understanding of human nature are all important aspects that must be carefully studied.

九地的变化，通便的利处，士卒心理的掌握，都是不可不加以考察的。

The principle governing occupation of hostile territory is: When an army penetrates deep into hostile territory, it will be more united and focused in battle; when it makes only a shallow penetration, its fighting spirit is likely to be threatened and diluted. When the army leaves its own country behind and crosses the border into another country for battle, it is on isolated ground. When an area is high accessible and communicative to various parties, it is focal ground. When an army penetrates deep into hostile territory, it is on serious ground. When an army makes only a shallow penetration into hostile territory, it is on frontier ground. When the area to the rear of the army is highly dangerous, and the area before it is very narrow, it is on constricted ground. An area from which there is no escape route is called death ground.

一般进攻敌国作战，进入敌国深则意志专一，进入敌国浅则意志溃散。离开本国进入敌境作战，称作绝地；四通八达的地区，称作衢地；进入敌国很深的地区，称作重地；进入敌国浅的地区，称作轻地；背有险固前为隘口，称作围地；无处可走的地区，称作死地。

On dispersive ground, the general must unite the determination of the army. On frontier ground, the general must keep the forces in close contact. When encountering key ground, the general must rush his forces forward to occupy it before the enemy does. On communicative ground, the general must be vigilant in defense. On focal ground, the general must strengthen his alliances. On serious ground, a general must ensure a continuous supply of food and provisions. On treacherous ground, a general must push his forces quickly forward so as to pass it. On constricted ground, a general must seal the points of entry and exit. On death ground, the general must fight as if he does not wish to live.

所以散地要使军队意志统一，轻地要使军队紧密连接，争地要使军队迅速迂回敌后，交地要固守关口，衢地要谨慎防守，重地要补充粮食，圮地要迅速通过，围地要堵塞缺口，死地则要显示死战的决心，殊死拼斗。

It is the intuitive nature of soldiers to resist when they are surrounded, to fight until death when they do not have any alternative and to obey when they are in a highly dangerous situation.

所以士卒的心理情况是，遭敌包围就会尽力抵抗，形势危急，迫不得已就会拼死决斗，深入困境就会听从指挥。

Thus, if the schemes and ploys of the neighboring warlords are not known, one should not be keen to enter into any alliances with them. Those who do not know the conditions of forested mountains, the dangerous terrain of mountain paths and the treacherous nature of swamps and marshes will not be able to conduct the movement of troops. Those who do not use local guides will not be able to gain the advantages of the terrain.

所以，不知道诸侯的谋略，不能与之结交；不知道山林、险阻、沼泽等地形，就不能行军；没有向导，则不能得地利之便。

If one fails to understand and exploit even one of the nine types of ground, one cannot claim to be the supreme commander of an all-conquering army. When a supreme commander attacks a large state, he ensures that it is impossible for the enemy to assemble all his forces against him. He will overpower his enemy convincingly and overawe the other states so much that none of the allies of the enemy would dare unite against him. Thus, he does not have to contend with securing alliances with other states. He does not have to foster or cultivate its power over other states. Rather, he relies on his supreme ability to overpower the enemy to achieve his own agenda and goals. Thus, he is able to conquer cities and overthrow the states in his enemies.

这几方面，如果有一方面考虑不到，就不能算是霸王之兵。霸王之兵，攻击大国，就会使敌方召集不到民众；威加于敌国，就能使敌国不能缔结外交。所以不必去争取于天下诸侯交结，也不必去培植自己在天下的势力，只要伸展自己的力量，施加威严于敌国，就可以拔取敌人城池，毁灭敌国国都。

In a war situation, bestow rewards that do not adhere to conventions and norms. Implement orders that do not conform to customary law and regulations. Direct the various forces of the army as if instructing one person. Order the officers and men to carry out tasks, but do not tell them the reason or intention. Order them to go after advantages and gains but do not divulge the dangers involved. Throw the officers and men on dangerous ground and they will attempt to survive. Place the troops on death ground and they will strive to remain alive. When the troops are thrown into situations of grave danger, they are capable of turning defeat into victory.

施行没有常规的奖赏,执行不用规定的指令,使用三军的官兵,如同使用一个人一样。令其执行任务,不要用言语申说;令其执行取利的命令,不要告之于不利条件。头士卒于死亡之地,然后他们才能转死为生,使士卒陷于危境,然后才能夺取胜利。

Thus the art of warfare is to pretend to accommodate the motives and desire of the enemy. Concentrate your forces on a single position of the enemy. Thus, even coming from a thousand *li*, you can still kill the generals of the enemy. This is what is meant by the art of accomplishing tasks in a skillful and capable manner.

所以,用兵作战,在于谨慎地审查敌人的意图,根据敌人意图,集中兵力指向敌军的一点,千里攻敌,斩杀敌将,这就叫做用巧妙的办法克敌制胜。

Thus, when the date for war is decided upon, close all border exits, cancel all travel permits and disallow the movement of emissaries from other states. Finalize and oversee closely all final preparations, plans and strategies for war in the temple of the ancestors.

所以,决定作战之日,要闭锁关口,销毁符节,禁止敌国使节往来,在庙堂上再三激励士卒,以责成具体任务。

When the enemy provides an opening, move in swiftly to exploit it. Capture first what the enemy treasures most, and do not let the enemy know the date of the attack. Military strategy must be adapted to the circumstances of the enemy so that actions and decisions can be determined accordingly. Thus, at the beginning of a battle, be as coy as a virgin girl so as to lure the enemy into providing an opening. As the battle progresses, be as swift as an escaping hare so as to catch the enemy unaware.

敌人打开门户,就要迅速进入。首先夺取敌人要害,暗地里透露会战期限。紧密跟随敌人,寻找进攻的机会。所以,战争开始时好像处女那样沉静,使敌人打开门户不加防范,然后就像撒开的兔子一样迅速敏捷,是敌人措手不及,无法抵挡。

Chapter 12
Attacking with Fire

There are five ways to use fire to attack the enemy. The first way is to burn the enemy soldiers in their camp. The second way is to burn enemy stockpiles and provisions. The third way is to burn the heavy military equipment and supplies of the enemy. Fourth is to burn the armory and warehouses of the enemy. The fifth way is to torch the transportation trains of the enemy.

火攻的形式有五种：一是烧敌人军队，二是烧敌人储备，三是烧敌人辎重，四是烧敌军军械仓库，五是烧敌军补充军队。

To launch attacks by fire, one must possess the necessary conditions. The materials and equipment needed to start and use a fire must be available at all times. There are opportunistic times for launching attacks by fire. There are also suitable days to start a fire. Opportunistic time refers to periods of dry and hot weather. Suitability of days refers to the location of the moon in relation to the four positions of the stars among the constellations. These four positions of the moon and stars among the constellation signal the days on which strong winds will arrive.

实行火攻要具备一定的条件，这些条件都要在平时就有所准备。点火要选择一定的天时和日子。天时，要选择气候干燥的天气。日子，要选择月亮行经箕、壁、翼、轸四个星宿的时候。月亮行经这四个星宿的时候，就是起风之日。

In assaults by fire, one must use the five ways of attacking interchangeably, depending on circumstances. When the fire breaks out within the camp of the enemy, prepare quickly to attack the enemy from outside. When fire breaks within the camp of the enemy and there is no confusion nor commotion among soldiers, wait patiently and do not be eager to attack. When the fire is burning ferociously with opportunities to be gained, follow through quickly with your attacks. When there are no opportunities to be gained and followed through, cease immediately. Fire can be started from outside the camp of the enemy. There is no need to wait for the fire to start within the camp of the enemy. Fires can always be started at suitable times and occasions.

凡是用火攻，必须根据五中火攻所引起的不同变化，在以兵力灵活地配合。火从里面烧起，就要预先派兵在外策应。火烧起来而敌军并无动静，要保持冷静和等待，不可贸然进攻，让火一直烧下去，然后可借火势发起进攻，不能借则停止。火可以在外面烧，不需内应起火，按天时发起。

When fire is burning in the windward direction, do not assault the leeward position. If the wind blows strongly, and continuously, during the day, it then tends to cease blowing during the night.

从上风点火时，不可在下风进攻。白天风刮得时间长了，夜晚就会停止。

The adept in warfare knows the five interchangeable methods of attacking with fire and would plan and prepare for their usage with vigilance. Thus, those who use fire as a means to support attacks are wise and shrewd. Those who use water as a means to support attacks are powerful. Water can be used to cut off and isolate an enemy, but it cannot be used to destroy and deprive him of his equipment, provisions and supplies.

军队必须懂得灵活运用物种火攻的变化，掌握好时机和分寸。所以用火来帮助军队进攻有明显的好处，在以水来帮助进攻会更强。但水攻只可以把军队隔绝，并不可以夺取。

Now in warfare, those who are able to win battles and secure land and cities but are unable to exploit the gains swiftly and expediently will jeopardize their interest. This is tantamount to a waste of time and resources. Thus, it is said that it is the enlightened leader who deliberates on the plan, while the capable general implements it. Move only when there are advantages to be gained. Strike only when there are definite chances of success. Fight only when there are definite dangers.

凡是打了胜战、夺取城邑，但不能巩固其成果，是很危险的，叫做耗费资财的"费留"。所以说，贤明的国君要慎重的考虑它，优秀的将领也会认真的处理它。没有利益就不行动，不能取胜就不使用，不到万不得已的危险之时就不决战。

A warlord must not embark on a military campaign simply out of anger. A general must not go into battle out of rage. Move when there are advantages to be gained. Cease when there are no advantages to be gained.

国君不可以因一时愤怒而发动战争，将领不可以因一时气愤而请求出战。符合国家利益就行动，不符合国家利益就停止。

Anger can return to happiness. Anger can return to joy. But a destroyed nation cannot be reinstated. A dead person cannot be resurrected.

愤怒可以从新变为喜悦，气愤也可以转变为高兴。但国家灭亡了却不能再复存，人死不可以再复生。

Thus, an enlightened ruler must always be prudent in matters of war, and a general must always be cautious and attentive. This is the way to ensure security for a nation and to preserve the strength and entirety of the army.

所以贤明的国君对战争极其慎重,优秀的将领对之也十分警惕,这是保证国家和军队安全的关键所在。

Chapter 13
Intelligence and Espionage

Raising an army of 100,000 for a distant military campaign will impose severe strains on the incomes of the people. This, together with the drain on the state treasury, will amount to a daily expenditure of 1,000 pieces of gold. There will be great commotion and disruption of peace at home and abroad, and people will be exhausted from transporting military supplies along supply routes. The disruption to work, jobs and various professions will affect 700,000 households.

凡兴兵十万，出征千里，百姓的耗费，国家的开支，每天要花费千金；全国上下动荡不安，运输军需物资的队伍疲惫于道路上，不能从事耕作的有七十万家。

Two opposing armies may be at war with each other for many years, seeking the ultimate day of victory. However, if one is reluctant to part with honors and ranks, money and gold for espionage purposes and remains ignorant of the situation of the enemy, he is extremely inhumane. Indeed such a person can never be a general of men, can never be a good assistant to the ruler and can never be a master of victories. Thus, the enlightened ruler and the capable general are able to secure victories for their military campaigns and achieve successes that surpass those of many others. The reason is because of foreknowledge.

战争双方相持数年，是为了取胜于一旦，如果吝啬爵禄和金钱不重用间谍，以致不能了解敌情而导致失败，那就是不仁到极点。这样的将帅，不是军队的好将帅，不是国君的好帮手；这样的国君不是能打胜战的好国君。英明的国君、良好的将帅，之所以一出兵就能战胜敌人，成功地超出众人，就在于事先了解敌情。

This foreknowledge cannot be obtained from the spirits or from the gods. It cannot be obtained by comparing with similar present or past events and situations. Neither can it be obtained from the study of astrology. This foreknowledge must be obtained from men who have knowledge of the situation of the enemy.

要事先了解敌情，并非祈求鬼神取得，并非用相似的事做推测，也并非观察日月星辰运行来验证，而是取于了解敌情的人。

There are five kinds of secret agents which can be used. They are local agents, inside agents, double agents, doomed agents and live agents. When these five types of agents are deployed simultaneously, their complex modes of operations will be beyond comprehension of the enemy. They are like mythical and divine schemes that can be deemed the most precious treasures and weapons of the ruler.

使用间谍有五种：有因间，有内间，有反间，有死间，有生间。物种间谍都用起来，能使敌人不知道我方用间的规律，这是它神妙之处，国君胜敌的法宝。

Local agents are ordinary people recruited from the homeland of the enemy and used as spies. Inside agents are officials of the enemy who are recruited and employed. Double agents are spies of the enemy who have been recruited to work. Doomed agents refer to our own spies who are unable to keep secrets and are then deliberately fed false information to leak to the spies of the enemy. Living agents are our spies who have returned safely from the territory of the enemy with information.

利用敌国乡里的普通人作间谍，称作为因间；收买敌国官吏做间谍，称作为内间；收买或利用敌方所派来的间谍，称作为反间；故意散布假情报，使我方间谍知道，然后传给敌方敌人上当后将间谍处死，称作为死间；派往敌方侦查后能活着回来报告敌情的人，称作为生间。

Thus, among all military relationships, none can be more intimate that those maintained with spies and secret agents. There can be no bigger rewards than those showered on spies and secret agents. There can be no greater secretive operations than those pertaining to espionage.

所以在军队人事中，没有比间谍更亲信，奖赏没有比间谍更优厚，事情没有比使用间谍更机密。

Only those who are wise will be able to use secret agents; only those who are benevolent, loyal and just are able to deploy and to use secret agents. Only those who are thorough and detailed will be able to decipher the truth embedded in espionage reports. Such is the intricacy and subtlety of espionage. Indeed, there is no location in which espionage cannot be used.

不是才智过人的人不能使用间谍，不是仁慈慷慨的人不能用间，不是用心微妙的人不能取得间谍真实的情报。微妙！真是无所不可使用间谍。

When espionage activities and secret operations have been leaked before their implementation, then the agents concerned and those whom they are in contact with must be put to death.

用间的计谋尚未实施，就被泄漏出去，间谍和知道机密的人都要处死。

There may be an army you wish to strike, cities you wish to conquer and key people you wish to assassinate. For such cases, there is a need to know beforehand detailed information on the identities of the garrison commander, his supporting officers, the visiting consultants, the guards and patrols, and various attendants. Your agents must be ordered to investigate these matters in great detail.

凡是要攻击的敌军，要攻取的城邑，要刺杀的敌方官员，必须先了解那些守城将官、左右亲信、掌管传达通报的官员、守门官吏和宫中近侍官员等姓名，指令我方间谍一定要侦查清楚。

The secret agents of the enemy who are spying among us must be actively sought out. Use incentives to bribe them, guide and counsel them and them pardon and release them. Thus, they can become double agents and be used and employed by us.

必须搜查出前来我方侦查的敌军间谍，依据情况用重金收买，优利款待，然后放他回去，这样反间就可以为我所用。

It is through information gained from double agents that the situations of the enemy can be known, and loyal and inside agents can be recruited and deployed. It is through the intelligence gained from the double agents that we are able to use doomed agents to carry false information to the enemy. It is through the efforts of the double agents that our living agents are able to return on time with important reports of the enemy. The ruler must know fully how to use and operate the five different kinds of agents and espionage activities. However, to know the situation and condition of the enemy, the ruler must depend on double agents. Thus double agents must be treated the most generously.

通过反间了解敌情，这样乡间、内间就可以为我所用了；通过反间了解敌情，这样就能使死间把虚假情报传给敌人；通过反间了解敌情，这样就可以使生间按预定时间，回来报告敌情。五种间谍的使用，国君都必须掌握，而要了解敌情的主要关键在于使用反间，所以反间不可不给予优厚的待遇。

In ancient times, the rise of the Shang Dynasty over the Xia Dynasty was because its military advisor Yi Yin, had served as an official in the kingdom of Xia. Similarly, the rise of the Zhou Dynasty over the Yin Dynasty was because its military advisor, Lu Ya, had served as an official in the kingdom of Yin. Thus, it is the enlightened ruler and the capable general who are able to use the most intelligent ones from within their ranks to be deployed as spies and secret agents so as to achieve the greatest and complete victories in war. Secret operations and espionage activities form an integral part of any military campaign; as the planning of strategies and the movement of troops depend heavily upon them.

从前商朝的兴起，是因为重用了曾经在夏为臣的伊尹；周朝的兴起，是因为重用了在殷为官的姜子牙。所以，明智的国君、贤能的将帅，能用高超智慧的人做间谍，一定能成就大业。这是用兵作战重要的一着，整个军队都要依靠他提供情报来采取行动。

Methods of War

Sima Rangju

司马法

The Methods of War (司马法) *is a military text attributed to Sima Rangju which discusses concepts of military theory, as well as administration and propriety: laws, regulations, discipline, tactics, and strategy. It is alternatively known as Sima Fa, Sima Art of War, Methods of Sima, or Principles of Sima. The title "Da Sima" is translated in this edition as "Minister of War". It is believed to have been developed in the state of Qi during the mid-Warring States period (c. 430 BCE).*

Chapter 1 - Benevolence as Foundation
Ideal Political Governance

In antiquity, taking benevolence as the foundation and employing righteousness constituted the Way of governance. However, when governance failed to attain the desired moral and political objectives, we have to resort to authority. Authority comes from waging warfare, not from the harmony among men. For this reason, if one must kill men to give peace to the people, then killing is permissible. If one must attack a state out of love for their people, then attacking it is permissible. If one must stop war with war, although it is war, it is permissible. Thus, if a ruler shows benevolence, he will be loved; if a ruler shows righteousness, he shall willingly be submitted to; if a ruler shows wisdom, he will be relied upon; if a ruler shows courage, he will be embraced; if a ruler shows integrity, he will be trusted. Thus within the state, the government gains the love of the people: the means by which the state can be preserved. Outside the state, it acquires a reputation of military greatness, the means by which it can wage war.

古人以仁爱为根本，以正义的方法处理国家大事，这就叫做政治。政治达不到目的时，就要使用权势。权势总是出于战争，而不是出于中和与仁爱。因而，杀掉坏人而
使大众得到安宁，杀人是可以的，进攻别的国家，出发于爱护它的民众，进攻是可以的，用战争制止战争，即使进行战争，也是可以的。因此，君主应该以仁爱为民众所亲近；以正义为民众所喜爱；以智谋为民众所倚重；以勇敢为民众所效法；以诚实为民众所信任。这样，对内就能得到民众的爱戴，借以守土卫国；对外就能具有威慑力量，借以战胜敌人。

Love the People

The Way of warfare: neither contravening the seasonal occupations, nor working the people to exhaustion, is the means by which to love our people. Neither attacking a state in national mourning, nor taking advantage of natural disaster, is the means by which to love their people. Not mobilizing the army in either winter or summer is the means by which to love both your own people and the enemy's people. Thus even though a state may be vast, if it is belligerent, it will inevitably perish. Even though calm may prevail in the realm, those who forget warfare will certainly be endangered. Thus, although all under heaven is peaceful, all under heaven is happy, one must still use hunting trips as war exercises; one must still train the army during the spring and summer. This is to make sure that the preparation of war will not be forgotten.

作战的原则是：不违背农时，不在疾病流行时兴兵作战，为的是爱护自己的民众；不乘敌人国丧时去进攻它，也不趁敌国灾荒时去进攻它，为的是爱护敌国的民众；不在冬夏两季兴师，为的是爱护双方的民众。所以国家虽然强大，好战必定灭亡；天下虽然太平，忘掉战争准备，必定危险。即使天下已经平定，全国欢腾，每年春秋两季还是要用打猎来进行军事演习，各国诸侯也要在春天整顿军队，秋天训练军队，这都是为了不忘战争准备。

Teaching the Six Virtues

In antiquity, they did not pursue a fleeing enemy more than 100 paces or follow a retreating enemy more than three days; thereby showing what the forms of propriety are. They did not exhaust the incapable and had sympathy for the wounded and sick; thereby showing what is benevolence. They awaited the completion of the enemy's formation, and then made the attack; thereby showing what is integrity. They contended for righteousness and not for profit, thereby showing what is righteous. Moreover, they were able to pardon those who submitted; thereby showing what courage is. They knew the end and the beginning of war; thereby showing what is wisdom. These six virtues are taught to the population at proper times and serve as a code of conduct for the masses. This is the rule of managing the army.

古时候(西周以前)，追击已逃的敌人不超过一百步，追踪主动退却的敌人不超过三天，这是为了表示礼让。不残杀丧失战斗力的敌人并哀怜它的伤病人员，这是为了表示仁爱。等敌人布阵完毕再发起进攻，这是为了表示诚信。争大义而不争小利，这是为了表示战争的正义性。赦免降服的敌人，这是表明军队的勇敢。能够预见战争开始和结局，这是表示统帅的智慧，根据"礼、仁、信、义、勇、智"六德按时集合民众进行教育，作为管理民众的准则，这是从古以来治军作战的方法。

Administrative Measures

The administrative measures of the Former Kings: they accord with the Way of Heaven; they establish at places which are beneficial. They place the virtuous in the office, create official posts and distribute work. They established feudal states and apportioned salaries according to rank. The feudal lords were pleased and embraced them. Foreign states also came to submit. Punishment and war was thus eliminated. That is how the Sage rules.

从前的君王治理天下，顺应自然规律，适合地理条件，任用贤德的人，设官分职，各司其事，分封诸侯，区分等级，按照爵位高低给以不同的俸禄。这样，使诸侯都心悦诚服，外国也向往归附，诉讼和战争也都没有了，这就是圣王用仁德治理的天下。

Punishing Offenders

Next came the Worthy Kings: they ordered the rites, music, and laws and measures, and then created the five punishments, raising armored troops to chastise the unrighteous. They made inspection tours of the feudal lands, investigated the customs of the four quarters, assembled the feudal lords, and investigated differences. If any of the feudal lords had disobeyed orders, turned his back on Virtue, or contravened the seasons of Heaven - endangering meritorious rulers - they would publicize it among the feudal lords, making it evident that he had committed an offense. They then announced it to the whole nation. Then they offered sacrifice to the Former Kings. Only thereafter would the Prime Minister charge the army before the feudal lords, saying, "A certain state has acted contrary to Tao. You will participate in the rectification campaign on such a year month and day. On that date, the army will reach the offending state and assemble with the Son of Heaven to apply the punishment of rectification."

The Prime Minister and other high officials would issue the following orders to the army:

When you enter the offender's territory, do not do violence to his gods; do not hunt his wild animals; do not destroy earthworks; do not set fire to buildings; do not cut down forests; do not take the domesticated animals, grains or implements. When you see their elderly or very young, return them without harming them. Even if you encounter adults, unless they engage you in combat, do not treat them as enemies. If an enemy has been wounded, provide medical attention and return him.

When they had executed the guilty, the king, together with the feudal lords, corrected and rectified the government and customs of the state. They raised up the Worthy, established an enlightened ruler and corrected and restored their feudal position and obligations.

其次，贤王制定礼乐法度，设置五刑[来治理国家]，
使用军队讨伐不义。亲自巡视各诸侯的领地，访察地方，会见诸侯，考核他们是否遵守"礼乐法度"。对那些玩忽命令、触犯法纪、败坏道德、逆天行事和迫害功臣
的国君，便通令各国诸侯，公布他的罪行，并上告于天地神灵和祖先。然后由冢宰向诸侯征调军队，发布命令说："某国无道，应出兵征伐他。各诸侯的军队应于某年某月某日到达某国，会同天子惩治罪犯。"冢宰又使百官向军队宣布命令说："进入该国的地区，不准亵渎神位，不准打猎，不准破坏水利工程，不准烧毁房屋建
筑，不准砍伐树木，不准擅取家畜、粮食和用具。见到老人和儿童，要护送他们回家，不准伤害。即使遇到少壮的人，只要他们不抵抗就不以敌人对待。对于受伤的
敌人，给予治疗，而后放他们回去。"惩办了首恶后，天子和诸侯们还要帮助整顿好那个国家，选用贤能，另立明君，调整、恢复其各级官职。

Governing Feudal Lords

The ways by which the kings and the hegemons governed the feudal lords were six:

1. With territory, they gave 'shape' to the feudal lords.
2. With government directives, they restrict the feudal lords.
3. With forms of propriety, they drew the feudal lords closer to them.
4. With gifts, they please the feudal lords.
5. With strategists, they regulate the feudal lords.
6. With weapons and armor, they gain the submission of the feudal lords.

By sharing weals and woes with them, they will unite the feudal lords, bringing harmony between smaller and larger states.

王霸治理诸侯的办法有六种：用调整封地的大小来控制诸侯，用政策法令约束诸侯；用礼仪威信亲近诸侯，用馈赠财物悦服诸侯，用有智谋的人去扶持诸侯，用强大的军队慑服诸侯。还要以共同的利害来使诸侯联合起来，大国亲近小国，小国尊敬大国，和睦相处。

Nine Prohibitions

The kings and hegemon will assemble the feudal lords in order to announce nine prohibitions:

1. Those who take advantage of the weak states or encroach upon them will have their borders reduced.
2. Those who murder the Worthy or harm the people will be deposed.
3. Those who are brutal within their state and bully those weaker states will be purged.
4. Those who cause the fields to be unused and the people to scatter will be reduced.
5. Those who rely on the terrain advantage, and refuse to submit, will be invaded.
6. Those who harm or kill kin will be punished.
7. Those who depose or slay their ruler will be exterminated.
8. Those who oppose orders and resist the government will be quashed.
9. Those who are rebellious and lustful, both within and without their border, acting like animals, will be extinguished.

会合诸侯颁发九项禁令。凡是恃强欺弱以大欺小的，就削弱他。虐杀贤良残害民众的，就讨伐他。对内暴虐对外欺凌的，就废除他。使田野荒芜民众逃散的，就削减封地。仗恃险固而不服从的，就兵临其境警告他。残杀骨肉至亲的，就按法律惩办他。驱逐或杀害君的，就诛灭他的同党，毁灭他的家园。违犯禁令不守法度的，就孤立制裁他。内外淫乱，行同禽兽的，就灭掉他的国家。

Chapter 2 - Duty of the Son of Heaven
Duty of the Son of Heaven

The duty of the Son of Heaven (the ruler) is to concentrate on modeling after Heaven and Earth, and observing the measures of the Former Sages. The duty of officers and common men must be to respectfully serve their parents and to be upright with their superiors and rulers. Even though there may be an enlightened ruler, if the officers are not first instructed properly, they cannot be used.

天子正确的思想行为，应当是取法天地，借鉴古代圣王。士氏的正确思想行为，应当是遵从父母教训，不偏离君主和长辈的教导。所以虽有贤明的君主，如果对士民不事先教育，也是不能使用他们的。

Education of the Population

When the ancients instructed the people, they would establish the relationships and fixed distinctions of noble and common - causing them not to encroach upon each other; the virtuous and righteous not to exceed each other; the talented and technically skilled can be used; and the courageous and strong will not clash with authority. Thus their strength will be united and their thoughts in harmony.

In antiquity, the rules governing the state cannot be used in the military; and those appropriate in the military may not be appropriate in governing the state. Thus righteousness and virtue do not infringe upon each other.

Superiors should value officers who are not boastful, for such officers are great talents. If he is not boastful, it shows that he is not contentious. When the ruler seeks the opinions of these officers for civilian affairs, he would get an accurate picture; for military affairs, they will be attended to properly. Thus, those who are talented and technically skilled will be used properly. For those who follow orders, they should be rewarded well; for those who defy orders, they should be severely punished. Then the strong and courageous will not clash with authority.

Only after effective instructions have been given to the people, can the state carefully select and employ them. Only after government affairs have been thoroughly ordered, can we say the offices have been sufficiently provided. When instructions are thoroughly examined and broken down so easily understood, the people can practice the teachings well. When practice becomes habit, the people will embody the customs. This is the pinnacle of transformation through instruction.

古代教育民众，必须制定上、下、尊、卑的人伦道德规范，使上下尊卑之间彼此不相欺凌，德和义不互相踰越，有才技的人不被埋没，有勇力的人不敢违抗命令，这样，大家就会同心协力了。古时候，朝廷的礼仪法度，不能用于军队，军队的礼仪法度，不能用于朝廷。所以德和义就不会互相踰越。君主必须敬重不自夸的人，因为不自夸的人，是君主所宝贵的人才，如能不自夸，就说明他没有奢望，没有奢望就不会和别人相争。朝廷听取这些人的意见，一定会掌握真实情况，军队里能听取这些人的意见，事情就会得到妥善处理，这样，有才技的人就不致被埋没了。对服从命令的人，上级要给予奖励，对违抗命令的人，上级要给予制裁，这样，有勇力的人就不敢违抗命令了。民众经受了这些教育，然后再慎重选拔任用他们。各项事业都治理得很好，各级官吏就尽到职责了。教育内容简明扼要，民众就容易学得好，习惯一经养成，民众就会按习俗行事了。这就是教育的最大成效。

Pursuing the Enemy

In antiquity, they did not pursue a fleeing enemy too far, nor follow a retreating army too closely. By not pursuing too far, they will not be ambushed; by not pursuing too closely, they will not be ambushed. They used the forms of propriety as the foundation of the army and benevolence as the foundation of their victory. After they are victorious, their teachings could then again be employed. Thus the gentleman would value these teachings.

古人用兵，追击败逃的敌人不过远，追踪主动退却的敌人不迫近。不过远就不易被敌人诱骗，不迫近就不易陷入敌人的图套。以礼制为规范，军队就能巩固，用仁爱为宗旨，就能战胜敌人。用这种方法，取胜以后，还可以反复运用，因而贤德的人都很重视这种方法。

Uniting the Masses

Shun made the official announcement of their mission within the state, because he wanted everyone to embrace his orders. The rulers of Xia Dynasty administer their oaths in the army, for they want their people to be mentally prepared. The rulers of Shang Dynasty swore their oaths outside the gates to encampments, for they wanted the people to understand their intentions first, before going into battle. King Wu of Zhou Dynasty made the oath just before the two armies clashed, in order to stimulate the people's will to fight.

虞舜在国内告诫民众，是为了使人们理解他的命令。夏启在军中誓师，是为了使军队事先有思想准备。商汤在军门之外誓师，是为了使军队事先了解他的意图以便行动。周武王在两军将要交锋的时候誓师，是为了激励士卒的战斗意志。

Governance and Weapons

The rulers of Xia acted in accordance with their Virtue and never employed weapons, so their weapons are not varied. The ruler of Shang relied on righteousness, so they first used weapons. The ruler of Zhou relied on force, so they invented and fully utilized all kinds of weapons.

夏禹用德取天下，没有使用武力，所以当时兵器种类比较简单。商汤用义取天下，开始使用武力和兵器。周武王用武力取天下，使用了各种各样的兵器

Promoting Virtue

In Xia Dynasty, the rulers bestowed rewards in court in order to make the good people more eminent. In Shang Dynasty, they carried out executions in the marketplace to warn the evil. In Zhou Dynasty, the rulers granted rewards in court and carried out executions in the marketplace to promote virtues and terrify the debauched. Thus, although the method is slightly different, the rulers of all three dynasties aim to manifest Virtue.

夏代在朝廷上奖励有功的人，是为了鼓励好人。商代在集市上杀戮有罪的人，是为了警告坏人。周代在朝廷上奖励有功的人，在集市上杀戮有罪的人，是为了勉励"君子"，震骇"小人"。三王的办法虽有不同，但是鼓励人们为善的精神是一致的。

Weapons

When the types of weapons are not used together, it will not be advantageous. Long weapons are for protection. Short weapons are for defending. If the weapons are too long, it will be difficult to wield against others; if they are too short, they cannot reach the enemy. If they are too light, they will be adroitly used and can easily lead to chaos. If they are too heavy, they will not be sharp and will never attain objectives.

各种兵器不配合使用，就不能发挥威力。长兵器用以掩护短兵器，短兵器用以抵近战斗。兵器太长就不便使用，太短就打击不到敌人。太轻就脆弱，脆弱就容易折毁。太重就不锋利，不锋利就不中用。

Chariots, Flags, Insignia

War Chariots: Those from Xia Dynasty are called 'Hook Chariots', and their advantage is in being smooth-riding. Those from Shang Dynasty are called 'Yin Chariots' and their advantage is speed. Those from the Zhou Dynasty are called 'Yuan Rong' and their advantage is structural strength.

Flags: The Xia Dynasty used a black one, representing the leader of men. The Shang's was white representing the righteousness of Heaven. The Zhou's was yellow, representing the Way of Earth.

Insignia: The Xia used the sun and the moon, to signify brightness. The Shang used the tiger to signify military greatness. The Zhou used the dragon, esteeming culture.

兵车：夏代叫钩车，注重行驶平稳；殷代叫寅车，注重行动迟速；周代叫元戎，注重结构精良。旗帜：夏代用黑色，取其象手持人头那样威武；殷代用白色，取其象天体那样皎洁；周代用黄色，取其象大地那样深厚。徽章：夏代用日月，表示光明；殷代用虎，表示威武；周代用龙，表示文采。

Military Superiority

If managing the troops with too much grandeur and authority, the morale of the troops will be affected. But if managing the troops without much grandeur and authority, it will be difficult to maneuver the troops to victory. When the superiors are not able to use the people well, and suitable people are not assigned to official positions, then the artisans are not able to profit from their work, oxen and horses are not able to fulfill their functions, while the officers insult the people. Such a situation is termed as "excessive grandeur" and the people will cower. When superiors do not respect Virtue, but employ the deceptive and evil; when they do not honor those who follow the Way but employ those who are tyrannical; when they do not value those who obey commands but instead esteem those who contravene them; when they do not value good actions but esteem violent behavior, then such situations are termed as "diminished grandeur". If the conditions of diminished grandeur prevail, the people will not be victorious.

治军过于威严，士气就会受到压抑，缺少威信，就难以指挥士卒克敌制胜。上级使用民力不适宜，任用官吏不恰当，有技能的人不能发挥其作用，牛马也不能合理地使用，主管者又盛气凌人地去强迫人们服从，这就是过于威严。过于威严，士气就感到受压抑。君主不尊重有德行的人而信任奸诈邪恶的人，不尊重有道义的人而任用恃勇逞强的人，不重用服从命令的人，而重用专横武断的人，不重用善良的人，而重用残暴的人，以致引起民众反抗官吏，这就会降低威信。缺少威信，就不能指挥士卒去战胜敌人。

Order in Formation

A campaign army takes measures as its prime concern so that the people's strength will be adequate. Then even when the blades clash, the infantry will not run and the chariots will not gallop. When pursuing a fleeing army, the troops will not break formation, thereby avoiding chaos. The solidarity of a campaign army derives from military discipline that maintains order in formation, does not exhaust the strength of men or horses and - whether moving slowly or rapidly - does not exceed the measures of the commands.

军队行动，以从容不迫为主，从容不迫就能保持士卒力量的充沛。虽各冲锋陷阵中，步兵也不要快步走，兵车也不要奔驰，追击敌人也不准超越行列，这样才不至扰乱战斗队形。军队的稳固性，就在于不打乱行列的秩序，不用尽人、马的力量，行动的快慢决不许超出命令的规定。

Military & Civilian Realms

In antiquity, the form and spirit governing civilian affairs would not be found in the military realm; those appropriate to the military realm would not be found in the civilian sphere. If the form and spirit appropriate to the military realm enter the civilian sphere, the Virtue of the people will decline. When the form and spirit appropriate to the civilian sphere enter the military realm, then the military spirit of the troops will weaken.

In the civilian sphere words are cultivated and speech is languid. In court, one is respectful and courteous and cultivates himself to serve others. Not summoned, he does not step fourth; unquestioned, he does not speak. When you want to speak, the forms of propriety are plenty; when you have finished speaking, the forms of propriety are few.

In the military realm, one speaks directly and stands firm. When deployed in formation, one focuses on duty and acts decisively. Those wearing battle armor do not bow; those in war chariots need not observe the forms of propriety; those manning fortifications, do not scurry. In times of danger, one does not pay attention to seniority. Thus civilian forms of behavior and military standards are like inside and outside, like left and right.

古时候，朝廷的礼仪法度不用在军队中，军队的礼仪法度，不用在朝廷内。如果把军队的礼仪法度用在朝廷内，民众的礼仪风气就会被废弛，把朝廷的礼仪法度用在军
队中，军队的尚武精神就会被削弱。因为在朝廷上说话要温文尔雅，在朝见君主时态度要恭敬谦逊，严以律己，宽以待人，国君不召不来，不问不说，朝见时礼节隆重，辞退时礼节简单。在军队中要昂首直立，在战阵中要行动果断，穿着铠甲不跪拜，在兵车上不行礼，在城上不急走〔以免惊扰士众〕，遇危险不惧怕[以免惑乱军心]。所以礼和法是相互为用的，文和武是不可偏废的。

Rewards and Punishment

In antiquity, the Worthy Kings made manifest the Virtue of the people and fully sought out the goodness of people. Thus they did not neglect the virtuous nor demean the people in any respect. Rewards were not granted, punishments were never even tried.

Shun neither granted rewards not imposed punishments, but the people could still be employed. This was the height of Virtue.

The Xia granted rewards but did not impose punishment. This was the height of instruction.

The Shang imposed punishment but did not grant rewards. This was the height of military ferocity.

The Zhou used both rewards and punishment, and Virtue declined.

Rewards should not be delayed beyond the appropriate time for you to want the people to quickly profit from doing good. When you punish someone, punish him immediately, for you want the people to quickly see the harm of doing what is not good.

Do not reward great victories, for then neither the upper nor lower ranks will boast of their achievement. If the upper ranks cannot boast, they will not seem arrogant, while if the lower ranks cannot boast, no distinctions can be established among the men. When neither of them boasts this is the pinnacle of deference.

In cases of great defeat, do not punish anyone, for then the upper and lower ranks will assume the disgrace falls on them. If the upper ranks reproach themselves, they will certainly regret their errors, while if the lower ranks feel the same, they will certainly try to avoid repeating the offense. When all ranks divide the responsibility for the detestable among themselves, this is the pinnacle of yielding.

古代贤明的君王，表彰民众的美德，鼓励民众的善行，所以没有败坏道德的事，也没有不遵守法度的人，因而无须用赏也无须用罚。 虞舜不用赏也不用罚，民众都能听他使用，这是由于有了高尚的道：德。夏代只用赏而不用罚，这是由于有了良好的教育。商代只用罚，而不用赏，这是由于有了强大
的威势。周代赏罚并用，这是由于道德已经衰败了。奖赏不要过时，为的是使民众迅速得到做好事的利益。惩罚要就地执行，为的是使民众迅速看到做坏事的恶果。
大胜之后不颁发奖赏，上下就不会夸功，上级如果不夸功，就不会骄傲了；下级如果不夸功，就不会向上比了。上下都能这样不夸功，这是最好的谦让风气。大败之
后不执行惩罚，上下都会认为错误是在自己。上级如果认为错误在自己，必定决心改正错误，下级如果认为错误在自己，必定决心不再犯错误。上下都象这样争着分 担错误的责任，也是最好的谦让风气。

Harmony and Peace

In antiquity, those on border duty were not required to serve labor duty for three years thereafter. This is because the ruler sees the people's labor. Upper and lower ranks look out for each other in this fashion, which was the pinnacle of harmony.

When they had attained their aim of pacifying the realm, they sang triumphal songs to show their happiness. They stored away the implements of war, erected the Spirit Terrace, and celebrate the end of labors of the people, and to show that time for rest had come.

古时对于守边防的军人，[服役一年后，]三年内不再征调他们，这是看到他们太辛苦了。上下这样地互相体恤，就是最团结的表现。打了胜仗就高奏凯歌，表达喜庆的心情。结束战争后，高筑"灵台"集会，慰劳民众，表示从此开始休养生息。

Chapter 3 - Determining Ranks
Before the Start of War

In general, to wage war: First determine the rank and position; prominently announce what are accomplishments and offenses; retain travelers with talents; publicize instructions and edicts; make inquiries among the populace; seek out artisans; apply methodology to planning; fully exploit things, change the people's hatreds; dispel doubts; nourish strength; search out and employ the skillful; take action in accordance with people's hearts.

凡是作战,先要确定军中各级官职爵位,宣布赏罚制度,收用各方游士,颁发军队教令,征询大众的意见,搜罗有技术的人才,多方考虑,弄清各种情况的根源,分辨和推究疑难问题,积蓄力量,寻求巧计,根据民心所向而采取行动。

Before the Start of War II

In general, to wage war, the following needs to be done: solidify the morale; analyze the advantages and gains; impose order on chaos; regulate the advancing and halting; accept legitimate remonstrance; nourish a sense of shame; simplify the laws to follow and limit the usage of punishment, minor offenses should be constrained, otherwise major offenses will be committed.

作战必须:巩固军心,明辨利害,治理纷乱,进止有节,服膺正义,激发廉耻,简约法令,少用刑罚,小罪就要制止,犯小罪的如果得逞,犯大罪的也就跟着来了。

Five Considerations and Weapons

Be in accord with Heaven; make material resources abundant; bring joy to the people; take advantage of the terrain; value the use of weapons. These are the "Five Considerations". Accord with Heaven means to make use of the weather and seasonal changes, or the opportunities that arise. To accumulate material resources, rely on seizing them from the enemy; to bring joy to the people, wage wars that are in accord with what the people want. To take advantage of terrain, defend strategic points. To value the use of weapons means using bows and arrows for withstanding attacks, maces and spears for defense, and halberds and spear-tipped halberds for support.

Now each of these five weapons has its appropriate use: The long protect the short, the short rescue the long. When they are used in turn, the battle can be sustained. When they are employed all at once, the army will be strong. When you see the enemy using new weapons, you should try to replicate them so that you can be a match for him.

顺应天时，广集资财，悦服人心，利用地形，重视运用兵器，这是作战必须考虑的五件事情。顺应天时，就是要利用天候季节，因时制宜地行事。广集资财，就是要利用敌人物资以增强我之实力。悦服人心，就是要顺应大众意志以勉励士卒杀敌。利用地形，就是要控制隘路、险要、阻绝等地形。重视运用兵器，就是战斗中要用弓矢掩护、殳矛抵御、戈戟辅助。

这五种兵器有五种用途，长兵器用以掩护短兵器，短兵器用以补救长兵器的不足。"五种兵器"轮番出战可以持久，全部出战就能形成强大力量。发现敌人的新兵器，就应该仿效制造，才能与敌保持力量平衡。

Unity and Strength

The commanding general should be good at motivating his troops, solidifying their morale. He also needs to monitor the changes in the enemy's camp and take necessary precautions. The minds of the troops and the general must be together as one. Horses and oxen are well-fed; chariots and weapons are maintained well, these are strengths for the army. Training should be done during peaceful times, and only then during war, would there be order in the army. The whole army is like a human, where the commanding general is the body, the general are the arms and limbs, and the troops are like the toes and fingers.

主将既要善于勉励士卒，巩固军心，又要仔细观察敌情变化，采取相应的行动。将帅的意志和士卒的意志必须统一，马、牛兵喂饱，休息好，车辆、兵器要妥善保养，这样，才有战斗力量。训练重在平时，作战重在指挥。将帅好比人的躯干，卒好比人的四肢，伍好比人的手指，〔必须象它们一样地协调一致，才能指挥运用自如。

Wits and Courage

In general, warfare is a battle of wits and combat is a matter of courage. The deployment of formations is a matter of skill. Employ what your men want and effect what they are capable of; abolish what they do not want and are incapable of. Do the opposite to the enemy.

作战指挥要用智谋，战斗行动要靠勇敢，军队布阵要巧妙灵活。要力求实现自己的意图，但也要量力而行，不要去做违反自己意图和力所不及的事。对于敌人则相反，(要使他去做他所不愿做或不能做的事。)

Heaven, Resources and Excellence

In general, for warfare, one must have Heaven, material resources and excellence.

Seize the opportunity. When divining by the tortoise shell predicts victory, start preparing for war in a secretive manner. This is termed as "having Heaven".

When the masses are rich and plentiful and so is the state, this is termed as "having resources".

When the men are practiced in the relative advantages of the formations, and they give their best in preparation for battle, this is termed as "having excellence".

When the people are encouraged and give their best in fulfilling their responsibilities, they are termed as "happy people".

凡是作战，应该有天，有财，有善。遇着好时机不要错过，占卜有了胜利的征兆就机密行动，这就叫"有天"。民众富足，国力充沛，这就叫"有财"。士卒训练有素，阵法熟练，物资器材预有准备，这就叫"有善"。人人都能尽力去完成战斗任务，这就叫"乐人"。

Army Preparation

Increasing the strength of the army and making the formations solid; making the numbers adequate and constantly training the troops; relying on the many talents to manage all military affairs; perceiving the nature of things and responding to the sudden events. This is termed as 'preparation for the foreseeable'.

Fast chariots and fleet infantrymen, bows and arrows, and a strong defense are that which is meant by 'increasing the army'. Secrecy and silence and increasing one's strength are that what is meant by 'making the formations solid'. On this basis, being able to advance or withdraw is what is meant by 'multiplying strength'. At times of little activity, the upper ranks instruct and constantly drill the lower ranks. This is what is meant by 'training in formations'. When there are appropriate offices, it is termed as 'all matters are well managed'. When accordance with these things is perceived and managed, it is referred to as 'simplifying administration'.

军队强大而阵势巩固，兵员充实而战法熟练，选拔各种人才去管理各项事务，洞察各种情况以应付突然事变，这就是预有准备。兵车轻快，步兵精锐，弓箭足以固守，这就是强大的军队。行动隐秘肃静，增强自身的战斗力，这就是巩固的阵势。凭借这样的阵势而又进退合宜，这就是增强了战斗力。主将利用闲暇时间教导士卒熟练阵法，这就是频繁排阵。各项事物，都有人负责，这就叫事事有人管。人人胜任职务而能分清事物的轻重缓急，这就是用人得当。

Disastrous Campaign

Determine the size of your troops according to the terrain, and deploy your formation according to the enemy's situation. When to attack, wage battle, defend, advance, retreat and stop; how the front and rear are ordered, and the chariots and infantry moving in concord; these are matters that need to be considered during war. Disobedience, not trusting each other, not in harmony, are lax, doubtful, weary, cower, low fighting spirit, arrogant towards upper ranks, grievances cannot be addressed, tired, unrestrained, disunity, slow; all these are disasters to the war. When they suffer from extreme arrogance, abject terror, moaning and grumbling, constant fear and show frequent regrets over taking actions; they are what caused the demise of the army. Being able to be large or small, firm or weak; to change formations, and to use large numbers or small groups, with respect to the enemy's situation, all these are termed as the 'control of war'.

衡量我军兵力，适应地形条件和敌人情况而确定我军阵形；掌握攻、战、守的变化，前进、后退或停止的时机，注意前后的顺序以及战车与步兵的协同，这些都是临战应该考虑的事情。对上级不服从、不信任、彼此不和睦、怠忽职守、互相猜疑、厌恶作战、畏惧敌人、军心涣散、互相责难、委屈难伸、疲劳困顿、肆无忌惮、分崩离析、纪律废弛、这些都是作战的祸患。骄傲已极，畏惧太甚，士卒呻吟吵闹，军心忧虑惶恐，朝令夕改，这会导致军队的覆灭。声势宜大宜小，战法用刚用柔，编组用参用伍，兵力用多用少，都必须从利害两个方面加以考虑，这是作战的权变。

Waging War

In general, to wage war, employ spies against the distant; observe the near; seize opportunities; take advantage of the enemy's material resources where possible. The army should esteem good faith and abhor the doubtful. Arouse the soldiers with fervor of righteousness. Undertake affairs at the appropriate time. Employ people with kindness. When you see the enemy, remain quiet; when you see turbulence, do not be hasty to respond; when you see danger and hardship, do not abandon the masses.

一般作战，侦察敌情远处用间谍，近处用观察。用兵作战要抓住时机，适应财力。军队内部要崇尚诚信，切戒猜疑。兴兵要合乎正义，做事要抓住时机，用人要施恩惠，遇敌必须沉着，遇着混乱必须从容，遇着危险和艰难不要忘掉部队。

Waging War II

Within the state, be generous and foster good faith. Within the army, be magnanimous but strict. When facing the enemy, be decisive and nimble. Within the state, there should be harmony across all ranks. Within the army, rules must be clear and strictly adhered to. When facing the enemy, investigate the situation well. Within the state, display the right virtues. Within the army, display uprightness. In battle, display good faith.

治国要施恩惠讲信用，治军要宽厚要威严，临阵要果断要敏捷。治国要上下和睦，治军兵法令严明，临阵要明察情况。治国要显露美德，率军要表现方正，作战要显示诚实。

Military Formations

For military formations, when advancing, the most important thing is for the ranks to be dispersed; when engaged in a battle, the formation should be dense, and the weapons should be mixed. Troops should be well-trained, and remain calm at all times, only then can the formation be well-ordered. When orders are clear and accurate, and the upper and lower ranks observe righteousness, only then will the troops be motivated properly. When many well-conceived plans prove successful, the people will submit. If people submit at all times, then affairs will be finished in the correct order. When the banners are bright and contrasting, the troops can see them clearly. When plans have been finalized, final determination should also be made. For enemies who are indecisive as to whether to advance or retreat, or without plans at all, attack them. Do not change your battle plans or the banner signals.

一般布阵，军队的行列既要求疏散[以便使用兵器]；又要求密集[以便于战斗]。兵器要多种多样配合使用，士卒要训练有素，要沉着镇静，阵形才能保持严整。威令鲜明准确，上下遵守信义，就能人人奋勉。谋划屡次成功就能使人信服。人人心悦诚服，事情就能依次办好。旗帜鲜明，部队才看得清楚。作战计谋既经确定，决心就应坚定。对那些进退不定，遇敌无谋的人，应予以惩罚。[临阵的时候]，不要随意乱用金鼓，不要轻易改变旗号，[以免引起错觉和迷乱。]

Making the Enemy Submit

Whenever affairs are well executed, they will endure; when they accord with the ancient ways, they can be made to happen. When the oath is clear, morale will be high and you can extinguish the enemy. The way to eliminate the enemy is either to use righteousness or power. One can use righteousness to gain the good faith of the enemy, uniting the realm. This allows one to use the people of the enemy's state as well. One can also use power to make the enemy submit. Rouse his arrogance and attack his weaknesses. Use troops to attack from outside and use spies to attack from within.

凡是好的事情就能保持长久，按照古法办事就能顺利推行。战斗誓词鲜明有力，士气就会旺盛，就能消灭一切敌人。消灭敌人的方法：一是用道义。就是以诚信感召敌人，以威力慑服敌人，造成统一天下的形势，使人人心悦诚服，这就能争取敌国的人为我所用。二是用权谋。就是设法助长敌人的骄横，夺取敌人的要害，用兵力从外部向它进攻；用间谍从内部策应。

Seven Military Affairs & Four Controls

First is management of talents; second is strict adherence to rules; third is the issuance of clear orders and cause; fourth is management of skill sets; fifth is skill in using fire; sixth is skill in marine battles; seventh is skill in using weapons. They are referred to as the Seven Military Affairs. Glory, profit, shame and death are referred to as the Four Controls; these will make people observe the rules.

Being tolerant and being strict are merely just ways to prevent transgressions and change intentions.

一是广罗人才，二是严肃法纪，三是注重宣传，四是讲求技巧。五是善用火攻，六是习于水战，七是改善兵器，这是七种军国大政。荣誉、利禄、耻辱、刑罚，这是四种令人遵守法纪的手段。和颜悦色地讲道理或严厉地予以管教，都不过是为了使人改恶从善。所有这些都是治军的方法。

Benevolence and Talents

Only benevolence can attract people; however if one is benevolent but not trustworthy, then he will vanquish himself. Treat men as men, be upright with the upright, employ the appropriate language, and use fire only when it should be used.

只有仁爱，才能使人亲近。但是只讲仁爱而不许信义，反会使自已遭到失败。用人要知人善任，正人必先正己，言辞必须严正，火攻必须用得适宜。

Setting Out for War

The principle of war is this, after you have rallied the troops, governmental measures must be set up. Treat your troops with a benign countenance and lead them with sincere words. Use their fear to warn them, use their desire to control them. When in enemy territory, control the strategic location and place the right people in the right positions.

一般作战的原则：已经鼓舞了士气，接着就要颁布纪律。对待士卒要和颜悦色，教导士卒要言辞恳切。利用他们畏惧的心理而告诫他们，利用他们的欲望而使用他们，进入敌境就要控制有利地形，并按将士的职位分派他们任务，这就是战法。

Setting Regulations & Policies

Protocols and policies of tasks and systems that are to be executed should come from the masses. They should be tested and evaluated to the furthest extent. If they cannot be done, then the general should lead by example on how the tasks and system should be executed. If they can be done, then make sure the troops know them. By executing them several times, in time people will remember them and they become true protocols and policies. And soon these protocols and policies will be known as the law.

凡是要求人们执行的规章制度，都应来源予大众的要求。在试行中检验其是否名副其实[卓有成效]。并力求妥善地、彻众地予以执行。如果有可以做到而没有做到的，将帅就要亲自带头去做。如果一切都做到了，就进而要求部队牢记这些准则，经过多次反复执行，就形成了规章制度，这些符合人们要求的规章制度，就叫做 "法"。

Managing Chaos

The way to manage chaos, or imposing order, consists of benevolence, credibility, straightforwardness, unity, righteousness, change wrought by authority and centralized authority.

治乱的方法，一是仁爱，二是信用，三是直率，四是统一，五是道义，六是权变，七是集中指挥。

Establishing Laws

The principles of establishing the law system are acceptance by the people, the laws must be clear, the laws must be strictly adhered to, must be executed at the earliest possible moment. Establish rankings, use colors to distinguish the rankings and all officers are to dress according to protocols.

建立法制，一要使人能接受。二要法令严明，三要有法必依，四要雷厉风行，五要规定各级服制，六要用颜色区别等级，七要使官吏按规定着装，不得混乱。

Centralized Authority & Law

When the power of authority falls solely with oneself, it is termed as 'centralized'. When those below the ruler fear the law, then it is termed as 'law'. In the army, troops should not listen to commands from dubious sources. When in battle, should not desire for small advantages, its plans should achieve results successfully, and should be executed in a subtle fashion.

治军，执行法令完全由将帅作主的叫做"专"。上下都一致遵守的才能叫做"法"。[军队要听从统一的指挥号令]而不要听信非正式的传说。作战时不要贪图小利，计划要能即日成功，行动要求隐密莫测，这才是治军之道。

Upper & Lower Ranks

When upright methods do not prove to be effective, then centralized control of affairs must be undertaken. If people do not submit to Virtue, then laws will have to be imposed. If they do not trust each other, then orders have to come from one source. If they are dilatory, motivate them. If they have doubts, try to change them. If people do not trust the ruler, then whatever is promulgated must not be revised.

This has been the administrative rule from antiquity.

一般作战时，用正常的办法行不通就要用专断，不服从的就用军法制裁。如果互不相信就要使之统一认识，如果军心懈怠就应加以鼓舞，如果下级产生疑惧就设法改变这种情况，如果下级不信任上级命令，更要坚决执行而不轻易改变。这些都是从古以来治军作战的方法。

Chapter 4 - Formational Discipline
Troop Formation Requirements

In general, for the principles of warfare: positions should be strictly defined; administrative measures should be strictly adhered to; movement should be nimble; the soldiers' disposition should be calm; and the minds of the officers and people should be unified.

作战一般的原则，战斗队形中士卒的位置要严格规定，号令要森严，行动要敏捷，士气要沉着，意志要统一。

Sitting and Squatting Formations

In general, for the principles of warfare: rank and appoint men to office based on their morals and ability. Establish companies and squads. Order the rows and files. Set the correct spacing between the horizontal and vertical. Investigate whether what is ordered is carried out.

Soldiers in standing formations should crouch down and advance; those who are in squatting formation should advance using their knees. If they are frightened, make the formation dense; if they are in danger have them assume a sitting formation. If the enemy is seen at a distance, after observations, they will not fear them; if the enemy is close, stay focused. Inside, the formations should use left, right, row and column to define the positions. When not advancing, troops should take the sitting formation. When giving out orders, how troops should be positioned and the weapons to carry in each formation's position should be taken into consideration. If the horses are aroused and the troops are afraid, tighten the formation and use either the sitting or squatting formations. The general should advance using his knees and calm the troops down. Have them get up, shout and advance using drums; signal a halt with the bells. When the troops are resting, ordered or having meals, have them sit down, and when there is a need to move, use knees to advance. Seize and summarily execute any deserters to stop the others from looking about to desert. Shout in order to lead them. If they are too terrified of the enemy, do not threaten them with execution and severe punishment but display a magnanimous countenance. Speak to them about the way to survive and achieve accomplishment; supervise them in their duties to complete the tasks.

作战的方法，要根据人们的德才分成等级，授予适当的职位，建立军队各级的编制，规定行列的次序，调整纵横队列，并检查是否名副其实。采用立阵时前进要弯腰，
采用坐阵时移动用膝行，军队有畏惧心理时，队形要密集。情况危急时，要用坐阵。对远处的敌人观察清楚了就不会惶恐；对近处的敌人，要目中无敌，就会集中精力，进行战斗。士卒在布阵中的位置，按左、右、行、列分布。屯兵驻止时用坐阵。从容下达命令，要规定每个甲士和徒手的具体位置，

兼顾各种兵器使用的轻重缓急,如果车震马躁,士卒畏惧,就应靠拢使队形密集,采用跪阵或坐阵,将领膝行前去用宽和的言词告诫他们,[使他们镇定下来]。如果要转入进攻就起立,高声呼喊,擂鼓前进。如果要停止,就鸣金。当士卒衔枚、受命或吃饭时,都应坐下实施,必须移动时,用膝行移动。在战场上要用杀戮来严禁顾盼不前,并高声喝令他们前进。如果士卒畏惧太甚,就不要再行杀戮,而应和颜悦色地把立功求生的办法告诉他们,使之各尽其职,完成任务。

Executing Punishment

Within the army: all punishment has to be imposed within half a day; confinement does not go beyond the rest period; do not cut the army's food supply as a form of punishment; when the enemy is in doubt, such is an opportunity to subdue him.

三军之中:惩罚兵众,半天以内就要执行;监禁士兵,不超过一息的时间;要乘敌人尚在疑惑不定的时候,用兵袭击,就可征服它。

Endurance & Victory

In general, during battles, one can endure if he has sufficient numerical strength, but achieve victory if morale is high enough; one can endure with solid defense but achieve victory when being endangered; one can endure if the troops genuinely want to fight but achieve victory when the fighting spirit is high; with the armor one is secure; with weapons, one attains victory.

一般作战:凡兵力充实就能持久,士气旺盛就能取胜;防守坚固就能持久,军队处于危地反能取胜。士卒真心求战就能稳固,朝气蓬勃就能取胜。用盔甲防护自己,用兵器战胜敌人。

Solid Defense

In general, the chariots will be secured in a close-knit formation; infantry will be solid in a squatting formation; armor is strong through toughness; weapons must be light and easy to wield to achieve victory.

兵车密集就能巩固,步兵用坐阵就能巩固,铠甲要坚实厚重才能牢固,兵器要轻巧应手才能取胜。

Mindset for Victory & Fear

When men have their mind set for victory, the next stage is to find out the situation of the enemy and see if there is a chance to attack. When men are filled with fear, the next stage is to find out what their fear is. Once feelings have been made clear, their consequences and cause should be treated the same. How the general handles both situations depends on his execution of authority.

人们都有了求胜之心,这时就应该着重研究敌情是否能打。人们都有畏惧之心,这时就应着重研究他们是畏惧什么?把求胜之心和畏惧之心都研究清楚,把两方面的利害关系看待如一。而对这两方面情况的掌握,就全在于将帅的权衡。

Troop Size

In general, in warfare: using small troops against the enemy's troops is dangerous. Using large troops against the enemy's large troops does not guarantee victory. Using small troops against the enemy's large troops is asking for failure. Using large troops against small troops can achieve swift victory. Thus war is also a comparison of strength and numbers.

一般作战:使用小部队对敌小部队可能有危险,使用大部队对敌大部队就可能不成功,使用小部队对敌大部队就要失败,使用大部队对敌小部队就要迅速决战,所以作战是双方兵力的对比和较量。

Encamped, On the Move, In Battle

When in encampment, be careful about the weapons and armors. When on the move, be cautious about the rows and files. When in battle, be careful about when to advance or stop.

驻军时要注意严整战备,行军时要注意行列整齐,作战时要注意进止有节。

Respecting Troops

In general, in warfare: if you respect the troops, the troops will be satisfied. If you lead in person, they will follow. When orders are not organized and clear, the troops will disregard the orders given and act on their own. If orders are issued in proper measure, they will be seriously regarded. When the drumbeat is rapid, troops will move swiftly. When the drumbeat is more measured, troops will advance in measured steps. When their uniforms are light, they will feel agile. If their uniforms are heavy, they will feel stalwart.

凡是作战,将帅恭敬待下就会让士兵满意,以身作则就能服众。上级政令烦杂士兵就会轻率行动,政令有间歇讲节制战士就能遇事持重。进攻时击鼓迅急就是号令疾速前进,击鼓舒缓则是号令缓攻徐进。服饰轻而薄将士行动就会便捷,服饰厚且重将士行动就迟钝。

From Small to Big

When the horses and chariots are sturdy, the armor and weapons are strong, then even a small force can perform like a big force.

只要马健康、兵车坚固，甲胄兵器精良，虽是小部队也能起大部队的作用。

Bad Characteristics of a General

If the general has the same knowledge and wisdom as his troops, they will not be able to achieve results. If the general always insists on his own decisions, a lot of his troops will be sacrificed. If the general is scared of death and not courageous, his troops will have many doubts. If the general fights without strategizing, he will not be victorious.

主将见识与众人同等，就不会取得战功。主将一味专横独断，战士就会多牺牲。主将贪生怕死，缺乏勇气，部下就会疑虑重重。主将只知拼死蛮战，有勇无谋，就不能夺取战争的胜利。

Some Causes of Death

In general, men will die for love and gratitude, out of anger, out of fear of military greatness or authority, for righteousness or greed. Thus in warfare, laws can regulate men, making them regard death lightly. Moral and a righteous cause can make men willing to die for righteousness.

人们有为感恩而效死的，有因激怒而拼死的，有被威逼而拼死的，有因仗义而效死的，有因贪利而拼死的。一般作战，用法令约束人，只能使人们不敢怕死，用道义感动人，才能使人们愿意为正义而死。

Timing, Terrain & Popular Support

In warfare, whether one wins or loses depends on whether he has the correct timing, in the right terrain and gains popular support.

一般作战。或者胜利，或者失败，都取决于是否顺应天时，顺应人心。

Alertness

In warfare, the whole army should not be on alert for more than three days; a single company should not be on alert for more than half of a day, and the guard duty of a single soldier should not exceed one rest period.

凡是战时，对三军的告诫命令不要超过三天，对兵众的警戒训令不要超过半天，对一人的禁卫职务不可超过一息时间。

Strategic Attack vs. Physical Attack

During war, strategic attack is the best way to achieve victory. Next is physical attack. The general should know the war situation well and pay attention to details. This is to allow him to decide whether a strategic attack or a physical attack can achieve victory. This is a question that the general needs to contemplate.

进行战争，最好的方法是用谋略取胜，其次才是用攻战取胜。将帅必须掌握全局的形势，抓住具体环节，[以决定]是用谋略取胜还是以攻战取胜，这是作战时应该权衡的问题。

Unity and Victory

Regarding victory, when the whole army unites as one, victory can be achieved.

凡是胜利，都是由于全军团结得象一个人，才能取得。

Drums and Drumbeats

In warfare, for drums, there are drums that direct the deployment of flags and pennants; drums for advancing the chariots, drums for war horses, drums for directing infantry, drums for taking over, drums for organizing or forming formations, drums for standing and sitting. All seven should be prepared.

一般指挥部队的鼓点，有命令旗帜开合的，有命令兵车驰驱的，有命令战马奔驰的，有命令步兵前进的，有命令交兵接刃的，有命整齐队形的，有命令起坐行动的。这七种鼓点都必须规定齐全。

Strength in Formation and Numbers

In warfare, when the formation is already solid, do not make it more solid. When you have numerical advantage, do not commit all of them to attack. Committing all of them to attack will endanger the effort.

凡是作战，已经坚固的阵容不要再加强。即使兵力雄厚、进攻时也不要把力量一次用尽，凡是把力量用尽了的都很危险。

Using Formations

In warfare, it is not the forming of a battle formation that is difficult; it is the point in which that the men can be ordered into a formation fast that is difficult. It is not the point in which that the men can be ordered into a formation fast that is difficult, it is the ability of the men to exercise flexibility in using formation that is difficult. All in all, it is not the knowledge of formation that is difficult, it is the appropriate implementation of the formations that is difficult.

一般作战；不是布阵难，而是使吏卒熟习阵法难。不是使吏卒熟习阵法难，而是使他们灵活运用难。总之，不是懂得阵法难，而是实际运用难。

Character and Culture

All men have their own nature, and nature can differ from region to region. Through teaching, these natures can become part of the culture. Culture differs from region to region. Through moral teaching, these cultures can come together.

各地的人各有其性格，性格随各州而不同。教化可以形成习俗，习俗也是各州不同。通过道德的教化就能统一习俗。

Basic Principles to Achieve Victory

In warfare, whether the troops are numerous or few, even though they have attained victory, they should act as if they have not achieved it. A general that does not require the weapons to be sharp, armor to be strong, chariots to be sturdy, horses to be strong or troops to be expanded have not acknowledged the basic principles to achieve victory

不论兵力大小，打了胜仗要和没有打胜仗一样不骄不懈。凡是不讲求兵器锋利，不讲求盔甲坚韧，不讲求车辆牢固，不讲求马匹良好，不努力扩充兵员，都是没有掌握打胜仗的道理。

Crediting Victory and Assuming Blame

In warfare, if you are victorious, share the achievement and praise with the troops. If about to re-engage in battle, make the rewards exceptionally generous, and the punishments heavier. If you failed to achieve victory, accept the blame yourself. If you fight again, assume a leading position and do not repeat the tactics used last time. Whether you win or not, do not deviate from this principle for it is the "True Principle".

凡是作战，胜利了要与众人分享荣誉。如果还要再进行战斗，就要着重赏罚。假使没有取得胜利，就要把错误归于自己。再战时，要决心身先士卒，不重复使用上次的战法。无论胜败都不要违反这个原则，因为这是正确的原则。

Treating the Population

With regard to people, rescue them from suffering with benevolence; engage them in battle with righteousness; make judgment with wisdom; fight with courage; lead them through credibility; encourage them with profits, and gain victory through honors. Thus the leader must embody benevolence and his actions accord with righteousness. He must make decisions wisely, be courageous in handling big matters and rule the state with credibility. If the leader is humble and friendly, his people will be deferential. If the leader attributes failings to himself, the people will follow the ways of previous wise people, following their principles. When the hearts of the population are won and they are happy, they will give their best for the state.

对所有的国民百姓。执政者要用仁爱去解救他们的苦难，用忠义去激发他们为国而战，用智慧判断他们的功过，用勇敢来率领他们去战斗，用诚信来使他们志向专一，用财富来勉励他们去效力，用功勋来鼓舞他们去取胜。所以执政者的心志要合乎仁爱，行为要合乎道义。掌管万物要靠智慧，处理大事要靠勇气，使国家长治久安要靠诚信。为政谦逊而和蔼，人心自然就融洽了；把过错的责任留给自己来承担，使民众取法前贤，以为处世之准则；悦服民众之心，使他们乐于为国效力。

To Attack or Avoid the Enemy

In warfare, attack the weak and quiet, avoid the strong and quiet. Attack the tired, avoid the well trained and alert. Attack those who are very afraid, avoid those who are alert. Since antiquity these have been the rules governing the army.

凡战，击其微静，避其强静；击其疲劳，避其闲窕；击其大惧，避其小惧，自古之政也。

Chapter 5 - Employing Masses
Employing Large or Small Forces

In warfare, when you employ a small number, their defense should be solid. When you employ a large mass they must be well-ordered. With a small force it is advantageous to win using Indirect methods; with a large mass, it is advantageous to use Direct tactics. When employing a large mass, they must be able to advance and stop; when employing a small number, they must be able to advance and withdraw. If your large mass encounters a small enemy force, surround them at a distance but leave one side open. Conversely, if you divide your forces and attack in turn, a small force can withstand a large mass. If their masses are beset by uncertainty, you should take advantage of it. If you are attacking an enemy occupying a strategic position, abandon your flags as if in flight, and when the enemy attacks, turn around to mount a counterattack. If the enemy is vast, then concentrate your force and let them surround you. If the enemy is fewer and fearful, avoid them at the moment and attack when opportunity arises.

指挥作战的要领，兵力弱小应力求营阵巩固，兵力强大，应力求严整不乱。兵力弱小利于变化莫测出奇制胜，兵力强大利于正规作战。兵力强大要能进能止[稳重如山]，兵力弱小要能进能退[出没无常]。用优势兵力与劣势敌人交战，应从远处形成包围并留个缺口"让他溃逃"。分批轮番攻击敌人，就要以少战多。用拐势兵力对付优势敌人，就要虚张声势迷惑敌人，采用出敌意外的方法争取胜利。如果敌人已占据了有利地形，就卷起军旗，假装败退引诱它出来，然后反击它。如果敌人兵力很多，应当察明情况并准备在被围攻的情况下作战。如果敌人兵少并害怕被灭，就应先退让一步，然后乘隙消灭它。

Movement of Troops

In warfare, keep the wind to your back, the mountains behind, heights on the right and defiles on the left. Pass through wetlands, cross over damaged roads. Select camping ground that is configured like a turtle's back.

凡是作战，要背着风向背靠高地，右边依托高地左边依靠险要，遇着沼泽地和崩塌地要迅速通过，宿营要选择四面有险可守、中间较高的地形。

After Deployment

In warfare, after deployment, observe the enemy's actions. Watch the enemy and then initiate movement. If they are waiting for our attack, then act accordingly. Do not drum the advance, but wait for the moment when their masses arise. If they attack, concentrate your forces and attack his weakness.

一般作战，先摆好阵势，不忙于作战，看敌人怎样行动，再采取相应的行动。如果发现敌人已准备好圈套，等待我去中它的计，为了适应这种情况，就暂不发起进攻，而等待观察敌人主力的行动。如果敌人进攻，就集中兵力看准敌人的破绽去打击它。

Testing the Enemy

In warfare, employ large and small numbers to observe their tactical variations; advance and retreat to probe the solidity of their defenses. Endanger them to observe their fears. Be tranquil to observe if they become lax. Move to observe if they have doubts. Mount a surprise attack to see their discipline. Mount a strike when they are in doubt. Attack when they are unprepared, so they are not able to fight with full strength. Attack his well-ordered formation to break down his deployment. Use their failure to attack them, preventing them from executing their strategies, forcing them to abandon them, and when they are fearful, attack them.

一般作战，应使用或多或少的兵力去试探敌人，以观察它的变化。用忽进忽退的行动，以观察它的阵势是否稳固；迫近威胁敌人，看它是否恐惧；按兵不动，看它是否
懈怠；进行佯动，看它是否疑惑；突然袭击，看它阵容是否整治。在敌人犹豫不决的时候打击它，乘敌人仓卒无备的时候选攻它，使敌人战斗力无法施展。袭击敌人并打乱它的部署，利用敌人冒险轻进的错误，阻止它实现其企图，粉碎它既定的计划，乘它军心恐惧时歼灭它。

Chasing the Enemy

In warfare, when pursuing an enemy, do not rest. If some of the enemy stops on the road, be wary.

凡是追击溃败的敌人，一定不要停息，敌人如果在中途停止，就要慎重考虑它的企图。

Planning Attack and Retreat

In warfare, when nearing an enemy's city, you must have a route of attack; when about to withdraw, you must ponder the retreat route.

凡是追近敌人都城的时候，一定要先研究好进军的道路。退却的时候，也一定要预先考虑好后退的方案。

Timing and Resting

In warfare, if you move too early, you will be exhausted easily; if you move too late, the men may be afraid. If focused on resting the men, the men would become lax, if you do not rest the men, they will be exhausted; yet if the men are allowed to rest too long, they may become afraid.

凡是作战，行动过早易使兵力疲惫，行动过迟易使军心畏怯，只注意休息会使军队懈怠，总不休息必然使军队疲困，但是休息久了，反而会产生怯战心理。

Troop Administration

Writing letters to families should be forbidden, this is to break focus on all the small troubles of life. Select the best and equip them with weapons; this is to increase the strength of the troops. Abandoning armor and carrying minimal rations, this is to motivate the troops. From antiquity, this has been the administration of troops.

禁绝士卒和亲人通信，以断绝他们思家的念头。选拔优秀人才，授予兵器，以提高军队的战斗力。舍弃笨重装备，少带粮食，以激发士卒死战的决心。这些，都是从古以来治军作战的方法。

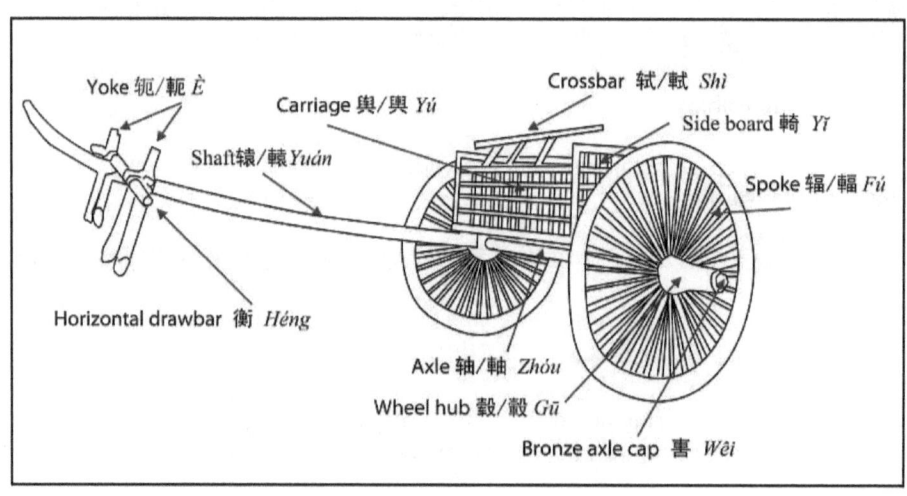

Chinese horse-drawn chariot design, c. 400 BCE

The Book of Wuzi

Wu Qi

吴子

The Book of Wuzi *(吴子) is attributed to Wu Qi. It is also sometimes referred to as The Wuzi or The Book of Wu Qi. In an ongoing dialogue, Lord Wen of Wei (魏文侯) and his son, Lord Wu of Wei (魏武侯) asked Master Wu Qi questions about war theory, strategy, exploiting the terrain to best advantage, and handling unexpected situations. It is believed to have been written during the middle of the Warring States period (c. 5th century BCE).*[1]

Part 1
Introduction - Strengthening the Nation
Need for Strengthening Domestic and External Issues

Wearing the attire of a Confucian scholar, Wu Qi attended an audience with Lord Wen of Wei to discuss military matters. At the outset of the audience, Lord Wen of Wei announced, "I do not have much interest in military matters."

Wu Qi replied, "From plain visible facts, I can deduce the hidden. From the past, I may foretell the future. How can your Lordship sincerely say that he has no interest in this subject?

"All through the four seasons, you have gathered the skins of wild animals, covered them with lacquer, painted them with colors and embellished them with glistening images of rhinoceros and elephants. Wearing these in winter does not keep one warm; wearing them in summer does not make one cool. Further, my Lord has ordered the making of twelve and twenty four feet long halberds, and has had the chariots covered in leather. These chariots are not grand and beautiful for ceremonies. These chariots are not mobile enough for hunting. If they are to not be used for war, I have no idea what use you might have for them. Your Lordship, however, does not seek capable people who are adept in using them. As such, it is

---

[1] "Zi" (子; "Tzu") was used as a suffix for the family name of a respectable man in ancient Chinese culture. It is a rough equivalent to "Sir" and is commonly translated into English as "Master".

similar to a nesting hen fighting against the fox, or a puppy fighting a tiger: although they have great fighting spirit, they will still perish.

"In times past, the Lord of the Cheng Sang Clan concentrated on improving the culture and domestic issues but neglected military matters, thereby leading to the extinction of the state. The Lord of the Yu Hu Clan was belligerent, thus he concentrated only on military matters and neglected domestic matters. He also led his state to extinction.

"An enlightened ruler would use such examples to remind himself that he should tend to both the domestic matters and military matters together. It does not count as righteousness when an enemy attacks and you do not fight back. It does not count as benevolence if you are only concerned with the lives of your soldiers after they have been killed.

Wu Qi's words were so impressive that Lord Wen personally laid a mat for Wu Qi and Lord Wen's wife presented Wu Qi with a goblet of wine. Later, Lord Wen invited Wu Qi to the ancestral temple where he appointed Wu Qi as the Commander for the defense of the Western River. From that time, Wu Qi fought a total of seventy six battles with other feudal lords and won sixty four of them decisively. Wu Qi expanded the territory of Wei in all directions, broadening its borders by a thousand *li*. Such were Wu Qi's accomplishments.[2]

吴起穿戴儒生的衣冠，以讨论治军打战的谋略谒见魏文侯。
魏文侯说："我对治军打战的事没兴趣。"
吴起说："臣根据所见来推断隐藏，以过去推断未来，君王为何言不由衷？现在君王一年四季派人杀兽剥皮以制革，并在革上涂红漆、画色彩，烙上犀牛和大象的图形。这些东西，冬天穿着不暖和，夏天穿着不凉快。君主又派人打造二丈四尺的长戟和一丈二尺的短戟；还用皮布覆盖战车，此战车并不华丽，用它来打猎也不轻便，不知君王要拿它们做什么？如果是用来准备作战，却又不寻求会使用它们的人，那就好比母鸡和狸猫搏斗，又好比哺乳的母狗去挑战老虎一样，为了孩子虽有拼斗，却肯定丧生。从前，承桑氏的国君因为只讲文德、废弃武备而丧国。有扈氏的国君因战恃兵多、好斗凶狠、不修文德，也丧国。有鉴于此，英明的君主必然内修明文治，对外加强武备。所以，当敌人来战而不进击，这算不上是义；看着死伤的将士才哀伤，这算不上是仁。"
于是魏文侯亲自安排席位，夫人捧着酒杯，在祖庙宴请吴起，任命吴起为大将，防守西河。后来，吴起与各诸侯国大战七十六次，大获全胜六十四次，其余十二次未分胜负。魏国因此向四面扩张领土达千里之广，都是吴起的功劳。

---

[2] The title, "Lord" is used, although the exact title is "Marquess". Lord Wen of Wei was succeeded at the time of his death by his son, the Lord Wu of Wei.

Unity and the People's Support

Wu Qi said: "In antiquity, an enlightened ruler, for the benefit of the state, would teach and enlighten the people. He would be seen to be close to the people and it would be known that he understood their hardships.

"There are four disharmonies of which the ruler should take note. If there is disharmony within the state, a military campaign should not be started. If there is disharmony within the army, it should not be allowed to enter into battle. If there is disharmony within a formation, it should not be used to lead an attack. If there is a lack of cohesion during the conduct of battle, a victory cannot be won.

"An eminent ruler, for this reason, will first unite his people before seeking to employ them to achieve great things. He will not venture to implement his plans without first seeking to formally divine the prospects and the appropriateness of the timing from Heaven at the ancestral temple. Only if all the signs are auspicious, then he will he proceed to mobilize the army.

The people will then know that the ruler values them and their lives. They will then be willing to share weal and woe together and, if necessary, to lay down their lives. Officers will feel that losing their lives while advancing is glorious and that clinging to life while retreating is disgraceful."

吴起说："从前想治理好国家的君主，首先必定教化民众，关心人民疾苦。有四种不和的因素须要多加注意：国内人心不统一，不可以出兵；军队内部不团结，不可上阵；临阵部伍不一致，不可以进攻；战斗动作不协调，不可能取胜。所以英明的君主，要征召百姓前，务求内部团结一致，才可一起成就大事。凡有所谋，君主还不敢偏信个人的谋划，一定要到祖庙祭告，用大龟占卜吉凶，并观测天时，是吉兆才敢行动。民众知道君主爱护他们的生命、不忍心看他们死，竟然周到至此，而且愿同他们生死存亡。所以他们就会以拼命死效命为荣，以退却偷生为耻。"

Four Virtues of a Ruler

Wu Qi said: "*The Way* is simply the proper manner in which things should be done.[3] It is the means by which one can return to the foundation and start from the beginning. Righteousness is simply a matter of ethical behavior. It is the means by which great accomplishments may be achieved. Strategizing is simply a means of keeping harm at a distance, and gaining benefits. Principles are simply the means of preserving duty and maintaining achievements. If one's behavior is not in accord with the Way and righteousness, but dwells in magnificence and the

---

[3] When capitalized or italicized, "The Way" refers to *Tao*, or *Dao*. *Tao* signifies the primordial essence or fundamental nature of the universe.

enjoyment of power, disaster will inevitably befall him. Thus the wise ruler will manage the state according to the Way, managing the state with righteousness, ordering the people with propriety and ruling the people with benevolence. Cultivating these virtues will cause the state to flourish; neglecting them will cause the state to decline.

"This was why the people of Xia rejoiced when Shang Tang exterminated Xia Jie, and why the people did not condemn King Wu of Zhou when he removed King Zhou from the Yin Shang Dynasty. The people saw that these actions were in accord with proper morals and were the mandate of Heaven. Thus they achieved success."[4]

吴起说："道,是一切行事的原则,可使人掌握根本,不会舍本逐末；义,是正当的行为,可使人成大事、立大功；谋,是深思熟虑,可使人趋利避害；要,是切中纲领,可使人保持业绩,守住成果。如果行为举止不合道义,只顾好大喜功,尽享荣华,必有后患。所以贤明的君主,以道安定天下,以义治理国家,以礼约束百姓,以仁爱抚人民。君主若能遵循道、义、礼、仁这四种德性,国家必然兴盛,反之,必然衰微。因此,古时商汤讨伐夏桀,而夏朝子民反而高兴；周武王讨伐商纣,而商朝人民视为正当。这是因为商汤和周武王,合乎天理和人伦,所以才有如此结果。"

Running the State and Victory

Wu Qi said: "In general, to govern the state and the army well, it is necessary to instruct them with propriety, to motivate them with righteousness and to instill a sense of shame in them. When men have a sense of shame, the enlightened ruler, in the grand scheme, can wage a great war or, more simply, preserve peace.

"Being victorious in battle is relatively easy compared to the difficulty of preserving the fruits of victory. Thus it is said that a ruler whose state gains five victories will meet with disaster; the ruler whose state gains four victories will see his state decline; the ruler whose state gains three victories can achieve hegemony; the ruler whose state gains two victories can claim to be a king and the ruler whose state gains merely one victory will become an emperor. Thus it may be seen that those who have achieved ultimate success following many victories are few and those who have ultimately failed following many victories are many.

吴起说："道,是一切行事的原则,可使人掌握根本,不会舍本逐末；义,是正当的行为,可使人成大事、立大功；谋,是深思熟虑,可使人趋利避害；要,是切中纲领,可使人保持业绩,守住成果。如果行为举止不合道义,只顾好大喜功,尽享荣华,必有后患。所以贤明的君主,以道安定天下,以

---

[4] The Shang Dynasty (商朝) ruled in the Yellow River valley sometime between 1600 BC and 1046 BC, succeeding the Xia Dynasty and followed by the Zhou Dynasty.

义治理国家，以礼约束百姓，以仁爱抚人民。君主若能遵循道、义、礼、仁这四种德性，国家必然兴盛，反之，必然衰微。因此，古时商汤讨伐夏桀，而夏朝子民反而高兴；周武王讨伐商纣，而商朝人民视为正当。这是因为商汤和周武王，合乎天理和人伦，所以才有如此结果。"

Reasons for War and its Counter Strategy

Wu Qi said: "There are five reasons why wars are started: to repair injustice, to win fame, to seek revenge, to gain wealth and to quell internal strife. The wars that are fought for these reasons are called: righteous, bully, anger, plundering and contrary wars.

"The 'righteous' army is raised to save people from disorder and chaos. The 'bully' army is raised to control, command and awe the people. The 'anger' army is raised by an intemperate ruler merely from some displeasure. The 'plundering' army is raised out of greed to seek profit without consideration for moral and ethics. The 'contrary' army is raised when the state is in turmoil, the masses exhausted and the morale of the people has been depleted.

"There are appropriate strategies to counter wars that have been started for these reasons. In the case of the 'righteous', you must use propriety and reason to subdue them. For the 'bully' you must be respectful and even deferential to subdue them. With the 'anger' army, you must use persuasion and patience to subdue them. Against the 'plundering' army you must use your wits and guile to subdue them. Against the 'contrary', you must confront them firmly and impose your authority to subdue them."

吴起说："战争发生的原因有五种，一是争取名位，二是争夺利益，三是仇恨，四是内乱，五是饥荒。而这五种起兵名称是义兵、强兵、刚兵、暴兵、逆兵。除暴救乱称为义；仗势欺人、以强凌弱称为强；因意气用事而发动战争称为刚；不顾利益、贪图利益称为暴；内政紊乱、人民困苦，却仍征调兵力发动战争称为逆。弭平这五种战争的办法如下：对义兵，应以礼相待，使之折服；对强兵，应以谦恭的心，使之折服；对刚兵，应以言辞说服之；对暴兵，应使用谋略摆平；对逆兵，应使用权势慑服。"

Managing Troops, Selecting Talent, Strengthening the Nation

Lord Wu said to Wu Qi: "I would like to hear your thoughts on managing troops, selecting talent and strengthening the nation."

Wu Qi replied: "From antiquity, it has been seen that enlightened rulers have always made every effort to deal righteously and with propriety to all; to observe the distinctions of rank, encouraging the officials and people to settle into the appropriate hierarchy in accordance with proper custom, and to select and recruit the talented in order to be prepared for emergencies."

"In years past, Duke Huan of Qi, Lord Wen of Jin and Lord Mu of Qin were each able to summon tens of thousands of men, and consequently they were able to achieve hegemony.[5] Foremost the enlightened ruler must be able to evaluate his people.

1. He must recognize that those who have courage and strength should be assembled into a unit.
2. Those who take pleasure in advancing into battle and exerting their strength, so as to manifest their loyalty and courage, should be assembled into another unit.
3. Those who are nimble and fleet should be assembled into another unit.
4. Officials who have lost their positions and are eager to make amends should be assembled into another unit.
5. Those who have lost in war and want to eradicate their disgrace should be assembled into a unit.

These five units will be the elite troops. With a contingent of a thousand of such men, one can then break any encirclement or breach the walls of any city."

武侯问吴起："愿听您对掌握军队、选拔人才、巩固国家的看法。"
吴起回答道："古来英明的国君，必定谨守君臣之间的礼仪，要求上下阶级的分际，使官吏和人民各安其位、顺应风俗，并且选拔人才，应付突发事件。
春秋时代，齐桓公、晋文公、秦穆公都曾征募勇士好几万，因而称霸。强国的君主，一定先了解人民的实力，选拔人才加以活用。有胆识、有力气的人，编委一队；乐于奋战，以表现忠勇精神的，编委一队；身手矫捷、能够越野的，编委一队；因故丢官去职，急于戴罪立功的，编委一队；曾经打败战，意图建功雪耻的，编委一队。这五队，是军中精锐，有了如此三千人，作战时，如果被敌人围困，必可由内而出，突破重围；如果向敌人进攻，必可由外而入，攻掠城池。"

Strength in Attack and Defense

Lord Wu then inquired: "I would like to hear your views on preparing stable battle formations, making impregnable defenses and gaining certain victory in battle."

Wu Qi replied: "My methods are more than mere talk; employing my methods will allow you to see immediate effects. When you have worthy men holding high

---

[5] Hegemony is an indirect form of imperial dominance in which the hegemon (leader state) rules subordinate states by the implied means of power rather than by direct military force.

positions and relatively less worthy men occupying lower positions, then your battle formations will be stable. When the people are satisfied with their respective positions and honor their officials, then the defense will be solid. When the people support the policies of their government and are not envious of the conditions in other states, then in battle you are certain to be victorious."

武侯接着问:"请问使阵营安定、反防守坚固、作战必胜的方法。"
吴起回答道:"这些方法岂止于说说听听而已,还可以立即见到成效。如果您能让有才能的人居于上位,而实力差的人置于下位,阵营便能安定;人民安居乐业,爱戴其官吏,防御便巩固;百姓支持政府所有措施,对邻国的施政不以为然,在战争中便稳操胜券。"

The Book of Wuzi — Wu Qi

Chapter 1 - Importance of Seeking Talent

There was once a time when Lord Wu was planning state affairs, and found that the advice offered by his ministers was not equal to his own considerations. After dismissing the court, he wore a pleased and self-satisfied countenance.

Wu Qi saw this and said: "There was a time when Lord Zhuang of Chu, who was planning state affairs with his ministers, discovered that none of his ministers were his equal in intelligence. After he had dismissed the court, he looked very troubled.

"His chief official, Shen, then asked him: 'Why does your Lordship wear such a troubled countenance?' Lord Zhuang replied: 'I have heard that there is no deficiency of Sages at any one time and there is not a deficiency of talent in any states. To have such as teachers would allow one to become a king, while having such as friends would allow one to achieve hegemony. Now I am not particularly talented, yet none of my ministers are equal to me. Our state is in deep trouble!'

"Lord Zhuang was troubled by this same circumstance but my Lordship seems to be rather proud of it. This worries me."

On hearing this, Lord Wu was ashamed.

武侯有一次召集大臣们，讨论国事，群臣所提出的意见都比不上武侯本身的想法。散会后，武侯显得很得意。
吴起看到此情形，便对武侯说："从前楚庄王也曾召集群臣商讨国事，群臣意见都不及他。会议结束后，楚庄王愁眉不展。楚国达夫申公问他为何心事重重。楚庄王回答道：'我曾经听说过，任何时代都有圣人，任何国家都有贤才。以他们为师，可以成王；与他们为友，可以称霸。如今我能力薄弱，而诸位大臣竟然比不上我，楚国前途堪忧。'楚庄王为此烦忧，而您却反而得意。这令臣俱之。"
武侯听到后，感到羞愧万分。

Military Strategy Classics of Ancient China

Chapter 2 - Knowing the Enemy
National Alertness

Lord Wu addressed Wu Qi: "In our current situation, the state of Qin threatens us on the west, Chu intrudes upon us in the south, Chao menaces us in the north, Qi trespasses upon us from the east, Yan endangers our rear and Han jeopardizes our front. Being surrounded by these six states worries me. We have no choice but to defend against them. What can be done about this precarious situation?"

Wu Qi said: "In general, vigilance in the face of danger is the true measure of good governance: it is essential to the security of state. Since you are alert to the danger and have recognized the importance of being cautious, you have already taken the first step in avoiding disaster. Now, I will describe the characteristic of each of the six states.

"Although Qi's formations have plentiful numbers and resources, they are not strong. Qin's formations are too diverse and incapable of fighting alone. Chu's formations are complete, but they cannot be maintained indefinitely. Yan's formations are adept at defense but they are immobile. Han's and Zhao's troops are well controlled but they are not effective."

武侯问吴起说："以目前形势来看，秦国威胁我国西方，楚国围在南方，赵国扼住北方，齐国在东方，燕国在后方阻绝，韩国在前方据守。这六国兵力，环绕在我国四周，形势对我极为不利，真是令人担忧，可有对策？"
吴起答道："维护国家安全，首先要有警觉心。如今您能体会到警觉心的重要，灾害便已远离。在此，让我分析六国的形势：齐国兵力充足，但其阵不坚固；秦国兵阵分散，各自为战；楚国兵阵完整，但不能持久；燕国防守阵型坚固，但机动性不足；韩、赵两国兵力训练有素，但在战场上很难发挥实际效用。"

Six States Characteristics & Counter Strategies

"Although the Qi people are strong and the country is prosperous, the ruler and officials are arrogant and do not care about the people. The state's policies are not uniform and not strictly enforcement. Salaries and wages are not fair. This causes disharmony and disunity. Although they are numerous, they are not strong. To defeat them, we should divide our army into three groups and have our left and right groups attack on the left and right wings of Qi's army. Once their battle formations are thrown into disarray, our central group will be in position to attack and victory will follow.

"The Qin people are a different matter. They are tough and their terrain is treacherous. The Qin government is well organized. They are strict and their orders are enforced. The people believe in their state's rewards and punishment systems. The Qin troops are brave and have a fighting spirit. They are able to scatter and engage in combat individually. In order to defeat them, we must entice various groups with small benefits; the greedy will abandon their posts to pursue them. We can then capitalize on this opportunity by hunting each group down individually and then capturing the generals that have been isolated. Finally, we must array our army to ambush their commander.

"The Chu people are not strong. Their lands stretch far and wide, and the government cannot effectively administer the expanse. Their troops are weary and although their formations are well-ordered, they do not have the resources to maintain their positions for long. To defeat them, we must strike swiftly, unexpectedly and retreat quickly before they can counter attack. This will create chaos in their formations and reduce their fighting spirit. If we strike repeatedly, it will wear them out. Thus, with persistence, their army can be defeated.

"The Yan are a sincere and straightforward people. They are cautious, love courage and righteousness and rarely employ deception. Thus they will defend their positions, but are immobile and incapable of innovation. To defeat them, we must be unconventional, by attacking them at the rear and flanks, where and when they least expect it. When they turn to face our attacks, we should keep a distance. When they withdraw to face another threat, chase them. This will confuse them and create fear in their ranks. If we avoid conflict against their strong points and use our armored chariots to set ambushes, we can capture their generals insure victory.

"The Han and the Zhao are gentle people. Their populations are weary from war and experienced in arms, but they have little regard for their generals. The soldiers' salaries are meager and their officers have no strong commitment to their countries. Although their troops are experienced, they cannot be expected to fight to the death. To defeat them, we must concentrate large numbers of troops in our attacks to present them with certain peril. When they counterattack, we must be prepared to defend our positions vigorously and make them pay dearly. When they retreat, we must pursue and give them no rest. This will grind them down.

"This, then, is the assessment of the six nations."

"齐国人性情刚烈，国家富足，但君臣骄奢，忽视民众利益，政治松弛，俸禄分配不均，一阵之中人心不齐，兵力部署前重后轻，所以阵势浩大，但不坚实。打击齐兵的方法是，宜将我军分为三路，两路夹击它的左右翼，另一路承势追击，他的阵势便可破了。秦国人性情强悍，它的地势险要，政令严明，赏罚分明，士卒临阵勇猛而斗志高昂，所以能在分散的阵势中各自奋战。打击秦兵的方法是，先施以小利引诱它的士兵脱离主将的指挥，此时，我军就可以逐一击破其分散队伍，并设置伏伺机取胜，就可以擒获它的将领。楚人性情柔弱，它的领土广大，政令混乱，民力疲惫，所以阵势虽然严整但不能持久。打击楚兵的方法是，要袭扰其驻地，先动摇其士气，然后突然进击再突然撤退，使其疲于应付，而不要急于和它决战。这样就能打败它的军队。燕国人性情诚朴，行动谨慎，好勇尚义，但缺乏诈谋，所以它的阵势长于防守而不善于灵活出击。打击燕兵的方法是，一交战就压迫它，打了一下又迅速撤退，同时还要袭击它的后方，这样会使其将帅疑惑而士卒恐惧，此时，我军车骑埋伏在敌人撤退的必经之路上，就可以虏获燕军将领。韩与赵是中原国家。其民性情温顺，它的政治平和，百姓不好战斗，而且轻视将帅，不满意自己的待遇，士卒没有拼死效命的决心与斗志，所以阵势虽然整齐但不中用。打击它们的方法是，可用强大的兵力压制，如果敌人兵众来犯就与它对峙，如果它退却就追击，这样一来它的军队便会疲惫不堪。以上就是六国方面的形势。"

Providing Opportunities for Talent

"Within the army, there are always soldiers who have the courage of the tiger, who have the strength that to lift tripods easily and who have the fleetness of a barbarian horse. Such men are needed to seize the enemy's flags and kill the enemy's generals. These men should be put into one select unit. These men you should honor and favor generously, for in their hands rests the fate of the whole army. Rank and prominence should be given to those who are expert in weapons, who are strong and quick and are capable and motivated to kill enemies. Their families should also be treated well, encouraged with rewards and warned with punishments. Because such warriors can defend positions resolutely, attack relentlessly and exterminate enemies, the ruler who can discern and employ such men can attack a force double his own number."

Lord Wu exclaimed: "Excellent!"

"此外，一军之中，必定有勇猛之士，臂力大，脚力够，战斗时勇冠三军，能夺取敌军军旗或敌军将领。这些有能力的士兵，应当加以提拔任用，并且珍惜。因为，这些人将是左右全军胜负命运的重要分子。还有士兵中，若有善于使用兵器，身手矫捷，体格健壮，志于杀敌立功之士，应该提拔，晋升其爵位，厚待其父母妻子，再以奖赏激励和处罚警惕。这些士兵就可以构成坚强的阵势，也可以歼灭敌人。国君能做到这点，
便可以迎击两倍于我的敌人。"
武侯听后说："好！"

The Enemy You Can Attack

"In general, there are eight conditions under which one may engage the enemy in battle without having to make prolonged assessments:

1. When in violent winds and extreme cold, they arise early and embark upon the march while barely awake, and have to break ice to cross streams.
2. When in the burning heat of the summer, they arise late and press forward with haste, through hunger and thirst, concentrating on reaching far off objectives.
3. When the army has been out in the field for an extended period; their food supplies are exhausted; the people are resentful and angry; numerous baleful portents arise among the officers unable to squash them.
4. When the army's resources have already been exhausted; firewood and hay are scarce; weather is frequently cloudy and rainy; and even if they wanted to plunder for supplies, there is nowhere to do it.
5. When the number of troops mobilized is not large; the terrain and water not advantageous; the men and horses are sick and worn out and no assistance is available from their allies.
6. When the road is far and the sun is setting; the officers and men have labored long and are fearful; they are tired and have not eaten and have just cast aside their armor.
7. When the generals are weak, the official irresponsible, the officers and troops are not solid, the whole army is frequently in fear and the troops lack support.
8. When their formations are not yet arranged; their encampment not yet finished or they are passing through dangerous territory, and only half of their troops are out of it.

In any of these eight conditions, you can confidently attack."

吴起说："不必占卜吉凶就能够与之交战的有八种情况：
第一是，在吹着烈风的寒冷冬天，一大早就开始行军，入夜还迁徒不定，并且不顾艰难，企图强行渡河。
第二是，在炎炎夏日，部队出发迟缓，中途又不休息，且不顾士兵饥渴，往远处行军。
第三是，军队长期出征在外，粮食匮乏，人民怨怒，凶吉祸福的谣言纷起，指挥官无力阻止。
第四是，军队的物资、燃料、粮秣用尽，偏逢连日阴雨，无法就地掠夺，补充军需。　第五是，士卒人数不多，水土不服，人马病倒，又孤立无援。
第六是，长途行军，；离目的地还有一段距离，但天色已晚，士兵疲劳、恐慌又饥饿，正解除武装休息。
第七是，指挥官没有权威，干部轻浮不实，而且军心涣散，精神不稳，一再虚惊骚动，全军彷徨无助。
第八是，开始部署阵营或扎营，但尚未完整；部队正行经险峻地形，但还没有完全走完，只有一半通过。
以上八种情况，我军可放心攻击，不必游移。"

The Enemy You Cannot Attack

"There are six circumstances in which, without performing too much assessment, you should avoid conflict.

1. When the land is broad and vast and the people are wealthy and numerous.
2. When the government loves the people and the ruler's kindness extends and flows to all.
3. When the rewards and punishment system is fair and transparent and is implemented in a timely fashion.
4. When people are rewarded according to their accomplishment, and the talented and able are employed.
5. When the forces are massive and well-equipped.
6. When they have the assistance of all their neighbors or the support of a powerful state.

In general, if you are no match for the enemy in these areas; without a doubt avoid them. This is what I meant by: see the possibilities and advance, know the difficulties and withdraw."

"敌人若有以下六种情况，不必占卜吉凶，即应回避，不可与之作战：
第一是，领土广大，人口众多，生活富足。第二是，政府爱护人民，广行德政，恩惠遍及社会各层。第三是，赏罚分明，执行赏罚适得其时。第四是，论功行赏，任用贤能。第五是，兵力强大，装备精良。第六是，有邻国或大国支助。
以上六项，如果比不上敌国，必须回避，无庸置疑。终的来说，有获胜把握时，应该断然进攻；反之，应避免冲突，立即撤退。这就是所谓，见可而进，知难而退。"

Detecting the Enemy's Situation

Lord Wu said: "From the external appearances, I should be able to know their internal situation. From their advance, I should be able to know their objective. Then, I should be able to predict victory or defeat. What do you think of this?"

Wu Qi replied: "When the enemy approaches in large numbers with their ranks in disarray, when their flags and formations are in disorder and when the troops frequently look around; by using one tenth of their strength, we can invariably immobilize them. When their reinforcements have not arrived, when there is disunity within the troops, when their preparations for defense have not been completed, when orders and rules have not been announced and when the morale of the army is shaken; then they can neither advance nor retreat. This enemy you can with half of its strength and never risk failure."

魏武侯向吴起问道："藉着观察敌人的外在表面，就能知晓敌人的内在虚实；观察敌人的前进方式，就能知晓敌人的目的，并以此来判断最后胜利属谁，你对着有什么看法？"

吴起答道："如果敌军来攻时，浩浩荡荡，漫无顾忌，且军旗杂乱，人马频频回顾。这种敌军，只要用十分之一的兵力，便能使其慌乱不知所措。若是敌方的援军尚未会合，君臣之间不团结，防御工事还没完成，法令规章并未发布，军心骚动，既不能前进，又不敢后退。这样的敌人，只要用一半的兵力，便能获胜。"

Weaknesses You Can Attack

Lord Wu asked "Under what circumstances can one invariably attack the enemy?"

Wu Qi replied: "When you know the enemy's strengths and weaknesses, these are the situations give you the opportunity to attack:

1. When the enemy has just arrived on the field and their battle formations are not yet properly formed and deployed, they can be attacked.
2. When they have just eaten and have not yet established their encampment, they can be attacked.
3. When they are on the move and their formation is in disarray, they can be attacked.
4. When they have labored hard and are exhausted, they can be attacked.
5. When they have failed to seize the advantages of the terrain, they can be attacked.
6. When they have not seized upon the critical timing, they can be attacked.
7. When their flags and banners move about chaotically, they can be attacked.
8. When they have just traveled a great distance, with their supplies and reinforcements having just arrived, and the troops have not rested, they can be attacked.
9. When they are crossing the river and only half of them have crossed, they can be attacked.
10. When they are on treacherous terrain or narrow roads, they can be attacked.
11. When their formations change frequently, they can be attacked.
12. When the general is distant from his troops, they can be attacked.
13. When they are frightened or afraid, they can be attacked.

It is wise to select the best troops to make a swift attack upon them; while dividing the remaining troops so as to attack in waves in order to deliver a continuous assault."

武侯问："什么情况下，敌人必定可为我所破？"

吴起说："制胜之道，在于观察敌人虚实，当敌人有机可乘，即针对其弱点攻击。譬如以下十三点种情况：

第一是：敌人由远方来，刚刚抵达，一切作战安排尚未就绪，可以攻击。
第二是：刚用完餐，尚未整顿进入备战状态，可以攻击。
第三是：部队正在移动，次序混乱时，可以攻击。
第四是：疲劳困惫时，可以攻击。
第五是：未得地利之便，可以攻击。
第六是：未能掌握天时，可以攻击
第七是：旗帜混乱摇动，显得举起不定，可以攻击。
第八是：长途跋涉，后续部队刚赶到，尚未休息，可以攻击。
第九是：全军渡河，一半已登岸，另一半还在水中，可以攻击。
第十是：正通过险道隘路时，可以攻击。
第十一届是：一再变换兵阵，可以攻击。
第十二届是：将领和士卒离散，军中无大将时，可以攻击。
第十三届是：心存恐俱时，可以攻击。
凡是以上状况，表示敌军有种种危机，应立即以精锐部队冲击，然后将兵力分为数波，持续攻击，不必迟疑。"

Chapter 3 - Managing Troops
Factors in Using Troops

Lord Wu asked: "In using troops, what is most important?"

Wu Qi replied: "First you need understand the four principles of 'lightness', the two principles of 'heaviness' and the one principle of 'integrity'."

Lord Wu asked: "And what are they?"

Wu Qi said: "The four principles of 'lightness' mean the terrain will feel that the horses are light, the horses will feel that the chariot is light, the chariots will feel that the soldiers on it are light and the soldiers will feel that the burden of war is light. The terrain feels the horses are light means that one should choose a suitable terrain that would not hamper the movement of the horses. If the horses are properly fed and rested, they will be strong and thus when they are pulling chariots, they will feel that the chariots are light. If the axles of the chariots are well-oiled, sturdy and properly maintained, they can move soldiers easily, and thus the chariots will feel that the soldiers are light. If the soldiers' weapons are sharp and their armor is sturdy, they will feel confident. Thus, the burden of war will feel lighter.

"Those courageous who advance should be rewarded 'heavily'. Those who retreat should be punished 'heavily'. These are the two principles of 'heaviness'. 'Integrity' refers to the consistency of the rewards and punishment system. When the enlightened ruler employs these principles, his troops will achieve victory."

武侯问："用兵的方法，以什么为先？"
吴起说："先要了解四轻、二重、一信的道理。"
武侯问："这是什么？"
吴起解释："四轻指得是，使地觉得马轻，马觉得车轻，车觉得人轻，人觉得战争轻。熟悉地形的险易，选择最佳的行军路线，地形不成为马的障碍，马跑起来就会觉得轻快，这叫地轻马；马侍养良好，按时喂养，自然体力强壮，拉车不觉得吃力，这叫马轻车；兵车保养维护得当，滑润、坚固，车上在人，不会负担过重，这叫车轻人；武器装备精良，坚甲利兵，士卒不会视战争为畏途，这叫人轻战。
至于二重、一信的意思是，勇敢前进有重赏，懦怯后退受重罚，这就是二重；令出必行，信赏必罚，这就是一信。
如能彻底实行四轻、二重、一信等要领，用兵必胜。"

Gain Control of the Army

Lord Wu asked: "What is most important in ensuing victory?"

Wu Qi replied: "'Control is of foremost importance.'"

Lord Wu asked: "It is not simply a matter of numbers?"

"When the laws and orders are not clear, when rewards and punishment not meted out, when sounding the gongs will not cause them to halt or when the beating the drum will not make them advance; even if you have a million men, of what use would they be? 'Control' is achieved by thorough training and good management. During war, when discipline is strict, the soldiers will move and attack with precision. In advance and withdraw their stride will be measured; the left and right will look out for each other. Even when a contingent is broken off from the main body, they will preserve the formations; even when scattered they will reform lines. When the whole army is united by having shared weal and woe together, if when deployed, they do not feel tired then, no matter where you dispatch them, no one can withstand them. Such armies are called 'The Father and Son Army'."

武侯问："用兵靠什么取胜？"
吴起说："用兵靠'治'取胜。"
武侯又问："不是兵力的多寡吗？"
吴起答道："若法令不严明，赏罚不确实执行。鸣金停止，军队不停；鸣鼓前进，军队不前进。纵然有百万大军，又有何用？
所谓'治'，指的是训练和管理。平时纪律严明，战时赫赫有威。前进无人能挡，后退无人敢追。不论进退都有节度，左右照应彼此，即使军队被冲散，断绝联系，依然能各自为战，阵容严整。官兵上下共危安，全军精诚团结，无法离间；全力以赴，不知疲倦。这种军队，投入任何战争，必定无人能挡，我们称之为'父子之兵'。"

Things to Note on Marching Armies

Wu Qi said: "Command an army on the march requires observing the proper timing of advancing and stopping; not missing the appropriate times for eating and drinking; and never completely exhausting the strength of the men and horses. These three are necessary for the troops to be able to execute the orders of their superiors. Only when the orders of the superiors are followed, is control achieved. If advancing and resting are not timely; if drinking and eating are not timely; if the horses are tired and the men are weary, then they will be unable to carry out the commander's order. If the orders are not carried out, the troops will be in turmoil while encamped, and defeated in battle."

吴起说："行军的要领是，不要违背前进和停止的节奏，不要耽误适时的供食，不要耗尽人马的体力。这三点做到了，才能保证完成上级授予的任务。完成了上级授予的任务，就达到了治军的要求。如果前进和停止不能节制，饮食不能适时供给，人马疲乏而不能休息，就不能完成上级授予的任务。上级授予的任务不能完成的军队，驻守之地必然混乱，开赴战场必定打败仗"

Decisiveness

Wu Qi said: "On the battlefield, which will soon to become a land of corpses, the soldiers who are committed to fighting to the death will live; whereas those who seek to stay alive will die. A good general will act as if his army is on a sinking ship or trapped in a burning building; he knows that there is not enough time for the wise to devise plans or the courageous to get angry. The only useful thought that one can have is to fight! Thus it is said that great harm can befall the army as the result of hesitation, while the greatest disaster that can befall the whole army is the deadly delay that results from too many doubts."

吴起说："战场是打仗流血的地方，只要抱着必死的决心就会闯出生路，若想侥幸偷生反而容易遭于死亡。善于指挥作战的将领，就像坐在漏船上，又像伏在燃烧的房屋下，即使平素机智过人的人，也来不及谋划；勇敢的人，也来不及惊慌忿怒，唯一能做的就是迎敌奋战。所以说，用兵打仗，最坏的是犹豫不决。全军失败的灾难，多半肇因是疑虑过多，使得行动迟缓。"

Education & Training of the Army

Wu Qi said: "In war, men perish from inability and are defeated by the unfamiliar. Thus, before men are deployed, training to make them capable warriors who are familiar with every aspect of battle should be given the highest priority. One man who has been trained can train ten men. Ten men who have been trained can train a hundred. A hundred men who have been trained can train a thousand. A thousand men who have been trained can train ten thousand. Ten thousand men who have been trained can train the whole army.

"Being near gives one an advantage over an enemy coming from afar. Being well-rested gives one an advantage over an enemy who is tired. Being satiated gives one an advantage over an enemy who is hungry. Being familiar with the maneuvers of an army gives one and advantage over the chaos of a mob. It is essential for the soldiers to be able to go from being deployed in circular formations to square ones, to be able to move in unison, to be able to divide then combine, unite then disperse. When all these changes are familiar, when the men have been provided with weapons and trained in using them, only then are they an army. All these matters are the responsibility of the general."

吴起说："士卒在战争中往往死于没有本领，败于不熟悉战法。所以用兵的法则总以训练为先。一人学会了战斗本领，可以教会十人；十人学会，可以教会百人；百人学会，可以教会千人；千人学会，可以教会万人；万人学会，可以教会全军。我以近待敌远来，以安逸待敌疲劳，以饱食待敌饥饿。即学圆阵如何改变成方阵；即学从坐下变起立；即学从行动变停止；既学从左转到右，既学从前进转为后退；既学从分散转为集中，从集中转为分散。各种变化都训练熟悉了，才发给兵器。这些都是将领应该做的事情。"

Placing Individuals in Appropriate Positions

Wu Qi said: "A basic rule of warfare that should be grasped is that of appropriate deployment: that men of short stature should carry spears and spear-tipped halberds, that the tall should carry bows and crossbows, that the strong should carry the flags and banners, that the courageous should carry the bells and the drums, that the weak should serve in logistics; that the wise should be involved in planning; that people from the same village or district should be grouped together, so that they can look out for each other.

"As for the orders from drum beats, to a single drum beat, they should equip and gather themselves together. To the second drum beat, they should be drilled in various deployments. To the third drum beat, they should have their meals. To the fourth drum beat, they should make a final inspection. To the fifth drum beat, they should move out. Upon only hearing the drum beat should the soldiers move in unison, raise the banners and set off."

吴起说："作战训练的法则是，让身材较矮小的人使用矛戟，身材较高大的人使用弓弩，强而有力的人掌握军旗，勇敢的人司号令，身体较弱的人充当后勤，有智谋的人担任参谋。让同乡邻里的士卒编在一起，相互合作。在鼓声号令方面，第一通鼓整装集结，第二通鼓演练阵法，第三通鼓用饭，第四通鼓最后总检查，第五通鼓出发前进。等全军在击鼓讯号下行动一致，才可举旗出兵。"

Principles of Marching & Stationing the Army

Lord Wu said: "What are the principles for advancing and halting the army?"

Wu Qi answered: "Avoid stationing at 'Heaven's Furnace' or 'Dragon's Head'. 'Heaven's Furnace' is the mouth of a deep valley. 'Dragon's Head' is the top of a high mountain. The left army should hold the Green Dragon Banner; the right army should hold the White Tiger Banner. The front should hold the Vermilion Bird Banner; the back should hold the Mysterious Military Banner and the central army should use banners to command the whole army. When considering whether to engage in combat, determine the wind direction. If upwind, yell and charge with the wind, if downwind, it is best to maintain your formation and await the opportunity to attack."

武侯问道："军队前进、停止，有一定的原则吗？"
吴起答道："不要在「天灶」或「龙头」停止。所谓「天灶」，就是大山谷的谷口；所谓「龙头」，就是大山的顶端。指挥军队，左军必用青龙旗，右军必用白虎旗，前军用朱雀旗，后军用玄武旗，而中军用招摇旗在上方指挥，部队在下面跟着信号行动。临战前，还要观测风向，顺风时乘势鼓噪而进，逆风时就坚守阵地，待机破敌。"

Maintenance of Horses

Lord Wu asked: "How should we care for our horses?"

Wu Qi replied: "The stables should be clean and comfortable. The horses should be given appropriate feed and water. Feeding should continue until they are neither too hungry nor too full. In the winter, they should have warm stables and during the summer, cool stables. Their manes and hair should be kept trimmed and their hooves properly tended. They should be trained to be familiar with all sights and sounds of battle so that they will not be easily startled. They should practice galloping and pursuit, learning to exercise restraint in advancing and halting. The bonds between the horses and the men should be strong before the horses can be employed.

"The equipment, such as saddles, bridles, bits and reins must be strong and durable. Usually, the horses are injured either at the start of war, or towards the ending. Similarly, they are either injured by hunger or by overfeeding. When the sun is setting and the road is still long, the men should alternate riding and walking in turns, for it is better for the men to be slightly weary than to tire the horses. This will allow for easy escape should the enemy attack unexpectedly. Understanding this will allow one to travel without severe hindrance or undue worry."

武侯问道："驯养马有什么要领？"
吴起回答说："一定要使马匹处所舒适，喝水吃草要合适，饥饱要有节制。冬天要保持马房的温暖，夏天要使它凉爽通风。随时剪刷马鬃，细心为它铲蹄钉掌，并训练它熟悉各种声音和颜色，使其不致惊骇，还要让它练习奔驰最追逐和熟悉前进和停止的动作。须做到人马互相熟悉，然后才能使唤它。驾车和骑马的工具，如马鞍、笼头、嚼子、缰绳等物。一定要完好坚牢。一般来说，马匹不是伤于使用之后，就是伤于之初；不是伤于饥饿，就是伤于过饱。当天色已晚而路途尚远时，应当骑马与步行交替进行。宁可让人疲劳一些，千万不要使马过度疲劳。要让马儿常保余力，以防备敌人的袭击。能够懂得这些道理的，就能让自己横行天下。"

Part 2

Chapter 1 - Selection of Generals

Wu Qi said: "Only a person who has both military capabilities and civility can be the commander of an army. He must be one who is strict and flexible as well. Normally, when people appraise generalship, they usually focus on courage. However, courage is but one of the many required characteristics of a general. Being only courageous, one would rashly rush into battle without a proper consideration for the gains and loss. Such action is not acceptable.

"The affairs the general must manage are five.

1. Control
2. Preparation
3. Commitment
4. Caution
5. Regulation

"Control is a matter of governing the masses, just as one controls the few. Preparation means always being ready to give battle; even during the journey to the battleground, always be prepared to be ambushed. Commitment means entering combat without any concern for one's life. Caution means that even after conquering, one maintains the same control and attitude as if just entering a battle. Regulation means that laws and orders are kept to a minimum and are not abrasive. The proper form of behavior for a general is to accept command without declining, destroy the enemy, and only afterward speak about returning. Thus when the army goes forth, a proper general will be determined to die in victory rather than live in disgrace."

吴起说：" 文武兼备的人，才能胜任军队的将领。能刚柔并用的人，才可以统兵作战。一般人评论将领，往往只看到他的勇敢，其实勇敢对一个将领来说，不过是应该具备的若干条件之一。只有勇气的人，必定轻率应战，轻易与敌交战而不顾及利害，是不可取的。所以，将领应当谨慎的五件事：一是理，二是备，三是果，四是戒，五是约。所谓理，就是治理众多的军队如同治理少数军队一样；所谓备，就是指挥军队出动就像随时会见到敌人一样的戒备；所谓果，就是临敌交战时不考虑个人生死；所谓戒，就是即使打了胜战，还是如同初战那样谨慎；所谓约；就是法令简明而不繁琐。此外，接受任命决不推辞，击败敌人后才说班师回朝的话，这是将领应该遵守的准则。所以，将领从率军出征那一天起，就抱定了只有光荣牺牲，决不忍辱偷生的决心。"

The Book of Wuzi – Wu Qi

Four Areas to Note & Characteristics of a Good General

Wu Qi said: "In warfare there are four vital points which a ruler must give careful consideration; these are: morale, terrain, covert affairs and strength. The vital point for good morale is that control and management of the army's movement lies entirely in the hands of one general alone. With only ten men at a mountain route where the road is narrow and perilous, a general can stop an army of thousands; that is a vital point of terrain. Being able to make full use of spies, to use light cavalry to harass the enemy, to sow discord between the enemy ruler and his officials so that and the higher ranks and lower ranks reproach each other, such is the vital point of covert affairs. When the chariots have been fitted with strong axles and secure pins; when the boats have been fitted with proper rudders and oars; when the officers and men have been thoroughly trained and are familiar with all the formations; and when the horses have been trained in pursuit and maneuvering, such is the vital point of strength.

"Only one who knows how to accomplish these four is qualified to be a general. Moreover he must be respected by his subordinates; able to calm the masses and able to frighten the enemy with his reputation alone. His reputation for virtue, benevolence, courage and decisiveness must be beyond reproach. When he issues an order, no one must dare to disobey him or rebel against him. With such a general, the state will grow strong and prosper; without such, the state will perish. This is what is called a good general."

吴起说："大凡用兵打战，有四个应当注意的关键；一是掌握士气，二是利用地形"，三是善于谋略，四是发挥兵力。三军之众百万之师，掌握轻重缓急，在于将帅一人，这就是掌握士气的关键；狭险的道路，名山要塞，十人防守，千人不能通过，这就是利用地形的关键；善于使用间谍，用轻骑频频搔扰敌人，以分散其兵，使敌人君臣不和，上下互相责怪，这就是善于谋事的关键；战车及其零件十分牢固，战船及其橹桨十分结实，士卒熟悉战阵，战马善于驰骋，这就是发挥兵力的关键。懂得这四个关键，才可以担任将领。而且它的威信、品德、仁爱、勇敢，都必须足以为全军之表率，而且能安抚士众，威慑敌人，决断疑难。他发布命令，部下不敢违背，所到之处，敌人不敢抵抗。得到这样的将才，国家就会强盛；失去他，国家就要灭亡。这就叫良将。"

Characteristics & Importance of Good Communication

Wu Qi said: "Good communication is of vital importance. The different drums, gongs and bells are the means to impress the ear; flags, banners, pennants are the means to impress the eye; and prohibitions, orders, punishments and fines are the means to impress the mind. Since the ear is impressed by sounds, the sounds must be clear and loud. Since the eye is impressed by color, the colors must be discriminating and bright. Since the mind is impressed by penalties, they have to be strict and impartial. If these three means of communication are not well established, the army will invariably be defeated. Thus it is said that wherever the general's banners go, the troops will go, and wherever the general points, everyone will attack without concern for his life."

吴起说："鼙鼓金铎是用来威慑耳朵；旌旗麾帜是用来威慑眼睛；禁令刑罚是用来威慑军心。耳朵听命于声音，不可不清脆响亮；眼睛听命于颜色，不可不鲜明；军心受制于刑法，刑罚不可不威严。三者如果不确立，虽有国家，必定被敌人打败。所以将领旌旗所在的地方，没有不依命令而行的；将领指向的地方，没有不拼死前进的。"

Knowing the Enemy General

Wu Qi said: "In general, it is essential to know the enemy commander and to be able to evaluate his ability. Depending on the situation, one may use deceits to achieve good results without much effort. If an enemy general is stupid and trusting he can be deceived and entrapped. If he is greedy and insensitive to honor, he can be given gifts and bribed. If he is indecisive and changes his mind easily, you can devise plans to labor and tire him. If his upper ranks are wealthy and arrogant and the lower ranks are poor and resentful, it will be easy to sow discord among them. If their maneuvers are hesitant and the troops have are poorly directed, they may be frightened into running away. If the officers dislike the commanding general and desire to return home, you should block off the easy roads and leave the treacherous ones open. Then they can then be attacked and captured. If the terrain over which they can advance is easy and their only route of retreat is difficult, wait for them to advance. If the terrain over which they must advance is difficult but the retreat route is easy, they can be pressed and attacked. If they encamp on low wetlands where there is no way for the water to drain off, you should pin them down and wait for heavy rain to flood and drown them. If they encamp in wild marsh or in fields that are dense with dry vegetation, where strong winds blow, you can use fire to destroy them. If the enemy remains encamped and undisturbed for a long period of time, the officers may allow discipline to become slack and negligently let their guard down, then you may defeat them with a surprise attack."

吴起说："一般来说，作战最重要的是，一定要预先探知敌人的将领是谁，观察其才能。根据情况，运用计谋，不废力气而大功告成。敌将愚昧而轻信于人的，可以使欺骗的手段诱惑他。敌将贪婪而不顾名誉，可以用金钱收买。敌将轻率而无谋略能力，可以使疲劳战术使他困顿。敌人上级军官富裕骄横，下级吏卒贫困而怨愤，可以用离间的手段来分化他。敌人进退忧疑不定，部队无所适从，可以用震撼的方式吓退他。士卒藐视其将领而思家，可以阻断平坦大道而开放险阻之路，引而截击消灭。敌人进路平易而退路艰难，可以让他前来并消灭他。敌人进路艰难而退路平易，可以逼近猛击他。敌人驻扎在低洼潮湿的地方，水道不通、大雨连日，可以放水淹他。敌人驻扎荒郊野泽、杂草丛生、环境污秽而常起风的地方，可以使用火攻烧死他。敌人久住一个地方而没有移动，官兵懈怠、戒备疏忽，可以视机偷袭他。"

Testing the Enemy General

Lord Wu asked: "If our two armies are facing each other and I do not know the enemy general, what methods can I employ to learn about him and his abilities?"

Wu Qi replied: "Test him with a probing attack. Send some shock troops with orders to withdraw after light initial contact. When the enemy responds to the attack, and the shock troops withdraw, the actions of the enemy troops will disclose the ability of the general. When they pursue our troops, if they move and stop in unison and their formations are well preserved; if they feign being unable to catch up; if when they are offered easy gains, they pretend not to realize it, their commander is termed as a 'wise general'. You should not engage him.

"If their troops should respond to the feigned attack by yelling and screaming, with their flags and banners in disarray, with some troops moving of their own accord with their weapons not held properly; and when they pursue, they pursue in haste, as though they are afraid they might not capture our men, or when they see an advantage they appear to be afraid of not gaining it, this is the mark of a 'stupid general'. Although his troops may be many, he can be engaged and taken."

武侯问道："两国对崎，不知敌将的才能，我想调查清楚，用什么办法呢？" 吴起答道："让地位低而勇敢的战士，率领轻装精锐的小部队去试探攻击敌人，务必要败退，不要求胜，然后观察敌人出战的行动。如果敌人的进退行止有条不紊，追击假装追不上，见到战利品假装没看见，这样的将领是有智谋的，，不要和他交战。如果敌人喧哗吵嚷，旌旗混乱，士卒行动不统一，兵器横七竖八，追我军唯恐不及，，见利唯恐不得，这样的将领是愚昧的，敌军众多，仍然可俘虏敌将。"

Chaos and Communication

Lord Wu asked: "Even though our chariots are sturdy, our horses well-bred, our generals courageous and our troops strong; and then they are suddenly confronted by the enemy, our army is thrown into chaos, what can be done?"

Wu Qi replied: "The general who commands the army must maintain discipline during daylight by the use of flags, banners and pennants to relay orders; and at night by the use the gongs, drums, horns and whistles. When the flags signal left, the troops should move left. When the flags signal right, they should move right. When the drum is beaten, they should advance and when the gongs are sounded, they should retreat. At the first sound of the horn, they should advance. At the second sound of the horn, they should reassemble. If anyone disobeys an order, he should be executed at once. Then, the officers and soldiers will not dare to disobey and order. Only in this way, will the army learn discipline and submit to authority. In combat, no enemy will be stronger nor will any defense remain impregnable."

武侯问："战车坚牢，马匹精良，将领勇猛，士卒强悍，突然遭遇敌军，军队顿时混乱，应该怎么办？"

吴起回答："一般指挥军队作战的方法是，白天用旌旗幡帜，夜里用金鼓笳笛。旗帜指挥向左则左，指挥向右则右，擂鼓即前进，鸣金就停止。第一次吹响笳笛就前进，第二次就集合。如有不服从命令的，就依法斩首。这样，三军就会听从指挥，畏服威严，士卒不敢违法，打起来就没有不能战胜的强敌，也没有不能攻破的坚阵。"

The Book of Wuzi – Wu Qi

Chapter 2 - Responding to Changes in War

When Outnumbered by the Enemy

Lord Wu asked: "What should we do if our troops are outnumbered?"

Wu Qi replied: "You should avoid engaging them on open flat terrain. Instead you should attack them in narrow quarters. Thus it is said, for one to attack ten, a narrow path is advantageous. For ten to attack one hundred, a deep ravine is superb. For hundreds to attack thousands, a dangerous pass is excellent. With only a small number of troops, you should endeavor to ambush your enemy on a narrow road while sounding the war drums and gongs. Even with superior numbers, they will be startled. Thus it is said, large numbers of troops are best employed in open flat terrain; smaller numbers of troops, are best employed on difficult confined terrain."

武侯又问:"如果敌众我寡,怎么办呢?"
吴起答道:"避免与它在平坦的地形上作战,要尽量在险要的地方拦击他们。所以,以一击十,没有比利用狭隘地形更好的;以十击百,没有比利用险要地形更好的;以千击万,没有比利用阻绝地形更好的。如果用少量的兵力,突然出击,在狭隘的道路上击鼓鸣金,敌人即便有众多的兵力,莫有不惊慌混乱的。因此,要指挥众多兵力作战,务必选择平坦的地形;要运用少数兵力打战,务必选择险要的地形。"

How to Win against a Strong Enemy

Lord Wu asked: "If the enemy forces are numerous, well trained and courageous; if there are dangerous high grounds behind them, if there are mountains on the right and a river on the left; if the enemy is well fortified and has many crossbows in defensive positions; if they are as steady a mountain when they withdraw; if they are like torrential rain when they attack; if their rations and supplies are plentiful, this makes them formidable. What can be done?"

Wu Qi replied: "This is a serious problem. An enemy such as this cannot be overcome by force alone, but by only by wise plans. By assembling one thousand chariots, ten thousand cavalry, and an appropriate number of foot soldiers and then dividing them into five groups, with each group traversing a different route, the enemy will certainly be confused and mystified by our actions. If the enemy has strengthened his defenses to stabilize the morale of his troops, we should send an emissary to inveigh him to surrender. If he listens to our appeals, he will abandon his position and leave. If he does not listen, he will kill our emissary and burn our treaties.

"In this event, we should use our five divisions to engage the enemy on five fronts all at once. Should they attempt to flee, we should not give chase. If we cannot defeat them by sheer force, we should feign a retreat to entice their troops to give chase. If they should take the bait, we should counterattack with one division engages their front, with another division moving to cut off their rear while our other two divisions flank them. If our five divisions strike simultaneously, we will certainly gain the advantage. In this way, we can attack the strong."

武侯又问道:"假使敌军人马众多、训练有素而且十分勇敢,背后依附着险要的高地,右面有山,左面临水,深沟高垒,又以劲弩固守阵地,后退时像山一样,前进时像风雨一样急速,粮食充足难以和它长期对抗,该怎么办呢?"

吴起答道:"这是一个重大问题啊!不是仅靠车骑的武力就能解决,而是需要高明的智慧来谋取。如果能装备战车千辆、骑兵万人,加上一定数量的步兵,分为五支军队。而五支军队各成一路,形成五路踪队,向五个方向前进,敌人必然因此产生疑惑,不知我方意图。敌人如果坚守阵地以稳定军心,便立刻派出军使去观察其动向。如果敌人听我劝说,便会撤兵离去;如果敌人不听劝说,反而杀我军使,烧我军书,我军则兵分五路进攻,打胜了不要穷追,不胜则急速撤退。如果要假装败退诱敌,则以一军稳妥行动,与之激战,一军从正面牵制敌人,一军断其后路,另外两队先衔枚而进,悄悄地左右两侧,袭击敌人据守的地方。这样五军合击,必然形成有利的形势,这就是攻击强敌的办法。"

When Surrounded by the Enemy

Lord Wu asked: "If the enemy is approaching, we have no way to retreat and our soldiers are frightened. What should be done?"

Wu Qi replied: "The way to deal with this situation, if we have the strength of numbers, is to divide ourselves and surround them. If we are outnumbered, we should concentrate our troops and continue attacking the enemy relentlessly. Then, even if his army is numerous, he can be defeated."

武侯问道:"但敌人逐渐逼近我军,我军想摆脱他们可是没去路,士卒都很恐慌,这怎么办呢?"

吴起答道:"应付这种情况,如果我众敌寡,可以分兵包围敌军;如果敌众我寡,可以集中兵力袭击它,不断地袭击它,如此一来,敌人虽多也可以制服。"

When Caught in Unfavorable Terrain

Lord Wu asked: "If I should encounter the enemy in a place such as a deep valley with dangerous terrain all around and I am outnumbered, what should be done?"

Wu Qi replied: "Dangerous terrain like hilly regions, forests, valleys, deep mountains and vast wetlands, should be crossed quickly, you depart from them promptly. Do not tarry. If you should encounter the enemy in high mountains or deep valleys, you should first beat the drums and attack the enemy with your archers and crossbowmen, taking prisoners if possible, while observe the enemy's formation. If the enemy's army is seen to be in chaos, do not hesitate to attack with your main body of troops."

武侯问道:"如果在溪谷之间与敌军相遇,旁边都是险阻的地形,敌众我寡,这怎么办?"
吴起答道:"遇到丘陵、森林、谷地、深山、大泽,要迅速通过,不得迟缓。如果在高山深谷地带与敌突然相遇,一定要先击鼓呐喊并乘势攻击敌人,再使用弓箭向前挺进,一面射杀,一面掳掠,同时仔细观察敌人的阵势,一旦发现敌军混乱,就毫不迟疑地发动攻击。"

When Caught in a Valley

Lord Wu asked: "If when we are in a narrow confined valley with high mountains on both the left and right, the enemy unexpected attacks us and we cannot advance or retreat, what should be done?"

Wu Qi replied: "This is called 'valley' warfare. It is difficult because even if your troops are numerous, they cannot be effective. You should summon your most talented officers and direct them to confront the enemy with the most nimble footed soldiers who are equipped with sharp weapons. Your chariots and cavalry should be concealed, several miles away if possible. Then, if they cannot see our chariots and cavalry, the enemy will not dare to attack for fear of ambush. They will then adopt a solid defense. You should immediately display your flags and array your banners, to allow time to withdraw outside the valley and encamp. Trapped inside the valley, the enemy will be frightened and we may use our chariots and cavalry to harass them continuously, permitting them no rest. This is the way to conduct valley warfare."

武侯问道:"如果左右都是高山,地形很狭窄,突然遇袭,既不敢前进,又不敢后退,该怎么办?"
吴起回答道:"这叫谷地战。兵力虽多也用不上,应该挑选精锐的士卒与敌对抗,用轻捷善走的步兵手持锐器作为先锋,把战车和骑兵分别埋伏在四周,与前锋相距约几里路,让敌人没见到战车和骑兵,而知道有伏兵,必然坚守阵地,不敢轻易进退。此时,我军张旗列旍,指挥部队走出山外扎营。这样敌人必生畏惧,我军则在用车骑袭击,使其不能休息。这就是谷地战的原则。"

Fighting in Wet Terrain

Lord Wu asked: "If we should encounter the enemy in wet terrain such as a watery marsh where chariot wheels sink down to the axles, where our chariots and cavalry are floundering and we are not equipped with boats and marine equipment, what should be done?"

Wu Qi said: "This is called the 'water' warfare. It is best to not employ the chariots and cavalry; have them remain at the side. You should seek a high vantage point to survey the situation. If you can discern the extent of the wet conditions; fathom its expanse, depth and movement, you may then conceive a plan for victory. For example, if the enemy begins to cross the water, you can advantageously attack when half of his troops have crossed."

武侯问道："假如我军在大水沼泽地带遇敌，战车都淹没，车骑也有被大水吞没的危险，同时又没有舟楫的设备。，进退两难，怎么办？"
吴起答道："这叫水战。水战用不上战车和骑兵，只好把战车和骑兵暂留一旁，一定要登上高处四面瞭望，观察水势，知道水势的大小、深浅、宽窄，然后才能想办法出奇制胜。敌人如果渡水而来，乘其军渡到一半时，迫近迎击。"

Wet and Dry Weather

Lord Wu asked: "When it has been raining continuously with the horses and the chariots stuck in the mud, we have been surrounded by the enemy and our troops are terrified, what should be done?"

Wu Qi said: "In general, it is best to suspend operations when the ground is wet and you cannot employ your chariots. Wait for the weather to clear and for the ground to dry. Avoid the enemy, calm and rest your troops. Seek higher ground since chariots are of more value on high ground which will dry more quickly than low ground. Only deploy chariots, whether advancing or halting, on dry ground. If the enemy withdraws, pursue them by following their tracks."

武侯问道："如果遇到阴雨连绵，车马举足艰难，而且四面受到敌人包围，全军恐慌，这怎么办？"
吴起答道："凡用兵车作战，一般在阴雨天气和泥泞的地面上就要停止行动，等到天晴而地面干燥时才行动。兵车利于高地行动，不利于低洼之地。作战的时候，迅速奔驰要用坚固的兵车，不论前进或停止，都要依从上述原则。如果敌人应战，要沿着它的车迹追逐。"

Fighting Plunderers

Lord Wu asked: "If a raiding band of soldiers should suddenly appear, plundering our lands and fields, seizing our cattle and horses, what should be done?"

Wu Qi said: "When a raiding force suddenly appears, you should not immediately attack them; you must first determine their number and strength. Take a defensive position and reconnoiter the enemy forces. After their raids, as they struggle with their loot, their armor will begin to feel heavy and they become afraid. They will try to withdraw quickly to avoid retaliation. This will result in stragglers, dividing their forces. You can then pursue and capture them piecemeal."

武侯问道:"如果残暴的敌寇突然来袭,掠夺庄稼,抢走牛羊,这怎么办?"吴起答道:"敌寇突然来袭,一定要考虑它实力的强弱,应先避其锐气,先作防守,不要急于应战。待它傍晚撤退时,其装备必然变得沉重不便,心里必有所恐,为求急于退还,必有不相接连的地方。这时我军如果乘机追击,就可以歼灭它。"

After Conquering Cities

Wu Qi said: "In general, there are a set of principle to follow after conquering an enemy's city. Immediately upon conquering the city, you should take charge of their public buildings, take control of the city's supplies and make use of the former bureaucrats for administration. You should prevent your soldiers from looting. Issue orders that troops are not to cut down trees, destroy houses, and take the grain, slaughter animals, or burn people's supplies. This will demonstrate to the populace that you do not have bad intentions. You should accept those who surrender and peacefully settle them."

吴起说:"一般围攻敌人的城池有一套基本原则,就是城池已被我军攻破后,应当分别进驻它的官府,控制和使用其原来的官吏,接管它的器材物资。军队所到之处,不可砍伐树木,不可毁坏建筑物,也不可掠夺老百姓的粮食、宰杀其牲畜、烧毁或积聚财物。应向百姓表明我军无残害无辜之意。如果请求投降归顺的,应允许并加以优抚。"

Military Strategy Classics of Ancient China

Chapter 3 - Motivating the Talented

After Conquering Cities

Lord Wu asked: "Is it adequate for victory to make punishments severe and rewards clear?"

Wu Qi replied: "As to these matters of severity and clarity, no can have all the answers, but it is certain that these alone cannot be totally relied upon. When you issue orders and the people willingly follow them; when you raise the army and mobilize the masses; when the people take pleasure in going to battle; when engaging the enemy, the people take honor in fighting to the death; these are what a ruler of men can rely upon."

Lord Wu inquired further: "How does one attain such conditions?"

Wu Qi replied: "It is necessary to recognize men of accomplishment. You should identify such men and honor them with a grand feast. You should also invite men who have not accomplished anything in order to stimulate them."

Thereupon Lord Wu had the ancestral temple prepared for a grand feast with sitting mats set out in main hall, arranged in three tiers for the officers and chief officials. Those who were distinguished by great achievement were seated in the first tier and feasted on the finest food and with the finest cutlery. Those who ranked next in accomplishment were seated in the middle tier, and feasted on fine food with less lavish vessels. Those who had not accomplished anything noteworthy were seated in the last tier, and feasted on fine food with ordinary utensils. When the feast was over and they came out of the temple, Lord Wu made it a point to honor the parents and families of the meritorious outside the temple gate, again according to their accomplishments. Annually he sent emissaries to call on the families of those who had died in service of the country, and bestowed aid on their parents. In so doing, he showed that they would not be forgotten. After performing such actions for three years, Qin happened to mobilize its army against Wei. When Wei's officers heard about it, without waiting for any official orders, they put on their armor, assembled and engaged the enemy.

Subsequently, Lord Wu summoned Wu Qi and said: "We have seen the results of what you previously told me about honoring accomplishment."

Wu Qi replied: "I have heard that 'to each his own strength and weakness.' Morale has its highs and lows. I humbly request that my Lord allocate fifty thousand previously undistinguished men to me and allow me lead them against the enemy. If we lose, we might be considered to a joke by his Lordship. Allow me to explain by drawing an analogy: if there were a villain who had been sentenced to death, but had escaped and was in hiding and one thousand men had been sent to look for him, they would most likely just look around aimlessly for him and make no serious attempt to find him. They would do this because each would be afraid that the villain would do him personal harm. Thus a man who has total disregard death can frighten a thousand. Now if I may assemble a body of fifty thousand such men, gather them into a single murderous unit, and personally lead them against the Qin, we surely will make it difficult for them."

Lord Wu agreed to Wu Qi's request, granting him five hundred strong chariots and three thousand cavalry. Wu Qi's band destroyed the Qin's army of one half a million troops by following the policy of encouraging the officers and men.

On the eve of the battle Wu Qi addressed the troops: "Everyone, including aides and officers, must personally confront and capture the enemy chariots, cavalry and infantry. If our chariots do not make prisoners of the enemy's chariots, if our cavalry does not make prisoners of the enemy's cavalry, if our infantry does not make prisoners of the enemy's infantry, then even if we command an overwhelming victory, no one will be credited with any achievement." On the day of the battle, Wu Qi's military greatness shook the world.[6]

武侯问道："刑罚和奖赏都很严明，是否足以打胜仗？"
吴起答道："关于赏罚严明的问题，臣不能尽到其详。但是，我认为不能完全依靠刑罚严明就可以打胜仗。只有发号施令，人人都乐意听从；兴师动众，人人都乐意出战；与敌交战。人人都乐意效死，这三项才是君主能够打胜仗的依靠。"
武侯又问道："如何才能做到乐闻、乐战、乐死者三点？"
吴起答道："君主可以选拔有功的将士设宴慰劳，让未曾建功的人也参加，并给予鼓励。"
于是武侯在宗庙的大殿设置了席位，分前、中、后三排宴请士大夫。建立上等功绩的人坐前排，宴席上加上贵重礼器；建次等功绩的人坐中排，席上的食品和礼器依次减等；未曾立功的人坐后排，席上无礼器。宴会结束以后从宗庙出来，又在庙门之外赏赐有功人员的父母妻室，也以功绩大小分别等级。凡是为国捐躯的将士家庭，朝廷每年派遣使者慰问、赏赐他们的父母，表明朝廷永远不忘烈士的功勋。此法实行了三年，碰上秦军来犯，兵临西河国境，魏国的将士知道了这个消息，不等朝廷发出号令，数万人便纷纷披甲戴盔投军上阵，奋勇杀敌。
武侯于是召见吴起，对他说道："你以前所说的『励士之道』近日见到成效了。"

---

[6] Wu Qi was later exiled from Wei, but was welcomed by King Dao of Chu (楚悼王), and appointed as Prime Minister. He implemented reforms aimed at changing the corrupt government dominated by the old nobility. Old nobles plotted to assassinate Wu Qi at King Dao's funeral. Wu Qi spotted the assassins and rushed to the side of King Dao's body. He was killed, but many arrows also struck the dead King. The new King Su (楚肃王), furious at his father's body being mutilated, ordered all nobles involved to be executed, along with their families.

吴起回答道："臣听说一个人的才能各有所短，也各有所长；士气民气有时旺盛，有时衰微。君王不妨试着派出毫无功绩的五万人，请允许我率领他们抵御秦军。倘若战而不胜，那就会被诸侯取笑，并且对时局失去举足轻重的地位。这就好比假使有一个犯了死罪的贼寇，潜伏在荒野之中，派一千人去追捕，但这一千人都瞻前顾后，原因何在呢？这是因为大家都怕这个贼寇会突然出其不意地伤害自己。所以一个舍命拼死，足以威慑千人。现在我把五万大军集合成像那个犯了死罪贼寇一样，率领他们去讨伐敌军，威力自然难以抵抗。"

于是武侯听从了吴起的建议，另拨战车五百辆，骑兵三千人，一战而击败秦军五十万，这都是励士之道的功效啊！

作战开始的前一天，吴起对三军发布命令，说："各级士吏听从命令，与敌人的车兵、骑兵、步兵作战，如果我方的车兵无法俘虏敌方的车兵，骑兵无法俘虏敌方的骑兵，步兵无法俘虏敌方的步兵，，全军虽然最终打了胜仗，也无功绩可言。"

所以开战那一天，下达的命令虽然极为简略，却威震天下。于是武侯听从了吴起的建议，另拨战车五百辆，骑兵三千人，一战而击败秦军五十万，这都是励士之道的功效啊！

作战开始的前一天，吴起对三军发布命令，说："各级士吏听从命令，与敌人的车兵、骑兵、步兵作战，如果我方的车兵无法俘虏敌方的车兵，骑兵无法俘虏敌方的骑兵，步兵无法俘虏敌方的步兵，，全军虽然最终打了胜仗，也无功绩可言。"

所以开战那一天，下达的命令虽然极为简略，却威震天下。

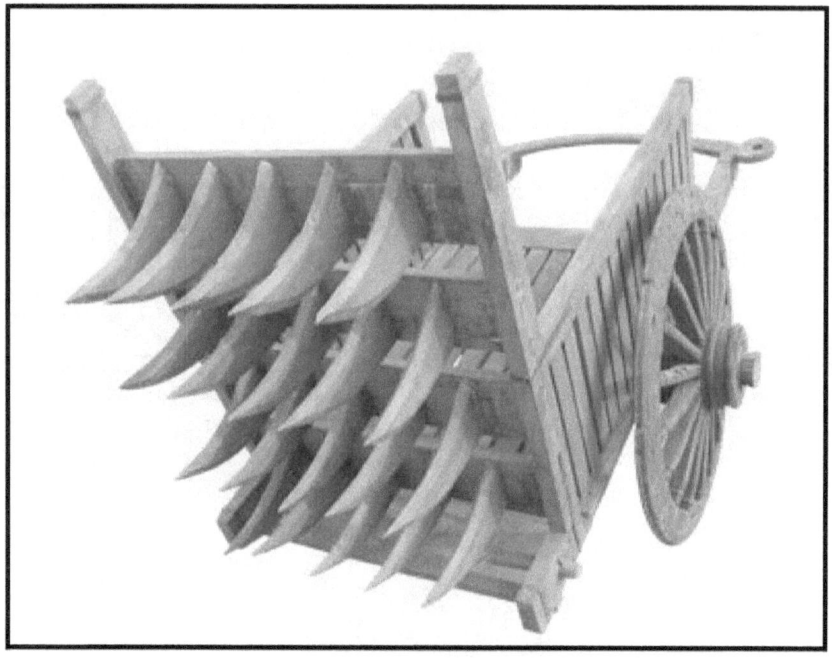

Spear-tipped cart

The Book of Wei Liaozi

Wei Liao

尉缭子

The Book of Wei Liaozi *(尉缭子) is a text attributed to Wei Liao which considers military strategy, while discussing both a civil and a military approach to conducting state affairs. It is sometimes also referred to as Wei Liaozi's Art of War. Recommendations are included for ruling over the army, managing differing types of cities, and how to preserve the state. Also discussed are the judicial responsibilities of both the general and the ruler. It is believed to have been written during the late Warring States period (c. 400 BC).*

Chapter 1
Heavenly Positions

Verse 1.1

King Hui of Liang State asked Wei Liaozi: "Is it true that the Yellow Emperor, through punishment and Virtue, could achieve a hundred victories without defeat?"

Wei Liaozi replied: "Punishment was employed to attack the rebellious, and Virtue was employed to stabilize peace. This is not what is referred to as 'Heavenly Positions' (astrology), auspicious times, yin & yang, or the appearance of comets. The Yellow Emperor's victories were a matter of human effort; that is all. Why do we say that? Now if there is a fortified city, and one attacks it from the east and west but cannot take it, and attacks it from the south and north but cannot take it, can it be that all four directions fail to accord with the auspicious moment? If you still cannot take it, it is because the walls are high, the moats deep, the weapons and implements fully prepared, the materials and grains accumulated in great quantities, and their soldiers are unified. If the wall is low, the moats shallow, and the defenses weak then it can be taken. From this perspective, 'moments', 'seasons' and 'Heavenly Positions' are not as important as human effort."

梁惠王问尉缭子说:""黄帝的兵书《刑德》的学说,据说根据它来用兵就可以百战百胜,有这回事吗?"

尉缭子回答说：" 所谓刑德，是说用武力征伐敌人，用仁德安定天下，不是指天官、时日、阴阳、向背等而说的。黄帝所说的，不过是强调人的作用罢了。为什么这样说呢？譬如现在有座城，从东西两方进攻，不能取胜；从南北两方进攻，也不能取胜，难道四方面都没有适应吉利时辰的方位吗？其所以攻不下来，是因防守者的城垣高，城壕深，武器装备完善，资财粮食充足，豪杰之士同心协力的原故。如果它的城垣低，战壕浅，守备弱，就能攻下来了。由此看来，相信天官时日，不如充分发挥人的作用。

Verse 1.2

"According to Heavenly Positions, deploying troops with water toward the rear is termed as 'isolated terrain'. Deploying troops facing a long ridge is termed as 'abandoning the army'. When King Wu attacked King Zhou of Shang, he deployed troops with the rear facing the Ji River and facing the ridge. With 22,500 troops, King Wu managed to defeat King Zhou's army of hundreds of thousands, and destroyed the Shang Dynasty. King Wu did not accord with Heavenly Positions."

"Chu's general Gong Zi Xin (Kung-tsu Hsin) was about to engage the State of Qi when the comet appeared with its tail pointing to the State of Qi. People believed that State of Qi would be victorious, and would never be defeated, so they refused to attack the State of Qi. Gong Zi Xin said: 'What does a comet know? To fight someone with a broom, of course we use the handle to fight to achieve victory.' The next day, Gong Zi Xin engaged Qi and achieved resounding victory. The Yellow Emperor said: 'Putting spirits and ghosts first is not as good as first investigating one's own knowledge.' This means that the Heavenly Positions are nothing compared to human effort."

按《天官》上，' 背水列阵是置军队于绝境，向坡列阵是把军队置于无用之地。'
但武王伐纣的时候，却背着济水，向着山坡列阵，以二万二千五百人，击败众多的纣军，灭亡了商朝，难道是纣王所布的阵势没有得到天官之利吗！楚将公子心与齐国作战，当时出现彗星，彗星的柄搦向齐国方面，有人认为柄所指的方向定会取得胜利，因而不能进攻。公子心说：' 彗星知道什么呢，用扫帚打人的，本来就应当倒转头来用柄去打才能取胜' 。第二天与齐国交战，果然大破齐军。黄立说：' 首先问神问鬼，不如首先问问自己的才智如何' 。与其说是天文星象的应验，不如说它是发挥了人的作用。

Chapter 2
Military Discussions

Verse 1

Measure the fertility and barrenness of the earth to decide where to build cities. Construct the city walls in accordance with the terrain. The size of the cities should be in accordance with the size of the population. The size of the population should be in accordance with the amount of grain available. When all three have been mutually determined, then internally, one can be solid in defense. And externally, one can be victorious in battle. Being victorious in battle externally is because one is well-prepared internally. Victory and preparations are mutually employed, like the halves of a tally exactly matching each other.

要衡量土地的肥瘠来确定建立城邑。城邑的兴建要和土地面积的大小相适应，城邑的大小要和人口的多少相适应，人口的多少要和粮食的供应相适应。三者互相适应，对内就可以进行固守，对外就可以战胜敌人。能够战胜敌人于国外，主要在于国内有充分的准备，胜利和准备的一致性，就象符节的相吻合一样，这是两者之间没有差异的原故。

Verse 2

Deployment of the army should be as secretive as the depths of the Earth; as obscure as the heights of Heaven, with a weak front but underneath lies great power. When the power is unleashed, one does not feel inadequate when the army is used vastly, or one does not feel vast when the army is used in a small manner. One who is enlightened about prohibitions, pardons, education and prevention will attract and settle displaced people, and bring more lands under cultivation. When the land is broad and under cultivation, the state will be wealthy; when the people are numerous and well-ordered, the state will be well governed. When the state is wealthy and well governed, although the people do not remove the blocks from the chariots, nor expose their armor, their military greatness instills order everywhere. Thus it is said that the army's victory stems from the political measures taken. When one is victorious without exposing his armor, it is the ruler's victory; when victory comes after deploying the army, it is the general's victory.

善于治兵的人，就像大地那样深藏不露，就像天空那样深邃莫测，表面无形无影却蕴藏着巨大的力量。作战时，大规模用兵不会感到兵力不足，小规模用兵也不会感到兵力过多。平时必须明确各种应兴应革的事项，对于流散的人民，应安托他们，对于没有利用的土地，应该充分利用起来。土地广大而又能充分利用，国家就富足；人民众多而又有良好的组织，国家就安定。富足而安定的国家，不必出动军队，凭借声威就可以使天下顺服。所以说，军事的胜利，取决于朝廷的政治措施。不使用武力就取得的胜利，是君主在政治上的胜利；经过战争而取得的胜利，是将帅在指挥上的胜利。

Verse 3

The army cannot be mobilized out of personal anger. If victory can be foreseen, then the troops can be raised. If victory cannot be foreseen, then the mobilization should be stopped. If trouble arises within a hundred miles, do not make preparation for a war that lasts a single day. If trouble arises within a thousand miles, do not make preparation for a war that lasts a single month. If the trouble lies within the country, do not make preparation for a war that lasts a single year.

进行战争，是不能意气用事的。预计有胜利的把握就采取行动；预计没有胜利的把握就坚决停止。祸乱发生在百里之内，不要只作一天的战斗准备；祸乱发生在千里之内，不要只作一月的战斗准备；祸乱发生在四海之内，不要只作一年的战斗准备。

Verse 4

As for the commanding general, above he is not constrained by Heaven; below he is not controlled by Earth; in the middle he is not managed by men. He should be composed so that he cannot be stimulated to anger. He should be pure so that he cannot be enticed by wealth. Now if the mind is deranged by emotions, the eyes are blind, and the ears are deaf: to lead men with these three perversities is difficult!

做将帅的人，必须上不受天时的限制，下不受地形的限制，中不受人为的限制。要气量宽宏，不可因刺激而发怒；要清正廉洁，不可被金钱所诱惑。如果任用态度轻狂，目光短浅，信息不灵的人来统帅军队，那就难于成功了。

Verse 5

Wherever a well-trained army ventures, whether it is along byways that wind about like sheep's intestines, along roads as bumpy as a saw's teeth, curling about the mountains, or entering a valley, it will be victorious. Whether deployed in a square formation or deployed in a round formation, it will be victorious.

A sturdy army is like the mountains, like the forests, like the rivers and great streams. A light force is like a roaring fire; like the earthen walls it presses upon them, like clouds it covers them. They cause the enemy's troops to be unable to disperse, and those who are dispersed, to be unable to reassemble. Those on the left are unable to rescue those on the right; those on the right are unable to rescue those on the left.

The soldiers should stand like trees; the effects of the crossbows should attack like the goat using its horn. Every man, without exception, should have high morale and display his courage. Casting off all doubts, fervently and determined, they go forth decisively.

训练有素的军队，在羊肠小道也能取胜，在高岩峻岭也能取胜，攀登高山也能取胜，深入谷地也能取胜。方阵也能取胜，园阵也能取胜。行动稳重时，要象山林那样沉着镇静，象江河那样一往无前；行助急骤时，要象火烧那样急剧猛烈，象墙倒那样有压顶之势，象云层履盖那样无可逃避。使集中的敌人来不及分散，分散的敌人来不及集中，左边的敌人来不及救援右边，右边的敌人来不及救援左边。军队刀枪剑戟如林立，万弩齐发如旋风，人人斗志昂扬，英勇果敢，一往无前地去决战决胜。

Chapter 3
Discussion of Regulations & Systems

Verse 1

As for the military arena, regulations must first be established. When regulations are established first, the soldiers will not be disordered. When the soldiers are not disordered, discipline will be well maintained. If wherever the gongs and drums direct them, 100 men all contend; when moving forward, penetrating the enemy's ranks and causing chaos among his formations, 1,000 men all strive; and to overturn the enemy's army and kill his generals, 10,000 men will raise their blades in unison. Thus no one under Heaven will be able to withstand them in battle.

凡是统率军队，必须预先建立各种制度。各种制度建立了，士卒就不会混乱。士卒不混乱，纪律就严明了。这样，命令一经发出，成百的人都尽力战斗。冲锋陷阵时，成千的人都尽力战斗。歼灭敌军时，成万的人都协力作战，这样，天下就没有任何力量能够与它抗衡了。

Verse 2

In antiquity, the soldiers were organized into squads of five and ten, the chariots into companies and rows. When the drums sounded and the pennants flew, it never happened that the first to scale the walls were not outstanding state soldiers of great strength! The first to die were also always outstanding state soldiers of great strength. If the enemy suffers a loss of one man and we lose a hundred, it enriches the enemy and greatly diminishes us! Through the ages, average generals have been unable to prevent this.

When conscripts have been assigned to the army, but they run off to their native places, or flee when they approach a battle, the harm caused by the deserters is great. Through the ages, average generals have been unable to prevent it.

What can kill men beyond a hundred paces are bows and arrows. What can kill a man within fifty paces are spears and halberds. When the general drums the advance but the officers and troops yell at each other, twist their arrows, breaking them, smash their spears, cradle their halberds, and find it advantageous to go to the rear; and when the battle commences and all these occur, it will be internally self-defeating. Through the ages, average generals have been unable to prevent this.

Soldiers breaking away from their squads of five and ten; chariots moving away from their companies and rows; indirect forces abandoning their generals and fleeing; the masses also running off; these are things which average generals through the ages have been unable to prevent. Now if a general can prevent these four situations, he will be able to traverse high mountains, cross over deep rivers, and assail strong formations. Being unable to prevent these four is like losing your boat and oars and crossing the Yangtze and Yellow rivers. It cannot be done.

古时，士兵有"什伍"的编制，战车有"偏列"的编制。当击鼓挥旗发起进攻时，首先登上敌人城堡的，往往只是那些乐于为日出力的勇士，首先战死的，也往往是那些为国出力的勇
士。如果只杀伤一个敌人而我军却损伤一百人，这就等于大大地加强了敌人而严重地损伤了自己，可是平庸的将领却不能避免。士兵应征入伍后，刚编入部队就逃亡回家，或者刚上战场就自行溃败，这就会出现大量的逃散伤亡，可是平庸的将领却不能制止。敌人在百步之外，就应当用弓箭杀伤他们；在五十步之内，就应当用矛、戟杀伤他们。但是将帅击鼓传令时，士兵们却互相吵闹，把箭、矛折断，把戈戟抛弃，面对敌人而畏缩不前，战斗中出现这些情况，就是自己先溃败了，可是平庸的将领却不能禁止。战斗时士兵脱离了队伍，战车脱离了"偏列"，机动部队抛弃他们的将领自行逃走，其他士兵也随之溃散，可是平庸的将领却不能制止。将帅如能制止这四种情况发生，那么高山可以攀登，深水可以跨越，坚固的阵地也可以摧破。如果不能防止这四种情况发生，要想战胜敌人，就好比没有船只而想渡
过江河一样，是不可能达到目的。

Verse 3

People do not take pleasure in dying, nor do they hate life, but if the commands and orders are clear, and the laws and regulations carefully detailed, you can make them advance. When, before combat, rewards are made clear, and afterwards punishments are made decisive, then when the troops move forth, they will be able to realize an advantage, and when they move, they will be successful.

人们本来并不是好死厌生的。只是由于号令严明，法制周详，才能使他们奋勇向前。既有明确的奖赏鼓励于前，又有坚决的惩罚督促于后，所以出兵就能获胜，行动就能成功。

Verse 4

Appoint a company commander for 100 men, a Sima (battalion commander) for 1,000 men, and a general for 10,000 men. This is how a small number can control a large number; a smaller authority can manage a large group of people. If they listen to my techniques of management of troops, he can control the whole army as well. If no single man can escape punishment, fathers will not dare conceal their sons and sons will not dare conceal their fathers, so how much more so the citizens of the state?

如今百人设一卒长，千人设一司马，万人设一将军，这是以少数人管辖多数人，以少数将吏去治理整个部队的事务。如果能听从我的统御方法，就可以驾驭三军之众。如果做到一个违犯者也不放过，就是父亲也不敢放过儿子，儿子也不敢放过父亲，何况对于一般的人呢！

Verse 5

If a warrior wields a sword to strike people in the marketplace, among 10,000 people, there will not be anyone who does not avoid him. If I say it is not that only one man is courageous, and that the 10,000 are useless, what is the reason? Being committed to dying and being committed to staying alive are not comparable. If you listen and use my techniques, you will find they are sufficient to cause the whole army to put their lives forward. No one will stand before them, no one will chase after them. They will be able to come and go without obstacles; the characteristic of an army that belongs to a king or hegemon.

一个亡命之徒，持剑在持市上杀人，众人没有不躲避他的。我认为这并不是由于这个人特别勇敢而众人都无能。为什么呢？因为抱必死决心的人和贪生怕死的人，本来是不相向的。如果依照我的办法行事，可以使三军之众，就象一个持剑的亡命之徒那样，前进时敌人不敢抵抗，后退时敌人不敢追击，而能做到进退无阻。能够进退无阻的军队，那就是图王称霸的军队了。

Verse 6

Who led a mass of 100,000 and no one under Heaven opposed him? Duke Huan. Who led a mass of 70,000 and no one under Heaven opposed him? Wu Qi. Who led a mass of 30,000 and no one under Heaven opposed him? Sun Tzu. Today among the armies led by commanders from the various feudal states, there is not one that does not reach a mass of 200,000 men. Yet they are unable to succeed in establishing their merit; it is because they do not understand prohibitions, pardons, education and prevention. If you make the ordinances clear so that one man will be victorious, then ten men will also thereby be victorious. Thus I say if you improve our weapons and equipment, nurture our martial courage, when you release our forces it will be like a bird attacking, like water rushing down a thousand-fathom valley.

Now, a state that finds itself in difficulty, sends its valuable treasure out with emissaries to other states, sends its beloved sons out as hostages, and cedes land along its borders. Although the troops coming to assist are said to have the strength of 100,000, but in actuality they do not exceed tens of thousands. When their troops come forth, there are no generals to whom the ruler has not said: 'Do not be the first to fight.' In reality, one cannot enter battle with them.

有统率十万军队而天下无敌的，是谁呢？是齐桓公。有统率七万军队而天下无敌的，是谁呢？是吴起。有统率三万军队而天下无敌的，是谁呢？是孙武子。现在各国一些杰出的将领，所统率的军队都不下二十万，其所以不能功成名就，就在于没有建立明确的奖惩制度。如果明确建立了这些制度，一个人取得胜利，就会带动十个人

取得胜利，十个人取得胜利，就会带动百人、千人、万人取得胜利。所以说，改善我们的武器装备，培养我们的战斗作风，军队一旦出动，就象鸷鸟捕食那样凶猛，像倾泻到深谷的急流那样势不可当。

如今有的国家遇到外患的时候，总是以贵重的珍宝作为礼品，以爱子作为人质，以国土割让给别人，用这些条件去乞求别国派兵援助，而派来的援军往往名为十万，其实不过几万罢了。而且当其出发的时候，他们的国君总是告诉他的将领说："不要在别人之前进入战斗"。他们是根本不可能为你奋力作战的。

Verse 7

If we want to manage the population within our borders, without the system of five, no one could order them. Through proper ordinances, the mass of 10,000 troops can then be used in battles. If such a mass has worn our uniform, eaten our food and still cannot emerge victorious, then it is not the fault of the soldiers. Rather, it is fault brought about internally. Even if we are aided by allied feudal states, and they behave like a slow horse, and the enemy acts like a strong horse, it would be like pitting a weak horse against a strong horse. How would it improve our disposition?

治理全国民众，没有什伍的制度，就没有谁能治理好他们。编成十万大军，就必能用它们去取胜。如果这些军队，穿了国家的衣服，吃了国家的粮食，战不能胜，守不能固，这不是士兵的罪过，而是由于军内没有建立良好的制度或指挥不当的缘故。在这种情况下，纵然有别国军队帮助作战，而敌人好象一匹飞驰的骏马，援兵却象一匹迟顿的劣马，劣马去和骏马较量，这怎能有助于我军的气势呢。

Verse 8

We should employ all resources available for our own use. We should study all the known regulations to create our own regulations. We should revise our commands and orders and make punishments and rewards clear. We should make clear that for those who do not engage in agriculture, there will be no means to eat; and for those who do not engage in battle or achieve battle merits, there will be no means to attain ranks. We should cause the people to compete to go out to the farms and into battle. Then we will remain invincible! Thus I say that when a command is promulgated, an order issued, its credibility will extend throughout the state.

利用天下的财富来充实我们的国力,参考天下的制度来修订我们的制度。整肃号令,严明赏罚,使天下都知道不耕种的人不能得食,无战功的人不能得爵。鼓励民众奋勇争先地投入生产和战斗,这样就可以天下无敌了。所以说,号令一经发出,就必须取信于民而风行全国。

Verse 9

If among the populace, there are those who say they can vanquish the enemy, do not allow them to speak idly but absolutely test their ability to fight. To look at people's lands and have a desire to gain them, to divide up other ruler's subjects and nourish them, one must be able to have the help of capable talents. If you are unable to bring in and employ your capable talents, but want to possess all lands, you must destroy armies and slay generals. In this way, even though you may be victorious in battle, the state will grow increasingly weak. Even though you gain territory, the state will be increasingly impoverished. All this proceeds from the state's bad regulations.

如果有人说他有战胜敌人的办法,可不能轻信他的空话,必须实践中考验他。要想兼并别国的土地,统治别国的人民,必须国内贤才辅佐。如果在国内没有贤才辅佐,
而想统一天下,必然招致兵败将亡的后果。即使侥幸获胜,国家也会因此而更加衰弱,即使攻占别国的土地,国家也会因此而更加贫困,这些都是由于国家制度有病,[不能选贤任能的缘故]。

Chapter 4
Combat Superiority

Verse 1

In general, in warfare, there are those who gain victory through the Way; those who gain victory through military greatness, and those who gain victory through strength. Holding careful military discussions and evaluating the enemy; causing the enemy morale to be lost and his forces to be disunited, so that even if his disposition is complete, he will not be able to employ it; this is victory through the Way. Being precise about laws and regulations, making rewards and punishment clear, improving weapons and equipment, causing the people to have minds totally committed to fighting; this is victory through military grandeur. Destroying armies and slaying generals, using all tools to attack the city, overwhelming the populace and seizing territory, returning only after being successful, this is victory through strength. When kings and feudal lords know these, their education in the three ways to victory will be complete.

战争有用道胜的，有用威胜的，有用力胜的。讲求军事准备，判明敌人虚实，设法促使敌人士气沮丧而内部分化，虽然军队的组织形式完整但却不能用来作战，这就是以道胜。审定法制，严明赏罚，改善武器装备，使人人都有必战的决心，这就是以威胜。击破敌军，斩杀敌将，使用各种攻城器械强攻敌人城邑，粉碎敌人防御，占领敌国土地，功成之后，班师回国，这就是以力胜。战争决策者明白这些，就能完全掌握三种胜利方式的具体运用了。

Verse 2

Now, the means by which the general fights is with the people; the means by which the people fight is their fighting spirit. When their fighting spirit is substantial they will fight; when their fighting spirit has been snatched away, they will run off. Before formation has been formed, before the soldiers have clashed, the means by which one overpowers the enemy are five:

1. Producing great strategy to pre-empt the enemy.
2. Giving the correct mandate to the correct person.
3. Being able to cross into an enemy's border.
4. Having a great defense, like deep moats and high walls.
5. Proper mobilizing, deploying, and applying punitive measures to the enemy.

In these five cases, first evaluate the enemy, and afterward move. In this way, you can attack their weakness and seize them.

One who excels at employing the army is able to seize men and not be seized by others. This requires wisdom. Orders unify the minds of the masses. When the masses are not understood by the general, the orders will have to be changed frequently. When orders are changed frequently, then even though orders are issued, the masses will not have faith in them. Thus the rule of thumb for giving commands is that small errors need not be rectified, minor doubts need not be cleared. Thus when those above do not issue doubtful orders, the masses will not listen to two different versions. When actions do not have any questionable aspects, the multitude will not have divided intentions. There has never been an instance where the people did not believe in the capability of their leader and the generals were still able to retain their strength. There has never been the case that the general did not make the masses voluntarily offer their services and still gain their services.

将军所赖以作战的是军队，军队所赖以作战的是士气。士气旺盛就勇于战斗，士气沮丧就会溃败。在军队还未行动，双方还未接触时就能够压倒敌人的条件有五个方面，一是朝廷的决策英明，二是将军选拔的人，三是进入敌境的迅速突然，四是本国防务的坚强充实，五是列阵决战的指挥正确。这五个方面都要先分析敌情，而后行动，用以实击虚的办法去压倒敌人。善于用兵的人，能压倒敌人。而不为敌人所压倒。压倒敌人，在于将帅的机智。号令是用来统一军队行动的，对军队情况不了解，号令就会经常变更，经常变更的号令，纵然下达了，大家也都不会相信。因此，下达号令的原则是，有小的缺点不必变更，有点不明确也不须重申。所以，上级没有可疑的命令，大众也就不会无所适从；行动没有犹豫不定的事情，大众就不会三心二意。从来就没有不取得大众衷心信任，而能得到他们自愿效力的，也没有不取得大众自愿效力，而能使他们拼命作战的。

Verse 3

A state must promote and practice etiquette, trust, familiarity, and love. And only then can it tolerate hunger and overcome problems. The state must first promote and practices of filial piety, parental love, honesty and shame. And only then would people be willing to use their life to protect the state. In antiquity, rulers ruled with respect and integrity, and then used rewards and ranks to motivate the people. They educated the populace first as to what was considered "honesty and shame", and punishments and fines afterwards; comfort the populace with benevolence and love, and impose constraints on the populace afterwards.

一个国家必须有崇礼守信相亲相爱的风气，民众才能忍饥耐饿克服困难。国家必须有孝顺慈爱廉洁知耻的习俗，民众才能不惜牺牲去捍卫国家。古代君王治理民众，必须先以礼信感化他们，然后用爵禄鼓励他们；先以廉耻教育他们；然后用刑罚督促他们；先用仁爱抚慰他们，然后用法律约束他们。

Verse 4

Thus, those who engage in combat must take the lead in person, in order to incite the masses and officers, just as the mind controls the four limbs. If the masses and officers are not incited, then they will not die for their country. When they will not die for their country, then the whole army cannot do battle. In order to stimulate the soldiers, the people's material welfare has to be ample. The ranks of nobility, the degree of comforting for the dead, the materials which the people chase after must be made evident. One must govern the people in accordance with their needs. One must govern the people by giving due credit for achievements. Actually giving people rewards for going into the field, feasting done together with relatives and friends, the mutual encouragement from fellow villagers, mutual assistance in times of crisis, marching off to war together – these are what stimulate the people. Ensure that the members of the five member squads and ten member squads take care of each other, as though they were relatives; the members of the companies and their officers behave like close friends. When they stop, they will be like a solid, encircling wall; when they move, they move like the wind and rain. The chariots will not make retreats; the soldiers will not turn around. This is the Way to establish the foundation for combat.

将帅指挥作战，必须用自己的表率行为来激励部队，这样才能象头脑指挥四肢一样的灵活自如。战斗意志不加激励，士兵就不会为国家效死，士兵不为国家效死，部队就没有作战能力。激励士气的方法，就是使民众都过富裕的生活。官职的等级，死丧的抚恤，民众所追求的，应该有明确的规定。必须根据民众的生活需要制定保障措施，根据民众的功绩给予表彰奖励，使他们在田地体禄方面得到实惠，起居饮食方面得到照顾，邻里互相鼓励，死生互相帮助，战时携手应征入伍，这就是激励民众的办法。使同什同伍的人，象亲戚那样互相关心，上下级关系象朋友那样亲密无间，军队驻止下来就象铜墙铁壁一样的坚固，行动起来就象急风暴雨一样的迅猛，战车一往直前，士兵绝不后退，这就是战胜敌人的根本原则。

Verse 5

Land is the means by which to nourish the populace; fortified cities, the means for defending the land; combat, the means for defending the cities. Thus if one concentrates on agriculture, the people will not be hungry; if one concentrates on defense, the land will not be endangered; if one concentrates on combat, the cities will not be encircled. These three were the fundamental concerns of the Former Kings, and among them military affairs were the most urgent. Therefore the Former Kings concentrated on five military affairs: When the food supply is not substantial, the soldiers do not set out. When rewards and salaries are not generous, the people are not stimulated. When military warriors are not selected based on capabilities, the masses will not be strong. When the weapons and implements are not prepared, their fighting strength will not be great. When punishments and rewards are not appropriate, the masses will not respect them. If one emphasizes these five, then at rest, the army will be able to defend any place it secures, and in motion it will be able to attain its objectives.

土地是用来养活民众的，城塞是用来保卫土地的，战斗是用来防守城塞的。所以，注重农业生产的，民众就不会受饥荒，注重边疆守备的，领土就不会被侵犯，注重机动作战的，城市就不会被围困。这件事是古代君王立国的根本问题，而其中军事问题又最为紧要。所以古代君王特别注意军事方面的五个问题：粮食储备不充分，军队就难以行动；奖赏待遇不优厚，民众就得不到鼓励；武士不经严格挑选，部队就不会坚强；武器装备不充实，战斗力就不会强大；赏罚不公正，民众就不会畏服。能够注意到这五个方面的问题，防守时就能守必固，行动时就能战必胜。

Verse 6

As for moving from the state from being motionless, to going forth to attack, the defense should be strong. In deploying your troops, you want the formations to be solid. In launching an attack you want to make the utmost effort. And in going forth to battle, you want to be of one mind.

要由防御转入进攻，防御就要稳定，阵地就要坚固，发起进攻要使用全部力量，战斗行动要协调一致。

Verse 7

The state of a king enriches its people; the state of a hegemon enriches its officers. A state that merely survives, enriches the high officials, and a state that is about to perish, enriches the king's own granaries and storehouses. Thus to satisfy the high ranks but neglect those at the bottom would result in a disaster with no means of rescue.

实行王道的国家，注意增加人民的收入；实行霸道的国家，注意增加武士的待遇；没落的国家，只图增加中上层贵族们的财富；濒于灭亡的国家，只图增加君王自己的库存财物。所以说，只满足上层而忽略下层，其祸患是无法挽救的。

Verse 8

Thus I say that if you hire the Worthy and give responsibility to the capable, even without selecting an auspicious time to do it, it will still be advantageous. If you make the laws clear and are cautious in issuing orders, then without performing divination, you will obtain good results. If you esteem achievement and nurture effort, without praying, you will still attain blessings. Thus it is said, 'Gaining the Heavenly timing is not as good as the advantages of terrain. Advantages of terrain are not as good as harmony among men.' What Sages esteem is human effort; that is all!

常言说，选用贤能，不须选择吉日良辰，也会顺利。法令明确，不必占卜吉凶，结果也会圆满。尊重功劳，不必祈祷也会得福。又说，天时有利不如地形有利，地形有利不如人心和睦。圣人所重视的，只在人的作为罢了。

Verse 9

Now when the army is toiling on the march, the general must establish himself as an example. In the heat, he does not set up an umbrella; in the cold, he does not wear thicker clothes. On difficult terrain, he must dismount and walk. Only after the army's well is finished does he drink. Only after the army's food is cooked does he eat. Only after the army's ramparts are complete does he rest. He must personally experience the same toil as his troops. Through this fashion, even though the army is in the field for a long time, it will be neither worn-out, nor exhausted.

勤劳的军队，将帅与士卒同甘苦，不先顾自己。天热不张伞，寒冷不加衣，路险必然下马步行，部队的井挖好了自己才饮水，部队的饭煮熟了自已才进餐，部队的营垒筑成了自己才休息，将帅必须与士兵同劳佚，共甘苦。这样，部队虽然长期作战，也能保持旺盛的士气而不致衰竭疲弊。

Chapter 5
Tactical Balance of Power in Attack

Verse 1

The military unit is victorious through being quiet and calm; a state is victorious through being united. One whose strength is divided will be weak; one whose minds have doubts will have their fighting spirit lowered. Now, when one's strength is weak, advancing and retreating will not be bold, and pursuing an enemy will not result in anyone being captured. Generals, commanders, officers, and troops should be a single body, both in action and at rest. But if the commander's mind is already doubtful, or the troops are inclined to disobey, then even though a plan has been decided on, they will not move; or if movement has been initiated, they cannot be controlled. When different mouths speak empty words, the general lacks the proper demeanor, and the troops have not been properly trained; if they set out to attack they will inevitably be defeated. This is what is referred to as army that is too sick to attack. It is inadequate for engaging in warfare. Now the general is the mind of the army, while all those below are the limbs and joints. When the mind is determined and focused, then the limbs and joints are invariably strong. When the mind moves in doubt, then the limbs and joints are invariably slow and weak. Now, if the general cannot have the cooperation of his troops, like the mind moving the limbs as when and where it wants them to be, then even though the army might be victorious, it will be a lucky victory, not the result of the tactical balance of power in attack.

军队以沉着冷静致胜，国家以统一团结致胜。部署分散力量就会削弱，决心动摇，士气就会涣散。力量薄弱，就不敢大胆进退，即使有好的战机也可能放走敌人。将吏士卒，一动一静，都象人的身体一样，如果决心摇思想混扎，就是计划决定了，也不能立即行动，行动起来了，又不能加以控制。军队中众说纷纭，空话连篇，将帅没有严肃的态度，士兵没有正规的训练，这样发动进攻，必然要招致失败，这就是颓废无用的军队，这种军队是不能同敌人战斗的。将帅好比人的首脑，部属好比人的四肢，首脑的决心坚定，四肢的动作必然有力，首脑的决心犹豫，四肢的动作必然迟疑。如果将帅指挥军队，不能象首脑控制四肢那样灵活自如，士兵不能象四肢那样按首脑的指挥行动，这样的军队，即使取得胜利，也是侥幸的胜利，而不是正确指挥的结果。

Verse 2

The troops should not fear the enemy and their general at the same time. If they fear us then they will despise the enemy; if they fear the enemy they will despise us. The general who is despised will be defeated; the general who establishes his military grandeur will be victorious. When the general is able to establish military greatness, his commanders will fear him. When the commander fears their generals, the troops will fear their commanders. When the troops fear their commanders, then the enemy will fear the troops. For this reason, those who would know the Way of victory and of defeat must first figure out the relationship between fearing and despising. Now, one who has only gained the goodwill of the troops through love, he cannot use the troops; one who is not respected and feared in the minds of his troops, he cannot use the troops. Love makes the troops follow orders, military grandeur is established from above. If they love their general they will not have divided minds; if they are awestruck by their general they will not be rebellious. Thus excelling at generalship is merely a question of exercising love and military greatness.

士卒是不会既畏惧敌人又畏惧自己将帅的。畏惧自己的将帅就会蔑视敌人，畏惧敌人就会蔑视自己的将冲。将帅被士卒蔑视，作战就会失败；将帅在士卒个有威信，作战就能胜利。凡将帅能掌握运用这个原则，军吏就会畏惧将帅；军吏畏惧将帅，士卒就会畏惧军吏；士卒畏惧军吏，敌人就会畏惧我军士卒。因此，要知道胜败的道理，首先就要懂得畏惧与蔑视两者的相互关系。如果不能以爱使士卒悦服、士卒就不会为我所用；如果不能以威信使士卒畏成，士卒就不会听我指挥。爱抚在于使下级驯服；威信在于上级自己树立。爱抚能使士卒不怀二心；威信能使下级不敢违令。所以善于带兵的人，就要善于掌握爱与威的运用。

Verse 3

One unsure of victory should not rush into battle. One unsure of capturing a city should not launch an assault on the city. Credibility must be established before the moment of need; affairs must be managed before the first signs appear. Thus the masses, once assembled, should not be dismissed. When the army has set forth, it should not return empty-handed. They will seek the enemy as if searching for a lost son; they will attack the enemy as if rescuing a drowning man, with haste.

作战没有必胜的把握，就不可以轻言作战，攻城没有必取的把握，就不可以轻言攻城。否则，即使采取严刑重赏也是不足以令人信服的。威信在于平素树立，事变要在事前预见。所以兵员一经集中，就不能随便解散，军队一经出动，就不能无功而返。寻求敌人要象寻找丢失的孩子那样志在必得，进攻敌人务象抢救落水的人那样奋不顾身地迅速行动。

Verse 4

One who long occupies strategic points lacks the mind to do battle. One who lightly provokes a battle lacks fullness of fighting spirit. One who is belligerent in battle lacks soldiers capable of victory.

分兵守险的，不会有决战的意图；进行挑战的，不会使用全部兵力；鲁莽作战的，不会有把握地取得胜利。

Verse 5

Now in general, one who starts a war in the name of righteousness values initiating conflict. One who contends out of personal animosity should respond only when it is unavoidable. Troops mobilized because of hatred, should await the enemy and act after them. Thus to start a war, one must look at the timing to start it. When the war has ended, one must still be alert and fully prepared.

凡是正义的战争，最好由我首先发动，为争私结怨的战争，应是出于不得已。因结怨而引起的战争，最好后发制人。所以说，发动战争，必须看准时机，战争结束，还是应当戒备。

Verse 6

There are wars that are victorious because of great plans from court; there are those who achieve victory in the plains and battlefields; and those who attain victory by attacking the cities. Those who fight can gain victory; those who submit are lost; and those fortunate enough not to be defeated, as in cases where the enemy is unexpectedly frightened and victory is gained by a turn of events, are said not to have achieved a complete victory. What is not a complete victory lacks any claim to having created a tactical imbalance in power. Thus the enlightened ruler, on the day of the attack, will concentrate on having the drums and horns sound in unison, and the army marching in unison as well. Thus without seeking victory, he can still be victorious. There are armies which, from the front look unprepared or weak, but are still able to achieve victory; because they have a strategy for victory, are well-prepared, have good execution of plans and are under great leadership. For five men there is a squad leader, for ten men a lieutenant, for 100 men a company captain, for 1,000 men a battalion commander, and for 10,000 men a general. This organization is already all-encompassing, already perfected. If a man dies in the morning, another will replace him that morning; if a man dies in the evening, another will replace him that evening. The wise ruler weighs the tactical balance of power with the enemy, evaluates the general, and only thereafter mobilizes the army.

战争有靠谋略取胜的，有靠野战取胜的，有靠强攻城市取胜的。总之，要敢于战斗才能胜利，屈服退让就会失败，即使侥幸不败，也是由于敌人意外地发生惊慌而偶然
胜利的。偶然的胜利不能算是真正的胜利。不能获得真正胜利的将领，就不合有真正的权威。所以英明的主帅在作战的时候，必须以正确的指挥，统一的行动来与敌决战，这样，虽不强求胜利而胜利也会自然到来。军队也有假装没有准备或故意表示怯弱而取胜的，这是因为它有巧妙的制敌办法，有充分的战斗准备，有周密的应战计划，有坚定的临战指挥的原故。按军队的编制，五人为伍设有伍长，十人为什设有什长，百人为卒设有卒长，千人为率

设有率长，万人为军设有将军，这样的编制已经是很周密很完善的了，战斗中指挥官早上战死，早上就有人接替，晚上战死，晚上就有人接替。战前要分析敌人的虚实，察明敌将的才能，然后才能起兵。

Verse 7

Thus in general, when assembling an army a thousand miles away, they must arrive within ten days and when a hundred miles away, they must arrive within one day; while the assembly point should be at the enemy's border. When the troops have assembled and the generals have arrived, the army should penetrate deeply into their territory, sever their roads, and occupy their large cities and large towns. Have the troops and the citizens ascend the walls and press the enemy into endangered positions. Know the configuration of the terrain and attack any strategic barriers. Occupy the terrain around a city or town and sever the various roads about it, follow up by attacking the city itself. If the enemy's generals and armies are unable to believe in each other, the officers and troops unable to be in harmony, and this situation happens up to a point where there are those unaffected by punishments, we will defeat them. Before the rescue party has arrived, a city will have already surrendered.

If fords and bridges have not yet been constructed, strategic barriers not yet repaired, dangerous points in the city walls not yet fortified, and the iron caltrops not yet set out, then even though they have a fortified city, they do not have any defense. If the troops from distant forts have not yet entered the city, the border guards and forces in other states not yet returned; then even though they have men, they do not have any men! If the domesticated animals have not yet been herded in, the grains not yet harvested, the wealth and materials for use not yet collected; then even though they have resources, they do not have any resources. Now when a city is empty and void and its resources are exhausted, we should take advantage of this vacuity to attack them. The 'Art of War' says, 'They go out alone, they come in alone. Even before the enemy's men can cross blades with them, they have attained victory.' This is what is meant.

大凡集中军队，远隔千里的，不能超过十天的时间，相距百里的，不能超过一天的时间，而且必须集中在敌人边境附近。兵员已经集中，将帅已经到达，就应立即深入敌人腹地，分别遮断它的交通，包围它的重要城市，迫使敌人困守孤城而处于危险的境地。同时驱使城内的男女居民也处于危险的境地，重层配置，分头抢占险要地形，向敌人要害突击。在敌人困守孤城、各方联系又被切断的情况下，再全面发起进攻，就可使敌军将冲丧失威信，官兵互不协力，虽用严刑峻法也不能迫使下级服从命令。这样就可以乘势打败敌人、不待敌人援军到达，而守城敌军就已投降了。
如果敌人交通设施没有战备，要塞没有修理，工事没有构筑，障碍没有设置，虽有城塞也是不能防守的。边境的堡垒没有部队占领，守边的部队没有调动就绪，虽有人也等于无人了。敌人应征集的牲畜没有集中，应征集的粮食没有征集。该征收的财物没有收齐，虽有资财也等于没有资财了。对这种城邑空虚而资财穷尽的敌人，我应乘虚进攻它。兵法上说，"我军行动自由如入无人之境，敌人不待交锋就已被打败"，就是指的这种情况。

Chapter 6
Tactical Balance of Power in Defense

Verse 1

In general, when the defenders do not occupy the outer walls of cities nor the borderlands, and when they retreat, do not establish watchtowers and barricades for the purpose of defensive warfare, they do not excel at defense. The valiant and brave sturdy armor and sharp weapons; powerful crossbows and strong arrows should all be within the outer walls; and then all the grain stored outside in the earthen cellars and granaries collected, and the buildings outside the outer wall broken down and citizens brought into the fortifications. This will allow the attackers to grow their fighting spirit, while the defenders' fighting spirit will be cut in half. The defenders will suffer heavy losses. Yet, generals through the ages have not used such principles.

凡是守城的军队，不在外城迎击敌人，不固守城郊险要据点，这样来进行防御战斗，不是好的办法。因为，把英雄豪杰，精锐部队，优良兵器，都集中在城内，并且收集城外的存粮，拆毁城外的房后，使民众统统退保城垣，这样就会使攻者气焰嚣张，而守者士气低落，一旦遭敌进攻，守军就会受到很大损伤。但是一般庸将却不懂得这个道理。

Verse 2

Now the defenders should not neglect their strategic points. The rule for defending a city wall is that for every *zhang* (3.5 miles), you should employ ten men to defend it – artisans and cooks not being included. Those who go out to fight do not defend the city; those who defend the city do not go out to fight. One man on defense can oppose ten men besieging them; ten men can oppose 100 men; 100 men can oppose 1,000 men; 1,000 men can oppose 10,000 men, Thus constructing a city's interior and exterior walls is not just accumulating loose soil and tamping it down, wantonly expending the strength of the people. It is truly for defense. If a wall is 1,000 *zhang*, then 10,000 men should defend it. The moats should be deep and wide, the walls solid and thick, the soldiers and people should have firewood and foodstuffs provided; the crossbows stout and arrows strong, the spears and halberds sharpened. This is the method for making a solid defense.

防守的军队绝不能放弃险要的地形，守城的方法，城墙每一丈，需要十人防守，勤杂人员还不计算在内。出击部队不担任守备，守备部队不担任出击。守城一人可挡敌十人，十人可挡敌百人，百人可挡敌千人，千人可挡敌万人。所以建筑城郭，并不是耗费民力去堆土玩，实际是为了加强防御。通常千丈之城需要万人防守，同时要求城壕深而宽，城墙坚而厚，人力充足，柴粮丰富；弓矢坚强，矛戟也同样锋利。这就是守城的方法。

The Book of Wei Liaozi

Verse 3

If the attackers number at least 100,000, while the defenders have a reinforcement outside that will certainly come to the rescue, it is a city that can be defended. If there is no reliable reinforcement to inevitably rescue them, then it is not a city that can be defended. Now if the walls are solid and rescue certain, then even ignorant men and women will all, without exception, give their all to defend the city. For a city to withstand a siege for one year, the strength of the defenders should exceed that of the attackers and the strength of the reinforcement exceed that of the defenders. Now if walls are solid but rescue uncertain or reinforcement cannot be depended upon, then the ignorant men and women – all without exception – will defend on the parapets, but they will weep. This is normal human emotion. Even if you then open the grain reserves in order to relieve and pacify them, you cannot stop it. You must incite the valiant and brave, with their sturdy armor, sharp weapons, strong crossbows, and stout arrows to exert their strength in the front and the young, weal, crippled, and ill to exert their strength together in the rear.

敌人使用十万以上的兵力进攻城市时，守城的军队如果有可靠的援军，城市就一定能守得住，如果没有可靠的援军，城市就不一定能守住。如果防者城垣坚固，又有可靠的援军，那么，民众就没有不竭尽全力守城的。要想坚守一年的城市，守军兵力多于进攻的敌人，而援军兵力多于防守的军队。如果城垣坚固但没有可靠的提军，那么，民众就没有不守着城垛而悲伤的，这是人之常情，即使散发财物和粮食来安抚他们，也不能消除这种悲观情绪。在这样的情况下，必须勉励豪杰英雄率领精锐部队，使用优良武器，奋力战斗于前，使老幼残弱者并力支援于后，才有希望坚持下去打开局面。

Verse 4

If an army of 100,000 is encamped beneath the city walls, the reinforcement must break open the siege, and the city's defenders must go out to attack. When they move forth, they must secure the critical positions along the way. But the reinforcement to the rear of the besiegers should not sever their supply lines; and the forces within and without should respond to each other. This sort of rescue displays a half-hearted commitment and we can wait for the opportunity to topple the attackers. To deal with the reinforcement, the enemy general will put their stalwarts in the rear, and place the old in the forefront. Then the enemy will not be able to advance, nor be able to stop the defenders from breaking out. This is what is meant by the 'tactical balance of power in defense'.

敌人十万大军兵临城下，援军必须能打开重围，守军也必须能乘机出去，抢占要点。援军也可以只在敌军的后方打开一条通路，使军的粮道不被切断，并与守军互相策应，这是为了表示救援不积极用以迷惑敌人，等待有利战机。敌人为了对付援军，只好把精部队撤到后方控制起来，而把战斗力差的部队配置在攻城前线，这样敌人攻城，就不可能有进展，而守军也可以出去了。这就是守城的权变。

Chapter 7
Twelve Cultivations

Military effectiveness lies in being firm in decisions. Beneficence lies in giving at the correct time. Adaptation lies in promptly responding to affairs. Warfare lies in controlling morale and fighting spirit. Attack lies in surprises. Defense lies in manipulating external appearance. Perfection lies in being detailed in planning. Not encountering difficulty lies in foresight and preparation. Caution lies in paying attention to details. Wisdom lies in controlling the 'larger picture'. Eliminating harm lies in being decisive. Gaining the masses lies in deferring to other men.

Regret arises from relying on what is doubtful. Evil lies in excessive executions. Prejudice comes from frequently following one's own desires. Non-accomplishment arises from hating negative performance feedback. Extravagance lies in exhausting the people's resources. Non-enlightenment lies in accepting advice which separates you from reality; being impractical stems from lightly initiating movements. Stubbornness and shallowness lie in staying away from the capable and Worthy. Misfortune lies in loving profits. Harm lies in drawing ruffians near. Demise lies in lacking preparation. Danger lies in lacking clear commands and orders.

立威在于坚定不移，施惠在于恰合时宜，机变在于适应情况，作战在于激励士气，进攻在于出敌不意，防守在于隐蔽部署，不犯错误在于考虑周密，无困难在于予有准备，慎重在于能警惕小事，明智在于能统筹全局，消除祸患在于勇敢果断，能得人心在于礼贤下士，后悔在于决心犹豫，罪恶在于滥行杀戮，偏袒在于私心过重，
办事不顺在于讨厌听到批评自己的过错，用度不足在于耗尽民财，是非不明在于受人离间，不切事实在于轻举妄动，固执浅薄在于疏远贤人，祸患在于贪财好利，受害在于接近坏人，灭亡在于没有战备，危险在于号令不明。

The Book of Wei Liaozi

Chapter 8
Military Discussions

Verse 1

In general, when employing the military, do not attack cities that have not committed transgressions or slay men who are innocent. Whoever kills people's fathers and elder brothers; whoever profits himself by plundering the riches and goods of other men; whoever makes slaves of the sons and daughters of other men is, in all cases, a brigand. For this reason, the military provides the means to execute the brutal and chaotic, and to stop the unrighteous. Wherever the army is applied, we must try to retain the farmers in the fields, the merchants in their shops and the officials in their offices: for the use of the military is to punish the one man who started the atrocities. Thus, even without the forces bloodying their blades, all will give their allegiance.

凡是用兵，不要进攻无过的国家，不要杀害无辜的人民。杀害人家的父兄，掠夺人家的财物，奴役人家的子女，这些都是强盗的行为。战争的目的是平定暴乱，制止不义行为。对于被讨伐的国家，要使农民不离开他们的土地，商人不离开他们的店铺，官吏不离开他们的机关，因为用兵的目的，只在于惩罚祸首一人，所以能不必经过流血战斗就可得到天下的拥护。

Verse 2

A state of 10,000 chariots concentrates on both agriculture and warfare. A state of 1,000 chariots focuses on being able to rescue and defend itself. A state of 100 chariots commits itself to be self-sufficient. For those engaged in agriculture and warfare, the ability to start battles depends on ability itself and not something external. Those who can rescue and defend themselves do not seek aid outside themselves, and those who can be self-sufficient do not seek material resources outside themselves. Now if one's resources are neither sufficient to go forth to wage battle, nor adequate to remain within the borders and defend the state, one must correct the insufficiency with commerce markets. The development of fair trade is a good way to increase taxes, the source of military spending. A state of 10,000 chariots may not collect revenue suitable for states holding only 1,000 chariots. It must develop commerce, taxation and revenue like a state of 10,000 chariots.

万乘之国实行农战结合，以足食足兵，千乘之国要能自救自守，百乘之国要能自给自足。农战结合，足食足兵的国家，战守之权操之在己而不仰仗他人；能自救自守的国家，就可不向外国乞求援助；能自给自足的国家，就可不向别邦乞求资财。[在国防经济上，]如果进不足以战胜敌人，退不足以进行固守的，就应该用发展集市贸易的办法来解决。发展集市贸易，是增加税收、供给军费的好办法。万乘之国虽然不像千乘之国那样求助于人,但必须像百乘之国那样,发展贸易,增加收入。

Verse 3

In general, executions provide the means to spotlight an army's military grandeur. If by executing one man, the entire army will be shaken into action, kill him. If by killing one man, 10,000 men will rejoice, kill him. In executing, start with those of high authority; in rewarding, start with those of low positions. If someone should be killed, then even though he is honored and powerful, he must be executed, for this will show that punishment goes all the way to the top. When rewards extend down to the cowherds and stable boys, this is reward flowing down to the lowest. Now the ability to implement punishments reaching all the way to the top and rewards flowing down to the lowest is known as the general's martial charisma. Thus rulers should value such generals.

杀戮,是用来整肃军威的。杀一人能使全军震动的,就杀掉他。杀一人能使万人高兴的,就杀掉他。需要杀人时,应该以地位高的人作典型,实行奖赏时应该以地位低的人做榜样。应该杀的虽然官高势大,也一定要杀,这就是"刑上究"的原则;奖赏及于下属的牛童马倌,这就是"赏下流"的原则。能够做到"刑上究","赏下流",这是将帅威武严肃的表现。所以君主应该尊重将帅的职权。

Verse 4

Now when the commanding general takes up the drum to direct an army that is going into battle, when the swords clash, if the general directs well, he will be rewarded for his achievements, and his fame will be established. If he does not direct well, he himself will die and the state will perish. For this reason survival and extinction, security and danger all lie in the ability of the general. How can one not value the general?

将帅击鼓指挥军队,使其在危难情况下与敌决战,当两军短兵相接的时候,如果指挥得当,就会建立功名,如果指挥不当,就会身死亡。由此看来,国家的存亡安危,在于将帅的指挥是否得当,这怎能不使人重视将帅的作用呢?

Verse 5

Now taking up the drums and wielding the drumsticks, having the soldiers collide and the blades clash, so that the ruler achieves great success through military affairs, all these I do not find to be difficult. The ancients said, 'Attacking without chariots with protective covering, defending without equipment such as the caltrops, this is what is meant by an army that does not excel at anything!'

Impoverished armies, lacking in equipment and supplies, stem from the state not having commerce. Commerce should be regulated by officers from the government. The government should buy items which are cheap in the market and sell those which are expensive in order to restrain the aristocrats and civilian people. People only eat one *dou* (roughly 2 pounds) of grain, and horses eat three *dou* of beans, so why is it that the people have a famished look and the horses an emaciated appearance? This is because the markets have goods to deliver but lack a controller. Now if you raise the best trained army but do not manage the markets, one would be unable to conduct warfare.

击鼓指挥军队，与敌人进行格斗，君主要取得军事上的胜利，我以为并不是困难的事。古人说："没有'蒙冲'去进攻，没有'渠答'去防守，这是装备不完善的军队"。军队由于营养不良，以致影响了视力，影响了听力，这是由于国家没有管好市场，以致供给缺乏的原故。市场，应对百货进行管理，用贱买贵卖的办法，以限制士民操纵物价。一般说，每人每天不过吃粮食一斗，每马每天不过吃饲料三斗，而弄得士卒
饥饿，马匹瘦弱，这是为什么呢？这是由于市场虽有各种物品，而无人管理的原故。要知道统率天下的军队，而没有对百货进行有效的管理，那是不能顺利进行作战的。

Verse 6

To be able to retain men in service, straight from their mobilization to the time when their armor and helmets have become worm infested (death), they must be men whom we can employ gainfully. This is like a bird of prey pursuing a sparrow which flies into a man's arm or enters someone's dwelling. It is not that the sparrow is casting away its life, but that to the rear, there is something worse to fear.

进行战争，能使军队坚持长期作战的，必然是由于军令严明，官兵不得不为我效力的原故。譬如凶猛的鸟追逐小雀，有时竟使小雀窜入人们的怀中，闯进人家的室内，这并不是它愿意舍生就死，而是怕后面的凶鸟追上来了。

Verse 7

When Tai Gong Wang was seventy, he butchered cows at Chao Ge and sold food in Meng Jin. He was more than seventy years old, but the ruler did not give an office to him and people all referred to him as a mad fellow. Then when he met King Wen of Zhou Dynasty he commanded a mass of 30,000, and with one battle, the country was settled. Without his wisdom and strategic planning, how could they have achieved this unification? Thus there is a saying, 'If a good horse is whipped, a distant road can be traversed; if Worthies and men of rank unite together, the way to good governance will be illuminated.'

太公望到了七十岁，还在朝歌宰牛为业，在盟津卖食品谋生。年过七十，还没有得到君主的任用，许多人都说他是放荡不拘的人。及至遇见了周文王，却能统帅三万之众，一战而平定天下。如果他没有高深的谋略，哪能得到这样的重用呢？所以常言说，良马得到鞭策就可以日行十里。贤士得到重用，就可使政治昌明。

Verse 8

When King Wu of Zhou attacked King Zhou of Shang, the army forded the Yellow River at Meng Chin. On the right was the king's pennant, on the left the axe of punishment, together with 300 warriors committed to die and 30,000 fighting men. King Zhou's formation deployed several hundred thousand men, with the infamous ministers, Fei Lian and E Lai personally leading against halberdiers and axe bearers. Their lines stretched across a hundred miles. King Wu did not exhaust the warriors or people, the soldiers did not bloody their blades, and they conquered the Shang Dynasty and executed King Zhou. There was nothing auspicious or abnormal; it was merely a case of perfecting oneself, or not perfecting oneself, in human affairs. Generals of the present generation investigate 'singular days' and 'empty mornings', divine about Xian Chi, interpret full and disastrous days, accord with the tortoise shell augury, look for the auspicious and baleful, and observe the changes of the planets, constellations, and winds – wanting to thereby gain victory and establish their success. I view this as very difficult.

武王伐纣，统帅军队在盟津渡河，他右手执白旄，左手执黄钺，指挥敢死之士三百人，士卒三万人同商军作战。这时商纣的军队有几十万，而又有飞廉恶来这些勇将，身先士卒，不避戟斧，阵势绵延百里不断。但武王并没有使士卒疲劳，也没有经过激烈的战斗，就打败了商军，诛灭了纣王。这不是由于什么吉凶灾祥预兆，而是由于人善与不善的必然结果。如今一般庸将，只知道考究时辰判定方位，求神问卜推测吉凶，以及观察星辰风云的变化来推断战争的胜败，想用这些方法来致胜立功，我以为是很难做到的。

Verse 9

Now the commanding general should not be governed by timing and trends, not controlled by the terrain below, nor governed by men. Weapons are evil implements. War is contrary to Virtue. The post of the general is an office of life and death. Thus only when it cannot be avoided does one employ these things. In directing a war, the general should not be restricted by timings and trends, should not be limited by terrain, should not be restricted by the ruler at the rear and restricted by an enemy in the front. The unified army, acting as one man, should be like the wolf and tiger, like the wind and rain, like thunder and lightning, with military grandeur and mysteriousness. All under Heaven should be terrified by it. The army that would be victorious is like water. Now water is the softest and weakest of things, but whatever it collides with – such as hills and mounds – will be collapsed by it, for no other reason than its nature is concentrated and its 'attack' is totally committed. Now if one has the sharpness of the famous sword *Mo Yeh*, the toughness of rhinoceros hide for armor, the large masses of the army, and using direct and indirect methods, then under Heaven, no one can withstand him in battle. Thus it is said that if you use the Worthy and employ the talented, even if the hour and day are not auspicious, your results will still yield the advantage. If you make the laws clear and are cautious about orders, without divining the tortoise shell or milfoil (superstitious practices) you will obtain propitious results. If you honor achievement and nurture effort, without praying, you will obtain good fortune. It is also said that 'timing and trends are not as good as the advantage of terrain; the advantages of terrain are not as good as harmony among men.' The sages of antiquity stressed human effort; that is all.

做将帅的人，必须上不受天时的限制，下不受地形的限制，中不受人为的限制。武器，是杀人的凶器，战争，是暴力的行动，将帅，是掌握生杀的官吏，所以只在不得已的情况下才能使用它。指导战争，要做到上不受天时的影响，下不受地形的限制，后面不受君主的制约，前不受敌人的阻抗。万众一心的军队，行动起来就象虎狼般的勇猛，风雨般的急骤，雷电般的突然，声势浩大，行动莫测，使天下惊惧。胜利的军队象水一样，水看来是最柔弱的，但它所冲击的地方，山陵也会崩塌，这不是别的原因，而是由于水总是流向一个方向，不断冲刷的结果。现在用莫邪那样锋利的武器，犀牛皮制成的坚固铠甲，装备起来的大量军队，再加上奇正的灵活运用，天下就没有任何力量可以同他抗衡了。所以说，只要任用贤能，不须选择吉日良辰事情也会顺利；只要法令严明，不须求神问卜也会获得吉祥；只要奖励战功优厚抚恤，不须祈祷也会得福。又说，天时有利不如地形有利，地形有利不如人心和睦。古代的圣人，不过是重视人的作用罢了。

Verse 10

When Wu Qi engaged Qin in battle, wherever he encamped, he would not flatten the ground where he slept. He used young saplings to provide protective covering against the frost and dew. Why did he act like this? He did this because he did not place himself higher than other men. If you want men to die, you do not require them to perform perfunctory acts of respect. If you want men to exhaust their strength, you do not hold them responsible for performing the rites. Thus in antiquity, an officer wearing a helmet and armor did not bow, showing people that he does not want trouble, or want to trouble anyone. Anger the people, and yet require them to die, to exhaust their strength - from antiquity till today has never been heard of as having achieved success.

吴起与秦军作战，就睡在不加平整的田埂上，只用树枝掩盖以遮蔽霜露。为什么这样呢？这是因为他不自视高人一等的原故。凡是要求人家为你效死，就不能要求人家对你必恭必敬；要求人家竭尽全力，就不能讲究那些繁文缛节。所以古时候穿戴盔甲的将士不行跪拜之礼，这是表示不愿因自己而增加别人的麻烦。给别人增添很多麻烦，而又要求人家为你效死尽力，是从古至今，没有听说过的。

Verse 11

When the commanding general receives his mandate, he forgets his family. When he commands the army and they encamp in the field, he forgets those close to him. When he takes up the drumsticks and drums the advance, he forgets his safety. When Wu Qi approached the time for battle, his attendants offered their swords. Wu Qi said: 'The general takes sole control of orders given. When a decision needs to be made, he makes it. He controls the troops and directs their blades. Such is the work of the general. Charging at the enemy, as a single soldier, that is not a general's affair.'

将帅奉命出征的时候，就忘掉自己的家庭，带领军队到达战场的时候，就忘掉自己的亲属，临阵指挥的时候，就忘掉自己的安危。从前吴起临战的时候，左右的人把宝剑呈送给他。吴起说：" 将帅的主要职责是发号施令。在危难的情况下，做出决断，以指挥军队去作战，这才是将帅的职责，直接拿起兵器与敌人格斗，不是将帅的职责。

Verse 12

When the army has assumed formation, they should advance for a day and complete a total of three days' distance. Beyond the three days' distance, they should be like a dammed river that has been released. Observing the enemy in front, one should employ their strengths. If the enemy's flags are white, we use white flags; if they are using red banners then we use red banners.

三军整队行军，先行三十里，接着走三天，走九十里。九十里以后，就要象决开江河一样势不可挡地前进。与敌人接近时，应根据敌人特点来对付他，如果敌人使用白色标记，我也用白色标记来欺骗它，敌人用红色标记，我也用红色标记迷惑它。

Verse 13

When Wu Qi engaged Qin in battle, before the armies clashed, one man – unable to overcome his courage – went forth to slay two of the enemy and return with their heads. Wu Qi immediately ordered his decapitation. An army commander remonstrated with him, saying: 'This is a skilled warrior. You cannot execute him.' Wu Qi replied: 'There is no question that he is a skilled warrior, but it is not what I ordered.' He had him executed.

吴起与秦军作战，两军尚未交锋，有一人自恃其勇，独自冲向前去，斩获敌人两个首级回来。吴起要立刻杀他。军吏请求说："这是个有本领的人，不可杀掉。"吴起说："他诚然是有本领的，但他违背了我的命令。"结果还是把他杀了。

Chapter 9
General, as Officer of the Law

Verse 1

A general is an officer of law and punishment, the manager of all matters. He should not favor anyone. When he does not favor anyone, everything is within his control and he can control anything. The perfect man does not stop a criminal more than five paces away. Even though they may have shot at him with barbed arrows, he does not pursue past vengeance. He excels at discovering the nature of a criminal's offense. Without relying on torture, he can obtain a complete understanding of the offender's situation. If you flog a person's back, brand his ribs, or break his fingers in order to question him about the nature of his offense, even a state hero could not withstand this cruelty and would falsely implicate himself.

将帅是掌管刑法的官吏，也是一切事务的主宰者，不应偏袒任何人。正由于不偏袒任何人，所以任何事情发生，都能公平裁决，任何情况出现，都能正确处理。贤德的人总是亲自询问，详察案情，避免错误，秉公审理，即使犯人与自己有深仇宿怨，也不追究前仇。所以善于审案的人，不必施行拷打，也可以把案情全部掌握。如果依靠鞭打犯人脊背，烧灼犯人两肋，捆夹犯人手指等办法来审讯，就是豪杰之士，也会因经不起这种酷刑，而被屈打成招了。

Verse 2

There is a saying in our age: 'One who has thousands of pieces of gold will not die; one who has hundreds of pieces of gold will not suffer corporal punishment.' If you listen to my suggestion and try them in practice, then even a person with the wisdom of Yao or Shun (sage kings) will not be able to avert a word of the charge against him, nor one with 10,000 pieces of gold be able to use the smallest silver piece to escape punishment. At the present, those in prison awaiting judgment number no less than several dozens in the smallest jails, no less than several hundred in the middle-sized jails, and no less than several thousand in the largest prisons. Ten men involved 100 men in their affairs; 100 men drag in 1,000; and 1,000 trap 10,000. Those who have become entangled first are parents and brothers; next relatives; and next those who are acquaintances and old friends. For this reason, the farmers all leave their occupations in the fields, the merchants depart from their stores, and the officials leave their posts. These good people have all been dragged in because of the nature of our criminal proceedings. The 'Art of War' says: 'When an army of 10,000 goes forth, its daily expense is a thousand pieces of gold.' Now when there are 10,000 good people thus entangled and imprisoned, yet the ruler is unable to investigate the situation – I take it to be dangerous!

现今的俗话说：″有千金的人，可以免死，有百金的人，可以免刑。″如能听取我的意见，采用我的办法，虽有尧舜的智慧，也不能矢说一句通融的话，虽有万全的财富，也不能用一″铢″钱行贿。现今审理案件，小案拘禁不下数十人，中等案件拘禁不下数百人，大案拘禁不下数千人。而且往往是十人的事牵连百人，百人的事牵连千人，千人的事牵连万人。所牵连的人，首先是父母兄弟，其次是亲属，再次是熟识的朋友。被牵连的农民被迫离开土地，商人被迫离开店铺，士大夫被迫离开官府。象这样众多的良民被牵连而矢进监狱，这就是当前拘禁囚犯的实际情况。兵法上说：″十万大军出征，一日托费千金。″现在十万良民被牵连入狱，而君王不能明察，我认为是很危险的。

Chapter 10
Officers and Rulers

Verse 1

Bureaucratic offices are the means to control affairs of state and are the foundation of state administration. Regulations on four groups derived according to their occupations are the parameters of administration. Honor, rank, riches and salaries must be appropriately determined by capabilities and character, for they are the embodiment of nobility and public service. Treating the good well and punishing the evil, rectifying the laws for organizing the people, and collecting taxes and penalties are implements for governing the people. Making land distributions equitable and restraining taxes and other impositions on the people provide measure to what is levied and bestowed. Regulating the artisans and preparing implements for use should be the contribution of the Master Artisans. Dividing the territory and occupying the strategic points is the work of eliminating any possible oddities and stopping potential chaos. Preserving the laws, investigating affairs and making decisions are the roles of subordinates. Illuminating the duties of the bureaucrats, setting responsibilities as light or heavy – these fall under the authority of the ministers and ruler. Making rewards and bestowals clear, being strict in executing and punishing are methods for stopping evil. Being cautious about what to undertake and what to give up, insisting on one united policy are the essentials of government. When information from below reaches up high, and the concerns of up high penetrate to below, this is the most ideal situation.

设置各级官吏，主管各项事务，是治理国家的根本措施。各种官制，按职守分管士、农、工、商各个部门，这是治理国家的分工。〔天官冢宰主管〕授予官爵俸禄必须与其德才相称，这是区别尊卑贵贱的体制。[地官司徒掌管]表扬好人，惩罚坏人，执行比法，以考核、统计人冒及其财产，均分土地，减轻赋税，以保障对民众取予的适度。[冬官司空掌管]分配工人的任务，供应物资器材，提高工作效率。[夏官司马主管]划分防区，守备要地，以防止和消灭各种变乱事件。执法严肃，处理果断，这是臣子的本分。制订法令，实行考核，这是君主的责任。明确属下的主管业务，区别政事的轻重缓急，这是各部大臣的职权。奖赏公正，惩罚严格，这是防止坏人活动的手段。研究应兴应革的事项，坚持统一的方针政策，这是治理国家的关键。下情上达，上情下通，这是全面了解情况的方法。

Verse 2

By knowing the extent of the state's resources, you can plan to use the surplus. Knowing the weakness of others is the way to strengthening oneself; knowing the movements of others leads to calmness. Officers are divided into the civil and martial, because these are the two areas for which the ruler administers the state.

The ceremonial vessels are all regulated, for they are being used by the Son of Heaven's (the king's) convocation. When itinerant persuaders and spies have no means to gain entrance, this is the technique for rectifying and preserving discussions. The feudal lords have their rites for honoring the Son of Heaven, and rulers and their people – generation after generation – continue to acknowledge the king's mandate to rule. If someone changes or creates new rites, alters what is normal, or contravenes the king's illustrious Virtue, then in accordance with the rites, the king can attack them. Officials with no affairs to administer, a ruler without rank or rewards that need to be bestowed, a populace without criminal cases or lawsuits, a state without traders or merchants – how perfected the king's rule! What I have so clearly proposed, and the ruler should heed and take actions to move towards, is because of the ruler's high morality.

了解国家资财的多少，这是量入为出，节约开支的根据。了解敌方的薄弱环节，这是让自己变弱为强的依据。了解对方的动态，这是我方冷静才能看透。设置文武官吏，分管政治、军事，这是王者治理国家的两种手段。祭祀的制度有统一的规定，这是天子会合诸侯的仪式。不听信游士的邪说和间谍的诡计，这是贯彻正确主张的保证。诸侯谨守天子的礼法，君臣关系，世代相传，这是承受天子之命的前提。如果改换国号变更制度，违背天子的德政，按礼就可以进行讨伐。要做到社会安定，不须官吏去管理，万民勤奋不需上级去鼓励，民众没有纠纷，国家没有商贩，造成最好的政治局面。我之所以坦率地陈述这些意见，也就是希望你能施行这种德政。

Chapter 11
Foundations of Governance

Verse 1

In general, what is the way to govern the populace? I say that without the five grains, you have nothing to fill their stomachs, without silk and hemp, nothing to cover their form. Thus to fill their stomachs, there are grains, and to cover their form there is thread. Husbands work at weeding and plowing, wives at weaving. If people do not have secondary occupations, then there will be goods accumulated in the storehouses. The men should not engrave nor make decorative carving; the women should not embroider nor do decorative stitching. Carved wooden vessels allow water to seep in; metal utensils have an offensive smell. The Sage drinks from an earthen vessel and eats from an earthen vessel. Thus when clay is formed to make utensils, there will be no waste.

治理民众用什么办法呢？回答是，没有五谷人们就没有饭吃，没有丝麻人们就没有衣穿，所以吃饭有了粮食，穿衣有了丝麻，男子从事耕种，女子从事纺织，人们专事耕织不受其他事务的影响，国家就有储备了。提倡男子不要从事奢侈品的雕刻，女子不要从事装饰品的刺绣。木制的食器容易渗水，金属的食器带有腥味，圣人的饮食用具都是来源于土，因而制作陶土用具，这就可杜绝天下的浪费了。

Verse 2

Today, people think the nature of metal and wood is not 'afraid' of cold, thus they embroider their clothes with them. The original nature of horses and oxen is to eat grass and drink water, but people feed the animals beans and grains. This is governing which has lost its foundation, and it would be appropriate to establish regulations to control it. In spring and summer, the men go out to the southern fields, and in the fall and winter, the women work at weaving cloth: the people will not be impoverished. Today, when their short, coarse clothing does not even cover their bodies, nor the dregs of wine and husks of grain fill their stomachs, the foundation of government has been lost. Since antiquity, the land has not become more fertile or barren; the people have not become more diligent or lazy. How could have the ancients attained a state of being well fed and well clothed, how could we have lost it now? The men do not finish plowing their fields; the women do not finish weaving cloths, so how could they not be hungry and cold? Probably, the administration of the ancients was fully effected while that of today stops before thorough implementation.

如今，金木本来是不知道寒冷的，却要给它披上锦绣，牛马本来是吃草炊水的，却要喂它粮食，这种做法完全违反了它们的本性，应该建立合理的制度才是。春、夏男子到田里耕种庄稼，秋、冬女子在家里染织布帛，这样人民就不会贫困了。现在人民穿的是粗布短衫，而且。还遮不住身体，吃的是粗劣食品，而且还填不饱肚子，这是没有把国家治理好的表现。古时候，土地的肥沃同今天没有两样，人民的勤惰同今天也没有两样，为什么古人丰衣足食，而今人缺吃少穿呀？主要是种田的人不能经常耕作，织布的人不能经常纺织，这怎能免于饥寒呢？总的来说，这是由于古代行之有效的耕织制度，到今天已经把它废止了的原故。

Verse 3

Now what is termed as good governance is causing the people not to have any selfish interests. If the people do not have selfish interests, then all will be one family. In the absence of private plowing and weaving, they will suffer the cold together, they will experience hunger together. Then, even if one has ten sons, they will not have the expense of even an extra bowl of rice, while if one has one son, their expenses will not be reduced by even one bowl. As such, would there be any clamoring and drunken indulgence ruining the good people? When the people stimulate each other to frivolity and extravagance, misfortunes, greed and competition spring up. When one person starts to hoard, then other people seek to selfishly accumulate some extra food and have some stored wealth. If this continues, crime will happen, arrests would then have to be made, and punishments have to be meted out. The ruler is then not fit to rule.

所谓良好的政治，在于教育民众不要自私。如果民众不自私，天下就象一家人一样，而不必进行私耕私织，大家都把别人的寒冷当作自己的寒冷，把别人的饥饿当作自己的饥饿。因此，有十个孩子的人，也不加重他的生活负担，只有一个孩子的人，也不减轻他的社会责任，这样人们哪里还会喧喧嚷嚷嗜酒作乐，以致败坏良好的风尚呢？如果民众不安分，私欲就会产生，争权夺利的祸患就随之而起了。如果有一个人违背了这种无私的准则，别人也跟着他把粮食储藏起来自己吃，把财物储藏起来自己用，发展下去就会犯禁了，而民众一旦犯紫，就逮捕治罪，这怎能配得上为万民之首呢？

Verse 4

Those who excel at governing take hold of the regulations, causing the people not to have any selfish interests. When those below do not dare to be selfish, there will not be any who commit evil. Return to the foundation; accord with unselfish principles, have all issues move along the Way, and then the greedy mind will be eliminated. Also, competition will be stopped, the jails will be empty, the fields full, the grains plentiful; the lives of the populace will be stable. All surrounding tribes will feel that they are cared for. Then outside your borders there will not be any difficulty, while within the state there will be neither violence nor turbulence. This is the perfection of administration.

好的政治，就是坚持法制，教育民众不要自私，大家不敢自私，就没有为非作歹的人了。如果人们恢复纯朴的本性，遵循无私的准则，那么，个人和私欲就会打消，争夺行为就会停止，监狱里就会没有囚犯，劳动的人就会遍布田野，生产的粮食就会增多，民众的生活就会安定，四方的民族也会受到关怀，国家没有外患，也没有内乱，这就可以称得上天下大治了。

Verse 5

The azure sky – no one know its extremity! Of the ancient emperors and Sage kings, who should be your model? Ages that have passed cannot be regained, future ages cannot be awaited. Seek them in yourself.

蓝蓝的天空，谁知道它的边际？五帝三王的政治，谁的方式可供效法呢？过去的时代不可能重现，未来的理想也不能只靠等待，只有求之于自己的创造

Verse 6

There are four qualities for one referred to as the Son of Heaven: great intelligence, great benevolence, vast accomplishment and invincibility. These are the aspects of the Son of Heaven.

能够称为天子的，要具备四个条件：一是智慧超人，二是恩布万民，三是功业宏伟，四是天下无敌。这都是天子应做到的事。

Verse 7

Wild animals are not used for sacrificial offerings; miscellaneous studies do not make a scholastic education.

不能把野生的动物作为祭品，不能把杂凑的学说当成真才实学。

Verse 8

There is a saying: "The hundred miles of the sea cannot quench one man's greed; a spring three feet deep can slake the thirst of the army." I say: "Desire is born from lack of self-knowledge; perversity is born from lacking prohibitions." The highest ruler transforms the spirit first, relies on trends as secondary, the third is not taking the people away from their seasonal work or seizing the people's wealth. Now prohibitions must be completed through security forces, rewards must be completed through the civil.

现今有人说："百里宽的大海，不够一个贪得无厌的人喝，三尺深的小泉，却够三军之众解渴。"我认为私欲的产生由于没有节制，邪恶的产生由于禁止不力。所以，要解决这个问题，首先是精神感化，其次是因势利导，再次

就是不误农时，不竭民财。禁止坏人坏事，必须使用强制手段才能成功；奖励好人好事，必须结合教育才能奏效。

Chapter 12
Tactical Balance of Power in Warfare

Verse 1

The 'Art of War' states: "1,000 men provide the means to exercise the war tactics, 10,000 men provide the means to exercise martial prowess. If you apply the force of tactical power to the enemy first, he will not be able to commit in strength. If you apply martial prowess first, the enemy will not be able to withstand your attack." Thus in warfare, it values the first to move the most. If one is able to understand and implement the principle, then it will conquer the enemy. If one is not able to understand and implement the principle, then it will not conquer them. Now when we attack, they will defend; when they attack, we will defend. These mutually produce victory and defeat. The pattern of battle is as such. Detailed planning comes from observing both the enemy and our side. Grabbing opportunities and advantages comes from being flexible in our plans. If you have something, pretend not to have it; if you lack something, appear to have it. Then how can the enemy trust appearances?

兵法上说，兵力小的可用权谋取胜，兵力大的可用威力取胜。先敌使用权谋，敌人有力量也无法使用，先敌使用武力，敌人有力量也无法抗拒，所以用兵最好先发制人。善于运用这一原则。就能战胜敌人，不善于运用这一原则，就不能战胜敌人。我去进攻敌人，敌人必然要反击，敌人来进攻我们，我们也必然要反击。不是我战胜敌人，就是敌人战胜我，这是战争的客观规律。精细周到的谋略在于明察敌我双方情况，机动权变的指挥在于灵活运用作战原则。有装做没有，没有却装做有，敌人怎么能摸清我们的真实情况呢？

Verse 2

The reason why the deeds of the Former Kings are passed down is that they entrusted the upright with responsibility and eliminated the deceitful. They always preserved the benevolent and congenial hearts, but were decisive, without delaying, in effecting punishments.

先王之所以为后世传颂的，在于能任用正直的人，清除奸诈的人，保护善良恭顺的人。而对于那些触犯刑法的人决不留情。

Verse 3

One who understands the Way of warfare will invariably first plan against the defeats, which arise from not knowing when to cease. Why must one always think that advancing would be successful? If you advance too recklessly and seek to engage the enemy in battle, should they – on the contrary – have plans in place to stop you going forth; the enemy will control the victory. Thus the 'Art of War' says: "If they seek us, engage them; when you see them, attack. When the aggressors dare not oppose us, press the attack, and they will inevitably lose their opportunity to control the situation."

所以懂得战争规律的人，必先考虑一味冒进的危险，怎能指望一往无前就能胜利呢？如果轻举冒进，寻求决战，敌人又有计划地加以阻止，这样我军的进攻一定会遭到失败。所以兵法上说，如果敌人求战，我就应战，或者见到敌人就去进攻，或者我军的力量本来不能阻挡敌人的进攻，而又轻率地交战，都必然会丧失战争的主动权。

Verse 4

Those from whom the initiative has been taken have low fighting spirit; those who are afraid are unable to mount a defense; those who have suffered defeat have no men to fight. They are all cases of an army general who is not able to command and manage his troops well. When you decide to go forth and have no doubts, follow your plan. When you take the initiative and attack the enemy and still no one confronts you, press the attack home. If you can have a clear picture of the enemy's situation and occupy the high ground, then overawe them into submission. This is the pinnacle of implementing the 'Art of War'.

军队处于被动地位就会挫伤士气，军心恐惧就不能坚守，遭受失败是由于指挥无方，这些都是用兵不得其法的原故。军队斗志昂扬而毫不犹豫，就同敌人进行决战，敌人动摇而又不敢前进，就乘机发动进攻，明瞭敌情而又居高临下，就利用威势压倒敌人。这就算是精通兵法了。

Verse 5

Those who are unguarded in their discussions can be clandestinely overheard. Those who plunder and bully without proper discipline can be destroyed. Those who are met with gushing waters or struck by lightning will be thrown into chaos. You must settle those of your troops who are in crisis, eliminate their worries and decide matters through wisdom. Plan properly during the planning phase in the court; emphasize on selecting the right general to be given the mandate; arouse the fighting spirit of the army when inside the enemy territory. Only then can the enemy state be forced to submit without fighting.

军队言语不谨慎，就会泄密。如果欺凌侵犯无节制，就会失败。士兵遇上洪水或雷电袭击，就会溃乱。必须要转危为安，消除祸源，机智地进行处置。朝延的决策要高明，将帅的选用要慎重，进入敌人国境要迅速，这就可以不经战斗而使敌国屈服了。

Chapter 13
Heavy Punishment

Verse 1

If a general commanding 1,000 men or more retreats from battle, surrenders his defenses, or abandons his terrain and deserts his troops, he is termed as a 'state brigand', someone who has stolen from the state. He should be executed, his family exterminated, his name expunged from the registers, his ancestral graves broken open, his bones exposed in marketplace.

If a commander of 100 or more men retreats from battle, surrenders his defenses, or abandons his terrain and deserts his troops, he is termed an 'army brigand'. He should be executed, his family broken, and his male and female children shall serve in government as slaves.

If you cause the people to fear heavy punishment within the state, then outside the state they will regard the enemy lightly. Thus the Former Kings made the regulations and measures clear before making their punishment heavy. When punishments are heavy, then they will fear them within the state. When they fear them within the state, then they will be stalwart outside of it.

统辖千人以上的将领,若有作战失败,守城投降,擅离防地,弃军逃跑的,叫做国贼。对这种人要处死抄家,取消他的官籍,挖掘他的祖坟,把尸骨暴露在大街上示众,全家男女收入官府作为奴隶。统辖百人以上的官吏,若有作战失败,守城投降,擅离防地,弃军逃跑的,叫做军贼。对这种人要处死抄家,把全家男女收入官府作奴隶。这样就会使全军将士对内畏惧重刑,对外轻视敌人了。所以从前英明的君主,都是首先中明法令,然后使用重刑。刑罚重则人心畏刑,人心畏刑就会坚强对敌了。

Chapter 14
Army Organizations

Within the army, the regulations for organizations should be as follows: five men comprise a squad of five, with all the members being mutually responsible for each other. Ten men comprise a squad of ten, with all the members being mutually responsible for each other. Fifty men compose a platoon, with all the members being mutually responsible for each other. 100 men comprise a company, with all the members being mutually responsible for each other.

If any member of the squad of five or ten violates an order or commits an offense, should the others report it, their punishment will be remitted. If they know about it but do not report it, then the entire squad will be punished. If any member of a platoon or company violates an order or commits an offense, should the others report it, their punishment can be remitted. If they know about it but do not report it, then the entire platoon or company will be punished. All the officers – from the level of the squad of five up to the top generals in command, superiors and inferiors – are mutually responsible for each other. If someone violates an order or commits and offense, those who report it will be spared from punishment, while those who know about it but do not report it will all share the same offense.

Now when the members of the squads of five and ten are mutually bonded and the upper and lower ranks are mutually linked, no perversity will remain undiscovered, no offense will remain unreported. Fathers will not be able to cover for their sons and elder brothers will not be able to cover for their younger brothers. How much less so will the people of the state, living and eating together, be able to violate orders and conceal each other?

军队的联保制度，是按五人编为一伍，伍内的人互相联保，十人编为一什，什内的人互相联保；五十人编为一属，属内的人互相联保；百人编为一闾，闾内的人互相联保。伍内如有触犯禁令的，同伍的人揭发了他，全伍免罪，知道而不揭发，全伍受罚。什内有触犯禁令的，同什的人揭发了他，全什免罪，知道而不揭发，全什受罚。属内有触犯禁令的，同属的人揭发了他，全属免罪，知道而不揭发，全属受罚。闾内有触犯禁令的，同间的人揭发了他，全闾免罪，知道而不揭发，全闾受罚。
将吏从什长以上到左、右将军，上下都互相联保，凡有触犯禁令的，揭发了的都免于治罪，知道而不揭发的，都与他同罪。同伍同什的人都互相具结，上下之间都互相联保，就没有不能破获的阴谋，没有不被揭发的罪恶。即使父亲也不能够包庇他的儿子，哥哥也不能够包庇他的弟弟，何况一般的人呢？既然同吃同住在一起，哪还敢有违犯禁令而私相包庇的呢？

Chapter 15
Exit and Entry

The Central, Left, Right, Forward and Rear armies all have their designated camping ground – each surrounded on all four sides by temporary walls – with no passage among them permitted. The general has his designated terrain; the regimental commander has his designated camping ground; and the company commander has his designated camping ground. They should all construct ditches and sluices, and make the orders for the passageways to be blocked, so that it is impossible for someone who is not a member of the company to pass through. If someone who is not a member of the company enters, then the commander should execute him. If he fails to execute him, he will share the offense with him.

Along the roads leading to the encampment, set up lookout posts every 120 paces. Survey the men and the terrain to make sure the lookout posts are within sight of each other. Prohibit crossing over the roads, and make sure the roads are always clear. If a soldier does not have a tally or token issued by a general or commanding officers, he cannot pass through. Wood gatherers, fodder seekers and animal herders need to form and move in squads of five. If they are not moving in squads of five, they cannot pass through. If an officer does not have a token, if the soldiers are not in orderly arrangement, the guards at the crossing gates should execute them. If anyone oversteps the demarcation lines, execute him. Thus if within the army, no one contravenes nor violates the prohibitions, then without there will not be any perversity that is not caught.

中军和左、右、前、后各军，都有分配的营地，营地四周围以矮墙，不能互相来往。将有营地，帅有营地，伯也有营地，各个营地周围都挖有界沟，并明确颁布营地的禁令，规定各"伯"
驻地，不是同"伯"的人不得进入。如有不同"伯"的人擅自进入，伯长应杀他们。伯长不杀他们，就和他们同罪。军中纵横方向的道路，每隔一百二十步设立一个岗哨，根据人数和地形使岗哨能够监视到各条道路，负责限制行人往来，保障交通顺畅，除非持有将吏的符节一律不准通行。打柴和放牧的人员，都要整队行动，不整队的不得通行。官吏没有符节，士兵没有整队的，都由担任营门警卫的军官惩罚他们。凡是越出自己营地范围，进入别人营地的，都应加以惩罚。这样，内
部就没有触犯禁令的人，外来的奸细也就不难查获了。

Chapter 16
Rewards & Punishment in War

The orders which bind the squad of five states: 'Five men comprise the squad of five. They collectively write an agreement that binds them together with the commander. If in battle they lose men, but capture or kill an equivalent number of enemies, they negate each other. If they capture members of an enemy squad without losing anyone themselves, they will be rewarded. If they lose members without capturing or killing an equal number of the enemy, they will be killed and their families implicated.

If they lose their squad leader but capture a squad leader, the two negate each other. If they capture a squad leader without losing their own, they will be rewarded. If they lose their squad leader without capturing an enemy squad leader, they will be killed and their families exterminated. However if they rejoin the battle and take the head of a squad leader, then their punishment will be lifted. If they lose their general or kill one, the two negate each other. If they capture a general without losing their own, they will be rewarded. If they lose their general and do not kill an enemy general, they should be considered according to the Law for abandoning their positions and fleeing.'

The martial law during war states: 'The leader of a squad of ten can execute the other nine. A company commander can execute double squad leaders. The general of 1,000 men can execute company commanders. The general of 10,000 men can execute the general of 1,000 men. The generals of the Left and Right Armies can execute the generals of 10,000 men. The Grand General has no one he cannot execute.'

束伍令规定，五人编为一伍，写一份五人联保凭征，保存在将吏那里。战斗时，伍内伤亡与斩获的数量相等的，功罪相当；有斩获而自己没有伤亡的，有赏；伍内有伤亡而没有斩获的，处死刑，并惩办他的家族。自己的什长伯长伤亡而能斩获敌人什长伯长的，功罪相抵；斩获敌人什长伯长而自己什长伯长没有伤亡的，有赏；自己
什长伯长伤亡而没有斩获敌人什长伯长的，处死刑，并惩办他们的家族；战时军规律军，能斩获敌人什长伯长的，可以免罪。将领伤亡而能斩获敌统率将领的，功罪相抵；斩获敌人将领而自己将领没有伤亡的，有赏；自己将领伤亡而没有斩获敌人将领的，按放弃防地，临阵脱逃论罪。战时军律规定，什长有权处死所属的任何一个人，伯长有权处死什长，统率千人的将领有权处死伯长，统率万人的将领有权处死统率千人的。将领，左、右将军有权处死统率万人的将领，大将军有权处死全军的任何人。

Chapter 17
Regulating & Ordering the Troops

To regulate the troops, segment them into three armies. The Left Army will have green flags, and the troops will wear green feathers. The Right Army will have white flags, and the troops will wear white feathers. The Central Army will have yellow flags, and the troops will wear yellow feathers.

The troops will have five emblems: the front line will have the green emblems, the second row red emblems, the third row yellow emblems, the fourth row white emblems, and the fifth row black emblems.

Next, anyone who loses his emblem will be punished. The first five lines place their emblems on their heads; the next five lines place their emblems on their necks; the next five on their chest, the next five on their stomachs and the last five on their waists. In this way, it will never happen that the troops will have someone other than their own officers or officers other than their own troops. If someone sees a case where it is incorrect but does not inquire about it, or sees confusion but does not act to stop it, his crime will be comparable to that of the offender.

When the drums sound for the troops to move and engage in battle, those lines that move forward confront the danger, while those who retreat to the rear are reviled. Those who venture forward past the five lines will be rewarded; those who retreat past the five lines to the rear will be executed. By this rule, it can be known that advancing and retreating, moving to the fore and rear are achievements. Thus it is said: 'If you beat the drum, they advance like thunderclap, they move like the wind and rain, no one will dare oppose you to the fore, no one will dare chase after you to the rear.' This speaks volumes about having regulations.

管理军队，就是依经手卒把军队区分为三军。左军用青旗，士兵戴青色羽毛；右军用白旗，士兵戴白色羽毛；中军用黄旗，士兵戴黄色羽毛。士兵的标记有五种，第一行用青色标记，第二行用红色标记，第三行用黄色标记，第四行用白色标记，第五行用黑色标记，按此次序规定，管理士兵，遗失标记的，要给以惩罚。第一个五行的标记佩在头上，第二个五行的标记佩在颈上，第三个五行的标记佩在胸前，第四个五行的标记佩在腹部，第五个五行的标记佩在腰间。这样，士兵就不会认错他的官长，官长也不会认错他的士兵。如果官长发现不属于自己的士兵而不加盘问，见到行列混乱而不加制止，就和犯错误的人同罪。开始进行格斗的时候，如果前行的奋勇前进，就是敢于战斗，后行的退缩不前，就是沾污军誉，超过前面五行而前进的有赏，越出后面五行而后退的就杀。这些规定都是为了分清吏卒们进、退、先、后的功过是非。因此可以说，命令一下，军队前进就象雷霆那样迅速，冲击就象风雨那样猛烈，没有哪个敌人敢于在前面阻挡，也没有哪个敌人敢于在后面尾追，这 就说明了经卒令的重大作用。

The Book of Wei Liaozi

Chapter 18
Regulating the Movement of Troops

Verse 1

Gongs, drums, bells and flags – these four instruments each have their methods of employment. When the drum sounds, the army should advance; when the drums are beat again, they should attack. When the gongs sound, they should stop; when the gongs are struck again, they should withdraw. Bells are used to transmit order. When flags point to the left, the army should go left; when the flags point to the right, then to the right. For non-regular units these signals should be mixed up. Beat the drum once and they may move to the left; beat it another time and they may advance to the left. For each step there is one beat, this is the pace beat. If for the ten steps, there is one beat, this is the quick march beat. If the drumming is unbroken, this is the racing beat. The *shang* note comes from the general's drum. The *jiao* note comes from that of a regimental commander's drum. The low pitch drum is that of a company commander. When the three drums sound together, the generals, regimental commander and company commanders are all of one mind. For the non-regular units, these signals should be mixed up. If a drummer misses a beat, he is executed. Those who set up a clamor are executed. Those who do not obey the gongs, drums, bells, and flags but move by themselves are executed. When combat methods are taught to 100 men, after their instruction is complete, unite them with other companies to comprise 1,000 men. When the instruction of 1,000 men is complete, unite them with other regiments to comprise of 10,000. When the tens of thousands have been instructed, assemble them into one army. When the masses of the army can divide and unite, they can then execute the methods of large scale combat. When the army's instructions are complete, test them with military maneuvers.

金鼓铃旗四种指挥工具各有各的用法。一次击鼓部队就前进，二次击鼓部队就冲击；一次鸣金部队就停止，二次鸣金部队就后退。铃是用来传达命令的。旗指向左边部队就向左，指向右边部队就向右。但使用奇兵时就应变换这些指挥信号。有时鼓声一阵是令一部分部队向左冲击的，有时鼓声一阵是令一部分部队向右冲击的。走一步敲一下鼓是慢步行进的鼓声，走十步敲一次鼓是快步行进的鼓声，鼓声不断是跑步行进的鼓声。发商音的鼓，是将使用的鼓；发角音的鼓，是帅使用的鼓；发音细小的鼓，是伯使用的鼓；三种鼓声同时响起，表示将、帅、伯意图一致。对奇兵应改换这些指挥信号。鼓音混乱的处死，大声喧哗扰乱鼓音的处死，不听金鼓铃旗指挥而擅自行动的处死。首先以百人为单训练作战，训练完成后，再以十个百人单位进行合练，十个百人单位训练完成后，以万人为单位进行合练，万人训练完成，就集合全军进行合综。全军吏卒都应学会有时分散，有时集中这种大军作战的方法。全军训练完成后，通过校阅，以检查训练的效果。

Verse 2

For a well-trained army: in a square formation, they are victorious; in a circular formation, they are also victorious; in a very uneven array, they are also victorious; and if they encounter difficult terrain, they will also emerge victorious. If the enemy is in the mountains, climb after him. If the enemy is in the depths, plunge in after him. Seek the enemy as if searching for a lost child, seek him without any doubt and fast. In this way, you will be able to defeat the enemy and control his fate. Now, one must make decisions early and determine plans beforehand. If plans are not determined first and if intentions are not decided early, then neither advancing nor retreating will be in order. When doubts arise, defeat is certain. Thus a direct army values arriving first. An indirect army values arriving second. Being first, being second – these are ways to control the enemy. Generals throughout the ages who have not understood these principles, after their first commission, rush to be first to launch an attack – relying on courage alone. There were none who were not defeated. Their actions should be hesitant but are not; their movements should be confident but are not; their movement should be at times slow, at times rapid but is neither slow nor rapid when it needs to be. These three situations drag on the army in battle.

有训练的军队，方阵也能取胜，圆阵也能取胜，在错综复杂的地形作战也能取胜，在险要阻绝的地形作战也能取胜。敌人在山上，就缘山进攻它。敌人在水上，就下水攻击它。搜找敌人要象搜找丢失的孩子一样追切，毫不迟疑地追击，所以能打败敌人，致敌于死命。用兵必须提早定下决心，预先确定作战计划，如果计划不预先制定，决心不及早定下，就会进退不定，疑虑丛生，这样必然招致失败。一般来说正兵贵在先发制人，奇兵应该后发制人，但是，哪个先用，哪个后用，都是为了战胜敌人。

一些庸将不懂得这种奇正变化的法则，一意孤行，以先击为勇，这就没有不失败的了。在出兵时，该考虑的不考虑；进军中，该有信心而又动摇；在战斗中，当快时不快，当慢时不慢，这三种都是对作战不利的。

Chapter 19
Orders of the General before the Start of the War

Before the commanding general is about to receive his commission, the ruler must first discuss military strategy in the ancestral temple, then issue the order in court. The ruler personally grants the Axe of Authority to the general, saying: "The Left, Right and Central Armies have their separate responsibilities. If anyone oversteps the boundary of their responsibility to seek the intercession of higher ranks, he shall be put to death. Within the army, there cannot be two sources of orders. Anyone who issues a second order shall be executed. Anyone who withholds orders shall be executed. Anyone who delays the implementation of an order shall be executed. Anyone who disobeys an order shall be executed."

The general makes the announcement: "To those about to go out beyond the gates of the state capital, the time for assembling is set as midday. Within the encampment, we shall set up a gnomon (form of sundial) and place it at the front gate. Those who arrive past the designated time will be subject to the provision of the law."

When the general has entered the encampment, he closes the gate and has the roads cleared. Anyone daring to enter or to leave the encampment without permission will be executed. Anyone daring to make a big clamor will be executed. Those not following orders will be executed.

将军奉命出征，君主必先在宗庙商定大计，然后在朝廷发布命令，并亲自把斧钺授予将军说："左、
右、中三军，皆有分掌的职权，如有越级报告的处死。军队中除将军外不得发布命令，擅自发布命令的处死。扣压命令的处死，贻误命令执行的处死。"将军受领任务后，向下级宣布说："出了京城以后，限于正午以前，树立营表，设置辕门，等待军队报到，如果超过规定时间而迟到的依法惩办。"将军入营以后，即关闭营门，禁止通行，有敢擅自通行的处死，有敢高声喧嚷的处死，有敢不服从命令的处死。

Chapter 20
Vanguards

What is referred to as the vanguard moves off from the main force about 100 miles, arriving at a designated place and an appointed time. It carries three days of supplies of prepared food. It moves in front of the main army. Only when they have confirmed the orders and signals, do they then move off. Before they move off, one should reward them to motivate them, and deploy them as the disposition of each army changes. This is the method to move the troops.

The advance army moves in front of the vanguard. When the order to move off is raised (the proper flag), it moves off from the main force to double the vanguard's distance – about 100 miles ahead of the vanguard, arriving at the designated place and time. They carry six days supply of prepared food. They are ordered to prepare for the battle and deploy troops to occupy strategic positions. If the battle turns to the army's advantage, they pursue the retreating enemy; if the forces are stalemated, they race into the enemy. If the vanguard encounters anyone who has turned back, they should execute him. What are termed the armies of generals, consist of four forces and they are the main, advance, vanguard and pockets of army, and using them would allow the general to seize victory.

The army has its squads of ten and five and the methods of dividing and reuniting. Before engaging in battle, duties are assigned, and designated units should occupy the strategic locations, passes, and bridges. When the order to engage in battle is raised, they should all assemble. The main army sets out with a fixed daily ration and their combat equipment all complete. The orders are issued and they move; anyone who does not follow orders is executed.

Now determine and assign forces to the strategic points within the borders of the state. After the advance army and vanguard have already set out, the people within the borders are not able to move about. Those who have received the king's commands and who have been given and carry the proper tallies and tokens are officers acting in accord with their duties. Officers who are not acting in accord with their duties, but yet move, should be executed. When the main army has moved off, these officers – acting in accord with their duties – travel about and are employed to ensure that army affairs are mutually regulated. Accordingly, one who wants to wage warfare must first secure the interior.

所谓踵军，通常与大军(主力部队)相距约一百里，按期到达会战地点，它应携带三天干粮，在大军的前面行进，还要预先规定好行动的信号，接到信号后就开始行动。踵军开始行动之前，应搞赏士卒，以激发他们的战斗意志。这就是踵军向战场前进的方法。
兴军，在踵军的前面行进，接到前进的信号就开始出发。它与大军的距离比距踵军远一倍，与踵军相距约一百里，也要按期到达会战地点，并应携带六天干粮，到达后作好战斗准备，同时派出分手(一部兵力)占领附近要点。战斗有利就追击败退的敌人，后续部队要急速跟进策应他们。踵军遇有从兴军逃回的应予惩办。一般地说，将领善于指挥大军、踵军、兴军、分卒，这四部分军队，使它们相互配合，首尾相应，就能胜利地行军作战了。

军队有什伍的编制，有分散有集中，事先区分任务，据守要害、关卡、桥梁，到了战期，根据号令向规定的地点会合。大军应按规定及时补充粮食和各种物资，接到命令就开始行动，不按照命令行事的应予惩办。

凡宣布戒严的地区，在它的范围之内，当兴军、踵军已经出发，而主力还未出发的时候，境内的民众，一概不许通行。奉有君主命令并持有符节的，叫做传达任务的军

官，这种人才准通行。不是传达任务的军官而擅自行动的应予惩罚。当主力出发以后，传达任务的军官才离开这个地区，回去参与军务。总之要进行战争，必须首先安定内部的秩序。

Chapter 21
Military Instructions I

Verse 1.1

Rules for instructing the soldiers: when dispersing them to their encampments, have the soldiers assume formation; those who advance or retreat contrary to orders should be punished for the crime of contravening instructions. The front lines are instructed by the commander of the front lines; the rear lines are instructed by the commander of the rear lines; the lines to the left are instructed by the commander of the lines to the left; the lines to the right are instructed by the commander of the lines to the right. When all five men in a line have been successfully instructed, their squad leader is rewarded. Failing to successfully instruct all of them will result in being punished as though one had committed the crime of contravening instructions. If someone who has fallen ill brings it to the attention of the squad himself, and the squad members jointly report it, they will then be spared from punishment.

军队的教令规定，在分设营垒或布列阵势中，凡有不按照教令进退的，都给以违犯教令的处分。教练的时候，前行的士兵，由前行的伍长教练。后行的士兵。由后行的伍长教练。左行的士兵，由左行的伍长教练。右行的士兵，由右行的伍长教练。教练好五个人，那个伍长应当受到奖励。教练不好，就应受到违犯教令的惩罚。因伤病不能参加教练的，自己先向伍内报告，伍内士兵为他作证，可以免受处罚。

Verse 1.2

In general, when the squad of five assumes formation for battle, if one of the men does not advance to attack the enemy, his instructor will be punished as if he had committed the crime himself. The squad of ten protects and bonds the ten men within it. If they lose a man and the other nine men do not fight to the death in a desperate battle with the enemy, then their instructor will be punished as if he had committed the crime himself. From the squad of ten up to the subordinate generals, if anyone does not follow the laws, their instructors will be punished as if they had committed the crime himself. In general, to make punishments and fines strict, and incentives and rewards fair, they must be incorporated within the laws for instructing the soldiers.

凡是同伍的人临阵交锋，如有一人不向前与敌死战，则负责教练的伍长，应和犯法的人同罪。什内的人互相联保，如有一人死亡，其余九人不尽力与敌死战，则负责教练的什长，应和犯法的人同罪。自什长以上直到裨将，有不按教令行动的，则负责教练的各级官吏，应和犯法的人同罪。凡是想做到刑罚严明，奖赏公平，必须在军队平时教练中贯彻实施。

Verse 1.3

Generals and the army have different flags, companies have different emblems. The Left Army wears their emblems on the left shoulder; the Right Army wears their emblems on the right shoulder; the Central Army wears their emblems on the front of the chest. Record on their emblems which part of the army they are from. From the front to the rear, for each platoon of five lines, the most honored emblems are placed on the head; the others accordingly place the emblem lower and lower on the body.

将吏使用不同的旗帜，士兵佩戴不同的徽章。左军的徽章佩在左肩，右军的徽章佩在右肩，中军的徽章佩在胸前，并在微章上写明部别姓名。此外，军队按照前后五行的顺序，佩戴五种不同颜色的微章，第一行把徽章戴在头上，其余各行依次降低佩戴的位置。

Verse 1.4

The squad leader instructs the other four men using a board as a drum, a piece of tile as a gong, and a bamboo pole as a flag. When he strikes a drum, they should advance; when he lowers the flag, they should race forward; when he strikes a gong, they should withdraw. When he points left, they should go left; when he points right, they should go to the right. When the gongs and the drums are struck together, they should sit.

When the squad leader has completed instructing the squad, they should be united with another squad, under a leader for a squad of ten. When the squad leaders have completed instructing them, they should be united under a platoon commander. When the platoon commander has completed instructing them, they should be united under a company commander. When the company commander has completed instructing them, they should be united under an army commandant. When the army commandant has completed instructing them, they should be united under a subordinate general. When the subordinate general has completed instructing them, they should be united under a commanding general.

When the commanding general has completed instructing them, he has them deploy in formation in the countryside. He sets up three large posts, one every hundred paces and has the army arrange into a formation before moving towards the first pole. They advance 100 paces and practice engaging the enemy. The army should quick-step for a hundred paces, and then race for another hundred paces. They practice battle tactics according to such plans. Afterward, rewards and punishments should be implemented according to how much they achieved during training.

伍长教练伍内四人，用木板代鼓，用瓦器代金，用竹竿代旗。击鼓就前进，把旗放低就快跑，鸣金就后退，指挥向左就向左，指挥向右就向右，金鼓齐鸣就坐下。伍长教练好了,由什长集合教练。什长教练好了,由卒长集合教练。卒长教练好了,由伯长集合教练。伯长教练好了,由兵尉集合教练。兵尉教练好了,由碑将集合教练。裨将教练好了,由大将集合教练。大将教练他们,在野外排成阵势,进行演习。演习时树立三个大标竿,每隔百步树立一个。军队列阵完毕,在距第一个标竿百步时演习决斗,在距第二个标竿百步时演习快步前进,在距第三个标竿百步时演习跑步急进。反复演练使军队完全掌握各种要领,然后根据演练好坏进行赏罚。

Verse 1.5

From the commandant on down, every officer has a flag. When the battle has been won, in each case, look at the rank of the flags that have been captured and reward accordingly. Such action will show that the commanding general is determined to reward based on accomplishments. Victory in war lies in military grandeur. Establishing military grandeur lies in uniting strength. Uniting strength lies in correct implementation of punishments. To implement punishments correctly, rewards system must be clear. Today when the people turn their backs to the border gates, facing life and death in war, if they have been taught to die without hesitation, there is a reason, and that is correct implementation of rewards and punishment.

军尉吏以下的军官都有指挥旗,凡是战胜敌人获得敌人指挥旗的,应按旗帜所代表的官爵,给予相应的奖赏,以表明有功必赏的决心。战胜敌人在于能树立军威,树立军威在于使人同心协力,使人同心协力在于刑罚公正。刑罚公正的目的,是为了突出奖赏的作用。要使士兵出国作战,在生死关头毫不犹豫地牺牲生命,靠的就是赏罚严明。

Verse 1.6

Instructed defenders set up a solid defense; those engaged in battle to inevitably fight; perverse plans not to be put in action; perverse people not to speak; orders effected without differing from the original orders given; the army to advance without doubt; and the light units to behave like a clap of thunder – to rush at the enemy like the stampede of horses. Raise those with merit; distinguish those with Virtue, making their distinction as clear as black and white. Cause the people to follow the orders of their superiors just as the four limbs respond to the mind.

要使防御的必能固守,进攻的必能备战,奸谋不会发生,奸人不敢造谣,命令贯彻不会走样,部队行动没有疑虑,轻装急进象雷电似的迅速,奋勇杀敌象惊马似的奔
驰。提拔有功的人,表扬有德的人,功过是非黑白分明,这就能使士兵按照上级的命令行动。如象四肢听从头脑的指挥一样灵活了。

Verse 1.7

If the forward units break up the enemy's ranks, penetrate the enemy's solid defense like water bursting through, there is a basis for it. This is the result of effective training. They provide the means to open sealed borders, preserve the altars of state, eliminate disaster and harm, and gain martial accomplishment.

前锋部队,能够打乱敌人行列,突破敌人坚阵,就象大水决堤似的不可抵御,绝不是偶然的,这是军队训练有素的结果。训练这样一支军队,目的是为了开拓疆土,保卫国家,消除祸患,成就"武德"。

Chapter 22
Military Instructions II
Verse 1.1

I have heard that once a ruler of men knows the way to achieve victory, he is then able to unite others and become expansive and great, to unify the ordinances and regulations, and have his military grandeur prevail in the world. There are twelve essential matters to look at to achieve victory:

1. The first is called 'joint punishment' and refers to the method of joint criminal responsibility for all members of the squad of five.
2. The second is called 'terrain restrictions' which refers to prohibiting and stopping passage along the roads in order to ensnare spies.
3. The third, 'chariots as a unit', refers to the chariot commanders and infantry leaders being mutually dependent, the three officers in the chariot and the squads of five being cohesive, all coming together to form a unit.
4. The fourth, 'defending strategic points', refers to dividing the terrain with boundaries and having each man securely defending his position till death.
5. The fifth, 'demarking boundaries', refers to the left and right restraining each other, front and rear awaiting each other and a wall of chariots creating a solid defense in order to oppose the enemy and stop them.
6. The sixth, 'commands are distinguished', refers to the forward rows concentrating on advancing, thereby being distinguished from those in the rear; who are not to compete to be the first to ascend, nor overstep their positions.
7. The seventh, 'five emblems', refers to distinguishing the rows, with emblems so that the troops will not be disordered.
8. The eighth, 'preserving the units', refers to units breaking up and following each other, each having their appointed sections.
9. The ninth, 'gongs and drums', refers to stimulating the troops to achievement and compelling them to great heights.
10. The tenth, 'arraying the chariots', refers to making the formation tight, with the spears deployed to the front and putting blinders on the horses' eyes.
11. The eleventh, 'warriors of death', refers to selecting the courageous and strong from among the masses of the army to ride in war chariots. They race forward and back, across and about, using tactics to gain mastery over the enemy.
12. The twelfth, 'strong troops', refers to regulating the flags and preserving the units. Without the flags signaling an order, they do not move.

When the instructions for these twelve rules have been successfully taught, anyone who contravenes an order should not be pardoned. As such, a weak army will be able to strengthen. If a ruler does not have a reputation, they will be able to know him. If orders become enervated, they will be able to revitalize them. If the people become migrants, they will be able to attract them. If the people are numerous, they will be able to govern them. If the territory is vast, they will be able to defend it. Without sending out the chariots or taking the armor from the storage bags, your military grandeur will still spread throughout the land.

我听说人君掌握了必胜的方法，就能兼并广大的土地，实行统一的制度，从而威震天下。其方法有十二条：一是"连刑"，即一个犯罪，全伍连坐；二是"地禁"，即是管制交通，以防止奸细；三是"全车"，就是说战车上的甲士和随车步卒都要在车长统一指挥下，协调一致地行动；四是"开塞"，即划分防区，各自尽忠职责以行坚守；五是"分限"，即营阵左右相互警卫，前后相互照顾，环列战车，形成坚固营垒，用以抗拒敌人和保障宿营安全；六是"号别"，即前列部队进战时，与后列界限分明，后列不得抢先突进，以免次序紊乱；七是"五章"，即用五种颜色的标记以区别行列；保持部队始终不乱；八是"全曲"，即各部队在行动中互相连系，保持自己在战斗队形中的关系位置；九是"金鼓"，即激励将士杀敌主功，为国牺牲；十是"阵车"，即驻止时用战车前后连结成阵，遮蔽马的双目以免惊驰；十一是"死士"，即从各军中选拔有才而能勇敢的人，乘着战车，忽左忽右、忽前忽后地出奇制胜；十二是"力卒"，即选用才力超群的人掌管军旗，指挥部队，没有命令不得擅自行动。按照以上十二条进行教育后，有效逼犯教令的决不宽容。这样，军队战斗力弱的可以增强，君主威望不高的可以提高，法令废弛的可以整顿，人民流散的可以归附，人口众多而庞杂的也可以治理好，土地广大的可以守得住，不必出兵打仗，也能威服天下。

Verse 1.2

Soldiers have five commitments: for their general, they forget their families; when they cross the border, they forget their relatives; when they confront the enemy, they forget themselves; when they are committed to die, they will live; urgently seeking victory is the lowest. 100 men willing to suffer the pain of a blade can penetrate a line and cause chaos in a formation. 1,000 men willing to suffer the pain of a blade can seize the enemy and kill its general. 10,000 men willing to suffer the pain of a blade can transverse anywhere at will.

对军队有五条要求：受命为将要忘掉家庭，出国作战要忘掉亲戚，临阵杀敌要忘掉自己，只有抱必死的决心，才可以求得生存，急于求胜，是不好的。百人死战，就可以摧破敌阵。千人死战，就可以擒敌杀将。万人死战，犹可以横行天下。

Verse 1.3

King Wu asked Tai Gong Wang: "I want to know the essence of employing men." Tai Gong Wang replied: "Your rewards should be like mountains, your punishments like streams. When carrying out punishment and rewards, make no errors; the next is to correct mistakes immediately, if any. As such, there would not be disputes. Now anyone who, when about to be punished, requests that he not be punished should die. Anyone who, when about to be rewarded, requests that he not be rewarded should die. Attack a country when it has major changes. Observe their display of riches in order to observe their poverty. Observe their display of weaknesses in order to determine their 'illnesses'. If the ruler is immoral and the people disaffected, in cases such as these, one has a basis for attack."

周武王问太公望说:" 我想用最少时间来了解用人的要领。
太公望说:" 奖励好人好事,要象高山那样的坚定不移,惩罚坏人坏事,要象溪水那样的通行无阻。执行赏罚最重要的是不发生差错,其次是有了差错及时纠正,这就不合使人背后议论了。凡是有罪当罚而请求不罚的处死,有功当赏而请求不赏的处死。讨伐别的国家,必须利用它国内的变乱。观察它的财政情况,看它是否穷困,观察它国内的弊端,看它有何危机,看它上层是否专横暴戾,下层是否离心离德,有了这些情况就是有了可以讨我伐的因素。

Verse 1.4

In general, whenever about to mobilize the army, you must first investigate the strategic balance of power both within and outside the borders, in order to decide whether to mount a campaign. You must know whether the army is well prepared or suffers from inadequacies, whether there is a surplus or shortage of food. You must determine the route for advancing and returning. Only thereafter can you mobilize the army to attack the weakest points and be certain of being able to enter his state.

If the territory is vast but the cities small, you must first occupy their land. If the cities are large but the land narrow, you must first attack their cities. If the country is vast, and the populace is small, isolate their strategic points. If the land is confined, but the people are numerous, then construct fortifications in order to attack them. Do not destroy their material gains nor delay people's scheduled agricultural activities. Be magnanimous towards government officials, stabilize the people's occupations, and provide relief for the impoverished, for then your virtuous deeds will be sufficient to spread throughout the land. Today, warring states attack each other and mount large assaults on the virtuous. From the squads to the platoons, from the platoons to the army, none have unified orders. They cause the people to have unsettled minds; these rulers incline toward arrogance and extravagance. Officials are constantly involved in disputes, spending their time investigating matters. These are entanglements that cause all parties to be tired and dispirited, thus bringing about defeat. After the sun has set, the road remains long, and when the soldiers return to camp, they are dispirited. The army is tired from the campaign, the general covetous. Thus the troops will plunder to seize material gains and will be easily defeated.

兴兵作战，必须详细研究敌我形势的变化，以计划军队的行动。敌我战备的程度，粮食的多少，比较双方进出道路的远近险易，然后出兵进攻，必能顺利攻入敌境。敌人地大而城小，必先占领广阔的土地。城大而地窄，必先攻占它的城市。土地广阔而人口少的，就要控制它的枢纽要害，城市狭小而人口稠密的，就构筑土山攻城。

对敌国不要损害其民众的利益，不要耽误民众的耕种，废除苛刻的法令，安定人民的生活，拯救民众的疾苦，这就是施恩于天下了。现今各国互相攻伐，往往仗恃强大，攻击施行德政的国家。军队从"伍"到"两"，从"两"到"师"，命令不统一，军心不安定。崇尚骄奢，惹事生非，官吏忙于处理这些事情，徒劳精力，招致战败。还师罢军，挫伤士气，久战疲惫，将帅贪功，士卒劫掠，这就很容易被战败了。

Verse 1.5

When the general is arrogant and obnoxious, the fortifications are low, and the troop's minds unstable, they can be attacked. If the general can be counted on, fortifications are high, but the masses are afraid, they can be encircled. In general, whenever you encircle someone, you must provide them with a prospect for some escape, causing them to become weaker day by day. When time passes, even if the defenders reduce their rations, they will have nothing to eat. When their masses fight with each other at night, it is a sign that they are terrified. If the masses avoid following instructions, they have become disaffected. If they just wait for others to come and rescue them, and when the time for battle arrives, they are tense; they have all lost their will and are dispirited. Being dispirited defeats an army; distorted plans defeat a state.

凡是敌人将帅轻浮、营垒低矮、军心动摇的，就可以进攻它。将帅稳重、营垒高大、军心恐惧的，可以围困它。围困敌人，必须给它展示一线希望，使它斗志逐渐削弱，时间一久，即使敌人节约粮食，也会陷于饥饿了。敌方士兵夜间自相攻击，是军队惊恐不安的表现。士兵不听指挥，是上下离心离德的表现。等待别国救援，会战前局促不安的，是信心丧失，士气沮丧的表现。士气沮丧，军队就会失败；谋略错误，国家就会败亡。

Chapter 23
Army Orders I

Verse 1.1

Weapons are implements for killing. War is contrary to Virtue. Plundering is an underhanded activity. Therefore when a true king attacks the brutal and chaotic, he takes benevolence and righteousness as the foundation for it. At the present time, the warring states, to establish their military grandeur, resist their enemies and plot against each other. Thus they cannot disband their armies.

兵器，是杀人的工具。战争，是违反道德的行为。掠夺，是卑鄙的手段。所以王者讨伐暴乱，是为了申张仁义的。战国诸侯为了树立自己的权威，抵抗外敌侵略，互相图霸称雄，因而战争。

Verse 1.2

War takes the military as its trunk and political gains as its seed. War can be seen as the exterior and politics as the interior. One who can investigate and fathom the two will know the difference between victory and defeat. Politics is the means to discern benefit and harm, to discriminate between security and danger. The military is the means to contravene a strong enemy, to forcefully attack and defend.

战争这个问题，军事是手段，政治是目的。军事是现象，政治是本质。能弄清这二者的关系，就懂得胜败的道理了。政治是用来明察利害，辨别安危的。军事是用来战胜强敌，保卫国家的。

Verse 1.3

One who is unified will be victorious; one who is beset by dissension will be defeated. When formations are tight, they are solid; when using weapons, it is better that the formations are loose. One whose troops fear their general far more than the enemy will be victorious. One whose troops fear the enemy far more than their general will be defeated. Thus to know who will be victorious and who defeated, measure your general with the enemy. If the general is settled and quiet, the troops are well-ordered; if the general is brutal and hasty, they are in chaos.

意志统一就能胜利，离心离德就会失败。布阵队形密集有利于巩固，行列疏散则便于使用兵器。士卒畏惧将帅超过畏惧敌人的就能胜利，士卒畏惧敌人超过畏惧将帅的就会失败，所以要预知胜败，就可以比较士卒畏敌还是畏将，用这个比较来预见胜败，就象用秤称物一样准确。将帅沉着，军队就会严整，将帅急躁，军队就会混乱。

Verse 1.4

Sending troops forth and deploying the army have standard orders; the dispersal and density of the lines and squads have standard methods; and arraying the rows from the front to rear has appropriateness and suitability. Standard orders are not employed when pursuing a fleeing enemy or suddenly striking a city. If the front and rear are disordered, then the army loses the ability to achieve victory. If anyone causes confusion among the lines, behead him.

出兵列阵有一般的法则，队形疏密有一定的标本，先后次序有适当的规定。这里所说的一般法则，不是用于追击和奔袭城邑的。前后次序紊乱了就会战败，所以对扰乱次序的人要处死。

Verse 1.5

The standard deployment for formations is always facing toward the enemy. There are also internally oriented formations, externally oriented formations, standing formations, and sitting formations. Internally oriented formations provide the means to preserve the center; externally oriented formations provide the means to defend against external threats. Standing formations are the means to move, sitting formations the means to stop or defend. Standing or sitting formations deployed in accordance with the need to move or stop, with the general being in command in the middle. The weapons of the seated soldiers are the sword and axes; the weapons of the standing soldiers are the spear tipped halberd and crossbow; the general also occupies the middle, in command.

布阵通常是面向敌人的，但根据情况也有向内的，也有向外的，有立阵，也有坐阵。向内是为了保卫中军的安全，向外是为了防备敌人的袭击，立阵是准备进攻的，坐阵是用于驻止和防守的。采取立阵还是坐阵，应该根据军队的进止攻守来决定，将帅总是居中指挥。坐阵的兵器主要使用剑斧以备近战。立阵的兵器主要使用戟弩以利远战，将帅也是居中指挥。

Verse 1.6

Those who excel at repelling the enemy, first join battle with regular troops, then use surprise strategies to control them. This is the technique for certain victory. Array Axes of Authority: make a display of the emblems and flags. Those who have merit must be rewarded; those who contravene orders must die. The preservation or destruction of the state and the life or death of the soldiers lies at the hands of the general. Even though there are those under Heaven who excel at commanding armies, no one will be able to repel an army whose general does the above.

善于抵御敌人的，通常先以正面兵力与敌作战，然后以机动兵力乘机打击它，这是必胜的方法。战斗时还要陈列斧钺，设置旗章，有功必赏，犯令必杀。国家的存亡，官兵的生死，全都系于将帅的指挥。能这样去指挥军队，纵然天下有善于用兵的人，也是不能抗拒他的。

Verse 1.7

Before arrows have been shot and cross in flight, before the long blades have clashed, if the enemy's front lines are noisy, it means their army is weak. If the back lines are noisy, it means they are strong in numbers. If both the front and the back lines are not noisy, it means there is a plan. All three situations are typical war situations.

在敌我双方还没有交锋的时候，如果敌人前军呼噪是它兵力虚弱的表现，后军呼噪是它兵力充实的表现，前后都不呼噪的是有秘密的企图。虚、实、秘三者都是作战的形态。

Chapter 24
Army Instructions II
Verse 1.1

Units are dispatched from the main army to undertake advance preparations for defense. They should set up observation posts along the borders every three to five miles. When they hear that the main army is making preparations to advance, mount a defense, and engage in battle, they should prohibit all movement in order to provide security to the state.

在主力前方担任警戒的部队，他们在彼此相距三至五里的地方，各自占领要点。一听到主力出动，就立即做好戒备措施。战时，边境一律要禁止通行，这是为了保障国家安全的缘故。

Verse 1.2

When troops from the interior are about to set out for border duty, have the commanding officer provide them with their flags, drums, halberds, and armor. On the day for issuing forth, anyone who leaves after the commanding officer has gone out beyond the district border shall be liable to the law, for late arrival for border duty.

The term of border duty for a soldier is one year. Anyone who leaves before being replaced shall be punished analogously to the law for deserting the army. If his parents, wife, or children know about it, they will share the crime with him. If they do not know about it, pardon them.

内地士兵去守卫边疆时，应使将吏发给旗鼓戈甲。到了出发的日期，如有士兵在将吏之后离开县界的，应以后期出境论罪。士兵守卫边疆一年，而不等到接替的人到来就擅自离开的，应同逃兵一样治罪，父母妻子知道情况的，与犯人同罪，不知道情况的，免罪。

Verse 1.3

If a soldier arrives at the headquarters of the Grand General a day after his commanding officer, his parents, wife and children should all share the crime with him. If a soldier abandons his post to return home for a day and his parents, wife, or children do not arrest him, hold him or report it, they should also share the crime with him.

士兵在将吏之后一日至大将处所报到的，父母妻子都与他同罪。士兵逃亡到家已过一日，父母妻子既不拘捕又不报告的，也与他同罪。

Verse 1.4

If they should abandon their commanding officer in battle, or if their commanding officer should abandon his troops and flee by himself, behead them all.

凡是在战斗中，士兵擅自脱离将吏的，以及将吏抛弃所属部队自逃跑的，都应处死。

Verse 1.5

If a forward officer should abandon his troops and flee, any officer to the rear who is able to kill him and reassemble his troops should be rewarded.

前方的将吏抛弃他所属部队逃跑的，后方的将吏能杀掉他，并把他的部队收容在一起的有赏。

Verse 1.6

Anyone among such troops who has not achieved merit within the army must serve three years at the border.

在战斗中没有立功的，罚戍守边疆三年。

Verse 1.7

If the army engages in a major battle and the commanding general dies, all of the subordinate officers whose commanding units of more than 500 men, who were not able to fight to the death with the enemy should be beheaded. All the troops near to the commanding general, on the left and right in protective formation, should be beheaded. As for the remaining officers and men in the army, those who have merit should be demoted by one grade. Those who do not have merit should be sent to three years' border duty.

三军大战，如果大将战死，其部下凡是带领五百人以上的将吏，没有与敌死战的都处死，大将左右的亲兵凡当时在阵中的，都一律死，其余士兵有军功的降一级，没有军功的罚戍边三年。

Verse 1.8

If the squad of five loses a man in battle, or if a squad member dies in battle but they do not retrieve his corpse, then take away all the merit of his squad members. If they retrieve his corpse, then their crimes should all be pardoned.

战斗时伍内有逃亡的人，以及伍内有人战死而不能夺回他的尸体的，同伍的人都要剥夺军功，能够收回死者尸体的，都赦免其罪。

The Book of Wei Liaozi

Verse 1.9

The army's advantage and disadvantage lie in the strength of the state. Today if a person's name appears as holding a particular military office, but in reality he is at home, then the office has not gained from his presence, and the household does not have the registration of his name. When troops are assembled to compose an army, it will have an empty name without substance. Outside of the state, it will be inadequate to repel enemies, while within the borders, it will be inadequate to defend the state. This is the way in which the army becomes insufficient; in which the general has his military grandeur taken away.

军队的利害得失，在于国家的编制名额与实际人数是否相符。现在不少士兵的名字列在军队，而本人却在家中，军队没有实际的兵员，家中没有本人的名字。国家调集士兵编成军队时，只有空的名额而无实际的兵员，对外不足以抵抗敌人，对内不足以守卫国家，这就是军队之所以战力不强，将帅之所以丧失威望的缘故。

Verse 1.10

In my opinion, when soldiers abandon their units and return home, the other members of their squad in the same barracks and their officers would be punished by taking their rations, to be put into the army's provisions. Thus a person is nominally with the army, but in reality, double the ration is taxed from the household. The resources of the state are then expended, and the harvest of the people is naturally exhausted. How can the disaster of defeat be avoided in such a case?

我认为现在士兵逃亡回家的，就对原籍同伍的五家人和主管官吏，罚以粮食，充实仓库，作为军需物资，这样一来，名义上是一支军队，而民众却有两倍的负担，弄得国内空虚，民不聊生，怎能避免失败的灾难呢？

Verse 1.11

Today, if the rules are able to stop deserters from returning home, this prevents the loss of an army and is the first military victory. When the squads of five and ten are mutually bound to the point that in battle, the troops and officer will aid each other, this is the second military victory. If the general is able to establish his military grandeur and set a great example, the soldiers to master and follow instructions, while the commands and orders are clear and trusted, and attacking and defending are both properly executed, this is the third military victory.

现在以法令禁止士兵逃亡，能禁止士兵逃亡，这是战争取得胜利的第一个因素。平时什伍之内能互相联保，战时官兵就能互相救援，这是战争取得胜利的第二个因素。将帅能够树立威信，士兵能够听从指挥，号令明确坚定，攻守运用得当，是战争取得胜利的第三个因素。

Verse 1.12

I have heard that in antiquity, those who excelled in employing the army could motivate half of their officers and soldiers to fight to death in war. The next could motivate a third of their officers and soldiers to fight to death in war. And the next could motivate a tenth of their officers and soldiers to fight to death in war. One who could motivate half his troops to fight till death will have his military grandeur spread throughout the land. One who could motivate one third of his troops to fight till death is equivalent to the strength of the warlord. One who could motivate a tenth of his troops to fight till death can thoroughly execute orders given to him.

Thus I say that a mass of a million that does not follow orders is not as good as 10,000 men who fight. 10,000 men who fight are not as good as 100 men who are truly aroused. Thus rewards should be as clear as the sun and moon, credibility should be given accurately, like the cycle of the four seasons; orders should be like the Axe of Authority that commands with authority, and regulations are as sharp and clear as the famous sword *Gan Chiang*. Only when such conditions are met, officers and troops will follow orders.

我听说古代善于用兵的人，能使半数士卒甘愿战死，其次能使十分之三的士卒甘愿战死，其下能使十分之一的士卒甘愿战死。能使半数士卒甘愿战死的，威势可以驾凌天下。能使十分之三的士卒甘愿战死的，武力可以驾凌诸侯。能使十分之一的士卒甘愿战死的，号令可使士卒贯彻执行。
所以说，百万之众如不贯彻执行命令，还抵不上一万人齐心协力去战斗。用万人进行战斗，如果不贯彻执行命令，还抵不上百人齐心战斗。因此，奖赏要象日月当空那样光明，守信要象四时交替那样准确，号令要象斧钺那样威严，决断要象干将那样锐利。这样，士兵不服从命令的，就不会有了。

The Book of Wei Liaozi

Huangdi, the Yellow Emperor

The Three Strategies of Huang Shigong

黄石公三略

The Three Strategies of Huang Shigong *(黄石公三略) is a legendary military text which focuses on concepts of government, the administration of forces, the characteristics of a capable general, and implementing a system of rewards and punishments. The strategies are divided into "Upper", "Middle" and "Lower". Although called 'The Three Strategies of Huang Shigong', there is no agreement on historical authorship. It has been variously attributed to Huang Shigong and Jiang Ziya. Other scholars believe it may be a complete forgery. It is believed to have been written during the Han dynasty (c. 210 CE).*

The Upper Strategy - Popular Support

The ruler should focus on winning the minds of the capable, rewarding those of merit and having his policies adopted by the people. Thus, if he has the same wishes as the people, there is nothing he cannot accomplish. If he has the same hatred as the people, there is nothing he cannot overturn. Governing the state, and providing security for one's family, is a matter of gaining the people's trust. Losing control of the state and endangering one's family is a matter of losing the people's trust. At the end of the day, all people want to realize their ambitions.

做主将的方法，务必收揽那些杰出人物的心，赏赐禄位给有功的人，使自己的意志成为众人的意志。所以，与众人有共同的愿望，就没有做不成的事业，与众人有共同的仇恨，就没有不可战胜的敌人。国治家安，在于得人心。国亡家破，由于失人心。因为人们总是务实现自己的愿望的。

The Upper Strategy - Being Resolute and Flexible

Military theory states: The soft can counter the hard; the weak can counter the strong. Being soft at the appropriate time can be a virtue; being hard inappropriately can be a fault. The weak is what the people will help; pretending to be strong is what people will resent. Soft, hard, weak and strong - each has its appropriate place, and one should combine these four and use them where it is most appropriate. When neither the beginning nor end is visible, no one is able to gain full understanding. Heaven and Earth, like the myriad of things, also changes and transforms. Thus the commander should make changes and be flexible when the situation warrants. He should change and transform in response to the enemy. He does not precede affairs; when the enemy realigns, he immediately adapts. Thus he is able to formulate inexhaustible strategies and methods of control to secure victory, sustain his gains, bring tranquility and order to the whole land, and settle the Nine Barbarians.[1] Such a strategist is a teacher for an emperor.

Everyone covets strength and power, but rare are those capable of using "soft" and "weak" appropriately. If one can use them well, he can protect his life. If the ruler can use them well, he will be able to adapt to change. Such principles can be promoted throughout the land, and threats can be met without requiring special accommodation. Using these principles, one can make enemy states submit.

Military theory states: If the ruler can be soft and hard, the future of his state will be increasingly bright. If the ruler can be weak and strong, his state will be increasingly prosperous. If purely soft and weak, his state will inevitably decline. If purely hard and strong, his state will inevitably be destroyed.

《军谶》说：柔能制刚，弱能制强。柔而恰当是美德，刚而不当是祸害，示弱的往往得到人们的同情和援助，逞能的常常遭到人们的怨恨和非难。柔有柔的用处，刚有刚的用处，弱有弱的用处，强有强的用处，应该把这四者巧妙地结合起来，因事制宜地加以运用。

还不知道事情的始末，人们就不能认识它。"天地神明"也是随着事物的推移而变化无常的。所以军事上也要根据敌情而变化，不要首先行动，而要随着敌人行动采取适当的对策。这样就能图谋制胜，无往不利，辅佐君主，树立天威，拯济天下，安定"九夷"。这样出谋划策的人，就能做帝王的老师。

所以说，人们没有不好强的，但却很少有人能掌握"柔能克刚，弱能胜强"这个微妙的道理。如果人们能掌握这个微妙的道理，就可以保全自己的性命，君主掌握了这个微妙的道理，就能够适应事物的变化。推行它可以遍布于天下，收起来可以藏之于心里，不须用房屋安置它，也不须用城郭保护它，只需在心中巧妙运用，就可以使敌国屈服了。

《军谶》说：既能用柔，又能用刚，国家就充满光明，既能用弱，又能用强，国家就更加昌盛。如果单纯用柔或单纯用弱，国家就必定削弱，单纯用刚或单纯用强，国家就必定灭亡。

The Upper Strategy - Talent and People

---

[1] Throughout history, the frontiers of China were periodically attacked by nomadic tribes from the north and west, referred to as "barbarians".

The basic principle of governing the state is to rely on those people who are capable. If you trust those who are capable, and employ them as if they were your four limbs, then all your plans will be accomplished. Your measures will follow each other as naturally as your four limbs, or the way the joints work with each other, without any hindrance.

治理国家的原则，在于依靠贤人和民众。信任贤人如腹心，使用民众如手足，就不会失策。这样，行动起来就象肢体相随，骨节相应，自然而然，巧妙得没有间隙。

The Upper Strategy - Handling People, the Enemy and Victory

The essence of governing the state and army lies in understanding the needs of the people and managing the affairs of the state.

Protect those who are in danger; bring happiness to those who are in fear; forgive and ask for the return of those who rebel; make right the injustice done to those who have been wronged; investigate all grievances that are submitted; raise up the lowly; suppress those who are strong and arrogant; destroy the enemy; enrich the greedy; use those who have desires; relieve those who are fearful; get close to good strategists; stay away from slanderers; check all negative comments; eliminate the rebellious; stifle those who act willfully; diminish the arrogant; summon and use those who turn their allegiance to you; settle those who submit to you; release those who surrender.

If you gain a strong position, defend it. If you gain a narrow defile, block it. If you gain a difficult position, encamp to hold it. If you secure a city, cut it up. If you seize territory, then divide it up. If you obtain spoils, distribute them.

When the enemy moves observe him; when he approaches, prepare for him. If the enemy is strong and morale is high, be deferential to make him more arrogant. If the enemy is well rested, avoid him. If the enemy has not made a move, be persistent with your resistance. If the enemy is a tyrant, use benevolence to comfort his people. If the enemy is rebellious, attack him in the name of righteousness. If your enemies are united, and in harmony, separate them. In accordance with the enemy's action, initiate relevant measures to repress him and use force to destroy him. Mislead him with false information; cause him to make mistakes and capture him when he does.

When you gain something, do not keep it for yourself. If you occupy a territory, do not set up a permanent defense. Do not occupy a city for too long. Establish a ruler within the population; do not take over the position. The governing direction should come from you but the credit should go to the officials. Such action is where the greatest benefit lies. Allow others to become the warlords, while you yourself become the emperor. Allow the warlords to run the states themselves and set their own taxation.

统军治国的兵诀，在于体察民心，处理各种事务。

对处境危险的人要予以保护；对心存畏惧的人要给与安抚；对叛国离乡的人要赦罪召还；对含冤受屈的人要予以昭雪；对有所申诉的人要为他查清；对才高位低的人要予以提拔；对恃强骄横的人要予以压制；对与我为敌的人要加以消灭；对爱财的人要多给些财物；对自愿效力的人要予以任用；对怕人揭短的人要予以隐讳；对有深谋远虑的人要加以亲近；听到谗言不要相信；听到坏话要反复核查；对谋反的人要杀掉他；对蛮横的人要挫折他；对骄傲自满的人要抑制他；对愿意归顺的人要招抚他；对已被征服的人要给予安置；对战败投降的人要给予宽恕。

占领了坚固的地方要守备，占领了险区的地方要阻塞，占领了难于攻取的要地要驻兵屯守，得到城邑要分赏给有功的人，得到土地要分封给出力的人，得到财物要分散给众人。

敌人行动时要注意侦察，敌人接近时要严加戒备，敌势强盛时要示弱使它骄傲，敌人以逸待劳就要避开它，敌人未犯就要坚决抵抗，敌人暴虐无道要用仁德安抚民众，
敌人背逆无理要用正义声讨，敌人和睦团结要使它分化。顺应敌之行动以挫败它，根据敌之形势而击破它，放出假情报使它发生过失，四面包围把它歼灭。

胜利不要归功于己，获得财物要分给众人，夺取城池不要旷日持久，立其国人为君，不要自取其位，决策出于自己，功劳归于将士；哪知这正是大利之所在啊！让别人当诸侯，自己当天子，使他们各保城邑，让他们各自征收赋税。

The Upper Strategy - How a Good Ruler Treats His People

Since ancient times, all rulers have venerated their ancestors, but few have treated the people as they should have been treated. Those rulers who venerated their ancestors did so because it was required of them by ancestral rules. Those who treated the people as they should have been treated showed the greatness of the ruler. A ruler who treats his people well concentrates on agriculture and silk production and does not disturb the people during their vital seasonal occupations. He also keeps taxes and impositions to a minimum, not exhausting the wealth of the people. If a ruler imposes few labor services and does not cause the people to be over-labored, the state will be prosperous and families will enjoy happiness. Only then, does the good ruler select officers to control and supervise the people.

Good officers are men of valor and character. Thus it is said that drawing men of valor and character from enemy states will impoverish the enemies. These valiant men are the pillars of the state and the commoners are the roots. Securing the pillars and the roots, the measures of the government can then be implemented without resentment.

世上的君主多能尊敬他的祖先，但很少能爱护他的民众。尊敬祖先只是家族的礼法，爱护民众才是君主的盛德。爱护民众的君主，重视农桑，不侵占农时，减轻赋税，不使民众贫穷，减少摇役，不使氏力疲困。这样，国家富足，家庭快乐了，然后选"士"去管理他们。所谓"士"，就是英雄人物。所以说，收罗了敌国的英雄，敌国就会陷于困窘。英雄是国家的骨干，民众是国家的根本，获得了骨干，掌握了根本，政令就会通行而不致引起民众的不满。

The Upper Strategy - Attracting the Capable

The essence of employing the army lies in respecting the forms of propriety and making salaries generous. When propriety is observed, wise officers will come. When salaries are generous, righteous officers will disregard death. Thus when granting salaries to the capable, do not begrudge the expense, and when rewarding them, do not delay. Only then, subordinates will unite together and then the enemy states will be reduced.

The way to employ those who are capable is to honor them with ranks, and remunerate them generously with material goods, and then the capable will come forward on their own accord. Welcome them according to the forms of propriety; stimulate them with righteousness, and then the officers will be willing to lay down their lives for the state.

用兵的要诀，在于有隆重的礼节和优厚的俸禄。礼节隆重，有智谋的人就会自动到来，俸禄优厚有义气的人就乐于效死。所以，用厚禄优待贤人，不要吝惜财物，奖赏有功的人不要拖延时间，这样，就能使部属同心协力而削弱敌国。用人的方法是，封爵位尊重他，给资财赡养他，"士"就会自愿投效。用礼节接待他，用大义鼓励他，"士"就会以死相报。

The Upper Strategy - How Good Generals Treat Their Armies

Those who command an army must share in the advantages and disadvantages of the officers and men; they must share in both safety and danger. Only then can they confidently confront the enemy, gain full victory and completely destroy the enemy. Once in antiquity, when a great general was presented with a cask of good wine, he ordered the wine poured into the river, and then he shared the drinking of wine with his officers and men as it flowed downstream. Although a cask of wine is unable to flavor a river of water, the men and officers of the army were motivated to fight to the death because their general's regard for them touched them personally.

Military theory states: When the wells have not yet been completed, the general does not mention his thirst. When the encampment has not yet been set up fully, the general does not speak of fatigue. When the army's stoves have not been lit, the general does not speak of hunger. In the winter he does not wear a fur robe; in the summer he does not use a fan; in the rain he does not use an umbrella. Such is how the general shares weals and woes with his men.

Together in danger, together in safety, his army will be united together and will never be split apart. The army can be exercised but cannot be tired out. This is because of the general's beneficence. He ceaselessly gathers them together, and with his plans he constantly unites them. Thus it is said that when you cultivate beneficence tirelessly with one man you can gain ten thousands more.

当将帅的，必须与士卒同甘苦、共安危，才可对敌作战，这样才可使战争获得全胜，全部俘获敌人。从前良将用兵，有人送他一坛美酒，他叫人把酒倒在河里，与士卒同流而饮，一坛美酒虽然不能佼一河的水都有酒味，但全军却因此愿为他效力死战，这是由于将帅与士卒同甘苦的缘故。《军谶》上记：军井还没有凿成，将帅不说渴。帐幕还没有架好，将帅不说疲倦。军灶还没有做好饭，将帅不说饥饿。冬天不穿皮衣，夏天不用扇子，雨天不独自张伞，这就是将帅与士卒同甘苦的准则。将帅能与士卒同安乐共患难，这种军队就能团结一致而不会离散，经常使用而不知疲倦，这是因为平时积蓄恩惠，思想一致的缘故。所以说，将帅经常不断地对士卒多施恩惠，就能争取到千千万万人的拥护。

The Upper Strategy - A General's Orders

Military theory states: The basis of the general's authority is in his commands and orders. The basis for achieving complete victory is in competent military administration. The reason why officers are not afraid of war is because they know they are following appropriate commands.

Thus the wise general does not rescind an order. Rewards and punishment must be carried out, much the way Heaven and Earth work, without fail. Only then can the general employ the men. Only when the officers and soldiers follow orders, can the army then be deployed.

《军谶》上说：将帅之所以有威严，在于号令。作战之所以获得全胜，在于军政。士卒之所以不怕打仗，在于服从命令。因此，将帅要令出必行，赏罚必信，象天地运行那样准确无误，才可统御众人。士卒服从命令，才可出国作战。

The Upper Strategy - Relationship between a General and His Army

The one who unifies the army and gains control of the situation is the general, while the ones who bring about conquest and defeat the enemy are the men of the army. Thus a general that is not able to command and control an army should not lead the men. A rebellious army should not be used against an enemy. They can neither conquer cities nor destroy a state. They would exhaust themselves without accomplishing anything. If the army were exhausted, the general would be isolated and the army would be rebellious. If they tried to hold a defensive position, their defense would not be strong; if they attacked, they would fail. They are then referred to as a dissipated army. When the army is dissipated, the general is no longer able to command and control it effectively. Once the general loses his authority to command and control, the officers and men will disdain punishment. If the officers and men disdain punishment, the army will become disorganized. If the army suffers the loss of organization, the soldiers will run away from battle. If the soldiers run away from battle, the enemy will seize the opportunity and profit from it, and the army will perish in the end.

统帅军队掌握形势的是将领，夺取胜利打败敌人的是士卒。所以，治军无方的将领不能让他统率军队，离心离德的军队不能用以攻伐敌人。因为它既不能攻占城池，也不能灭亡敌国，这两件事都做不到，必公军力疲弊。军力疲弊，会使将领孤立，士卒抗命，用来防守必不能巩固，使其出战也必致溃败。这叫"师老兵疲"。师老兵疲，将领就没有威信，将领没有威信，士卒就不怕刑罚。士卒不怕刑罚，军队必然混乱。军队混乱，士卒扰会逃亡，士卒逃亡，敌人就会乘机进攻，敌人乘机进攻，军队必致丧败。

The Upper Strategy - How Good Generals Treat Their Armies II

Military theory states: The exemplary general, in his command of the army, governs men as he would wish to be treated himself. Spreading his benevolence and kindness, the strength of his men is renewed daily. In approaching battle, they act like the wind arising; in attack, they act like the release of a pent-up river.

Thus the army can be seen but not withstood, can be tendered but not be conquered. If the general leads the men in person, the soldiers will become the most valiant under Heaven.

《军谶》上说：良将统军队，能够对待部下，如同希望别人怎么样对待自己。广施恩惠，军队的战斗力就会一天比一天增强，作战就象暴风骤雨那样迅速猛烈，进攻就象江河决堤那样汹涌澎湃。因此，这个军队就能使敌人望风逃窜而不敢抵抗，只有降服而不能求胜。将领能身先士卒，他的军队就能称雄于天下。

The Three Strategies of Huang Shigong

The Upper Strategy - Rewards and Punishment

Military theory states: The army employs rewards and punishments and these two are like inside and outside; they are two opposite sides and are inseparable.

When rewards and punishments are clear, then the general's authority is assured. When the proper administration of reward and punishment is employed, then the officers and men are obedient. When those who are capable are entrusted with this responsibility, enemy states will be fearful.

《军谶》上说：军队既要有赏，又要有罚，二者互为表里不可缺一。赏罚严明，将领的威信才能树立。官吏称职，士卒才会悦服。重用了德才兼备的人，敌国就会震动。

The Upper Strategy - Treating Officers, Generals and Plans

Military theory states: Where capable officials preside, the state will have no internal enemies.

Thus capable officers can be deferred to and must not be treated arrogantly. The generals can be congenial, but must never be doubted. Plans can be complex but must never be doubted. If officers are treated arrogantly, their subordinates will not be submissive. If the generals are doubted, there will be mistrust. If his plans are doubted and not acted upon promptly, the enemy will take the opportunity to attack. If a general is mistrusted and proceeds to mount an attack under such conditions, chaos will result. In this regard, the general holds in his hands the fate of the state. If he is capable, he will be able to lead the army to victory and the state will be secure.

《军谶》上说：贤人所归附的国家就所向无故。所以，对士要谦恭而不可傲慢，对将领充分信任而不可使他有遭到陷害的顾虑，对谋略要深思熟虑，而不可犹豫不决。
对士傲慢，下级就不会悦服，对将领疑虑，君将之间就互不信任，谋略犹豫，敌国就会乘隙进击。这样去打仗，必然招致祸乱。将领是国家的命脉，将领能率军战胜敌人，国家才能安定。

The Upper Strategy - Characteristics of Good Generals

Military theory states: The general should be of high integrity; able to be calm when needed; able to be fair and strict; able to accept criticism; able to judge disputes; able to attract and employ capable men; able to select and accept advice; able to know the customs of states; able to map mountains and rivers; able to discern defiles and obstacles; and able to exert military authority.

Thus it is said that the wisdom of the benevolent, plans of the Sage, words of the wood carriers, opinions of court officials and the affairs of ascension and decline - all these are what the general should seek out and hear. If the general has a thirst for the capable, then strategies can be executed. If the general refuses to ask and listen to advice, then those who are capable will leave. If he refuses to take into consideration any plans set out by strategists, the strategists will leave. If good and evil are treated alike, the meritorious will grow weary. If the general is stubborn, his subordinates will shirk all responsibility. If he brags, his assistants will not make accomplishments. If he believes slander, he will lose the hearts of the people. If he is greedy, treachery will be unchecked. If he is licentious, his officers and men will follow suit. If the general has one of the faults mentioned before, the masses will not submit. If he has two of them, the army will lack discipline. If he has three of them, his subordinates will not fight. If he has four of them, the entire state is in danger.

《军谶》上说："将领应该廉明，能镇静，能公正，能严肃，能接受规劝，能明断是非，能容纳人才，能博采众议，能知各国风俗，能通晓山川形势，能明了地形险阻，能掌握军队权柄。"所以说，"仁贤"的智谋，"圣明"的远虑，民众的议论，官员的意见，存亡兴衰的史迹，都是将领应当知道的。将领能思"士"
如渴，就会使有谋略的人归从。如果将领拒绝规劝，杰出的人物就会散去。不采纳其计策，谋士就会叛离。善恶不分，有功的人就会消极。一意孤行，下级就会归咎于上。自我夸耀，下级就不积极立功。听信谗言，众人就会离心离德。贪图财物，就无法禁止坏人坏事。迷恋女色，士卒就会淫乱无度。[以上八条]将帅身上有
了一条，就会众心不服。有了两条，就会军无法纪。有了三条，就会全军溃败，有了四条就会祸国殃民。

The Upper Strategy – The Necessity to Keep Plans Secret

Military theory states: The general's plans must be kept secret. The officers and masses must be kept united. Attacks on the enemy must be swift.

If the general's plans are kept secret, enemy spies cannot be effective. If the officers and men are united, then the heart of the army is one. If the attack is swift, the enemy will not be prepared. When the army has these three, their plans will not be thwarted. If the general's plan is leaked out, the army will not be able to achieve their strategic disposition. If internal affairs are spied out, disasters, beyond control will befall the army. If ill-gotten gains are brought into the camp, a myriad of evildoers will assemble. If the army is marked by these three, defeat is inevitable.

《军谶》上说：将领的谋略要保密，士卒的思想要统一，进攻敌人行动要迅速。将领的谋略秘密，奸细就不能得逞。士卒的思想统一，军队就固结一致。进攻行动迅速，

敌人就猝不及防。将领做到这三点，计划就不会遭破坏。将领的谋略泄露了，军队就会丧失有利的形势，敌人侦察到我内部情况，祸患就不可制止。非法的财货进入了军营，一切坏事都会发生。将领有了这三点，军队一定要溃败。

The Upper Strategy - Character and Temperament of Good Generals

Military theory states: Contemplation and courage are critical characteristics of the general; deployment and anger are tools of the general.

These four are the general's most valuables assets. If the general does not carefully contemplate the course of actions, his strategists will abandon him. If the general is not brave, his officers and men will be fearful. If the general moves the army recklessly, the army will not be imposing. If his anger implicates the innocent, the whole army will be in fear.

将领没有深谋远虑，有智谋的人就会离去。将领不勇敢，官兵就会恐惧。将领轻举妄动，军队不被敌人重视。将领迁怒于人，全军就会畏惧。《军谶》上说："深谋远虑，坚定勇敢，是将领宝贵的品德。适时而动，当怒而怒，是将帅用兵的艺术。" 这四项，都是将领应当谨慎从事的。

The Upper Strategy - Motivating and Keeping Talents

Military theory states: If the army lacks material resources, the officers will not come. If the army does not have ample rewards, the officers will not go into war.

When there is bait, there will certainly be fish; when the rewards are generous, there will certainly be courageous officers. Thus, what will gain the loyalty of the officers will be the appropriate forms of propriety. What will induce the officers to fight are the rewards. Treat them with appropriate propriety, reward them with what they love, then those you seek will come. But if you treat them well at first, but later regret doing so, they will not remain with you. If you reward them well at first, but later regret doing so, then officers will not listen to your commands. If you tirelessly confer appropriate propriety and rewards, the officers will fight and lay down their lives for their commander.

《军谶》上说："军中没有资财，士就不来归附。军中没有奖赏，士就不会勇往作战。"《军谶》也说："香饵之下，必有鱼上钩；重赏之下，必有勇夫。"

所以，使士衷心归向的是礼，使士乐于效死的是赏。士喜好礼就以礼相招；士喜爱赏就用赏相示，这样，所求的人就会来到。所以，先以礼相待，但过后又后悔，士就不愿留下来；先以赏相示，但过后又后悔，士就不愿受驱使。只有不断以礼相待、以赏相示，士才能争着为他效死。

The Upper Strategy - Preparation for War

Military theory states: A state preparing to mobilize its army, concentrates first on making its beneficence ample. A state preparing to attack concentrates on nurturing its people.

Conquering many with few is a matter of beneficence. Conquering the strong with weak is a matter of loyalty. The good general, in nurturing his officers, treats them no differently than himself. Thus he is able to unite, in a common purpose, all his people and gain complete victory.

《军谶》上说："要兴兵打仗的国家，必先多施恩惠。要采取攻势的国家，必先与民休息。"
能以少胜多，是广施恩惠的缘故。能以弱胜强，是与民休息的结果。所以，良将爱护士卒，要象爱护自己一样，才能使万众一心，取得全面胜利。

The Upper Strategy - Knowing the Enemy

Military theory states: The key to using the army is to first know the enemy's situation. Look into his granaries and armories, make an estimation of his food stocks, make a judgment of his army's strength and seek out his natural advantages. Do all these things to seek out and attack his weaknesses.

Thus if the state does not have the hardship of war and yet is transporting grain, the state must be suffering from lack of food. If the people have a sickly look, the state is impoverished.

If they are transporting food from a thousand miles, the people would have a hungry look. If they are gathering wood and grass for food, the army does not have enough food to last one night. If someone transports provision a thousand miles, he lacks one year of food; two thousand miles, he lacks two years of food; three thousand miles, he lacks three years of food. This is what is referred to as an empty state. When the state is empty, the people are impoverished. When the people are impoverished, then the government and the population are estranged. While the enemy attacks from outside, the people will plunder from within and the state will inevitably collapse.

《军谶》上说：用兵的要诀，是必须首先查明敌情。了解其库存的物资，估计其粮食的多少，判断其兵力的强弱，查明其天候和地形，以寻求敌人可乘之隙。所以，国家没有战事而运粮，说明国家缺粮。民众面黄饥瘦，说明国家贫穷。从千里之外送粮食，民众就会挨饿。临时打杂草做饭，军队就不能按时吃饱。运粮千里，国家就会缺少一年的粮食；运粮二千里，就会缺少二年的粮食；运粮三千里，就会缺少三年的粮食，这就会使国家空虚。国家空虚，民众就贫困。民众贫困，上下就不会相亲。敌人从外面进攻，民众在内部抢掠，国家定会崩溃。

The Upper Strategy - If a Ruler Is a Tyrant

Military theory states: If the ruler is a tyrant, his subordinates will be hasty to implement harsh measures. Taxes will be onerous, fines and punishments will be imposed by whim and fancy, and the people will mutually injure and steal from each other. This is called a demised state.

《军谶》上说："君主暴虐，臣属就会急躁苛刻，赋税繁重，滥用刑罚，民众就会互相残害、行贼，这样就会亡国。"

The Upper Strategy -Thieving from the State

Military theory states: When those who are secretly greedy display the appearance of incorruptibility; when people feign proper countenance to gain high posts; when they prevaricate to gain fame; when they steal from the state by distributing the state's resources as personal beneficence, they cause confusion in the ranks. All these thieving actions are the beginnings of chaos.

《军战》上说："暗中贪污伪装廉洁，制造假象骗取名誉，盗用朝廷爵禄以行私，使上下昏暗，假装正派，骗取高官，这便是盗国的开端。"

The Upper Strategy - Source of Chaos

Military theory states: If the officials form cliques, each advancing the interest of those with whom they are in league; the state attracts and appoints the evil and corrupt while suppressing the benevolent and capable; officials turn their backs on the state and establish their own individual interests; and men of equal rank slander each other, this is the source of chaos.

《军谶》上说："百官结党营私，各自引用亲信，拉拢坏人，压制好人，背弃公道，树立私恩，同事之间，互相诽谤。这便是国家祸乱的根源。"

The Upper Strategy - Chaos at the Roots

Military theory states: When clans come together to plan evil; when a person without title acts in high prominence, and there are none who oppose him; when an image of virtue is created through false beneficence and propaganda; and when these practices proliferate and intertwine, they can subvert the authority of the existing officials. When they then abuse the populace causing upheaval within the state, while the officials conceal the truth from the ruler, this causes chaos at the roots.

《军谶》上说："豪门大族成党为奸,虽无爵位却很喧赫,成风十足,无不震恐。党羽勾结有如葛藤相连,私布小恩小惠,篡夺朝廷大权,欺压广大民众,国内议论哗然、群臣蒙蔽君主,不愿直言,这就是带灾祸的到根源。"

The Upper Strategy - Treachery to State

Military theory states: When clans, generation after generation, act treacherously, encroaching upon and robbing district offices; when they forge and distort documents; when all their actions only serve to promote their own benefit, thus endangering the ruler, they are referred to as the state's treacherous ones.

《军谶》上说："世世代代作恶,侵盗县官,一举一动只求便利自己,舞文弄墨,歪曲诡辩,以危害国君,这就是国贼。"

The Upper Strategy - Misfortune to the State

Military theory states: When officials are many and the people are few; when there is no distinction between the honored and lowly; when the strong and the weak insult each other; and when such action cannot be stopped, then the whole state will be injured and will reap misfortune.

《军谶》上说："官多民少,尊卑不分,强弱相互欺虏。不能禁止,必波及到军主与子民,国家便会受害。"

The Upper Strategy - Harming the State

Military theory states: When the ruler loves those who are good, but does not advance them; when he hates those who are evil, but does not dismiss them, those who are capable will go into seclusion, and those who are otherwise disposed will hold important positions. Such a situation will bring harm to the state.

《军谶》上说："喜爱好人而不进用,厌恶坏人而不除掉,有才有德的人隐退,无才无德的人当权,国家就会受到危害。"

The Upper Strategy - Powerful and Royal Families

Military theory states: When the ruler's relatives and powerful families are strong and large; when they form cliques and occupy positions of authority; when they grow more powerful with the passing of time; when they abuse those who are of higher authority and the ruler cannot bear to dismiss them, then the state will suffer defeat.

《军谶》上说："朝廷宗室权力强大，结党营私，窃据高位，以下犯上，时间愈久、势力愈大，君主不忍除掉他，国家就会遭到败坏。"

The Upper Strategy - When Deceitful Officials Hold Superior Positions

Military theory states: When deceitful ministers hold superior positions; when these ministers rely on their authority to grant personal favors and act in a manner that offends the masses; when they monopolize appointments for themselves; when advancement and dismissal lacks a solid basis; when, in advancements and dismissals, they boast of their own merits; when they seek gain by any means possible; when they slander and vilify those of great virtue and make false accusations against the meritorious; when, whether good or evil, all are treated the same by them; when they create a harsh government, changing the customary ways from antiquity and altering what was common practice; when they hinder the affairs of government so that proper commands and orders are not put into effect; when the ruler employs such deceitful ministers and fails to dismiss them, then the entire state will be clamoring and contentious, and will certainly suffer disaster and calamity.

《军谶》上说："用花言巧语谄媚取宠的人当权，全军都会指责，他们倚仗权势，夸耀自己，动辄违背众意。他们一举一动都按上级脸色行事。他们刚愎自用，夸功自傲，诽谤品德高尚的人，把他们诬蔑为庸碌无能的人。他们好坏不分，只求符合己意。他们挤压政事，上令不能下达。标新立异，变更古制，改易常法。君主任用这种佞臣，必受祸害。"

The Upper Strategy - Causes of Harm to Ruler

Military theory states: When audacious men of standing in the ruler's court praise each other, they cover the ruler's eyes, blinding his wisdom. When they present both slander and praise together, they block the ruler's ears, making him deaf to good and bad. When these evil men support each other and thus deceive the ruler, the ruler will lose the loyalty of the people.

《军谶》上说："奸雄互相标榜，蒙蔽君主的眼睛，使其分不清是非。诽谤与吹捧同时盛行，堵塞君主的耳朵，使其分不出邪正。他们各自庇护其亲信，使君主失去忠臣。"

The Upper Strategy - How to Get Rid of the Causes of Harm

Accordingly, if the ruler carefully investigates these slanders, he will discover the beginnings of chaos. If he respectfully invites capable recluses to take positions, he will attract those who are really capable. If he engages the capable and virtuous, then evil men will stay away. If the ruler appoints virtuous men with experience and judgment, the myriad affairs will be well managed. If the plans can be brought to down to all levels, then victory can be predicted. Then the ruler will not lose the heart of the people and his state will flourish.

所以，君主能明察诡辩的言论，才能看出祸乱的萌芽。君主聘请有德有才的人，奸雄就会远遁。君主信任年高德助的老臣，万事都能治好。君主征聘隐士，就能得到有真才实学的人。君主谋事能深入下层与大众商量，事业就会成功。君主不失掉人心，德政就能传播四万。

The Middle Strategy - Governing Subordinates

The Three August Ones never spoke[2], but the populace lived with high morality, thus there is no one to whom to attribute this accomplishment. The Five Emperors understood how the Heaven and Earth work, spoke and gave orders and thus the world gained great peace. Great officers will not yield credit to themselves, yet great peace will prevail and the populace will not know how it came about. Therefore, in employing subordinates, they did not rely on customs or rewards. Such is accomplishment without harm.

Kings governed men in the acceptable way, causing their hearts to be compliant and their wills submissive, while also establishing restrictive measures and making preparations against decline. When the feudal lords gathered at court, the duties of kingship were not neglected. They made military preparations, but they never suffered the misfortune of war. The ruler did not doubt the subordinates, while the subordinates had faith in their ruler. When the state is settled and the rule secure, the officers can retire with accomplishment.

The rulers governed their officers by virtue of his authority, bonding with them through trust, motivating them with rewards. When that trust declined, the officers grew distant, and when rewards were inadequate, they would not submit to orders.

三皇没有什么言论，而良好风气自然流布于四海，所以天下的人都不知道应归功于谁。五帝顺应自然规律，设教施令，使天下太平。君臣谦让而不争功，教化传播于四海，百姓不知道为什么会这样太平。使用臣属并不依靠"礼赏有功"，君臣之间就能和谐无间。王者以道德治人，使人心悦诚服，制定各种法规以防衰乱，诸侯按时朝见，各项政事不废，虽有军备，却无战祸。君不疑臣，臣不疑君，国家安定，君权巩固，臣下功成分退，君臣之间也能

---

[2] The Three Sovereigns and Five Emperors (三皇五帝) were a group of semi-mythological rulers and culture heroes during the period circa 3000 BC to 2100 BC. In myth, the three sovereigns were demigods who used their abilities to help create mankind and impart essential skills and knowledge. The five emperors were exemplary sages possessed of great moral character.

和诸无问。五霸统御"士"用权术，结交"士"靠信任，使用"士"靠奖赏。信任差了"士"就会疏远他；奖赏少了"士"就不听命。

The Middle Strategy - Full Authority on General

Military theory states: When the army is mobilized and advances into the field, the sole authority lies with the general. If the court interferes with advancing or withdrawing decisions, the general will have great difficulty attaining success.

《军势》上说："出兵打仗，重在将帅机断行事。如果进退都要受君主的控制，那就很难成功。"

The Middle Strategy - Using Each Type of Man

Military theory states: Employ the wise, courageous, greedy and stupid. The wise take pleasure in establishing their accomplishments. The courageous take pleasure in putting their ambitions into effect. The greedy fervently pursue gains. The stupid have little regard for death. Employ each through their unique character; such is the military's subtle exercise of authority.

《军势》上说："使用有智谋的人、勇敢的人、贪婪的人和愚笨的人，各有不同的方法。有智谋的人乐于建立功业，勇敢的人渴望实现他的志愿，贪婪的人追求利禄，愚笨的人不惜性命。根据他们各自的特点来使用他们，这是治军用人的妙术。"

The Middle Strategy - Using the Expressive and the Benevolent

Military theory states: Do not allow officers who are expressive to discuss the enemy's good points, as that will dishearten the army. Do not allow the benevolent to control finances, for they will dispense excessive rewards to those of lower rank.

《军势》上说："不要使能说善辩的人谈论敌人的长处，因为这会扰乱军心。不要用仁慈的人主管财物，因为他会多施财物以迎合下级。"

The Middle Strategy - No Divination

Military theory states: Prohibit seers from divining about the army's good or bad fortune on behalf of the officers and men.

《军势》上说："军队中要禁止巫祝，不准其为官兵卜问军事上的吉凶祸福。"

The Middle Strategy - Employing the Righteous and Wise

Military theory states: One does not employ righteous officers using solely material wealth. This is because those who are righteous will not die for those who are malevolent; the wise do not make plans for an incompetent ruler.

《军势》上说:"使用仗义的人不能单靠钱财。因为正义的人,不会为不仁的人去效死;聪明的人,不会为昏庸的君主出谋划策。"

The Middle Strategy - Virtuousness and Nobility

The ruler cannot be without virtue, for if he lacks virtue his ministers will rebel. He cannot be without some nobility, for if he lacks dignity, he will lose his authority. A minister cannot be without virtue, for if he lacks virtue, then he has nothing with which to serve his ruler. He cannot be without dignity, for if he lacks dignity, the state will decline. But if he is too grandiose, then he himself will stumble.

君主不可以没有道德,若没有道德,臣下就会叛离,也不可以没有威望,若没有威望,就会丧失权力。臣下不可以没有道德,没有道德就不能辅佐君主,也不可以没有威势,没有威势国家就会衰弱,但是威势过盛。自己就会栽筋斗。

The Middle Strategy - How Ancient Order was Established and Destroyed

The ancient Sages, in governing the world, observed success and decline; their contemplations of gains and losses created the forms of administration. Thus the feudal lords have two armies, the regional lords have three armies and the Emperor has six. When the world is in chaos, when rebellions are widespread, when the Emperor has lost his influence, then the feudal lords will form alliances or fight against each other.

When states are of similar strength, neither state can overcome the other. There is then a need to win the minds of valiant, sharing their likes and dislikes, and only after this, the stratagems should be used. Without stratagems, there is no means to resolve uncertainties and settle doubts. Without being shrewd and imaginative, there is no means to destroy evildoers. Without calculating, there is no means to be successful.

古时"圣王"统治天下,观察盛衰的变化,考虑得失的原因,从而建立制度。规定诸侯辖二师,方伯辖王师,天子辖六师。后来天下混乱,叛逆逐渐发生,人们忘记了天子恩泽而目无天子了,诸侯之间结盟立誓互相攻伐。由于政治军事势均力敌,谁也没有办法消灭谁。于是设法收揽"英雄"之心,与他们同好同恶,然后再运用权术。所以,不计议分析就无法决嫌定疑,不诡诈出奇就不能破奸灭寇,不施阴谋诡计就不能成功。

The Three Strategies of Huang Shigong

The Middle Strategy - The Three Strategies

The Sage can embody Heaven and model the laws of the Earth. The learned can find their lessons in antiquity. Thus the *Three Strategies* has been written for periods of decadence. The *Upper Strategy* establishes the forms of propriety and rewards, discriminates between the evildoers and the valiant, and makes clear what is success and defeat. The *Middle Strategy* marks out the differences in virtue and behavior and manifest changes in the balance of power. The *Lower Strategy* arrays virtue and morals, looks into security and danger, and makes clear the calamity of harming the capable.

Thus if the ruler thoroughly understands the *Upper Strategy* he will be able to employ the capable and seize his enemies. If the ruler thoroughly understands the *Middle Strategy*, he will be able to employ and control his generals, unite his people. If he thoroughly understands the *Lower Strategy*, he will be able to discern the sources of success and decline and understand the regulations for governing a state. If his subordinates thoroughly understand the *Middle Strategy*, they will be able to achieve merit and preserve themselves.

When the soaring birds have all been slain, then good bows are stored away. When the enemy states are extinguished, ministers should be lost. Lost does not mean killing them, but taking away their power and removing their authority. The ruler grants them fiefdoms, establishes them in his court, at the highest ranks of his subordinates, in order to manifest their merit. He presents them with excellent lands in the central region in order to enrich their families, and bestows beautiful and valuable treasures to please them.

Now once the armies have been brought together, they cannot be hastily separated. Once military authority has been granted, it cannot be easily rescinded. When armed forces return home from victory it puts the ruler in a critical situation. He should weaken the commander by appointing him to new position and taking away his military authority, by means such as granting him a vassal state. This is called the 'hegemon's strategy' of managing generals. The reasons for creating the hegemony are very complex. Preserving the structure of the state, gathering the valiant and courageous are what comprise the *Middle Strategy* and make up the ruler's most important and difficult strategic choices.

"圣人"能够体天之道，"贤者"能够法地之理，"智者"能够以古为师。所以《三略》一书是为处乱世而作的。《上略》是说设置礼赏、辨别奸雄、显示成败的。《中略》是区别德行、明察权变的。《下略》是阐述道德、分析安危、说明迫害"贤人"的利害。所以君主深通《上略》就能任用贤人，战败敌人。深通《中略》，就能驾御
将帅统率士众。深通《下略》，就能明白盛衰的根源，熟悉治国的纲纪。人臣深通《中略》，就能成就功业保全身家。

高飞的鸟死了,良弓就要收藏起来。敌国灭亡了,谋臣就要被消灭。所谓消灭,并不是消灭他们的肉体,而是要削弱他们的威势,剥夺他们的权力。然后在朝廷上封赏他,给他极高的爵位,以表彰他的功劳。赐与中原最肥沃的土地,使他家财富足。赏给他美女珍宝,使他心情愉快。

军队一经编成,就不能仓促解散。兵权一经授予,就不能马上收回。战争结束将帅班师回朝,这是君主存亡的关键时刻。所以,要削弱将帅的实力而给他爵位,剥夺他的兵权而封给他土地,这是"霸者"统御将帅的策略。因此,"霸者"的作为,其道理是很复杂的。

保全国家,收罗英雄,就是《中略》所论的权变。这是历代做国君的的奥妙。

The Lower Strategy - The Capable and the Sages

A ruler who can save the people from peril can attain security and peace for the people. A ruler who can quiet distress in the populace can enjoy the happiness of the populace. A ruler who can rescue society from misfortune will gain from the prosperity of the society. Therefore, if the ruler's beneficence extends to all the people, the capable will give their allegiance. If the ruler's beneficence extends to every part of his kingdom, the Sages will ally with him. Where the capable go, the state will be strong. Where the Sages go, all will be united. One seeks the capable through virtue and the Sages through the 'Way'. If the capable depart from the state, it will become weak. If the Sages depart from the state, the state will grow depraved. Weakness is a step towards danger, and depravity is a sign of doom.

能挽救天下于危亡的,就能使得天下安宁。能消除天下忧患的,就能享有天下的快乐。能拯救天下灾祸的,就能获得天下的幸福。所以恩泽及于民众,贤人就会归向他;恩泽及于万物,圣人就会归向他。贤人归向他,这个国家就会强盛。圣人归向他,天下就会统一。使贤人来归要凭"德",使圣人来归要凭"道"。贤人离去,国家就会衰弱。圣人离去,国家就会混乱。衰弱是走向危险的阶梯,混乱是即将灭亡的征候。

The Lower Strategy - Bringing Harmony to the Populace

Governance by the capable causes men to submit by action. Governance by the Sages causes men to submit whole-heartedly. When men submit by action, the beginning can be planned and started. When men submit whole-heartedly, the end can be preserved. Physical submission (through action) can be attained through forms of propriety. Mental submission can be attained through harmony.

The harmony mentioned here is not the sound of instruments but is the result of people taking pleasure in their families, clans, occupations, states, practicing virtues and supporting the orders of the government. One who rules the people in this fashion creates a harmony in order to bring balance to their activities. Thus the virtuous ruler creates a harmony to give pleasure to his populace; a debauched ruler uses his power not to create harmony, but merely to amuse himself. One who provides pleasure for the people lasts and prospers; one who provides pleasure only for himself does not last, but will perish.

贤人执政，能使人行动顺从，圣人执政，能使人心悦诚服。行动顺从，可以创业。心悦诚服，可以全始全终。使人行动顺从要靠"礼"，
使人衷心悦服要靠"乐"。所谓"乐"，不只是金、石、丝、竹等乐器，而是使人爱家庭、爱宗族、爱职业、爱国家，拥护政令，讲究道德。这样治氏的君主，还要作"音乐"来陶治人们的感情，使其不失和谐。所以有德的君主，是用"乐"来使民众快乐。无德的君主，只知用"音乐"使自己快乐。使民众快乐的，国家才能保
持长久。只图自己快乐的，国家不久便会灭亡。

The Lower Strategy - Internal Stability and External Expansion

One who does not ensure internal stability but focuses instead on external expansion, will labor without success. One who focuses on internal stability instead of external expansion, will labor with ease and attain lasting results. A government marked by ease has many loyal ministers. A government marked by labor has many resentful people. Thus it is said that one who concentrates on expanding his territory, will impoverish his state; one who concentrates on spreading his virtue and beneficence will be strong. One who is able to hold what he possesses will feel secure; one who is greedy for what others have is seeking disaster. A government on the verge of being destroyed will burden later generations. The ruler, who enacts policies beyond proper measure, even though successful, inevitably will be defeated.

不搞好内政而图谋向外扩张的，会劳而无功。不从事向外扩张而只顾搞好内政的，会逸而有成。实行休养生息的政治，是由于有许多忠臣。实行劳民伤财的政治，必然产生许多怨民。所以说，热衷于扩张领土的，内政必然荒废。着意广施恩德的，国家就会强盛。能保持自己所当有的，会得到安宁，贪图别人所有的，会招未祸殃。
残暴的政治，世世代代都将受害。所作所为超过限度，即使成功也终必失败

The Lower Strategy - Setting the Example

One who indulges himself while instructing others is contrary to natural order. One who rectifies himself and transforms others is in accord with the Way. Contrariness is summoning chaos; following the Way is the essence of order.

不先正自己而去教育别人是违背常理的，先正自己而后教育别人才顺乎常理。违背常理是致乱的根源，顺乎常理才是安定的关键。

The Lower Strategy - Way, Virtue, Benevolence, Righteousness, Propriety

The Way, virtue, benevolence, righteousness and forms of propriety are one body. The Way is a common set of principles that men follow. Virtue is what men learn and gain when they follow the Way. Benevolence is love and care among the people. Righteousness is how people should behave. Forms of propriety regulate the behavior of people. None of these can be ignored.

Thus, everyday our actions should be regulated by forms of propriety. Punishing brigands and stopping injustice are decisions of righteousness. The compassionate heart is an expression of benevolence. To right oneself and gain the respect of others is the path of virtue. Ensuring that all people are equal and do not lose what they have gained, this is the work of the Way.

道、德、仁、义、礼，这五者是相互联系的一个整体。"道"是人们所应遵循的普遍规律。"德"是人们入"道"所领悟的心得体会。"仁"是人与人之间的相互亲爱。"义"是人们所应当做的事情。"礼"是人们所应遵守的规范。这五者缺一不可。所以，人们每天的生活行动，都要受礼的约束，讨贼报仇是正义的决定。同情之心是仁爱的发端；正己正人是修德的途径。使人平均，各得其所，是道的教化。

The Lower Strategy - Commands and Orders

What proceeds from the ruler and descends to the ministers is termed a command. What is recorded on bamboo strips and silk is termed an order. When rules are initiated and implemented, it is termed governance. When commands are not conveyed correctly, then orders are not carried out. When orders are not carried out, then governance cannot work. When governance cannot work, then the effect of governance cannot extend far and wide. If the effect of governance cannot be extended far and wide, then evil ministers will prevail. If evil ministers prevail, then the ruler's authority is damaged.

君主给臣下的指示叫"命"，把它写在竹帛上叫"令"，执行命令叫"政"。"命"有错误，"令"就不能推行。"令"不能推行，政务就不能确切施行。政务不能正确施行，指导政务的原则就行不通，原则行不通，奸邪就会得势。奸邪得势，君主的威信就要受到损害。

The Lower Strategy - Benefits of Getting the Capable

To gain the capable, the process is long. To gain the incapable, the process is short. Thus the wise ruler would rather take the long process than the short process, so that he is able to complete his aims by respecting the capable and having his subordinates do their best for him.

千里之外去聘请"贤人",路途是遥远的。招引奸佞之徒,路途却是近便的。所以,英明的君主宁愿舍近求远,这样就能保全功业,尊崇"贤人",下级也就会乐于尽心竭力了。

The Lower Strategy - Treating Good and Evil

If a ruler dismisses one good man, then good people will lose heart. If a ruler rewards an evil person then more evil persons will be drawn to him. When the good are rewarded and the evil suffer punishment, the state will then be secure and multitudes of good people will come.

废除一个好人,许多好人都会丧气。奖励一个坏人,许多坏人都到来。好人得以保护,坏人受到惩罚,国家就安宁而许多好人都会到来。

The Lower Strategy - Deluding and Creating Doubts in the Populace

When the masses are doubtful of those in control, the state is unstable. When the masses are deluded, they cannot be governed. When doubts are cleared and delusions are removed, then the state can be secured.

民众都对上级怀有疑虑,国家就不会安定。民众都对法令迷惑不解,他们就不会守秩序。只有疑虑消除,迷惑澄清,国家才能安宁。

The Lower Strategy - Implementing Orders and Policies on the Populace

When one order goes against the will of the people, then other orders will be disobeyed. When one evil act is committed, then other evil acts will follow. Thus if you put a good order into effect amidst compliant people and impose harsh measures on wicked people, orders can be executed without discontent.

Using laws that incur the wrath of discontented people is contrary to Heaven. Using measures that incur the wrath of the vengeful, to suppress the vengeful will cause an irreversible disaster. The ruler governs the people by making them peaceful. To make them peaceful, governance must be transparent and of high integrity. When the people gain what they want, the world will be tranquil.

一项法令违背民意,其它法令也会失去效用。一件坏事施行了,就会结下许多恶果。所以,对"顺民"要给予好处,对"凶民"要加以制裁,这样,法令就能推行,众人也无怨言。用民众所怨恨的法令,去治理心有怨恨的民众,这叫逆天行事。用民众所仇恨的措施,去治理胸怀仇恨的民众,其祸患不可挽救。治理民众要使他们平服，要做到民众平服，必须凭借政治清明，这样，民众就各得其所而天下太平了。

The Lower Strategy - Creating a Well-Ordered Government

If those who oppose the ruler are honored, while the greedy and uncivilized are enriched, then even if there is a Sage ruler, he cannot realize a well-ordered government. If those who oppose the ruler are punished, while the greedy and uncivilized are punished, then good moral conduct will prevail in the society and evil will be eliminated.

Pure, incorruptible officers cannot be enticed with rank and salary. Self-constrained, righteous officers cannot be coerced with threats. Thus the wise ruler, when employing the capable, must observe what will attract them. To attract the pure and incorruptible, one must observe strictly the forms of propriety. To attract the self-constrained and righteous, one must practice self-constraint and righteousness. Only then can the capable be attracted and the ruler's reputation preserved.

犯上的人反而高官，贪鄙的人反而富足，这样，虽有圣王也不能把国家治好。犯上的人受到诛戮，贪鄙的人受到拘禁，这样，良好的风气才能树立，坏人坏事才能清除。高尚纯洁的人，是不能用爵禄收买到的。有正义有气节的人，是不能用威刑胁迫的。所以圣明的君主征求贤人，必须依照他们的志趣而罗致他。罗致高尚纯洁的人，要讲究礼貌，罗致有正义有气节的人，要讲究道义。然后"士"才可以请到，"圣名"也就可以保全了。

The Lower Strategy - The Knowledge of Sages

The Sage perceives the sources of success and failure, understands what causes victory and defeat, understands the crux of governing chaos and knows the measure of going and coming. Though in poverty, a Sage would not hold a position in a doomed state. Though lowly, he would not accept a salary from turbulent state. He would go into reclusion, with his ideas on good governance, and take an official position when the time came. When they meet rulers that have the same ambition and goals, they can accomplish extraordinary ends. Since their goals are lofty, their names will be praised in later generations.

才德出众的人，能明察盛衰的根源，通晓成败的端倪，详察治乱的关键，深知进退的节度，虽然穷困也不当即将亡国的官吏，虽然贫来也不领混乱之邦的俸禄。匿名隐居，胸怀安邦治国之道的人，时至而动，就能住极人臣。遇到志同道合的君主，就能建立卓越的功勋。由于他的道德高尚而流芳后世。

The Lower Strategy - When to Use the Army

The Three Strategies of Huang Shigong

The wise ruler does not take pleasure in using the army. He mobilizes it to eliminate the violently perverse and punish the rebellious. Using righteousness to execute unrighteous is like releasing the pent-up river to extinguish a torch, or pushing one who is teetering at the edge of a cliff; success is inevitable. The wise ruler does not send troops rashly, because war can cause serious injury and damage to many things. War is not a good thing and it is something Heaven abhors. War should be a last resort and only when it is in accord with Heaven. When the ruler is in accord with Heaven, he is like a fish in water; when he is not, he will perish. Thus the ruler should constantly strive to be in accord with Heaven.

圣王用兵，不是好战，而是用以讨伐暴乱。以正义讨伐不义，就象决开江汀，让大水去淹灭微弱的火炬，就象在深渊的岸边去推下一个摇摇欲堕的人，其胜利是必然的。"圣王"之所以悠闲安静而不急于进兵，是不愿过多地造成人和物的损伤。战争不是好事，是"天道"所不容的。只在不得已时进行战争，才顺乎"天道"。人之顺乎天道，就好象鱼在水中一样，得水使生，离水便死。所以君子要时刻警惕自己而不敢背离天道。

The Lower Strategy - Powerful Families

When prominent, powerful families gain control of governance, the ruler's authority is diminished. If the power to decide life and death lies in the hands of the powerful families, the state is near its demise. If the powerful families submit to the ruler then the state can long endure. If the power to decide life and death lies in the hand of ruler, the state is secured. When people of all levels are poor, the state is impoverished. When people of all levels enjoy abundance, then the state will be prosperous and happy.

豪强执政，国君的威望就会受到削弱。生杀大权操在豪强手中，国君的威望就会完全丧失。豪强俯首听命，国家才可长久。生杀大权操在君主手中，国家才能安宁。民众穷困，国家就没有储备，民众富裕，国家才能安乐。

The Lower Strategy - Capable and Depraved Officers

When the capable officers are brought into the government, depraved ones will be left out. When depraved officers are brought into the government instead, capable officers will depart. When those who should be in are not in, those who should be outside are not outside; it is the start of disaster that can last through generations.

贤臣被亲近，奸臣就会被疏远。奸臣被亲近，贤臣就会被陷害。亲疏倒置，祸乱就要延传到后世。

The Lower Strategy - Rules and Officers

When the senior ministers doubt the ruler, evil will accumulate and gather. If ministers usurp the respect that should be due to the ruler, then there will be confusion in the ranks. When the ruler occupies the position of a minister, the ranks have lost their order.

大臣怀疑君主的能力，众奸就会乘机聚集，臣属居于君主的地位，上下地位就混乱了。君主处于臣位，上下地位就颠倒了。

The Lower Strategy - Treating the Capable

If harm is done to those who are capable, such action can harm three generations. If the ruler does not use those who are capable, he himself will suffer. If he is jealous of those who are capable, his reputation will be tarnished. When those who are capable are promoted or recommended, blessings will flow to future generations. Thus the wise would seek out and advance those who are capable, thereby making his name illustrious.

伤害贤人的，祸患延及三世。埋没贤人的，本身就会受害。嫉妒贤人的，名誉不得保全。推荐贤人的，造福子孙、后代。所以君子积极推荐贤人，因而美名显扬。

The Lower Strategy - Treating the Populace

If the ruler profits one person at the expense of a hundred, hundreds of people will leave the city. If the ruler profits one person at the expense of ten thousand, the whole populace will be in chaos and consider fleeing. If the ruler deposes one person and profits a hundred, the people will remember his munificence. If the ruler deposes one person and profits ten thousand, the government will be secure.

利一人而害及百人，民众就会离开城郭。利一人而害及万人，全国就会分裂。除去一人而利及百人的，人们就会仰慕他的恩泽。除去一人而利及万人，政治就不会混乱了。

The Three Strategies of Huang Shigong

Replica of Han Dynasty armor

The Thirty Six Stratagems

三十六計

***The Thirty Six Stratagems** (三十六計) is a text used to illustrate a series of stratagems used in conflict, politics and war, often through improvised or deceptive means. The stratagems are divided into six groups: stratagems of advantage, opportunity, attack, confusion, deception and disadvantage. Each individual stratagem is presented with examples from Chinese history. The stratagems were originally taken from the Book of Qi, and formally written during the Southern Qi Dynasty (c. 400 CE).*

Chapter 1 – Stratagems of Advantage

1. *Deceive Heaven to Cross the Sea*

We tend not to be suspicious of familiar things that we see often. Therefore secrets should be made to look like familiar things and not like something that is incompatible with the obvious. In this way, the obvious can be used as a vessel in which to hide secrets.

自认为防备周到，就容易产生麻痹松懈的情绪；平常看惯的就不在怀疑。秘密蕴藏在暴露的事物中，而不是与暴露的事物相排斥。所以那些公开的事物，也可以蕴藏非常机密的东西。

In the year 643 BC, seventeen years into his reign, Taizong, the Emperor of Tang, received a request for military assistance from a small country. The Emperor decided to personally lead his army of 300,000 men. His loyal advisors tried to dissuade him from going, as the trip required them to cross the sea, but the Emperor was adamant. On seeing the immensity of the sea however, the Emperor lost courage to make a crossing. He then summoned his subjects to think of an alternative way, but none was able to offer a good plan.

When the Emperor asked again, it was reported that an old but rich peasant living by the sea had requested an audience. The old man claimed that he would be able to provide food for the entire army for their journey across the sea. On hearing this, the Emperor was delighted. The old man invited the Emperor to his house for entertainment. Emperor Taizong happily agreed and went with his men.

After traveling for a few miles, the Emperor and his men were then led into an enormous tent. The tent was beautifully decorated inside and there were many servants. There the feasting began with fine wine, food and music. After a while, the Emperor and his subjects heard strong winds blowing and the thundering sounds of waves. The Emperor was suspicious and ordered some of his men to open the tent. He then realized that they were not in the house of the old man, but on a boat out at sea. The old man was actually Xue Ren Gui in disguise, and the creator of the strategy, "Deceive Heaven to Cross the Sea."

见《永乐大典—
薛仁贵征辽事略》。唐太宗贞观十七年，御驾亲征，领三十万大军以宁东土。一日，浩荡大军东进来到大海边上，帝见眼前只是白浪排空，海茫无穷，即向众总管问及过海之计，四下面面相觑。忽传一个近居海上的豪民请求见驾，并称三十万过海军粮此家业已独备。帝大喜，便率百官随这豪民来到海边。只见万户皆用一彩幕遮围，十分严密。豪民老人东向倒步引帝入室。室内更是绣幔彩锦，茵褥铺地。百官进酒，
宴饮甚乐。不久，风声四起，波响如雷，杯盏倾侧，人身摇动，良久不止。太宗警惊，忙令近臣揭开彩幕察看，不看则已，一看愕然。满目皆一片清清海水横无际涯，哪里是什么在豪民家作客，大军竟然已航行在大海之上了！原来这豪民是新招壮士薛仁贵扮成，这"瞒天过海"计策就是他策划的。

2. *Besiege Wei to Rescue Zhao*

To defeat a stronger enemy, one should try to make the enemy spread out his forces and then attack each of the small units separately. Instead of making a direct attack into the enemy's strength, one should attack in places like the rear, where the defenses are weaker.

如果要打击强大的敌人，应当设法使之分散兵力，然后各个击破。与其向敌人面前进攻，不如在他空虚的后方给以痛击。

This strategy derives its name from a famous incident that occurred in 354 BC. At this time, one of China's most renowned strategists, Sun Bin, a descendent of Sun Tzu (Sun Zi), was an advisor to the Lord of the State of Qi. Sun Bin had previously been at the court of the State of Wei, but another minister, Pang Juan, who is believed to have had the same teacher as Sun Bin, became jealous of his cleverness. He had Sun Bin framed as a spy, sentenced to the mutilation of having his kneecaps removed, and imprisoned; but Sun Bin escaped and fled to the State of Qi.

Several years later, the Lord of the State of Wei appointed the same Pang Juan as commander of the army, and sent him to attack the capital of the State of Zhao. The Lord of Zhao, Han Dan, appealed to the State of Qi for help. When the Lord of Qi consulted his advisors, they all spoke in favor of immediately sending aid to their ally. Only Sun Bin recommended against attacking immediately. Sun Bin advised: "To intervene between two warring armies is like trying to divert a tidal wave by standing in its path. It would be better to wait until both armies have worn themselves out." The Lord agreed to wait.

The siege of Zhao had lasted more than a year before Sun Bin decided the time was ripe to come to Zhao's aid. The King of Qi appointed prince Tian Ji as general and Sun Bin as military advisor. Tian Ji planned to attack the Wei forces directly to lift the siege of Zhao, but again Sun advised against direct intervention saying: "Since most of Wei's troops are out of the country engaged in the siege, their own defenses must be weak. By attacking the capital of Wei, we will force the Wei army to return to defend their capital; thereby lifting the siege of Zhao. This will provide the opportunity to destroy the Wei forces." Tian Ji agreed to the plan and divided his army into two parts, one to attack the capital of Wei, and the other to prepare an ambush along the route to the capital.

When the Wei general, Pang Juan, heard that the capital was being attacked, he broke off the siege of Wei and rushed his army back to defend his capital. Weakened and exhausted from the year long siege and the forced march, the Wei troops were caught completely by surprise in the ambush and suffered heavy losses. Zhao was thus rescued, while Pang Juan barely escaped back to Wei to recoup his losses.

事见《史记·孙子吴起列传》，是讲战国时期齐国与魏国的桂陵之战。公元前354年，魏惠王欲释失中山的旧恨，便派大将庞涓前去攻打。这中山原本是东周时期魏国北邻的小国被魏国收服，后来赵国乘魏国国丧伺机将中山强占了，魏将庞涓认为中山不过弹丸之地，距离赵国又很近，不若直打赵国都城邯郸，既解旧恨又一举双得。魏王从之，欣欣然似霸业从此开始，即拨五百战车以庞涓为将，直奔赵国围了赵国都城邯郸。赵王急难中只好求救于齐国，并许诺解围后以中山相赠。齐威王应允，令田忌为将，并起用从魏国救得的孙膑为军师领兵出发。这孙膑曾与庞涓同学，对用兵之法谙熟精通。魏王用重金将他聘得，当时庞涓也正事奉魏国。庞涓自觉能力不及孙膑，恐其贤于己，遂以毒刑将孙膑致残，断孙两足并在他脸上刺字，企图使孙不能行走，又羞于见人。后来孙膑装疯，幸得齐使者救助，逃到齐国。这是一段关于庞涓与孙膑的旧事。

且说田忌与孙膑率兵进入魏赵交界之地时，田忌想直逼赵国邯郸，孙膑制止说：解乱丝结绳，不可以握拳去打，排解争斗，不能参与搏击，平息纠纷要抓住要害，乘虚取势，双方因受到制约才能自然分开。现在魏国精兵倾国而出，若我直攻魏国。那庞涓必回师解救，这样一来邯郸之围定会自解。我们再于中途伏击庞涓归路，其军必败。田忌依计而行。果然，魏军离开邯郸，归路中又陷伏击与齐战于桂陵，魏部卒长途疲惫，溃不成军，庞涓勉强收拾残部，退回大梁，齐师大胜，赵国之围遂解。

3. *Kill with a Borrowed Knife*

When the enemy has been identified, and the intentions of one's allies are unclear, it is advisable to use the allies to attack the enemy. This will establish the loyalty of the allies and fight off the enemy without incurring any costs.

敌方已经明确，而盟友的态度还未明朗，那诱使盟友去消灭敌人，自己不必付出代价。

Toward the end of the Spring and Autumn Era, Lord Jian of the State of Qi was preparing to send an expedition against the State of Lu. The State of Lu was no match for the State of Qi. Therefore, the State of Lu was in a panic. Zi Gong, a disciple of Confucius, analyzed the situation and came to the conclusion that only the State of Wu was a match for the State of Qi. Thus he thought of using Wu to attack Qi.

Zi Gong went to see Tian Chang, who was then one of the highest ranking officials in Qi, one who wished to obtain more power from the Lord of Qi. Zi Gong advised Tian Chang that since he was opposed by the Commander of the Army, he should make things difficult for the Commander. Instead of having the Commander of the Army gain credit by defeating Lu, why not get him to attack State of Wu instead, which would be more difficult. Tian Chang liked the idea, but since Qi was prepared to attack Lu, he wondered how he could change the mind of the Lord of Qi. Zi Gong said, "This is easy. Let me persuade the State of Wu to save Lu. This will give the Lord of Qi reasons to change the target."

So Zi Gong traveled to the State of Wu. There Zi Gong said to the Lord of Wu, Fu Chai, "When the State of Qi has defeated Lu, their next target will be State of Wu. Why not make the first move and attack the State of Qi now?" Fu Chai agreed but was worried about being attacked from his rear by the State of Zhao. So, Zi Gong went to the State of Zhao, and managed to persuade them to join in the battle, thus securing the rear for Wu.

After travelling to the three states, Zi Gong had apparently achieved his goal, but after further analysis, he realized that the future of Lu was still not secure. So he went to the State of Jin and spoke to Lord Ding. He told Lord Ding, "If the State of Wu manages to conquer Qi, their next target would be State of Jin, so please make preparation for an expedition from Wu."

In 484 BC, Lord Fu Chai of the State of Wu led his army of 103,000 men on an expedition against State of Qi. The Qi army was ambushed by Wu, and several generals including the Commander of the Army were killed. Qi suffered huge losses and brokered for peace. As expected, Lord Fu Chai, after winning the battle, wanted to use his momentum to attack Jin and then Lu. However, on the advice of Zi Gong, Jin was prepared, and managed to fend off Wu. Zi Gong had finally achieved his goal by using the strategy twice: First by using State of Wu to save Lu and second by using the State of Jin to fend off the State of Wu.

春秋末期，齐简公兴兵伐鲁。鲁国实力不敌齐国，形势危急。孔子的弟子子贡分析形势，认为唯吴国可与齐国抗衡，可借吴国兵力挫败齐国军队。于是子贡游说齐相田常。田常当时蓄谋篡位，急欲铲除异己。子贡以"忧在外者攻其弱，忧在内者攻其强"的道理，劝他莫让异己在攻弱鲁中轻易主动，扩大势力，而应攻打吴国，借强国之手铲除异己。田常心动，但因齐国已作好攻鲁的部署，转而攻吴怕师出无名。子贡说："这事好办。我马上去劝说吴国救鲁伐齐，这不是就有了攻吴的理由了吗？"田常高兴地同意了。子贡赶到吴国，对吴王夫差说："如果齐国攻下鲁国，势力强大，必将伐吴。大王不如先下手为强，联鲁攻齐，吴国不就可抗衡强晋，成就霸业了吗？"子贡马不停蹄，又说服赵国，派兵随吴伐齐，解决了吴王的后顾之忧。子贡游说三国，达到了预期目标，他又想到吴国战胜齐国之后，定会要挟鲁国，鲁国不能真正解危。于是他偷偷跑到晋国，向晋定公陈述利害关系：吴国伏鲁成功，必定转而攻晋，争霸中原。劝晋国加紧备战，以防吴国进犯。

公元前484年，吴王夫差亲自挂帅，率十万精兵及三千越兵攻打齐国，鲁国立即派兵助战。齐军中吴军诱敌之计，陷于重围，齐师大败，主帅及几员大将死于乱军之中。齐国只得请罪求和。夫差大获全胜之后，骄狂自傲，立即移师攻打晋国。晋国因早有准备，击退吴军。子贡充分利用齐、吴、越、晋四国的矛盾，巧妙周旋，借吴国之刀"，击败齐国；借晋国之"刀"，灭了吴国的威风。鲁国损失微小，却能从危难中得以解脱。

4. *Conserve Energy while Exhausting Enemies*

Put the enemy in difficult situations; avoid a direct attack in the initial stage. Reduce the advantages of your enemy; turn him from strong to weak

要使敌人处于困难的境地，不是直接出兵攻打，而是采取能消耗敌人锐利的方法，令敌人由盛变衰、由强变弱。

At the end of the Warring States Period, the State of Qin sent an expedition, with Li Xing as the Commander of the Army, to attack the State of Chu. At first the aggressive Li Xing was able to capture several cities in Chu, but then met with strong resistance from the Chu army, which was headed by Xiang Yan, who was able to ambush Li Xing's army and dealt them heavy losses.

Before long, the Lord of Qin replaced Li Xing with Wang Jian, an old and experience general. Wang Jian had no intention of launching further attacks right away. Instead he concentrated on building up his defenses. The Chu army was on high alert and anxious to ward off further attacks by the Qin army; but for a year there were no attacks. The Qin army had dug in and was resting and eating well.

When the Chu forces saw that the Qin had no intention of attacking, but were merely prepared to defend, they begin to let their guard down, and Xiang Yan began to pull back the Chu army to their capital. On seeing the Chu army's movement, Wang Jian seized the opportunity to let loose his army onto the unsuspecting Chu. Being well-rested, the Qin army was unstoppable. They dealt a huge blow to the Chu. Riding on the momentum, the Qin army marched into the heart of Chu state and, in 223 BC, the Qin annexed Chu.

以逸待劳，语出于《孙子·军争篇》：以近待远，以佚（同逸）待劳，以饱待饥，此治力者也。"又，《孙子·虚实篇》："凡先处战地而待敌者佚（同逸），后处战地而趋战者劳。故善战者，致人而不致于人。"
原意是说，凡是先到战场面等待敌人的，就从容、主动，后到达战场的只能仓促应战，一定会疲劳、被动。所以，善于指挥作战的人，总是调动敌人，而决不会被敌人调动。

战国末期，秦国少年将军李信率二十万军队攻打楚国，开始时，秦军连克数城，锐不可挡。不久，李信中了楚将项燕伏兵之计，丢盔弃甲，狼狈而逃，秦军损失数万。后来，秦王又起用已告老还乡的王翦。王翦率领六十万军队，陈兵于楚国边境。楚军立即发重兵抗敌。老将王翦毫无进攻之意，只是专心修筑城池，摆出一派坚壁固守的姿态。两军对垒，战争一触即发。楚军急于击退秦军，相持年余。王翦在军中鼓励将士养精蓄锐，吃饱喝足，休养生息。秦军将士人身强力壮，精力充沛，平时操练，技艺精进，王翦心中十分高兴。一年后，楚军绷紧的弦早已松懈，将士已无斗志，认为秦军的确防守自保，于是决定东撤。王翦见时机已到，下令追击正在撤退的楚军。秦军将士人人如猛虎下山，只杀得楚军溃不成军。秦军乘胜追击，势不可挡，公元前223年，秦灭楚。

5. *Loot a Burning House*

When the enemy is in a difficult situation, one must seize the opportunity to attack, and use the momentum to obtain victory.

敌方出现危难时，就要乘机进攻夺取胜利。这是强大者利用优势，抓住战机，制服弱敌的策略。

During the Spring and Autumn Era, the State of Wu and the State of Yue were constantly fighting each other. After many years of fighting, Yue finally succumbed to Wu. The Lord of Yue, Gou Jian, was captured and sent to the Wu as a slave. He vowed to resurrect his state. So, on the surface, he pretended to be obedient towards Lord of Wu, Fu Chai and ultimately managed to gain his trust.

Finally, Gou Jian was released back to Yue as its administrator. At Yue, Gou Jian continued his presence, paying tribute to Wu every year. This behavior relaxed Fu Chai's guard against Yue, and allowed its military and economy to be strengthened.

In the meantime, Fu Chai was so impressed by his repeated victories that he became very arrogant. He began to build lavish palaces and appointed deferential and incompetent officials. He suppressed advice and opinions against him, causing great disarray in Wu. In 473 BC, Wu suffered poor a harvest. During that time, the stronger lords would attend an annual celebration that was, in actual fact, a show of strength of each state. Wu being one of the strong states was no exception. Although provisions were scarce due to the poor harvest, Fu Chai brought most of his army to the ceremony. Gou Jian took the opportunity to launch an attack on Wu and managed to seize it without much effort.

春秋时期，吴国和越国相互争霸，战事频繁。经过长期战争，越国终因不敌吴国，只得俯首称臣。越王勾践被扣在吴国，失去行动自由。勾践立志复国，十年生聚，十年教训，卧薪尝胆。表面上对吴王夫差百般逢迎，终于骗得夫差的信任，被放回越国。因国之后，勾践依然臣服吴国，年年进献财宝，麻痹夫差。而在国内则采取了一系列富国强兵的措施。越国几年后实力大大加强，人丁兴旺，物资丰足，人心稳定。吴王夫差却被胜利冲昏了头脑，被勾践的假象迷惑，不把越国放在眼里。他骄纵凶残，拒绝纳谏，杀了一代名将忠臣伍子胥，重用奸臣，堵塞言路。生活淫靡奢侈，大兴土木，搞得民穷财尽·公元前473年，吴国颗粒难收，民怨沸腾。越正勾践选中吴王夫差北上和中原诸侯在黄池会盟的时机，大举进兵吴国，吴国国内空虚，无力还击，很快就被越国击破灭亡。勾践的胜利，正是乘敌之危，就势取胜的典型战例。

6. *Feign East and Attack in the West*

By feigning in one direction and attacking in another, the enemy will be in chaos and will have no idea what might happen next. This is similar to the *Cui* sign in the *Book of Changes*. One should seize the opportunity to attack the enemy when he is thus unprepared.

敌人乱得像野生的草，意料不道所要发生的事，这是《易经》萃卦中所说的那种混乱溃败的象征。因此，要利用敌人不能自主的机会去夺取胜利。

During the period of the Eastern Han Dynasty, Ban Chao was sent to Xiyu with the goal of persuading the smaller countries to join forces with the Han forces to attack Xiongnu. In order for the alliances to work, the Han forces, together with their allies the Yu Tian, would have to create a north-south corridor, which cut across the small country of Sha Che. No friend to Han, Sha Che had been trying to rally the other smaller countries to succumb to Xiongnu and go against the Han. So, Ban Chao decided to attack Sha Che.

On becoming aware of the situation, Sha Che sought reinforcements from Gui Ci, who sent a force of 50,000 men. Ban Chao, together with his ally, the Yu Tian, had only 25,000 soldiers and, thus, was no match for Sha Che. So, Ban Chao hatched a plot to achieve victory in spite of the numerical inequity.

Ban Chao spread rumors within his camp that he was contemplating a retreat because they were seriously outnumbered. This rumor was intentionally spread to the captured Sha Che soldiers. That very night, the Han troops started to retreat to the east together with their allies the Yu Tian. As they retreated, they pretended to be retreating hastily and in disarray. The Sha Che prisoners took this 'fortunate opportunity' to escape and reported the matter to Gui Ci.

Gui Ci was pleased to hear the news and was confident that the Han and Yu Tian forces were afraid of him. Gui Ci led his 10,000 of his men on a chase after the retreating Han and Yu Tian forces. But, Ban Chao had merely used the darkness of night to help him hide his forces. Gui Ci, being very eager for victory, rushed his soldiers to find Ban Chao and, thus, very soon they were some distance away from Sha Che. Once Gui Ci had gone far enough, the Han and Yu Tian armies turned back and launched an attack on Sha Che. The troops defending Sha Che were caught by surprise and the King of Sha Che surrendered to the Han. After an unfruitful night, Gui Ci heard that Sha Che had suffered huge losses and had surrendered to the Han and Yu Tian forces. Knowing he was fighting a lost cause, Gui Ci gathered what remained of his army and returned home.

东汉时期，班超出使西域，目的是团结西域诸国共同对抗匈奴。为了使西域诸国便于共同对抗匈奴，必须先打通南北通道。地处大漠西缘的莎车国，煽动周边小国，归附匈奴，反对汉朝。班超决定首先平定莎车。莎车国王北向龟兹求援，龟兹王亲率五万人马，援救莎车。班超联合于阗等国，兵力只有二万五千人，敌众我寡，难以力克，必须智取。班超遂定下声东击西之计，迷惑敌人。他派人在军中散布对班超的不满言论，制造打不赢龟兹，有撤退的迹象。并且特别让莎车俘虏听得一清二楚。这天黄昏，班超命于阗大军向东撤退，自己率师向西撤退，表面上显得慌乱，故意放俘虏趁机脱逃。俘虏逃回莎车营中，急忙报告汉军慌忙撤退的消息。龟兹王大喜，误认班超惧怕自己而慌忙逃窜，想趁此机会，追杀班超。他立刻下令兵分两路，追击逃敌。他亲自率一万精兵向西追杀班超。班超胸有成竹，趁夜幕笼罩大漠，撤退仅十里地，部队即就地隐蔽。龟兹王求胜心切，率领追兵从班超隐蔽处飞驰而过，班超立即集合部队，与事先约定的东路于阗人马，迅速回师杀向莎车。班超的部队如从天而降，莎车猝不及防，迅速瓦解。莎车王惊魂未定，逃走不及，只得请降。龟兹王气势汹汹，追走一夜，未见班超部队踪影，又听得莎车已被平定，人马伤亡稍重的报告，大势已去，只有收拾残部，悻悻然返回龟兹。

Chapter 2 – Stratagems of Opportunity

7. *Create Something from Nothing*

Using a small deception to deceive the enemy; this deception would then grow bigger and eventually becomes a fact.

用假象欺骗敌人,但不是弄假到底,而是巧妙地由虚变实。也就是说开始用小的假象,继而用大的假象,最后假象变成真相。

In 755 AD, during the Tang Dynasty, military governor An Lu Shan revolted against the Emperor: this was the infamous An Shi rebellion. Under An Lu Shan's command was General Ling Hu Chao, who led an army and besieged the city of Yong Qiu. Defending the city against the rebels was General Zhang Xun, who had only a small troop and limited weapons. Zhang Xun ordered his soldiers to make many dummies of straw, each the size of a man and dress them in black. They then fastened them with ropes and lowered them down the outside of the city walls in the night. When Ling Hu Chao's army saw the straw dummies, they thought the enemies were scaling down the wall and immediately unleashed a volley of arrows upon them.

By the time Ling Hu Chao's army realized that it was a ruse, they had already "given" thousands of arrows away. Subsequently, General Zhang Xun commanded 500 real soldiers to scale down the city walls during the night. Ling Hu Chao's army ignored the move, thinking that Zhang Xun was up to his old tricks. The 500 soldiers stormed into Ling's camp, setting the tents on fire, creating chaos and panic. Ling Hu Chao's army was then bitterly defeated.

唐朝安史之乱时,许多地方官吏纷纷投靠安禄山、史思明。唐将张巡忠于唐室,不肯投敌。他率领二三千人的军队守孤城雍丘(今河南杞县)。安禄山派降将令狐潮率四万人马围攻雍丘城。敌众我寡,张巡虽取得几次突击出城袭击的小胜,但无奈城中箭只越来越少,赶造不及。无有箭只,很难抵挡敌军攻城。张巡想起三国时诸葛亮草船借箭的故事,心生一计。急命军中搜集秸草,扎成千余个草人,将草人披上黑衣,夜晚用绳子慢慢往城下吊。夜幕之中,令狐潮以为张巡又要乘夜出兵偷袭,急命部队万箭齐发,急如骤雨。张巡轻而易举获敌箭数十万支。令狐潮天明后,知已中计,气急败坏,后悔不迭。第二天夜晚,张巡又从城上往下吊草人。贼众见状。哈哈大笑。张巡见敌人已被麻痹,就迅速吊下五百名勇士,敌兵仍不在意。五百勇士在夜幕掩护下,迅速潜入敌营,打得令狐潮措手不及,营中大乱。张巡乘此机会,率部冲出城来,杀得令狐潮大败而逃,损兵折将,只得退守陈留(今开封东南)。张巡巧用无中生有之计保住了雍丘城。

8. *Use the Secret Chen Chang Passage*

Intentionally expose movements, so as to lure the enemy to defend certain positions. Then make a detour to the rear of the enemy and attack, taking him by surprise.

故意暴露我方的行动，以牵制敌方在某地集结固守，然后我方迂回到敌人后面发动攻击，攻其不备，出其不意。

In 200 BC, before Liu Bang became the Emperor of China and founded the Han Dynasty, he was once under the control of Xiang Yu and had to retreat to Han Zhong. Later, Liu Bang managed to break free from Xiang Yu's control and led troops into Si Chuan. To strengthen his defenses against Liu Bang, Xiang Yu deployed General Zhang Han, a former Qin General, and his troops to monitor Liu Bang's movement. Liu Bang's army was stationed at a place call Shu, surrounded by steep mountains. The main route out of Shu was through wooden bridges. Under the advice of General Zhang Liang, Liu Bang ordered that all the wooden bridges be burnt. They did this to prevent an attack from Xiang Yu and also to assuage Xiang Yu's fear that he would ever return to take his place.

In the days that followed, Liu Bang appointed Han Xin as his general and began preparing his army for retaliation against Xiang Yu. Just before they were ready to retaliate, Liu Bang ordered soldiers to prepare the burnt bridges. Xiang Yu's general, Zhang Han who had stationed his troops on the other side was aware of the movements. So, while the wooden bridges were gradually restored, Zhang Han got ready for the attack from Liu Bang's troops. However, there was no sign that Liu Bang's army was charging forward through the almost completed bridges.

General Zhang Han became suspicious and ordered some men to spy on Liu Bang's camp. The men brought back bad news for Zhang Han. Liu Bang had left with all his men, leaving behind empty tents. The truth was finally out. Liu Bang had used the restoring work as a decoy, so that General Zhang Han would not suspect his main intention. Liu Bang had led his main force secretly out of Shu via a small road to Chen Cang, opposite where General Zhang Han was stationed. Liu Bang's army then launched a surprise attack and defeated Zhang Han's army.

此计是汉大将军韩信创造。"明修栈道，暗渡陈仓"是古代战争史上的著名成功战例。

秦朝末年，政治腐败，群雄并起，纷纷反秦。刘邦的部队首先进入关中，攻进咸阳。势力强大的项羽进入关中后，逼迫刘邦退出关中。鸿门宴上，刘邦险些丧命。刘邦此次脱险后，只得率部退驻汉中。为了麻痹项羽，刘邦退走时，将汉中通往关中的栈道全部烧毁，表示不再返回关中。其实刘邦一天也没有忘记一定要击败项羽，争夺天下。公元前206年，已逐步强大起来的刘邦，派大将军韩信出兵东征。出征之前，韩信派了许多士兵去修复已被烧毁的栈道，摆出要从原路杀回的架势。关中守军闻讯，密切注视修复栈道的进展情况，并派主力部队在这条路线各个关日要塞加紧防范，阻拦汉军进攻。

韩信"明修栈道"的行动，果然奏效，由于吸引了敌军注意力，把敌军的主力引诱到了栈道一线，韩信立即派大军绕道到陈仓（今陕西宝鸡县东）发动突然袭击，一举打败章邯，平定三秦，为刘邦统一中原迈出了决定性的一步。

9. *Observe the Fire from the Other Side of the River*

When the enemy has internal disputes, and is agitated, we should monitor their movements. When the dispute has aggravated to the point where they are infighting, we should use the opportunity to deal a heavy blow.

在敌人内部冲突激化、分崩离析之时，我方应等待地方形势的恶化。届时，敌人横暴凶残，相互厮杀，必将自取灭亡。我方顺应其势，见机行事，坐收渔利。

During the period of the Three Kingdoms, around 200 AD, the major forces in the region were divided between Yuan Shao and Cao Cao. When Yuan Shao died, his wife, Liu, divided his kingdom among his three sons, Yuan Tan, Yuan Xi and Yuan Shang. As Yuan Shang was borne by Liu, she gave him the power to control the important cities. The eldest son, Yuan Tan, was unhappy and contemplated staging a war against his brother. He decided against this idea, only for fear that Cao Cao might take advantage of the situation to conquer them. Nevertheless, the animosity amongst the brothers persisted.

Three years later, a fierce battle broke out between Cao Cao and the Yuan brothers, and the Yuan brothers were badly defeated and managed to escape to Liao Dong, under Gongsun Kang. Cao Cao's general asked Cao Cao to ride the winning momentum to annexed Liao Dong, and capture the Yuan brothers, which at this moment left only Yuan Shang and Yuan Xi. Cao Cao laughed and said, "There is no need to pursue them. Gongsun Kang will bring their heads to me." With that he ordered the troops to head back home.

Now Gongsun Kang had always been suspicious of the Yuan family because of their ambition to capture Liao Dong. Now the two Yuan brothers sought refuge under him because they had no choice. Gongsun Kang thought that if he took the two Yuan brothers under him, there would be no guarantee they will not rebel against him. Moreover, taking the two Yuan brothers under him, he would definitely incur the wrath of Cao Cao, who was more powerful than him. The only use of these two Yuan brothers to Gongsun Kang would be when Cao Cao came to attack him. But on hearing that Cao Cao had returned with his troops to Xu Chang and had no intention to attack him, he realized that keeping the two brothers was meaningless, and would bring more harm than benefit. In the end,

Gongsun Kang ambushed the two brothers, beheaded them and presented their heads to Cao Cao.

东汉末年，袁绍兵败身亡，几个儿子为争夺权力互相争斗，曹操决定击败袁氏兄弟。袁尚、袁熙兄弟投奔乌桓，曹操向乌桓进兵，击败乌既，袁氏兄弟又去投奔辽东太守公孙康。曹营诸将向曹操进君，要一鼓作气，平服辽东，捉拿二袁。曹操哈哈大笑说，你等勿动，公孙康自会将二袁的头送上门来的。于是下令班师，转回许昌，静观辽东局势。

公孙康听说二袁归降，心有疑虑。袁家父子一向都有夺取辽东的野心，现在二袁兵败，如丧家之犬，无处存身，投奔辽东实为迫不得已。公孙康如收留二袁，必有后患，再者，收容二袁，肯定得罪势力强大的曹操。但他又考虑，如果曹操进攻辽东，只得收留二袁，共同抵御曹操。当他探听到曹操已经转回许昌，并无进攻辽东之意时，认为收容二袁有害无益。于是预设伏兵，召见二袁，一举擒拿，割下首级，派人送到曹操营中。曹操笑着对众将说，公孙康向来俱怕袁氏吞并他，二袁上门，必定猜疑，如果我们急于用兵，反会促成他们合力抗拒。我们退兵，他们肯定会自相火并。看看结果，果然不出我料。

10. *Sheath a Dagger in a Smile*

Show a friendly stance to the enemy, so that they will let down their guard against you. Meanwhile, prepare yourself for battle and take extreme care not to let your enemy know your true intention.

设法让敌方相信我方是善意友好的，从而对我方降低戒备。我方则暗中策划，积极准备，见机行事，不要让对方有所察觉而采取应变措施。是一种暗藏杀机、外表示柔的计策。

During the Warring States Period, the State of Qin wanted to expand their territories, so they sent out an army to attack the State of Wei, being led by General Gongsun Yang. They came to the Wu City which was very difficult to attack because of the terrain and strong fortresses. Gongsun Yang was thinking very hard about how to capture the city given all the difficulties until he got the information that the person leading the defense of the city was Gongzi Xing, a friend of his. Delighted, he sent a letter to Gongzi Xing, indicating that he actually wished for a truce on account of their friendship. In the letter, Gongsun Yang also indicated a time and venue to discuss the truce. After the letter was sent out, Gongsun Yang asked his troops to pose a retreating stance. On seeing that the Qin troops were retreating, Gongzi Xing agreed to the meeting to discuss the truce.

On the day of discussion, Gongzi Xing brought with him 300 men to the venue. On seeing that Gongsun Yang brought fewer men and were also unarmed, Gongzi Xing strongly believed that Gongsun Yang sincerely wanted a truce. The discussion was carried out in an amiable atmosphere. After the discussion, Gongsun Yang threw a feast for Gongzi Xing. But before Gongzi Xing could sit down, Qin troops came out from everywhere and had Gongzi Xing and his men surrounded and captured. Gongsun Yang later used the captured soldiers to trick those who were defending Wu city to open the city gates. In the end, Gongsun Yang managed to capture the Wu city.

战国时期，秦国为了对外扩张，必须夺取地势险要的黄河崤山一带，派公孙鞅为大将，率兵攻打魏国。公孙鞅大军直抵魏国吴城城下。这吴城原是魏国名将吴起苦心经营之地，地势险要，工事坚固，正面进攻恐难奏效。公孙鞅苦苦思索攻城之计。他探到魏国守将是与自己曾经有过交往的公子行，心中大喜。他马上修书一封，主动与公子行套近乎，说道，虽然我们俩现在各为其主，但考虑到我们过去的交情，还是两国罢兵，订立和约为好。念旧之情，溢于言表。他还建议约定时间会谈议和大事。信送出后，公孙鞅还摆出主动撤兵的姿态，命令秦军前锋立即撤回。公子行看罢来信，又见秦军退兵，非常高兴，马上回信约定会谈日期。公孙鞅见公子行已钻入了圈套，暗地在会谈之地设下埋伏。会谈那天，公子行带了三百名随从到达约定地点，见公孙鞅带的随从更少，而且全部没带兵器，更加相信对方的诚意。会谈气氛十分融洽，两人重叙昔日友情，表达双方交好的诚意。公孙鞅还摆宴款待公子行。公子行兴冲冲入席，还未坐定，忽听一声号令，伏兵从四面包围过来，公子行和三百随从反应不及，全部被擒。公孙鞅利用被俘的随从，骗开吴城城门，占领吴城。魏国只得割让西河一带，向秦求和。秦国用公孙鞅笑里藏刀计轻取崤山一带。

11. *Let the Plum Die in Place of the Peach*

When the situation has come to a point where sacrifices have to be made, sacrifice a battle to achieve victory in war.

当局势发展必须有所损失的地步时，应该牺牲局部以换取全局的胜利。

During the Warring States period, General Tian Ji of the state of Qi had a very good advisor, Sun Bin. Often Tian Ji would race and bet his horses against those of Lord of Qi, and most of the time his horse would fail to win. Sun Bin had knowledge that the horses are split into three categories, Upper, Middle and Lower with the Upper horse being the fastest. Sun Bin told Tian Ji he had a plan and asked Tian Ji to put in high stakes for the next race. Tian Ji followed Sun Bin's plan to pit Tian Ji's Lower Class horse against Lord's Upper Class horse, pit Tian Ji's Upper Class horse against Lord's Middle Class horse and pit Tian Ji's Middle Class horse against Lord's Lower Class horse.

In the end, Tian Ji won the two out of the three races and emerged the winner of the races and won thousands of pieces of gold from the Lord; and Sun Bin also gained favor from the Lord as well.

齐国将军田忌赏识孙膑的才能，收他为门客。田忌经常与齐王赛马，却屡次败阵。孙膑在得知赛马分上中下三等进行后，便向田忌建议，要与齐王赌上千金，并且保证必胜。田忌信任孙膑，照其话做了。孙膑便叫田忌以其下等马装作上等马与齐王的上等马比赛，这场会大败，接着，将其上等马装作中等马，将其中等马装作下等马，分别与齐王的中等马及下等马比赛，便可反胜两场，获得最终胜利。田忌结果赢了这场赛马，得了齐王千金，而孙膑亦因此名震齐国。

12. *Steal a Goat along the Way*

Try to take advantage of the enemy's weaknesses where possible, no matter how small they are. Use their weaknesses to achieve minor victories.

敌人出现的小漏洞也必须趁机利用。在微小的利益，也要力争获得。把敌人的小漏洞变为我方的小胜利。

In 383 AD, during the Sixteen Kingdoms period, the ruler of Former Qin, Emperor Fu Jian had plans to destroy the Eastern Jin. He sent his younger brother Fu Rong to lead as vanguard, and Fu Rong won the first battle. Judging that the Jin did not have adequate forces and their supplies were low, Fu Rong suggested to Fu Jian to hasten his attack on Eastern Jin. Fu Jian, on hearing it, did not wait for the rest of the army to arrive to launch an attack on the Shou Yang City. The general guarding Shou Yang was Xie Shi. Xie Shi, on knowing that the Qin vanguard did deal a blow to the Qin, sent General Liu Lao with 50,000 troops to deal with the Qin vanguard, and Liu Lao won, killing Qin General Liang Cheng. Xie Shi, on seeing their victory, rode out with his troops and reached the banks of the Fei Shui River. Camping on the opposite bank of the river were the Qin main forces. Fu Jian, on seeing how well-organized and well-defended Xie Shi's troops were, decided to wait for more reinforcements to arrive.

Xie Shi saw that he was outnumbered and knew that he needed to win this battle, by wits. He sent a letter to Fu Jian, trying to provoke him. In the letter he wrote, "I want to battle with you, winner takes all. If you do not dare to take up the challenge, my advice is that you surrender early. If you dare to take up my challenge, move your troops back, let my army cross the river and we can battle each other." Fu Jian was furious when he read the letter, so he ordered his troops to retreat, so as to allow Xie Shi's troops to cross the river. He wanted to attack Xie Shi's troops when they were busy crossing the river. Little did Fu Jian realize that, because they had lost their vanguards, the morale of the Qin troops was very low. Upon hearing the retreat order, the Qin troops panicked and there was chaos everywhere in the Qin's camp. Xie Shi, on seeing the situation, led his troops across the river and attacked the retreating Qin troops. Fu Jian, on seeing the battle was lost, retreated back to Luo Yang. The reason why Qin lost was because the Jin forces were able to take advantage of the situation.

公元383年，前秦统一了黄河流域地区，势力强大。前秦王苻坚坐镇项城，调集九十万大军，打算一举歼灭东晋。他派其弟苻融为先锋攻下寿阳，初战告捷，苻融判断东晋兵力不多并且严重缺粮，建议苻坚迅速进攻东晋。苻坚闻讯，不等大军齐集，立即率几千骑兵赶到寿阳。东晋将领谢石得知前秦百万大军尚未齐集，抓住时机，击败敌方先锋，挫敌锐气。谢石先派勇将刘牢之率精兵五万，强渡洛涧，杀了前秦守将梁成。刘牢之乘胜追击，重创前秦军。谢石率师渡过洛涧，顺淮河而上，抵达淝水一线，驻扎在八公山边，与驻扎在寿阳的前秦军隔岸对峙。苻坚见东晋阵势严整，立即命令坚守河岸，等待后续部队。

谢石看到敌众我寡，只能速战速决。于是，他决定用激将法激怒骄狂的苻坚。他派人送去一封信，说道，我要与你决一雌雄，如果你不敢决战，还是趁早投降为好。如果你有胆量与我决战，你就暂退一箭之地，放我渡河与你比个输赢。苻坚大怒，决定暂退一箭之地，等东晋部队渡到河中间，再回兵出击，将晋兵全歼水中。他哪里料到此时秦军士气低落，撤军令下，顿时大乱。秦兵争先恐后，人马冲撞，乱成一团，怨声四起。这时指挥已经失灵，几次下令停止退却，但如潮水般撤退的人马已成溃败之势。这时谢石指挥东晋兵马，迅速渡河，乘敌人大乱，奋力追杀。前秦先锋苻融被东晋军在乱军中杀死，苻坚也中箭受伤，慌忙逃回洛阳。前秦大败。淝水之战，东晋军抓住战机，乘虚而入，是古代战争史上以弱胜强的著名战例。

Chapter 3 – Stratagems of Attack

13. *Strike the Grass to Startle the Snake*

If something looks suspicious, seek to find out the truth. Take action only when the truth has been found. Only by analyzing your enemy carefully, can you find the critical point in their strategy.

发现可疑情况就要弄清实情，只有在侦查实情以后才采取行动；反复了解和分析敌情，发现阴谋的重要地方。

In 627 BC, Lord Mu of State of Qin decided to launch an attack on the State of Zheng. Beforehand, Lord Mu had placed a spy inside the State of Zheng. Advisor Jian Shu advised against the expedition, as the Qin troops would have to travel a very long distance to the State of Zheng. By the time the Qin forces reached the State of Zheng, the Zheng forces would be well-prepared. But the advice fell on deaf ears; Lord Mu sent Meng Ming as the commander-in-chief of the expedition.

When the Qin troops were setting off, Shuo Shu cried and said, "I am afraid you might not come back victorious, and worse, may be ambushed by the State of Jin at Xiao Mountain." As expected by Jian Shu, when the State of Zheng heard about the expedition, they expelled the spy planted by Qin and made preparations. On seeing that they were unlikely to be victorious, Meng Ming decided to retreat.

On reaching the Xiao Mountain, Meng Ming remembered what Jian Shu had said. He did not make any preparation because the State of Qin had a strong relationship with the former Lord of State of Jin. Little did he realize that there were a lot of Jin troops lying in ambush at the Xiao Mountain. One hot afternoon, the Qin forces discovered a small troop of Jin. Meng Ming was furious and ordered his troops to chase them. They lost sight of the Jin troop when they reached a narrow valley of the Xiao Mountain. On seeing the terrain was very treacherous, Meng Ming realized his mistake; but it was too late. Jin soldiers came out from hidden places and captured most of the Qin forces and its general, including Meng Ming. Why the Qin forces lost was because they startled the "snake", which is the State of Zheng, leading to their defeat at the hand of the Jin forces.

公元前627年，秦穆公发兵攻打郑国，他打算和安插在郑国的奸细里应外合，夺取郑国都城。大夫蹇叔以为秦国离郑国路途遥远，兴师动众长途跋涉，郑国肯定会作好迎战准备。秦穆公不听，派孟明视等三帅率部出征。蹇叔在部队出发时·痛哭流涕地警告说，"恐怕你们这次袭郑不成，反会遭到晋国的埋伏，只有到崤山去给士兵收尸了。"果然不出蹇叔所料，郑国得到了秦国袭郑的情报，逼走了秦国安插的奸细，作好了迎敌准备。秦军见袭郑不成，只得回师，但部队长途跋涉，十分疲惫。部队经过崤山时，仍然不作防备。他们以为秦国曾对晋国刚死不久的晋文公有恩，晋国不会攻打秦军。哪里知道，晋国早在崤山险蜂峡谷中埋伏了重兵。一个炎热的中午，秦军发现晋军小股部队，孟明十分恼怒，下令追击。追到山险险要处，晋军突然不见踪影。孟明一见此地山高路窄，草深林密，情知不妙。这时鼓声震天，杀声四起，晋军伏兵蜂涌而上，大败秦军，生擒孟明视等三帅。秦军不察敌情，轻举妄动，"打草惊蛇"终于遭到惨败。当然，军事上有时也可故意"打草惊蛇"而诱敌暴露，从而取得战斗的胜利。

14. *Borrow a Corpse to Resurrect a Soul*

A person that is capable would not ask for help. A person who is incapable would ask for help. By using those who are incapable, I am able to control people and not be controlled by people.

有作为的，不求助于别人；没作为的，求助于别人。利用无所作为的并顺势利用它，不是我受别人支配，而是我支配别人。

Towards the end of the Qin Dynasty, most of the people hated the tyranny of the Qin, but there was no one to gather and lead the people to rebel against Qin, until the first year of the second Qin Emperor.

Cheng Sheng and Wu Guang were conscripted and sent to Yu Yang. During the journey, their group encountered heavy rain and a flood. So, there was no way they could arrive at their destination on time. During that time, the Qin laws stated that for those who are conscripted, if they are not able to reach the designated destination on time, the whole group will be beheaded. Cheng Sheng and Wu Guang, on seeing that it was impossible to reach Yu Yang on time, decided to fight for their lives instead. They knew that the rest of the group members also had such thoughts, so it was a good time to gather them to revolt against Qin.

But Cheng Sheng realized that he had no power or authority to lead these people to revolt against Qin. During that time, there were two popular figures among the population and they were the eldest prince of the first Qin Emperor, and the other was General Xiang Yan, from the former State of Chu. So both Cheng Sheng and Wu Guang decided to use the superstitious mindset of the people.

When the group was preparing fish for dinner, they found a note inside the belly of the fish. On the note was written: "Emperor Chen Sheng". The group was shocked and news of it spread within the group. During the night, Wu Guang mimicked the cry of the wolf. People on hearing the wolf cry could vaguely hear the words: "Revive Chu, Emperor Cheng Sheng." With both of these things happening, most of the group members thought that Cheng Sheng must be somebody sent from Heaven to lead them. On seeing the opportunity was ripe, Cheng Sheng and Wu Guang shouted, "Since death awaits us, if we go to Yu Yang, let us revolt now and fight for a chance to live!" Cheng Sheng proclaimed himself as the General and together with Wu Guang started the first peasant rebellion in China's history.

秦朝实行暴政，天下百姓"欲为乱者，十室有五。"大家都有反秦的愿望，但是如果没有强有力的领导者和组织者，也就难成大事。秦二世元年，陈胜、吴广被征发到渔阳戍边。当这些戍卒走到大泽乡时，连降大雨，道路被水淹没，眼看无法按时到达渔阳了。秦朝法律规定，凡是不能按时到达指定地点的戍卒，一律处斩。陈胜、吴广知道，即使到达渔阳，也会误期被杀，不如一拼，寻求一条活路。他们知道同去的戍卒也都有这种思想，正是举兵起义的大好时机。

陈胜又想到，自己地位低下，恐怕没有号召力。当时有两位名人深受人民尊敬，一个是秦始皇的大儿子扶苏，温良贤明，已被阴险狠毒的秦二世暗中杀害，老百姓却不知情，另一个是楚将项燕，功勋卓著，爱护将士，威望极高，在秦灭六国之后不知去向。于是陈胜，公开打出他们的旗号，以期能够得到大家拥护。他们还利用当时人们的迷信心理，巧妙地作了其它安排。有一天，士兵做饭时，在鱼腹中发现一块丝帛，上写"陈胜王"（这个王字是称王的意思），士兵大惊，暗中传开。吴广又趁夜深人静之时，在旷野荒庙中学狐狸叫，士兵们还隐隐约约地听到空中有"大楚兴，陈胜王"的口号。他们以为陈胜不是一般的人，肯定是"天意"让他来领导大家的。陈胜、吴广见时机已到，率领戍卒杀死朝廷派来的将尉。陈胜登高一呼，揭竿而起。他说：我们反正活不成了，不如和他们拼个你死我活，就是死，也要死出个样儿来。于是，陈胜自号为将军，吴广为都尉，攻占大泽乡，天下云集响应，节节胜利，所向披靡。后来，部下拥立陈胜为王，国号"张楚"。

15. *Lure a Tiger from its Mountain Lair*

Wait for the natural conditions to be unfavorable to your enemy; use deception to lure the enemy to attack you, since attacking him would be dangerous.

等待自然条件对敌人不利时在去围困敌人，用人为的假象去诱惑敌人，向前进攻有危险，那就想办法让敌人来攻我。

Towards the end of the Eastern Han dynasty, just before the Three Kingdoms Period, there was intense fighting among warlords for territories. One young warlord was Sun Ce, who was only seventeen when he took over his father's ambitions. In 199 AD, Sun Ce wanted to expand north, eyeing Lu Jiang. The problem was that Lu Jiang had the Yangtze River and the Huai River as natural barriers, thus making the region very difficult to attack. Moreover, the warlord occupying the Lu Jiang region was Liu Xun, who wielded great power but was extremely greedy.

So Sun Ce discussed with his advisors the strategy he should use, and they decided to use the "to lure a tiger from its mountain lair" strategy. Sun Ce wrote a letter heaping praises on Liu Xun and together with the letter included a very expensive gift. At the end of the letter, after much praises at the start, he sought help from Liu Xun. Sun Ce wrote, "The army from Upper Liao always plunders my territories. As we are weak, we are not able to send our troops to expel them. Can you please help us? Your help is greatly appreciated." Being praised to the sky by Sun Ce, Liu Xun was more than happy to help Sun Ce; because he had plans to take over Upper Liao, because of the huge wealth that the people had gathered. And seeing that Sun Ce was 'weak', he did not have to fear that he would be attacked from the rear. Liu Ye advised against the move, but Liu Xun was too mesmerized by the praises and gifts sent by Sun Ce to take in his advice.

Sun Ce monitored Liu Xun's movements. When he saw that Liu Xun had left with his troops to Upper Liao, leaving the city defenseless, he seized the opportunity to take over the city. With the weak city defense, it was too easy for Sun Ce's men. Liu Xun, on the other hand, was not able to conquer Upper Liao, and when news travelled to his ears that Lu Jiang has been captured by Sun Ce, he knew all was lost and went to seek refuge at Cao Cao.

东汉末年，军阀并起，各霸一方。孙坚之子孙策，年仅十七岁，年少有为，继承父志，势力逐渐强大。公元199年，孙策欲向北推进，准备夺取江北卢江郡。卢江郡南有长江之险，北有淮水阻隔，易守难攻。

占据卢江的军阀刘勋势力强大，野心勃勃。孙策知道，如果硬攻，取胜的机会很小。他和众将商议，定出了一条调虎离山的妙计。针对军阀刘勋，极其贪财的弱点，孙策派人给刘勋送去一份厚礼，并在信中把刘勋大肆吹捧一番。信中说刘勋功名远播，今人仰慕，并表示要与刘励交好。孙策还以弱者的身份向刘勋求救。他说，上缭经常派兵侵扰我们，我们力弱，不能远征，请求将军发兵降服上缭，我们感激不尽。刘勋见孙策极力讨好他，万分得意。上缭一带，十分富庶，刘勋早想夺取，今见孙策软弱无能，免去了后顾之忧，决定发兵上缭。部将刘晔极力劝阻，刘勋哪里听得进去？他已经被孙策的厚礼、甜言迷惑住了。

孙策时刻监视刘勋的行动，见刘勋亲自率领几万兵马去攻上缭，城内空虚，心中大喜，说："老虎已被我调出山了，我们赶快去占据它的老窝吧！"于是立即率领人马，水陆并进，袭击卢江，几乎没遇到顽强的抵杭，就十顺利地控制了卢江。刘勋猛攻上缭，一直不能取胜。突然得报，孙策已取卢江，情知中计，后悔已经来不及了，只得灰溜溜地投奔曹操。

16. *Release the Enemy Only to Capture Him Later*

If you force your enemy into a desperate situation, he will fight with all he has. If you give your enemy an escape route, he will focus on escaping rather than fighting. When he is escaping, try to follow him, but not force him to attack. While escaping, it reduces his strength and fighting spirit. Once they are tired and have low morale, you can capture them easily without too much bloodshed.

如果把敌人逼的无路可走，他就会拼命反扑。让敌人跑路反而可以让他的气势减弱。对逃跑之敌要紧紧跟随，不能过于逼迫，借以消耗其体力，瓦解其斗志。等到敌人士气低弱、军心涣散时在去逮捕他，这样就会避免不必要的流血牺牲。总之，不进逼敌人，并让他相信这一点，就能赢得光明的胜利。

In 225 AD Zhuge Liang had plans for the Northern Territory, but first had to deal with Meng Huo, the leader of the Southern Tribes to secure his rear. Meng Huo led an army of 10,000 men to invade the Shu Kingdom. So, Zhuge Liang personally led an army to fend off Meng Huo. The first time they met, Zhuge Liang lured Meng Huo to a valley and ambushed him. Meng Huo was caught unaware and was captured.

Since the leader had been captured, the mission could be considered accomplished; but Zhuge Liang considered that Meng Huo had high standing among the Southern tribes, and thus had strong influence on them. So instead, it would be wiser to make Meng Huo succumb to him whole-heartedly. So Zhuge Liang decided to release Meng Huo. Before Meng Huo left, he said to Zhuge Liang that the next time they met, Zhuge Liang would be on the losing side. When Meng Huo went back to the army camp, he removed all the boats from the Lu River to prevent the Shu army from advancing, and stationed his base on the southern bank. Zhuge Liang instead crossed the river where Meng Huo's defense was the weakest, and attacked his supplies depot. Meng Huo was furious and punished his generals. The generals being punished were angry, so they captured Meng Huo and surrendered him to Zhuge Liang. Seeing that Meng Huo was not convinced of his defeat, he released Meng Huo again. This went on for another four times, captured and released. Until the seventh and the last time, when Zhuge Liang set fire to Meng Huo's bamboo-armored soldiers and defeated him, did Meng Huo submit himself to Zhuge Liang, and vowed not to rebel again.

诸葛亮七擒孟获，就是军事史上一个"欲擒故纵"的绝妙战例。蜀汉建立之后，定下北伐大计。当时西南夷酋长孟获率十万大军侵犯蜀国。诸葛亮为了解决北伐的后顾之忧，决定亲自率兵先平孟获。蜀军主力到达泸水（今金沙江）附近，诱敌出战，事先在山谷中埋下伏兵，孟获被诱入伏击圈内，兵败被擒。

按说，擒拿敌军主帅的目的已经达到，敌军一时也不会有很强战斗力了，乘胜追击，自可大破敌军。但是诸葛亮考虑到孟获在西南夷中威望很高，影响很大，如果让他心悦诚服，主动请降，就能使南方真正稳定。不然的话，南方夷各个部落仍不会停止侵扰，后方难以安定。诸葛亮决定对孟获采取"攻心"战，断然释放孟获。孟获表示下次定能击败你，诸葛亮笑而不答。孟获回营，拖走所有船只，据守沪水南岸，阻止蜀军渡河。诸葛亮乘敌不备，从敌人不设防的下流偷渡过河，并袭击了孟获的粮仓。孟获暴怒，要严惩将士，激起将士的反抗，于是相约投降，趁孟获不备，将孟获绑赴蜀营。诸葛亮见孟获仍不服，再次释放。以后孟获又施了许多计策，都被诸葛亮识破，四次被擒，四次被释放。最后一次，诸葛亮火烧孟获的藤甲兵，第七次生擒孟获。终于感动了孟获，他真诚地感谢诸葛亮七次不杀之恩，誓不再反。从此，蜀国西南安定，诸葛亮才得以举兵北伐。

17. *Toss out a Brick to Get Jade*

Use a decoy to trick the enemy, putting him in a confused state, and he will fall into the trap.

用类似的东西诱惑敌人，使敌人懵懵懂懂地上当受骗。

In the year 700 BC, the State of Chu sent out an army to conquer and annex the State of Jiao. Their movement was very fast and when they reached the city walls, their morale was extremely high. The Lord of Jiao knew that going out to fight with the Chu troops was asking for death, so they decide to defend the city within the walls. The terrain surrounding the State of Jiao was a place easy to defend, but difficult to attack. The Chu troops repeatedly attacked the city walls, but to no avail. So this went on for more than a month. One advisor from the State of Chu analyzed the situation and thought that they should use wits, instead of numerical strength, to conquer the city; so he hatched up a plan and let the Lord of Chu in on it. Since the city had been surrounded for a very long time, they would have a shortage of firewood. The plan was to get soldiers to pose as woodcutters to collect firewood from the nearby forest. The Jiao soldiers, on seeing that the woodcutters were defenseless, would ride out to capture these woodcutters together with their firewood. So they could use the 'woodcutters' to lure out the Jiao soldiers and capture the city, while they were out.

The Chu soldiers carried out the plan. The first few days, they let the Jiao soldiers plunder the firewood from the 'woodcutters' successfully. After several successful attempts, the Jiao soldiers became complacent. On the sixth day, a large group of the Jiao soldiers rode out to chase after the 'woodcutters' again. This time, they were lured into an ambush. The Jiao soldiers were totally caught unaware when Chu soldiers came out of their hiding. They tried to retreat, but their retreat route was cut off. Most of the Jiao soldiers were either captured or killed. On seeing that they had destroyed most of the Jiao soldiers, the Lord of Chu ordered another attack on the State of Jiao. Seeing that there was no way of winning, the Lord of Jiao decided to surrender.

公元前700年，楚国用"抛砖引玉"的策略，轻取绞城。这一年，楚国发兵攻打绞国（今湖北郧县西北），大军行动迅速。楚军兵临城下，气势旺盛，绞国自知出城迎战，凶多吉少，决定坚守城池。绞城地势险要，易守难攻。楚军多次进攻，均被击退。两军相持一个多月。楚国大夫莫傲屈居瑕仔细分析了敌我双方的情况，认为绞城只可智取，不可力克。他向楚王献上一条"以鱼饵钓大鱼"的计谋。他说："攻城不下，不如利而诱之。"楚王向他问诱敌之法。屈瑕建议：趁绞城被围月余，城中缺少薪柴之时，派些士兵装扮成樵夫上山打柴运回来，敌军一定会出城劫夺柴草。头几天，让他们先得一些小利，等他们麻痹大意，大批士兵出城劫夺柴草之时，先设伏兵断其后路，然后聚而歼之，乘势夺城。楚王担心绞国不会轻易上当，屈瑕说："大王放心，绞国虽小而轻燥，轻躁则少谋略。有这样香甜的钓饵，不愁它不上钩。"楚王于是依计而行，命一些士兵装扮成樵夫上山打柴。

绞侯听探子报告有挑夫进山的情况，忙问这些樵夫有无楚军保护。探子说，他们三三两两进出，并无兵士跟随。绞侯马上布置人马，待"樵夫"背着柴禾出山之机，突然袭击，果然顺利得手，抓了三十多个"樵夫"，夺得不少柴草。一连几天，果然收获不小。见有利可图，绞国士兵出城劫夺柴草的越来越多。楚王见敌人已经吞下钓饵，便决定迅速逮大鱼。第六天，绞国士兵象前几天一样出城劫掠，"樵夫"们见绞军又来劫掠，吓得没命的逃奔，绞国士兵紧紧追赶，不知不觉被引入楚军的埋伏圈内。只见伏兵四起，杀声震天，纹国士兵哪里抵挡得住，慌忙败退，又遇伏兵断了归路，死伤无数。楚王此时趁机攻城，绞侯自知中计，已无力抵抗，只得请降。

18. *Disband the Thieves by Capturing their Chief*

If the enemy's power base is destroyed, and his leaders captured, then the whole organization would be disintegrated. Just like a sea dragon having to fight on land, it will face severe difficulties.

摧毁敌人的主力，擒住他的首领，就可以瓦解他的整体力量。就好像龙离开大海到陆地作战而面临绝境一样。

In 757 AD, during the Anshi Rebellion, Tang Su Zhong, the Emperor of the Tang Dynasty, commanded General Zhang Xun to guard the city of Sui Yang from the rebels. Zhang Xun's army eventually had a fierce fight with the troops of the rebel General Yin Zi Qi.

General Zhang Xun's army fought bravely and killed 5,000 enemy soldiers. The enemy camp was thrown into confusion. Nobody could locate General Yin Zi Qi. General Zhang Xun then hatched a plan to lure the rebel general from his hideout. He ordered his men to use fake arrows made of straw to shoot at the enemy. When the enemy soldiers saw this, they thought that they had defeated Zhang Xun's army and rushed to report to General Yin Zi Qi. Thus, they disclosed the location of the general. General Zhang Xun ordered his men to shoot at General Yin Zi Qi, who was wounded in his left eye. Although General Yin Zi Qi managed to escape after a fierce struggle, his troops were thoroughly defeated.

唐朝安史之乱时，安禄山气焰嚣张，连连大捷，安禄山之子安庆绪派勇将尹子奇率十万劲旅进攻睢阳。御史中丞张巡驻守睢阳，见敌军来势汹汹，决定据城固守。敌兵二十余次攻城，均被击退。尹子奇见士兵已经疲惫，只得鸣金收兵。晚上，敌兵刚刚准备休息，忽听城头战鼓隆隆，喊声震天，尹子奇急令部队准备与冲出城来的唐军激战。而张巡"只打雷不下雨"，不时擂鼓，象要杀出城来，可是一直紧闭城门，没有出战。尹子奇的部队被折腾了整夜，没有得到休息，将士们疲乏已极，眼睛都睁不开，倒在地上就呼呼大睡。这时，城中一声炮响，突然之间，张巡率领守兵冲杀出来·敌兵从梦中惊醒，惊慌失措，乱作一团。张巡一鼓作气，接连斩杀五十余名敌将，五千余名士兵，敌军大乱。张巡急令部队擒拿敌军首领尹子奇，部队一直冲到敌军帅旗之下。张巡从未见过尹子奇，根本不认识，现在他又混在乱军之中，更加难以辨认。张巡心生一计，让士兵用秸杆削尖作箭，射向敌军。敌军中不少人中箭，他们以为这下玩了，没有命了。但是发现，自己中的是秸杆箭，心中大喜，以为张巡军中已没有箭了。他们争先恐后向尹子奇报告这个好消息。张巡见状，立刻辨认出了敌军首领尹子奇，急令神箭手、部将南霁云向尹子奇放箭。正中尹于奇左眼，这回可是真箭只见尹子奇鲜血淋漓，抱头鼠窜，仓皇逃命。敌军一片混乱，大败而逃。

Chapter 4 – Stratagems of Confusion

19. *Remove the Firewood from Under the Cooking Pot*

Direct confrontation may not be advisable when facing a strong opponent. It may be better to use tactics to destroy his morale.

直接面对敌人的锋芒，而是间接瓦解敌人的气势，也就是说以柔克刚的方法转弱为强。

Towards the end of the Eastern Han Dynasty, the warlords were fighting amongst each other. At the northern part of China, the Hebei region, one warlord stood out: Yuan Shao. In the year 199 AD, Yuan Shao attacked Xu Chang with 100,000 troops. At that time, Cao Cao was at Guan Du with only 20,000 troops to defend against Yuan Shao. The stand-off between Cao Cao and Yuan Shao lasted for a long time, and supply provisions became an issue during the war. Yuan Shao sent for another 10,000 carts of provisions from his base and stationed it at Wu Cao.

On hearing that Yuan Shao did not have enough troops to defend Wu Cao, Cao Cao immediately led 5,000 men disguised as Yuan Shao troops to Wu Cao. Under the cover of night, Cao Cao's troops surrounded Wu Cao, and before long, raided the supply depot and set fire to many of the provision there. Yuan Shao on hearing the attack, and knowing that his large troops needed large amounts of provisions, was lost for action. News of the attack also spread through the Yuan Shao camp, and the morale of the soldiers was affected. Cao Cao took this opportunity to deal a huge blow to the Yuan Shao troops. Yuan Shao was badly defeated and managed to escape back to Hebei with only 800 soldiers.

东汉末年，军阀混战，河北袁绍乘势崛起。公元199年，袁绍率领十万大军攻打许昌。当时，曹操据守官渡（今河南中牟北），兵力只有二万多人。两军离河对峙。袁绍仗着人马众多，派兵攻打白马。曹操表面上放弃白马，命令主力开向延津渡口，摆开渡河架势。袁绍怕后方受敌，迅速率主力西进，阻挡曹军渡河。谁知曹操虚晃一枪之后，突派精锐回袭白马，斩杀颜良，初战告捷。

由于两军相持了很长时间，双方粮草供给成了关键。袁绍从河北调集了一万多车粮草，屯集在大本营以北四十里的乌巢。曹操探听乌巢并无重兵防守，决定偷袭乌巢，断其供应。他亲自率五千精兵打着袁绍的旗号，衔枚急走，夜袭乌巢，乌巢袁军还没有弄清真相，曹军已经包围了粮仓。一把大火点燃，顿时浓烟四起。曹军乘势消灭了守粮袁军，袁军的一万车粮草，顿时化为灰烬，袁绍大军闻讯，惊恐万状，供应断绝，军心浮动，袁绍一时没了主意。曹操此时，发动全线进攻，袁军士兵已丧失战斗力，十万大军四散溃逃。

袁军大败，袁绍带领八百亲兵，艰难地杀出重围，回到河北，从此一蹶不振。

20. *Fish in Troubled Waters*

When the enemy is in a state of confusion, one should take advantage, and gain control when he is weak and without proper direction. The best way to control the enemy is to let nature takes its course, as all men have to eat and rest.

趁敌人内部纷乱之际，利用其虚弱而无主见的条件，迫使敌人随从我方的意志，就像人到了夜晚要入睡一样。

During the first year of the Tang Dynasty, the Qi Dan people from the north continuously made incursions into the Tang Territories. The court of the Tang Dynasty appointed Zhang Shou Gui as the Governor of Youzhou to settle the problem of the Qi Dan's incursions. The Qi Dan general in charge of conquering Youzhou was Ke Tu Gan. Ke Tu Gan tried many times to take over Youzhou, but to no avail. So he decided, as a ruse, to ask for a truce and seek to be under the Tang Court. Zhang Shou Gui knew immediately it was a ruse, given the fact that the Qi Dan's strength was still strong. He decided to set a counter-ruse instead. The next day, Governor Zhang sent Wang Hui as an envoy to Ke Tu Gan's camp on the pretense of accepting the truce, but it was actually to seek out enemy information.

At the camp, Ke Tu Gan threw a feast for Wang Hui, and all the Qi Dan generals were there. During the feast, Wang Hui noticed that not all the generals were hostile towards the Tang Court. Wang Hui also managed to find out there was a Qi Dan general called Li Guo Zhe who was at odds with Ke Tu Gan.

After the feast, Wang Hui went to look for Li Guo Zhe. Pretending not to know the relationship between he and Ke Tu Gan, Wang Hui heaped praises on Ke Tu Gan in front of Li Guo Zhe. Li Guo Zhe was boiling inside when he heard the compliments, until he got so angry, he blurted out everything, including the fact that Ke Tu Gan was about to attack Youzhou with the new reinforcements.

Wang Hui then tried to persuade Li Guo Zhe to switch sides, promising that the Tang Court would hire him and make full use of him. Li Guo Zhe was persuaded, and made his intention on switching sides known to Wang Hui. Wang Hui, on completing his mission, went back to Youzhou. The next evening, Li Guo Zhe led his own troops and stormed Ke Tu Gan's camp. Before he was able to react, Ke Tu Gan was killed by Li Guo Zhe. The camp was thrown into total chaos. The Tang troops took the opportunity to rout Qi Dan's troops and scored a decisive victory. Governor Zhang took the opportunity and was able to capture Qi Dan's King, thus completing his mission of stopping Qi Dan's incursions.

唐朝开元年间，契丹叛乱，多次侵犯唐朝。朝廷派张守圭为幽州节度使，平定契丹之乱。契丹大将可突干几次攻幽州，未能攻下。可突干想探听唐军虚实，派使者到幽州，假意表示愿意重新归顺朝廷，永不进犯。张守圭知道契丹势力正旺，主动求和，必定有诈。他将计就计，客气地接待了来使。第二天，他派王悔代表朝廷到可突干营中宣抚，并命王悔一定要探明契丹内部的底细。王悔在契丹营中受到热情接待，他在招待酒宴上仔细观察契丹众将的一举一动。他发现，契丹全将在对朝廷的态度上并不一致。他又从一个小兵口中探听到分掌兵权的李过折一向与可突干有矛盾，两人貌合神离，互不服气。王悔特意去拜访李过折，装作不了解他和可突干之间的矛盾，当着李过折的面，假意大肆夸奖可突干的才干。李过折听罢，怒火中烧，说可突干主张反唐，使契丹陷于战乱，人民十分怨恨。并告诉王悔，契丹这次求和完全是假意，可突干已向突厥借兵，不日就要攻打幽州。王悔乘机劝说李过折，唐军势力浩大，可突汗肯定失败。他如脱离可突汗，建功立业，朝廷保证一定会重用他。李过折果然心动，表示愿意归顺朝廷。王悔任务完成，立即辞别契丹王返回幽州。第二天晚上，李过折率领本部人马，突袭可突干的中军大帐。可突干毫无防备，被李过折斩于营中，这一下，契丹营大乱。忠于可突干的大将涅礼召集人马，与李过折展开激战，杀了李过折。张守圭探得消息，立即亲率人马赶来接应李过折的部从。唐军火速冲入契丹军营，契丹军内正在火并，混乱不堪。张守圭乘势发动猛攻，生擒涅礼，大破契丹军。从此，契丹叛乱被平息。

21. *Shed the Skin of the Cicada*

Preserve the original formation and stance, such that the allies will not suspect and the enemy will not be aroused to action. But in actual fact, one is secretly diverting main forces to attack other targets.

保留阵地原有外形，保持原有气势，使友军不怀疑，使敌人不敢轻举妄动。我方却秘密转移主力，攻打其他目标。

During the Three Kingdoms Period, Zhuge Liang died during the sixth Shu's expedition against the Northern Territories. Before Zhuge Liang died, he passed instructions to his disciple Jiang Wei on how to retreat the troops, so that they would not be attacked by the Wei soldiers. When Zhuge Liang died, Jiang Wei ordered that no funeral should be held, and for the Shu soldiers to make a retreat. Sima Yi, on hearing that the Shu troops were retreating, personally led his troops to chase after the Shu army.

Before the retreat, Jiang Wei had sculptors carve out a wooden statue of Zhuge Liang, dressed the statue up and placed the statue on Zhuge Liang's chariot. Jiang Wei then ordered General Yang Yi to get a small army to await Sima Yi's troops.

Sima Yi, from afar, saw that the retreat was orderly and Zhuge Liang was among the troops. Knowing Zhuge Liang's character and intelligence, Sima Yi did not want to take chances, so he ordered his troops to head back to camp. On seeing the movement of the Wei army, Jiang Wei then ordered the main troops to increase their retreating speed and managed to reach Hanzhong safely. When the news of Zhuge Liang's death reached Sima Yi, it was all too late.

三国时期，诸葛亮六出祁山，北伐中原，但一直未能成功，终于在第六次北伐时，积劳成疾，在五丈原病死于军中。为了不使蜀军在退回汉中的路上遭受损失，诸葛亮在临终前向姜维密授退兵之计。姜维遵照诸葛亮的吩咐，在诸葛亮死后，秘不发丧，对外严密封锁消息。他带着灵柩，秘密率部撤退。司马懿派部队跟踪追击蜀军。姜维命工匠仿诸葛亮摸样，雕了一个木人，羽扇纶巾，稳坐车中。并派杨仪率领部分人马大张旗鼓，向魏军发动进攻。魏军远望蜀军，军容整齐，旗鼓大张，又见诸葛亮稳坐车中，指挥若定，不知蜀军又耍什么花招，不敢轻举妄动。司马懿一向知道诸葛亮"诡计多端"，又怀疑此次退兵乃是诱敌之计，于是命令部队后撤，观察蜀军动向。姜维趁司马懿退兵的大好时机，马上指挥主力部队，迅速安全转移，撤回汉中。等司马懿得知诸葛亮已死，再进兵追击，为时已晚。

22. *Shut the Door to Catch the Thief*

The best way to capture a weak enemy is to have him surrounded. It is not advisable to pursue a weak enemy because it is agile in movement. This will only exhaust one's strength and make one vulnerable.

对于弱小之敌，应包围起来歼灭。小股敌人力量虽弱，但行动灵活，不宜穷追不舍。

During the Warring States period, The Qin army set out to attack the State of Zhao and they were stopped at Chang Ping. The Zhao general in charge of defense was General Lian Po. General Lian Po saw that the Qin army was large, so he ordered his troops to stay in defense position, and avoid fighting the Qin army head-on. There was no fighting for four months. The Lord of Qin was getting impatient, so he sought the advice of his advisors. Fan Sui suggested sowing discord between the Lord of Zhao and the General Lian Po. Lord of Zhao fell for the plot and ordered that General Zhao Kuo to take over for General Liao Po, who was believed to be a prodigy in war strategies then, but lacked experience severely.

When General Zhao Kuo took over, he took an offensive position instead. Now Qin General Bai Qi pretended to lose to General Zhao Kuo on the first few battles. This made Zhao Kuo very haughty, so much so, that he sent a letter to the Qin army and proposed a final battle where winner takes all. This fitted the plan of General Bai Qi very well, and Bai Qi ordered several troops to surround the Zhao's camp. The next day, Zhao Kuo rode out of the camp with his main troops.

Being arrogant, Zhao Kuo did not detect that the Qin army was luring them deeper into Qin's territory, away from their camp. When they reached the Qin camp, the Qin army 'hid' inside their camp and refused to come out and engage the Zhao's army. The stalemate went on for a few days, then news traveled to Zhao Kuo, that the Zhao's camp had been taken over by the Qin troops, and their supply route had been cut off. With the Zhao's supply route cut off, the Qin army had the Zhao's army surrounded for forty six days. During this time, the Zhao army had to kill each other for food and Zhao Kuo made unsuccessful attempts to break through the tight barricade. In the end, Zhao Kuo died during the last attempt and with the general dead, the 400,000 troops surrendered to Qin army. But alas, the Zhao army was too large an army for Qin to take it as its own, so all of them were buried alive. The State of Zhao never recovered from this bitter defeat.

战国后期，秦国攻打赵国。秦军在长平（今山西高平北）受阻。长平守将是赵国名将廉颇，他见秦军势力强大，不能硬拼，便命令部队坚壁固守，不与秦军交战。两军相持四个多月，秦军仍拿不下长平。秦王采纳了范雎的建议，用离间法让赵王怀疑廉颇，赵王中计，调回廉颇，派赵括为将到长平与秦军作战。赵括到长平后，完全改变了廉颇坚守不战的策略，主张与秦军对面决战。秦将白起故意让赵括尝到一点甜头，使赵括的军队取得了几次小胜。赵括果然得意忘形，派人到秦营下战书。这下正中白起的下怀。他分兵几路，指挥形成对赵括军的包围圈。第二天，赵括亲率四十万大军，来与秦兵决战。秦军与赵军几次交战，都打输了。赵括志得意满，哪里知道敌人用的是诱敌之计。他率领大军追赶被打败了的秦军，一直追到秦壁。秦军坚守不出，赵括一连数日也攻克不了，只得退兵。这时突然得到消息：自己的后营已被秦军攻占，粮道也被秦军截断。秦军已把赵军全部包围起未。一连四十六天，赵军绝粮，士兵杀人相食，赵括只得拼命突围。白起已严密部署，多次击退企图突围的赵军，最后，赵括中箭身亡，赵军大乱。可惜四十万大军都被秦军杀戮。这个赵括，就是会"纸上谈兵"，在真正的战场上，一下子就中了敌军"关门捉贼"之计，损失四十万大军，使赵国从此一蹶不振。

23. *Befriend the Far and Attack the Near*

Sometimes, it is more beneficial to attack a nearby enemy than a distant one because of geographic constraints. So it is advisable to form an alliance with a distant enemy to destroy the nearby one.

地理位置受到限制，形势发展受到阻碍，攻击近处之敌对自己有利，攻击远处之敌对自己有害。火焰是向上蹿，水是向下流的，天地万物的发展变化莫不如此。

During the end of the Warring States Period, there were only seven states left. The Qin states had very notable growth, both military and economically, after it adopted the teaching of Shang Yang in its state administration. In 270 BC, Lord

Zhao of Qin wanted to annex the State of Qi. Fan Sui suggested the "befriend the far and attack the near" strategy. Fan Sui said, "The State of Qi is strong and it is far away from Qin. If we were to attack it, we need to pass by the State of Han and Wei. If we send too few troops, we will not be able to win. If we send in too many troops, we cannot concretely annex the land we conquer. Why not attack the nearby States of Han and Wei instead? To prevent the State of Qi from forming an alliance with State of Han and Wei, we proposed an alliance with Qi first." Lord Zhao agreed with Fan Sui and carried out his plan. With that, this became the main focus of Qin's foreign policy for the next forty years. Thus the State of Qin was later able to annex the other six states and united ancient China.

战国末期，七雄争霸。秦国经商鞅变法之后，势力发展最快。秦昭王开始图谋吞并六国，独霸中原。公元前270年，秦昭王准备兴兵伐齐。范雎此时向秦昭王献上

"远交近攻"之策，阻秦国攻齐。他说：齐国势力强大，离秦国又很远，攻打齐国，部队要经过韩、魏两国。军队派少了，难以取胜；多派军队，打胜了也无法占有齐国土地。不如先攻打邻国韩、魏，逐步推进。为了防止齐国与韩、魏结盟，秦昭王派使者主动与齐国结盟。其后四十余年，秦始皇继续坚持"远交近攻"之策，远交齐楚，首先攻下韩、魏，然后又从两翼进兵，攻破赵、燕，统一北方；攻破楚国，平定南方；最后把齐国也收拾了。秦始皇征战十年，终于实现了统一中国的愿望。

24. *Borrow a Passage to Attack Guo*

A smaller state situated between an enemy and oneself should be given immediate support when the enemy threatens to attack it. In this way, one will earn the trust of the smaller state, and may eventually exert one's influence on it. Words without action will not win the trust of the small state in a precarious situation.

地处敌我两大国之间，当敌方胁迫它屈服的时候，我方要立即援助，并借机把自己的势力渗透进去。对于处于困境的国家，只有空话而无实际的援助，是不能取得信任。

During the Spring and Autumn Period, the State of Jin was eyeing two smaller states beside it, the State of Yu and Guo. The problem was that the relationship between these two states was strong; whoever is attacked, the other people will definitely send reinforcements. A Jin advisor, Xun Xi, suggested sowing discord between the two states, by bribing the Lord of Yu with a prized horse and a precious jade piece that the Lord Xian of Jin was holding. Since these were prized possessions of the Lord of Jin, thus was he hesitant. Xun Xi persuaded Lord of Jin, "My lord, there is no need to worry. You will get back your prized possessions once you have annexed the two states. You are just entrusting them temporarily to the Lord of Yu." Lord Xian was convinced and sent someone to present the gifts to the Lord of Yu. The Lord of Yu was overjoyed when he received the gifts.

For the next step of the plan, Lord Xian sent someone to create trouble at the border of the States of Jin and Guo, thus creating an excuse to send an army against Guo. Lord Xian requested safe passage through the State of Yu to attack the State of Guo. As the Lord of Yu had initially accepted the gifts from Jin, he felt obliged to accede to the request, but his advisors were against it. The Lord of Yu rationalized his decision by saying, "It would be stupid to honor the alliance to a weak state by sacrificing the relationship with a strong state."

So the Jin troops used the path to attack Guo and they scored a decisive victory. When they returned past the State of Yu, they shared their bounty with the Lord of Yu. The Lord of Yu was immensely happy and even allowed the Jin troops to rest near the capital. A few days later, Lord Xian of Jin arrived with a large army and the Lord of Yu went out to welcome Lord Xian. Lord Xian invited the Lord of Yu for a hunting trip, and the latter obliged. Before long, the capital of Yu was captured by the large Jin army that was left behind. Thus both the States of Yu and Guo were captured.

春秋时期，晋国想吞并邻近的两个小国：虞和虢，这两个国家之间关系不错。晋如袭虞，虢会出兵救援；晋若攻虢，虞也会出兵相助。大臣荀息向晋献公献上一计。他说，要想攻占这两个国家，必须要离间他们，使他们互不支持。虞国的国君贪得无厌，我们正可以投其所好。他建议晋献公拿出心爱的两件宝物，屈产良马和垂棘之璧，送给虞公。献公哪里舍得？荀息说：大王放心，只不过让他暂时保管罢了，等灭了虞国，一切不都又回到你的手中了吗？献公依计而行。虞公得到良马美璧，高兴得嘴都合不拢。

晋国故意在晋、虢边境制造事端，找到了伐虢的借口。晋国要求虞国借道让晋国伐虢，虞公得了晋国的好处，只得答应。虞国大臣宫子奇再三劝说虞公，这件事办不得的。虞虢两国，唇齿相依，虢国一亡，唇亡齿寒，晋国是不会放过虞国的。虞公却说，交一个弱朋友去得罪一个强有力的朋友，那才是傻瓜哩！

晋大军通过虞国道路，攻打虢国，很快就取得了胜利。班师回国时，把劫夺的财产分了许多送给虞公。虞公更是大喜过望。晋军大将里克，这时装病，称不能带兵回国，暂时把部队驻扎在虞国京城附近。虞公毫不怀疑。几天之后，晋献公亲率大军前去，虞公出城相迎。献公约虞公前去打猎。不一会儿，只见京城中起火。虞公赶到城外时，京城已被晋军里应外合强占了。就这样，晋国又轻而易举地灭了虞国。

The Thirty Six Stratagems

Chapter 5 – Stratagems of Deception

25. *Replace Good Beams with Rotten Timber*

Find a chance to change the enemy's battle formation frequently, and try to take away its main source of power. Wait until it is unable to cope with the situation before attacking it. This is similar to taking control of the wheels of a wagon; one can then control the direction of the wagon as well.

频繁的变动敌人的阵容，抽调开敌人的精锐主力，等待它自行败退，然后乘机取胜。这就好像拖住了大车的轮子，也控制了大车的运行一样。

Liu Bang emerged the victor when he fought Xiang Yu, and established the Han Dynasty as a result. During the start of the Han Dynasty, Liu Bang perceived that those who did not share his surname were potential dangers, and saw that dealing with them would be a major issue during his reign. Of all these lords that Liu Bang conferred, Han Xin was the greatest threat, as Han Xin was the chief commander of his army when Liu Bang fought Xiang Yu. With this in mind, Liu Bang made up an excuse to reduce Han Xin's rank, by conferring the title "Duke Huai Yin" to him and ordered him to stay in the capital.

During the power struggle between Liu Bang and Xiang Yu, Han Xin gained a lot of achievements under Liu Bang. During that time, one advisor, called Kuai Che suggested to Han Xin to rebel against Liu Bang, splitting the kingdom into three parts, each held by Liu Bang, Xiang Yu and Han Xin. But Han Xin did not take the advice which he regretted after his 'demotion'.

In 200 BC, Liu Bang appointed Chen Xi as the Commander-in-Chief for border defense against the Xiongnus. Han Xin went to see Chen Xi secretly and reminded Chen Xi to use him as an example of what would happen. He said to Chen Xi, "See what has happened to me? Liu Bang would not trust you. Why not take the opportunity to revolt against Liu Bang and I will assist you from the inside?" Chen Xi agreed and planned the uprising for when the correct opportunity arose.

In 197 BC, Chen Xi revolted and Liu Bang personally led an army to suppress the rebellion. Han Xin acted according to plan. The plan was to fake the edict of Liu Bang, which was to order the killing of Empress Lu and the Crown Prince, and then ride out with the army to attack Liu Bang from the rear. But the plan was discovered by the Lu Empress.

Empress Lu consulted with advisor Chen Ping to counteract Han Xin's plan. Empress Lu began spreading rumors in the capital that Liu Bang had successfully suppressed the rebellion, killed Chen Xi and that all the officials should be in court to celebrate Liu Bang's victory. The order was conveyed to Han Xin as well. Han Xin did not know whether to believe the rumor so he attended court with

Chen Ping. On his way, he was captured and was killed. Han Xin never realized that all were rumors, and the actual Chen Xi's rebellion was only suppressed two years later.

楚汉相争，以刘邦大胜，建立汉朝为结局。这时，各异姓王拥兵自重，是对刘氏天下潜在的威胁。翦灭异姓诸王，是刘邦日夜考虑的大事。异姓诸王中，韩信势力最大。刘邦借口韩信袒护一叛将为由，把他由楚王贬为淮阴侯，调到京城居住，实际上有点"软禁"的味道。韩信功高盖世，忠于刘邦。当年楚汉相争，战斗激烈之时，谋士蒯彻曾建议韩信与刘邦分手，使天下三分。韩信拒绝了蒯彻的建议，辅佐刘邦夺得天下。而今却落得这样的下场，心中怨恨至极。

公元前200年，刘邦派陈豨为代相，统率边兵，对付匈奴。韩信私下里会见陈豨，以自己的遭遇为例，警告陈豨，你虽然拥有重兵，但并不安全，刘邦不会一直信任你，不如乘此机会，带兵反汉，我在京城里接应你。两个人秘密地商量好，决定伺机起事。

公元前197年，陈豨在代郡反汉，自立为代王。刘邦领兵亲自声讨陈豨。韩信与陈豨约定，起事后他在京城诈称奉刘邦密诏，袭击吕后及太子，两面夹击刘邦。可是，韩信的计谋被吕后得知。吕后与丞相陈平设下一计，对付韩信。

吕后派人在京城散布：陈豨已死，皇上得胜，即将凯旋。韩信听到这个消息，又没有见到陈豨派人来联系，心中甚为恐慌。一日·丞相陈平亲自到韩信家中，谎称陈豨已死，叛乱已定，皇上已班师回朝，文武百官都要入朝庆贺，请韩信立即进宫。韩信本来心虚，只得与陈平同车进宫。结果被吕后逮捕，囚系在长乐宫之钟室。半夜时分，韩信被杀。后世称"未央宫斩韩信"。盖世英名的韩信至死也不知道，陈豨已死的消息，完全是谎言。陈豨叛乱，是在韩信死了两年之后才平定的。

26. *Point at the Mulberry but Scold the Locust Tree*

A stronger force can use warning or admonishment to control a weaker force. A suitable display of power will receive support and the use of a decisive method will demand reverence. It is not necessary to destroy the smaller force when one is much stronger.

强者慑服弱小者，要用警戒的方法加以诱导。威严适当，可以获得拥护。手段高明，可以使人顺服。

During the Spring and Autumn Period, the Lord Jing of the State of Qi appointed Sima Rangju as the commander-in-chief to lead an expedition against the States of

Jin and Yan, and sent one of his favored officers, Zhuang Jia as the supervisor. Sima Rangju, on knowing the appointments, arranged with Zhuang Jia to meet at the campsite at exactly noon. The next day, Sima Rangju arrived at the camp very early and ordered that a wooden pole be placed at the campsite as a time dial.

When noon was reached, there was still no sign of Zhuang Jia. Sima Rangju sent several messengers to hurry Zhuang Jia, but to no avail. It was finally evening when Zhuang Jia made his way to the campsite, in a drunken stupor. Sima Rangju asked Zhuang Jia, "Why are you late?" Zhuang Jia replied nonchalantly, "A few of my friends and relatives came to send me off, so we had a few rounds of drinks. Since so many people came, I had to entertain them, right? That is the reason why I am late." Sima Rangju was furious and scolded, "As the appointed supervisor of the army, instead of putting state military matters ahead of everything else, you rather bothered with your family affairs." Zhuang Jia, taking advantage of the fact that he was a favored official, took no heed of the scolding.

Sima Ranju ordered the disciplinary officer to come forward and asked, "To be late without reason, what is the punishment according to martial laws?" The disciplinary officer replied, "Execution!" Sima Rangju immediately asked men to arrest Zhuang Jia. Seeing the seriousness of the matter, Zhuang Jia's followers rushed back to look for Lord Jing.

Before the messenger of Lord Jing arrived, Zhuang Jia was executed on the spot. The soldiers were stunned and scared stiff. Everyone understood the consequences of not following orders. Later, the messenger of Lord Jing came rushing into the camp with his chariots, carrying with him the order to release Zhuang Jia. But Sima Rangju said, "When the general is outside (the court), there are orders that the general can choose not to follow." And on seeing that the messenger was arrogant, he again summoned the disciplinary officer and asked, "To rush into the camp with a chariot in a disorderly manner, what is the punishment?" The disciplinary officer again replied, "Execution." Once the word was uttered, the messenger's face turned white.

Sima Rangju said, "Since you are a messenger sent by Lord Jing, we shall not execute you." Sima Rangju ordered that the messenger's follower and three horses from the chariot be executed, and let the messenger go. With this showing, the soldiers knew that they must follow what Sima Rangju ordered, thus the army was very disciplined and went on to win many victories.

春秋时期，齐景公任命田穰苴为将，带兵攻打晋、燕联军，又派宠臣庄贾作监军。穰苴与庄贾约定，第二天中午在营门集合。第二天，穰苴早早到了营中，命令装好作为计时器的标杆和滴漏盘。约定时间一到，穰苴就到军营宣布军令，整顿部队。可是庄贾迟迟不到，穰苴几次派人催促，直到黄昏时分，庄贾才带着醉容到达营门。穰苴问他为何不按时到军营来，庄贾无所谓，只说什么亲威朋友都来为我设宴饯行，我总得应酬应酬吧？所以来得迟了。

穰苴非常气愤，斥责他身为国家大臣，有监军重任，却只恋自已的小家，不以国家大事为重。庄贾以为这是区区小事，仗着自己是国王的宠臣亲信，对穰苴的话不以为然。穰苴当着全军将士，命令叫来军法官，问："无故误了时间，按照军法应当如何处理？"军法官答道："该斩！"穰苴即命拿下庄贾。庄贾吓得浑身发抖，他的随从连忙飞马进宫，向齐景公报告情况，请求景公派人救命。在景公派的使者没有赶到之前，穰苴即令将庄贾斩首示众。全军将士，看到主将杀违犯军令的大臣，个个吓得发抖，谁还再敢不遵将令。这时，景公派来的使臣飞马闯入军营，拿景公的命令叫穰苴放了庄贾。穰苴沉着地应道："将在外，君命有所不受。"他见来人骄狂，便又叫来军法官，问道："乱在军营跑马，按军法应当如何处理？"军法官答道："该斩。"

来使吓得面如土色。穰苴不慌不忙地说道："君王派来的使者，可以不杀。"于是下令杀了他的随从和三驾车的左马，砍断马车左边的木柱。然后让使者回去报告。穰苴军纪严明，军队战斗力旺盛，果然打了不少胜仗。

27. *Pretend to be a Fool*

It is better for one to pretend that he knows nothing, and take no action, rather than pretending to know everything, and rush into a situation. One should prepare his forces in the dark and not let others know of his secret, waiting for an opportunity to strike, just as lightning and thunder wait to strike in winter.

宁可假装糊涂而不次采取行动，也绝不假装聪明而轻举妄动。要沉着冷静，深藏不露，就像雷电在冬季蓄力待发一样。

During the period just before the Three Kingdom Periods, where the many warlords were fighting for territories, two prominent heroes were outstanding. They were Liu Bei and Cao Cao. When Liu Bei was serving under Cao Cao, he hid his ambitions by drinking and tending to his vegetables every day. Once, Cao Cao invited Liu Bei over for a drink, and the topic that came up during the chat concerned who were the heroes of that time. Liu Bei listed several names, but was denounced by Cao Cao. Cao Cao said, "The only people that can be considered heroes of our time are you and me." This shocked Liu Bei, till he dropped the chopsticks he was holding, because he thought all along he had hid his ambition from Cao Cao very well. At the right moment, the lightning struck and immediately, Liu Bei used it as an excuse for dropping his chopsticks, saying, "I was scared stiff by the lightning. That is why I dropped the chopsticks." With that explanation, Cao Cao laughed and thought that since Liu Bei was so cowardly, it was unlikely he would achieve his ambition. Cao Cao, from then onward, let down his guard on Liu Bei. In the end, Liu Bei managed to break free from Cao Cao, and formed one of the three kingdoms, vying with Cao Cao.

三国时期，曹操与刘备青梅煮酒论英雄这段故事，就是个典型的例证。刘备早已有夺取天下的抱负，只是当时力量太弱，根本无法与曹操抗衡，而且还处在曹操控制之下。刘备装作每日只是饮酒种菜，不问世事。一日曹操请他喝酒，席上曹操问刘备谁是天下英雄，刘备列了几个名字，都被曹操否定了。忽然，曹操说道："天下的英雄，只有我和你两个人！"一句话说得刘备惊慌失措，深怕曹操了解自己的政治抱负，吓得手中的筷子掉在地下。幸好此时一阵炸雷，刘备急忙遮掩，说自己被雷声吓掉了筷子。曹操见状，大笑不止，认为刘备连打雷都害怕，成不了大事，对刘备放松了警觉。后来刘备摆脱了曹操的控制，终于在中国历史上干出了一番事业。

28. *Burn the Bridge after Crossing the River*

Pretend to expose one's weakness to lure the enemy into one's trap. When the enemy is within your control, cut off the supply routes, and eventually destroy him. Do not go for the small advantage, when one can go for the kill, as it may result in one's destruction.

故意露出破绽，给敌人提供方便条件。诱使敌人深入我方阵地，然后切断其前应与后援，使其陷入困境。敌人贪图不应得的利益，必遭祸患。

Towards the end of the Han Dynasty, when the warlords were fighting amongst each other for territories, there was one warlord by the name of Liu Biao. He favored his youngest son, Liu Zhong, and did not like his eldest son, Liu Qi. Liu Qi's stepmother, who is Liu Zhong's natural mother, was afraid that Liu Qi would inherit the power and wealth from Liu Biao, since the eldest son was bent on harming him. Liu Qi knew that his situation was precarious, so he sought advice from Zhuge Liang many times, but to no avail. So Liu Qi thought of a plan.

Liu Qi invited Zhuge Liang to the second floor of a restaurant for a meal. When they were in the midst of the meal, Liu Qi arranged beforehand for someone to remove the ladder that led to the second floor. Liu Qi again sought advice from Zhuge Liang, "We are now neither near the Earth nor Heaven, what you said would only enter the ears of Liu Qi, please advise me on my situation." Zhuge Liang, seeing that he could not get out of the circumstance, told Liu Qi a story, "During the Spring and Autumn Period, Concubine Li of Lord Xian of the State of Jin wanted to do harm to two of her stepsons; Shen Sheng and Zhong Er. Knowing her intention, Zhong Er escaped to another state. Shen Sheng on the other hand was filial, and wanted to stay and serve his father. One day, Shen Sheng came back with delicious food to be presented to his father. But Concubine Li had the food laced with poison.

"When Lord Xian was about to eat the food, Concubine Li said, 'Since the food came from outside, it would be better to let someone try the food to see if it has gone bad.' So, one of the attendants tried the food and died on the spot. On seeing this, Lord Xian was furious and accused Shen Sheng of being not filial, and that he wanted to kill him to usurp his position. Lord Xian ordered that Shen Sheng be executed. Shen Sheng, on hearing it, knew there was no way of defending himself, so he committed suicide. Shen Sheng stayed and he was killed, Zhong Er left and he lived."

Liu Qi on hearing the whole story knew what to do, he hurried back and requested from his father to be deployed to Jiang Xia, thus avoiding his stepmother.

后汉末年，刘表偏爱少子刘琮，不喜欢长子刘琦。刘琦的后母害怕刘琦得势，影响到儿子刘琮的地位，非常嫉恨他。刘琦感到自己处在十分危险的环境中，多次请教诸葛亮，但诸葛亮一直不肯为他出主意。有一天，刘琦约诸葛亮到一座高楼上饮酒，等二人正坐下饮酒之时，刘琦暗中派人拆走了楼梯。刘琦说："今日上不至天，下不至地，出君之口，入琦之耳，可以赐教矣"诸葛亮见状，无可奈何，便给讲一个故事。春秋时期，晋献公的妃子骊姬想谋害晋献公的两个儿子：申生和重耳。重耳知道骊姬居心险恶，只得逃亡国外。申生为人厚道，要尽孝心，侍奉父王。一日，申生派人给父王送去一些好吃的东西，骊姬乘机用有毒的食品将太子送来的食品更换了。晋献公哪里知道，准备去吃，骊姬故意说道，这膳食从外面送来，最好让人先尝尝看。于是命左右侍从尝一尝，刚刚尝了一点，侍从倒地而死。晋献公大怒，大骂申生不孝，阴谋杀父夺位，决定要杀申生。申生闻讯，也不作申辩，自刎身亡。诸葛亮对刘琦说："申生在内而亡，重耳在外而安。"刘琦马上领会了诸葛亮的意图，立即上表请求派往江夏（今湖北武昌西），避开了后母，终于免遭陷害。

29. *Put Flowers on the Tree*

Borrow a setting to boost one's image. Although one may be on the weak side, one's battle array can appear to be strong.

借助别人的局面布成有利的阵势，兵力虽少，但气势颇大。鸿雁在高空飞翔，全凭其丰满的羽翼助成气势。

Towards the end of the Han Dynasty, when Liu Biao, one of the warlords had died, Liu Bei was entrusted with the Jing province; but he was very weak then. On seeing the situation, Cao Cao brought an army to attack Liu Bei towards Wang city. Liu Bei, together with the peasants and army, retreated to Jiang Ling. Because the number of peasants and troops retreating was huge, the retreat was very slow. Cao Cao managed to reach the rear of the retreating contingent and had a small battle with Liu Bei's army. Liu Bei lost and had to retreat, asking his sworn brother, Zhang Fei, to cover his rear flank. But Zhang Fei had only twenty or thirty cavalry soldiers with him; there was no match at all. But Zhang Fei came up with a plan. He ordered his cavalry soldiers to cut down some branches, tie them to the back of their horses and run in large circles in the forest. Zhang Fei, himself riding on his black steed, went to the middle of the bridge at Chang Ban Slope, to wait for Cao Cao's army.

When Cao Cao arrived, he saw that Zhang Fei was alone at the bridge and was curious why, till he saw the dust clouds rising above the forest. Cao Cao suspected that there might be an ambush, thus decided to stop advancing. Zhang Fei was thus able to stop Cao Cao's large army with only twenty or thirty cavalry soldiers by using the "Putting flowers on Tree" ruse. This bought time for Liu Bei's contingent to retreat successfully to Jiang Ling.

无人不知张飞是一员猛将，而他却是一个有勇有谋的大将。刘备起兵之初，与曹操交战，多次失利。刘表死后，刘备在荆州，势孤力弱。这时，曹操领兵南下，直达宛城，刘备荒忙率荆州军民退守江陵。由于老百姓跟着撤退的人太多，所以撤退的速度非常慢。曹兵追到当阳，与刘备的部队打了一仗，刘备败退，他的妻子和儿子都在乱军中被冲散了。刘备只得狼狈败退，令张飞断后，阻截追兵。

张飞只有二三十个骑兵，怎敌得过曹操的大队人马？那张飞临危不惧，临阵不慌，顿时心生一计。他命令所率的二三十名骑兵都到树林子里去，砍下树枝，绑在马后，然后骑马在林中飞跑打转。张飞一人骑着黑马，横着丈二长矛，威风凛凛站在长板坡的桥上。

追兵赶到，见张飞独自骑马横矛站在桥中，好生奇怪，又看见桥东树林里尘土飞扬。追击的曹兵马上停止前进，以为树林之中定有伏兵。张飞只带二三十名骑兵，阻止住了追击的曹兵，让刘备和荆州军民顺利撤退，靠的就是这"树上开花"计。

30. *Switch the Roles of the Host and the Guest*

Try to put the foot in where there is a crack and eventually, gain control of the brain of enemy. This involves a logical sequence.

乘着空隙插足进去，设法控制敌人的要害，这必须循序渐进。

This happened during the end of the Han Dynasty, when warlords were fighting amongst each other for territories.

Yuan Shao and Han Fu used to be allies, and they were in the group of warlords aiming to overthrow Dong Zhuo; but the campaign failed in the end. After the campaign, the strength of Yuan Shao grew, together with his ambitions as well. He stationed troops in Hebei for expansion purposes, but his provision supply was inadequate. On seeing that his ally lacks provision, Han Fu decided to lend a hand by sending provisions to Yuan Shao.

But Yuan Shao was not satisfied; he did not like the idea of depending on someone to send him provisions. On heeding the advice of his advisor Feng Ji, he decided to grab the provision depot at Ji Zhou. The governor of Ji Zhou was Han Fu himself, but Yuan Shao was desperate to solve his provision problem. Yuan Shao wrote a letter to Gongsun Zan, suggesting that they attack Ji Zhou together. This proposal suited Gongsun Zan very well, because for a long time, he had the intention of attacking Ji Zhou. So Gongsun Zan accepted Yuan Shao's proposal.

Yuan Shao also sent another messenger to Han Fu informing him that Yuan Shao and Gongsun Zan has allied together to attack Ji Zhou. The messenger suggested, "Since Yuan Shao is your good friend, and you have sent him provisions before, why not ask him to come over to your side? Ally with him to fend off Gongsun Zan instead." Han Fu agreed with the proposal and sent a letter to Yuan Shao. Yuan Shao agreed to change sides and went to Ji Zhou with his troops. Yuan Shao was let into the city and slowly he replaced critical defense positions with his own generals. When Han Fu realized that this invited "guest" has taken over the "host", it was too late, so Han Fu escaped from Ji Zhou.

袁绍和韩馥，应当是一对盟友，当年曾经共同讨伐过董卓。后来，袁绍势力渐渐强大，总想不断扩张，他屯兵河内，缺少粮草，十分犯愁。老友韩馥知道情况之后，主动派人送去粮草，帮袁绍解决供应困难。

袁绍觉得等待别人送粮草，不能够解决根本问题。他听了谋士逢纪的劝告，决定夺取粮仓冀(jì)州。而当时的冀州牧正是老友韩馥，袁绍顾不了那么多了，马上下手，实施他的锦囊妙计。他首先给公孙瓒写了一封信，建议与他一起攻打冀州。公孙瓒早就想找个由头攻占冀州，这个建议，正中下怀。他立即下令，准备发兵攻打冀州。

袁绍又暗地派人去见韩馥，说："公孙瓒和袁绍联合攻打冀州，冀州难以自保。袁绍过去不是你的老朋友吗？最近你不是还给他送过粮草吗？你何不联合袁绍，对付公孙瓒呢？让袁绍进城，冀州不就保住了吗？"
韩馥只得邀请袁绍带兵进入冀州。这位请来的客人，表面上尊重韩馥，实际上他逐渐将自己的部下一个一个似钉子扎进了冀州的要害部位，这时，韩馥清楚地知道，他这个"主"被"客"取而代之了。为了保全性命，他只得只身逃出冀州去了。

The Thirty Six Stratagems

Chapter 6 – Stratagems of Disadvantage

31. *Use the Tender Trap*

With regards to a strong enemy, one should aim to control its general. Against an intelligent enemy general, one should plot to dampen his morale and will to fight. Once the general's fighting spirit is quenched, the army will be weakened. Therefore, one should try to hit the enemy at its weakest point while conserving one's energy.

如果敌人的兵力强大，就设法打击将领；如果敌人的将领足智多谋，就要挫败他的意志。敌人将领斗志衰弱，兵卒士气低落，敌军的战斗力酒会丧失殆尽。充分利用敌人弱点进行控制和分化瓦解，就可以保存自己，扭转局势。

In Strategy No. 5 we mentioned the fight between the State of Wu and State of Yue. Gou Jian, the lord of Yue, was defeated by Fu Chai, the Lord of Wu first and became Fu Chai's subordinate. Gou Jian was subservient to Fu Chai, gaining his trust in the process. In the end, after a long humiliating period, Gou Jian was allowed to go back to the State of Yue. When he went back to Yue, Gou Jian was determined to avenge his humiliation. One Yue official spoke to Gou Jian saying, "A bird that flies high can die because of food. A fish that swims deep can die because of bait. To seek revenge, we should first reduce their fighting spirit. Only then can are we able to achieve our aim."

Noting this, Gou Jian sent two ladies, considered to be the most beautiful during that time, Xi Shi and Zheng Dan, to Fu Chai. Gou Jian also sent tribute to Fu Chai every year. These actions gained more of Fu Chai's trust. And when Fu Chai led an expedition against the State of Qi, Gou Jian even loaned him an army to achieve his goal. Gou Jian went to congratulate Fu Chai on his victory as well. This reduced Fu Chai's guard against Gou Jian.

Fu Chai, being licentious, was indeed smitten by the two ladies, so much so that he did not listen to the advice of his important official, Wu Zixu anymore or even attend to court matters. In the end, in the year 482 BC, when the State of Wu was met with a serious drought, Gou Jian led a strike against State of Wu and defeated Fu Chai.

前面曾讲到春秋时吴越之战，勾践先败于夫差。吴王夫差罚勾践夫妇在吴王宫里服劳役，借以羞辱他。越王勾践在吴王夫差面前卑躬屈膝，百般逢迎，骗取了夫差的信任，终于放他回到越国。后来越国趁火打劫，终于消灭了吴国，逼得夫差拔剑自刎。

那所趁之"火"是怎样烧起来的呢？原来勾践成功地使用了"美人计"。勾践被释回越国之后，卧薪尝胆，不忘雪耻。吴国强大，靠武力，越国不能取胜。越大夫文种向他献上一计："高飞之鸟，死于美食，深泉之鱼，死于芳饵，要想复国雪耻，应投其所好，衰其斗志，这样，可置夫差于死地。"于是勾践挑选了两名绝代佳人：西施、郑旦，送给夫差，并年年向吴王进献珍奇珠宝。夫差认为勾践已被他臣服，所以一点也不加怀疑。夫差整日与美人饮酒作乐，连大臣伍子胥的劝谏也完全听不进去。后来，吴国进攻齐国，勾践还出兵帮助吴王伐齐，借以表示忠心，麻痹夫差。吴国打胜之后，勾践还亲自到吴国祝贺。

夫差贪恋女色，一天比一天厉害，根本不想过问政事。伍子胥力谏无效，反被逼自尽。勾践看在眼里，喜在心中。公元前482年，吴国大旱，勾践乘夫差北上会盟之时，突出奇兵伐吴，吴国终于被越所灭，夫差也只能一死了之。

32. *Drop Defenses to Feign a Trap*

It may sometimes be better to deliberately display weakness, to confuse the enemy and make the latter abandon the attack for fear of trickery. In a situation where the enemy is strong and you are weak, proper use of this strategy can appear extraordinary.

如果兵力空虚，就故意显示出更加空虚的样子，使敌人在疑惑之中更加疑惑。在敌强我弱的情况下，运用这种策略会奇妙莫测。

During the period of the Three Kingdoms, Zhuge Liang was in the city of Yang Ping. He sent his general Wei Yan with the majority of the Shu soldiers, leaving only 10,000 men behind to defend the city. The 200,000-strong Wei army was led by General Sima Yi. However, due to miscalculation, the Shu army missed the Wei army.

When the Wei army was about sixty miles from the city, Sima Yi learned from his spy the strength left in the city. Zhuge Liang also received news that the enemy was near, but it was too late to summon Wei Yan back. The town was in a panic, but Zhuge Liang remained calm. He ordered his soldiers to keep all the army flags flying and to not leave the tents without permission. He then summoned men to open the gates and pretend to sweep the ground next to the gates.

When Sima Yi arrived, he was shocked by what he saw. He knew Zhuge Liang to be a good strategist with many tricks up his sleeve. So when he saw that the gates were opened up instead of closed, his suspicion was aroused. He suspected that Zhuge Liang might have laid an ambush, waiting for him. His suspicion was further aroused when he saw that Zhuge Liang was sitting leisurely on top of the city walls playing his zither and sipping tea.

The Thirty Six Stratagems

Sima Yi paid attention to the chords played by Zhuge Liang and they were placid, showing no signs of a troubled mind. He therefore concluded that the empty city was definitely a scheme to lure his troops in. Sima Yi ordered his men to turn around and retreat. Thus Zhuge Liang was able to salvage the situation using the "Empty City" scheme.

诸葛亮北伐中原，由于错用了"言过其实，不可大用"的马谡，结果致使街亭这个战略要地失守，再无法进军取胜，而且随时有被魏兵堵截归路、全军覆灭的危险。诸葛亮顿足长叹："大势去矣，这全是我的过错造成的！"为避免更大损失，忙安排人马，布置撤退。为防魏军乘势追击，赶紧把关兴、张苞两员小将唤到帐前："你们二人各带三千人马，在武功山小路两侧布置疑兵。如果魏军来到，敌众我寡，切不可战，只大声击鼓呐喊，用疑兵计吓退他们即可。然后，急奔阳平关，撤回国内！"
又把张冀叫来布置："引部分军兵，快速修理剑阁通道，以为大军准备退路。" 然后传令：大军悄悄收拾行装，分别从各自驻地快速撤回国内。

诸葛亮的中军营地现在西城县内，这是个弹丸小城，易攻难守。待诸葛亮把身边人马分派出去执行紧急命令之后，城中就近于空地了。正要拔寨撤离，忽然十几匹马飞跑进城来，马上士兵大汗淋漓、气喘吁吁地报告："司马懿亲率十五万大军，已向西城扑来，而且马上就要到了！"
这时，诸葛亮身边只剩下一些文官，连一员武将也没有。士兵也大多派出去，只留有两千老幼病残，根本无法作战。

众官员听到这消息，一个个吓得面无血色，一句话也说不出来。很明显，战不能战，逃也逃不掉——
此地路径狭窄，惟一大道已为司马懿占住。再加上辎重行李多，马匹、车辆少，逃不出几里，就会被魏军铁骑追杀殆尽。诸葛亮也十分紧张，忙登上城楼向外望。果然，西北方向尘埃冲天蔽日，已隐隐有大军奔走声如沉雷般动地而来；尘头起处更不时闪现魏军旗号，招摇挥动。

诸葛亮稍一沉吟，马上传下命令：把城内所有旗帜全放倒，藏匿起来！城内士兵，各自隐在驻地房舍、围墙内，不许乱动乱叫，如果违令不遵者，立斩！然后，又下令：大开东南西北四面城门，每一门前，派二十名老少军兵打扮成老百姓模样，洒水扫街，不许神色慌张，举措不当。如果魏军冲到城前，也不能退入城内，仍要一如既往。众人不解其意。诸葛亮微微一笑，胸有成竹地说："我自有退兵之法，你们不必惊慌。"说罢，披一件印有仙鹤图案的宽大长衫，戴一顶绸布便帽，让两个小童抱着一张琴、一只香炉，随他登上城楼，贴着楼上栏杆端端正正地坐下，点燃香。然后，闭目养了会儿神，再缓缓睁开眼，虚望前方，安然自得弹起琴来。

这时，司马懿统领的大兵已来到城下。先头部队见到这种情形，都不敢贸然前进，急忙向司马懿报告。马司懿不相信，以为部下看花了眼：诸葛亮怎么打扮成道士模样，不领兵拒敌，反而悠闲地在城头弹起琴来？于是命令三军暂且停止行动，自己则飞马跑到城下，远远观望。果然，城楼上诸葛亮笑容可掬地端坐，在袅袅上升的香烟间，旁若无人、安然自得地正沉浸在自己所弹奏的琴音中。他左边的童子，手捧一把宝剑；右边的童子，则拿着一把尘尾。城门口处，有二十余老少百姓正低头洒扫街道，有条不紊，不惊不慌。

司马懿看了许久，听了很长时间，无论从对方人物的表情动作还是诸葛亮所弹出的琴声中，都看不出丝毫破绽。其子司马师道："我们应即刻冲杀进去，活捉诸葛亮！他分明是故弄玄虚——城肯定是座空城！"
其他将士也纷纷要求进兵攻城。司马懿凝然不动，仍静静谛听。忽然他神色一变，露出紧张模样，忙下令："后队改作前锋，先锋变为后队，马上撤退！"
众人不解：眼前并没有什么异常情况。司马懿怒道："马上撤退。违令者斩！" 众将士狐疑不明，却只好遵令撤退。

直到撤离西城远了些，司马懿才心有余悸地解释："诸葛亮这个人和我打过多年仗了。他一生最是谨慎，从不做没把握的事，更甭说干冒险的事了！今天大开城门，故意显出是座空城，让我们白白拿走并轻易把他捉住，这里就肯定有埋伏，是个骗局！我军若贸然轻进，必中其计。"
司马师问："父亲一直凝听静立，后来并无动静，您为什么突然神色大撤军呢？"
司马懿冷笑："当统帅、做大将的人，必须善于观察天地之间的运行变化，了解人间世上的各种知识！我听到诸葛亮琴音，初始平和恬淡，却突然昂扬激烈，渗出一股杀机！分机要动手、出兵了！再不走，让他围住，四面挨打不成？！"
司马师及众将觉得有理，但仍不十分信服。不料，才走不远，刚进入武功山，猛听得山坡后杀声震天，鼓声动地，伏兵顿起。众将大惊。司马懿道："刚才若不及时撤退，必中其计了！"话音未落，只见旁边大道上一军杀来，旗上大字："右护卫使虎翼将军张苞"。

一见是西蜀有名战将、当年威震寰宇的张飞张翼德的儿子打杀过来，魏兵心惊胆战，纷纷弃甲抛戈而逃。逃不多远，山谷中又喊杀声起，鼓角喧天、尘埃万丈。一杆大旗上写着："左护卫使龙骧将军关兴"。魏兵一见是关云长之子，更是魂飞魄散！哪敢接战？！
本是山地，喊声杀声因在谷中回荡，似乎漫山遍野均有蜀国兵马。烟尘大起蔽日遮天，内中旗帜招展，刀枪闪耀，更似乎是天兵大将！
魏军不敢久停，忙丢掉辎重粮草，仓皇而逃。
张苞、关兴也不追赶，只将魏军丢弃的辎重物资拣起，迅速撤退了。

再说西城中的诸葛亮，见司马懿带兵疾忙退去，轻轻长吁一口气，用手拭了额上的冷汗，笑了起来。诸葛亮笑道："兵法云，知已知彼，方可百战不殆。司马懿知我一生谨慎，从不弄险，所以见今天这情况，就判断我在用计、骗他入城。所以反慌忙退走了。而我知司马懿了解我的这一贯作风，所以便借用这种心理，而乘机算计了他！也是知已、知彼才敢如此啊！若换上司马昭或曹操统兵，我绝不会如此的！" 众人叹服。

"不过，司马懿也确是知我之人。如果不是实在没别的办法，我也不会用这险计的！实在是万不得已呢！"

诸葛亮道。众人佩服得五体投地，又后怕不已。

司马懿退兵，一直又退回街亭，和曹真的大军汇合在一起时，才放下心来。而此刻，蜀国各路军已安然无恙地撤回本国了。司马懿于是又带一支人马来到西城。及问当地居民，才明白自己"聪明反被聪明误"，误中诸葛亮之计。当得知当时诸葛亮所处的危险境地，他的所作所为及张苞、关兴其实只有少数人马，只是虚张声势而并不敢真正交锋时，不觉由衷叹赞："诸葛孔明之才，我不如也！"

33. *Provide Disinformation to Enemy Spies*

When an enemy lays traps, set traps within his traps, to create internal chaos. When one secures assistance within an enemy's ranks, one will not lose the battle.

在敌人给我布置的疑阵中再反设一层疑阵。如果利用敌人内部的策应去争取胜利，那么我方就不会遭受损失。

During the Three Kingdoms Period, one of the great illustrations of the Double Agent Scheme is seen in Battle of the Red Cliff. Cao Cao initially had Cai Mao and Zhang Yun as his chief marine commanders for his 830,000 troops. As Cao Cao's troops came from the northern side, his soldiers did not have any experience in marine battles, so Cai Mao and Zhang Yun were extremely precious to Cao Cao.

On the other side of the battle was the alliance of Liu Bei and Sun Quan with Zhou Yu as the commander-in-chief. Zhou Yu was very talented and intelligent, thus Cao Cao had the intention of pulling Zhou Yu to his side. Zhou Yu, knowing that Cai Mao and Zhang Yun were the chief marine commanders, was not happy. He was thinking of a plan to get rid of them when he heard that Jiang Gan was coming.

Jiang Gan served Cao Cao and was a former classmate of Zhou Yu. Zhou Yu knew that Jiang Gan's intention was to persuade him to switch sides, but he intended to use Jiang Gan to remove Cai Mao and Zhang Yun. Zhou Yu threw a feast for Jiang Gan and ordered that during the feast, military affairs should not be mentioned. The feast went into the middle of the night. After the feast, Zhou Yu pretended to be very drunk and invited Jiang Gan to spend the night in his tent. Jiang Gan, on seeing that he had not achieved his goal, was not able to sleep so he wandered around in Zhou Yu's tent. He stumbled upon a letter that was written by Cai Mao and Zhang Yun, stating that they were willing to work with Zhou Yu to defeat Cao Cao.

Suddenly, Zhou Yu talked in his dreams. It scared Jiang Gan. He kept the letter in his sleeves and went back to his bed. After a while, someone came to wake up Zhou Yu. Zhou Yu woke up and spoke to the messenger while keeping his eyes on Jiang Gan. Jiang Gan strained his ears to listen to the conversation but he could only vaguely hear the words, "Cai" and "Zhang". Jiang Gan then confirmed his suspicions.

Jiang Gan hurried back to Cao Cao's camp after he made sure that Zhou Yu had fallen asleep. He showed the 'fake' letter to Cao Cao and told Cao Cao about the conversation. These infuriated Cao Cao and he ordered the execution of Cai Mao and Zhang Yun. After a short while, Cao Cao realized his mistake, but it was too late, he had lost two precious marine commanders.

三国时期，赤壁大战前夕，周瑜巧用反间计杀了精通水战的叛将蔡瑁、张允，就是个有名例子。

曹操率领号称的八十三万大军，准备渡过长江，占据南方。当时，孙刘联合抗曹，但兵力比曹军要少得多。

曹操的队伍都由北方骑兵组成，善于马战，可不善于水战。正好有两个精通水战的降将蔡瑁、张允可以为曹操训练水军。曹操把这两个人当作宝贝，优待有加。一次东吴主帅周瑜见对岸曹军在水中排阵，井井有条，十分在行，心中大惊。他想一定要除掉这两个心腹大患。

曹操一贯爱才，他知道周瑜年轻有为，是个军事奇才，很想拉拢他。曹营谋士蒋干自称与周瑜曾是同窗好友，愿意过江劝降。曹操当即让蒋干过江说服周瑜。

周瑜见蒋干过江，一个反间计就已经酝酿成熟了。他热情款待蒋干，酒席筵上，周瑜让众将作陪，炫耀武力，并规定只叙友情，不谈军事，堵住了蒋干的嘴巴。

周瑜佯装大醉，约蒋干同床共眠。蒋干见周瑜不让他提及劝降之事，心中不安，哪里能够入睡。他偷偷下床，见周瑜案上有一封信。他偷看了信，原来是蔡瑁、张允写来，约定与周瑜里应外合，击败曹操。这时，周瑜说着梦话,翻了翻身子,吓得蒋干连忙上床。过了一会儿,忽然有人要见周瑜,周瑜起身和来人谈话,还装作故意看看蒋干是否睡熟。蒋干装作沉睡的样子,只听周瑜他们小声谈话,听不清楚,只听见提到蔡、张二人。于是蒋干对蔡、张二人和周瑜里应外合的计划确认无疑。

他连夜赶回曹营,让曹操看了周瑜伪造的信件,曹操顿时火起,杀了蔡瑁、张允。等曹操冷静下来,才知中了周瑜反间之计,但也无可奈何了。

34. *Pretend to be Injured*

No one would intentionally harm himself. Therefore, if someone is hurt, others would believe that he has been injured by others. Pretense will thus gain the enemy's trust and sow discord among enemy members. This is similar to playing with an innocent child. As long as you act according to his wishes, you will be able to trick him.

人们通常不会自己伤害自己。如果受到伤害必定不受怀疑。我方以假做真,令敌人信假为真,这样离间的计谋就能实现了。要像欺骗幼童那样迷惑敌人,顺势进行活动。

During the Spring and Autumn Period, Ji Guang killed the Lord of Wu, Liao, and declared himself the lord of State of Wu. He gave himself the title He Lu. The deceased lord's son Qing Ji was gathering capable men to overthrow He Lu. As Qing Ji was courageous and intelligent, he posed a great threat to He Lu's life. Wu Zixu, He Lu's trusted advisor recommended Yao Li, an assassin, to him.

Yao Li was small in size but this disadvantage was made up for with his courage and intelligence. He revealed to He Lu his plan for befriending Qing Ji, "Qing Ji is now looking for capable men. I will pretend to be an exile from your kingdom who wishes to join his camp. To obtain his trust, Your Lordship will have to chop off my right arm and execute my whole family." Such drastic actions! He Lu was reluctant at first but finally agreed to the plan. Yao Li was arrested and imprisoned on the pretext of having offended the Lord and had his right arm chopped off as punishment. Later, Yao Li was secretly released but He Lu announced that he had escaped from prison and had his family beheaded.

Yao Li went to Qing Ji. When Qing Ji saw Yao Li's amputated arm and learned that his wife and children had been executed, he believed Yao Li's story and kept him as his aide.

When Qing Ji planned to attack Wu, Yao Li volunteered to be the guide, convincing Qing Ji that he was the best person for the job. Troops were sent both by land and sea and Yao Li sailed on the same boat as Qing Ji. When the boat was in the middle of the sea, Yao Li took out a spear and ran it through Qing Ji.

Qing Ji, an experienced fighter himself, caught Yao Li and pushed his head into the water. When his men came forward to kill Yao Li, Qing Ji said, "This man is a courageous fighter. No one should kill two courageous fighters in a day." Qing Ji then pulled the spear from his body and bled to death. As for Yao Li, after completing the mission, he too committed suicide.

春秋时期，吴王阖闾杀了吴王僚，夺得王位。他十分惧怕吴王僚的儿子庆忌为父报仇。庆忌正在卫国扩大势力，准备攻打齐国，夺取王位。

阖闾整日提心吊胆，要大臣伍子胥替他设法除掉庆忌。伍于胥向阖闾推荐了一个智勇双全的勇士，名叫要离。阖闾见要离矮小瘦弱，说道："庆忌人高马大，勇力过人，如何杀得了他？"要离说："刺杀庆忌，要靠智不靠力。只要能接近他，事情就好办。"阖闾说："庆忌对吴国防范最严，怎么能够接近他呢？"要离说："只要大王砍断我的右臂，杀掉我的妻子，我就能取信于庆忌。"阖闾不肯答应。要离说："为国亡家，为主残身，我心甘情愿。"

吴都忽然流言四起：阖闾弑君篡位，是无道昏君。吴王下令追查，原来流言是要离散布的。阖闾下令捉了要离和他的妻子，要离当面大骂昏王。阖闾假借追查同谋，未杀要离而只是斩断了他的右臂，把他夫妻二人关进监狱。

几天后，伍子胥让狱卒放松看管，让要离乘机逃出。阖闾听说要离逃跑，就杀了他的妻子。这件事不断传遍吴国，邻近的国家也都知道了。要离逃到卫国，求见庆忌，要求庆忌为他报断臂杀妻之仇，庆忌接纳了他。

要离果然接近了庆忌，他劝说庆忌伐吴。要离成了庆忌的贴身亲信。庆忌乘船向吴国进发，要离乘庆忌没有防备，从背后用矛尽力刺去，刺穿了胸膛。庆忌的卫士要捉拿要离。庆忌说："敢杀我的也是个勇士，放他走吧！"庆忌因失血过多而死。要离完成了刺杀庆忌的任务，家毁身残，也自刎而死。

35. *Use Multiple Interconnected Ploys*

If the enemy has a strong and powerful army, a head-on confrontation is not advisable. Instead, one should utilize a few connected strategies to decrease the enemy's power. With good leadership and planning, it will be easy to win the battle, as if Heaven is on one's side.

敌人兵力强大时，就不要去硬拼。应当运用计谋使他们自我牵制，借以削弱它的力量。主帅如能巧妙地运用计谋，克敌制胜就如同有天神帮助一样。

During the Three Kingdoms Period, Zhou Yu and Pang Tong set up "chain schemes" or a series of related schemes to trap Cao Cao. First, when Cao Cao sent his man, Jiang Gan to spy on Zhou Yu, Zhou Yu used the "Double Agent Scheme" to lure Cao Cao into killing two of his best marine commanders, Cai Mao and Zhang Yun. This weakened Cao Cao greatly and eventually led to Cao Cao losing the Battle of Red Cliff.

Next Zhou Yu used the "Self-Injury Scheme" to punish one of his best generals, Huang Gai, to make Cao Cao believe that there was internal chaos in Zhou Yu's camp. Therefore, when Jiang Gan visited Zhou Yu for the second time, he "accidentally" bumped into Pang Tong. Jiang Gan was taken in when Pang Tong said that he had plans to defect Cao Cao's camp.

Pang Tong's "surrender" to Cao Cao triggered the final plan. Cao Cao was pleased to see Pang Tong and exchanged views with him on war strategies. As Cao Cao had lost his best marine commander, he was desperate to seek advice from Pang Tong. Cao Cao's men could not swim and suffered seasickness. Pang Tong said, "Although your men are well-trained, they are not used to traveling at sea so they get seasick, especially in strong currents. You should tie your ships together, thirty or fifty in a row. This way the ships will be stable and the soldiers can walk on the decks freely."

Cao Cao thanked Pang Tong for his great suggestion and ordered his blacksmiths to chain all the ships together in their next attack on Zhou Yu. However, Zhou Yu learned of Cao Cao's plan and set fire to Cao Cao's ships. With all the ships chained together, it was almost impossible for the soldiers to escape from the burning ships. Thus Cao Cao suffered a bitter defeat at the Battle of the Red Cliff.

赤壁大战时，周瑜巧用反间，让曹操误杀了熟悉水战的蔡瑁、张允，又让庞统向曹操献上锁船之计，又用苦肉计让黄盖诈降。三计连环，打得曹操大败而逃。

在"反间计"那一章里，我们讲了周瑜让曹操误杀蔡、张二将之事，曹操后悔莫及，更要命的是曹营再也没有熟悉水战的将领了。

东吴老将黄盖见曹操水寨船只一个挨一个，又无得力指挥，建议周瑜用火攻曹军。并主动提出，自己愿去诈降，趁曹操不备，放火烧船。周瑜说："此计甚好，只是将军去诈降，曹贼定生疑。"黄盖说："何不使用苦肉计？"周瑜说："那样，将军会吃大苦。"黄盖说："为了击败曹贼，我甘愿受苦。"
第二日，周瑜与众将在营中议事。黄盖当众顶撞周瑜，骂周瑜不识时务，并极力主张投降曹操。周瑜大怒，下令推出斩首。众将苦苦求情，，老将军功劳卓著，请免一死。"周瑜说："死罪既免，活罪难逃。"命令重打一百军棍，打得黄盖鲜血淋漓。

黄盖私下派人送信曹操，大骂周瑜，表示一定寻找机会前来降曹。曹操派人打听，黄盖确实受刑，现正在养伤。他将信将疑，于是，派蒋干再次过江察看虚实。

周瑜这次见了蒋干，指责他盗书逃跑，坏了东吴的大事。这次过江，又有什么打算？周瑜说："莫怪我不念旧情，先请你住到西山，等我大破曹军之后再说。"把蒋干给软禁起来了。其实，周瑜想再次利用这个过于自作聪明的呆子，所以名为软禁，实际上又在诱他上钩。

一日，蒋干心中烦闷，在山间闲逛。忽然听到从一间茅屋中传出琅琅书声。蒋干进屋一看，见一隐士正在读兵法，攀谈之后，知道此人是名士庞统。他说，周瑜年轻自负，难以容人，所以隐居在山里。蒋干果然又自作聪明，劝庞统投奔曹操，夸耀曹操最重视人才，先生此去，定得重用。庞统应允，并偷偷把蒋干引到江边僻静处，坐一小船，悄悄驶向曹营。

蒋干哪里会想到又中周瑜一计：原来庞统早与周瑜谋划，故意向曹操献锁船之计，让周瑜火攻之计更显神效。曹操得了庞统，十分欢喜，言谈之中，很佩服庞统的学问。他们巡视了各营寨，曹操请庞统提提意见。庞统说："北方兵士不习水战，在风浪中颠簸，肯定受不了，怎能与周瑜决战？"曹操问："先生有何妙计？"庞统说："曹军兵多船众，数倍于东吴，不愁不胜。为了克服北方兵士的弱点，何不将船连锁起来，平平稳稳，如在陆地之上。"曹操果然依计而行，将士们都十分满意。

一日，黄盖在快舰上满载油、柴、硫，硝等引火物资，遮得严严实实。他们按事先与曹操联系的信号，插上青牙旗，飞速渡江诈降。这日刮起东南风，正是周瑜他们选定的好日子。曹营官兵，见是黄盖投降的船只，并不防备，忽然间，黄盖的船上火势熊熊，直冲首营。风助火势，火乘风威，曹营水寨的大船一个连着一个，想分也分不开，一齐着火，越烧越旺。周瑜早已准备快船，驶向曹营，只杀得曹操数十万人马一败涂地。曹操本人仓皇逃奔，捡了一条性命。

36. *Escape or Flee When All Else Fails*

In a situation where the enemy is obviously stronger, total retreat may be the best option. There is nothing wrong with retreating to avoid confrontation with a stronger enemy.

全军退却，避开强敌，以退为进，待机破敌，这部违背正常用兵法则。

During the Spring and Autumn Period, the State of Chu was a very strong state. Chu was getting ready to attack the State of Jin and it even coerced the State of Chen, Cai, Zheng and Xu to join in the attack. At the same time, Lord Wen of the

The Thirty Six Stratagems

State of Jin had just conquered State of Cao, a state that is near State of Chu. Lord Jin knew that a battle between Jin and Chu was inevitable.

The commander-in-chief for Chu was Zi Yu and he led his troops towards State of Cao. Lord Wen analyzed the situation and found the odds against him, so he decided to retreat first, to avoid the stronger Chu troops. Lord Wen retreated to Chen Pu, a place that is at the border of the State of Jin. There, the terrain was more suitable for defending, and Lord Wen sent messengers to the State of Qin and Qi for help.

Zi Yu arrived at Chen Pu and saw that Lord Jin has made preparations for the battle. Lord Wen, on the other hand, heard that the right wing of Chu's troops were the weakest, because they consisted of soldiers from the State of Chen and Cai. Zi Yu ordered the right and left wing to launch an attack on Lord Wen with the central troops following behind. Lord Wen beat a retreat. On seeing the situation, the Chen and Cai soldiers thought that Lord Wen was retreating again, so they gave chase. Out of nowhere, a group of chariots with horses wearing tiger skins rode out. The horses that the Chen and Cai soldiers were riding thought that the tigers were there. The whole troop was immediately thrown into chaos. Lord Wen had some of his men mixed into the crowd. These men reported to Zi Yu that the Chu troops had scored a victory. On hearing that and checking out the dust cloud, Zi Yu ordered that the left wing should attack further.

Lord Wen pretended to retreat again, and the left wing of Chu's troops fell into an ambush and was exterminated by Lord Wen's army. When Zi Yu's main force arrived, it was too late; he was surrounded by Lord Wen's army. Battle cries sounded and Zi Yu's troops fought with Lord Wen's army but they were outnumbered and caught by surprise. Zi Yu suffered heavy losses, but managed to escape back to Chu.

春秋初期，楚国日益强盛，楚将子玉率师攻晋。楚国还胁迫陈、蔡、郑、许四个小国出兵，配合楚军作战。此时晋文公刚攻下依附楚国的曹国，明知晋楚之战迟早不可避免。

子玉率部浩浩荡荡向曹国进发，晋文公闻讯，分析了形势。他对这次战争的胜败没有把握，楚强晋弱，其势汹汹，他决定暂时后退，避其锋芒。对外假意说道："当年我被迫逃亡，楚国先君对我以礼相待。我曾与他有约定，将来如我返回晋国，愿意两国修好。如果迫不得已，两国交兵，我定先退避三舍。现在，子玉伐我，我当实行诺言，先退三舍。（古时一舍为三十里。）"

他撤退九十里，已到晋国边界城濮，仗着临黄河，靠太行山，足以御敌。他已事先派人往秦国和齐国求助。

子玉率部追到城濮，晋文公早已严阵以待。晋文公已探知楚国左、中、右三军，以右军最薄弱，右军前头为陈、蔡士兵，他们本是被胁迫而来，并无斗志。子玉命令左右军先进，中军继之。楚右军直扑晋军，晋军忽然又撤退，陈、蔡军的将官以为晋军惧怕，又要逃跑，就紧追不舍。忽然晋军中杀出一支军队，驾车的马都蒙上老虎皮。陈、蔡军的战马以为是真虎，吓得乱蹦乱跳，转头就跑，骑兵哪里控制得住。楚右军大败。晋文公派士兵假扮陈、蔡军士，向子玉报捷："右师已胜，元帅赶快进兵。"子玉登车一望，晋军后方烟尘蔽天，他大笑道："晋军不堪一击。"其实，这是晋军诱敌之计，他们在马后绑上树枝，来往奔跑，故意弄得烟尘蔽日，制造假象。子玉急命左军并力前进。晋军上军故意打着帅旗，往后撤退。楚左军又陷于晋国伏击圈，又遭歼灭。等子玉率中军赶到，晋军三军合力，已把子玉团团围住。子玉这才发现，右军、左军都已被歼，自己已陷重围，急令突围。虽然他在猛将成大心的护卫下，逃得性命，但部队丧亡惨重，只得悻悻回国。

这个故事中晋文公的几次撤退，都不是消极逃跑，而是主动退却，寻找或制造战机。所以，"走"，是上策。

Liu Bei, also known as Luo Guanzhong in *Romance of the Three Kingdoms*

Questions & Replies

Tang Taizong & Li Jing

唐太宗李卫公问对

Questions and Replies: Tang Taizong and Li Jing (唐太宗李卫公问对) *is an ongoing set of dialogues between Tang Dynasty Emperor Taizong and Li Jing, a prominent Tang general. In analyzing military strategy, centuries after the Warring States period, Tang Taizong and Li Jing discuss previous military works such as Cao Cao's Xin Shu, Wu Qi's Book of Wuzi, Sun Tzu's The Art of War, Sima Rangju's Methods of War and Jiāng Ziyá's The Six Secret Teachings. Although no clear authorship has been established, the text is believed to have been written in the late Tang Dynasty (c. 599-649 CE).*

Part 1
Question 1

Tang Taizong asked: "Gao Li has encroached upon Xian Luo[1] several times. I dispatched an emissary commanding an end to this, but my edict has been defied. I am considering sending forth a putitive expedition. What are your thoughts?"

Li Jing replied: "According to what we have been able to find out, Gai Su Wen relies upon his own knowledge in military affairs. He thinks that China lacks the capability to mount a punitive expedition, thus he defies your edict. I request an army of 30,000 men to capture him."

Tang Taizong said: "Your troops will be few, while the place is distant. What type of strategy will you employ?"

Li Jing said: "I will use *indirect* troops."

Tang Taizong said: "When you pacified the Tu Jue, you employed *direct* troops. Now you speak about *indirect* troops. Why is that?"

Li Jing said: "When Zhuge Liang captured Meng Huo seven times, it was not through any other means. He employed *indirect* troops; that's all."

---

[1] This area is also known as Silla (新罗), one of the Three Kingdoms of Korea, and one of the longest sustained dynasties in Asian history.

Questions and Replies

Tang Taizong said: "When Ma Long of the Jin Dynasty conducted a punitive campaign against Liang Zhou, it was also in accord with the 'Diagram of Eight Formations' and he built narrow chariots. When the terrain was broad, he deployed 'deer-horn chariot' encampments, and when the road was constricted he built large wooden boxes and placed one each upon individual chariots, so they could both fight and advance. I believe it was *indirect* troops which the ancients valued!"

Li Jing said: "When I conducted the punitive campaign against the Tu Jues, we travelled west for several thousand miles. If they had not been *indirect* troops, how could we have gone so far? Narrow chariots and 'deer-horn chariot' encampments are essentials to the deployment of troops. They allow controlling the expenditure of energy, provide a defense to the fore, and constrain the regiments and squads. These three advantages, when gained interchangeably, can improve the prowess of the troops. This is what Ma Long learned so thoroughly from the ancients."

太宗问：高丽几次侵略新罗，我派使臣前去谕令息兵，可是高丽不从，我想出兵讨伐，你以为怎样？
李靖答：据调查了解盖苏文自以为精通军事，认为中国没有能力讨伐他，所以敢于违抗命令，请给我三万兵把他擒来。
太宗问：兵力这样少，距离那样远，用什么方法对付他呢？
李靖答：使用正兵。
太宗问，你平定突厥的时候是用奇兵制胜的，现在征高丽却说使用正兵，是什么道理？
李靖答：诸葛亮七擒孟获，不是用的别的方法：只是运用正兵器了。
太宗说：晋将马隆讨平凉州的[树机能]时，也是依照孔明的八阵图用偏箱车布阵。在开阔的地形上，就用偏箱车结成鹿角车营；在狭窄的道路上，就架设木屋于偏箱车上，这样，一面战斗，一面进，[因而取得了胜利。]毫无疑义，正兵的运用是古人所重视的。
李靖说：我讨伐突厌时，西行数千里，如果不是用正兵，怎能从事这样的远征呢，使用偏箱车、鹿角车营作战，是用兵的要则。既能保持战力，又能抗拒敌人，还能约束队伍，这三种长处结合使用，便可发挥它的威力了。

Question 2

Tang Taizong said: "At the battle in which I destroyed Sung Lao Sheng, when the fronts clashed, our righteous army retreated somewhat. I then personally led our elite cavalry to race down the Southern Plain, cutting across in a sudden attack on them from the flank. After Lao Sheng's troops were cut off from the rear, we severely crushed them and subsequently captured him alive. Were these *indirect* troops, or *direct* troops?"

Li Jing replied: "Your majesty is a natural military genius, not one who only learns by studying. I have examined the 'Art of War' as practiced from the Yellow Emperor on down. First be *indirect*, and afterwards, *direct*; first be benevolent and righteous, and afterward employ strategy and craftiness. Moreover, in the battle at the Huo Yi, the army was mobilized out of righteousness, so it was *indirect*. When Qian Cheng fell off his horse and the Right Army withdrew somewhat, it was *direct*."

Tang Taizong commented: "At that time, our slight withdrawal almost led to the failure of our great affair, so how can you refer to it as *direct*?"

Li Jing replied: "In general, when troops advance to the front, it is *indirect*. When they deliberately retreat to the rear, it is *direct*. Moreover, if the Right Army had not withdrawn somewhat, how could you have gotten Lao Sheng to move forward? The 'Art of War' states: "Entice the enemy with baits he cannot resist. Keep him on the move and ambush him." Lao Sheng did not know how to employ his troops. He relied on courage and made a hasty advance. He did not anticipate his rear being severed or being captured by your Majesty. This is what is referred to as 'using the *direct* as the *indirect*.'

"As for Huo Qu Bing's tactics unintentionally agreeing with those of Sun Tzu and Wu Qi, was it really so? When our Right Army withdrew, Gao Zu turned pale. But then I attacked vigorously and, on the contrary, it became advantageous for us. This coincidentally agreed with Sun Tzu and Wu Qi. My Lord certainly shows his knowledge."

大宗问：我在霍邑击破宋老生的战斗中，刚刚交锋，我军稍向后退，敌人乘机进击，这时我亲率精锐骑兵，由南原急驰而下，予以侧击，切断了老生军队的后路，使其大败，因而活捉了宋老生。这是正兵呢，还是奇兵呢？
李靖答：陛下的英明神武是天赋的，不是一般人所能学得来的。按兵法所说，自黄帝以来，〔用兵的方略〕都是首先运用正兵，而后讲求出奇制胜；首先讲求仁义，而后运用权谋诡诈。霍邑之战，我军因仗义而兴师，这是正兵；因建成坠马，右军稍向后退，这是奇兵。
太宗问：当时右军稍向后退，几乎坏了大事，怎么说是奇兵呢？
李靖答：大凡作战，用正规的战法，向前攻击便是"正兵"，有计划地退却使敌陷于不利便是"奇兵"，如果右军不后退，怎能诱致老生全力进攻呢！兵法上说："以小利去引诱敌人，乘其混乱然后攻取它。"老生不知兵法，恃勇急进，不料被陛下断绝后路，为陛下所擒。这就是所谓变奇兵为正兵了。
太宗说：从前霍去病用兵作战，能与孙吴兵法不谋而合，这确有其事吗？当右军稍向后退，高祖大惊失色，我从侧后乘机公击，反而造成我军的胜利，这与孙吴兵法也是不谋而合的，你说的话实在有见识。

Question 3

Tang Taizong said: "Whenever an army withdraws, can it be termed as *direct*?"

Li Jing said: "It is not so. Whenever the soldiers retreat with their flags confused and disordered, the sounds of the large and small drums not responding to each other and their orders shouted in a clamor, this is true defeat, not *direct* strategy. If the flags are in order, the drums respond to each other and the commands and orders seem unified, then even though they may be retreating and running, it is not a defeat and must be a case of *direct* strategy. The 'Art of War' says: 'Do not pursue an enemy who pretends to retreat in desperation.' It also says: 'When you are capable, feign incapability.' These all refer to the *direct*."

Tang Taizong said: "At the battle of Huo Yi, when the Right Army withdrew somewhat, was this a question of Heaven's effort? When Lao Sheng was captured, was this due to the effort of man?"

Li Jing said: "If the *indirect* troops had not changed to *direct* and the *direct* to *indirect*, how would you have gained the victory? Thus for one who excels at employing the army, *direct* and *indirect* lie with man, that is all! He changes them from one form to the other so often that it becomes difficult to discern them, which is the reason they are attributed to Heaven."

Tang Taizong nodded his head.

太宗问：凡是军队退却，都能说是奇兵么？
李靖答：不是的。军队退却的时候，如果旗帜参差而不整齐，鼓音大小而不应和，号令喧嚣而不统一，这是真正败退而不是奇兵，如果旗帜整齐，鼓声应和，号令统一，人马纷纭，[似乱非乱，]虽然退走，但不是真正败退，其中必定有奇。兵法上说："不要追击假装撤退的敌人。"又说："能而假装不能。"这些都是用奇的说法。
太宗问：霍邑之战，右军稍向后退，这是天意吗？老生被擒，这是人力所为吗？
李靖答：若不是[陛下]将正兵变为奇兵，奇兵变为正兵，怎能取得胜利呢！所以善于用兵的，或奇或正，在于人的运用罢了。由于奇正变化达到神妙莫测的地步，所以人们常常把它归之于天意。
太宗表示赞成。

Question 4

Tang Taizong said: "Are the *indirect* and *direct* distinguished beforehand or are they determined at the time of battle?"

Li Jing said: "According to Duke Cao's Xin Shu, 'If you outnumber the enemy two to one, then divide your troops into two, with one section being *indirect* and the other being *direct*. If you outnumber the enemy five to one, then three sections should be *indirect* and two sections should be *direct*.² This states the general point. As Sun Tzu said: 'In war, there are only the *direct* and *indirect* forces. However the combinations and changes between the two are infinite. Their interactions and combinations are like two never-ending, interlocking rings where possibilities of its beginning and endings cannot be determined.' This captures it. So how can the distinction be made beforehand?

"If the officers and troops are not yet trained in my methods, if the assistant generals are not yet familiar with my orders, then we must break the training into two sections. When teaching battle tactics, in each case the soldiers must recognize the flags and drums, dividing and combining in turn.

These are the techniques for teaching warfare. When the instructions and the evaluation of their implementation have been completed, and the masses know my methods, only then can they be raced about like a flock of sheep, following wherever the general points. Who then makes a distinction of *direct* and *indirect*? What Sun Tzu refers to as 'Thus, if I can uncover the dispositions of the enemy while remaining concealed myself' is the pinnacle in employing the *direct* and *indirect*. Therefore, such a distinction beforehand is merely for the purpose of instruction. Determining the changes at the moment of the battle, the changes are inexhaustible."

Tang Taizong said: "Profound indeed! Duke Cao must have known it. But what the Xin Shu teaches is only what he conveyed to his generals, not the fundamental method of the *direct* and the *indirect*."

太宗问：奇兵与正兵是平时就先行区分的，还是临时根据情况而决定的呢？
李靖答：按《曹公新书》上说："[在兵力对比上]我为二敌为一时，我就分兵为二，
以一部分为正兵，一部分为奇兵；我为五敌为一时，我就以五分之三为正兵，五分之二为奇兵。"这仅是大概的说法。只有孙武说过："作战不过"奇"和"正"，可是"奇""正"相互的变化，就像圆环旋转那样，无始无终，能穷尽吗？"这才算真正懂得了运用奇、正的道理，哪有平时就加以区分的呢！如果士卒没有学会战法，部将没有熟习号令，就必须区分为奇、正二部分来教练他们。教战时，使各队识别指挥的旗帜和鼓音，按指挥反复进行分合变化的
演习。所以说奇正区分和分合变化，只是一种教战的方法。训练完成，士卒都熟习了战法，然后就能象驱赶群羊一样，任由将帅指挥他们，谁还能认清奇正的分别呢！孙武所说的"若知敌人兵形而我方兵形不被敌方所知"，正

---

² Cao Cao was a famous warlord of the Three Kingdoms period (c. 200 BCE). Cao Cao should not be confused with Cao Gui, a wondering military scholar who stood against Bao Shuya, the leader of the troops of Duke Huan of Qi in a battle, during the Spring and Autumn period (c. 630 BCE).

是奇正运用到了最高的境界。所以平时区分[奇正]是为了进行训练，而临阵对敌时的奇正变化则是没有穷尽的。
太宗说：[奇正的运用，]真是深奥啊！深奥啊！[以上的道理]曹公是一定知道的。但《新书》的说法只是教给诸将一般的法则罢了，不是专门论述奇正的原则的。

Question 5

Tang Taizong said: "Duke Cao states, '*direct* troops attack from the flank.' My Lord, what do you have to say about this?"

Li Jing replied: "I recall that, in commenting on Sun Tzu, Duke Cao said: 'Going out first to engage in battle is *indirect*; going out afterward is *direct*.' This is different from his discussion of flank attacks. I humbly refer to the engagement as *indirect*, and those which the general himself sends forth to capture opportunity as *direct*. Where is the restriction of first, or later, or flank attack?"

Tang Taizong said: "If I cause the enemy to perceive my *indirect* as *direct*, and cause him to perceive my *direct* as *indirect*, then is this the meaning of, 'displaying a form'? Is employing the *direct* as *indirect*, the *indirect* as *direct*, unfathomable changes and transformation, what is meant by Sun Tzu as 'being formless'?"

Li Jing bowed and said: "Your Majesty is indeed wise. Your understanding has passed those of the ancients, and beyond what I can attain."

太宗问：曹公说：奇兵就是从侧面打击敌人。你认为怎样？
李靖答：曹公注释《孙子兵法》时还说："先向敌人交战的是正兵，以后出敌不意的是奇兵。"这和[奇兵就是]从侧面打击敌人的说法不同。我认为两军正面交锋是正兵，临时捕捉战机出奇制胜的是奇兵。那有拘泥于先后、侧击的说法呢。
太宗说：我的正兵，使敌人误认为是奇兵，我的奇兵，使敌人误认为是正兵，这就是孙子所说的"形人"吧！善于变奇兵为正兵，变正兵为奇兵，这样变化莫测，这就是孙子所说的"无形"吧！
李靖再拜说：陛下圣明，您的说法实在远远超出了古人，不是我所能及的。

Question 6

Tang Taizong said: "If 'dividing and combining are changes,' wherein lies the *direct* and *indirect*?"

Li Jing said: "For those who excel at employing troops, there are none that are not *indirect*, none that are not *direct*, thus they cause the enemy never to be able to discern them. Thus with the *indirect*, they are victorious, with the *direct*, they are also victorious. The officers of the army only know they achieve victory; none knows how it is attained. Without being able to fully comprehend the changes, how could the outstanding generals attain this? As for where the dividing and combining come from to create the *indirect* and *direct*, only Sun Tzu was capable of comprehending it. From Wu Qi on, no one has been able to attain it."

Tang Taizong said: "What was Wu Qi's strategy like?"

Li Jing said: "Permit me to speak about the general points. The Marquess Wu of Wei asked Wu Qi about the strategy to be employed when two armies confront each other. Wu Qi said: 'Gather some lower ranks men who are courageous and have them lead some light shock troops to test him. When the enemy responds to the attack, they, the shock troops, should pretend to run off. When they flee, do not punish them, but observe whether the enemy advances to take the bait. If they sit as one and arise as one, and do not pursue your fleeing troops, the enemy has good strategists. If all their troops pursue the fleeing forces, some advancing, some halting, in disordered fashion, the enemy is not talented. Attack them without hesitation.' I think that Wu Qi's strategy is generally of this sort, not what Sun Tzu would refer to as 'In battle, use the *direct* forces to match the enemy, and use the *indirect* forces to win the enemy.'

"My Lord, your uncle Han Qing Hu once said you could discuss Sun Tzu and Wu Qi with him. Was he referring to the *indirect* and *direct*?"

Tang Taizong said: "How could Qing Hu know about the pinnacle of deploying *indirect* and *direct*? He only took the *direct* as *direct*, and *indirect* as *indirect*! He never knew about the 'mutual changes of the *direct* and *indirect* into each other, the inexhaustible cycle.'"

太宗问：军队在进行分合变化的时候，奇正表现在哪里？
李靖答：善于用兵的人，无处不用正兵，无处不用奇兵，使敌人无法判断，所以正也能胜，奇也能胜。全军官兵，只知道胜利了，而不知道为什么能够取得胜利，如果不是把奇正变化灵活运用到了极点，怎能做到这样地步呢？由分合而产生奇正的变化只有孙武才能做到，吴起以下都比不上他。
太宗问：吴起用兵的方法怎样？
李靖答：请让我概略说明一下。魏武侯问吴起：两军对垒时，要知道敌方将领的才能，应该采用什么方法？吴起答：令勇敢的下级军官率领部队前往攻击，刚一交锋就败退，败退了也不要加以制止，借以观察敌军进攻的动作。如敌人前进、停止都有节制，见到我军败退也不追击，这是敌将有智谋的表现。如果敌人全军进行追击，士卒行动毫无秩序，这是敌将没有才能的表现，要立即进击
不可迟疑。我认为吴起的方法大都是这一类的，不是象孙武所说"以'正'兵求合，而以'奇'兵求胜"的原则。

Questions and Replies

太宗说：你的舅父韩擒虎曾说，你可以和他谈论孙吴兵法，也是指奇正说的吗？
李靖答：擒虎怎能知道奇正变化的奥妙，他仅仅知道以奇为奇，以正为正罢了，从来不知道奇正相互变化循环无穷的道理。

Question 7

Tang Taizong said: "When the ancients approached enemy formations and then sent forth *direct* troops to attack where unexpected, were they also using the method of 'mutual changes' for *indirect* and *direct* troops?"

Li Jing said: "In antiquity, most battles were a question of minimal tactics, conquering those without any tactics, and of some minor degree of excellence conquering those without any capabilities. How can they merit being discussed as the 'Art of War'? An example is Xie Xuan's destructions of Fu Jian. It was not because of Xie Xuan's excellence but probably Fu Jian's incompetence."[3]

Tang Taizong ordered the attending officers to find Xie Xuan's biography and read it. After reading the biography, he said: "Fu Jian's management in this area was not good."[4]

Li Jing said: "I observe that Fu Jian's biography records that 'Qin's army had all been broken and defeated, with only Mu Rong Chui's single force still intact. Fu Jian the Qin king, leading more than a thousand cavalry, raced over to join him. Chui's son Bao advised Chui to kill Fu Jian but without results. From this, one sees that when the Qin's armies were in turbulence, only Mu Rong Chui's forces remained intact, so it is obvious that Fu Jian was probably betrayed by Chui's treachery. Now to be betrayed by others and yet still hope to conquer the enemy, is that not difficult? Thus I say that men such as Fu Jian lacked tactics."

Tang Taizong said: "Sun Tzu said that one who plans extensively will conquer one who does less planning, so thus we know some planning will conquer no planning. All affairs are thus."

太宗问：古人临阵出奇，攻敌不意，这也是奇正变化的法则吗？
李靖答：古代的战斗，多是一些稍有智谋的人战胜没有智谋的人，一些稍有能力的人战胜没有能力的人，这些人哪能谈得上懂兵法呢？如东晋时谢玄在淝水击破了符坚，不是谢玄善于用兵，而是符坚不善于用兵的缘故。
太宗命侍臣拣出谢玄的传记阅览以后说：符坚哪些地方处理不善呢？

---

[3] Xie Xuan (謝玄) was a Jin Dynasty general who is best known for repelling the Former Qin army at the Battle of Fei River, preventing the Former Qin emperor Fu Jiān from destroying Jin and uniting China.
[4] Fú Jiàn (Chinese: 符健) was the founding emperor of the Chinese state Former Qin.

李靖答：我看《苻坚载记》说：淝水之战时，秦各军都溃败，只有慕容垂一军[三万人]独能保持完整。苻坚率领残兵千余骑，来到慕容全的营地，慕容垂的儿子慕容宝劝垂杀坚，垂未杀。从秦军溃败和慕容垂一军独能保持完整的情况来看，苻坚被慕容垂所陷害就是很明显了。既为人所陷害，还想战胜敌人，不就难了吗。所以我说，没有智谋的就是苻坚这一类的人。

太宗说：《孙子》说策划多的可以战胜策划少的，这样看来，策划少的就可以战胜没有策划的了。一切事情都是这样。

Question 8

Tang Taizong said: "The Yellow Emperor's 'Art of War' has been transmitted by previous generations as the 'Classic of Grasping the *Direct*' and as the 'Classic of Grasping Opportunities' as well. What do you have to say about this?"

Li Jing said: "The pronunciation of the character '*direct*' is similar to that for 'opportunity'. Thus some have transmitted the title as the latter, but the meaning is the same. If we investigate the actual writing, it says: 'Four formations as *indirect*, four formations as *direct*. The remaining forces are for grasping opportunity.' Here the character '*direct*' means troops, because pronunciation of the character '*direct*' is the similar to that for 'opportunity'. My humble opinion is that in war there are opportunities everywhere, so we should stress the word 'grasping' in speaking about it. It ought to be focused to excess; then it would be correct.

"Now *indirect* troops receive their mission from the ruler, while *direct* troops are ordered forth by the general. Sun Tzu said: 'When orders are regularly enforced and used to train the soldiers, they will be obedient.' This means that orders for *indirect* troops are what are received from the ruler. Moreover, he says: 'The employment of the troops cannot be spoken of beforehand.' and 'there are commands from the ruler which are not accepted.' These are orders that the general himself issues.

"For the generals: If they employ *indirect* tactics without any *direct* ones, they are defensive generals. If they employ *direct* tactics without any *indirect* ones, they are aggressive generals. If they employ both, they are generals to preserve the state. Thus 'grasping opportunity' and 'grasping the *direct*' are not fundamentally the same methods. Students of military strategy thoroughly understand this point!"

太宗问：黄帝的兵法，一般传说叫"握奇文"，或者叫"握机文"，究竟怎样说法？
李靖答："奇"
可以读为"机"，所以有人将"奇"传为"机"，它们的意义是一样的。按《握奇经》上说："[天、地、风、云]四阵为正，[龙、虎、鸟、蛇]四阵为奇，剩下的'奇'〔由大将掌握〕，称为'握机'"。所谓"奇"就是剩余的兵力[中军]，因"奇"可读为"机"，〔所以有人把"握奇"当作"握机

"。]我认为用兵无处不是战机，哪能只就掌握而言，应当理解为掌握机动力量[随机应便]才是正确的。正兵是受命于君主的，奇兵是：决定于大将的。兵法说："平时能认真贯彻命令、教育士卒，士卒就能养成服从的习惯。"

这是说兴兵作战的正兵是受命于君主的。又说："作战行动，君主不能预为约束。君主的命令如不适应战场情况也可以不接受。"这是说[临敌制胜的]奇兵是决定于大将的。大凡将领只知用正而不知用奇的，是墨守成规的将领；只知用奇而不知用正的，是鲁莽从事的将领；奇正都运用得当的，才是辅国的良将。所以说"握机"、"握奇"，本来没有两种方法，在于学者融会贯通罢了。

Question 9

Tang Taizong said: "The Classic of Grasping Opportunities states: 'The number of formations is nine, with the center formations under the commanding general's control. The four sides and eight directions are all regulated by the center unit. Within the main formation, reside smaller formations; within the platoons, reside smaller platoons. They can take the front to be the rear, the rear to be the front. When advancing, they do not run quickly; when withdrawing, they do not race off. There are four heads, eight tails. Wherever they are struck is made the head. If the enemy attacks the middle, the adjoining two heads will both come to the rescue. The number begins with five and ends with eight.' What does all this mean?"

Li Jing said: "Zhuge Liang used stones to make eight rows. The layout for the square formation is similar. When I instructed the army, we invariably began with this formation. What generations have passed down as 'The Classic of Grasping Opportunities' only includes a rough outline."[5]

Tang Taizong said: "Heaven, Earth, wind, clouds, dragons, tigers, birds, and snakes – what is the meaning behind these eight formations?"

Li Jing said: "There was an error made by those who transmitted them to later generations. The ancients wanted to secretly conceal which orders were given to which troops, so they craftily created these eight names. The eight formations were originally one, then being divided into eight. For example, 'Heaven' and 'Earth' originated in flag destinations; 'wind' and 'clouds' originated in the pennant names. 'Dragons,' 'tigers', 'birds' and 'snakes' originated in the distinctions of the platoons and squads. Later generations erroneously transmitted them. If they were cleverly creating formations in the image of animals, why would they just stop at eight?"

---

[5] Zhuge Liang (諸葛亮) was a chancellor of the state of Shu Han during the Three Kingdoms period of Chinese history, famous for his military strategy.

太宗问：握机阵分为九个阵，
[外有四正四奇，]中央的一阵由大将掌握，周围各阵都以他的号令为准。大阵之中包括了许多小阵，大队之中包括了许多小队。可把前阵作为后阵，后阵作为前阵。由于进退都是齐一的，所以进不速奔，退不急走。四头八尾，敌人触犯的部分都可作为首部，敌若冲击中间，首尾都来救应。布阵的数目最初是五个，以后演变到八个。 这是什么道理呢？
李靖答：诸葛亮用石头纵横排列成八行[垒成八升阵]，这和[黄帝九军]方阵之法一样。我过去训练部队，必先教会这种这阵法。世人所传的握机文，仅仅说明了它的概略罢了。
太宗问：以天、地、风、云，龙、虎、鸟、蛇，作为八阵的名称，它的含义是什么？
李靖答：这是后人传说的错误。古人为了保守这一阵法的秘密，所以故意设立八种奇怪的名称。其实八阵本来是一个整体，不过区分为八个部分罢了。象天阵、地阵是根据旗号命名的，风阵、云阵是根据幡名命名的，龙、虎、鸟、蛇各阵是根据部队代号而命名的。后人传[龙阵象龙，虎阵象虎……]，如果各降都要假设各种物象，其何止八种呢？

Question 10

Tang Taizong said: "The numbers of formations begin with the five and ends with eight, so if they were not set up as images of animals, then they are really ancient military systems. Would you please explain them for me?"

Li Jing said: "I observe that the Yellow Emperor governed the army according to the methods by which he first established the 'village and well' system. Thus the 'well' was divided by four roads, and eight families occupied it. Its shape was that for the Chinese character for 'well' (井), so nine squares were opened therein. Five were used for formations, four were empty. This explains why the numbers started with five.

"The middle was left vacant to be occupied by the commanding general, while around the four sides the various companies were interconnected, so this is what is meant by the number of formation ends with eight. As for the changes and transformations to control the enemy: intermixed and turbulent, their fighting appeared chaotic, but their method was not disordered. In a nice flow of movement, from their deployment of circular transformation to square formation, their formations are not dispersed. This is what is meant by 'when they dispersed and become eight, reunite and again become one'."

Tang Taizong said: "The Yellow Emperor's governance of the army was profound indeed! Even if later generations have men with the wisdom of Heaven and great planning ability, none will be able to exceed his scope! After him, who came near to him?"

Li Jing replied: "When the Zhou Dynasty first flourished, Jiang Ziya substantially copied his methods. He began at the Qi state capital by establishing the well acreage system, constructing three hundred chariots, and training three hundreds Tiger Guards in order to establish a military organization. They practiced advancing 'six paces, seven paces' making 'six attacks, seven attacks,' so as to teach them battle tactics. When he deployed the army at Mu Ye, with only a hundred officers as vanguard, Jiang Ziya controlled the army and established his military achievements. With 45,000 men, he conquered King Zhou's mass of 700,000.

"In the Zhou dynasty, 'Sima Fa' was based upon Jiang Ziya. When Jiang Ziya died, the people of Qi (岐) obtained his bequeathed strategies. When Duke Huan became hegemon to the Zhou Kingdom, he relied on Guan Zhong who again cultivated the Jiang Ziya methods. Their army was referred to as a 'restrained and governed' and all the feudal Lords submitted."

Tang Taizong said: "The Confucians mostly say that Guan Zhong[6] was merely the minister of a hegemon, so they truly do not know that his military methods were founded upon the ancient military system. Zhuge Liang had the talent to be a king's right hand man, and he compared himself with Guan Zhong and Yue Yi. From this we know that Guan Zhong was also the true talent to a king. But when the Zhou declined, the king could not use him, so he allied with the state of Qi, under Duke Huan, and mobilized an army there."

Li Jing bowed twice and said: "Your Majesty is indeed wise, since you understand people well. Being able to serve you, giving my best until death, I would not be ashamed to meet the ancient Worthy (ancestors).

"I would like to speak about Guan Zhong's methods for organizing the state of Qi. He divided Qi to compose three armies. Five families comprised the fundamental unit, so five men made up a squad of five. Ten fundamental family units composed a hamlet, so fifty men composed a platoon. Four hamlets constituted a village, so 200 composed a company. Ten villages constituted a town, so 2,000 composed one battalion. Five towns made up an army, so 10,000 men composed one army. It "all proceeded from the *Sima Fa*' means that one army consists of five battalions, while one battalion consists of five companies. In actual fact, these are all bequeathed methods of Jiang Ziya."

---

[6] Guǎn Zhòng (管仲) (c. 720-645 BCE) was a chancellor and reformer of the State of Qi during the Spring and Autumn period of Chinese history.

太宗问：布阵的数目最初是五个，最终演变到八个，非因物象而设，其实这是古代的制度，你可以谈谈这个问题。

李靖答：黄帝最初实行井田制，创立"丘井之法"[以治理人民]，并根据井田制建立了军事制度。一井用四条道路分开，八家环绕，共处一井，[中间作为公田，]它的形状象个井字，分开则为九块方地。[开始，以前、后、左、右、中]五处用作布阵，四个角落作为空地，这就是所谓阵数起于五个的由来；其后空出中央部分，由大将居中指挥，以前后左右及四个角落相连环绕在四周[成为八阵]，这就是所谓阵数演变成八个的由来。等到分合变化打击敌人的时候，则旌旗纷纷，人马纭纭，战斗似乱而阵法不乱，部队行动，有如奔流，由方阵变为圆阵，而阵势仍然不散；这就是所谓分散开就成为八小阵，合起来就成为一大阵的说法。

太宗问：黄帝建立的军事制度，意义很深奥啊！后人虽有很高的智慧，很深的谋略，也没有能够超出他的范围的，从他以后又有谁能继承他的兵法呢？

李靖答：周朝初兴的时候，太公就继承了黄命的制度，开始在岐都建立井田制度，并召集兵车三百辆，虎贲三百人，以建立周朝的军制。训练时，以六步七步、六伐七伐教练战法。牧野之战，太公先以勇士百人进行挑战，[继之以主力冲击，]成就了武功，于是以四万五千人战胜了商纣的七十万军队。周《司马法》是根据太公所立的制度而作，太公死后，齐国人得到他的遗法。至齐桓公称霸于天下，用管仲为宰相，重新整理太公的军事制度，使齐国军队成为节制之师，天下诸侯没有不畏服的。

太宗说：儒家多说管仲不过是霸者的谋臣罢了，殊不知管仲的兵法就是根据周朝的制度来的。诸葛亮有辅佐帝王的才能，常将自岬比作管仲、乐毅，由此可知管仲也有辅佐帝王的才能。但在周室衰微的时候，周王不能任用他，所以凭借齐桓公兴师以匡正天下。

李靖再拜说：陛下圣明，知人如此深刻，老臣虽尽力至死亦必求无愧于先贤。我愿谈谈管仲治理齐国的方法：他将齐国的人民区分为三部分，立为三军。[行政上]以五家为一轨，所以[兵制上相应以]五人为一伍；十轨为一里，所以五十人为一小戎；四里为一连，所以二百人为一卒；十连为一乡，所以二十人为一旅；

五乡为一师，所以万人为一军。这也是根据《司马法》一师分为五旅，一旅分为五卒的意义演变来的。其实这些都是来源于太公的遗法。

Question 11

Tang Taizong said: "People say that the 'Sima Fa' was composed by Sima Rangju. Is this true or not?"

Li Jing said: "According to the Biography of Rangju, in 'Records of the Grand Historian', he excelled in commanding the army at the time of Duke Jing of Qi, defeating the forces of Jin and Yan. Duke Jing honored him with the post of Commander of Horses (known as Sima), and from then on he was called Sima

Rangju. His sons and grandsons were then surnamed Sima. In the time of Duke Wei of Qi, they sought out and talked about the methods of the ancient Commanders of the Horse and also narrated what Rangju had studied. This subsequently became a book in ten chapters called 'Methods of the Sima', or 'Sima Rangju'. Moreover, what has been transmitted from the military strategists and remains today is divided into four categories: 'balance of power and plans', 'disposition and strategic power', 'yin and yang', and 'techniques and crafts'. They all come out of the 'Sima Fa'."

Tang Taizong said: "During the Han, Zhang Liang and Han Xin ordered the compilation of books on military art. Altogether, there were 182 thinkers, but after they collated and edited them to select the important ones, they settled on thirty five. Now we have lost what they transmitted. What about this?"

Li Jing said: "What Zhang Liang studied was Jiang Ziya's 'Six Secret Teachings' and 'The Three Strategies'. What Han Xin studied were the books of Sima Rangju and Sun Tzu. But the main principles do not go beyond the 'Three Focus' and 'Four Schools'; that is all."

Tang Taizong asked: "What is meant by the 'Three Focus'?"

Li Jing said: "I find that in the eighty one chapters of the 'Plans of Jiang Ziya', military strategies cannot be exhausted; the seventy chapters of the 'Sayings of Jiang Ziya', troops cannot be exhausted; and the eighty five chapters of the 'Warfare of Jiang Ziya', resources cannot be exhausted. These are the 'Three Focus'."

Tang Taizong asked: "What is meant by the 'Four Schools'?"

Li Jing said: "These are what Ren Hong from Han has discussed: four classes of military strategists, 'strategies and tactics', 'circumstances and developments', 'yin and yang' and 'techniques and crafts'."

太宗问：有人说《司马法》是穰苴所著，是不是？
李靖答：根据《史记·穰苴列传》记载，齐景公时，穰苴善于用兵，曾击败燕国和各国的军队，景公加封他为司马，于是人皆称为司马穰苴。他的子孙、也号称司马氏。到齐威王时，命大臣追论、整理古《司马法》，并将穰苴的兵法附记于内，遂有司马穰苴兵书数十篇。现在所有的兵家流派分为权谋、形势、阴阳、技巧四种，都出自《司马法》。
太宗问：汉张良、韩信将古兵法排列为一百八十二家，经过甄别删去芜伪，择其精要可用的选定了三十五家，现在为什么失传了呢？

李靖答：〔没有完全失传，〕张良所学的就是太公的《六韬》《三略》，韩信所学的就是穰苴、孙武的兵法，然而这些兵书的内容，大体不外三门四种。
太宗问：什么叫三门？
李靖答：太公谈政治外交的"阴谋"有八十一篇，所谓阴谋的意义，不是"言"篇所陈的善言能够说明的；太公谈品德修养的"言"有七十一篇，其中的意义不是"兵"篇所讲的兵法能够说明的；太公谈军事原理的"兵"有八十五篇，其中的意义不是所讲的富国之道能够说明的。这就是三门。
太宗问：什么是四种？
李靖答：汉成帝时任宏所论述的就是这个问题，他把兵家流派区分为权谋、形势、阴阳、技巧四种。

Question 12

Tang Taizong said: "The 'Sima Fa' begins by mentioning the Spring and Winter ceremonial hunts. Why?"

Li Jing answered: "To accord with the seasons and the ritual of paying respect to the spirits, then put in the schedule for training; this is to pay attention to priorities. Thus agriculture and rituals that pay respect to spirits are the most important government affairs, according to the Zhou Rites. King Cheng held the Spring Hunt on the southern side of Mount Qi. King Kang held the assembly at Feng Palace. King Mu held the assembly at Mount Tu. These are affairs of the Son of Heaven.

"When the Zhou rule declined, Duke Huan of Qi assembled the armies of the feudal state at Zhao Ling, while Duke Wen of Jin made his alliance with the feudal Lords at Jian Tu. In these cases, the feudal Lords respectfully performed the affairs of the Son of Heaven. In actuality, they used the Law of Nine Attacks to overawe the irreverent. They employed the pretext of the hunt to hold court assemblies, accordingly conducting tours and hunts among the feudal Lords, as well as conducting military exercises. The 'Sima Fa' states that unless there is a national emergency, the army should not be wantonly mobilized, but that during the times between the agricultural seasons, they should certainly not forget military preparations. Thus it is not profound that it placed the hunts of Spring and Winter at the beginning chapters!"

太宗问：《司马法》首先便叙述春天和冬天狩猎的事，是什么缘故？
李靖答：利用农闲季节[进
行田猎以教练战法]，并祭祀宗庙托之于神，这是为了郑重其事，所以《周礼》
[将田猎]列为最重要的制度。周成王时曾在歧山的南面进行过田猎，周康王曾借田猎在酆宫受过诸侯的朝见，周穆王亦在涂山田猎会合过诸侯，这都是

天子亲自主持的事。周室衰微以后，齐桓公曾与诸侯会师于召陵，晋文公曾与诸侯结盟于践土，这都是诸侯假天子之命所行之事。其实都是用"九伐之法"来威慑不遵王命的诸侯。假借朝会的名义，利用巡狩的机会，进行军事训练，是说国家无事不要轻易动兵，必须利用农闲季节[举行田猎]，这就是不忘备战的意思。所以《司马法》首先叙述田猎，不是有很深远的意义吗！

Question 13

Tang Taizong said: "During the Spring and Autumn period, the 'Methods for the Double Battalion of King Zhuang of Chu' stated that 'the hundred officers should act in accord with the symbolization of things, military administration should be prepared without official instructions.' Did this accord with the Zhou regulations?"[7]

Li Jing said: 'According to the *Zhuo Zhuan*, 'King Zhuang's chariot battalions consisted of thirty chariots per battalion. Each chariot in the battalion had a company of infantrymen plus a platoon for the flanks.' When the army was advancing, the battalion on the right was deployed by flanks. They took their flank as their defining measure. Thus they stayed close to the flanks to fight. These were all Zhou regulations."

"In the case of Chu, I refer to 100 men as a company, while fifty men are called a platoon. Thus each chariot is accompanied by 150 men, many more than in the Zhou organization. Under the Zhou, each chariot was accompanied by seventy two infantry men and three armored officers. Twenty five men, including an officer, formed one platoon, so three Zhou platoons were seventy five men altogether. Qi is a country of mountains and marshes; chariots were few, men numerous. If they were to be divided into three platoons, then they would be functionally the same as the Zhou."

太宗问：按春秋《左传》所载，楚庄王的军队有二广的编制，其规定说："军中百官根据旗鼓的号令而行动，军队的事情不待命令就有所准备。"这也是来自周朝的制度吗？

李靖答：根据《左传》上说："楚庄王的亲兵广(车队)三十辆，每辆车士卒人数为一卒(一百人)比周制每车人数多一倍。步卒在车的右边行动，以车的右辕为准，在两车之间进行战斗。"这都是周朝的制度。我认为：按百人为一卒，五十人为一两，这样，楚国的战车，每求是用士卒一百五十人，比周制人数加多了。周制一乘车只有步卒七十二人，甲士三人；以二十五人为一甲，三甲共七十五人。楚国多高山大泽，车少人多，也[将一百五十人]区分为三队，这种三队区分法与周朝的制度是一样的。

---

[7] King Zhuāng of Chǔ (楚莊王) was a monarch of the Zhou Dynasty State of Chu during the Spring and Autumn period.

Question 14

Tang Taizong said: "During the Spring and Autumn period, when Sun Tzu attacked the Di, he abandoned his chariots and used infantry units instead. Were they also *indirect* troops? Or *direct* troops?"[8]

Li Jing said: "Sun Tzu used strategy for chariot warfare; that is all. Although he abandoned the chariots, his strategy is still found therein. One force acted as the left flank, one force acted as the right flank, and one resisted the enemy in the front. Dividing them into three units, this is one tactic for chariot warfare. Whether 1,000 or 10,000 chariots; it would be the same. I observe that in Duke Cao's 'Xin Shu' it states: 'Attack chariots are accompanied by seventy five men. To the fore, to oppose the enemy is one unit; to the left and right corners are two more units. The defense chariots have an additional unit. It consists of ten men to prepare the food, five to repair and maintain the equipment, five to care for the horses and five to gather firewood and fetch water – altogether twenty five men. For a pair of attack and defense chariots, altogether there are 100 men.' If you mobilize 100,000 men, you would employ 1,000 each of the light attack and heavy defense chariots. This is the general outline of Sun Tzu's old methods."

"Moreover, I observe that in the period from Han to Wei, army regulations had five chariots comprise a platoon, with a supervisor to command them. Ten chariots formed a regiment, under a chief commandant. For 1,000 chariots, there were two men, a general and lieutenant general. If more chariots, the organization followed this pattern. If I examine it in comparison with our present methods, then our probing force is the old cavalry; our frontal assault troops are the old infantry and cavalry, half and half; and our holding force goes forth with combined chariot tactics."

"When I went to the west to correct and punish the Tu Jue, we crossed several thousand miles of treacherous terrain, I never dared change this system for the constraints and regulations of the ancients can truly be trusted."

太宗问：春秋时，晋国的荀吴领兵伐狄于大卤地方，舍弃车战，改为步战，这是正兵，还是奇兵呢？
李靖答：荀吴是用车战的方法。他虽然舍弃车战改用步战，但仍然是用车战的方法。[在进战时]以一队为左角，一队为右角，一队为前拒，共分三队，这是一乘车的作战方法，就是千乘万乘都是一样的。　　　　　　　　我按《曹公新书》说：攻车一乘有七十五人，分为前拒一队，左右角各一队；守车一队，包括有炊事人员十人，守护装具的五人，饲养马匹的五人，砍柴担水的五人，
共计二十五人，攻守两车共有士卒百人。所以动员十万军队，就需要战车千

---

[8] The "Di" refers to various ethnic groups who lived in northern China during the Zhou Dynasty.

乘，也就是需要轻、重车二千乘，这是荀吴旧法的大概情况。再从汉魏的军制来看，通常
以五车为一队，设仆射一人；十车为师，设率长一人；兵车千乘设正副将领二人，如兵车再增多也是仿效这样的办法。我现在的方法是参照古来使用的，跳荡队，由
骑兵组成，战锋队，由步骑各半的混合部成，驻队则由步兵和车辆组成。我西讨突厌时，越过险阻转战数里，这种制度也未敢轻易变动。因为古时的战法严整不乱，确实应当重视。

Question 15

Tang Taizong said: "Zhuge Liang once stated that: 'A well-trained army cannot be defeated by its enemies, even when the general is incapable in commanding. However, when the army is lacking in training, no matter how talented the general is, the army would still be unable to conquer its enemies.' However, I doubt that this conclusion may not necessarily be the absolute certainty under such circumstances."

Li Jing answered: "Zhuge Liang made this statement out of personal feelings. According to Sun Tzu's 'Art of War', 'When the general is weak and lacking of authority, when his orders are unclear and not distinct, when the duties and not fixed and assigned to men and officers respectively, and the ranks are formed in a slovenly haphazard manner, the result is utter disorganization.' Since ancient times, an enemy's victory is caused by our own disarray, and chaos has occurred numerous times in the history. The so-called 'When the general is weak and lacking of authority, when his orders are unclear and distinct' refers to the military training not following the traditional method; What we called 'there are no fixed duties assigned to men and officers' refers to a frequent change in duties of soldiers. What we called 'Our own chaos cited our enemies victory' refers to the fact that when our army is in disarray and unorganized, our losses are caused by our chaos, and not by our enemies. Therefore, Zhuge Liang stated that 'A well-trained army cannot be defeated by its enemies, even when the general is incapable in commanding. However when the army has fallen into their own chaos and disorganization, no matter how talented the general is, he still could not save the army from peril.' There is no doubt about this statement."

Tang Taizong said: "The importance of methods used for military training and inspecting must not be ignored."

Li Jing answered: "When the training method truly works, the soldiers will happily serve us and follow the commands given; however, when our training method fails, even though we inspect them day and night, it would not serve any purpose. The reason why I need to focus and study the traditional training system, and compile them into drawings is to educate our soldiers to become a highly organized and well-trained army."

Tang Taizong said: "I need you to choose for me an ancient battle formation, illustrate all of your choices and send them to me."

太宗曰：诸葛亮说："训练有素的军队，即使将帅没有才能，也不会被敌人打败，没有训练的军队，即使将帅有才能，也不会战胜敌人。"我怀疑这种说法，不一定是很正确的论断。

李靖答：武侯[这种说法]是有所感而发的。按《孙子》说："教道不明，吏卒无常，陈兵纵横，曰乱。"

自古以来，由于自己混久而造成敌人胜利的不可胜数。所谓"教道不明"，是指军队教育没有遵照古法；所谓"吏卒无常"，是指将吏士卒时任用经常变动，所谓"乱军引胜"，是指敌人取得的胜利是由于我们自己的混乱所造成

的，而不是敌人打胜的。所以武侯说："军队训练有素，虽然将帅没有才能，也不会被敌人打败；如果军队自己溃乱，即使将帅有才能，也不能挽救于危亡。"这有 什么可疑的呢！

太宗说：教育和校阅的方法，实在不能忽视。

李靖答：教育得法，士卒就乐于为我所用；教育不得法，纵然早晚督促责备也无济于事。我所以要专心研究古制并把它编纂成图，是希望教育官兵使之成为有训练的军队。

太宗说：你为我选择古代阵法，全部绘制成图送上来。

Question 16

Tang Taizong asked: "When an army from another kingdom is warring, they choose to use running, powerful and strong horses to create a huge impact. Is this considered *indirect* tactics in military strategy? Han's army uses strong bows with coordination, is this considered as *direct* tactics in military strategy?"

Li Jing answered: "According to Sun Tzu's 'Art of War': 'A clever combatant looks to the effect of combined energy and does not require too much energy from each individual; hence, he is highly capable of utilizing the combined strengths in individuals who would be suitable under different circumstances.' The so-called 'choosing individuals who possess different strengths' refers to adapting the strengths of a foreign army and Han's army to carry out the combat. The foreign army is good at riding skills, therefore is more suitable for speedy battle; Han's army is adept in using bow and arrow, therefore is beneficial to launch slow-paced wars. We are naturally adapting with different situations, while utilizing our own strengths; but this is not the difference between *direct* tactics and *indirect* tactics. I said before that a foreign army or Han's army change their flags and costumes to fool their enemy, this is the true form of applying *indirect* strategies. In horse wars, *direct* and *indirect* strategies are used simultaneously, as is so in a war of bows; therefore things will constantly change and nothing will remain the same!"

Tang Taizong said: "Please explain further the method used."

Li Jing replied: "First, we have to make a false impression to lure the enemy, causing the enemy to obey my commands. This is the approach used."

Tang Taizong said: "I can understand this kind of spirit now. Sun Tzu's 'Art of War' stated that: 'In making tactical dispositions, the highest point you could attain is concealing them' and 'How victory may be produced for them out of the enemy's own tactics—that is what the multitude cannot comprehend.' Are these the same idea of *indirect* tactics?"

Li Jing bowed again and said: "What Sun Tzu stated is very obscure! But my wise majesty has understood more than half of it."

太宗问：番兵作战常用劲马奔驰冲击，这是奇兵吗？汉兵作战常用强弩互相配合，这是正兵吗？
李靖答：按《孙子》说："善
于用兵的人，要从所造成的有利形势上去手求取胜之道，不可责于人，要能选择具有不同长处的人，去适应不同的形势。"所谓选择不同长处的人，也就是利用番汉
兵卒的特长而进行战斗。番兵善于乘马，所以利于速战；汉兵长于用弩，所以利于缓战，这就自然地适应了不同的形势，然而这并不是奇兵和正兵的区别。我以前曾
讲过番汉变更旗号，更换服装，这才是奇兵和正兵相互为用的方法。马战有奇也有正，弩战有正也有奇，哪有固定不变的呢！
太宗说：你再详细地解说一下这种方法。
李靖答：先做出假象引诱敌人，使敌人听从我的调动，就是这种方法。
太宗说：我领悟这种精神了。《孙予》说："欺骗敌人的行动巧妙到了极点，就会看不出形迹来。"又说："运用各种欺骗敌人的方法以取得胜利，但许多人还不知道胜利是怎样得来的。"就是这样的道理吗？
李靖再拜说：孙子所说的很深奥啊！陛下英明，已领会过半了。

Question 17

Tang Taizong said: "Recently, the two tribes Khitan and Xi have come to pledge allegiance. I have named captaincy for these two places, Song Mo and Rao Le and they are supposed to follow the orders of the Protectorate General of the North. I am thinking about assigning Xue Wan Che for the position, and I would like to hear your opinion on this."

Li Jing answered: "Xue Wan Che is not as talented as Ashina She'er, Zhi Shi Si Li and Qi Bi He Li; among all of our foreign minister these three understand military strategies the most. I know about their talents because I have discussed with them the topography around Song Mo and Rao Le, the road conditions and the loyalty of the tribes. Their opinions are clear and trustworthy even when we are talking about the dozens of tribes in the West.

"When I teach them about battle formations, they all nodded with admiration. I hope my majesty could assign the task to them without hesitation. Xue Wan Che is just foolhardy; he can't carry such heavy responsibilities alone."

Tang Taizong said with a smile: "You can even use the help of foreign people. There is an ancient saying, 'Use the barbarians to control barbarians, China has been like this since the ancient times.' I see you understand this principle now."

太宗说：最近契丹、奚两个部落都来归顺，我已设置松漠、饶乐二都督，使其隶属于安北都护，我想任用薛万彻担任都护之职，你的意见怎样？
李靖答：薛万彻的才能不如阿史那社尔、执失思力和契苾何力，这三人都是番臣中懂得军事的。因为我曾经同他们谈论过松漠、饶乐的山川形势、道路状况和番人顺逆的情况，甚至达到西域的十数个部落，他们谈起来都是清楚可信。我教他们阵法，无不点头佩服，希望陛下任用他们不要怀疑。薛万彻有勇无谋，难以独自胜任。
太宗笑着说：番人都能为你所用。古人说：" 以蛮夷制蛮夷，中国历来是这样的。" 你已经懂得这个道理了。

Part 2
Question 2.1

Tang Taizong said: "Among all the military books I have read, so far not a single one of them could exceed Sun Tzu's 'The Art of War'; even if the thirteen chapters of Sun Tzu do not go beyond the scope of discussing weak points and strengths. When we have come to the state of being at war, we could win endless victories if we are capable of recognizing our enemies' weak points and their strengths. Nowadays our generals could only drone about 'avoiding the enemy's strength and attack their weak points'; however when they are facing the actual situation, only very few of them are capable of identifying the enemy's weakness. The underlying factor causing such a situation is because they are incapable of affecting their enemies; instead they are very much affected by their enemies. What do you think about this situation? You could also explain the essential points on how to identify our enemies' strengths and weaknesses."

Li Jing answered: "We start with teaching them how to deal with the changes of *indirect* and *direct* methods in military strategy; next we should teach them how to identify the strengths and weaknesses of enemies. Then their understanding would improve. At this time, our generals could not understand the difference between *direct* and *indirect* strategies; therefore, they are not able to understand the principle: an enemy's strengths are also their weaknesses and vice versa.

Tang Taizong asked: "By analyzing the situation of our enemy, we could truly understand the motives, strengths and weaknesses of our enemy. Agitating and putting our enemy in an emotional state will help us understand their patterns of movement. By means of using reconnaissance, we would have a better understanding about which type of terrain is more favorable or unfavorable for our enemy. Launching probing attacks against our enemy could help us gain an understanding about their strengths and weaknesses. Is this our *direct* and *indirect* methods toward understanding our enemy's strengths and weaknesses?"

Li Jing answered: "What we call *indirect* and *direct* methods are used to cope with our enemy's strengths and weaknesses. If our enemy is strong, we will use the frontal advance to fight against them. On the contrary, if they are weak, we should use a surprise attack to deal with them. If the generals could not understand the rule of varying these two strategies, they won't be able to conquer our enemy, even if they understand the enemy's strengths and weaknesses. After receiving their orders, our generals should truly understand the art of varying these two methods, and how to combine *direct* and *indirect* methods. Then they will naturally understand the strengths and weaknesses of the enemies they are facing.

Tang Taizong said: "When I change from using the *direct* method to using the *indirect* method, the enemy will wrongly think that I am still using the *direct* method, and they will launch an attack using an *indirect* method. When I change to using a *direct* method, the enemy will think that I am still using the *indirect* method; but I will launch an attack by using a *direct* method instead. Following these varying rules, we could place our enemy into a disadvantageous situation, and secure ourselves into a favorable situation. You should teach these ways to all of our generals, so that they can easily understand this principle."

Li Jing said: "Even thousands and thousands of words could not exceed Sun Tzu's saying, 'I impose my will on the enemy, but do not allow the enemy's will to be imposed on me.' I will keep this spirit in mind and let it become the core of my teachings to the generals."

太宗说：我看过的各种兵书中，没有超过《孙子兵法》的，《孙子》十三篇，没有超出虚实的范围。用兵作战，如果能认识到虚实的形势，就能无往而不胜利。现在的将领中，只能空谈"避实击虚"，到了临敌作战的时候，则又很少能识破敌人虚实的，这是由于他们不能左右敌人，而反为敌人所左右的原故，你以为怎样？你尽可能为诸将讲解一下认识虚实的要领。
李靖答：先教他们奇正相互变化的方法，然后再讲如何认识虚实的形势就可以了。现在诸将领多数不知以奇为正以正为奇的变化，又怎能认识到敌人的虚是实，实是虚呢！
太宗问：分析敌情，就会知道敌人的利害得失；激动敌人。就会知道敌人动静的规律；使用各种侦察手段就会知道敌人所处的地形哪里有利或不利；对敌试探攻击，就会知道敌人的强处和弱处。这就是以我的奇正察知敌人虚实的方法吗？
李靖答：所谓奇正，是用以对付敌人虚实的。敌强，我就用正兵；敌弱，我就用奇兵。如果将帅不知奇正的变化，就是知道敌人的虚实，又怎能战胜敌人呢！我奉命后，只要先教诸将学会奇正的用，然后他们对于敌人的虚实自然就知道了。
太宗说：我把奇兵变为正兵使用时，敌人还以为我是奇兵，而却以正兵打击它；我把正兵变为奇兵使用时，敌人还以为我是正兵，而我却以奇兵打击它。这样就能使敌人经常处于不利的态势，自己常处于有利的态势。你应以此法传授给各将领，使他们容易明由。
李靖说：千章万句，不外乎《孙子》说的"我能左右敌人，而不为敌人所左右"罢了，我当本着这种精神教育诸将。

Question 2.2

Tang Taizong asked (after conquering Gaochang): "I had assigned a Jade Pool captaincy to follow the orders of the An Xi protectorate, but the native soldiers there have different customs from the Han soldiers and could not cope with the changes. In your opinion what arrangement should be made?"[9]

---

[9] Gaochang was built in the 1st century BCE, and was an important site along the Silk Road.

Questions and Replies

Li Jing answered: "All humans should be the same; supposedly there are no differences between the foreigners and Han's people. But these foreigners live in a remote desert area on the border; they have to hunt for a living, therefore they are used to fighting. If we could comfort them with kindness and provide them sufficient living necessities, then we could use their help, just like we used the Han. Considering that Your Majesty has already established the An Xi protectorate, I propose that we should withdraw the army from the borders, back to the mainland. This could help in reducing the transportation of food supplies; this is the way to maintain our combat forces in military maneuvers. Meanwhile, we have to choose someone who is familiar with the situation of these foreigners, among our Han officials, to guard every checkpoint outside the mainland, to ensure that everything is secure and in order. If there is an emergency at the border, we immediately send our Han soldiers for aid."

Tang Taizong asked: "What is the way to maintain combat capability according to Sun Tzu?"

Li Jing answered: "'Use the army that is near to the battlefield to fight with the enemy that has traveled far; use the army that could leisurely prepare, and awaits their enemy, to fight the tired enemy; use the well-supplied army to fight with the starving enemy.' This is roughly the way, according to Sun Tzu. Those who are skillful in military traps further extend these three meaning into six strategies. These include: entice the enemy into coming to invade our territory; use calmness to deal with the impetuous enemy; treat the rash enemy sedately; use rigor to deal with the slack enemy; use orders and formations to deal with chaos; and use defense to deal with the enemy's offensive attack. If we do not follow these ways, our combat capability cannot be unleashed. Therefore, how could we beat our enemy, if we do not preserve our combat power?"

Tang Taizong said: "Nowadays, the people that study Sun Tzu's 'Art of War' can only recite the provisions of it; very few of them could apply it to actual situations. These ways of preserving our combat power should be widely spread to our generals."

太宗问：[灭高昌以后，]我设置瑶池都督使隶于安西都护，但那里的番兵和汉兵[习性不同]，你看应如何处置？
李
靖答：天之生人，本无番汉之别，但番人居住于边远荒漠的地方，必须以打猎为生，因此常常习惯于战斗。我若以恩信抚慰他们，以衣食周济他们，就能使他们象汉
人一样为我所用了。陛下既设立了安西都护，我建议将驻守边境的汉兵撤至内地，以减少粮食的补给运输，这就是兵家所说的保持战斗力的方法。同时在汉族官吏

中，选择熟悉番人情况的，使其散守塞外各城堡，这样就可以长久无急。一旦边境有事，就派遣汉兵出塞应援。

太宗问：《孙子》所说保待战斗力的方法如何？

李靖答："以靠近战场的军队对待远来的敌人，以从容休整的军队对待疲劳的敌人，以补给充裕的军队对待饥饿的敌人"，这是《孙予》所说的大概含义。善于用兵的人，从这三种含义引申为六种办法，那就是：以诱诈对待来犯的敌人，以冷静对待急躁的敌人，以稳重对待轻率的敌人，以严谨对待懈怠的敌人，以整齐对待混乱的人，以防守对待进攻的敌人。不这样，战斗力就不能发挥。[如此看来，]不采取保持战斗力的方法，怎能临敌制胜呢！

太宗说：现在学习《孙子兵法》的人，只能背诵条文，很少能解其精神实质而有所发挥的。这种保持战斗力的方法，你应当普遍知诸将。

Question 2.3

Tang Taizong asked: "There are not many experienced old soldiers left and the existing army is now newly established, and without any prior war experience; which type of training should we give them?"

Li Jing answered: "Usually I will divide the army into three stages. First, group five people to train them with the Wu method; after they have learned the method, send them for training in military schools. This is another stage. The method used in military schools is that once they have been trained successfully under a Wu (a five person group), they will be trained ten times under a Wu, and next they will be trained 100 times under a Wu. This will be another stage. After that, they will be trained by the lieutenant. The lieutenant will combine all the battle formations in the military schools and train them; this is yet another stage. When the army has completed all three stages, the general would hold a major examination: examine the various systems, dividing the army for frontal advance and surprise attack, warn the soldiers, and give punishment to those who violate the military orders. The last stage will be Your Majesty examining the army from the top, according to your preference."

太宗问：有作战经验的旧将老卒剩下的不多了，现有的军队是成立的，没有经过战斗，如今训练应该采取什么办法才好？

李靖答：我以往训练军队分为三个阶段。先以五人编为一位进伍法的训练，伍法学成后，交由军校训练，这是一个阶投。军校训的方法，是一伍学成以后再教十伍，十伍学成以后再教百伍，这又是一个阶段。以后再交由副将刘练，副将乃总合各军校的队伍进行阵法的训练，这又是一个阶段。大将军看到这三个阶段的

教练完成以
后，于是进行大阅，检查各种制度，区别奇兵和正兵，告戒将士，对违犯军令的给以处罚。然后陛下登高检阅，无论怎样指挥都是可以的。

Question 2.4

Tang Taizong asked: "There are several types of arrangements of Wu from the ancients, which of these are the main ones?"

Li Jing answered: "According to "Chun Qiu Zuo Shi Zhuan" (*Chronicle of Zuo*)[10], the method is, 'First we compile and next we train in Wu'. The 'Methods of Sima' mentioned to 'Group five soldiers into a Wu.' Wei Liaozi said, 'Bundle the Wu order.' In the Han dynasty, there was the 'Chi Ji Wu Fu' system (a system that records the military orders, the achievements and credits of the soldiers, and the codes that must be followed for each members in a Wu). Later, the books of these codes were written on paper; however this system was gradually lost. After I studied these theories, I thought that we should start with a group of five soldiers, gradually increase them into a group of twenty five, and from twenty five, increase to seventy five. This is the compilation system in Chun Qiu, where a platoon consists of seventy two infantry and three armored soldiers. If we don't use the platoons and choose to use cavalry, then twenty five infantry could be used as eight cavalry. This calculation is according to the method of 'Wu Bing Wu Dang' on the use of platoons, infantry and cavalry. Therefore every type of military strategy is all based on the method of Wu. If you choose to use infantry, you can arrange them into 'small columns' of five people, 'big columns' of twenty five people. If we arrange three 'big columns', there will be a total of seventy five people. We multiply this by five and we get 375 people. 300 of them will be the infantry and the rest will be cavalry. Among the cavalry, 150 will be the left part, used in frontal advance. The rest become the right part. Among the sixty cavalry, each left and right will have thirty cavalry to be used for the surprise attack. When we are launching an attack, our forces on both sides will be equal. I still use the approach of 'Five people as a Wu and ten times a Wu will be a team' according to Sima Rangju; these are the basics of the Wu theory."

太宗问：伍的编纽方法古人有数家，哪家是主要的？
李靖答：据《春秋左氏传》说，"先
偏后伍"；《司马法》说，"五人为伍"；《尉缭子》有"束伍令"；汉朝有"尺籍位符"的制度。后世的符籍是用纸写的，于是这种制度就逐渐失传了。我参考这
些说法后，认为：由五人逐渐变为二十五人，又由二十五人变为七十五人，这就是春秋时一求战车有步卒七十二人和甲士三人的编制。若不用战车而用

---

[10] Chunqiu Zuo Zhuan, or the Chronicle of Zuo, is among the earliest Chinese works of narrative history, covering the period from 722 to 468 BCE.

骑兵，则二十
五名步卒相当于八骑使用。这就是根据"五兵五当"运用在车、步、骑的办法。所以各家兵法，部是以伍法为基础的。[若舍车进行步战，可以]排成"小列"为五
人，排成"大列"为二。十五人，排成三个"大列"别为七十五人，再五倍之则为三百七十五人。〔除甲士十五人外，〕其余三百人为正，六十人为奇，[三百人
中]各以一百五十人为左右二正。[六十人中]各以三十人为左右二奇，前进时使左右兵力相等。司马穰苴所说五人为伍，十伍为队，我现在仍然沿用这种办法，这 就是伍法的大要。

Question 2.5

Tang Taizong asked: "When I discussed military strategies with Li Ze, what he said is basically quite similar to your approach; it's just that he didn't study the sources of them. The 'Liu Hua Battle Formation' that you have developed is based on what foundation?"

Li Jing answered: "My 'Liu Hua Battle Formation' was developed based on Zhuge Liang's 'Eight Tactical Formations'. Inside the big formation, there are small formations; inside the big camps there are small camps. The four sides and four corners are all inter-connected. The turning-points and cross-points are all symmetrical to each other. That is the ancient 'Eight Tactical Formations'. My 'Liu Hua Battle Formation' is developed on that foundation: the outside (six arrays) will be arranged into a square shape, while the inside (one array) will be arranged into a round shape. The shape of it is similar to six braided flowers; therefore I named it 'Liu Hua (six flowers) Battle Formation'."

Tang Taizong asked: "What is the purpose of arranging the array at the outside into a square shape and the inside array into a round shape?"

Li Jing answered: "The square formation is determined by the interval distance, measured by the count of steps; while the round formation is determined by the size of troops. The square formation is used to regulate the scope of movement of each team, while the round formation is for forming a seamless defense. Therefore, the count of steps of the square formation must be as fixed as the ground, and the round formation must cycle like the seamless cycling of the celestial stars. When the count of steps and the cycles can be done perfectly, we can achieve changes in the formation without being in disarray. From the 'Eight Tactical Formation' evolving into 'Liu Hua Battle Formation', it is still basically the old formation developed by Wu Hou."

太宗问：处我与李{责力}谈论兵法，他所说的很多与你相同，只是李{责力}的没有考究出处罢了。你所制定的六花阵法是根据什么？

李靖答：我的六花阵法是根据诸葛亮的八阵法演变而成。大阵中包含小阵，大营之中包含小营，四方四角，相互连系，转弯和交叉的地方彼此对称，古八阵法就是这样的。我制定的阵图是仿效这种法，把外面[的六阵]画成方形，内面[的一阵]画成圆形。其形象六个花瓣，所以称为六花阵。

太宗问：内面画成圆形，外面画成方形，是什么意思？

李靖答：方阵是由间隔距离的步数决定的，圆阵是由中军兵力的大小决定的。方阵是用来规整各队行动范围的，圆阵是为了联成环无间的防御的。所以方阵的步数要象大地一样的固定，圆阵的旋回象天体一样的循环无间，步数固定，旋回整齐，就可以变化而不乱。从八阵变为六花阵，仍然是武侯的旧法。

Question 2.6

Tang Taizong asked: "The outer square formation shows the advancing and retreating steps of soldiers, while the inner round formation indicates the range of weapons used. In order to achieve the most accurate pace, we have to train the flexibility of their feet; in order to achieve flexibility in using weapons, we have to train their hands. When the soldiers achieve a certain degree of flexibility in using their feet and hands, haven't we figured out most of the ways the ancients used to battle?"

Li Jing answered: "Wu Qi said 'Isolation of the team doesn't separate them, the troops are still in order while retreating.' This is the result of the usual foot training, which enables them to move at the same pace. Educating the soldiers is like arranging chess pieces on the chessboard; if we don't think of a route beforehand, how is the chess piece going to move? Sun Tzu said: 'On the battlefield we run analysis on the topography; from the analysis of the topography, we gather the information about the capacity of the surroundings; and from the capacity, we conclude the size of the troops. From the troop size of our enemy, we could understand better if our enemy is weak or strong, and from that we could find out the strategy to conquer them. When we use superiority to deal with the inferior, it's like lifting something light with something heavy and vice versa.' This is all due to the judgment that had been made beforehand, on the troop size of the enemy and the terrain of the battlefield."

Tang Taizong asked: "Sun Tzu's theory is indeed profound! Without considering the distance, troop size and terrain, how can the military operations move in orderly rhythms?"

Li Jing said: "The mediocre commander rarely knows about rhythm. Those who are good at commanding small battles would cause a dangerous situation in a large war; their rhythms of movements are short and brief. The warring situation is like the bow which has been pulled to the fullest extent; the rhythm will be like the arrow shooting out suddenly.

"I have studied this way, in the deployment of an army. It is appropriate to leave an interval of ten steps between every team; the stationed team is away from the frontal team for an interval of twenty steps. At the interval of every team, set up a domain team. Every advance should be made on the standard of fifty steps. When the horn is blown for the first time, each team stands separately: the interval between them should not exceed ten steps; until the fourth blow of the horn, the teams should hold their weapons and squat down simultaneously. The drumming will be the signal; each team will do the shouting for three times, followed by three times of hitting and hacking, until we have left only an interval of thirty or fifty steps between the enemy. The cavalry should come from behind; also note that they should approach the enemy until a distance of about fifty steps, when they should stop. The frontal advance army should move in the front, while the army for surprise attack should move behind. This is for the purpose of understanding the enemy's strengths and weaknesses. Hit the drum again, and the surprise attack army will change to the front, and the frontal advance army should move to the back. We should then lure our enemy out and beat them using their weaknesses. These are the basics of 'Liu Hua Battle Formation'.

太宗问：外画方形以显示士卒进退的步数，内画圆形以显示兵器运用的范围，要步度准确就应教以足法，要兵器运用灵活就应教以手法，手足便利，则古人布阵的方法不就思考到多半了吗？
李靖答：吴起说："隔
绝而队形不分离，退却品行列不散乱。"这就是平时进行步法训练的结果。教育士卒，如在棋盘上摆布棋子一样，若不画好路线，棋子向那儿移动呢！
孙武说："从
作战地区进行地形判断，从地形判断估计战场容量，从战场容量计算军队数目，从军队数目对比敌我强弱，从强弱对比找出致胜方法；以优势对劣势好象以重举轻，
以劣势对优势好象以轻举重。"这都是由于首先判断一国的幅员和地形的缘故。
太宗问：孙武的话，意义十分深刻啊！不考虑距离的远近、幅员和地形的广狭，怎么能够使军队的行动有节奏呢！
李靖说：庸将很少懂得节奏的。"善
于作战的人，其所造成的战势是险疾的，其行动的节奏是短促的，战势就象拉满的弓一样，节奏就象把箭突然射出一样。"我研究过这种办法，凡部署军队，各队以
间隔十步为宜，驻队距前队二十步，每隔一队设一域队，前进一次以五十步为准。吹第一次角声，各队同时分散而立，其间隔不超过十步的规定，到第四次角户，各
队抱枪蹲跪于地。于是击鼓为号，各队三次呼喊，三次击刺，前进到距敌三

Questions and Replies

十步至五十步，以对付敌人的变化。马军从后跃土，亦注意临到距敌五十步时即行停止。

正兵在前，奇兵在后，以观察敌人的虚实。[了解敌人虚实以后]再次击鼓，则奇兵在前，正兵在后，再把敌人引诱出来，乘机打击敌人弱点。六花阵法大概就是这样。

Question 2.7

Emperor Tang Taigong asked: "Cao Cao's Xin Shu mentioned: 'In embattlement, to fight our enemies, we must establish a mile post before everything else; then lead the army to arrange the battle formation according to the mile post. If any team is suffering from the attack of the enemy, the rest who didn't go for their rescue will be beheaded.' What kind of way is this?"

Li Jing answered: "The theory of establishing the mile post at the very last minute, when we are facing our enemy is not correct; this is just the usual teachings of war. Those who were skilled in using military strategies in ancient times only taught their army about the *indirect* method, but didn't teach them the *direct* method. Commanding the army is like driving a flock of sheep; they should advance when they are commanded, and retreat while receiving their orders. Because of the ego of Zhou Yu[11], the generals at that time dared not correct him. If we follow Zhou Yu's way to establish the mile post at the last minute of a battle, isn't it a little bit too late? I studied the 'Po Zhen Yue Wu' that was developed by Your Majesty: raise four flags at the front, arrange eight long streamers at the back; the fleet-footed move to either left or right, then rotate. Twist and turns are started with a quick pace and gradually change into slower pace. Hitting the cymbals and drums, there is rhythm for everything. All of this is imitating the Eight Tactical Formation's 'Four Heads and Eight Tails strategy'. Others can only focus on the spectacular music and footwork; who would have known that there is a battle formation underlying in it?"

Tang Taizong said: "In the past when Emperor Han Gaozu unified the whole of China, he wrote this song called Da Feng Ge. One of the lines is 'Where could I find a strong general to secure the peace of our country.' This means that in peace they want to leave war behind. Military strategies can only be understood by thoughts, and cannot always be explained with words. Only you can understand what I intended to express. The later generations may also understand that I created it for a specific purpose."

---

[11] Zhou Yu, also known as Cao Gong, was a military general and strategist during the late Han Dynasty period of Chinese history. Zhou Yu was assigned by Sun Quan, to be the naval commander for the defensive forces, defeating Cao Cao's forces at the Battle of Red Cliffs in 208 CE.

太宗问：《曹公新书》说：" 布阵对敌，必先设立标柱，然后率领军队根据标柱布列阵势。若一部遭受敌人攻击，其余不去救援的斩首。" 这是什么方法呢？

李靖答：临到与敌对阵才设立标柱的说法是不对的，这不过是平时教战的方法罢了。古人善于用兵的，只教正兵的戏法，不教奇兵的战法，指挥军队要象驱赶群羊一样，叫它进就进，叫它退就退，使它们不知要到哪里去。因曹公骄而好胜，当时奉行《新书》的将领，不敢指出他的短处。如按曹公所说临敌之时才设立标柱，不是太晚了吗？我看陛下所制定的"破阵乐舞"，前面举起四面旌旗，后面排列八幅长幡，舞蹈的人或左或右，曲折旋转，疾趋缓步，鸣金击鼓，各有节奏，这就是模仿八阵图四头八尾的方法。人们只见到音乐舞蹈的盛况，哪里知道这里面包含有阵法的内容呢！

太宗说：从前汉高祖平定天下后，曾作大风歌，其中一句是："安得猛士兮守四方"，[这是安不忘危的意思。]兵法可以意会，不可以言传。我作的"破阵乐舞"，惟有你已知道它的用意了，后来的人也将知道我不是随便创作的。

Question 2.8

Tang Taizong asked: "Using a single color of flags to command the army in five different directions, is this considered an *indirect* method? Using long streamers and small flags to command in a cross-cutting way; is this considered the *direct* method? When every team is separating and changing, what is the appropriate number of teams?"

Li Jing answered: "I follow the way of the ancients: gather the three teams into a group; the flags should lean against each other but do not cross each other. Five teams are then combined into one; then we should use two flags crossing one another. Ten teams are combined into one; we should then use five flags crossing each other. If separated, blow the horn once, and separate the five crossing flags. Then separate into ten teams again. When we are separating two crossed flags, then separate into five teams again; the non-crossing flag which leans against each other will separate into three again. When the army is separate, the combination will be the *direct* army and vice versa. After the three orders and five commands, three combinations and separations, we will get back to our usual training of frontal advance. By this time, the 'coaching four heads and tails' battle formation could be started. These are the steps that should be followed in training the army for battle formation."

Tang Taizong praised Li Jing's statement.

Questions and Replies

太宗问：在五个方位，各用一种颜色的旗子指挥军队的行动，这是正兵吗？用长幡、小旗相互交叉进行指挥，这是出奇吗？各队分合变化，其队数怎样才能适宜呢？

旗相靠而不交叉；五队合为一队，则用两旗交叉；十队合为一队，则用五旗交叉。[分散时]吹角一声，分开交叉的五旗，则[由十队合为]一队的又分为十队；分开交叉的两旗，则[由王队合为]一队的又分为五队；分开相靠而不交叉的两旗，则

[由三队合为]一队的又分为三队。军队分散的时候，则以合为奇，集合的时候，则以散为奇。经过三令五申，三散而三合，然后再回到正兵的操练，这样四头八尾

的阵法就可开始进行教练了，这是训练队形变化所应采取的步骤。

太宗说很好。

Question 2.9

Tang Taizong asked: "Zhou Yu has three types of cavalry: there are Zhan Qi, Xian Qi and You Qi. What is the difference between the use of cavalry today and in ancient times?"

Li Jing answered: "According to Xin Shu, Zhan Qi are the cavalry in the front; Xian Qi stay in the middle, while the back are You Qi. These are just names that separate the three types of cavalries given different tasks. Approximately twenty four infantries and soldiers on military chariots are equivalent to eight cavalries, twenty four cavalries are equivalent to seventy two infantries and soldiers on military chariots; this is the ancient military system. The infantries and soldiers on the military chariots are usually educated by the *indirect* method (therefore called the *indirect* army), while the cavalries are taught by *direct* method. The Zhou Yu method of separating cavalries into frontal, middle and back are not used then. The method did not discuss the separation of cavalries into left and right sides. This arrangement was made to deal with a single situation. The later generations don't understand and have the misconception that Zhan Qi must be placed somewhere between Xian Qi and You Qi. How could they use the cavalry correctly? I always use the following way: when the army is changing the battle formation, use You Qi as the frontal, while using Zhan Qi as the back part. Xian Qi should be used according to the situation. This is also the way used by Zhou Yu."

Tang Taizong said, while smiling: "Countless people have been fooled by Zhou Yu in this situation."

太宗问：曹公有战骑、陷骑、游骑三种，现在骑兵的使用和那时相比有何不同？

李
靖答：按曹公《新书》说：战骑在前，陷骑居中，游骑在后，这只是根据任务的不同各立名称，分为三类罢了。大约骑队的八骑相当于车徒二十四人，二十四骑相当
于车徒七十二人，这是古时的兵制。车徒通常教以正兵的战法，骑兵通常教以奇兵的战法。按曹公把骑兵分为前、后、中三复未使用，而没有谈到左右两厢，这是仅
就一种部署来说的。后人不理解三复的真正意义，以为战骑必定在陷骑、游骑之前，这怎么能使用得好呢？我经常使用下述方法：当回军转阵时，用游骑在前，战骑 在后，陷骑则根据情况的变化而使用，这也是曹公的方法。
太宗笑着说：[在这个问题上]不知道有多少人为曹公所迷惑。

Question 2.10

Tang Taizong asked: "If the method to use military chariots, cavalry and infantry is the same, then is the human factor the sole factor in deciding the effectiveness of the use of that method?"

Li Jing answered: "During the period of Chun Qiu, Zheng Zhuang Gong developed the 'Yu Li Battle Formation'. It uses the military chariots as the army's frontal assault, while the infantry stays behind. In this instance, there are only infantry and platoons but not cavalry. The separation of battle formations was named as 'Juo You Ju'; the sole purpose of it was for defense. It was not for the use of surprise attacks. When Xun Wu of Jing Dynasty conquered Di, they abandoned the use of military chariots and used only infantry. This could increase the number of infantries and make the battle easier. The purpose of making such arrangements was for surprise attacks, but not only for the purpose of defense. I concluded that all these methods, assuming that one cavalry is equivalent to three infantry, should be an appropriate ratio between the numbers of infantries and chariots. Combining the chariots, cavalries and infantries into teams, and cooperating in military operations, while using them effectively, how could our enemy know where the platoons will attack? Where will the cavalry come from and where will those infantry march out? Commanding the army should be either like being hidden under the unknown ground or suddenly dropped from the sky, therefore unable to be avoided. This kind of wit could only be possessed by Your Majesty. How would I know about the secret that lies within?"

太宗问：对车、步、骑三者运用的方法既然是一样的，那么，其运用的好坏在于人为吗？
李靖答：春秋时，郑庄公作"鱼
丽阵"，是用兵车在前，步卒在后[与周桓王作战]，那时只有兵车和步卒而没有骑兵，其阵的区分叫做左右拒，只是说用方阵抵御敌八，并非用以出奇制胜。晋苟

Questions and Replies

吴代狄时，曾舍弃车战改为步战，这样能增多骑兵就更便于作战了，其目的专在出奇制胜，不仅为抵御而已。我综合这些办法，以一个骑兵相当于三个步兵，战车与

步兵的数目也有适当比例；将车、步、骑三者混合编组配合行动，并加以巧妙地运用，敌人怎能知道我战车从那里驶出，骑兵从邻里袭来，步兵从那里进攻呢？指挥

军队的行动或象潜藏于九地之下[而不可知]，或象陡降于九天之上[而不及避]。这种机智如神的天才，只有陛下才有，我怎能知道这种奥妙呢！

Question 2.11

Tang Taizong asked: "Jiang Ziya's teachings on war mentioned: 'The field of battle should be arranged into a square; each side should have a width of 600 or sixty steps and should be labeled according to the sequence of the twelve Shi Chen.' What is your opinion on this method?"[12]

Li Jing answered: "Arranging the basics of a battle formation, four sides have a total count of 1,200 steps, forming a perfect square. Every team occupies the square land having a width of twenty steps. At the horizontal direction, every five steps, there will be one soldier occupying the space; for the vertical direction, there should be one soldier at the interval of every four steps. In total, there would be 250 separated into five formations and the four angles would have four empty spaces. This is what we call 'another formation inside a battle formation'. When the Emperor of Zhou Dynasty, Zhou Wu Wang defeated the Shang Dynasty, the brave soldiers (otherwise called Hu Ben Zhi Shi) led 3,000 soldiers from each team. At that time, every battle formation had 6,000 soldiers. Five battle formations have a total count of 30,000 soldiers. This is the way Jiang Ziya battled."

Tang Taizong asked: "What is the perimeter of your 'Liu Hua Battle Formation'?"

Li Jing answered: "During the large-scale examination of the army, the perimeter will be 1,020 steps, forming a square shape. The method is: separate the army into six formations. Every formation should occupy a perfect square, having a perimeter of 400 steps. The six battle formations should be separated into two sides, east and west. The central empty space should occupy 1,200 steps for the space of the commanding area. I have tried to train 30,000 soldiers with this formation. Every formation has 5,000 soldiers, one among all will practice the way of camping. The other five will be trained in square, round, curved, straight and sharp formation changes. Every formation should change five times and five formations could change twenty five times."

---

[12] One Shi Chen is equivalent to two hours.

Tang Taizong asked: "What is the significance of 'Wu Xing Formation'?"

Li Jing answered: "Wu Xing Formation was originally named using five different colors to represent five different directions, while the five kinds of formations (square, round, curved, straight and sharp) were designed to suit the different kinds of terrain. If the army was unfamiliar with these five kinds of formations, how could they fight their enemy? The use of military force is deceitful; therefore it was purposely named as 'Wu Xing Formation'. It is to cover up how deceitful it is, while practicing the theory of Shu Shu's counteraction of each other. Actually, the movements of the army are like the flowing of water; it follows the terrain to decide the direction it flows. This is the true meaning of 'Wu Xing Formation'."

太宗问：太公兵书上说，"把布阵的地方画为方形，每边长六百步，或六十步，并按十二时辰的顺序标示出来"，其方法如何？
李靖答：画定阵基，四边共一千二百步，成为一个正方形。每一部占纵横各二十步的方地，横方向每五步占一人，纵方向每四步占一人，共二十五百人分布成〔东、西、南、北和中央]五个方阵，四角有空地四处。这就是所谓阵里有阵。周武王伐商纣时，虎贲之士由各部掌握的共三千人，当时每阵六千人。五阵共三万人。这就是太公画地布阵的方法。
太宗问：你的六花阵画地多少？
李靖答：在大规模检阅军队的地方画周长一千二百步的正方形，其方法是：区分为六阵，每阵各占地周长为四百步的正方，并将六阵分为东西两厢，中间空地一千二百
步作为教战的场所。我曾用士卒三万人进行教练，每阵五千人，其中以一阵演练驻营的方法，其余五阵演练方、圆、曲、直、锐各种阵形的变化，每阵变化五次，五 阵共变化二十五次。
太宗说：五行阵的意义如何？
李靖答：五行阵本来是根据用五种颜色代表五个方位而定的名称，方、圆、曲、直、锐是根据地形而定的五种阵形。军队如不熟习这五种阵形，怎么可以临敌作战呢！用兵是诡诈的，所以故意称为五行阵，以掩饰其诡诈和渲染术数相生相克的道理。其实军队的行动象水一样，是因地势而制约其奔流方向的，这就是五行阵的意义。

Question 2.12

Tang Taizong asked: "Did the strategy of ambush known as the 'Pin Mu' strategy exist in the ancient times?"

Li Jing answered: "The Pin Mu strategy originated from tradition; it is basically the same idea as Yin Yang. Fan Li once mentioned that 'To revolt after the enemy's attack, we need potential; for a preemptive attack against the enemy, we need edge and courage.[13] Take the edge of the enemy's spirit and exert our fullest potential to conquer our enemy.' This is the wonder of military strategy, about potential and edges. There is another saying of Fan Li: 'Arranging the right formation as Pin and the left formation as Mu, the time to launch our operation depends on the situation.' Therefore, the left and right side of the formation in battle, and the timing to launch a military operation varies according to the situation. Underneath are the changes of the *indirect* and *direct* methods. The left and right refer to human Yin and Yang (right refers to Yin while left refers to Yang); day and night refers to the sky's Yin and Yang (night refers to Yin while day is Yang). Qi Fan refers to the varying of left and right or day and night Yin and Yang. If we are reluctant to make changes, then Yin Yang would be meaningless; how could we maintain the form of Pin Mu? Therefore the *direct* army is used to deceive our enemy, but not our *indirect* army. The army that wins victories is the *indirect* army, but not our *direct* army. This is the varying of *indirect* and *direct* armies.

"Ambushing does not solely refer to ambushing using the valleys and the surroundings. The real art of ambushing refers to the use of the *indirect* army as steady-going as the mountains; use the *direct* army as swift as the lightning. Although the enemy is in front of us, they are unable to determine the location of our *indirect* and *direct* armies. If we can apply these two methods to this level, what signs could then be determined?"

太宗问：李{责力}说的牝牡、方圆、伏兵之法，古时有吗？
李靖答：牝牡之法，出于世俗所传，其实就是阴阳的意思。我范蠡说："后发制人要用潜力，先发制人要用锐气；把敌人的锐气折到最低限度，把我们的潜力发挥到最大程度去消灭敌人。"这是亨家运用潜力和锐气的奥妙之处。范蠡又说：
"布设右阵为牝，再左阵为牡，行动的早晚要顺乎天时。"就是说布阵的左右、行动的早晚是因情况而不同，这就在于奇正的变化了。左右是指人的阴阳，(右为
阴，左为阳)早晚是指天的阴阳，(晚为阴，早为阳)奇反是指左右、早晚相互变化的阴阳，如果固执不变，明阳就没有意义了，怎能守牝牡的形式呢。所以欺骗敌
人的，是用奇兵迷惑它，而不是我的正兵，战胜敌人的，是用正兵打击它，而不是我的奇兵，这就是奇正的相互变化。
伏兵，不仅指利用山谷草木设伏而言，所谓真正的伏兵，是说运用正兵象山岳那样稳重，运用奇兵象雷霆那样急剧，敌人虽在对面，亦无法判断我奇正之所在。如果运用奇正到这种程度，那里还有什么形迹可以看得出来呢。

Question 2.13

---

[13] Fan Li (范蠡) was an ancient Chinese advisor in the state of Yue in the Spring and Autumn Period. He is best known for his *Twelve Golden Rules* and *Twelve Safeguards*.

Tang Taizong asked: "The battle formations of the 'Four Beasts' (dragon, tiger, bird and snake) also use the four sounds: Shang, Yu, Wei and Jiao to represent it. What is the theory behind this?"

Li Jing answered: "This is an example of the deceit of military strategies."

Tang Taizong asked: "Could it be abolished?"

Li Jing answered: "The reason to retain the names of the four beasts, and the design of the four sounds to represents the four beasts, is that if we abolish it, then there will be other, more deceitful ways."

Tang Taizong asked: "What is the principle behind this?"

Li Jing answered: "Under the guise of the name of the formations of four beasts, are the sky, the land and the wind; then add Shang Jin, Yu Shui, Zhen Huo, Jiao Mu's cooperation. All these exist in the ancient military strategies which mention deceit. Retaining its name would prevent the addition of other deceitful ways; abolishing it could lead to foolish people eager to battle, but who have no accurate ways to study anymore."

After a long consideration, Tang Taizong said: "You must not leak this secret; keep it tight."

太宗问：(龙、虎、鸟、蛇)四兽之阵，又用商、羽、微、角四音末代表它，这是什么道理？
李靖答：这是兵家诡诈的方法。
太宗问：可以废除吗？
李靖答：保存四兽的名称和代表四兽的四音正是为了废除它，如果果废而不用，其他诡计的方法就更多了。
太宗问：这是什么道理？
李靖答：假借[龙、虎、鸟、蛇］四兽的阵名和天、地、风、的称号，再加上商金、羽水、徵火、角木的配合，这都是兵家自古来的说诈方法，保留其名，其他诡诈的方法不会再增加；废除它，驱使贪婪愚昧的人还有什么方法可施呢。
太宗考虑很久才说：你要保守秘密，不可泄露出去。

Question 2.14

Tang Taizong asked: "I doubt the way about using draconian laws in military orders, so that the army fears us more that the enemy. In the past, Emperor Guang

Questions and Replies

Wu resisted Wang Mang's large troop with a small one. The emperor didn't use severe penalties. What is the cause of this?"[14]

Li Jing answered: "Military victories could be caused under totally different conditions; we could not use a single condition to deduce the outcome. For example, the victory of Chen Sheng and Wu Guang against the Qin Empire; can you say that the laws that were set by Chen Sheng and Wu Guang are even more stringent than Qin Empire's? When Han Guang Wu launched military operations to unify China, it conformed to the hopes of the people who hated Wang Mang. Not to mention that both Wang Xun and Wang Yi did not understand military strategies; they could only boast about the size of their troops, therefore causing their own defeat. I follow what was told in Sun Tzu's 'Art of War': 'If you give punishment when the soldiers have not yet supported you, how could you make people support your cause? But when the soldiers have supported you, and the army is unable to execute punishment accordingly, they would rarely achieve success."

Tang Taizong said: "The theory of Sun Tzu's 'Art of War' is unlike *Shang Shu*.[15] Shang Shu mentioned: 'If the dignity is more that the benevolence, the army could achieve victory; however when the benevolence exceeds dignity, the army could not succeed. What is the meaning of the statement?"

Li Jing answered: "We must place benevolence in front of dignity, use benevolence first and punishment next. The sequence should not be mistaken. If you give punishment first, making things up with benevolence will not help. Shang Shu's saying of 'weigh dignity more than benevolence' means that, he who governs people should consider the importance of dignity, but it does not mean that it is an educating method. Therefore, the sayings of Sun Tzu should not ever change."

太宗问：用严刑峻法，使三军怕我而不怕敌人的说法，我很怀疑。从前光武皇帝以孤军抵挡王莽百万之众，并没有使用严刑峻法，这是什么原因呢？
李靖答：兵家胜败的条件千差万别，各有不同，不可用一种条件去推断。如陈胜、吴广击败秦军，能说是陈胜、吴广的刑法比秦二世更为严苛吗？汉光武起兵定天下，是因为顺应了人民怨恨王莽的心理，何况王寻、王邑又不懂兵法，只夸军队众多，所以自取失败。我按《孙子》说："士卒尚未拥护。就使用刑罚。别人心不服；已经取得拥护而刑罚不能正确执行，这种军队就不能使用。"这是说，为将的必须先用恩爱和士卒建立良好的感情。然后才

---

[14] Emperor Guangwu is also known as Guang Wu and Han Guang Wu. He ruled only parts of China at first, and through suppression and conquest of regional warlords, the whole of China was consolidated by the time of his death in 57 CE.
[15] The title *Shu Shang* is translated in western texts variously as "Classic of History", "Classic of Documents", "Book of History", "Book of Documents" or "Book of Historical Documents", and it was formerly romanized as *Shu-king*.

可以实施严厉的刑罚,如果和士卒尚未建立良好的感情,便单纯使用严刑峻法,是很少能够成功的。

太宗说:[《孙子》听说的道理跟《尚书》不同,]《尚书》说:"威严超过仁爱,就可以成功;仁爱超过成严,就不会成功。"这是什么意思?

李靖答:先施仁爱,后用刑罚。次序不可颠倒。若是用弄罚,后用仁爱去补救,对事情就没有补益了。《尚书》说的[重威轻爱],是指在事情发生以后告戒人要慎重考虑法令的威信,不是说以此作为事先的教育方法。所以孙子的说法是万世不能更改的。

Question 2.15

Tang Taizong said: "After you conquered Xiao Xian, all generals and commanders would have liked to confiscate the properties of Xiao Xian's civil and military officials to reward the soldiers, and only you thought that it was inappropriate. You persuaded them by citing the allusion of Han Gao Zhu not killing Kuai Tong. After that, the people of Jiang Han were submissive. This incident really makes me think of what the ancients said about 'Scholarly talent could earn the support of the army, while the martial talents could make the enemy submissive.' I think you are the person being described."

Li Jing said: "When Han Guang Wu conquered the Che Ju army, he rode into the Che Mei camp to examine the situation. He rode slowly, representing that he was not suspicious or fearful; therefore the Che Mei army said 'King Siao has come to confide in us.' His daring was due to his analysis of the character of the Che Mei people. He was, of course not going to go in there blindly, without analysis beforehand! Not long ago, when I conquered Tu Jue, I was commanding two types of armies: foreign and Han. I didn't kill Yang Gan, but decapitated Zhuang Jia. I was just treating people honestly and fairly. Your Majesty is over confident of my abilities, and has promoted me to such a high position. I really dare not accept the compliment that I possess both scholarly and martial talents; it is too much of an honor."

太宗说:你平定萧铣之后,各将领都想没收萧铣部下文武官员的家财以搞赏士卒,只有你认为不可,并引用了汉高祖不杀蒯通之事,加以说服。以后江汉人民果然归顺了。我因此想到古人说过:"文才能使士众拥护,武功能使敌人慑服",可以说就是这样的人了。

李靖说:汉光武平定赤局军以后,乘马进入赤眉营中巡视检阅,按辔缓缓而行,[以
示对赤眉并无疑惧之心],因而赤眉军说:萧王此来是推心置腹,开诚相见。这是由于事先判断赤眉的人情本不是坏的,岂是没有分析而轻率进入赤眉军营的呢!我
不久以前征讨突厥时,统率番汉两部人马,出塞千里,并末杀一"扬干",

斩一"庄贾",也不过是推诚待人,大公无私罢了。陛下过分信任,把我提拔到这样高的 地位,如果说我是文武兼备实不敢当。

Question 2.16

Tang Taizong asked: "In the past, I sent Tang Jian as an envoy to Tu Jue, but you took the advantage at this time to conquer Tu Jue. There are people who said that you have made Tang Jian a 'dead envoy'. I still have doubts on this; why did you did you pick that particular time?"

Li Jing bowed again and continued with answering: "Tang Jian and I assist Your Majesty together. I had already predicted that Tang Jian would be unable to persuade Tu Jue; therefore, I took the advantage for which Tu Jue had been slack. This was for the good of the country and all commoners; therefore, I couldn't care about the private affairs between Tang Jian and myself. There were people who said I used Tang Jian as a sacrifice, but that was not my intention. According to Sun Tzu, the use of spies is not always the best strategy. I have given my comments on the last pages of the chapter about using spies: 'The water that bears the boat is the same that swallows it.' Or, if something is used correctly, it will be of benefit, and if used incorrectly, will do harm. Therefore there are people who use spies successfully, and there are people who don't. If the ministers could assist the monarch early, be fair in solving the affairs of the state, be loyal and do their best as ministers - honest in giving opinions - with this, even the best spies would be of no use. The matter involving Tang Jian is just a private affair. Your Majesty has no need to be suspicious of this action."

Tang Taizong said: "This is indeed true; the people who are not good cannot use spies. Is this something that can be done by a mediocre enemy? Even the Duke of Zhou could kill his relatives for a virtuous cause, not to mention an envoy; now I understand truly."

太宗问:我从前派遣唐俭出使突厥,你却乘此袭击,大败突厥,有人说你这是把唐俭做了死间,我到现在尚有怀疑,究竟如何?
李靖再拜答:我与唐俭同在朝廷并肩辅佐君主,预料唐俭必然不能说服突厥,所以来突厥懈怠之际纵兵进攻它,这是为了消除自家大患,也顾不得保全与唐俭的私人小义了。有人说我把唐俭作为死间,这不是我的本意。按《孙子》用间之说最为下策,我在用间篇之末曾这样论述过:"水能载舟亦能覆舟,所以有用间成功的,也有因用间而失败的。假如为臣的从年轻时就辅佐君主,参与朝政公正无私,忠心耿耿能尽臣节,信实不欺,竭诚相见,这样虽有善于为间的人,又怎能发生作用呢?象唐俭这样的事乃是小义问题,陛下何必怀疑呢!
太宗说:确是这样,不是仁义兼备的人不能使用间谍,这岂是平庸小人所能做到的吗。周公尚又为大义而灭亲,何况对于一个使者呢。现在我明白无疑了。

Question 2.17

Tang Taizong asked: "In war, it is better to be the host and not the visitor in the land. It is better to win quickly, but not to engage in protracted battles. Why is this?"

Li Jing answered: "War is launched because we have no other option; therefore it is not beneficial to be the visitor to the land, and launch protracted wars. Sun Tzu's 'Art of War' stated, 'If we are transporting food on the journey, it signifies that the commoners are poor.' This tries to explain the disadvantages of being the visitor in a war. Another saying is 'The skillful soldier does not raise a second levy, neither are his supply-wagons loaded more than twice.' His statement concluded that war should not be protracted. Analyzing the concept of the host and visitor force in war, it follows that it is possible that there could be a war that could turn the host force into the invaders, and vice versa."

Tang Taizong said: "What is this based on?"

Li Jing answered: "The army must depend on the food supplies of its enemy. This is the way to change from being the invading force into the main force. 'Make the full enemy hungry, make the strong enemy fatigued.' Therefore, military operations should not rigidly stick to the concept of 'main and invading forces', and the speed of the operations. If we command the whole military operation correctly, we can always still achieve victory."

Tang Taizong asked: "Are there cases of this which existed in the ancient times?"

Li Jing answered: "In the past, when the King of Yue was conquering Wu, he used the left and right army (hitting the drums at midnight) to attack. The army of Wu separated their troops for defense, but the King of Yue stopped hitting the drums and sneaked to attack the army of Wu with Yue's middle army. This is also an example of changing from the invading force to the main force.

"When Shi Le was warring with Ji Dan, Ji Dan was bringing his army from the far side. Shi Le assigned Kong Chang as the striker to attack Ji Dan's army, but Kong Chang retreated purposefully, to lure Ji Dan's army to chase them. Meanwhile, Shi Le arranged an ambush attack. They defeated Ji Dan's army; this is a case of changing the strong enemy into a fatigued one. Such cases happened all the time in history."

太宗问：用兵作战，贵为主，不贵为客；贵速胜，不贵持久，道理何在？
李靖答：兵是不得已才用的，故不宜为客和持久。《孙子》" 运道运输粮食，则百姓贫困。" 这是说为客的害处。又说："不可征调两次，粮食不应输送三回。"这是总结了不可恃久的经验。仔细分析主客的形势，从而有了变主为客，变客为主的方法。
太宗问：这是指什么说的？
李靖答："军队取粮于敌"，就是变客为主；"敌饱能使它饿，敌佚能使他疲劳"，这就是变主为客。所以用兵作战不必拘泥主客、迟速，只要能指挥得当，就能取胜。
太宗问：古人有这种事例吗？
李靖答：从前越王勾践伐吴，用左右两军[末夜]击鼓进战，吴军分兵抵抗，越王用中军息鼓偷渡袭击，打败了吴军，这是变客为主的例子。石勒与姬澹作战，姬澹率兵远未，石勒派孔苌为前锋迎击姬澹的军队，孔苌故意退却，引诱澹军来追，石勒则用伏兵夹击，大败澹军，这是变劳为佚的例子。古人这种事例是很多的。

Question 2.18

Tang Taizong asked: "I have heard that caltrop and wooden fences were designed by Jiang Ziya himself. Is that true?"

Li Jing answered: "Yes, but that is just for the purpose of defending against the enemy's attack. In battle, the main purpose is to defeat our enemy, but not only for the sole purpose of defending. The caltrop and wooden fence mentioned in Jiang Ziya's 'Liu Tao' were just defending tools; they aren't for use in attacks."

太宗问：铁蒺藜和行马，听说是太公所创制的，是吗？
李靖答：是的，然而那只是用以拒御敌人而已，用兵作战重要的是击破敌人，不仅是为了拒止敌人。太公《六韬》所说的铁蒺藜、行马是防守的工具，不是进攻所使用的。

Part 3
Question 3.1

Tang Taizong said: "Jiang Ziya's 'Six Strategies' mentioned: 'When infantrymen engage the chariots and cavalrymen in battle, they must take advantage of the hills, tomb mounds, rugged steeps and defiles.' But, in Sun Tzu's 'Art of War', it is said that the 'army forces should not be situated in places like ravines, hills, tomb mounds and old abandoned cities.' These seem to disagree; why?"

Li Jing replied: "The key in controlling the troops in battle is to unify the whole army, and the key to unification of minds in the troops is to prohibit superstition, and dispel doubts. If the commanding general has doubts, the morale of the troops will be sapped, and once the morale of the troops is sapped, the enemy would take this opportunity to act when we are off guard. Setting up camps and holding positions must be convenient enough for the army to maneuver. Terrain with precipitous cliffs, with torrents running between, deep natural hollows, confined places, tangled thickets, quagmires and crevasses are not convenient for an army to maneuver. Therefore, strategists tend to stay away, and try to avoid such places, so as to prevent the enemy from taking advantage to attack. As for the hills and tomb mounds, these are not places that are too dangerous to approach, and these places are strategic and beneficial for us. Why should we stay away from these places? What Jiang Ziya said is one the most important principles in military operations."

太宗问：太公说："用步兵对战车和骑兵作战，必须依托丘陵、基地以及险峻阻绝的地形。"孙子又说：天隙之地和丘陵、基地、以及无人居住的城池废墟，军队不可停驻。[两种说法不同，]为什么？
李
靖答：用兵作战，在于统一意志，统一意志，在于禁止谣言，消除疑忌。假使主将有所疑忌，那军心就动摇，军心动摇，那敌人就会乘隙而来了。安营札寨，据守阵
地，应当便利军队的行动。如绝涧、天井、天陷、天隙、以及天牢、天罗等地形，都是不便于军队行动的，所以用兵时应当避开它，以防止敌人乘隙攻我。至于立
陵、墓地和城池的废墟不是很险阻的地方，我得了对我有利，那怎能放弃而不利用呢。太公的说法是用兵最重要的原则。

Question 3.2

Tang Taizong said: "I think there is nothing more violent and dangerous in the whole world than war; once we discover an act that could be beneficial for our side in a war, how could we be hesitant only because of Ying Yang divination? From now on, if any of our generals are still confined to the theories of Ying Yang divination, and lose the best timing in combat, you should warn and exhort them repeatedly."

Li Jing bowed and said: "According to Wei Liao Zi: 'Huang Ti rules the land with benevolence and kindness, while using armed forces against the enemy.' This is the 'punishment and benevolence' referred to in military theories, but not the auspicious theories regarding time and days according to Yin Yang methodologists. However, we should make people use the method of deception, but not allow them to understand why they should do it. In later days, some incompetent generals commonly confined themselves with the theories of Yin Yang divination; this is why they suffered so many defeats. This is a lesson from which we must learn. I will immediately announce Your Majesty's sage instructions to all the generals."

太宗说：我想天下凶恶的事情没有超过战争的，作战时只要有利于军队的行动，那能因为避讳阴阳术数而犹豫不决呢。今后诸将如因拘泥于阴阳木数而失去机宜的，你当再三地告诫他们。

李靖再拜谢说：我按《尉缭子》所说："黄帝用仁德安定天下，用武力讨伐敌人"兵家所说的刑与德就是这样，不是阴阳家所讲的天官时日等迷信说法。然而诡诈之道，可以使人去做，但不可以使人知道为什么要那样去做。后来平庸无能的将领往往拘泥于阴阳术数，因而多有失败，不可不以此为戒。陛下的刘海。我立即宣示各将领。

Question 3.3

Tang Taizong asked: "In war, sometimes there is a need to divide the forces, while other times we need to merge the forces. It depends on the actual needs, based on changing situations. Having examined all the records in the past, who excelled at the tactics of dividing and merging the forces?"

Li Jing answered: "Fu Jian had an army of a million people but was finally defeated at the Feishui River. This was because he only used his forces together in a combined way and never divided them. When General Wu Han of the Eastern Han Dynasty was on a punitive expedition against Gongsun Shu, he separated with the adjutant general Liu Shang, and they camped their forces twenty miles apart. When Gongsun Shu attacked Wu Han, Liu Shang reunited with Wu Han and defeated Gongsun Shu in a pincer attack. This is the result of an army dividing and reuniting. Jiang Ziya also mentioned that 'An army that should divide but does not, is an entangled army; an army that should be united but does not is an isolated army.'"

Tang Taizong said: "Yes, when Fu Jian appointed Wang Meng, who knew a lot about commanding an army, he ruled the mainland. When Wang Meng died, Fu Jian was defeated at Fei Shui as expected. This is due to the army being entangled.

Wu Han was trusted by Emperor Guang Wu and was not remotely controlled by the government to command in the battle; therefore, Wu Han was able to suppress the Shu region. This was because the force was not isolated during that battle. The history records of victories and losses should be used as reference in the future."

太宗问：兵力的使用有分散有集中，必须各得其当，从过去的事迹来看，谁运用得最好？
李靖答：前秦苻坚统率百万大军，被谢玄击败于把水，这是用兵能合不能分的结果。汉光武命吴汉讨伐公孙述，吴与副将刘尚分处扎营，相距二十里，当公孙述进攻吴汉时，刘尚出兵合击，大败公孙述，这是用兵分而能合的结果。太公说过：
"当分散而不能分散，就是被束缚的军队；当集中而不能集中，就是被孤立的军队。"
太
宗说：是这样。苻坚最初因为任用深知兵法的王猛，所以取得中原，王猛死后，苻坚果然在淝水失败，这是军队被束缚住的缘故啊！吴汉受到光武的信任，用兵作战
不受朝廷的牵制，所以吴汉果然平定了蜀地，这是军队未陷入孤立境地的缘故呀！前代这些得失的事迹，很可作为后世的借鉴。

Question 3.4

Tang Taizong said: "I observe that of the innumerable sentences and words in all the military books, none has gone beyond the statement 'use various methods to cause your opponent to make mistakes.'"

After a long while, Li Jing said: "Yes, it is exactly like Your Majesty has said. Generally, in any military operations, if the enemy does not make any mistakes, how can we defeat them? It is just like playing a chess game where two players are equal in strength; if either one of them makes a mistake and he loses the whole game, then there will be no way to save the situation. In fighting for victory, most wins and losses are determined by a single mistake, not to mention many mistakes!"

太宗说：我看了很多兵书，千章万句，没有超出"使用多种方法以造成敌人的错误"一句话。
李靖考虑了很久说：确如陛下所说的。大凡用兵作战，若是敌人没有错误，那我军能取得胜利呢。譬如下棋，双方势均力敌，若一着失误，则全局无救。威信争胜负，大都是由于一着失误，又何况多次失误呢。

Question 3.5

Questions and Replies

Tang Taizong said: "Attacking and defending are actually two methods used for the same purpose; there are methods of 'warfare' to obtain victory in a war. Sun Tzu's 'Art of War' mentioned: 'One who excels at attacking makes the enemy unable to know where to defend; one who excels in defending would make the enemy unable to know where to attack.' But it did not mention if the enemy is taking an attack position; our side must also take an attack position. If our side takes a defensive position, the opponent also takes a defensive position. In such a way of both sides assuming mutual attack and defense positions, what techniques should we employ in order to obtain victory?"

Li Jing said: "There are many cases in history of both parties in a war taking mutual attack or defense positions. In all these cases, people would claim that 'One takes a defensive position when his strength is inadequate; whereas one attacks when the strength is abundant.' Assuming that 'being inadequate' also means weakness and 'being abundant' means great strength is the sign of one who does not really understand the essence of the attack and defense method. I follow the saying in Sun Tzu's 'Art of War': 'When one cannot conquer the enemy, take the defensive position; when one can conquer the enemy, take the attack position.' It means that, when there is no chance of defeating the opponent, I will temporarily assume a defensive position; when the conditions that will create my victory have surfaced, we will attack. It is not solely depending on the weakness or strength of the force. Later generations failed to understand the true meaning of this theory, therefore, when they should defend, they attacked and when they should attack, they defended. When they have infringed the principle of attack and defense, they are unable to unite both methods into one."

Tang Taizong said: "That is true. People have assumed that 'being abundant' and 'being inadequate' are also equal to strengths and weaknesses. They did not understand the principle in defending: that it is to appear in the eyes of the enemy as weak and with inadequate strength. The principle in attacking is to pretend to be abundant in strength. If we appear in the eyes of the enemy as weak, the enemy will definitely take the attack position. Pretending to be abundant in strength will definitely make the enemy assume the defensive position; this will make the enemy unable to assume the right position in war. Attacking and defense are both methods in acquiring victory; but in spite of our army and the opponent's, they are separated, and each side in the war will assume either a defense or attack position. If we use our position wisely, the enemy will be defeated. If the enemy uses their position wisely, we will be defeated. The outcome of the war will determine which of us is using the right strategy in the war. Attacking and defense are merely approaches to obtain victory. If we could master these methods, that could help us in obtaining victory and we could win in every war in which we are involved. Therefore 'If you know yourself and your enemy, you will never lose a battle' means we need to understand the true meaning of the attack and defense methods."

Li Jing bowed again and said: "The military strategies of the sages are very profound. Attack is the transformation of defense, while defense is the means of attacking; both ways are approaches to defeat the enemy. If in attacking we do not know how to defend, and in defending we fail to attack, we are not only separating both methods completely from each other, but isolating the application of defense and attack. Even though one could recite the words from Sun Tzu's 'Art of War', if he could not understand how to apply these methods in practice, and set attack and defense against each other, how can he get to know the mysterious subtleties of both attack and defense?"

太宗说：进攻和防守两件事情，其实都是用以致胜的方法罢了。《孙子》说："善于进攻的，能使敌人不知道在那里防守才好；善于守的，能使敌人不知道从那里进攻才好。"但是不曾讲到，敌人若来攻我；我也进攻敌人；我若防守，敌人也进行防守。这样相攻相守，要想取胜应采用什么方法？
李靖答：从前相攻相守的战例甚多，他们都说"防守是力量不足，进攻是力量有余"。认为兵力不足便是力量薄弱，兵力有余便是力量强大，这是没有领会运用攻守的方法。我按《孙子》说："不能取胜时，就采取防守；可以取胜时，就实施进攻。"也就是说，还没有战胜敌人的可能时，我就暂时防守；等到创造了取胜的条件，然后再进攻，并不是专就力量强弱来说。后人不了解这种意义，应当进攻反而防守，应当防守反而进攻，既然违反了攻守运用的原则，便不能把进攻和防守的方法统一起来。
太宗说：就是这样。有余或不足使人怀疑为力量的强弱。那里知道防守的原则要对敌假装力量不足，进攻的原则要对敌假装力量有余。对敌假装力量不足，敌人必然要来进攻，这是使敌人不知其不当进攻。对敌假装力量有余，敌人就必然采取防守，这是使敌人不知其当防守。进攻和防守本来都是致胜的方法，但从敌我双方说来就分一攻一守两个方面了。我若运用得当，敌人就会失败；敌若运用得当，我就会失败，从得失成败的结局看就可以分出敌我运用的好坏了。攻和守不过是致胜的方法而已，掌握了这种致胜的方法，就能百战百胜。所以说："知己知彼，百战不殆。"就是说要懂得攻守之法的道理。
李靖再拜说：圣人的兵法是很深奥的。进攻是防守的转化，防守是进攻的手段，两者都是为了战胜敌人。若攻不知守，守不知攻，这不仅是把攻守截然看作两回事，而且是把攻守的运用各自孤立起来了。虽然口诵孙、吴兵法，但不能理解其运用的奥妙，而把攻守对立起来，他怎能知其所以然呢！

Questions and Replies

Question 3.6

Tang Taizong said: "The 'Methods of Sima' stated that 'even though a state is large, it will definitely perish if it is constantly involved in war' and that 'even though a state is at peace, it could be endangered if it is not prepared for war.' Is this also a theory regarding attack and defense?"

Li Jing said: "Whenever a state and home territory are involved, they definitely involve attack and defense. Attacking is not restricted to attacking the enemy cities or battle formations. It also includes the way to defeat the enemy's strategic intention and further shake the morale of his troops. Defending, does not only involve perfectly intact city walls and solid formations, but also needs the high spirit and morale of the troops, as well as waiting for the best opportunity to defeat the enemy. Speaking in big terms, these concepts of attacking and defending are the concepts that a ruler should understand, and in small terms, are methods that generals ought to master. To be able to defeat the enemy's strategic intention and shake the enemy troop's morale is the so-called 'knowing the enemy' and to be able to keep the spirits high of your own troops is the so called 'knowing yourself'."

Tang Taizong said: "That is true! Whenever I was about to prepare for a battle, I would compare the strategy of the enemy's with ours and see whose is more prudent, then I would understand his strength better. I would also compare the enemy troops' morale with the morale of our troops and see whose morale is stronger. With that, I would understand the strength or weaknesses of our troops. Therefore, understanding the enemy and yourself is an important principle in military matters. The generals nowadays, even though they are not able to understand their enemy, if they are able to know themselves, how can they still be defeated?"

Li Jing said: "What Sun Tzu meant by: 'First, create the conditions that would make your troops unconquerable' is knowing yourself; 'Wait for the opportunity where you can defeat the enemy' is knowing the enemy. He also mentioned that 'being unconquerable depends on one's self, while being able to win lies with the mistakes made by the enemy.' During battle, I never dare to go against this strategy."

太宗问：《司马法》说：" 国虽大，好战必亡；天下虽安，忘战必危。" 这也是攻守的道理吗？
李靖答：凡是有国有家的，何尝不讲求攻守之道呢！进攻，不仅是攻打敌人的城池和冲击敌人的营阵，还必须有瓦解敌人军心的方法。防守，不仅要有完善的壁垒和坚固的营阵，还必须保持旺盛的士气，持机破敌。[以上、所说的]，从大的方面讲，是为君的应该懂得的道理。从小的方面讲，是为将的应掌握的方法。瓦解敌人的军心，就是所谓的知彼；保持我旺盛的士气，就是所谓的知己。

太
宗说：是这样。我每逢临敌作战，必先判断敌方的策划和我方的策划谁比较周密，然后敌方的虚实就可以知道了；察明敌方的士气和我方的士气谁比较旺盛，然后我
方的强弱就可以知道了。所以知彼知已是兵家的重要原则。现在的将领，即使不知道敌人情况，如果能够了解自己的情况，怎么还会失利呢。
李靖说：孙武所谓"首先造成不可被敌战胜的条件"，这就是知已；"等待可以战胜敌人的机会"，这就是知彼。又说："不可被敌战胜，在于自己的主观努力，可以取得胜利，在于敌人是否产生缺点和错误。"我用兵时一点也不敢违背这一教诲。

Question 3.7

Tang Taizong asked: "According to Sun Tzu's 'Art of War', the way to make the enemy's troop loses their morale is 'In the morning, the spirit of the enemy is high; in the afternoon, the troop becomes indolent; while at dusk, it may be exhausted.' Therefore a smart commander should avoid the enemy when they are high in morale and spirit, and attack them when they become indolent or exhausted in morale. "What do you think about this statement?"

Li Jing said: "All soldiers would fight their enemy with great courage and would not fear death; this is the great effect of controlling morale and spirit. Thus a good commander must start with observing the morale of his troops and encourage them to fight and to win victoriously; then we could start attacking the enemy. Among the vital points according to Wu Qi, morale is placed at the foremost. There is no other way. If you can raise the morale of the soldiers and make them eager to fight, then the whole army would become unbeatable. The saying of 'spirit is high in the morning' is not only restricted to the timing, but is using the beginning and the end of a day as an analogy. If the enemy's morale has neither declined nor depleted after three assaults, how can you make it indolent or exhausted? People who study the military strategies and principles are only reciting the words and text from military books; as a result, they will be tempted by the enemy in a war. If a general is able to make the enemy lose their spirit and morale, he could be entrusted to lead troops and command military operations."

太宗问：《孙子》上说，使敌军长失士气的方法是："朝气猛锐，昼气怠惰，暮气衰竭；善于用兵的人，要避开敌人的锐气，等待敌人懈怠衰竭的时候再打击它。"这种说法怎样？
李
靖答：凡有血气的人，能鼓起勇气与敌斗争，至死也不知道惧怕，这是气势所起的作用。所以用兵的方法，必须首先察明我士卒斗志，激励其战胜敌人的勇气，这样
才可以进击敌人。吴起所说的机，把气机放在首要地位，没有别的道理，就

Questions and Replies

是说只要能使人人勇于自斗，其猛锐的力量是不能阻当的。所谓朝气猛锐，并不是限于时
刻来说的，而是拿一天的早晚作比喻的。敌人经过三次冲击，而士气没有衰竭，又怎能一定使它懈怠衰竭呢！学兵法的人，只是背诵空洞条文，结果为敌人所诱惑， 假如能懂得使敌人丧失士气的道理，就可叫他统兵作战了。

Question 3.8

Tang Taizong asked: "You once said that Ze Li is knowledgeable in military strategies, but should he be used from a long-term point of view? If I am no longer around to direct and control him in person, I am afraid he could no longer be controlled. How could Crown Prince Zi control him in the future?"

Li Jing answered: "As for planning for the Crown Prince, Your Majesty might consider removing Ze Li from his position, so the Crown Prince could reappoint him in the future. Then he will feel gratitude and return the hospitality he has received. There is no permanent damage done, in terms of using Ze Li this way."

Tang Taizong said: "Good! I have no doubts on that matter anymore. However, if I appoint Ze Li and Zhang Wu Ji to administer the national affairs together, what would the future be like?"

Li Jing answered: "Ze Li is a loyal minister. I can guarantee that he would be competent in that position. As for Zhang Wu Ji, he helped Your Majesty a lot in building the empire, and Your Majesty appointed him sincerely as the assistant minister. But although he looks humbly corporal from the surface, he is actually jealous of more virtuous people at heart. Yu Chi Jing De once criticized him face to face, and then, fearing Zhang Wu's revenge, he decided to retire early. Hou Jun Ji hates him for forgetting the good old relationships in the past, therefore, participated in the rebellion of the deposed Crown Prince Cheng Qian. These were all caused by Zhang Wu Ji. Since Your Majesty asked me, I dare not avoid talking about it."

Tang Taizong said: "Do not let this leak out. I will have to consider how to settle this problem."

太宗问：你曾记过李{责力}深知兵法，天长日久还可以任用他么？如果不是我亲自控御恐怕就不能用了。将来太子治怎样控制他呢？
李靖答：为陛下打算，不如由你免去李{责力}的职务，将来由太子再来起用他，那他必定会感恩图报，这对于情理有什么损害呢！
太宗说：好！我没有怀疑了。
太宗问：若用李{责力}和长孙无忌共同掌管国家大事，将来会怎么样呢？
李靖答：李{责力}为忠义之臣，我可以保证他能胜任。至于长孙无忌有辅佐陛下创业的大

功，陛下又以肺腑至亲委任他做辅相。但是他表面上虽然谦恭下士，其实内心嫉能{女后}贤。所以尉迟敬德曾经当面指责过他的短处，[因为怕他报复]就引退了。侯君集恨他忘怀旧好，因而参加了废太子承乾的谋反。这都是长刃无忌造成的。陛下 既然问到我，我不敢避而不谈。

太宗说：不要泄露，待我从长考虑后再作处理。

Question 3.9

Tang Taizong asked: "Emperor Gao Zu of Han Dynasty was good at governing generals, but later on, Han Xin and Peng Yue were both executed by him, and Xiao He was imprisoned. Why would he treat them in such a manner?"

Li Jing answered: "In my opinion, neither Liu Bang nor Xiang Yu was a good ruler, proficient at governing generals. When the Qin Dynasty collapsed, Zhang Liang intended to avenge Chen Ping for the sake of Han. Han Xin resented Xiang Yu because he failed to assign them to important tasks; therefore, they went to Liu Bang to take advantage of his power and influence to reach their respective goals. As for Xiao He, Cao Sen, Fan Kuai and Guan Ying, they were actually desperadoes seeking refuge from Liu Bang. Emperor Gao Zu conquered the nation because he was able to assign them to key positions wisely. However, if the descendants of the six states are allowed to reestablish their old states, these people would exclusively embrace their old states and ruler. By then, even if Liu Bang had the ability to command these generals, how could they render their service for him? So I think that Liu Bang's victory should be attributed to Zhang Liang's brilliant plans and strategies, and Xiao He's effort and achievements. From this point of view, Han Xin and Peng Yue being executed, and Fan Zen no longer being appointed with any key positions are the same in nature. Therefore, I think neither Liu Bang nor Xiang Yu was a ruler capable of controlling generals."

Tang Taizong said: "When Emperor Guang Wu restored the Han Dynasty, he maintained his meritorious generals but did not entrust them with civil affairs. Is this being capable of controlling generals?"

Li Jing answered: "Although Emperor Guang Wu's victory is more easy to attain based on what had been achieved by his ancestors formerly, still Wang Meng was no less powerful than Xiang Yu, and Kou Xun and Deng Yu were much less capable than Xiao He and Han Xin. However, Emperor Guang Wu was honest and sincere with his subordinates, governed the state with softer policies and maintained his generals. So he was much wiser than Liu Bang. If we are to discuss the ability of controlling generals based on this, I would say that Emperor Guang Wu was successful."

太宗问：汉高帝善于统御将帅，后来韩信和彭越被杀，萧何又下狱，为什么这样对待功臣呢？

李
靖答：我看刘邦、项羽都不是善于统御将帅的君王。当秦二将灭亡时，张良本来是想为韩国报仇，陈平、韩信都怨恨楚项王不肯重用，所以他们惜刘邦的势力来为自

己谋求出路。至于萧何、曹参、樊哙、灌婴都是亡命之徒，投奔刘邦，高祖因为用了这些人才得了天下。假若当时使六国的后代重新复国，这些人必因怀念旧主而离

去，刘邦纵有御将才能，他们又怎能为汉所用呢！我认为刘邦之所以能得天下，是由于张良借箸之谋和萧何漕{车免}之功。以此来说，韩信和彭越的被杀，以及范增的不被重用，这两件事情是相同的。所以说刘邦和项羽都不是善于统御将帅的君王。

太宗问：光武中兴以后，为了保全功臣，不让他们主管朝政，这是善于统御将帅吗？

李靖答：光武虽然凭籍前人的基业容易成功，然而王莽的权势不下于项羽、邓禹和寇恂的才能也没有超过萧何和张良，可是光武独能以至诚待人，使用温和的政策保全功臣，这就比高祖贤明多了。以这样事例来评论统御将帅的方法，我认为光武是成功的。

Question 3.10

Tang Taizong asked: "In ancient times, when dispatching an army and appointing a commanding general for the troops, the ruler would perform a fast that lasted for three days, and then ritually hand the general a Yue[16], announcing: 'Every matter from here on to the highest of Heavens, will be decided by the general'. After that, the ruler would also give the general an ax which symbolized the power to execute punishment, or to kill, announcing that 'Every matter, from here to the deepest Earth, will be decided by the general.' The emperor will then push the general's chariot forward and say: 'The general will have total power in deciding whether to advance or retreat the army, in accordance with the situation.' After the army has set off, all affairs regarding the army would be put under the command of the general, not the ruler. I noticed that these ceremonies have long been abandoned. Now I would like to discuss and work out some new ceremonies to appoint the commanding general, with reference to the ancient ones. What do you think of it?"

Li Jing answered: "In my opinion, the ceremonies designed by the Sages in the past are performed in the temples because they want to draw strength from the spirits. The purpose of Yue and Ax passed to the general, and the push of the chariot is because the ruler wants to grant the general the authority to command. Nowadays, whenever Your Majesty is about to begin an expedition, you should discuss the matter with court officials, and hold ceremonies at the temple before

---

[16] A Yue is an ancient weapon in the shape of a broad ax symbolizing authority.

appointing a commanding general. This is an earnest request for the blessing of the gods. Whenever Your Majesty appoints a general, the appointed shall be granted with the power of making his own decisions, and take actions on the spot as they find suitable. By this, Your Majesty is giving the appointed general the highest authority. This is completely in accords with the ancient rites and the essence is all the same, without fasting."

Tang Taizong said: "Good." Then he ordered his attending courtier to record the two practices as a norm of appointing commanding generals to be followed by people in the future generations.

太宗问：古时出兵作战任命大将时，君王必先斋戒三天，然后将钺授给他说：从此上至天的事情由将军全权处理。又将斧投给他说：L从此下至地的事情由将军全权处理。又推着他的车子说：军队进退由你根据情况决定。出发以后，军中只听将军的指挥，不等待君王的令。我以为这种礼仪早已废弃了。现在想和你参照古礼制定遣将的礼仪，你看如何？
李靖答：我认为圣人所制定的在宗庙斋成的礼仪。是为了假借神威；授给斧钺和推毂，是为了授给将军以军权。现在陛下每当出师作战，必先与公卿商议，并祭告宗庙
而后派遣大将，这样假威于神的礼仪算是做到了；每当任命大将，必使他们见机行事，就是给了他们很大的权力。这与斋戒推教有什么区别呢！这是完全符合古札 的，其义也相同，所以不须再来参照制定了。
太宗说：好。于是就命近臣记载上这两件事做为以后遣将的法度。

Question 3.11

Tang Taizong asked: "Can the practices of Yin and Yang be abandoned?"

Li Jing answered: "No, they should not. Deception is of utmost importance in warfare. With Yin and Yang practices, we could manipulate the greedy and stupid, so these should not be abandoned."

Tang Taizong said: "You once mentioned that selecting astrologically auspicious seasons and days are methods that are not used by wise generals. Only stupid ones would stick with this sort of practice. So it should be abandoned?"

Li Jing said: "In the past, King Zhou of Shang Dynasty perished on a day designated as Jiazi,[17] but King Wu of the Zhou Dynasty succeeded on the same day. If one has to observe astrologically auspicious seasons and days, why on the same day of Jiazi should the Shang Dynasty perish, while the Zhou Dynasty

---

[17] Jiazi would be: Heavenly stem one and earthly branch one in the sixty-year cycle of traditional Chinese chronology.

triumphed? What a great difference! Another example is when Liu Yi, Emperor Wu Di of Northern and Southern Song Dynasties, was about to go on an expedition against the state of Southern Yan. The day he chose to set off was a day considered by the Yin and Yang diviners as an ominous 'shall perish day'. All of his generals thought he should not set off on that day, but the Emperor said: 'I will attack, and the enemy shall perish.' What he said was true, he defeated the state of Southern Yan and took the city of Guang Gu. From these cases, we can know that things such as Yin and Yang practice, and selection of astrologically auspicious seasons and periods can be abandoned. However, when Tian Dan, the general of the state of Qi, was besieged in Ji Mo by the army of Yan, he ordered a soldier to disguise himself as a god and enshrined and worshiped him. This disguised soldier said: 'The army of Yan can be defeated.' Then Tian Dan launched an attack with flames and oxen and completely defeated the army of Yan. This is what we know as military deception."

Tang Taizong said: "Tian Shan resorted to the spirits, ghosts and gods and defeated Yan while Jiang Ziya burned the yarrows and tortoise shells for divination and exterminated King Zhou of Dynasty Shang. The two affairs are contradictory to each other but produced the same results. Why?"

Li Jing answered: "They share the common aim to boost morale; however, there are people who employ the opposite way to acquire the same success. Some follow the situation and take favorable actions in accordance to the situation. In the past, when Jiang Ziya assisted King Wu of Zhou on an expedition against Zhou of Shang, they reached Mu Ye, where they faced a thunderstorm. As a result, their flags and drums were all either broken or destroyed. San Yisheng made a suggestion to divine first before taking any other actions. He felt that when the doubts and fears grew in their troops, they had to rely on divination and help from gods and spirits, in order to calm the troops down. But Jiang Ziya thought that the rotted grass and dry bones were not worth asking for. Moreover, in their case, the King Wu of Zhou was on an expedition as a subordinate against his ruler, how could people wait for an auspicious day to conduct such an operation? In this case, however, it appears that San Yisheng's suggestions of divination at the beginning and Jiang Jiang Ziya's rejection of the suggestion subsequently were contrary to each other, but their final motives were the same. They wanted to keep the troops united. When I stated previously that Ying and Yang practices should not be abandoned, I meant that these practices could be used for psychologically controlling our troops, before things begin to manifest themselves. Whether one could be successful in using these practices is mainly dependent on our own efforts."

太宗问：阴阳术数可以废除吗？
李靖答：不可。用兵是讲求诡诈之道的，假托阴阳术数，是使贪婪愚昧之人的一种办法，所以不可废除。

太宗说：你曾说过天官时日，明智的将领不以为法，是不用的，而愚昧的将领却往往受它拘束，废除了也是应该的。

李靖说：从前商纣在甲子日出兵遭到灭亡，而周武王在甲子日出兵获得成功，按天官时日讲，同是一个甲子日，结果是殷乱周治，光亡不同。又宋武帝在"往

亡日"兴兵讨伐南燕，将吏们以为不可，宋武帝说："我一前往，他就灭亡。"后来果然战胜了南燕。由此来说，阴阳术数可以废除是很明显的了。然而齐将田单在

即墨被燕军围困时，命一人假装神师，亲自礼拜词祭，神师说："燕军可以破。"于是田单以火牛出击，大破燕军。这就是兵家诡作之道。天官时日的说法，也是这 样的。

太宗问：田单假托神怪破了燕军，可是太公焚毁蓍龟而灭了商纣，二事相反[但都获得成功]，是什么缘故呢？

李

靖答：其巩固军心的动机是一致的，不过，有的采用相反的办法而取得成功，有的顺应当时的情况而采取有利的行动就是了。从前太公辅佐武王伐纣，进军到牧野，

忽然遇到宙雨，旗鼓都被折毁，谋臣散宜生想占卜问吉然后行动，这是因为当时军心疑俱，必须假借占卜问神以安军心。太公认为腐草枯骨没有请问的必要，况且反

这是以臣伐君，怎能等待吉日再行举事呢。看起来散宜生产生用占卜巩固军心的动机于前，太公采用毁蓍龟成全巩固军心的动机于后。逆顺虽然不同，道理却是一样

的。我在前面所说的阴阳术数不可废除，是为了用这种办法来防忠于未然。至于一切事情的成功，主要还决定于人的努力。

Question 3.12

Tang Taizong said: "At present, the commanding generals we have are Ze Li, Dao Zhong and Xue Wan Che. Among these three, who could be entrusted with great responsibility?"

Li Jing answered: "Your Majesty once mentioned that Ze Li and Dao Zhong wouldn't achieve great victories, but neither would they suffer disastrous defeats in commanding a war; while Xue Wan Che would either achieve victorious outcome or suffer a disastrous defeat. I consider this, according to a statement Your Majesty's made. A force that doesn't strive for great victories, but will also not suffer disastrous defeats is a well-trained army; while an army that may achieve great victories but also may suffer from disastrous defeats is an army relying on good fortune to achieve success. Thus Sun Tzu once said: 'A wise commander always ensures that his forces are put in an invincible position, and at the same time will be sure to miss no opportunity to defeat the enemy'. The power of controlling and commanding wholly belongs to the general."

太宗问：现在的将帅，只有李{责力}、道宗、薛万彻。这三人中，除了道宗是亲属之外，那个可以童用呢？
李靖答：陛下曾说李{责力}、道宗用兵不大胜也不会大败。薛万彻芳不大胜就是大败。我考虑圣上的话，不求大胜也不会大败的，是有节制的军队；或者大胜或者大败的，是凭侥幸成功的军队。所以孙武说：
"善于指导作战的人，使自己常处于不败的地位，而不失去任何击败敌人的机合"，指挥掌握在我而已。

Question 3.13

Tang Taizong said: "When two armies are against each another, in order not to fight, how should we manage it?"

Li Jing answered: "In ancient times, when the army of the state of Jin and Tai were at war, both of them withdrew at the moment they approached each other. The 'Method of Sima' stated that 'Do not chase after a fleeing army too far and do not follow the retreating army too tight.' I think that this refers to the reins of a horse. If our army is well-trained and controlled, the enemy's formation is well organized: how would we dare to start a battle rashly? That is why they met and then withdrew, with neither of them pursuing after each other. They just wanted to defend themselves from being defeated. Sun Tzu said: 'Desist from attacking an army whose formations are in an impressive array, and refrain from intercepting an enemy whose banners are in perfect order.' When we and the enemy are equal in terms of strength, we should move bravely and give the enemy an opportunity to suffer a disastrous defeat. This is common sense. At war, sometimes, you must not fight, and at others time, a war is inevitable. You must not fight when you have no confidence to win, and when the enemy has created mistakes which created advantages for you, you must take them."

Tang Taizong said: "If 'you have insufficient advantage in that battle, do not fight the enemy.' What does this mean?"

Li Jing answered: "Sun Tzu said: 'If I do not want to fight with the enemy, because we do not have advantage on the ground, the enemy would also be unable to fight with me. This is because the enemy would be caught confused and overwhelmed.' If the enemy has an excellent commander, when the two armies are at war, it is very hard to achieve victory in that war. Therefore, the saying of 'do not fight with the enemy' is only because we do not have the sufficient advantage over the enemy to win victory. As for fighting with the enemy, the best time is when the enemy has committed some mistakes and thus created an advantage for us to take. Sun Tzu said: 'He who is excellent at arousing the enemy is capable of sending all sorts of deceitful illusions, in order to lure the enemy into believing false news, and take actions in accordance with the false information. He will offer some bait, and the enemy who is lured will come and take it. Use these small benefits to arouse the enemy, and use the main force to wait for the perfect opportunity to defeat the enemy's force.' If the enemy does not have a good commander, they will certainly attack rashly, and we should take the advantage and attack him. Therefore, the saying that 'the war with the enemy is inevitable' is because there is an advantage you could take that could lead to victory."

Tang Taizong said: "This concept regarding a well-disciplined army is very profound! One will succeed by mastering this principle; going against this law will cause disastrous defeat. You should compile the deeds of the generals throughout history who excelled at constraining the army and present them to me with diagrams. I will select the quintessential ones and pass them down to the future generations."

Li Jing answered: "The diagrams I presented previously regarding Huang Ti, Jiang Ziya's 'Two-Array Diagram', 'Method of the Sima' and Zhuge Liang's '*Indirect* and *Direct*' methods are already very detailed. They are many famous generals in history who could achieve victories only by using one or two strategies from these military classics. However, most historians have limited knowledge in military affairs. Therefore, they are unable to record the real deeds in a war. I will definitely comply with the order and submit the record of deeds of wars in history after codification."

太宗问：双方对阵，要想不战，怎能办得到呢？
李靖答：从前晋国与秦国作战，刚一接触双方就退兵了。《司马法》说："追
击败退的敌人不要追得太远，跟踪撤退的敌人不要跟得太紧。"我所说的"绥"，就是驾御马的缰绳。我军的行动既有节制，敌军的队伍也很严整，这样怎敢轻于交
战呢？所以才有两军临战而退，退而不追的情况，这都是为了预防各自的失败。刊、武说："不要攻击阵容强大的敌军，不要袭击旗帜整齐的敌人。"
假若双方势均
力敌，一旦轻举妄进，为敌所乘，就会大败，这是很自然的道理。所以，用兵有不战，有必战的说法。不与敌人作战，是由于我的条件不足；必与敌人作战，是在于 敌人有隙可乘。
太宗问：不与敌人作战，是由于我的条件不足，这是指什么说的呢？
李靖答：孙武说："我
不想和敌人作战，虽然画地而守，敌人也无法同我作战，那是因为使敌人陷于迷惑而不知所措的缘故。"如果敌方有善于指挥的人，在两军交战时，就难于取胜，所

以说不与敌战，是因为自己的条件还不具备。至于必与敌人作战，是在于敌人有隙可乘，孙武说："善于调动敌人的，是显示各种假象，使敌人信以为真听从调动；

给敌人一些好处，敌人就会贪利来取，用小利调动敌人，用主力待机打击它。"如果敌方没有善于指挥的人，必然轻率来战，我便乘隙击破它。所以说必与敌人作战，是在于敌人有隙可乘。

太宗说：节制之师的道理很深奥啊！掌握这个法则就会胜利，违背这个法则就会失败。你可去编纂历代善于节制军队战斗行动的战例，并绘制成图呈送上来，我要选择其中最好的传于后世。

李靖答：我以前呈送的黄帝、太公二阵图和《司马法》以及诸葛亮的奇正之法，都已经很详细了，历代名将运用其中一、二而取得的为数很多。但史官懂得用兵的很少，因此，他们不能记载战争实事迹。我一定遵照命令编纂上报。

Question 3.14

Tang Taizong asked: "Amongst all the ancient war strategies and tactics, which is the most profound?"

Li Jing replied: "I divided the strategy of wars into three levels to allow the learners of military tactics to learn in an orderly and gradual manner. The first is 'Dao', the second is 'Heaven and Earth', third is 'Principles of Generalship'. The so called 'Dao' is very profound and subtle concept. It is what 'The Book of Changes' refers to as the greatest wisdom of all. It could convince people without using punishment; the 'Heaven' refers to the night or day, while the 'Earth' refers to danger or safe. A person who is good at controlling his army could seize the opportunity at night, and obtain the victory harder to achieve during the day. He can utilize an unfavorable terrain to attack his enemy who is at a favorable position. This is the theory of 'weather and geography' mentioned by Mencius. As for the 'Principles of Generalship', this is referring to the capability of appointing talented personnel and using the right weapons, which is as mentioned in 'Three Strategies', the phrase: 'you are able to obtain victory once you have the best generals' and what Guan Zhong meant by 'the equipment must be sturdy and sharp' in his theory.

Tang Taizong said: "Yes. I think that having the enemy give in without starting a war is the best strategy. Being victorious in every battle is next, and defending with high walls and trenches is lowest in grade. According to such a comparison, Sun Tzu includes all three grades of these solutions in his military books."

Li Jing said: "After reading the articles of the ancients, and deducing the deeds of the ancients, we can see the difference. For example, after the success of Zhang Liang, Fan Li and Sun Tzu, they were able to retire without any worries. They disappeared from the scene. If the generals don't understand the real meaning of

'Dao', how could they be able to remain uninvolved? As for Yue Yi, Guang Zhong and Zhuge Liang who were able to obtain victories in every battle, and defend toughly every time, if they don't clearly grasp the changes of environment and terrain, they could not achieve such victories! Secondarily, Wang Meng who stabilized the Qing Dynasty, Xie An who defended Eastern Jin Dynasty - if they didn't understand the art of appointing and selecting great and talented generals, and the art of repairing and preparing the right armaments in order to have the best protection, how would they be so successful? Therefore, learning the art of warfare must start from the lowest to the medium and then proceed to the highest. They can only learn, beginning with the easiest then proceeding to the toughest. Otherwise, everything is nothing but plain, useless talk. Reciting every word from the principles would prove to be useless; it would not help them to achieve anything."

Tang Taizong said: "According to the sayings of the Daoists, three generations of generals is a taboo and should be prevented. This also means that military tactics shouldn't be passed on presumptuously, but must be passed on cautiously."

Li Jing bowed again before exiting, he handed all his military strategies and tactics books to Ze Li.

太宗问：古人的兵法，哪家是最深奥的？
李靖答：我曾把兵法分为三等，使学习的人循序渐进，逐步达到精通。一是"道"，
二是"天地"，三是"将法"。所谓"道"是极为精深微妙的，就是《易经·系辞》所说的最有智慧的人，是不用刑杀而能服人的；所谓"天"是指夜间和白画而
言；所谓"地"是指险易而言。善于用兵的人，能够利用夜间以夺取白天难以取得的胜利，能够利用不利地形去进攻处于有利地形的敌人。孟子所说天时、地利就是
这个道理。所谓"将法"，是指善于任用贤能和使用优良的兵器，就是《三略》所说的"得到贤能之士就能胜利"，和管仲所说的
"器械必须坚固锋利"的道理。
太宗说：是这样。我认为不战而使敌人屈服的是上等，百战百胜的是中等，深沟高垒坚阵防守的是下等。按这样比较，孙武兵法三说法都有了。
李靖说：看了古人的文章，推究古人的事迹，也就可以看出差别了。如张良、范蠡、孙武三人成功以后，就毫无牵挂地超然引退，不知去向，若不是懂得"道"
的微妙，怎能那样呢！如乐毅、管仲、诸葛亮能够战必胜，守必固，若不是明察天时地利，怎能那样呢！其次如王猛的安定前秦，谢安的捍卫东晋，若不是善于任用
良将选择才，修备甲兵以求自固，怎能那样呢！所以学习兵法，必须先由下

到中等，由中等到上等，就能逐渐由浅入深了。不然的话，就不过是只尚空谈，只知道背 诵兵法的条文，那是不足取法的。

太宗说：道家的说法，忌讳三代为将，是说兵法不可妄传，但不可不传，你应慎重传授。

李靖再拜后退出，将他的全部兵书传授与李{责力}。

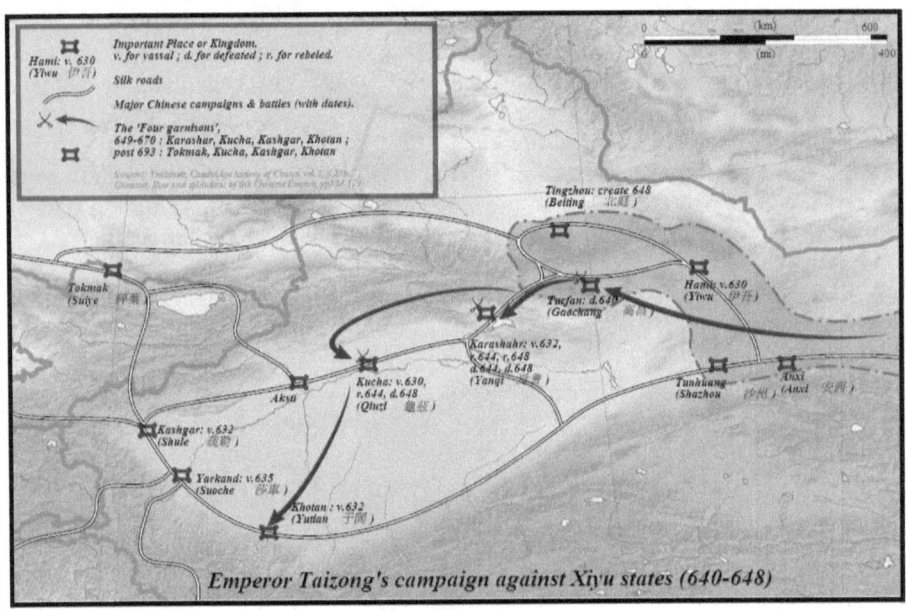

Bibliography

Army, U. S. (1985). Military History and Professional Development. U. S. Army Command and General Staff College, Fort Leavenworth, Kansas: Combat Studies Institute. 85-CSI-21 85.

Giles, Lionel. (2007) "The Art of War by Sun Tzu - Special Edition". Special Edition Books.

Griffith, Samuel B. (2005) "The Illustrated Art of War". Oxford University Press.

McNeilly, Mark. (1996) "Sun Tzu and the Art of Business : Six Strategic Principles for Managers. Oxford University Press.

Sawyer, Ralph D.; Mei Mei-chün Sawyer (1993). "The Seven Military Classics of Ancient China". Westview Press.

Watson, Burton. (1958). "Beginning of Chinese Historiography". Ssu Ma Ch'ien Grand Historian of China. Columbia University Press.

Yang, Lihui, et al. (2005). Handbook of Chinese Mythology. Oxford University Press.

www.ingramcontent.com/pod-product-compliance
Lightning Source LLC
Chambersburg PA
CBHW030213170426
43201CB00006B/68